Shakespeare's Plants and Gardens

ARDEN SHAKESPEARE DICTIONARIES

SERIES EDITOR
Sandra Clark (Birkbeck College, University of London)

Class and Society in Shakespeare Paul Innes
Military Language in Shakespeare Charles Edelman
Shakespeare's Books Stuart Gillespie
Shakespeare's Demonology Marion Gibson
Shakespeare's Insults Nathalie Vienne-Guerrin
Shakespeare and the Language of Food Joan Fitzpatrick
Shakespeare's Legal Language B. J. Sokol and Mary Sokol
Shakespeare's Medical Language Sujata Iyengar
Shakespeare's Musical Language Christopher R. Wilson
Shakespeare's Non-Standard English N. F. Blake
Shakespeare's Political and Economic Language Vivian Thomas
Shakespeare's Theatre Hugh Macrae Richmond
Women in Shakespeare Alison Findlay

FORTHCOMING TITLES:
Shakespeare and National Identity Christopher Ivic
Shakespeare and Visual Culture Armelle Sabatier

Shakespeare's Plants and Gardens

A Dictionary

Vivian Thomas and Nicki Faircloth

Bloomsbury Arden Shakespeare
An imprint of Bloomsbury Publishing Plc

B L O O M S B U R Y
LONDON · OXFORD · NEW YORK · NEW DELHI · SYDNEY

Bloomsbury Arden Shakespeare
An imprint of Bloomsbury Publishing Plc

Imprint previously known as Arden Shakespeare

50 Bedford Square	1385 Broadway
London	New York
WC1B 3DP	NY 10018
UK	USA

www.bloomsbury.com

BLOOMSBURY, THE ARDEN SHAKESPEARE and the Diana logo are trademarks of Bloomsbury Publishing Plc

First published in 2014, this revised paperback edition published 2016
Reprinted 2016

British Library Cataloguing-in-Publication Data
A catalogue record for this book is available from the British Library.

ISBN:	HB:	978-1-4411-4370-9
	PB:	978-1-4742-7387-9
	E-Pub:	978-1-4725-5857-2
	Web pdf:	978-1-4725-5858-9

Library of Congress Cataloging-in-Publication Data
A catalog record for this book is available from the Library of Congress.

Typeset by Fakenham Prepress Solutions, Fakenham, Norfolk NR21 8NN
Printed and bound in Great Britain

the secrets of nature
Have not more gift in taciturnity.

Troilus and Cressida (4.2.72–3)

In nature's infinite book of secrecy
A little I can read.

Antony and Cleopatra (1.2.10–11)

Contents

Acknowledgements

We wish to acknowledge the considerable and varied help that we have received in the course of researching and writing this volume. Our greatest debt of gratitude is to Audrey Thomas whose critical acumen has been inestimable; she has also prepared the manuscript, steering it through all its stages. James Heath has been most generous both with his dissertation and his botanical expertise. John Sutton cast a practised eye over the botanical sections. Bill Bryson, Richard Mabey and Roy Vickery have all given botanical and plant-lore advice and information via email. Professor Joscelyn Godwin, the modern translator of *Hypnerotomachia Poliphili,* has been most helpful. Patrick Smith's critical scrutiny has done much to improve clarity and precision of expression. We are indebted to Len Rix for his perceptive observations. The guidance, patience and encouragement of the Series Editor, Professor Sandra Clark has been much appreciated. Margaret Bartley, who besides effecting a smooth transition from Continuum to Bloomsbury has given enormous support to this project, especially in the closing phase. Emily Hockley, as assistant editor, has been assiduous in finessing the completion of the original volume and in effecting its transition to the paperback edition.

The London Library has proved an excellent source of extensive and esoteric information. The access provided by the Wellcome Library to databases and electronic resources has been invaluable. IT support has been provided by Richard Spires and Will Thomas. Any remaining omissions and errors are our own.

Series Editor's Preface

The Arden Shakespeare Dictionaries aim to provide the student of Shakespeare with a series of authoritative guides to the principal subject areas covered by the plays and poems. They are produced by scholars who are experts both on Shakespeare and on the topic of the individual dictionary, based on the most recent scholarship, succinctly written and accessibly presented. They offer readers a self-contained body of information on the topic under discussion, its occurrence and significance in Shakespeare's works, and its contemporary meanings.

The topics are all vital ones for understanding the plays and poems; they have been selected for their importance in illuminating aspects of Shakespeare's writings where an informed understanding of the range of Shakespeare's usage, and of the contemporary literary, historical and cultural issues involved, will add to the reader's appreciation of his work. Because of the diversity of the topics covered in the series, individual dictionaries may vary in emphasis and approach, but the aim and basic format of the entries remain the same from volume to volume.

Sandra Clark
Birkbeck College
University of London

Conventions

Headwords and Entries

In order to facilitate cross-referencing, each headword appearing in any other entry is printed (once) in **bold**. This principle does not apply to quotations. We have adhered to the usual practice in these dictionaries of generally dividing entries into three sections. Section (A) provides definitions; (B) explores examples of the ways in which the headword is used; (C) signposts relevant contemporary commentary and offers guidance to further reading. Brief entries have been conflated but the same principle prevails. Although titles are not included in references, authors' names and the date of publication is generally followed by the relevant page number: Smith (1980: 23). Modern plant identification has been checked with Stace. The main sources for the iconography of flowers are Ferguson and Hall.

Entries: criteria

Entries include all named plants, specific or generic (rose, grain), individually or grouped (hedge, wood); aspects of plants (husk, leaf); features of nature that aid or imperil plant-growth or fertility (bees, frost); processes required for maintenance or propagation (pruning, grafting); implements used in gardening (rake, sickle); the medium for growth (soil, dung); features of gardens (arbours; walks); and activities enjoyed in gardens (hunting, music). Terms relating specifically to landscape, such as 'champaigns' (*LR* 1.1.64), signifying open countryside, are not included. Landscape is featured, however, because of the presence of plants such as reeds and flowers that grow outside the garden.

Quotations

All quotations are indicated by means of an abbreviated title with act and scene divisions (*PER* 2.1.45) unless the title of the play is evident from the discussion. All citations relate to *The Riverside Shakespeare,* second edition, ed. G. Blakemore Evans, 1973. As a general rule, if a quotation consists of four full lines or more it appears in block quotes. Editorial commentary is usually drawn from the Arden editions, and takes the following form with page numbers of footnotes in brackets: *TMP,* Arden 2 (241). *Riverside's* American spelling is adopted in all quotations. Early botanical titles are printed in their original form. Page references for Gerard's *Herbal* (1597) are from the revised edition of 1633.

Division of Labour

Thomas has written the Introduction, the (B) sections in all entries, the Shakespeare component of the undivided brief entries, contributed occasionally to (A) sections and more widely (mainly secondary references) to (C) sections. Faircloth has written most of (A) sections (all the botanical information) and a large part of (C) sections (especially primary references), and compiled the Works Index. The project was brought to fruition by Thomas.

Abbreviations

1. Shakespeare's Works

ADO	*Much Ado About Nothing*
ANT	*Antony and Cleopatra*
AWW	*All's Well That Ends Well*
AYL	*As You Like It*
COR	*Coriolanus*
CYM	*Cymbeline*
E3	*Edward III*
ERR	*The Comedy of Errors*
HAM	*Hamlet*
1H4	*The First Part of Henry IV*
2H4	*The Second Part of Henry IV*
H5	*Henry V*
1H6	*The First Part of Henry VI*
2H6	*The Second Part of Henry VI*
3H6	*The Third Part of Henry VI*
H8	*Henry VIII*
JC	*Julius Caesar*
JN	*King John*
LC	*A Lover's Complaint*
LLL	*Love's Labour's Lost*
LR	*King Lear*
LUC	*The Rape of Lucrece*
MAC	*Macbeth*
MM	*Measure for Measure*
MND	*A Midsummer Night's Dream*
MV	*The Merchant of Venice*
OTH	*Othello*
PER	*Pericles*
PHT	*The Phoenix and the Turtle*
PP	*The Passionate Pilgrim*
R2	*Richard II*
R3	*Richard III*
ROM	*Romeo and Juliet*
SHR	*The Taming of the Shrew*
SON	*Sonnets*

STM	*Sir Thomas More* (the parts ascribed to Shakespeare)
TGV	*The Two Gentlemen of Verona*
TIM	*Timon of Athens*
TIT	*Titus Andronicus*
TMP	*The Tempest*
TN	*Twelfth Night*
TNK	*The Two Noble Kinsmen*
TRO	*Troilus and Cressida*
VEN	*Venus and Adonis*
WIV	*The Merry Wives of Windsor*
WT	*The Winter's Tale*

2. Others

Arden 2	Arden Second Series
Arden 3	Arden Third Series
Cho.	Chorus
ed.	editor(s) or edited by
esp.	especially
F1	the 'First Folio' edition of Shakespeare's collected plays, 1623
fn	footnote
Ind.	Induction
LN	long note
OED	*Oxford English Dictionary*
Q	Quarto
SOD	*Shorter Oxford Dictionary*
SQ	*Shakespeare Quarterly*
trans.	translated by
vol.	volume

List of Headwords

aconitum

acorn, acorn-cups, full-acorn'd

Adonis flower, Adonis' garden

alley

almond, marchpane

aloe

angelica

apothecary

apple

apple-john

apricock

Arabian tree, date

arbour

ash

aspen

balm

balsamum, balsom

bank

bark

barley

barren

bay

bean

bee, drone, hive, honey

beech

berry

bilberry

birch

bitter sweeting

blackberry

bloom

blossom

blow, blown

bosky

bough

bower

bowls

box-tree, box

brake

bramble, brier

branch

brier, rose

brook

broom

Bucklersbury

bud

bulrush

bur

burnet

bush

buttons

cabbage

camomile

canker

caper

caraway

carduus benedictus, holy-thistle

carnation

carrot, caret

caterpillar

cedar

centaury

chaff

chase

cherry

chestnut

chimney-sweeper

cicely

circummur'd

clove

clover, honey-stalk
cockle
cod, codling
coloquintida
columbine
compost, composture
corn
costard
coulter
covert, coverture
cowslip
crab
crop
crow-flower
crown imperial
cuckoo-bud
cuckoo-flower
Cupid's flower
cyme
cypress

daffodil
daisy
damask
damson
darnel
dead men's fingers, see long purples
deracinate
dew
dewberry
Dian's bud
dibble
dig
distil
dock
dogberry
dove house, dove-cote
draff, see husk
dung, dunghill, ordure

ear, earing, unear'd
earth

ebony
Eden
eglantine
elder
elm
eringo
estate

femetary, femiter, fumitory
fennel
fern-seed
fertile
fescue
fetch
field
fig, fico, figo
filbert
flag
flax, flaxen
Flora
flower
flower-de-luce, fleur-de-lys
fluellen
forest, forester
forthright
fountain, fount
fragrant, see smell
frost
fruit, fruitful
furrow
furze, gorse, goss

gallery
garden
gardener
garden-house
garland
garlic
germain
gillyvor
ginger
glade

gooseberry
gorse see furze
gourd
graft, graff
grain
grape
grass
green
ground
grove
grow

hade
hardock
harebell
harrow
harvest
hawthorn
hay
hazel
heath
hebona
hedge
hemlock
hemp
hep
herb, herb-woman
hermit
hew
holly
honey-stalk, see clover
honeysuckle
hunt
husbandry
husk, draff
hyssop

imp
insane root
iris
ivy

kecksies
kernel
knot
knot-grass

labyrinth
lady-smock
land, landlord
larks'-heels
laund
laurel
lavender
lawn
leaf
leathercoat
leek
lemon
lettuce
lily
limb
limbeck
lime, line-grove
locust
lodge
long heath
long purples
lop
love-in-idleness

mace, see nutmeg
mallow
mandrake, mandragora
manor
manure
marigold
marjoram, marjorum
marrow
mary-buds
mast
mattock
maze
mead, meadow

medlar
mildew
mint
mistletoe
moss
mulberry
mushrumps, mushroom
music
musk-rose
mustard, Mustardseed
myrtle

narcissus
nature
nettle
nosegay, posy
nut, nut-hook
nutmeg, mace

oak
oat
olive
onion
orange
orchard
osier
oxlip

Padua
palm
pansy
park, dispark'd
parsley
parsnip
peach
pear
pease, peascod, Peaseblossom
peony, see pioned
pepper, peppercorn, peppered
perfume, see smell
pig-nut
pimpernel

pine
pink
pioned, peony
pippin
planched
plane
plant
plantain, plantan
plantation
pleached
plough, plow
plum, prune, pruin
pomander
pomegranate
pomewater
pond, pool
poperin, pop'rin
poppy
postern
potato
primrose
prune
pumpion, pumpkin

quince

radish, redish
raisin, flapdragon
rake
rank, see smell
reed
reek, see smell
rhubarb
ripe
root
rose
rosemary
rot
rue, herb of grace
rush
rye

saffron
salad, sallet
samphire
sap
sapling
savory
scent, see smell
scion
scythe
sedge
seed
shade
shrub
sickle
simple(s)
slip
smell, fragrant, perfume, rank, reek, scent
soil
sow
spade
speargrass
spray
squash
stalk
statue
stem
stock
stover
straw
strawberry
strew, strewments, strow
sycamore

tennis
thicket, coppice, copse

thistle
thorn
thyme, time, tine
till, tillage, tilth
toadstool
tree
trowel
turf
turnip
twig
twilled

vegetive
verdure
vine, vineyard
viola
violet

walk
wall
walnut
warden
weed
wheat, wheaten
wilderness
willow
wither
wood
woodbine
worm
wormwood
wreath

yew

Introduction

The purpose of this study is to specify and examine all the plants and aspects of gardens that appear in Shakespeare's work and to explore the ways in which they are deployed in both literal and figurative contexts. Headwords include every plant in the canon designated by its name whether specific or generic (oak, grain), or by its fruit (apricock, almond); or by the many aspects or appendages (leaves, seeds, chaff), groupings or configurations (brake, glade); conditions or circumstances relating to growth (bees, fertile, frost, barren); processes attaching to plants (lop, graft, plough, winnow); implements employed in cultivation or control (coulter, rake); features relating to gardens (arbours, fountains, chase) and their leisure activities (bowls, tennis, music). Plant habitat requires that landscape beyond the garden is represented: river banks abound in reeds and flowers; the sole mention of samphire brings an entire landscape into view (*LR* 4.6.11–24). Agriculture gains prominence through the plants that nurture human existence or conversely impede productive activity. This is vividly portrayed by Burgundy who catalogues both life's sustaining plants and the weeds the 'coulter' should 'deracinate' (*H5* 5.2.32–55); even in a scene of revelry Mark Antony provides an account of the fecundity of Egyptian agriculture (*ANT* 2.7.17–23).

The language of plants, a common currency of the rural world, was augmented in Shakespeare's London by 'green desire', a new-found passion for plants and gardens. The formation of a network of enthusiasts embracing a variety of professions and occupations, the development of markets in seeds and plants, the emergence and development of botanical gardens, the construction of hugely expensive private gardens and an outpouring of related literature all testify to the magnitude of intellectual and financial investment in botanical capital. In the words of Ryden (1978), 'plants were, to an extent unknown today, in the centre of everyone's life'.[1] Responding to this heightened sensibility the dramatist was able to absorb and express conceptually and figuratively the proliferation of ideas and discoveries in the botanical world, confident that the intended resonances would be acknowledged. The vigour of folklore and the variety of colourful local plant names offered a rich source of suggestion and imagery. Plants were freighted with meaning, spiritual, emotional and medicinal: they possessed a voice which could be simple and direct, or multivalent and perplexing. Here was a distinctive language at the disposal of the dramatist: conceptual and analytical; sensuous and symbolic. The volumes referred to here, and others included in the bibliography, enable the reader to bring into view a *physical* landscape that exerted a powerful influence on the landscape of the *mind*. In mapping the relationship between the exploration of the plant world and the simultaneous outpouring of publications Knight (2009) in her wide-ranging and insightful study notes, 'The second half of the sixteenth century corresponds with an

English botanical renaissance', adding 'it was during the 1590s that English botanical and horticultural literature was most prolific'.[2] Ryden's opinion is that Shakespeare's 'primary, printed sources of his botanical knowledge, including plant names, seem to have been Gerard's and Lyte's herbals. In all probability he was also familiar with the gardening literature of the day and with such works as Tusser's *Five Hundreth Pointes of Good Husbandrie*, Holland's translation of Pliny's *Naturalis historia* and Cooper's dictionary.'[3] What is certain is that in a London steeped in a vigorous plant culture, he would have imbibed botanical knowledge from diverse sources.

The emergence of a plant culture: Identification and nomenclature

Enthusiasm for exotic plants and a new-found dedication to celebrating and cataloguing domestic flora is illustrated by Harkness (2007), who delineates the intellectual and social world of a scientific community: 'Elizabethan Londoners were sophisticated and cosmopolitan, living cheek by jowl with immigrants from France, the Netherlands, Spain, Portugal and Italy. The city's residents included Africans, Ottoman Turks and Jewish *conversos*.' In this city of 'naturalists, medical practitioners, mathematicians, teachers, inventors and alchemists', the epicentre of the botanical project lay on Shakespeare's doorstep: 'behind garden walls, inside the apothecary shops, and within the well-appointed houses of the merchants lived an important community of naturalists. Lime Street was the English outpost of a Europe-wide network of students of nature – including plant hunters, gardeners, rock and fossil collectors, and scholars interested in animals and insects.'[4] At a time when enthusiasm for finding, propagating and naming plants was unprecedented, the plethora of local names, the absence of any agreed method of taxonomy, and the unsatisfactory descriptive and pictorial representations of plants, resulted in frustrating confusion. The problem was compounded by variant spellings and the multifarious indigenous names. Several plants mentioned in this study are denoted by two or more names: bay/laurel, blackberry/bramble, clover/honeystalks, cuckoo-flower/lady-smocks, Cupid's flower/ love-in-idleness/pansy, furze/gorse, flag/iris, honeysuckle/woodbine, long purples/ dead men's fingers, marigold/mary-bud, osier/willow/palm tree, rue/herb of grace, mandragora/mandrake, medlar/open-arse. Sometimes one name is applied to two different plants. 'Bramble' can signify a blackberry bush but can also intimate the wild rose; 'woodbine' can be 'honeysuckle' or a totally separate plant; the 'palm' can allude to the leaf of a willow or that of a palm tree. 'Gillyflower' presents particular difficulties because the name is used for different flowers: generally, however, it refers to 'carnation' or 'pink'. 'Lady-smock' and 'cuckoo-flower' are names that emerge in Elizabethan times. Many named plants have defied all efforts at identification. Several, such as 'long purples' or 'dead men's fingers', 'cuckoo-buds', 'Dian's bud', 'kecksy', 'hardock', 'hebona', names first recorded in Shakespeare, give rise to uncertainty and speculation, whereas there is general agreement about other first usages like 'eringo' (sea-holly), 'honeystalks' (clover) and 'mary-bud' (marigold). Some plants, 'Cupid's flower', 'Arabian tree', 'crow-flower' and 'cuckoo-bud', defy definitive identification; 'chimney sweeper' and 'centaury' pose the question as to whether *any* plant is alluded to. 'Pioned' is sometimes glossed as 'peony' – a well-known flower of the period described by Gerard – but a woven structure supporting the river bank is a more likely meaning. There is debate about which plant Iago refers to in *Othello* (1.3.322). Q1 has the herb 'thyme' whereas F1 has 'time', which is taken by some editors to signify 'tine' meaning 'tares', an invasive weed. Thomas (1983) provides an extensive list of plants that were known by several names, noting that 'No less than fifty different local names have been recorded for *Caltha palustris,* the marsh marigold.' Particularly germane to this study is his observation that 'At least ten different species were known in one place or another as cuckoo flower; over twenty were bachelor's buttons or dead man's fingers.'[5] Despite their best endeavours, the plantsmen of the early modern period failed to achieve a satisfactory system of identification and classification.[6]

For the modern editor, problems of identification are particularly frustrating when symbolism is implicated. Notable examples are Ophelia's carefully allocated flowers and herbs, the plants included in Gertrude's narration of Ophelia's drowning and Lear's floral crown. Though plant identification is not always possible, each entry lays open the various interpretations and the associated meanings of the plants. Some plant names are used to designate characters (Viola, Fluellen, Cicely, Pimpernel, Dogberry, Costard); the case of Angelica is unique – being uncertain as to whether the appellation refers to the culinary herb or to a person. The quince, intrinsic to marriage feasts, is employed for culinary purposes in *Romeo and Juliet* (4.4.2); in *A Midsummer Night's Dream* the fruit is celebrated in the name of Peter Quince who directs the mechanicals in their marriage entertainment. Cordelia's instruction 'a century send forth' (*LR* 4.4.6) probably refers to military personnel but *centaury* is also a flower and, as suggested in Arden 3 (322), may be an enigmatic conflation. 'Costard', a variety of apple, is deployed only as a character's name or as a word meaning 'head'. There is a discrepancy, therefore, between the number of *named* plants (almost 200 individual names plus c. 10 generic names) and the number of plants that are *present* in Shakespeare's work. Whilst *Edward III* does not figure in the *Harvard Concordance*, examples from that play have been included in this study in the belief that this is, indeed, a Shakespeare play. This pragmatic approach is also taken for *Henry VIII* and *The Two Noble Kinsmen* where Fletcher has long been recognized as co-author. Likewise, the scene in *Sir Thomas More* generally ascribed to Shakespeare is also drawn on. Some passages contain numerous plants and consequently appear in several entries: Burgundy's description of the French landscape (*H5* 5.2.23–67); the celebrated garden scene in *Richard II* (3.4.29–107); Ophelia's gifts of flowers and herbs (*HAM* 4.5.175–86) and Gertrude's description of her drowning (5.1.166–83); Perdita as the incarnation of Flora (*WT* 4.4.116–29) and her horticultural disputation with Polixenes (4.4.73–108); Iago's moralizing analogy in which he proposes 'Our bodies are gardens' (*OTH* 1.3.320–33); Lear's crown vividly realized by

Cordelia (*LR* 4.4.1–10); Oberon's bank (*MND* 2.1.249–52); and perhaps surprisingly, the Wooer's description of the desolate and frantic Jailer's Daughter wandering around the margins of a lake (*TNK* 4.1.52–93). Many of the plants mentioned in these speeches are clearly symbolic – though interpretation is often elusive.

'What's in a name?': Imagery and poetic associations

Flowers are especially important not only because of their symbolic significance, but also for the colour and poetic potential carried in their names – often heightened by the epithets Shakespeare attaches to them: 'pale primroses', 'bold oxlips', 'freckled cowslip', 'azur'd harebell', 'daisies pied'. The gillyflower is 'streaked', violets are 'dim' or 'blue veined', the rose is 'crimson', 'vermillion', 'blushing', 'milk-white', 'fragrant'. The visual and atmospheric frequently cohere: 'daffodils/That come before the swallow dares, and take/The winds of March with beauty' (*WT* 4.4.118–20). The water iris, subject to the sway of the current, is designated 'the vagabond flag' (*ANT* 1.4.45). Often the focus is on the fruit of a plant: aloe, almond, blackberry, chestnut, apple, dewberry, damson, fig, gooseberry, grape, hazel, locust, mulberry, pear (popperin, warden), plum, quince, strawberry. Here again epithets can be significant: the 'rubied cherry' and 'clust'ring filberts' catch both the eye and the ear. The peach is mentioned only for its colour. Trees both native and exotic abound: apricot, Arabian tree (date/palm), ash, aspen, balsamum, bay, beech, cedar, cypress, ebony, elder, elm, holly, myrtle, oak, olive, palm, pine, plane, pomegranate, sycamore, willow. References to groupings or to configurations of trees and shrubs are numerous: arbour, coverture, glade, grove, laund, lime-grove, orchard, thicket, wood, forest. Adjuncts or elements of plants are numerous: bark, branch, blossom, leaf, grain. Weeds exert strong symbolic pressure: 'hateful docks', 'rough thistles' and 'rank femetary'.[7] A plant is sometimes mentioned for just one aspect: ginger is specified as a culinary ingredient; ebony is celebrated for its black, lustrous quality. Blackberries and gooseberries have mundane associations because their easy availability represented cheapness or worthlessness. Some plants have generally accepted symbolic significance: the willow is the emblem of forsaken love; the lily represents purity; both cypress and yew are linked to sadness, death and graveyards; the sycamore signifies sadness or melancholy; the palm is a symbol of victory but also serves to validate a pilgrimage; the oaken garland commemorates triumph; rosemary is for remembrance. On occasion contrasting, even antithetical meanings are ascribed to some plants. The strawberry can represent abundance, chastity, fertility, humility, modesty, purity and paradise but can also symbolize sensuality and eroticism. Weeds, besides implying neglect, were imaged as emblematic of the fallen world. Nevertheless, they were valued for their medicinal properties.

In her seminal study devoted to Shakespeare's imagery, Spurgeon (1935) observed, 'With Shakespeare, nature images are always the most frequent, especially those relating to growing things in a garden or orchard: trees, plants, flowers and fruits.'[8] The dramatist uses the natural world as analogy, simile, metaphor, and as a contributor to other rhetorical devices. Chastising Wolsey for burdening the populace with excessive taxation, Henry VIII delivers his economic analysis by way of an arboreal analogy: 'why, we take/From every tree, lop, bark and part o'th'timber,/And though we leave it with a root, thus hack'd,/The air will drink the sap' (*H8* 1.2.95–8). Acknowledging his irrevocable loss of power, Cardinal Wolsey expresses his predicament in terms of the growth, blossoming and blighting of plants:

> This is the state of man: to-day he puts forth
> The tender leaves of hopes, to-morrow blossoms,
> And bears his blushing honors thick upon him;
> The third day comes a frost, a killing frost,
> And when he thinks, good easy man, full surely
> His greatness is a-ripening, nips his root,
> And then he falls as I do.
>
> *(3.2.352–8)*

Audley presents the whole process of life in similar terms: 'First bud we, then we blow, and after seed,/Then presently then we fall' (*E3* 4.4.138–9). Plants and their immediate environment are frequently a source of delicate imagery: Antony's makeshift ambassador likens himself to 'the morn-dew on the myrtle leaf' (*ANT* 3.12.9); Lavinia's 'lily hands/Tremble like aspen leaves upon a lute' (*TIT* 2.4.44–5); Aufidius claims Coriolanus 'watered his new plants with dews of flattery' (*COR* 5.6.22); Imogen's birthmark is 'cinque spotted, like the crimson drops/I'th'bottom of a cowslip' (*CYM* 2.2.38–9); later, as the seemingly dead Fidele, Imogen is promised, 'Thou shalt not lack/The flower that's like thy face, pale primrose, nor/The azur'd harebell, like thy veins; no nor/The leaf of eglantine, whom not to slander/Outsweet'ned not thy breath' (4.2.220–4). The tradition of the cherry symbolizing closeness or twinning, usually feminine, is best captured in *A Midsummer Night's Dream* where 'two in oneness' is the conceptual nucleus of the play: 'a double cherry, seeming parted,/But yet a union in partition' (3.2.209–10). Vigour and vitality are also significant features in both literal and figurative representations of plants: the Athenian wood is replete with flora – plants collude like those described by Oberon: 'over-canopied with luscious woodbine,/With sweet musk-roses and with eglantine' (2.1.251–2); Hamlet reviling the burgeoning corruption of the world reflects, ''tis an unweeded garden/That grows to seed, things rank and gross in nature/Possess it merely' (*HAM* 1.2.135–7). The dramatist generates pressure not only through imagery but also by his orchestration of sound values and the associated potential of plants. Exploiting the assonance and alliteration of two soporifics, Iago savours Othello's anguish: 'Not poppy nor mandragora,/Nor all the drowsy syrups of the world/Shall ever medicine thee to that sweet sleep/Which thou ow'dst yesterday' (*OTH* 3.3.330–3). Iago also extracts maximum effect from his deployment of richly resonant sounds when assuring Roderigo that Othello's passion for Desdemona will be short-lived: 'The food that to him now is as luscious as locusts shall be to him shortly as a acerb as coloquintida' (1.3.347–9). Again luxuriating in assonance, Iago's contrast between the sweet locust fruit of the Cyprian carob tree and the equally exotic 'bitter apple' creates plausibility through verbal alchemy.

Medicines and poisons

Increasing plant availability stimulated scientific experimentation in both curative medicine and poisons by physicians, apothecaries and those simply curious for knowledge. London's Bucklersbury, a thriving market-place for herbs (alluded to by Falstaff (*WIV* 3.3.72)), was indicative of demand for and a ready supply of these plants for culinary, aromatic and medicinal uses. Returning to Stratford-upon-Avon Shakespeare would have found himself in the herb garden of his son-in-law, Dr. John Hall, who perhaps unusually, combined the functions of physician and apothecary. A division of labour is apparent in *Pericles* where the skilful physician Cerimon hands a prescription to a servant, 'Give this to the apothecary/And tell me how it works' (3.2.9–10). Here is also an indication of empiricism central to the scientific project. Doctors and apothecaries, like the magus Prospero, thirst to unravel 'the secrets of nature' – a term current in the period and employed metaphorically by the dramatist in *Troilus and Cressida* (4.2.72). Central to this engagement with 'great creating Nature' (*WT* 4.4.88) is the world of plants. The Friar in *Romeo and Juliet,* fully aware of the duality possessed by plants integral to pharmacopoeia, distinguishes between 'baleful weeds and precious-juiced flowers', and acknowledges that within a single flower, 'Poison hath residence and medicine power' (2.3.8–24). He is a hands-on practitioner rising early to gather herbs at the optimum time. The drug he provides to produce Juliet's state of death-like unconsciousness is described in great detail (4.1.93–106). The impoverished apothecary who provides Romeo with poison is subject to strict legal constraints (5.1.66–7). Laertes acquires his deadly poison from an unlicensed 'mountebank' (*HAM* 4.7.141). Appreciated for his knowledge of plants by the mendacious Queen, the doctor in *Cymbeline* is affronted by her proclivity for practising with poisons (1.5.12–44). Pollard (2005) explores the shared anxiety attaching to drugs and to the theatre. Both could be represented as 'curative, soporific, poisonous, narcotic, addictive, aphrodisiac, soothing, intoxicating'. Highlighting the intricate role of drugs in the plays – poisons and cures, both literal and metaphoric, permeate the drama of the period – she points out, 'in contrast to most contemporary portrayals of doctors as sinister and malicious, Shakespeare's doctors tend to be competent and kindly and his observations about current medical treatments for the most part very accurate'.[9]

Perdita and the secrets of nature

The most significant botanical exchange in Shakespeare foregrounds the relationship between art and nature.[10] Perdita's reluctance to grow 'carnations and streak'd gillyvors/ (Which some call Nature's bastards)' arises from her understanding that 'There is an art which in their piedness shares/With great creating Nature'. Unconvinced by Polixenes' assurance that techniques used to enhance plant variety are rational she links such artifice with the impropriety of face painting (4.4.79–103). As Bushnell points out, 'The gillyflower, or July-flower, an umbrella (and confusing) category of flowers that often embraced pinks, carnations and stock, came to obsess many gardeners from the sixteenth century to the end of the seventeenth century', so that, 'Even though they did not understand what they were doing, like the Dutch breeders of tulips responding to tulipmania, growers of gillyflowers tried every imaginable technique to make new varieties.'[11] Polixenes was over-estimating the prevailing state of horticultural knowledge or 'art'.[12] Where diversity occurred it owed nothing to these endeavours but was the result of Nature's promiscuity – though in the case of the tulip a virus was responsible. The divergent views of Polixenes and Perdita reverberated throughout the seventeenth century and became the subject of theological unease for another two centuries. Andrew Marvell's poem 'The Mower, Against Gardens' is a severe indictment of human arrogance and duplicity: 'The pink grew then as double as his mind'. Mankind contaminates nature: simplicity becomes meretriciousness; purity, promiscuity: 'The flowers themselves were taught to paint./The tulip white did for complexion seek,/And learned to interline its cheek'.[13] Perdita is clearly visible in Marvell's mirror.

Botanical perspectives: Classicism to modernism

The earliest building block in what was to become known as the discipline of botany was Theophrastus' *Enquiry into Plants* c. 300 B.C. His work survives in two collected volumes *Historia plantarum* and the *De causis plantarum*. Pliny plundered his work to produce the *Historia naturalis* in 77 A.D. Together with *De materia medica* by the contemporaneous Greek physician Dioscorides they were the bedrock for botanical studies into the sixteenth century. Pavord, in *The Naming of Names: The Search for Order in the World of Plants* (2005), traces the story of botanical research from ancient to modern times and provides a chronological table of the important contributions and events, together with brief biographies of the major players. Although the medieval period is sometimes dismissed as contributing little to botanical knowledge, documentary and pictorial representations reveal a deep-seated feeling for plants and gardens with aesthetic appreciation married to a utilitarian approach. These are featured beautifully and conveniently by Landsberg in *The Medieval Garden*

(1996); in Harvey's seminal study, *Medieval Gardens* (1981), and in his essays in the Garden History Society's journal which are characterized by vivid description and critical acuity. Interesting perspectives are provided by Pearsall and Salter, *Landscapes and Seasons of the Medieval World* (1973), Clarke's *Literary Landscapes and the Idea of England: 700–1400* (2006) and McLeod's *In a Unicorn's Garden* (2008). The Reformation, with the dissolution of the monasteries and redistribution of land, changed the physical and intellectual landscape. Recent studies that provide a detailed account of the evolution of horticultural discoveries, practices and publications include Knight, *Of Books and Botany in Early Modern England: Sixteenth Century Plants and Print Culture* (2009), and Willes, *The Making of the English Gardener: Plants, Books and Inspiration 1560–1660* (2011). Harkness, *The Jewel House: Elizabethan London and the Scientific Revolution* (2007) gives a wider scientific context to horticultural developments. A volume occupying an important place in the discourse relating to 'green Shakespeare' is Bruckner and Brayton, eds, *Ecocritical Shakespeare* (2010). This collection of insightful essays includes chapters on Ophelia and Perdita and their complex relationship with plants. Charting the changing perspectives between 1500–1800, Thomas' influential study *Man and the Natural World* (1983) engages with natural history, botany, theology, economics, politics and aesthetics. The physical, social and aesthetic pathways that animated the world of horticulture are articulated with insight and élan in all these studies. Young, *The Heart's Forest: A Study of Shakespeare's Pastoral Plays* (1972), is admirable in its exploration of Shakespeare's engagement with the world of pastoral. Hattaway's *Renaissance and Reformations* (2005), Pettegree's *Europe in the Sixteenth Century* (2002), Brotton's *The Renaissance Bazaar* (2002) and Jardine's *Worldly Goods* (1996) provide a physical, cultural, economic, religious and political mapping of the early modern period. Two volumes which provide valuable documentary material are Hadfield, *The English Renaissance 1500–1620* (2001) and Pallister, *The Age of Elizabeth* (1992). Fitzpatrick's *Shakespeare and the Language of Food* (2011) and Iyengar, *Shakespeare's Medical Language* (2011), both in this series of dictionaries, complement entries in this volume.

The herbal and garden manuals

Continental Europe was the crucible of botanical enquiry during the first half of the sixteenth century.[14] The dominant botanical text was the herbal. First and foremost it was a *medical* bible defined as 'an encyclopaedia, often richly illustrated, and consisting primarily of prose describing the appearance, habitat, known names, and purported "virtues" or curative powers of plants'.[15] The seminal studies in the field of the illustrated herbal were Brunfels' *Herbarum vivae eicones* (1530) celebrated for its 'living images of plants' by Weiditz (a pupil of Dürer), and Fuchs' *De historia stirpium* (1542). Brunfels and Fuchs produced their important books in Germany, 'but almost all the other important discoveries and innovations happened in Italy'.[16] The Counter-Reformation was instrumental in moving the axis of botanical enquiry from Italy to Northern Europe. The dominant figures in the latter part of the sixteenth century were from the Low Countries: Rembert Dodoens, Clusius or Charles de L'Ecluse, and Matthias de L'Obel. Their publisher in Antwerp was the Flemish printer Christophe Plantin who incorporated 2,173 illustrations in the compendium *Icones stirpium seu plantarum tam exoticarum* of 1591. L'Obel and Pena, refugees from religious persecution, published their register of plants *Stirpium adversaria nova* (1571) in London. The first book in English devoted to herbs was a small quarto printed by Richard Banckes in 1525 (later known as *Banckes' Herbal*). Publishing scientific works in the vernacular continued with the first *illustrated* herbal in English: *The Greate Herball* (1526).

By happy coincidence England's first plant book of genuine originality, the final part of Turner's *A new herball* (1564), was published in the year of Shakespeare's birth. William Turner (c. 1508–68) is regarded as the father of English botany. By the age of thirty he had published his glossary of plant names, *Libellus de re herbaria novus* (1538) listing 144 plants and providing their names in Latin, Greek and English. In *The Names of Herbes* (1548) he records almost 400 plants with German and French names accompanying English and Latin designations. This herbal was the first to provide detailed descriptions of British native flora, locating each plant in its natural habitat. His commitment to empiricism and field-work, both in England and the Continent, is reflected in his international correspondence and engagement in an exchange network of seeds and plant samples. The leading botanical figures of the day – mainly of Continental origin – shared Turner's belief in disseminating medical and theological knowledge by publishing in the vernacular. His 1564 herbal registered another important change of direction when he transcended his classical progenitors by analysis of species not mentioned by them. This physician, theologian, botanist and prolific author, who travelled widely in Italy, France and Germany, also cultivated gardens in England. He was closely associated with Syon House which was, in 1547, an outstanding centre of horticultural developments. Turner may have inspired the young William Cecil who became an avid collector of rare species and creator of spectacular gardens.

Gerard's *Herbal* of 1597 – dedicated to William Cecil, Lord Burghley – commandeered the endeavours of a generation of botanical writers referencing around 2,000 plants. This massive horticultural tome was a pictorial and literary cornucopia – 'a celebration of plants, their variety and beauty'.[17] It embodies the spirit of the age. Gerard, who did not benefit from a university education or from the extensive travels of his fellow plantsmen, produced a massively popular herbal which represents a cultural and publishing landmark. He had a wide circle of influential friends and associates including the generous Flemish scholars who had settled in London. Leaning heavily on the scholarship of others, the herbal represented the culmination of English absorption of plant culture. From 1577 Gerard was superintendant of Burghley's gardens in

London and Theobalds; he became curator of the physic garden of the College of Physicians at its inception in 1586, continuing in this position until 1603. A year later he became surgeon and herbalist to James I. His fame, however, rests on his herbal. This vast volume, which celebrates many new and spectacular arrivals, is best described as a gallimaufry, with careful observation sitting alongside fanciful accounts by poets, classical authorities, contemporary botanical scholars and folklore.[18] Its popularity may well be ascribed as much to its colourful observations as to its undoubted erudition. Even Gerard's greatest detractors – he has been accused of plagiarism and egregious errors – acknowledge his facility with language. Knight (2009) provides a vigorous and persuasive defence which incorporates a fascinating critique of this work in both botanical and literary terms. She notes that 'Gerard creates a sense of his text as provisional, one draft in an ongoing and broadly anthological process'.[19] Fortuitously, his timing was perfect. The book was 'printed in English, in a fine, light type, less daunting on the page than the heavy, Germanic black letter type that had been the norm in Turner's day'.[20] Marketing was also facilitated by his wide circle of influential contacts. When Thomas Johnson published a revision of Gerard's herbal in 1633 he added 800 plants to the original 2,000. Another figure of distinction, the apothecary John Parkinson, meticulous in his pursuit and dissemination of horticultural knowledge, commenced his gardening activities at Cripplegate in 1589. He produced a volume of over 600 pages, *Paradisi in sole paradisus terrestris* (1629). His *magnum opus,* the monumental *Theatrum botanicum* (1640) consisting of 1,775 pages, contained descriptions of around 3,800 plants, and was the culmination of the project that had illuminated Shakespeare's cultural world.

A fascinating aspect of the physical and linguistic engagement with plants and gardens was the creation of a common cultural capital: knowledge of private collections was rendered public by means of catalogues, herbals and manuals – crucially in the vulgar tongue. Gerard's catalogue of plants grown in his Holborn garden (1596) – the first catalogue printed in English – was a notable example. Whilst herbals and expensive gardening books catered to a leisure class there was also a ready market for publications aimed at more fundamental needs. The earliest gardening manual, published by Wynkyn de Worde c. 1520, was the anonymous *The crafte of graffynge and plantynge of trees.* However, the first major figure to enter this field was Thomas Hill, whose *A most briefe and pleasaunte treatise, teachying how to dresse, sowe and set a garden* (1558) was followed a decade later by *The Proffitable Arte of Gardening.* His final volume, *The Gardeners Labyrinth* (1577) was published posthumously under the pseudonym Didymus Mountain. It was frequently reprinted. 1578 witnessed Lyte's commercially successful translation of Dodoens' *A Niewe Herball* via the French intermediary (Clusius). A translation of a volume by Estienne and Liebault, *La Maison Rustique,* appeared in 1600. Most popular of all was Thomas Tusser's *A Hundreth pointes of Good Husbandrie,* first published in 1557. It became *Five Hundreth pointes* by 1573. Mascall's successful manual appeared in 1569. Hugh Platt, who was an advocate of root vegetables, published *Sundrie new and Artificiall Remedies against Famine* (1596) in response to bad harvests which began in 1595. Richard Gardiner's *Instructions for manuring, sowing, and planting of Kitchin Gardens* (1599) was also a response to the needs of the poor. Gervase Markham published the first part of his *English Husbandman* in 1613. The influx of Dutch and Flemish gardeners to East Anglia and Kent in the 1570s gave an impetus to horticulture. By 1600 there were Dutch gardeners in Surrey and by 1650 London was ringed by market gardens and orchards. The importance of orchards was signalled by the success of William Lawson's *New Orchard and Garden* (1618). Reginald Scot's *A perfite platforme of a hoppe garden* (1574) reflected the new-found popularity of hops, again indebted to the influence of these immigrants. James I granted the first royal charter to gardeners and fruiterers in 1605.

Investment in botanical capital

While plants have inevitably played a practical and symbolic role in all cultures, Shakespeare's England experienced a new-found passion for plants and gardens. There was a developing curiosity, an urgent desire to probe 'the secrets of nature'. Individuals and groups established networks to create order in the plant kingdom – precise identification, accurate pictorial representation and meaningful nomenclature. For the status-conscious courtiers of the day, gardens were a marker of wealth, power and sophistication; for the technical experts, plantsmen and gardeners who enabled them to realize their dreams, profit and delight went hand-in-hand; writers and publishers of the widely read herbals, manuals, catalogues and pamphlets achieved financial rewards and fame – which was both a stimulant to and a beneficiary of improved literacy. Here was a community embracing Continental ideas for the creation of gardens and absorbing new plants sourced from places as far away as Turkey and the New World. Plant hunters, researchers, apothecaries, herb-women, physicians and the grandees were caught up in a cooperative enterprise. Plants and gardens captured the imagination as never before. The passion for exotics was stimulated by the French nurseryman and entre-preneur Pierre Belon. The account of his sojourn in the Levant between 1546 and 1548 disseminated knowledge of the botanical treasures to be found in the East. Introduced from Turkey in the 1570s, the most recently arrived exotic mentioned in Shakespeare is the 'crown imperial' (*WT* 4.4.126). One of the first to report on the botanical riches of the Americas was the Spaniard Monardes (1569) – a work translated into English by John Frampton as *Joyfull newes out of the new-found worlde* (1577). In the network of distribution and exchange, cross-fertilization between agents can be illustrated by two examples: de Busbecq, instrumental in introducing the first wave of exotic plants into Western Europe, was an ambassador; Hugh Morgan was in touch with fellow apoth-ecaries on the Continent, but it was through intimacy with merchants and sea captains that he gained expert knowledge of imported plants. A cargo arriving in 1568 included caraway, cucumber, hemp, oranges, lemons, almonds, nutmeg and aniseed.[21]

The garden as theatrical space

The culture of plants and gardens expressed in embroidery, wall paintings, architecture and heraldic devices linked disparate aspects of Shakespeare's world. The stories of Shakespeare's favourite poet Ovid, animated the gardens and their architecture as much as they exerted their influence on page and stage. As Samson (2012) observes, 'With the concept of the garden as a work of art came iconography, gardens that told a story through their intertwining of motifs, themes, and complex mythological schema.'[22] Allied to delight in plants, patterning and embellishing gardens replete with architectural wonders, was a deep-seated empiricism, impatient to understand and to fashion the world of plants. The garden represented the ultimate aesthetic experience, a marriage between the sensory and the symbolic. Encompassing the idea of paradise intrinsic to Christianity, Islam and their classical counterpart Elysium, the garden had become a place for solace, contemplation, exercise, play and display. Greenery evoked ideas of purity and passion: a sanctified space for expression, spiritual and erotic. Compartments consisting of plants, sculpture, fountains and sundials reflected an ordered cosmos while at the same time celebrating human ingenuity. This Janus-like creation was consistently dualistic. Symbolic representation, articulated in sculptures of marble or topiary, was expressed through mythology. Ovid's tales, the chief inspiration, metamorphosed into dramatic images. In the world of plants and gardens novelty had never been more esteemed or sought after, causing some to echo the disguised Duke in *Measure for Measure,* 'Novelty is only in request' (3.2.224).[23] Along with this aesthetic craving for variety and the exotic there was a quasi-religious veneration for the properties of plants, their healing powers and their ability to speak symbolically. The comingling of the literary and botanical is characteristic of this period, but there is one book which occupies a peculiar position owing to its sensuous engagement with plants, gardens, architecture and eroticism. Francesco Colonna's *Hypnerotomachia Poliphili* (1499), part of which was translated into English by Robert Dallington as *The Strife of Love in a Dream* in 1592, succeeds in creating gardens where nature is luxuriant, opulent and resplendent but also restrained. Moreover, the harmonious collaboration of plants with marble sculptures ornamented with precious stones fashioned by master craftsmen is more than earthly, yet humanity is present in this highly eroticized theatre of dreams. A phantasmagoria, free from blemish, every leaf and bloom so perfectly formed and articulated that the most passionate and skilled plant lover could only marvel at such variety and perfection, this book captivates rather than instructs, but its popularity conveys the imaginative hold plants and gardens exerted on those seeking to create their own paradisal domains.[24]

Although Shakespeare does not identify the trophy garden *per se,* most of the elements – orchards, arbours, parks, wilderness, mazes, walks, fountains and galleries – are drawn on and subtly integrated into settings, action and discourse. 'Forthright', meaning a straight path, is mentioned twice (*TMP* 3.3.3; *TRO* 3.3.158), though it probably had little currency outside the trophy garden. A hunting ground of an estate is called a 'wilderness'. It figures prominently but enigmatically in *Titus Andronicus* (2.2; 2.3): inviting and treacherous. The dramatist, however, reserves the *term* 'wilderness' for remote and desolate geographical places. *Much Ado about Nothing* abounds in garden spaces – arbours, alleys and orchards – providing intimate areas which accommodate both playful and cynical deceptions, and musical entertainment. Here nature is fashioned to suit multifarious pleasures and activities. The green world of this play is as sophisticated as its social universe. In Belmont, a place of opulence, largesse and urbanity, Shakespeare creates a garden scene of intimacy, simplicity and lyricism that is generative: multiple narratives and music combine to reach out into history and the cosmos (*MV*.5.1.1–120). Shallow's orchard is a little realm of bucolic business and pleasure. The texture of the scenes is informed by the surroundings: discursive conversations draw on the mundane activities that register the heartbeat of this community (*2H4* 3.2; 5.1; 5.3). In *Henry VI, Part 2* Alexander Iden's walled garden is a retreat from the world: 'Lord, who would live turmoiled in the court/And may enjoy such quiet walks as these?/This small inheritance my father left me/Contenteth me, and worth a monarchy' (4.10.16–19). As he lies dying on the battlefield Warwick provides an inventory of the property that he must now relinquish: 'My parks, my walks, my manors that I had,/Even now forsake me; and of all my lands/Is nothing left me but my body's length' (*3H6* 5.2.24–6). The conflation of identity with possession is present, too, in Bolingbroke's indignant protestation: 'you have fed upon my signories,/Dispark'd my parks and fell'd my forest woods,/From my own windows torn my household coat,/Ras'd out my imprese' (*R2* 3.1.22–5). The single example of transference of gardens from the status of private property to a public leisure space occurs in *Julius Caesar*. Revealing the contents of Caesar's will, Antony pays tribute to his friend's munificence: 'Moreover, he hath left you all his walks,/His private arbors and new-planted orchards,/On this side Tiber; he hath left them you/And to your heirs forever – common pleasures,/To walk abroad and recreate yourselves' (3.2.247–51).

Recreating Eden and the Golden World: The emergence of the great gardens

Outstanding in their exploration of the diverse facets of this transformative period are Bushnell, *Green Desire: Imagining Early Modern English Gardens* (2003), Knight, *Of Books and Botany in Early Modern England: Sixteenth-Century Plants and Print Culture* (2009), Tigner, *Literature and the Renaissance Garden from Elizabeth I to Charles II: England's Paradise* (2012) and Samson, ed., *Locus Amoenus: Gardens and Horticulture in the Renaissance* (2012). Paula Henderson's impressive volume, *The Tudor House and Garden* (2005) provides descriptive and visual representations of the great gardens and houses of this period with the addition of a Gazetteer of gardens and ancillary buildings. The development of magnificent gardens, although drawing inspiration from their royal precursors were strongly influenced by Italian and French models. Unlike its Continental counterparts, sixteenth-century England lacked the valuable support of university departments and botanical gardens devoted to the study of plants (the first established in Europe were those of Pisa (1544) and Padua (1545); their prestigious counterpart at Leiden was founded in 1592). The Oxford Botanical Garden was not instituted until 1621though there were several private collections of rare and unusual plants. The Duke of Somerset's Syon House in London was a hub of horticultural activity. Impressive, too, was Lord Zouche's London garden which was overseen by Lobelius.

The progenitors of the Elizabethan gardens were the palaces of the first Tudor kings. As Henderson observes 'Renaissance classicism had been introduced in ornament and sculpture early in the Tudor period by Italian artists working at court'. Henry VII's interest in gardens (his rebuilt Richmond Palace possessed the first of England's extensive formal gardens) was inherited by his son, Henry VIII. [25] With almost reckless abandon he acquired and developed almost 60 houses and gardens including Nonsuch, Greenwich, Richmond Palace and Hampton Court (commandeered from Cardinal Wolsey in 1528). Wolsey's York House with its fine gardens was also confiscated by the monarch who, as we are reminded in Shakespeare's *Henry VIII* (4.1.95–7), changed its name to Whitehall. Thomas More had a splendid garden on the bank of the Thames at Chelsea. It was visited but not appropriated by the monarch. The Duke of Buckingham began, but never completed, an elaborate garden at Thornbury Castle in Gloucestershire.

The royal gardens set the standard for those created by Elizabeth's courtiers, some of whom might be described as 'the violets now/That strew the green lap of the new-come spring' (*R2* 5.2.46–7). Inspired by French and Italian models, they exchanged plants and ideas when engaging in the design and development of their estates. Their passion led them to the investment of huge financial and human resources, sometimes aimed to impress and to secure favour. Robert Dudley, later Lord Leicester, who received Kenilworth Castle as a gift from the Queen, created a garden integrated with its surrounding landscape. His prodigious achievements were demonstrated during the famous festivities in 1575. Fellow enthusiast and rival, William Cecil, later Lord Burghley, starting in the 1560s, created magnificent gardens at Burghley House in Northamptonshire, at his house on the Strand, and at Theobalds in Hertfordshire, where the Queen, who sojourned there on several occasions, was the most famous of many visitors. John Gerard was the supervisor of plants there from the 1570s. On Cecil's death in 1598 the property passed to his son Robert who was later obliged by James I to exchange it for Hatfield House. His other son, Thomas, created a spectacular garden at Wimbledon House modelled on the Italian Renaissance gardens. Elizabeth visited at least five times between 1592 and 1602. These interconnections were braided together by the familial, social and professional associations of the major participants. The vigour of this network, abetted by foreign travel and by international ties, both formal and informal, ensured that plants and ideas were easily assimilated. Just as

Marlowe's eponymous Jew of Malta relishes being at the centre of a global trading and financial nexus (1.1.1–48), these horticulturalists and makers of gardens revelled in the commerce of a botanical universe.

The rebuilding of Sir Christopher Hatton's hereditary home, Holdenby in Northamptonshire, begun in 1578 was 'dominated by great windows that glittered in the sun' and 'overlooked an equally dramatic garden'. It left him bankrupt. Bess of Hardwick's spectacular developments in Derbyshire at Chatsworth House, Hardwick Old Hall and Hardwick New Hall – 'a building more glass than wall', affording panoramic views of the garden – took place between the 1560s and 1590s.[26] Thomas Tresham, a familiar of Cecil and Hatton, refashioned the family estate at Rushton Hall. He also commenced a project at Lyveden in 1594. The creation of Lyveden New Bield included what was probably the most famous orchard in England. Tresham did not survive to complete his vision. Francis Bacon, William Cecil's nephew, eminent lawyer and natural philosopher, purchased the lease for Twickenham Park in1595 and made a fine garden there. In 1597 he planted walks at Gray's Inn. Acquiring Gorhambury from his mother he again indulged his passion for creating elaborate gardens. His essay, 'Of Gardens', published in 1625, famously extolled the garden as 'the purest of human pleasures'.[27] By 1600 the gardens at Nonsuch, established by Henry VIII, were deemed 'the finest in the whole of England'. They had been developed first by the twelfth Earl of Arundel (starting in 1556) and then by his son-in-law John, Lord Lumley, who created an allegorical garden between 1580 and 1609. His 'Grove of Diana' drew on Ovid's *Metamorphoses*.[28] Royal engagement was rekindled with the ascent of James I in 1603. The outstanding gardens at this time 'are best represented by those of Robert Cecil' who 'created or altered a number of gardens, at Pymmes, Theobalds, Cranborne, Hatfield and London'.[29] James indulged his consort, Anne of Denmark, with her elaborate scheme at Somerset House in 1606 (renamed Denmark House). The heir apparent, Henry Stuart (1594–1612), was endowed with a prodigious talent for gardens and architecture. His premature death entailed a serious cultural loss, not only for what he might have achieved as a garden-maker. The reign of his brother, Charles I, culminated in the civil war which effectively brought to an end this age of great gardens.

Thomas Tresham's library of 2,600 volumes containing more than 20 books by the leading Continental figures in architecture and design, together with the 200 surviving books from Sir Christopher Hatton's library at Holkham Hall in Norfolk, bear witness to the importance ascribed to academic guidance in the design and execution of these great schemes. Palladio is among the authors that featured in this library, and it is believed the peerless trio, Vitruvius, Alberti and Serlio were closely consulted.[30] These were not 'castles in the air' or the contrivances of dilettantes, but meticulously planned and carefully executed projects drawing heavily on the expertise of the leading academic treatises and the most skilled engineers, architects and garden designers in Europe. Technological innovations were harnessed, and the developing mastery of hydraulics put to the service of creating magical and playful effects. It is in two of the Late Plays that Shakespeare brings into sharp focus the relationship between magic and science. *The Winter's Tale* engages with botanical manipulation and magical effects of moving statuary (4.4.79–103; 5.3.87–98); *The Tempest* accommodates the entire panoply of garden entertainments: in addition to the pyrotechnics of the storm scene mirroring fireworks displays, there are labyrinths, music, chess and the culinary delights of the mystical banquet. As Tigner observes, 'In *The Tempest,* of all the spectacles that refer to mechanical tricks, the banquet table is the one that appears not simply as an allusion to both garden and stage machinery but is an actual automated device.'[31] Of course, Prospero's island garden does not leave such trickery there. The *coup de théâtre* is provided by the masque which foregrounds plants as the harbingers of fertility, botanical and human.

Vivian Thomas

Notes

1   Mats Ryden, *Shakespearean Plant Names: Identifications and Interpretations*, Stockholm: Almqvist & Wiksell International, 1978: 17.
2   Leah Knight, *Of Books and Botany in Early Modern England: Sixteenth Century Plants and Print Culture*, Farnham: Ashgate Publishing Limited, 2009: 6, 8.
3   Ryden, *op. cit.*, 18.
4   Deborah E. Harkness, *The Jewel House: Elizabethan London and the Scientific Revolution*, New Haven and London: Yale University Press, 2007: 2, 21.
5   Keith Thomas, *Man and the Natural World: Changing Attitudes in England 1500–1800*, Middlesex: Penguin, 1984: 83.
6   This diversity of names stimulated the pursuit of a more reliable and meaningful nomenclature, a development nurtured by academic need alongside popular engagement with plant culture. John Ray's *Synopsis methodica* (1690) lay in the future while Linnaeus's binomial nomenclature elaborated in his *Species plantarum* (1753), though eventually gaining universal acceptance was still further away. For a succinct summary of these important developments see Anna Pavord, *Naming of Names: the Search for Order in the World of Plants*, London: Bloomsbury, 2005: 395–402.
7   See Richard Mabey, *Weeds*, London: Profile Books Ltd, 2010, for a fascinating discussion.
8   Caroline Spurgeon, *Shakespeare's Imagery and What it Tells Us*, Cambridge: Cambridge University Press, 1935: 16.
9   Tanya Pollard, *Drugs and Theater in Early Modern England*, Oxford: Oxford University Press, 2005: 19, 165(fn).
10 For an interesting discussion on this topic see Frances E. Dolan, 'Taking the Pencil out

of God's Hand: Art, Nature, and the Face-Painting Debate in Early Modern England',
PMLA, vol. 108, No. 2, (March, 1993): 224–39. She says of Perdita, 'In her view,
the art that produces the gillyflower does not embellish nature but competes with and
effaces it ... For Montaigne, as for Perdita, the issue becomes the moral one of purity
versus corruption', 227–8.

11 Rebecca Bushnell, *Green Desire: Imagining Early Modern English Gardens*, Ithaca and
London: Cornell University Press, 2003: 150–1, See also 132–60 for a discussion of this
topic. She also highlights the social standing of Gerard and Parkinson, 26.

12 Noel Kingsbury, *Hybrid: The History and Science of Plant Breeding*, Chicago and
London: The University of Chicago Press, 2009, provides a useful summary of the
steps taken towards a genuine understanding of hybridization, especially 73–86.
The first plant to be successfully 'hybridized' was the 'gillyvor' effected by Thomas
Fairchild in 1717. This was a cross between a sweet william (*Dianthus barbatus*) and
a carnation (D. *caryophyllus*). However, it was a limited achievement because the plant
was sterile. See Martin Hoyles, *The Story of Gardening*, London: Journeyman Press,
1991: 249–56.

13 Andrew Marvell, 'The Mower Against Gardens', in *Andrew Marvell*, Frank Kermode
and Keith Walker (eds), Oxford: Oxford University Press, 1990.

14 The inspirational Rondelet created a vibrant centre at the University of Montpellier.
Among the celebrated figures benefiting from his tutelage were Gesner, Clusius
(Charles de l'Écluse) and Leonhard Rauwolff.

15 Knight, *op. cit.*, 22.

16 Pavord, *op. cit.*, 'At Padua in 1533, Francesco Buonafede, the university's former
professor of medicine, became the first ever professor of *simplicia medicamenta* –
plants for medicine ... In the 1540s, the first botanic gardens were established at Pisa,
Padua and Florence ... At Pisa, the brilliant teacher Luca Ghini (1490–1556) found
an entirely new way of studying plants when he made the earliest *hortus siccus.* By
pressing plants and sticking the dry skeletons into a book, he invented the herbarium',
205–6. It was, however, the least gifted scholar, Mattioli, who achieved the greatest
publishing success with his *Commentari* in 1544.

17 *Ibid.*, 338.

18 Knight, *op. cit.*, 'A single chapter turns into a veritable anthology of ancient poets
– Ovid, Virgil, Catullus, Prudentius – all mustered in order to prove a point about
a pine tree.' On one occasion he 'explains the origins of a disagreement among
Galen, Dioscorides, and Pliny, respectively the chief ancient authorities on medicine,
herbalism, and natural history', before proceeding 'to cite two poets, Virgil and
Catullus, demonstrating how their poetry can help to resolve the dispute', 102.

19 *Ibid.*, 82.

20 Pavord, *op. cit.*, 340.

21 *Ibid.*, 267.

22   Alexander Samson, ed., *Locus Amoenus: Gardens and Horticulture in the Renaissance*, Chichester: Wiley-Blackwell, 2012: 4.

23   Justus Lipsius, in *De Constantia* (78–80), complains of those who 'hunt after strange herbs and flowers, which having got, they preserve and cherish more carefully than any mother does her child; these are men whose letters fly abroad into Thracia, Greece, and India only for a little root or seed'. Cited by Samson, ed.: 13.

24   Colonna mentions the carob tree for which Cyprus was celebrated, a 'weeping gum-tree' and the 'Anthropophagi', all present in *Othello*, albeit the carob is represented in the play by its fruit, 'locusts' (1.3.348; 5.2.350–1; 1.3.144).

25   Paula Henderson, *The Tudor House and Garden: Architecture and Landscape in the Sixteenth and Seventeenth Centuries*, New Haven and London: Yale University Press, 2005: 19; 76–9.

26   Margaret Willes, *The Making of the English Gardener: Plants, Books and Inspiration 1560–1660*, New Haven and London: Yale University Press, 2011: 27; 125–7.

27   Francis Bacon, 'Of Gardens', Memphis, Tennessee: General Books, 2010. See David Jacques 'The Chief Ornament of Gray's Inn: The Walks from Bacon to Brown', *Garden History*, vol. 17, no. 1 (Spring 1989): 41–67.

28   Henderson, *op. cit.*, 94, observes 'By the end of Elizabeth's reign, familiar elements from medieval gardens remained. Gardens were still divided into individual compartments by walls or hedges. There were arbours and bowers, mounts, ponds and fountains … Ornament, which still included heraldic motifs, was increasingly related to classical texts: Ovid, in particular, was a favourite.' (Also informative are two essays by Elisabeth Woodhouse, 'Spirit of the Elizabethan Garden' and 'Kenilworth, the Earl of Leicester's Pleasure Grounds Following Rober Laneham's Letter', both in *Garden History*, vol. 27, no 1. Tudor Gardens (Summer, 1999): 10–31; 127–44.)

29   *Ibid.,* 107.

30   Willes, *op. cit.*, 37.

31   Amy L. Tigner, Literature and the Renaissance Garden from Elizabeth I to Charles II: England's Paradise, Farnham, Ashgate Publishing Ltd., 2012: 149. See also this author for the significance of horti-colonial trade in relation to the 'pursuit of luxury' (173).

A

aconitum (A) *Aconitum napellus* L., also aconite, wolf's bane, helmet **flower**, monkshood. Long known to be toxic, narcotic and analgesic, aconitum was a plant of witchcraft, thought to give the illusion of flying. In antiquity its juice was used as a poison in war, and when hunting. Its medicinal applications included its use as an antidote to poison.

(B) The only reference occurs in *2H4*. Conscious that family cohesion is imperative for survival of the dynasty, the dying Henry IV, a usurper whose reign has been dogged by rebellion, counsels his son, Thomas of Clarence:

> Learn this, Thomas,
> And thou shalt prove a shelter to thy friends,
> A hoop of gold to bind thy brothers in,
> That the united vessel of their blood,
> Mingled with venom of suggestion
> (As, force perforce, the age will pour it in),
> Shall never leak, though it do work as strong
> As aconitum or rash gunpowder.
>
> *(4.4.41–8)*

Its virulence makes aconitum an appropriate metaphor for the poisonous influence of insinuation.

(C) Aconitum was synonymous with poison: Greene records its properties when writing of a jealous husband, 'he will leave no confection unsearched, no mineral untried, no Aconitum unbruised, not herb, tree, root unsought' (1592, vol. 11, *Philomela*, 131). Jonson's Tiberius speaks of its power as an antidote to other poisons: 'I have heard that aconite,/Being timely taken, hath a healing might/Against the scorpion's stroke' (1603: *Sejanus:* 3.3.29). Ellacombe (1896) and Singleton (1922) propose aconitum as the plant sold by the **apothecary** to Romeo (*ROM* 5.1.59), a possibility supported by the pharmacologist Macht (1949). Mabey (1996) provides a modern commentary on its toxicity.

acorn, acorn-cups, full-acorn'd (A) An oval **nut** growing in a shallow, woody cup or *cupule,* the **fruit** of the **oak tree**, *Quercus robur* L. and *Q. petraea* L. Fallen acorns were known as **mast,** and were important for foraging pigs particularly in autumn and winter. By extension, acorn indicated fruit generally, something very small and insignificant, or a small container. It was a **fertility** symbol with the cup as the feminine and the acorn as the masculine parts. It had medicinal and cosmetic applications. The oak was Jove's tree, symbolizing strength; the acorn could assume the parent virtues.

(B) Celia, teasing Rosalind, says of her encounter with Orlando, 'I found him under a tree, like a dropp'd acorn', eliciting the playful response, 'It may well be call'd Jove's tree, when it drops such fruit' (*AYL* 3.2.234–7). Small and seemingly insignificant, the acorn is represented as contemptible by Lysander when rejecting Hermia for the taller Helena: 'Get you gone, you dwarf;/You minimus, of hind'ring knot-grass made;/You bead, you acorn' (*MND* 3.2.328–30). Earlier in the play the quarrel between the Fairy King and Queen is described by Puck as so fractious, 'that all their elves for fear/Creep into acorn-cups, and hide them there' (2.1.30–1). Establishing his authority, Prospero threatens Ferdinand, 'thy food shall be/The fresh-brook mussels, wither'd roots, and husks/Wherein the acorn cradled' (*TMP* 1.2.463–5). Though the acorn husks constitute a rough diet, the verbal music of the island asserts itself with 'cradled' and 'fresh-brook'. Believing the blameless Imogen has betrayed him, Posthumus' jealous outburst occasions an ugly simile:

> This yellow Jachimo, in an hour – was't not? –
> Or less – at first? Perchance he spoke not, but
> Like a full-acorn'd boar, a German one,
> Cried 'O!' and mounted;
>
> *(CYM 2.5.14–17)*

Arden 2 (72) has a long footnote on this but the drift seems straightforward. In his rancid imagination Posthumus visualizes a well-fed, over-lusty boar, greedy in copulation, with 'full-acorn'd' signifying testicles.

(C) Acorns were dismissed by Erasmus in his *Adages* – 'acorns have had their day' – as something to be left behind, because man had moved on from eating mast to grains (1536, vol. 31). With considerable forethought, Hill (1577) writes of the importance of sowing acorns to provide oak trees for the future. Levin (1970) suggests acorns were the food of the golden age. They featured frequently in embroidery and jewellery.

Adonis flower, Adonis' garden (A) While not named as such in *VEN,* many commentators include 'Adonis flower' in their list of Shakespeare's plants. A definitive identification is impossible, not least because contextually the flower could be red or purple. The generally accepted suggestion for a purple **flower** is *Anemone pulsatilla* L. formerly *A. purpurea* the windflower, but the description of its being chequered with white raises the possibility of *Fritillaria meleagris* L., the fritillary. Adonis was also a common name for pheasant's eye anemone, now *Adonis annua* L., a **weed** of cultivated and waste ground which has a red flower consistent with Ovid's account. 'Adonis' gardens' reflected the belief in Adonis as a deity of vegetation.

(B) As part of the myth recreated in *VEN,* this flower achieves a distinctive presence without being named. Solitary and grief-stricken, Venus witnesses Adonis' transmutation:

> By this the boy that by her side lay kill'd
> Was melted like a vapor from her sight,
> And in his blood that on the ground lay spill'd,
> A purple flow'r sprung up, check'red with white,
>> Resembling well his pale cheeks and the blood
>> Which in round drops upon their whiteness stood.
> She bows her head, the new-sprung flow'r to smell,
> Comparing it to her Adonis' breath,
>
> *(1165–72)*

The last two lines add to the problem of identification as none of the proposed flowers carries a **scent**. However, the scent may be subtle, because a few lines later Venus addresses the flower as 'Sweet issue of a more sweet-smelling sire' (1178). The snake's-head fritillary with its pale-purple, freckled, down-cast head appeals on visual grounds. Although the flower's identity remains a mystery, the appellation 'Adonis flower' is richly evocative.

The Dauphin, the only character to invoke 'Adonis' garden', does so when praising Joan Pucelle for recapturing Orleans:

> Divinest creature, Astraea's daughter,
> How shall I honor thee for this success?
> Thy promises are like Adonis' garden,
> That one day bloom'd and fruitful were the next.
>
> *(1H6 1.6.4–7)*

(C) The Adonis legend can be found in full in Chapter 10 of Ovid's *Metamorphoses*; Colonna (1499) describes the crimson Adonis flower growing round the fountain of Venus. Gerard identifies it as a weed which grows in the west of the country, as pernicious in corn as mayweed, but pretty enough for him to sow seeds in his garden. His illustration appears to show *Adonis annua* L. (1597: 310). Frazer's *The Golden Bough* (1922) includes a chapter on the symbolism of the Adonis gardens, noting the survival of the idea in Eastern Europe into modern times. Wilson (2004) sets Shakespeare's reference to the Adonis flower in the context of his possible Catholic allegiance, suggesting it invoked the martyrdom of young English Catholics. Tigner (2012) comments on Spenser's Garden of Adonis. Samson (2012: 10) sees the Garden of Adonis as the 'antitype' of Spenser's 'Bower of Bliss'. Mabey (2010) includes a chapter on the persistent survival of the Adonis flower.

alley (A) Alleys, sometimes allies, were **walks** or paths in formal and informal parts of the **garden**, including the wider **park**, **orchard**, **maze** and **wood**. They could be straight or winding, open as paths between beds of **flowers**, or enclosed with climbing **plants** for protection from the sun. Affording privacy, they suggested somewhere hidden and secret.

(B) *ADO* epitomizes a world of leisure. Antonio confides to Leonato, 'The Prince and Count Claudio, walking in a thick-pleach'd alley in my orchard, were thus much overheard by a man of mine' (1.2.8–11). In a play deeply engaged with 'noting' this garden is designed for intimate conversation, inadvertently overheard or contrived. Engaging in subterfuge to gull Beatrice, Hero instructs her gentlewoman:

> Now, Ursula, when Beatrice doth come,
> As we do trace this alley up and down,
> Our talk must only be of Benedick.
> When I do name him, let it be thy part
> To praise him more than ever man did merit.
>
> *(3.1.15–19)*

The alley, a natural amenity for congenial exercise, provides a stage-set for Hero. Intriguingly, she is more articulate and at ease in role-playing than being herself in formal situations. Both performance and location liberate her. Dromio of Syracusa makes the only literal reference to alley as a narrow passage: 'The passages of alleys, creeks, and narrow lands' (*ERR* 4.2.38). (See '**laund**'.) Describing the progression of the poison through his body, the Ghost uses a compelling image: 'That swift as quick-silver it courses through/The natural gates and alleys of the body' (*HAM* 1.5.66–7).

(C) Hill (1577) includes a chapter with illustrations on planning and making of allies, saying they should be designed to frame the garden; Markham (1613) writes of allies as the formal walks bisecting and surrounding the **knot** garden. Bacon (1625) gives detailed instructions on how to construct extensive alleys in the formal garden, the **heath** and **wilderness** with space for four people to walk abreast, recommending under-planting with **burnet**, **thyme** and **mint** for a refreshing smell when walking; he describes a 'covert alley, upon carpenter's work'. Massinger's Ramble jokes about the seamier side of gardens and allies where encounters with prostitutes are to be had in 'the garden alleys' (1632, *The City Madam*, 3.1.43–5). See also **forthright, gallery.**

almond, marchpane (A) *Prunus amygdalus* L., possibly a Roman introduction, the almond **tree** is the cultivated form of the highly toxic wild or bitter almond; it was not recorded in cultivation in England until the mid-sixteenth century. Gerard attests to its popularity for its **blossom**, and **nuts**, which were used in cooking for their sweet flavouring and particularly for the dessert of marchpane or marzipan. Almonds had medicinal and cosmetic applications. Symbolically they represented **fruitfulness**. In folklore the tree suggested fertility, both financially and sexually. In mythology Nana conceived her son Attis after gathering the blossom of an almond tree which had sprung from the severed genitals of Agdistis/Cybele.

(B) The single use of 'almond' is brief but pointed. It provides a footnote to a sordid and voyeuristic scene in which Cressida's surrender to Diomed is observed by multiple witnesses including Troilus, Ulysses, the prurient Thersites, and the compromised audience in the theatre. Anticipating Cressida's next amour Thersites muses: 'Patroclus will give me anything for the intelligence of this whore. The parrot will not do more for an almond than he for a commodious drab. Lechery, lechery, still wars and lechery' (*TRO* 5.2.192–5). Thersites neatly encapsulates Patroclus' licentiousness as the almond was the ultimate temptation for a parrot, the very acme of desire. The reference to 'marchpane' (marzipan) provides local colour in *ROM*. The First Servant calls out, 'Good thou, save me a piece of marchpane' (1.5.7–8).

(C) Turner records it in domestic cultivation in 1548. Peacham (1612) draws on its variable flowering habit, suggesting that emblematically it represented forwardness; Hawkins (1633) calls it 'the almond of fruitfulness'. Alderman Parrot's widow is notorious for her association with almonds: 'Shee would eate nought but Almonds, I assure you' and 'O fine Lady Pol! an Almond for a Parrat', taken to be indicative of her eagerness to remarry (Jonson, 1641, *The Magnetick Lady*, 5.5.5–7). Chancellor (1982: 20) notes the almond's biblical association with age and decay.

aloe (A) Usually *Aloe barbadensis*, sometimes *A. vera* L., the bitter aloe is a succulent **plant** from Asia and India, imported as solidified dried juice extracted from its fleshy **leaves**; from classical times aloes were synonymous with bitterness. It is not the biblical aloes, *Lignum aloes,* a resinous **tree**, which provided incense.

(B) Its sole use is in *LC* and alludes to its bitterness. Narrating the progression of her fall, the forsaken young woman recounts her seducer's expression of the power of love:

> When thou impressest, what are precepts worth
> Of stale example? When thou wilt inflame,
> How coldly those impediments stand forth
> Of wealth, of filial fear, law, kindred, fame!
> Love's arms are peace, 'gainst rule, 'gainst sense, 'gainst shame,
> And sweetens, in the suff'ring pangs it bears,
> The aloes of all forces, shocks and fears.

(267–73)

Love overbears bitterness (aloes); it has ascendancy over every oppositional influence. The purgative property of aloes may also be present because love is cathartic: it exorcizes 'all forces', physical, psychological and social.

(C) Bullein (1595) is clear on the difference between the two plants, recommending bitter aloes for medicinal purposes. Chancellor (1982: 9) notes that the aloe of the Old Testament differs from that of the New Testament: the former had soft and fragrant inner wood; the bitter aloe was used as a **spice** for embalming. Langham (1597) includes dozens of remedies using aloes, most of which relate to its use as a purgative. Some of the compounds he prescribes must have been extremely powerful as they also include such other bitter **herbs** as **coloquintida** and **wormwood**. Aloes now appears on the United States Government Food and Drug Administration food and additive list as a banned substance because of the adverse effects of its powerful constituents (www. fda.gov). Useful critical commentary and bibliographic information on *LC* is provided by Rowe in Cheney (2007: 144–60).

angelica (A) *Angelica archangelica* L. is an introduction from Syria or mainland Europe in the mid-sixteenth century. Seen as a harbinger of spring, angelica was named for the archangel Michael whose feast day was on 8 May; it had Marian associations, and was thought to offer protection against plague and witchcraft. Its dried **root** was employed medicinally and incorporated into **posies** for its sweet **smell**. Angelica was a candied sweetmeat, and was distilled as 'water of angelica'.

(B) Delectably aromatic, the plant's appearance in Capulet's kitchen is unsurprising given its culinary and medicinal properties. The hastily arranged marriage feast includes 'spices' and 'dates and quinces in the pastry'. Capulet, encouraging the kitchen staff to greater urgency, calls out, 'Look to the bak'd meats, good Angelica,/Spare not for cost' (*ROM* 4.4.1–6). Some editors propose that 'Angelica' is the name of one of the kitchen maids, and in F1 the name is italicized as are those of various characters. Others propose it is a teasing reference to the Nurse: 'for Angelica was the pagan princess of exquisite beauty and heartless coquetry who came to sow dissention among the Christian princes in Ariosto's *Orlando Furioso*' (Spenser, cited by Arden 2 (207)). Ferguson *et al.* (*SQ* 35–6) make a compelling case for the plant being flavouring for the 'bak'd meats', or 'its stalks may be sugared and served as a confection as was more usual'. They perceive 'good' not as an endearment, but 'because it is garden angelica that is wanted rather than "angelica sylvestris", the wild variety, apparently far smaller and less flavourful than its cultivated cousin'. Exploring the language and punctuation they propose a semi-colon rather than the more usual comma after meats and make the telling point that, 'As a marvellous panacea, angelica, known as the "root of the Holy Ghost", contrasts evocatively with the mandrakes mentioned by Juliet some fifteen lines earlier.' In the very next scene Juliet will be found 'dead'. Hence angelica informs the play's multiple ironies.

(C) Angelica features on most sixteenth-century plant lists for use against both the plague and witchcraft. Turner (1551) writes of it being sourced in Denmark, suggesting a new introduction, although Hill (1577) gives instructions on its cultivation indicating that it was a commonly available plant. Langham (1597) prescribes it particularly for colds, in time of plague, and against poisons, noting that 'It quencheth all carnall rage of youthfull lust', perhaps making it inappropriate for a wedding feast. Greene also has a character called Angelica (1588, vol. 7, *Perimedes*). Bate (1982) suggests that, if a recent introduction, it would have been more expensive than the meats with which it is juxtaposed. Potter (2003) considers its use as an appetite stimulant.

apothecary (A) A maker of drugs, preservatives, spices and cosmetics from component **herbs** or **simples,** the apothecary was usually supplied with the raw ingredients by others, possibly **herb-women**. He could trade through a shop, or in backstreet premises. Often early botanists, apothecaries had no formal academic training, unlike physicians who usually studied at Oxford, Cambridge, or on the Continent, and who were dependent on the apothecaries to make the plants into potions or pills. Apothecaries were not licensed until 1700, and while they may have offered informal advice, they generally did not diagnose illness. Although they jealously guarded their own sphere of power and influence, any charlatan could set up on a street corner, and most neighbourhoods had their own range of practitioners.

(B) Of the four references to apothecaries, two are purveyors of poison; one makes up a prescription supplied by a medical practitioner; and one is required to supply a remedy for delirium. Having played a leading role in the assassination of the Duke of Gloucester, the Bishop of Winchester is haunted by the spectre of his victim:

> Comb down his hair; look, look, it stands upright,
> Like lime-twigs set to catch my winged soul.
> Give me some drink, and bid the apothecary
> Bring the strong poison that I bought of him.

> *(2H6 3.3.15–18)*

Warwick maintains that Gloucester was strangled in his bed (3.3.160–78) so when the machiavellian Bishop summons the apothecary the poison is presumably for himself. Though not designated 'apothecary', Friar Lawrence is profoundly engaged with plants as medicines (*ROM* 2.3.1–26), crucially providing the drug that induces Juliet's illusory death (4.1.89–108). It is a *bona fide* apothecary who supplies Romeo with poison. What is remarkable about this incident is its exposure of an underclass:

> I do remember an apothecary –
> And hereabouts 'a dwells – which late I noted
> In tatt'red weeds, with overwhelming brows,
> Culling of simples; meagre were his looks,
> Sharp misery had worn him to the bones;

> *(5.1.37–41)*

Intriguingly, Laertes resorts to a 'mountebank' to secure his lethal 'unction' (*HAM* 4.7.141).

In *PER*, Cerimon, a healer of exceptional ability, revives the seemingly dead Thiasa. To one supplicant he hands a prescription saying, 'Give this to the 'pothecary,/And tell me how it works' (3.2.9–10). The mad Lear, overwhelmed by images of disease and rampant sexuality, pleads: 'Give me an ounce of civet; good apothecary,/Sweeten my imagination' (*LR* 4.6.130–1).

(C) The ready availability of newly printed *Herbals* made information more accessible to a wide range of practitioners. Turner notes the gardens of some London apothecaries and their interest in 'good and strange herbs' (Raven, 1947). Vaughan (1617: 124) suggests apothecaries should be regarded with some suspicion: 'Why will they comber themselves with Apothecary-drugs, when they may be delivered from diseases without danger, onely by observing a competent diet?'. Pollard (2005) examines the apothecary's role in the context of drugs in the early modern theatre. Knight (2009: 15–16) notes 'one result of the division of labour between plant collectors and the physicians was that those who, with their extensive formal education, might have known most about plants were instead often the least acquainted with them in their unprocessed form'. Willes (2011: 204–6) provides the background to the conflicts and tensions between apothecaries and physicians. For comment on the potential ambiguity in *PER* see Arden 3, fn, (290–1). Iyengar (2011) provides further details on the medical role of the apothecary.

apple (A) *Malus pumila* M., the apple was one of the earliest **fruit trees** cultivated for food, medicinal and ornamental purposes; it was accessible to all sections of the population. Shakespeare refers to several of the very many available varieties, most now lost to cultivation, including **apple-john, bitter sweeting, codling**, and **costard**, the last also an old name for the head, giving its name to costardmongers, later costermongers, **leathercoat, pippin** and **pomewater**. 'Apple' could be a generic term for fruit; it carried associations of good and evil from identification with the Garden of Eden. In classical tradition the apple was a love token, an attribute of Venus. It had wide proverbial and metaphorical usage, particularly with reference to rot and decay; apple could designate the pupil or centre of the eye, the apple of one's eye suggesting something precious.

(B) There is an explicit reference to Eve's apple in the closing lines of *SON* 93: 'How like Eve's apple doth thy beauty grow,/If thy sweet virtue answer not thy show'. Responding to Shylock's biblical disquisition on profit as a 'blessing', Antonio is vitriolic:

> Mark you this, Bassanio,
> The devil can cite scripture for his purpose.
> An evil soul producing holy witness
> Is like a villain with a smiling cheek,
> A goodly apple rotten at the heart.
> O, what a goodly outside falsehood hath!
>
> *(MV 1.3.90–102)*

Sebastian, exercising his acerbic wit at the expense of Gonzalo, says to Antonio, 'I think he will carry this island home in his pocket, and give it to his son for an apple' (*TMP* 2.1.91–2). Malvolio, announcing the pert 'young fellow' carrying Orsino's love missive to Olivia, describes Cesario/Viola as being 'Not yet old enough for a man, nor young enough for a boy; as a squash is before 'tis a peasecod, or a codling when 'tis almost an apple' (*TN* 1.5.139–58). The comic incongruity of Malvolio's excursion into the realm of horticultural metaphor emanates from this indoor-man resorting, with determined precision, to the language of the outdoor world. When the twins Viola and Sebastian come together in the closing scene, the amazed Antonio, saviour of Sebastian, exclaims, 'How have you made division of yourself?/An apple, cleft in two, is not more twin/ Than these two creatures' (5.1.222–4). A glimpse into contemporary life is provided in *H8* when a porter complains of the crowd jostling to see the coronation procession: 'These are the youths that thunder at a playhouse and fight for bitten apples' (5.3.60–1). Hortensio, expressing distaste for Katherine the shrew, despite the attraction of her dowry, has recourse to the proverbial phrase, 'there's small choice in rotten apples' (*SHR* 1.1.134–5). In *MND*, a play profoundly engaged with seeing and perspective, the transformative love juice, the cause of so much confusion and comedy, is administered by Oberon: 'Flower of this purple dye,/Hit with Cupid's archery,/Sink in apple of his eye' (3.2.102–4). The apple of the eye is also present in *LLL* (5.2.475).

(C) Andrews (1993) documents contemporary ornamental use of apples in Burghley's garden at Theobalds, recording hundreds of apple trees planted in **thorn hedges,** in **alleys** lined with trees and around the summerhouse. Cogan (1584: 88) details the apple's edible and medicinal properties: 'all apples generally are unwholesome in the regiment of health, especially if they be eaten raw before they be full ripe'. He suggests they are best eaten **rotted**, baked or stewed, and served at the end of a meal for good effect on digestion. Eaten raw, he recommends the pippin and costard. Drayton (1622) lists many of Shakespeare's varieties in his list of apples in the Kent orchards. William Lambarde in his *Perambulation of Kent* (1576) gives an account of the emergence of the Kentish orchards and the impetus provided by a policy of import substitution (see Willes 2011: 48–9). Palter (2002) provides extensive details of apples in classical, biblical, artistic and literary traditions. Chancellor (1982: 22) identifies the biblical apple as the apricot (*Prunus armeniaca)*. In their encyclopaedic study Morgan and Richards (2002) suggest that virtually all apple cultivars derive from a single species *Malus sieversii* which grows in the mountains of Kazakhstan.

apple-john The apple-john became a metaphor for age or for anything shrivelled. It was said to keep for two years and improve in the keeping. Falstaff is identified with the apple-john. Bewailing his physical shrinking he complains to Bardolph, 'do I not bate? do I not dwindle? Why, my skin hangs about me like an old lady's loose gown; I am wither'd like an old apple-john' (*1H4* 3.3.2–4). In *2H4* Francis a drawer rebukes a colleague for bringing in these same apples: 'Thou knowest Sir John cannot endure an apple-john'. The chastened second Drawer responds, 'Mass thou say'st true. The Prince once set a dish of apple-johns before him, and told him there were five more Sir Johns, and putting off his hat, said, "I will now take leave of these six dry, round, old, wither'd knights". It ang'red him to the heart' (2.4.2–9). Littlewit and Quarlous employ 'apple-john' in a pun on apple-squire or pimp (Jonson, 1614, *Bartholomew Fair* 1.2.50–2).

apricock (A) *Prunus armeniaca* L. was an introduction from Spain or Italy, probably after 1540; it was called *armeniaca* from its supposed Armenian origin, but it is likely the apricot travelled the silk road from China. It provided **scent**, early spring beauty, longevity, and productivity both for flavour and cosmetics, adding variety and novelty as a **fruit** for the wealthy. The apricot was considered an agent of diagnosis, most specifically in regard to pregnancy, perhaps because it was originally described as *praecox,* an early flowering **tree.**

(B) All three mentions are arresting. The imprisoned Palamon, having observed Emilia in the garden, alights on the apricot tree as the epitome of delicate beauty and as a natural servitor to her:

> Blessed garden,
> And fruit and flowers more blessed, that still blossom
> As her bright eyes shine on ye, would I were,
> For all the fortune of my life hereafter,
> Yon little tree, yon blooming apricock!
>
> *(TNK 2.2.232–6)*

The enchanted Titania exhorts her entourage to pander to her newly acquired amour, Bottom: 'Feed him with apricocks and dewberries,/With purple grapes, green figs, and mulberries' (*MND* 3.1.166–7). The names of the fruits, accentuated by alliteration and assonance, promote a richly sensual atmosphere. Moreover, both 'apricocks' and 'figs' are sexually suggestive. In a quintessentially emblematic scene the Queen and her ladies overhear the gardeners contrasting Richard II's misgovernment of the body politic with good **husbandry**:

> Go bind thou up young dangling apricocks,
> Which like unruly children make their sire
> Stoop with oppression of their prodigal weight;
> Give some supportance to the bending twigs.
> Go thou, and like an executioner
> Cut off the heads of too fast growing sprays,
> That look too lofty in our commonwealth:
> All must be even in our government.
>
> *(R2 3.4.29–36)*

(C) Perhaps the most famous apricots in early modern drama are those greedily devoured by the Duchess of Malfi, an action which confirms Bosola's suspicion that she is pregnant (Webster 1613, *Malfi*, 2.1.134–63). Bushnell (2003: 148–9) has a comment on the incident. This play is the inspiration for of the title of Palter's wide-ranging study of fruits in literature (2002). Harvey (1992) quotes Hakluyt as saying the apricot was introduced from Italy by Henry VIII's **gardener** Wolf. Turner (1548) notes that 'abricok we have very fewe of these trees as yet', but within 50 years cultivation of the apricot appears to be quite widespread. Lawson (1618), confirming their tenderness, writes that apricots were not suitable for growing in northern Europe, but Drayton (1622) lists them among the Kent fruit trees. The 1650 Parliamentary Survey of the Cecil house at Wimbledon records the survival of apricot trees in the garden (see Amherst (1896)). Chancellor (1982: 22) identifies the apricot as the 'apple' of the Bible. For observations on its introduction, propagation and status see Tigner (2012: 87).

Arabian tree, date (A) Probably the date or **palm** tree, *Phoenix dactylifera*, but the reference may possibly be intended to be mysterious and exotic rather than specific. The idea that the tree housed the mythical phoenix predates its botanical name. The dried **fruits** were imported from the Middle East as confectionery, but were also valued for their medicinal virtues.

(B) As the King's party marvel at the strange banquet set before them by mystical figures accompanied by 'Marvellous sweet music!' the cynical Sebastian comments: 'Now I will believe/That there are unicorns; that in Arabia/There is one tree, the phoenix' throne, one phoenix/At this hour reigning there' (*TMP* 3.3.19–24). The association of the Arabian tree with the phoenix and the unicorn distinguish it as occupying a place alongside the most egregious fictions that make up travellers' tales. Nevertheless, the resonance of this myth permeates the air, contesting the scepticism of the speaker. An engaging poetic reference is occasioned by Othello's plea to Desdemona's kinsmen that, in communicating the circumstances of his disgrace to the Venetian state, they 'nothing extenuate,/Nor set down aught in malice', but speak 'of one whose subdu'd eyes,/Albeit unused to the melting mood,/Drops tears as fast as the Arabian trees/Their medicinable gum' (*OTH* 5.2.342–51). The peculiar status of the tragic hero is encapsulated in the title, *Othello, The Moor of Venice*. The Moor, who has become a Christian and the bulwark of Venice against the Ottomans, possesses a highly distinctive and richly exotic mode of speech. The vivid image of the Arabian trees is embedded in assonantal lines that flow with the copious fluency of the 'medicinable gum'. Overwhelmed by grief and remorse he commits suicide within a few lines of his allusion to the Arabian trees' lachrymation. The perfection of love in 'The Phoenix and the Turtle' – the second line of which has a single reference to 'the sole Arabian tree' – suggests a tragic power inherent in a mythology that impregnates Othello's Arabian trees. This short poem celebrating the consummate fidelity of these birds immortalizes them.

(C) The *OED* confirms the use of 'phoenix' for palm in Old English. Both Gerard (1597) and Parkinson (1640) recognize its Middle Eastern origin, the importation of dried fruit for ease of transportation, and give its medicinal and culinary uses. The *Shakespeare's Poems* Arden 3 (421) commentary on 'The Phoenix and the Turtle' traces the connection between the phoenix and the Arabian tree back to Pliny. Greene suggests the mysterious connections of the tree: 'Be *(Philador)* in secrecy like the Arabick-tree, that yeelds no gum but in the darke night' (1616, vol. 9, *Greene's Mourning Garment,* 139).

arbour (A) Possibly derived from *herber,* a **turf** seat, itself from Latin *herbarium* or **garden,** or from *arbor,* Latin for **tree,** an arbour was a free-standing constructed feature to offer **shade** in summer. Often temporary, these wooden structures were covered with climbing **plants, roses** or trained trees. They provided space for informal eating, privacy in business and sexual affairs, and were places of relaxation and seclusion. **Flowers** added the dimensions of colour and intense **scent**; arbours were also found in the wider garden context in **orchards.** Arbours could provide a substitute for banqueting or **garden-houses.**

(B) *ADO* is notable for two playful garden scenes. Benedick and Beatrice are, in turn, subjected to artful deceptions designed to disrupt their 'merry wars'. The approach of Don Pedro and Claudio persuades Benedick, the arch-critic of love and marriage, to eavesdrop: 'I will hide me in the arbor' (2.3.36). He emerges from his hiding place a man now fiercely in love. Edward III's passion for the Countess of Salisbury causes him to sequester the services of his secretary Lodowick, drawing him into an inspirational place for penning a love missive: 'Then in the summer arbor sit by me,/Make it our council house, or cabinet:/Since green our thoughts, green be the conventicle' (*E3* 2.1.61–3). The 'conventicle' suggests secrecy; the green thoughts are those of love – anticipating Andrew Marvell's 'green thought in a green shade'. But unlike 'Thoughts in a Garden', which celebrates **nature** and the **gardener's** art, the ensuing dialogue in the arbour is dedicated to creating a language of love. Indeed, this is one of the finest seminars on language in the canon – as well as being one of the most entertaining. The warmly atmospheric scene in a Gloucestershire orchard opens with Justice Shallow's pressing invitation to Falstaff: 'Nay, you shall see my orchard, where, in an arbor, we will eat a last year's pippin of mine own graffing, with a dish of caraways, and so forth' (*2H4* 5.3.1–3). Capitalizing on the changing mood of the Roman populace, Mark Antony reads Caesar's will to demonstrate his private and public largesse. Announcing the 75 drachmas bequeathed to every citizen, Antony reveals,

> Moreover, he hath left you all his walks,
> His private arbors and new-planted orchards,
> On this side Tiber; he hath left them you,
> And to your heirs for ever – common pleasures,
> To walk abroad and recreate yourselves.

(JC 3.2.247–51)

Caesar's beneficence transforms private ownership into a public resource.

(C) Arbours leave few archaeological traces, although recent research into Tresham's remote and undisturbed garden at Lyveden New Bield indicates they could be up to 25 metres in length, providing extensive shady walking and sitting space (Eburne 2008). Their significance at Holdenby is reported by John Norden in 1595 and is quoted by Willes (2011: 27). Hill (1577) includes a chapter on constructing an arbour, suggesting a framework of poles bound together to support plants – his woodcut of the process of construction is reproduced in Willes (2011: 132). The modern edition of Hill contains a delightful woodcut of 'A garden repast', reprinted in *Riverside Shakespeare* (973), which could have been designed especially for *2H4* 5.3. Browne suggests arbours are not simply for the wealthy: 'And found an arbour by the shepheards made/To frolicke in (when Sol did hotest shine)' (1616: *Book 1, Song II*). Stubbes (1585) recognizes the potential for misbehaviour in arbours: 'they have gardens, either palled, or walled about very high, with their harbers and bowers fit for the purpose therein sumpteously erected: herein they may (and doubtlesse doe) many of them play the filthie persons'. Henderson (2005) gives the most comprehensive modern overview of Tudor arbours. See also **bower**.

ash (A) *Fraxinus excelsior* L. is a native timber **tree**, famed for its resilience and fast growth, the close-grained un-splintering wood providing shafts for farm tools as well as staves and spears. An emblem of strength, the ash was thought to guard against witch-craft, to have power to repel serpents, and to have medicinal applications.

(B) The Volscian military leader Aufidius, welcoming his old adversary, makes a striking comparison between the strength of the ash spear and the even more formidable Coriolanus: 'Let me twine/Mine arms about that body, where against/My grained ash an hundred times hath broke,/And scarr'd the moon with splinters' (*COR* 4.5.106–9). This vivid image of physical encounter should catch the ear as hyperbole but is so compelling that we *see* the 'splinters' of the 'grained ash' hurtle towards the moon. The only other mention also prizes the ash as weaponry. King David reassures Lorraine that Scotland's hostile actions against England will be remorseless: the Scots will not, 'hang their staves of grained Scottish ash/In peaceful wise upon their city walls' (*E3* 1.2.30–1).

(C) Hill (1577) recommends ash poles to frame an **arbour**. Lyly (1580, *Euphues*) emphasizes its power against serpents, a belief not limited to England as Colonna (1499) writes of 'the wild ash that vipers shun'. Sidney (1580) says the ash was for spears, while for Heresbach (1596) its main use is support for the **vine**. Peacham (1612) concludes his book of emblems with the idea that the strength of the ash was part of nature's bounty for the making of staves. Norden (1618) marks it down as one of the staple timber trees with **oak** and **elm**, preserved under statute by Henry VIII and Elizabeth. Mabey (1996) includes detail on its local associations and usage.

aspen *Populus tremula* L., a native **tree** of **woods** and hedgerows was possibly more common in Shakespeare's day. Its main characteristic was the permanently shaking **leaves**, hence *tremula,* and under the doctrine of signatures it was used to treat fevers. The two mentions could hardly be more different. In *TIT* the aspen leaf vitalizes an anguished speech of great beauty when Marcus encounters his mutilated niece Lavinia:

> O, had the monster seen those lily hands
> Tremble like aspen leaves upon a lute,
> And make the silken strings delight to kiss them,
> He would not then have touch'd them for his life!

> *(2.4.44–7)*

The emotional charge and tenderness in this example suggests that the aspen leaf exemplified delicacy. The incongruity of its use by the garrulous hostess of the Boar's Head Tavern creates a comic moment. Agitated at the prospect of Pistol crossing her threshold Mistress Quickly draws attention to her nervous disposition: 'Feel, masters, how I shake, look you, I warrant you...Do I? Yea, in very truth, do I, and 'twere an aspen leaf. I cannot abide swagg'rers' (*2H4* 2.4.105–9). Harrison (1587) records aspen as the wood for making arrows. Spenser (1596) uses the imagery of the shaking tree: 'tremble like a leaf of aspen greene' (*Faerie Queene,* Book 1, canto ix, stanza 51, line 4). Mabey (1996: 138) explains that its quivering is particularly notable because the leaves have serrated edges, and so rustle as they rub against each other. For discussion of the theory of signatures see Willes (2011: 211).

B

balm (A) *Melissa officinalis* L., bawm, or bee-balm, a rampant medieval Mediterranean introduction, was used medicinally as an elixir of life; metaphorically it suggested something soothing and calm. This **herb**, often interchangeable with **balsamum**, the holy oil, was used to treat a wide range of symptoms, was a healing ointment for wounds, and served to embalm a corpse; its lemon **scent** favoured its use for **strewing**. It was thought to have the secret of eternal youth, bring love, and guard against witches.

(B) Balm as an agent of purification is used by Mistress Quickly in *WIV* during the final humiliation of Falstaff. In her role as Queen of the Fairies she commands the children, 'The several chairs of order look you scour/With juice of balm and every precious flow'r' (5.5.61–2). Its association with eternal youth may add a layer of comic irony given Falstaff's presence in the centre of the circle. In the same scene Anne Page, despite the contrivances of her parents, guilefully secures a love match by marrying Fenton. So balm as a bringer of love is effective here too. This one seemingly trivial example reveals how the multiplicity of a plant's allusions invigorates a situation. On his return from the Irish campaign, Richard II is confronted with news of Bolingbroke's challenge. At the heart of an elaborate response his defiance is encapsulated in a formula that confirms the ritual potency of holy oil: 'Not all the water in the rough rude sea/Can wash the balm off from an anointed king' (*R2* 3.2.54–5). Balm as soothing, medicinal oil is employed in *COR*. Responding to the bloodied Cauis Martius' appeal for permission to lead another assault, Cominius gives way with the comment, 'Though I could wish/You were conducted to a gentle bath/And balms applied to you, yet dare I never/Deny your asking' (1.6.62–5). Likewise, in *TNK* the magnanimous Theseus gives instructions that his courageous adversaries, Arcite and Palamon, be treated with the most efficacious medicines: 'All our surgeons/Convent in their behoof, our richest balms,/Rather than niggard, waste; their lives concern us/Much more than Thebes is worth' (1.4.30–3). Always carrying singular force, balm as a soothing agent is employed metaphorically on several occasions. Macbeth refers to sleep as 'Balm of hurt minds' (*MAC* 2.2.36). Lear's sudden rejection of Cordelia leads France to wonder why, 'That she, whom even but now was your best object,/The argument of your praise, balm of your age' (*LR* 1.1.214–5) should now be reviled. Henry VI is confident that his benign reign will ensure fealty: 'My pity hath been balm to heal their wounds,/My mildness hath allay'd their swelling griefs' (*3H6* 4.8.41–2). Cleopatra's final words embrace death as painless and easeful: 'As sweet as balm, as soft as air, as gentle' (*ANT* 5.2.311).

Opening the chest washed up on the shore Cerimon discovers Thaisa's body, 'Shrouded in cloth of state, balm'd and treasur'd/With full bags of spices!' (*PER* 3.2.65–6). The ritual of anointing a body with valuable oils indicates a person of standing. The dirge in *TNK,* includes the lines, 'Balm, and gums, and heavy cheers,/ Sacred vials fill'd with tears' (1.5.4–5). The adjective 'balmy' appears twice in *OTH.* After he has calmed the uproar orchestrated by Iago, Othello prepares to return to bed: 'Come, Desdemona, 'tis the soldiers' life/To have their balmy slumbers wak'd with strife' (2.3.257–8). Towards the close of the play Othello, recovering his supple eloquence, kisses the sleeping Desdemona: 'O balmy breath, that dost almost persuade/ Justice to break her sword! One more, one more' (5.1.16–17). The dramatist has taken the word 'balm' with all its associations, to render an adjective sublime in its delicacy, refinement and alluring tenderness. The only other occurrence is in *SON* 107 which speaks of 'this most balmy time' (9).

(C) For a discussion of the tensions or incongruities associated with the closing **forest** scene in *WIV* see White (1991: 44–7). *Pericles,* Arden 3 (297–8), has an interesting note on shrouding and the inclusion of spices in the coffin. Rowland (1981) notes the use of balm in medieval post-natal care. Plat (1594) and Markham (1631) use distilled water of balm in several medicinal compounds. No mention has been found in contemporary writings of its use for embalming. Knight (2009: 81) cites Gerard's reaction to receiving **seeds** from 'a kind of Balme or Balsame tree' from 'the West Indies'. Iyengar (2011) conflates balm and balsamum; she includes an extensive entry largely relating to balsamum, but does not mention the plant *Melissa* as balm.

balsamum, balsom (A) *Commiphora opobalsamum*, a small, rare evergreen **tree**, the balm of Gilead, native to Arabia and Somalia, was known for its aromatic resin; **balm**, balsam and balsamum were used interchangeably at the time. Balsamum had medicinal applications from Greek times. In early modern times it was used mainly to ease childbirth; it was also a massage oil. Sacred since the Queen of Sheba brought balsamum to Solomon, it had extensive ceremonial functions.

(B) Its only appearance is in *ERR*, a play that teems with references to trade and commerce. Having been instructed by his master Antipholus of Syracuse to prepare for their immediate departure from Ephesus, Dromio announces his success: 'Our frautage, sir,/I have convey'd aboard, and I have bought/The oil, the balsamum, and aqua-vitae' (4.1.87–9). This play focusing on the triangle of Epidamium, Ephesus and Syracuse conveys a sense of the sea as a busy highway supporting a complex network of commercial transactions.

(C) Knight (2009: 81) cites Gerard's reaction to receiving **seeds** from 'a kind of Balme or Balsame tree' from 'the West Indies'. Rowland (1981) notes its place in medieval gynaecology and as a fragrant oil, while Parkinson (1640: 1528) calls it 'the true balme or balsame tree of the ancients' giving a wide range of its medicinal applications. Culpeper (1653) describes the method of obtaining oil and gum and its various medicinal uses. Colonna (1499: 306) speaks of 'every sort of balsum-bearing tree'. Chancellor (1982: 16) notes that Mark Antony gave Jericho to Cleopatra 'because of its splendid gardens, whose palm groves and balsam trees were an important source of revenue'. For discussion of the trading nexus and significant aspects of cultural exchange, see Brenner (1993), Gillies (1994), Jardine (1996), Brotton (2002), Stanivukovic (2007), Sebek and Deng (eds), (2008).

bank (A) The edge of a river, a shelf in a river or sea, a raised shelf or ridge of **ground**, a bank could also define a space for growing **flowers**, the sea-shore, or in a rare and obsolete form, it could delineate a country's coastline. A bank can provide a boundary, demarcation, barrier or division between **land** in private ownership, or delineate geographical features; banks require management or care to maintain their identity and function.

(B) The bank as a mound or as a defined space conducive to flowering is pervasive. So too is the river bank, whose chief attribute is agency: active rather than passive, it binds in the river, shaping it and responding to it. There is also a single ambiguous figurative example in *MAC* where a sand bank may be intimated. *STM* contains the only mention of bank as boundary or limit. Characteristic of the bank as inviting and decorative is Venus', 'Witness this primrose bank whereon I lie' (*VEN* 151). More expansive is Oberon's, 'I know a bank where the wild thyme blows,/Where oxlips and the nodding violet grows' (*MND* 2.1.249–50). Orsino's vividly imagined connection between **music** and **scent** is subtly captivating: 'That strain again, it had a dying fall;/O, it came o'er my ear like the sweet sound/That breathes upon a bank of violets,/ Stealing and giving odor' (*TN* 1.1.4–7). Arden 3 (162) reverts to Pope's emendation of 'south' for 'sound'. Florizel's playful response to Perdita's exuberant naming of flowers for his adornment – 'What? like a corse?' – accords with the play's insistent juxtaposition of life and death. Taking his deflationary riposte in her stride, she persists in her ebullience: 'No, like a bank, for love to lie and play on;/Not like a corse; or if – not to be buried,/But quick and in mine arms' (*WT* 4.4.129–32). Iris' description of Ceres' bounty includes the river-bank's provision of flowers for **garlands**: 'Thy banks with pioned and twilled brims,/Which spungy April at thy hest betrims,/To make cold nymphs chaste crowns' (*TMP* 4.1.64–6). What emerges is a picture of the river bank conducive to water-loving **plants**, particularly appropriate as emblems of chastity. It is tempting to think of **'pioned'** as **peonies** and **'twilled'** as petals, but 'pioned' is a term for 'excavated' while 'twilled' can signify intertwined or plaited **osiers**. So what seems to be implied is the interlacing of **branches** or **roots** as supporting structures of the bank – either natural or man-made. Moreover, as neither season nor situation is appropriate to peonies, the evidence seems to be against the flower here.

With a deft touch, Hotspur seeks to persuade Henry IV that Mortimer was taken prisoner only after long and courageous combat with Owen Glendower:

> When on the gentle Severn's sedgy bank,
> In single opposition hand to hand,

> He did confound the best part of an hour
> In changing hardiment with great Glendower.
> Three times they breath'd and three times did they drink,
> Upon agreement, of swift Severn's flood,
> Who then affrighted with their bloody looks,
> Ran fearfully among the trembling reeds,
> And hid his crisp head in the hollow bank,
> Blood-stained with these valiant combatants.
>
> *(1H4 1.3.98–107)*

Hotspur's imaginative recreation of the scene fails to persuade the King. The representation of the river as a vitalizing agent, pictorial and aural, finds powerful expression when the tribunes chastise the plebeians for celebrating Caesar's triumph over Pompey's sons. Re-creating a scene of their devotion to Pompey, Murellus protests:

> And when you saw his chariot but appear,
> Have you not made an universal shout,
> That Tiber trembled underneath her banks
> To hear the replication of your sounds
> Made in her concave shores?

Flavius follows up by instructing them to do penance:

> Go, go, good countrymen, and for this fault
> Assemble all the poor men of your sort;
> Draw them to Tiber banks, and weep your tears
> Into the channel, till the lowest stream
> Do kiss the most exalted shores of all.
>
> *(JC 1.1.43–60)*

The relationship between the river and its banks is conceived as symbiotic. No mere physical entity, the Tiber and its banks possess spirituality and articulacy.

Commending the proposed marriage alliance between Lady Blanch and the Dauphin to promote amity between England and France, Hubert employs a telling metaphor: 'O, two such silver currents when they join/Do glorify the banks that bound them in' (*JN* 2.1.441–2). Seldom prosaic, the river and bank as genuinely expressive is neatly embodied in a conceit in *CYM*. Iachimo, describing a tapestry in Imogen's bedchamber, comments, 'the story/Proud Cleopatra, when she met her Roman,/And Cydnus swell'd above the banks, or for/The press of boats or pride' (2.4.69–72). 'Bank' in *MAC* is ambiguous. Contemplating the assassination of Duncan the eponymous hero balances its rewards and penalties: 'that but this blow/Might be the be-all and end-all – here,/But here, upon this bank and shoal of time,/We'ld jump the life to come' (1.7.4–7). F has 'school', thus taking 'bank' to mean 'bench', possibly the judicial bench. Most editors, however, accept Theobald's emendation of 'shoal', perhaps suggesting an elevated piece of land like a sand bank in an estuary. The conception of bank as part of an estuary may also be present in *SON* 56.10–11.

(C) For excellent summaries of the debates and contributions on 'pioned and twilled brims' see *TMP*, Arden 2 (97–8); *TMP*, Arden 3 (247); Fox (1957: 202); Harrison (1943: 422–6). For a summary and analysis of 'bank and shoal/school' see *Macbeth*, Arden 2 (37–8). Mabey (2010: 113–15) provides engaging commentary on Oberon's bank.

bark (A) The outer sheath or protective covering of a **tree**, which if it is stripped off can leave the tree vulnerable to infection and **canker**; bark can also harbour pests. It can be the skin or covering of a person and also a ship. Figuratively it suggests closeness, intimacy or the provision of assurance.

(B) Although the word 'bark' is used more frequently as a synonym for a ship, there are numerous literal and metaphorical examples of the bark of trees. Decorating trees with verses, Orlando also inscribes their barks: 'O Rosalind, these trees shall be my books,/And in their barks my thoughts I'll character' (*AYL* 3.2.5–6). Later, Rosalind, disguised as Ganymede, teasingly upbraids him for desecrating **nature**: 'There is a man haunts the forest, that abuses our young plants with carving "Rosalind" on their barks; hangs odes upon hawthorns, and elegies on brambles; all, forsooth, deifying the name of Rosalind' (3.2.359–63). Expressing the connectedness of body and soul in terms of the tree and its bark Lucrece contemplates the implications of her defilement: 'Ay me, the bark pill'd from the lofty pine,/His leaves will wither and his sap decay;/So must my soul, her bark being pill'd away' (*LUC* 1167–9). Octavius Caesar recounts how the heroic Antony of the past endured near starvation: 'thy palate then did deign/The roughest berry on the rudest hedge;/Yea, like the stag, when snow the pasture sheets,/The barks of trees thou brows'd' (*ANT* 1.4.63–6). The centrepiece of a richly atmospheric passage taken from Plutarch, this vivid detail of an indomitable Antony contrasts sharply with the hero's later acknowledgement that his power and authority are at an end: 'and this pine is bark'd,/That overtopp'd them all' (4.12.23–4). The bark as preserver of the precious **sap** finds expression in *H8*. Henry VIII chastises Wolsey for imposing punitive taxes that will inflict damage on the economy: 'Why, we take/From every tree, lop, bark, and part o'th'timber;/And though we leave it with a root, thus hack'd,/The air will drink the sap' (*H8* 1.2.95–8). Perdita's objection to human intervention in Nature is challenged by Polixenes: 'You see, sweet maid, we marry/A gentler scion to the wildest stock,/And make conceive a bark of baser kind/By bud of nobler race'(*WT* 4.4.92–5). See *WT*, Arden 3 (265).

Maria, joining her associates in mockery of their suitors declares with proverbial economy, 'Dumaine is mine, as sure as bark on tree' (*LLL* 5.2.285). For a comic-romantic moment in *MND* Shakespeare coins the term 'barky'. Titania envisages her amorous embrace of Bottom as mimicking **nature**: 'So doth the woodbine the sweet honeysuckle/Gently entwist; the female ivy so/Enrings the barky fingers of the elm' (4.1.42–4).

(C) Markham (1631) emphasizes the need to protect the bark during the **grafting** process. Parkinson (1629: 550) recognizes the protective value of bark: 'The canker is a shrewd disease when it happeneth to a tree; for it will eate the barke round, and so kill the very heart in a little space.'

barley (A) *Hordeum vulgare* L. (cultivated) or *H. dystichon* L. (wild), is a hardy cereal **crop** for making poor-quality bread whereas **wheat** was the choice of the rich. Barley was also used in brewing. Barley bread was considered less nourishing, but it was readily available and would be eaten by all in times of shortage. English barley, thought superior to that from the continent, was used extensively in early modern medical practice particularly to cool the blood, and in cosmetics to soften the skin. It gave its name to barley-break, a game of 'catch' played by couples which was also a metaphor for sexual activity.

(B) Opening the pre-nuptial masque Iris welcomes Ceres, goddess of agriculture: 'Ceres, most bounteous lady, thy rich leas/Of wheat, rye, barley, fetches, oats, and pease' (*TMP* 4.1.60–1). The twin themes of **fertility** and purity permeate the masque. Less elevated is the French courtiers' discourse on the English army's unfettered march through their territories. They express surprise that the 'nook-shotten isle of Albion' breeds such formidable adversaries: 'Can sodden water,/A drench for sur-rein'd jades,/their barely-broth,/Decoct their cold blood to such valiant heat?' (*H5* 3.5.14–20). The reference to 'barley-break' in *TNK* is fascinating. The Jailer's Daughter, reminiscent of Ophelia, loses her sanity through her unreciprocated love for Palamon. Imagining playing the young lovers' game where one couple is in 'hell', she reflects on its horrors: 'Faith, I'll tell you; sometime we go to barley-break, we of the blessed. Alas, 'tis a sore life they have i'th'tother place, such burning, frying, boiling, hissing, howling, chatt'ring, cursing! O, they have shrowd measure! take heed: if one be mad, or hang or drown themselves, thither they go' (4.3.30–5).

(C) Cogan (1584) considers barley bread less nourishing than that made of wheat. Drayton recommends native barley 'whose faire and bearded eare/Makes stouter English Ale, or stronger English Beere', and suggests the sexual connotations of the game:

> The frisking Fairy there, as on the light ayre borne,
> Oft runne at Barley-breake upon the eares of Corne;
> And catching drops of dew in their lascivious chases,
> Doe cast the liquid pearle in one anothers faces.
> *(1622, Polyolbion 16, 233–4, 21, 97–100)*

TNK Arden 3 (283) provides a helpful entry on the game and its sexual connotation. Blake (2006) suggests it is merely a game of tag.

barren (A) A negative quality in all respects, barren can suggest unproductive, fruitless, and by extension childless, empty, bare, unresponsive, spiritless, useless, bleak, uninhabited or deserted. Money may be perceived as barren, rendering the charging of interest unjustified.

(B) The use of 'barren' in its horticultural sense is outweighed by its other meanings. Justice Shallow caught between the desire to impress Falstaff and fearful of being perceived as flush with cash, craftily responds to his guest's comment, ''Fore God, you have here goodly dwelling and rich', with the over-insistent riposte: 'Barren, barren, barren, beggars all, beggars all, Sir John! Marry, good air. Spread, Davy, spread, Davy' (*2H4* 5.3.6–9). Before the battle of Crecy King John of France, disparaging England, describes the invader Edward III as: 'inhabiting some barren soil,/Where neither herb or fruitful grain is had' (*E3* 3.3.55–6). This slight resonates, because moments earlier the Black Prince has reported the devastation he has inflicted on the French landscape: 'leaving at our heels/A wide apparent field and beaten path/For solitariness to progress in' (3.3.21–3). In the same play the Countess of Salisbury deploys copious diction when making a distinction between outer appearance and inner substance: 'The ground, undeck'd with nature's tapestry,/Seems barren, sere, unfertile, fructless, dry' (1.2.150–1). Perdita expresses her regret that she is unable to proffer anything more suitably colourful than **rosemary** and **rue** for her mature guests, Camillo and Polixenes:

> the fairest flow'rs o'th'season
> Are our carnations, and streak'd gillyvors
> (Which some call Nature's bastards). Of that kind
> Our rustic garden's barren, and I care not
> To get slips of them.
>
> (*WT* 4.4.81–5)

'Barren', here, means 'devoid of'. The closest metaphorical use of barren in this sense occurs in Richard II's defiant speech to Northumberland. Richard ascribes the confidence of his adversaries to their belief that 'we are barren and bereft of friends' (*R2* 3.3.84). Barren as applied to a landscape that is bleak, inhospitable and uninviting occurs in several places. Announcing the death of Hermione, Paulina claims Leontes is beyond redemption: 'A thousand knees,/Ten thousand years together, naked, fasting,/Upon a barren mountain, and still winter/In storm perpetual, could not move the gods/To look that way thou wert' (*WT* 3.2.210–14). A desolate place bereft of sustenance or any fortifying elements is also present in Henry IV's rejection of Hotspur's plea on behalf of Mortimer: 'No, on the barren mountains let him starve' (*1H4* 1.3.89). It is the bleakness of a frozen landscape that is employed in the Duke of Gloucester's consolatory speech: 'Thus sometimes hath the brightest day a cloud,/And after summer evermore succeeds/Barren winter, with his wrathful nipping cold' (*2H6* 2.4.1–3).

(C) Peacham (1612) compares the **plane tree** proverbially famed for its **shade**, but barren of **fruit**, to people who excel in virtue rather than wealth, and Spenser (ed. 1999, *The Shepheardes Calendar*) uses barrenness as an image of winter. Norden (1618) in his land survey believes that the **land** is naturally barren, and claims man's God-given duty is to make it useful through **husbandry** and **manuring**.

bay (A) **Laurel** and bay were used interchangeably for *Laurus nobilis* L., the bay, or sweet bay, a small evergreen **tree**, possibly a Roman introduction; it is unlikely to be **cherry** laurel, *Prunus laurocerasus* L., which was introduced c. 1600. Confusingly *Laurus* is the modern bay, and *Prunus* the laurel. The bay tree was sacred to Apollo, giving rise to its symbolism of immortality, and its use as the crown of victory; it was associated with celebration especially at Christmas, and was thought to offer protection from lightning. The **plant** had medicinal applications, and the **berries** were a long-known abortifacient. Bay also served as a fragrant **strewing herb**.

(B) Of three botanical uses the most explicitly symbolic occurs in *TNK*. Acknowledging Chaucer's tale as the play's source, the Prologue expresses anxiety:

> How will it shake the bones of that good man,
> And make him cry from under ground, 'O, fan
> From me the witless chaff of such a writer
> That blasts my bays and my fam'd works makes lighter
> Than Robin Hood!' This is the fear we bring;
>
> *(17–21)*

Frustrated by Marina's unwillingness to embrace prostitution, Bawd censures her decorum: 'Will you not go the way of womenkind? Marry, come up, my dish of chastity with rosemary and bays!' (*PER* 4.6.149–51). Rosemary and bay as garnishes for elaborate dishes imply affected behaviour. It is the mystical dimension of the plant that arises in *R2*. Just before the arrival of Richard from Ireland the Welsh Captain refuses to delay his departure citing strange natural phenomena: ''Tis thought the King is dead; we will not stay./The bay-trees in our country are all wither'd,/And meteors fright the fixed stars of heaven' (2.4.7–9). As the bay or laurel was associated with victory, the **withering** of the bay trees was seen as ominous. Interestingly, Holished's account of the withering bay trees related to England and to a time prior to this incident. Moreover, the consternation arose from their sudden re-greening.

(C) For a useful note on the withering and re-greening of the bay trees see *R2* Arden 3 (307); their withering may have been symbolic as bays are known to reshoot after withering in the cold. The use of bay to induce an abortion is documented from Anglo-Saxon times, suggesting a Roman survival (Grattan and Singer, eds: 1952). Gerard (1597) writes of the 'bay or laurel', but his culinary recommendations clearly indicate the sweet bay; he writes that it helps women achieve their 'desired sickness'. Bacon (1625) lists bay with the other evergreens that are so important in the winter garden, and in his **wilderness** or **heath,** actually a cultivated part of the **garden**. He recommends planting bay trees as trimmed stands of **bushes**.

bean (A) Usually identified as an early form of broad bean, *Vicia faba* L., one of several cultivated beans, it was possibly a Roman introduction. An ancient **crop**, it was often dried to supplement the limited winter diet of the poor. It was an essential component of pottage, and of animal fodder. Notorious for its propensity to produce wind, and hence shunned by the wealthy, it was also used medicinally. In proverbial usage the bean suggested poverty. It was considered unlucky and even thought to bring death.

(B) In a highly atmospheric scene in *1H4*, but one frequently dropped in performance, the carriers complain, 'Peas and beans are as dank here as a dog, and that is the next way to give poor jades the bots. This house is turn'd upside down since Robin Ostler died' (2.1.8–11). Damp fodder gives rise to intestinal worms. That fodder containing beans is a good conditioner is apparent in *MND* when Puck narrates, 'I jest to Oberon and make him smile/When I a fat and bean-fed horse beguile,/Neighing in likeness of a filly foal' (2.1.44–6). 'Beguile', here, means 'deceive'. The inference is that a 'bean-fed' horse's libido is raised so much that he is easily duped.

(C) Boorde (1547) is scathing about the nutritional qualities of bread made of beans, equating it to horse-bread, and warning that beans could provoke 'venerious acts'. Cogan (1584) says beans were more suitable for ploughmen than students because they caused wind. Camden (1605) writes 'hunger maketh hard beanes sweet' suggesting their value in times of famine.

bee, drone, hive, honey (A) All were essential to the early modern economy although the pollination process was not fully understood. Bees supplied beeswax, sealing wax, candles, and honey as a sweetener before the ready availability of sugar, which also made medicine more palatable or more easily administered. Bees were thought to be ruled by a king rather than a queen. The parasitical role of the drone was already a subject for jest. Hybla bees were believed to come from three Sicilian towns named for the goddess Hybla. Bees were decorative symbols of virtue, industry and social order in embroidery; they provided emblematic, proverbial, decorative, and sometimes anthropomorphic parallels with human society and the well-governed state. They were a rich source of imagery and allusion in contemporary poetry.

(B) The bee image is present in tragic, comic and political contexts. Lucrece, lamenting her violation at the hands of Tarquin, is mindful of her husband:

> My honey lost, and I, a drone-like bee,
> Have no perfection of my summer left,
> But robb'd and ransack'd by injurious theft.
>> In thy weak hive a wand'ring wasp hath crept,
>> And suck'd the honey which thy chaste bee kept.
>>> *(LUC 836–40)*

An unrepentant Edward III recognizes that his pursuit of the Countess of Salisbury is unprincipled:

> O that I were a honey-gathering bee,
> To bear the comb of virtue from this flower,
> And not a poison-sucking envious spider,
> To turn the juice I take to deadly venom!
>> *(E3 2.1.282–5)*

41

The scene of Cade's rebellion in *2H6* teems with social criticism, strange inversions, fantastic proposals and violent action. The humble bee enters the discourse through Cade's indictment of legal processes which have the capacity to dispossess the common man. He cites the seal, the bee's wax, as the ultimate authentication of legalized fraud: 'Some say the bee stings, but I say, 'tis the bee's wax; for I did but seal once to a thing, and I was never mine own man since' (4.2.81–3). This bizarre scene of the world turned upside-down may be comic and frightening in equal measure, but Cade's comment would have produced knowing nods. Responding sceptically to Warwick's assurance that Prince Hal's indulgence in the low-life of taverns is a sojourn, part of his education, Henry IV makes an obscure observation: ''Tis seldom when the bee doth leave her comb/In the dead carrion' (*2H4* 4.4.79–80). The analogy of the bee's commitment to the honeycomb is perhaps an allusion to Judges 14.8 (see below). Henry, again drawing on the bee analogy, interprets Hal's removal of the crown from his pillow as eager anticipation of his demise. He complains to his other sons how the efforts of thoughtful fathers are met with ingratitude:

> When like the bee tolling from every flower
> The virtuous sweets,
> Our thighs pack'd with wax, our mouths with honey,
> We bring it to the hive, and like the bees,
> Are murd'red for our pains.
>
> *(4.5.74–8)*

The image of the industrious bee belies the true nature of Henry's craft, glossing over his political machinations, usurpation and regicide. A perverse use is adopted by the Archbishop of Canterbury to induce Henry V to invade France and lay claim to his 'rightful' inheritance. Beginning with the concept of the division of labour he proceeds:

> for so work the honey-bees,
> Creatures that by rule in nature teach
> The act of order to a peopled kingdom.
> They have a king, and officers of sorts,
> Where some, like magistrates, correct at home;
> Others, like merchants, venter trade abroad;
> Others, like soldiers, armed in their stings,
> Make boot upon the summer's velvet buds,
> Which pillage they with merry march bring home
> To the tent-royal of their emperor,
> Who busied in his majesty surveys
> The singing masons building roofs of gold,
> The civil citizens kneading up the honey,
> The poor mechanic porters crowding in

Their heavy burthens at his narrow gate,
The sad-ey'd justice, with his surly hum,
Delivering o'er to executors pale
The lazy yawning drone.

(H5 1.2.187–204)

The bees make 'boot upon the summer's velvet buds', their symbiotic activity equated with 'pillage'. The harmony embodied in this paradigm is the very antithesis of Burgundy's description of the desolation of France by Henry V (5.2.31–67). The Hybla bee has two mentions. Falstaff, in expansive mood, asks Hal, 'And is not my hostess of the tavern a most sweet wench?' provoking an ironic riposte to Falstaffian hyperbole, 'As the honey of Hybla, my old lad of the castle' (*1H4* 1.2.39–42). Prior to the battle of Philippi, Antony's denunciation of Caesar's assassins leads Cassius to respond, 'Antony,/The posture of your blows are yet unknown;/But for your words, they rob the Hybla bees,/And leave them honeyless' (*JC* 5.1.32–5).

(C) Virgil, *Georgics IV* provides the main source of references to bees. Bee **husbandry** featured in the new technical and decorative gardening books: Heresbach (1596) and Lawson (1618) include extensive detail on the care of bees, the plants they were thought to like and dislike, and their housing. Their economic importance cannot be overestimated. Lyly (1580, *Euphues*) writes of the imagery of bees, and their organization as a commonwealth, while Whitney (1586) explores bee metaphors with reference to Pliny and Ovid. Hawkins (1633) in his chapter on the bee as an impresa includes classical authority, as well as moral and political analogies, particularly in the context of Marian belief and iconography. Arnold (1988) lists bees and honeycomb as decorations on Queen Elizabeth's clothing, a reflection of her virtue and the iconography of the well-ordered state. With reference to bees wax, *2H6*, Arden 3 (304) points out that 'Included in the "Complaints of the Commons of Kent" was the notorious "Green Wax" which sealed summonses and fines extortionately exacted by the likes of Crowmer (see Holinshed, 222)', adding that 'Cade probably alludes to signing one's name on a legal document as security for another person, thus "I was never mine own man [master] since". See *OED* Seal v 4 and c.f. *MV* 1.2.74'. Apropos Henry IV's reference to honey and the carrion, *2H4*, Arden 2 (143) cites the relevant passage from Judges 14.8 – 'he [Samson] turned out of the way to see the carkeise of the Lion: and beholde, there was a swarm of Bees and hony in the carkeise of the Lion'. Dent (1981:B205, 208, 211).

beech *Fagus sylvatica* L., is a native **tree** of chalk and limestone in south-east England. Planted and naturalized elsewhere it was cultivated in deer-**parks** to provide winter grazing. The timber was used for woodworking, charcoal and gunpowder. Most importantly, its **fruit** or **mast** was common food for foraging pigs and poultry. In times of famine it was used by the poor to make bread. The single reference occurs in *TNK* where the cousins Arcite and Palamon observing a prickly truce recall happier days.

Arcite comments, 'There was a time/When young men went a-hunting, and a wood,/ And a broad beech; and thereby hangs a tale' (3.3.39–41). This sexual innuendo fails in its purpose but confirms the beech as a romantic canopy for young lovers. Drayton (1622) writes of the Chilterns that crowned the Thames with 'beechen wreaths'; of the 'softer beech' growing in the Wealden **forest** which 'to the savage swine let fall our larding mast' and that in Essex the Thames was lined with 'vast beechy banks'. Culpeper (1653) comments on its value as fodder for deer and pigs in **parks, forests** and **chases**.

berry (A) An old English name for **grape**, berry also denoted any **fruit**, particularly wild, even if not technically a berry. Berries were easy to reproduce in embroidery, and they provided a metaphor for scavenging or something ordinary.

(B) There are several generic references to berries. For Caliban, berries are a delicacy. Alluding to their initial friendship he upbraids Prospero for inconstancy: 'When thou cam'st first,/Thou strok'st me and made much of me, wouldst give me/Water with berries in't' (*TMP* 1.2.332–4). Ingratiating himself with his new master, Stephano, Caliban promises, 'I'll show thee the best springs; I'll pluck thee berries' (2.2.160). Chastised for greed the bandits in *TIM* reject the eponymous hero's injunction to feast on Nature's bounty: 'We cannot live on grass, on berries, water,/As beasts and birds and fishes' (4.3.422–3). This conception of berries as sustenance of last resort is also present in *ANT* when Octavius Caesar admiringly describes Antony's desperate retreat over the Alps: 'thy palate then did deign/The roughest berry on the rudest hedge' (1.4.63–4). The brutal Aaron, cradling his infant son, promises him a diet conducive to moulding a warrior: 'I'll make you feed on berries and on roots,/And feed on curds and whey, and suck the goat' (*TIT* 4.2.177–8). The aesthetic delight and artistic inspiration afforded by berries is apparent in *PER* when Gower describes Marina's artistry: 'and with her needle composes/Nature's own shape of bud, bird, branch, or berry,/That even her art sisters the natural roses' (5.Cho. 5–7). Connectedness is the theme of Venus' comparisons: 'Even as the wind is hush'd before it raineth,/.../Or as the berry breaks before it staineth' (*VEN* 458–60). On other occasions when 'berries' are mentioned they are preceded by references to a specific fruit, such as cherries in *MND* (3.2.209–11), strawberries in *H5* (1.1.60–1), mulberries and cherries in *VEN* (1103–4) or the 'painted grapes' that deceive the birds in *VEN* (601–4).

(C) See **bilberry, blackberry, dewberry, gooseberry, strawberry**.

bilberry Also whortleberry, whinberry or blueberry is *Vaccinium myrtillus* L. Native to heaths, moors, and woods, this low-growing **shrub** is probably an ice-age survival. It is less common in south and central England though as 'hurts', a derivation of 'whorts', it can be found in the Surrey hills. It grows extensively in Scotland, on the Welsh mountains and on the Quantock Hills in Somerset. The intense blue colouring of the **fruit** stains the teeth and hands. The slightly acid fruit is the size of a blackcurrant. As the 'fairies' in *WIV* descend on Falstaff the disguised Pistol provides the single reference to this fruit. He directs the 'Elves', 'Where fires thou find'st unrak'd and hearths unswept,/There pinch the maids as blue as bilberry;/Our radiant Queen hates sluts and sluttery' (5.5.44–6). Here the bilberry is convenient both for colour and verbal rhythm. Mabey (1996) provides details of its continuing use. See also **dewberry**.

birch *Betula* L., species *alba,* or *pubescens*, is a common native family; it is not possible to distinguish which modern **tree** was indicated. Birch timber was used widely for lighter or temporary building; a tough and flexible wood, 'the birch' was used for flogging. Birch brooms served for sweeping and were associated with witches. Its **sap** was used in tanning, and medicinally it served to treat rheumatism, eczema and ulcers. Both references are to birch-twigs as instruments of chastisement. Explaining his temporary withdrawal from public life, the Duke claims to have undermined the law by being too permissive:

> Now, as fond fathers,
> Having bound up the threat'ning twigs of birch,
> Only to stick it in their children's sight
> For terror, not to use, in time the rod
> Becomes more mock'd than fear'd;
>
> *(MM 1.3.23–7)*

Duke Theseus and his party are accosted by a schoolmaster who introduces himself and his troupe: 'And I, that am the rectifier of all,/By title paedagogus, that let fall/The birch upon the breeches of the small ones' (*TNK* 3.5.109–11). Turner (1551) records its sole purpose as bound birch twigs for flogging, and Gerard (1597: 1478) notes that magistrates' rods were made of birch: 'and in our time also schoolmasters and parents do terrify their children with rods made of birch'. Parkinson (1640) recommends it when green and flexible to make the structure of **arbours,** and to bind casks; he gives its further uses as faggots for fuel, and for rods to beat children.

bitter sweeting Sometimes simply 'sweeting', bitter sweeting is a sweet variety of **apple,** possibly a cider apple. Mentioned only once, 'bitter sweeting' forms part of word-play in *ROM*. As Mercutio and Romeo make words and double meanings dance between them, with 'goose' gaining prominence, Mercutio asserts, 'Thy wit is a very bitter sweeting, it is a most sharp sauce', provoking the riposte, 'And is it not then well serv'd in to a sweet goose?' (2.4.79–82). Apple sauce was the traditional accompaniment to goose. The presence of the bittersweet apple is apt in more ways than one. Mercutio's chief pleasure in life is to engage Romeo in a verbal game: it is, indeed, his sweetest pleasure. There are four mentions of 'sweeting' but it is almost certain the word simply means 'darling' or 'sweetheart'. In his comments on the Kent apple orchards Drayton suggests the value of this variety: 'The sweeting for whose sake the plow-boys oft make war' (1622, *Polyolbion*, 18.683). McLean (1981) says that it was prized in medieval times for making cider.

blackberry (A) *Rubus fruticosus* L. agg., the most common British wild **fruit** was available to all sections of the community; it is a **plant** of woodland and wasteland, which is sometimes interchangeably called **bramble** and **brier**. Definitions for all these plant names overlap, and it is often not possible to decide which is intended: modern botany has distinguished nearly 300 different species in the *R.* genus. The blackberry continues to provide some of the same medicinal remedies used in Shakespeare's time. It has several associations in folklore and in proverbs, and also many culinary uses.

(B) Two of the three references to the fruit are provided by Falstaff in *1H4*. On the first occasion Falstaff is being successfully interrogated about his cowardly escape at Gad's Hill. Asked to explain how, in the pitch dark, he could distinguish men in Kendal green, he responds: 'Give you reasons on compulsion? if reasons were as plentiful as blackberries, I would give no man reason upon compulsion, I' (2.4.238–40). Falstaff is even wittier than might appear at first sight. As Spier and Anderson (1985: 455fn) observe, 'raison and reason' were the source of 'homonymic puns'. In the same tavern scene he enacts the role of the King when preparing Hal for the impending meeting with his father. Deploying rhetorical questions or a mock catechism he asks, 'Shall the blessed sun of heaven prove a micher and eat blackberries? a question not to be ask'd' (2.4.407–10). Falstaff couples the truant ('micher') and delinquency with an image of the sun/son – the heir apparent. Thersites, temperamentally even less reverential than Falstaff, provides a ruthless dissection of the conduct of the Trojan war, including the failed schemes of the Greek leadership: 'the policy of those crafty swearing rascals, that stale old mouse-eaten dry cheese, Nestor, and that same dog-fox, Ulysses, is not prov'd worth a blackberry' (*TRO* 5.4.9–12). However much enjoyed, the easy availability of the blackberry made it synonymous with low value.

(C) Knight (2009: 90–1) quotes both Gerard and Harrison expressing frustration at the casual disdain shown by many towards plants growing abundantly in the locality yet willingly paying high prices for inferior imports. Colonna (1499: 32) refers to blackberries as 'fragrant'. While Langham (1597) lists the blackberry for a wide range of medicinal applications, most writers comment on it as the bramble or brier probably because the blackberry was almost ubiquitous and uncultivated. Hunt (1989) suggests there was a considerable overlap of names at the time: blackberry could designate **mulberry**, **bilberry** and blueberry; bramble could equally refer to the blackberry, mulberry, **eglantine**, dog rose, and **hawthorn**, making accurate identification virtually impossible. Mabey (1996) details its country use and associations. Biddle (1999) notes that blackberries were planted in the **wilderness** at Nonsuch: a symbol both of **fruitfulness**, and of art overcoming nature. See also **berry, hep.**

bloom (A) Bloom designates the **blossom** or **flower** of a **plant**, the flower for its own sake, which is more delicate than blossom and holding the promise of fruit; it is often a poetic reference to a flower. Bloom can indicate all the flowers of a plant; figuratively it suggests a state of the greatest beauty, a flourishing condition, vulnerability or fragility. 'In bloom' is a synonym for 'in flower', 'flowering' or 'blossoming', and 'to bloom' is 'to bear flowers, to come into flower'; bloom on fruit is the sheen of ripeness.

(B) Figuratively bloom is the embodiment of burgeoning youth. Despite the disparity in age and condition Leonato challenges Claudio to a duel: 'I'll prove it on his body, if he dare,/Despite his nice fence and his active practice,/His May of youth and bloom of lustihood' (*ADO* 5.1.74–6). This Chekhovian moment, both painful and comic, takes extraordinary life from the twin phrases of the last line. Queen Elinor encourages King John to accept the offer made by France to ensure the removal of young Arthur as a contender for the English crown: 'That yon green boy shall have no sun to ripe/The bloom that promiseth a mighty fruit' (*JN* 2.1.472–3). Charles the Dauphin expresses his gratitude to Joan for driving the English out of Orleans: 'Thy promises are like Adonis' garden,/That one day bloom'd and fruitful were the next' (*1H6* 1.6.6–7). *TNK* has two delicate examples. Arcite, the outsider, reflects on an Athenian ritual: 'This is a solemn rite/They owe bloom'd May, and the Athenians pay it/To th'heart of ceremony' (3.1.2–4). Looking out from his prison cell into the garden Palamon images his desire for Emilia:

> Blessed garden,
> And fruit and flowers more blessed, that still blossom
> As her bright eyes shine on ye, would I were,
> For all the fortune of my life hereafter,
> Yon little tree, yon blooming apricock!
> How I would spread, and fling my wanton arms
> In at her window!
>
> *(2.2.232–8)*

The conception of blooming and fruiting animates politics, culture and love.

(C) Poetic examples from Ault (1949) include Surrey's 'The soote (sweet) season that bud and bloom forth brings', Sackville's 'every bloom down blown' by winter, and Griffin's contrast between his 'all-withering age' and the 'flowers of blooming years' which are green and fair. Campion (ed. David, 1969) writes 'Ever blooming are the joys of heaven's high paradise'.

blossom (A) The **flowers** of any **plant** can be called blossom; blossoming can signify the process of flowering, or the entire plant or **tree** in blossom, where **bloom** commonly describes a single fragile flower. Symbolic of spring, bloom, **blow** and blossom were interchangeable. Metaphorically blossom can suggest the flowering of love or a relationship, a state of loveliness, growing to maturity, the peak of manhood, a beautiful child, one of great promise, full of or in the prime of life. A blossom out of season means the opposite, possibly indicating death.

(B) The vulnerability of blossom to capricious weather is imaged by Warwick to convey the diminished beauty of his daughter, the Countess of Salisbury: 'As a

May blossom with pernicious winds,/Hath sullied, wither'd, overcast, and done' (*E3* 1.2.96–7). Contemplating his loss of office, Cardinal Wolsey alights on the image of blossom and frost to universalize his situation:

> This is the state of man: to-day he puts forth
> The tender leaves of hopes, to-morrow blossoms,
> And bears his blushing honors thick upon him;
> The third day comes a frost, a killing frost,
> And when he thinks, good easy man, full surely
> His greatness is a-ripening, nips his root,
> And then he falls as I do.
>
> *(H8 3.2.352–8)*

Wolsey's reflective acceptance of his fall, objectifying the political process, contrasts markedly with Antony's agitated, blame-shifting disgust at his undoing. Nevertheless, the Roman hero draws on the same image to produce a phrase of compelling beauty:

> The hearts
> That spannell'd me at heels, to whom I gave
> Their wishes, do discandy, melt their sweets
> On blossoming Caesar; and this pine is bark'd,
> That overtopp'd them all.
>
> *(ANT 4.12.20–4)*

Blossoms are integral to the configuration of the Temple Garden scene. Vying for support, Richard Plantagenet and Somerset seek to distinguish adherents by inviting them to signal favour by choosing a white or red rose. Vernon supporting Richard says: 'I pluck this pale and maiden blossom here,/Giving my verdict on the white rose side'. Somerset's defeat intensifies the invective, motivating Richard to elevate his emblem: 'Now, by this maiden blossom in my hand,/I scorn thee and thy fashion, peevish boy' (*1H6* 2.4.47–76). This 'maiden blossom' will become associated with a spiral of antagonism and violence.

A simile of singular beauty is present in *MM*. Charged with the task of informing Isabella that her brother is under sentence of death for making his fiancée pregnant, Lucio behaves with unusual circumspection and delicacy:

> Fewness and truth, 'tis thus:
> Your brother and his lover have embrac'd.
> As those that feed grow full, as blossoming time
> That from the seedness the bare fallow brings
> To teeming foison, even so her plenteous womb
> Expresseth his full tilth and husbandry.
>
> *(1.4.39–44)*

Another rascal, Autolycus, muses on his involvement in the elevation of the Old Shepherd and his son: 'Here come those I have done good to against my will, and already appearing in the blossoms of their fortune' (*WT* 5.2.124–5). The most peculiar metaphorical example occurs when the Ghost, confronting Hamlet, delivers a vivid description of the bitter consequences of his untimely death: 'Thus was I, sleeping, by a brother's hand/Of life, of crown, of queen, at once dispatch'd,/Cut off even in the blossoms of my sin' (*HAM* 1.5.74–6). Here, uniquely, blossoming is inimical.

(C) Lyly's *Euphues* (1580: 140) illustrates the vulnerability of blossom: 'The bud is blasted as soon as the blown rose, the wind shaketh off the blossom as well as the fruit.' Greene suggests that love is transitory: 'Lovers are like to the Heban blossomes that open with the deawe, and shut with the sunne' (1590, vol. 8, *Never Too Late*: 85). Spenser (ed. 1999, *The Shepheardes Calendar,* 1596 *The Faerie Queene*) includes the blossom of courtesy, blossom of tender years, of youth, blossom as a sign of the abundance of spring, and blossoms lost to both lust and winter.

blow, blown (A) Often a poetical reference to **flowers** at or past their best, or **withering**, as a noun (*OED* blow *n.3*) blow is sometimes a synonym for **bloom** or **blossom**, hence a potential ambiguity. 'Blown' can signify blown by wind, swollen, inflated, and has sexual connotations of loss of virginity. A contrast can be drawn between bloom as the freshness of youth, and blow indicating maturity or age.

(B) Which of the distinctive meanings of 'blown' is intended is generally made clear by the context, and writers of the period seem reasonably assured that there is little danger of confusion on the part of the reader or audience. The conjunction of **bud**, **canker** and blown, so frequent in the literature of the time, is deployed by Valentine and Proteus as they dispute the merits of succumbing to love. Proteus defends his status as a lover with the claim, 'Yet writers say: as in the sweetest bud/The eating canker dwells, so eating love/Inhabits in the finest wits of all', to which Valentine responds:

> And writers say: as the most forward bud
> Is eaten by the canker ere it blow,
> Even so by love the young and tender wit
> Is turn'd to folly, blasting in the bud,
> Losing his verdure, even in the prime,
> And all the fair effects of future hopes.
>
> *(TGV 1.1.42–50)*

'Blow' here evidently means reaching maturity. The opening line of Oberon's list of flowers is unexpected – 'I know a bank where the wild thyme blows' (*MND* 2.1.249) – because wild thyme, a ground hugging plant with tiny flowers, is admired more for the pungent scent emanating from its leaves than for the blown bloom. This encourages a sense of 'blown' as both being in flower and caressed by a gentle breeze. The courtly Boyet in *LLL* delights in verbal duels, especially with the Princess. Advising the ladies to remain masked, and to exchange their 'favours' so that the young men will each woo the wrong partner, Boyet says, 'Blow like sweet roses in the summer air', provoking the quizzical response, 'How blow? how blow? speak to be understood'. The query opens the door to Boyet's conceit: 'Fair ladies mask'd are roses in their bud;/Dismask'd, their damask sweet comixture shown,/Are angels veiling clouds, or roses blown' (5.2.293–7). 'Dismask'd' or unveiled, a woman reveals her beauty in full bloom. Perhaps confusingly, '*veiling* clouds' implies lowering or removing them. Claudio, denouncing Hero as promiscuous, declares he had thought her 'As chaste as is the bud ere it be blown' (*ADO* 4.1.58). A virgin bride is the bud of the flower; marriage alone should lead to full flowering. Having described Hamlet as 'Th'expectation and rose of the fair state' Ophelia perceives him now as, 'That unmatch'd form and stature of blown youth/Blasted with ecstasy' (*HAM* 3.1.152–60). When Cleopatra comments tartly on the sudden lapse of protocol, she is imaging the rose in its overblown state: 'What, no more ceremony? See, my women,/Against the blown rose may they stop their nose/That kneel'd unto the buds' (*ANT* 3.13.38–40). Precise and brutal, this depiction exposes the cynical response of those detecting imminent loss of power. Antony draws on a closely related image twice (3.13.20–1; 4.12.22–3). Prince Edward pleads for encouragement as he is about to enter a major battle as a novice. Part of Audley's counsel includes a stoical disquisition on life and death: 'First bud we, then we blow, and after seed;/Then presently we fall, and as a shade/Follows the body, so we follow death' (*E3* 4.4.138–40). Fearing for the fate of her sons at the hands of Richard III, Queen Elizabeth laments, 'My unblown flow'rs, new-appearing sweets!' (*R3* 4.4.10).

(C) Contemporary uses are largely poetical: Tottel (1557: 4) includes the description of the restless state of a lover: 'Her beauty hath the frutes opprest,/Ere that the buds were sprong and blowne'. Lyly (1580: 231) suggests youth is more attractive than age: 'A rose is sweeter in the bud than full-blown, young twigs are sooner bent than old trees.' Ault includes similar comparisons:

A maid is so modest, she seemeth a rose
When it first beginneth the bud to unclose;
But a widow full-blowen ful often deceives,
And the next wind that bloweth shakes down all her
    leaves.

(1949, Anon, 1557–8, 38)

bosky Possibly derived from the French *bosquet*, bosky means covered in **bushes, shrubs,** underwood and **thickets**. In Prospero's masque Ceres commends Iris, who 'with each end of thy blue bow dost crown/My bosky acres and my unshrubb'd down,/Rich scarf to my proud earth' (*TMP* 4.1.80–2). 'Bosky acres' is a more seductive image than are shrubs and thickets. This is the first recorded example of 'scarf' being used in a figurative sense.

bough (A) Sometimes interchangeable with **branch**, a bough is a large **limb** or offshoot of a **tree**. By transference it can designate a family line, or anything metaphorically referred to as a tree. Boughs of **laurel** or **bay** were said to crown a victor's head. Boughs could be personified; the bough could also represent a gallows, which itself was often made from the bough of a tree.

(B) The 'bough' is notable for the frequency with which some peculiar aspect or character is ascribed to it. In *AYL*, Duke Senior and his companions are encountered by Orlando, 'Under the shade of melancholy boughs' (2.7.111). His love poems that decorate the trees proclaim, 'But upon the fairest boughs…/Will I "Rosalinda" write' (3.2.135–7). Oliver relates how he was discovered 'Under an old oak, whose boughs were moss'd with age/And high top bald with dry antiquity' (4.3.104–5). The bough that proves so treacherous to Ophelia resonates with peculiar poetic significance:

> There is a willow grows askaunt the brook,
>
> …
>
> There on the pendant boughs her crownet weeds
> Clamb'ring to hang, an envious sliver broke,
> When down her weedy trophies and herself
> Fell in the weeping brook.
>
> *(HAM 4.7.166–75)*

The emblem of broken faith the **willow** inadvertently participates in Ophelia's death, and so shares in the sorrowful response of the 'weeping brook'. Pleading with Theseus to spare Palamon and Arcite, Emilia deploys a probing analogy: 'Do men proin/ The straight young boughs that blush with thousand blossoms,/Because they may be rotten?' (*TNK* 3.6.242–4). Cautioning Guiderius and Arviragus against the corruption of the Court, Belarius cites his own undeserved fall from trusted soldier to exile:

> Then was I a tree
> Whose boughs did bend with fruit; but in one night,
> A storm or robbery (call it what you will)
> Shook down my mellow hangings, nay, my leaves,
> And left me bare to weather.
>
> *(CYM 3.3.60–4)*

Defending himself against Apemantus' charge that his predicament arose from egregious folly, Timon protests:

> But myself,
> Who had the world as my confectionary,
> The mouths, the tongues, the eyes, and hearts of men
> At duty, more than I could frame employment;
> That numberless upon me stuck as leaves

> Do on the oak, have with one winter's brush
> Fell from their boughs, and left me open, bare,
> For every storm that blows –
>
> *(TIM 4.3.259–66)*

This section of a magnificent speech from Shakespeare's most underrated play makes telling use of this arboreal metaphor. A notable political application arises in *R2*. The Gardener, reflecting on Richard's kingship, concludes his extended gardening analogy with the comment, 'Superfluous branches/We lop away, that bearing boughs may live;/ Had he done so, himself had borne the crown,/Which waste of idle hours hath quite thrown down' (3.4.63–6). The bough as small offshoot occurs in *TIT* where the eponymous hero makes his victorious return to Rome, 'bound with laurel boughs' (1.1.74).

(C) Contemporary writers frequently ascribe human characteristics to boughs: Spenser (ed. 1999, *The Shepheardes Calendar*) has tears raining from boughs, bared boughs beaten by storms, and sharp boughs. Drayton (1622) notes fogs dripping from boughs, proud aspiring boughs, boughs ready for garlands, limbs that in battle were lopped like boughs, and stocky boughs.

bower (A) Often poetical for a shelter, an **arbour**, or **tree**-enclosed place, a bower is a **shady** recess usually with leafy cover. Arbours and bowers could be temporary or semi-permanent structures for displaying **statues**, used for assignations, private conversations or sexual encounters. By extension bower could suggest other forms of hiding place or shelter, somewhere for the court and aristocracy to exchange their structured world for one of make-believe, or play at a pastoral life.

(B) The period between the engagement of Hero and Claudio and their marriage ceremony is pleasantly filled by schemes designed to unite the principal verbal combatants, Beatrice and Benedick. Devising a strategy to entrap Beatrice, Hero brings together the elements of romantic love and playful entertainment by setting the scene in a bower. Her instructions to Margaret capture both atmosphere and situation with playful lightness of touch, even incorporating a political simile:

> Whisper her ear, and tell her I and Ursley
> Walk in the orchard, and our whole discourse
> Is all of her. Say that thou overheardst us,
> And bid her steal into the pleached bower,
> Where honeysuckles, ripened by the sun,
> Forbid the sun to enter, like favorites
> Made proud by princes, that advance their pride
> Against the power that bred it.
>
> *(ADO 3.1.4–11)*

Titania's bower is quite unlike the carefully manufactured structure in Leonato's Sicilian garden. Bottom's utterances are hardly conducive to dalliance but Titania creates her own verbal music: 'lead him to my bower./The moon methinks looks with a wat'ry eye;/And when she weeps, weeps every little flower,/Lamenting some enforced chastity' (*MND* 3.1.197–200). The bower's association with protection and liberation is confirmed by Puck's allusion to Titania's 'close and consecrated bower' (3.2.7). After winning the battle of wills with Titania, Oberon receives the changeling child: 'Which straight she gave me, and her fairy sent/To bear him to my bower in fairy land' (4.1.60–1). A space created to be secret and inviolable, he, too, has his own bower.

The beleaguered Countess of Salisbury is no sooner relieved by Edward III than she finds herself besieged by him. Rejecting the proposal that she 'lend' him her body 'to sport withal' she responds with a closely reasoned representation of the body as the bower of the 'intellectual soul':

> My body is her bower, her court, her abbey,
> And she an angel pure, divine, unspotted.
> If I should lend her house, my lord, to thee,
> I kill my poor soul, and my soul me.
>
> *(E3 2.1.234–42)*

Here is the clearest example of the bower as a consecrated space, divine and sublime. Attempting to persuade her son to soften his attitude towards the plebeians, Volumnia divests the bower of its more elevated aspects: 'I know thou hadst rather/Follow thine enemy in a fiery gulf/Than flatter him in a bower' (*COR* 3.2.90–2). Distressed by news of Tybalt's death Juliet, employing 'bower' as a verb, attempts to reconcile her love for Romeo with the horror of his deed: 'O nature, what hadst thou to do in hell/When thou didst bower the spirit of a fiend/In mortal paradise of such sweet flesh?' (*ROM* 3.2.80–2).

(C) In Ault's anthology (1949) 'bower' is the preferred poetic word: he has 18 examples, in contrast to just one for 'arbour'. Bower is the secluded place of love, honour, chastity, and safety; as a **garden** or banqueting-**house** it could be a place for eating. Spenser (1596) employs it as a place of safety, or for feasting in seclusion. Stubbes (1585) in his Puritan rants against any forms of pleasure sees bowers offering temptation and potential evil, often in a sexual context, but for Raleigh they represent heavenly glory and safety:

> There the holy paths we'll travel,
> Strewed with rubies thick as gravel,
> Ceilings of diamonds, sapphire floors,
> High walls of coral, and pearl bowers.
>
> *(Ault 1949,* The Passionate Man's Pilgrimage, *360)*

Drayton (1622) writes of **sedgy** or watery bowers, secret, ivy-sealed and woody bowers, sumptuous, delightful and gloomy bowers, and dainty summer-bowers. Biddle (1999) notes a 1582 bower for Diana at Nonsuch between the banqueting house and the **wilderness**.

bowls (A) The game of bowls featured frequently in early modern **gardens**, either as a discrete area set aside as a bowling **green**, or in a covered bowling **alley**; both were usually attached to a great house in town or country, and could sometimes be open to the public. As now, bowls were weighted to one side giving them a bias, so providing opportunities for word-play.

(B) 'Bowls' as a pleasurable pastime is present in *R2*. The Queen and her ladies seek distraction while awaiting news of Richard's plight:

> Queen: What sport shall we devise here in this garden
> To drive away the heavy thought of care?
> Lady: Madam, we'll play at bowls.
> Queen: 'Twill make me think the world is full of rubs,
> And that my fortune runs against the bias.
>
> *(3.4.1–5)*

There is dread as well as comeliness in this scene. The metaphor of the bowl and its bias might suggest randomness, though this is negated by the gardeners' commentary on Richard's neglect. That bowls could be taken seriously is intimated by the irate response of Cloten: 'Was there ever man had such luck? when I kissed the jack upon an up-cast, to be hit away! I had a hundred pound on't'. Consoled that due retribution has been exacted – 'You have broke his pate with your bowl' – and informed of the arrival of a visitor at Court, Cloten's spirits revive. Continuing the financial locution, he says, 'Come, I'll go see this Italian. What I have lost to-day at bowls I'll win to-night of him' (*CYM* 2.1.1–49). That bowling is perceived as a refined activity is conveyed by the Servant in *WT*. Seeking admission to the sheep-shearing feast for some vigorous dancers he promises, 'they themselves are o'th'mind (if it be not too rough for some that know little but bowling) it will please plentifully' (4.4.329–31). After Hortensio confirms that Kate has been tamed – 'go thy ways, the field is won' – Petruchio responds with a bowling metaphor: 'Well, forward, forward, thus the bowl should run,/And not unluckily against the bias' (*SHR* 4.5.24–5). Menenius also resorts to the image when attempting to talk his way past the Volscian guards. Having expatiated on his role as the chief chronicler of Coriolanus' deeds, he admits to occasional exaggeration: 'Nay, sometimes,/Like to a bowl upon a subtle ground,/I have tumbled past the throw' (*COR* 5.2.19–21). The implication here is that some bowling greens were designed to make the game more demanding by means of undulations. This example is apt for a speaker who spends most of the play employing verbal subtleties in his political manoeuvring. A world away, Costard defends the disgraced Nathaniel for abandoning his role as Alexander the Great in the 'Pageant of the Nine Worthies': 'a foolish mild man, an honest man, look you, and soon dash'd. He is a marvellous good neighbour, faith, and a very good bowler; but for Alisander – alas, you see how 'tis – a little o'erparted' (*LLL* 5.2.581–4). Both moving and amusing this description affords us a glimpse of a world outside the action of the play.

(C) Lawson (1618) recommends a bowling-alley in the **orchard** for health and recreation, but inevitably Stubbes (1585) inveighs against bowls, as against all other forms of pleasure. Husselby and Henderson (2002) worked on a plan of Cecil House in the Strand, only discovered at Burghley in 1999, which throws new light on the role of bowls in early modern times. There appears to have been a 'sporting complex', accessible from the outside, facilitating independent use, an early private 'health club' with bowling and tennis which were 'increasingly associated with gambling, drinking and delinquent behaviour'. Henderson (2005) documents the ubiquity of bowling greens and alleys in palaces and great houses, with detailed reference to contemporary plans, and demonstrates how they were an integral part of the newly designed gardens.

box-tree, box (A) *Buxus sempervirens* L., a native small **shrub**, box has been grown as an ornamental plant since classical times; it is usually carefully clipped into topiary shapes. Box was associated with funerals, immortality and eternity, and thought to be a plague preventative. Initially disliked in Tudor times for its **rank** smell when clipped, it became a general **hedging** plant for **knot** gardens into the seventeenth century; as a freestanding tree it could be clipped into topiary, grown in a pot or as hedging for an **arbour**.

(B) Appearing only once, its presence as a stage-prop in one of Shakespeare's great comic scenes is memorable. Maria directs Sir Toby Belch, Sir Andrew and Fabian to conceal themselves so that they can observe Malvolio's response to her forged letter: 'Get ye all three into the box-tree; Malvolio's coming down this walk' (*TN* 2.5.15–16). The box-tree is the visual centre-piece of this scene, as the observers, increasingly agitated, indignant and sportive, respond to the Steward's display of egotism and ambition. *TN* constantly juxtaposes death with lovemaking and mirth so that the emblematic significance of the box-tree may apply here, as well as promoting awareness of Olivia's fine garden.

(C) Colonna (1499) shows that the fashion for box was Europe-wide: he includes clipped box trees, **fountains** surrounded by columns of box, a box-tree in a container of lapis lazuli, a box hedge, and complicated topiary of box-trees in the shapes of crescent moons or balls. Bartholomeus (1582) notes its use for topiary, gives its medicinal virtues, comments on the density of its wood and its value as an evergreen. Parkinson (1629) writes of variegated box, of a small and large form, the latter of which could provide the required shelter in *TN,* noting its efficacy against the 'French disease' or syphilis.

brake (A) Brake can be bracken, the native *Pteridium aquilinum* L., or other forms of large fern. It can also refer to a clump of **bushes, thicket, covert,** or a path through **briers,** and by extension an entanglement as in briars or **thorns.**

(B) Shakespeare's applications of 'brake' are indeterminate. Employed five times in *MND* three of the mentions are probably of the same brake, designated surprisingly as **hawthorn**, which is prickly. This could be a **hedge** but a thicket is more likely. Peter

Quince is the first character in the play to use the word when he declares: 'here's a marvail's convenient place for our rehearsal. This green plot shall be our stage, this hawthorn brake our tiring-house' (3.1.2–4). A little later Peter Quince again directs them, 'When you have spoken your speech, enter into that brake' (3.1.74–5). Having witnessed the transformed Bottom, the rest of the Mechanicals, fleeing in panic, are tormented by Puck: 'I'll follow you,/I'll lead you about a round,/Through bog, through bush, through brake, through brier' (3.1.106–7). Here by inference 'brake' is irritating, perhaps a thicket or bracken. Later, narrating his trickery, Puck describes how Bottom, 'ent'red in a brake;/When I did him at this advantage take,/An ass's nole I fixed on his head' (3.2.15–17). Taking flight from Helena, Demetrius threatens, 'I'll run from thee, and hide me in the brakes,/And leave thee to the mercy of wild beasts' (2.1.227–8). The function of brakes as places of concealment is present also in *3H6*. The First Keeper announces to his colleague, 'Under this thick-grown brake we'll shroud ourselves,/ For through this laund anon the deer will come' (3.1.1–2). '**Laund**' means **glade**, so this convenient cover facilitates seeing while being unseen. The qualification, 'thick-grown', implies that brakes are not always dense. Wolsey provides an interesting metaphorical example when defending himself against widespread criticism for his imposition of heavy taxes. He claims that such misrepresentation is the price to be paid by those occupying high office: ''Tis but the fate of place, and the rough brake/ That virtue must go through' (*H8* 1.2.75–6). Here is an imputation that *some* brakes are dense and hard to negotiate. The only really ambiguous case arises in *MM* where Escalus expresses dismay at Angelo's determination to execute Claudio for the crime of fornication:

> Well; heaven forgive him! and forgive us all!
> Some rise by sin, and some by virtue fall;
> Some run from brakes of ice and answer none,
> And some condemned for a fault alone.
>
> *(2.1.37–40)*

Editors grapple with what Riverside (590) refers to as 'A famous crux'. Rowe's emendation 'brakes of *vice*' signifying 'thickets of crimes' makes good sense as the contrast is with 'fault alone'. Arden 2 (29), however, rejects 'brakes' as 'thicket', exploring other possible emendations and interpretations.

(C) Bracken was universally regarded as a nuisance, except when used as fuel; brake as hiding place suggested sanctuary. Bullein (1595: 11) compares the need to discipline children with weeding crops: 'For men haue smal profite of their corne, which be choked and ouercome with Thistles, Bryers, and Brakes which were not weeded in time, much lesse of their children, which haue receyued neyther correction nor honest learning in due season.' Spenser (1596) writes of flight through the hindering wood which includes brakes and briers, and Norden (1618) records brakes (bracken) as a sign of unprofitable land, and difficult to eradicate. Drayton describes the denseness of a brake, which might be a thicket or a large clump of bracken, of the deer hiding from the huntsman where 'He in the broom and brakes had long time made his lair', and of his being driven by the hounds from this place of safety (1622, *Polyolbion* 13, 27–8). Markham (1631) comments that brakes (bracken) provide good fuel for the malting process in making beer.

bramble, brier (A) *Rubus fruticosus* L. agg. **blackberry**, the name often inter-changeable with bramble or brier, a plant of woodland and wasteland, is the most common British wild **fruit**, accessible to all sections of the community. Brier can also indicate the wild **rose**, *Rosa canina* L., or **hawthorn** or blackthorn in hedging; all were sometimes called **thorns**. Thorns and briers, used by countrymen to designate any thorny plant, could provide a metaphor for troubles. Brambles and briers are threat-ening, symbolic of usurpation, decay, worthlessness, lowliness or entanglement owing to the quick growth of their long thorny stems. *R. fruticosus* has medicinal applications; it appears frequently in folk-lore and can be associated with the devil.

(B) Bramble/brier is personified in *VEN*. So intimidating is the wild boar in flight that plants recoil to allow it easy passage: 'The thorny brambles and embracing bushes,/ As fearful of him, part, through whom he rushes' (629–30). The faint-hearted bramble, however, becomes a pitiless brier to the vulnerable. Attempting to imbue Adonis with the tactics of the hare, Venus describes the creature's manoeuvres:

> Then shalt thou see the dew-bedabbled wretch
> Turn, and return, indenting with the way;
> Each envious brier his weary legs to scratch,
> Each shadow makes him stop, each murmur stay,
>
> *(VEN 703–6)*

For Orlando the thorns serve as convenient hooks for displaying his love poems. Rosalind affects displeasure at the author who 'hangs odes upon hawthorns, and elegies on brambles' (*AYL* 3.2.361–2). The vexatious plant is used by Puck to cause the Mechanicals maximum discomfort: 'I'll lead you about a round,/Through bog, through bush, through brake, through brier' (*MND* 3.1.106–7). Capable of enduring extremes of violence but unable to tolerate praise, Caius Martius dismisses Menenius' description of the 'wounds his body bears' as, 'Scratches with briers,/Scars to move laughter only' (*COR* 3.3.50–2). Adriana, excoriating her husband, draws on the brier's propensity to snare and cling: 'If aught possess thee from me, it is dross,/Usurping ivy, brier, or idle moss' (*ERR* 2.2.177–8).

(C) Contemporary writers focus on the bramble/brier rather than on the ubiquitous and uncultivated blackberry, emphasizing its practical use as a thorn, its nuisance value to farmers, and its associated imagery. Colonna (1499) uses comparable symbolism of danger and threat with woodlands full of briers and brambles. Erasmus (1536: vol. 33) considers something particularly stubborn, as 'harsher than a dry bramble'. Spenser (ed. 1999, *The Shepheardes Calendar*) writes of the 'spiteful' and 'solitary brere'. In his survey of the country in 1618, Norden records briars with

weeds, thistles, brakes and **thorns** as obstacles to cultivation, symbols of idleness and a curse on the land.

branch (A) An offshoot of a **tree** or other **plant**, a **branch** grows out of the main stem or out of a **bough**; though a branch is smaller than a bough, the terms can sometimes be interchangeable. By transference it can refer to anything resembling a branch of a tree such as an offshoot or division, a river, road or human artery, a family tree or, rarely, the human arm. As branches can be **pruned** or disbranched to restrain their growth, so too a human being can be pruned by discipline or mutilated by violence. Bare or stripped branches of both trees and human beings attract considerable pity. 'Branch' was a technical term for a pattern in embroidery with gold or needlework of flowers or foliage (*OED* 'branch' *n*.3.).

(B) Of numerous references only two are literal. Describing Marina's remarkable gifts the Chorus in *PER* praises her exquisite needlework: 'Deep clerks she dumbs, and with her needle composes/Nature's own shape of bud, bird, branch, or berry,/That even her art sisters the natural roses' (5.Cho. 5–7). The other case occurs in the garden scene in *R2* where, though literal, it is used by way of analogy to critique Richard's reign: 'Superfluous branches/We lop away, that bearing boughs may live;/Had he done so, himself had borne the crown,/Which waste of idle hours have quite thrown down' (3.4.63–6). Declining Warwick's proposal that he take the office of Protector to Henry VI, Clarence resorts to symbolism:

> No, Warwick, thou art worthy of the sway,
> To whom the heav'ns in thy nativity
> Adjudg'd an olive branch and laurel crown,
> As likely to be blest in peace and war;
> And therefore I yield thee my free consent.
>
> *(3H6 4.6.32–6)*

The majority of applications pertain to the family tree. Nominating a husband as reward should she cure the King, Helena makes an important caveat:

> Exempted be from me the arrogance
> To choose from forth the royal blood of France,
> My low and humble name to propagate
> With any branch or image of thy state;
>
> *(AWW 2.1.195–8)*

Characteristic of the family tree image is Richard Gloucester's insistence, despite Edward's proposed amnesty, that the wounded Clifford be put to death:

> Revoke that doom of mercy, for 'tis Clifford,
> Who not contented that he lopp'd the branch
> In hewing Rutland when his leaves put forth,

> But set his murth'ring knife unto the root
> From whence that tender spray did sweetly spring,
> I mean our princely father, Duke of York.
>
> *(3H6 2.6.46–51)*

WT has two interesting examples. Camillo makes light of Sicilian hospitality by emphasizing the intimacy that binds the two kings: 'Sicilia cannot show himself overkind to Bohemia. They were train'd together in their childhoods; and there rooted betwixt them then such an affection, which cannot choose but branch now' (1.1.21–4). Evidently the intended meaning is to continue to grow and flourish. Within minutes, however, Leontes succumbs to a fit of jealousy and plots the death of his dear friend. Like so many 'snare' words in this play – e.g. 'commit', 'satisfaction', the first collocating naturally with 'adultery', the second with 'sexual' – 'branch' can also mean 'divide' or 'separate'. Perdita provides a simple but unusual usage when wishing she had flowers of spring, appropriate to the young women at the sheep shearing: 'That wear upon your virgin branches yet/Your maidenheads growing' (4.4.115–6). Antony, naturally inclined to employ plant imagery, is the only character to use the term 'branchless'. Justifying his response to her brother's political manoeuvres, he protests to Octavia: 'If I lose mine honor,/I lose myself; better I were not yours/Than yours so branchless' (*ANT* 3.4.22–4).

(C) Erasmus (1536: vol. 32) records removing something 'root and branch' suggesting radical destruction or deletion. Spenser (ed. 1999, *The Shepheardes Calendar*) draws many human parallels, including 'the branch of youth', 'my budding braunch thou wouldest cropp', 'thy father, had he lived this day,/To see the braunch of his body displaie', and 'the braunch once dead, the budde eke needes must quail'. Writing to his mother about a wayward youth, Peacham asks:

> Why then dispaire yee Madame, of your sonne,
> Whose wit, as in the sappe, doth but abound
> These branches prun'd, that over rancklie runne,
> You'le find in time, the bodie inward sound.
>
> *(1612,* Minerva Britanna*, 32–5)*

Arnold (1988) lists flower work, gold honeysuckle, a gold holly bush, and green hawthorn in gold on the Queen's clothing as one example of branches in embroidery.

brier, rose (A) Brier indicates the **thorny** characteristics of any **rose**, sometimes called the brier-rose although this is not a technical designation; sometimes synonymous with rose, it generally suggests a wild **plant**, and can include **blackberry** or **bramble**. The **eglantine** or sweet brier, *Rosa rubiginosa* L., is a plant species in its own right with its discrete iconography. Figuratively, brier suggested the dark side of any rose, the spoiling of perfection, in contrast to its beauty, fragrance, purity or depth of colour, often with the implication of transience.

(B) During rehearsals Flute, in the role of Thisbe, delivers the delightfully incongruous lines, 'Most radiant Pyramus, most lily-white of hue,/Of color like the red rose on triumphant brier' (*MND* 3.1.93–4). Theatrical in quite a different way is Richard Plantagenet. Quarrelling with Somerset in the Temple Garden, he encourages his supporters, 'From off this brier pluck a white rose with me' (*1H6* 2.4.30). The bandits, justifying their delinquency as 'want', lead Timon to remonstrate, 'the oaks bear mast, the briers scarlet heps' (*TIM* 4.3.419). This is the single mention of the fruit of the brier. Throwing into disarray the rehearsals of the Mechanicals, a delighted Puck boasts, 'briers and thorns at their apparel snatch' (*MND* 3.2.29). Pining for love, Rosalind sighs, 'O how full of briers is this working-day world!' (*AYL* 1.3.12). Gratified by Diana's willingness to engage in the bed-trick, Helena promises happier times to come: 'But with the word the time will bring on summer,/When briers shall have leaves as well as thorns,/And be as sweet as sharp' (*AWW* 4.4.31–3). The paradox of the rose loved for its beauty but disliked for its thorns is resolved by Emilia:

> It is the very emblem of a maid;
> For when the west wind courts her gently,
> How modestly she blows, and paints the sun
> With her chaste blushes! When the north comes near her,
> Rude and impatient, then, like chastity,
> She locks her beauties in her bud again,
> And leaves him to base briers.
>
> *(TNK 2.2.137–43)*

(C) The beauty of roses is everywhere in early modern England. Fulfilling a wide range of culinary and medicinal purposes, roses frequently appear in plays and poetry, and are celebrated in every gardening book. Their darker side – the thorny stems or briers – is equally ubiquitous. Greene suggests that everything carries a hidden threat 'for the fairest Roses have prickes, the purest Lawnes their moles' (1590, *Never too Late*, 45). When Dowsabell 'picked of the bloomie Bryer' she was presumably plucking a wild rose (Drayton, vol. 2, Eclogues 536). Hawkins (1633) gives the Catholic rose iconography describing Mary as the mystic rose. Potter (2010: 131–59) discusses the rose in the Elizabethan context.

brook (A) A small stream or rivulet; used as a verb 'to brook' something or someone is to put up with or bear or tolerate.

(B) Generally used prosaically, the brook can exert contextual or poetic pressure. Prospero conveys a sense of brooks as intrinsic to the landscape: 'Ye elves of hills, brooks, standing lakes, and groves' (*TMP* 5.1.33). Earlier, Iris animates a scene by describing the meandering streams so vital to the non-human inhabitants: 'You nymphs, call'd Naiades, of the windring brooks,/With your sedg'd crowns and ever-harmless looks,/Leave your crisp channels, and on this green land/Answer your summons; Juno does command' (4.1.128–31). Shakespeare's coinage 'windring' gives a sense of winding, wandering and meandering. The French King in *E3* refers to the 'wand'ring brooks' (4.5.4). *TIM* provides another fascinating example. Criticizing Timon for his self-imposed exile from the comforts of the city, Apemantus unintentionally elevates the natural world: 'Will the cold brook,/Candied with ice, caudle thy morning taste/To cure thy o'ernight's surfeit?' (4.3.225–7). The image of the brook 'candied with ice' is exhilarating in its beauty. The paradox of the superfluous 'caudle' – Timon needs no cure for a hangover – colludes with 'candied' to intensify a musicality that reinforces the visual impact. Whereas Apemantus' brook is imaged to support his philosophical argument, the brook becomes agent and mourner in Gertrude's framed description of Ophelia's death:

> There is a willow grows askaunt the brook,
> That shows its hoary leaves in the glassy stream,
>
> …
>
> When down her weedy trophies and herself
> Fell in the weeping brook.

(HAM 4.7.166–75)

The association of the brook with the **willow** is a strong one and occurs again in *PP*: 'Cytherea (all in love forlorn)/A longing tarriance for Adonis made/Under an osier growing by a brook,/A brook where Adon us'd to cool his spleen' (6.3–6). Perhaps the neatest metaphorical example occurs in *2H6* where the Machiavellian Earl of Essex seeks to persuade the King that Gloucester, despite his seeming honesty, is a dangerous schemer who aspires to kingship: 'Smooth runs the water where the brook is deep,/And in his simple show he harbors treason' (3.1.53–4).

(C) Drayton (1622) employs 'brook' extensively throughout *Polyolbion*.

broom *Cytisus scoparius* L., a low-growing **shrub**, is a relatively short-lived native **plant** of **heaths**, waste ground and sandy **soil**. Broom **buds** were pickled and eaten in **salads**, apparently a favourite food of James I; broom was widely prescribed in **herbal** and folk medicine including its use as an abortifacient. Emblematic as the *planta genista* of Henry II and the Plantagenets, it attracted superstition, and was regarded as unlucky indoors. Broom was associated with witchcraft, probably from the idea that witches' broomsticks were made from the plant. *TMP* has the clearest reference to this plant. Specifying Ceres' diverse domains, Iris cites 'thy broom-groves,/Whose shadow the dismissed bachelor loves,/Being lass-lorn' (4.1.66–8). It would seem that 'broom-groves' afford forsaken lovers isolation for peaceful contemplation. In her madness the abandoned Jailer's Daughter claims to be able to sing 'The Broom' (*TNK* 4.1.107). Arden 3(362) prints the opening verse which refers to 'bonnie Broom' and 'Birchen Broom', the latter implying a broom for sweeping. Norden (1618) records broom as a nuisance on an **estate**, a curse on the **land**, useful for fuel but difficult to eradicate even through ploughing and burning. Nares (1859) suggests that broom is not tall enough or long-lived enough to form a proper grove: he proposes **birch** as an alternative.

Bucklersbury (A) A short street between modern Queen Victoria Street and Walbrook, which was inhabited at least from Roman times; in early modern London Bucklersbury, a mixed residential and commercial area, was very close to the river. It was well-known for housing **apothecaries** and those selling drugs whether fresh and green, or dry.

(B) The single reference to Bucklersbury arises during Falstaff's attempt to stir the passions of Mistress Ford as a means of gaining access to her husband's coffers. With only the slightest nod in the direction of his lack of lovers' language, his mature years and his body odour, Falstaff protests, 'Come, I cannot cog and say thou art this and that, like many of these lisping hawthorn buds, that come like women in men's apparel, and smell like Bucklersbury in simple time – I cannot' (*WIV* 3.3.70–3). Bucklersbury evidently is at its most odoriferous when fresh **herbs** or **simples** are most abundant.

(C) Stow (1598) records it as 'Bucklesbury', and Nares quotes Dekker: 'Go into Bucklersbury and fetch me two ounces of preserved melounes; look there be no tobacco taken in the shop while he weighs it' (1859: vol. 1, 116). Blench (1964: 125) cites *Certain Sermons appointed by the Queen's Majesty*: 'Some worldly people cannot abide the sweetness of preaching as they that be used to stinking savours can not live in Bucklersbury, or in the poticaries shoppe', suggesting that the name provided a ready metaphor for smell. Ackroyd (1998) draws on Dekker, Stow and Shakespeare to give the history of Thomas More's connection with the site: he owned a large house in Bucklersbury in which he raised his family, and which he later leased to his adopted daughter Margaret Giggs. The Grocers' Company had shops in Bucklersbury where they stored and sold spices, confectionery, perfumes, spiced wines, herbs and drugs which they compounded and dispensed to the public: the street's historical role is confirmed on www.apothecaries.org.

bud (A) The rudimentary, immature state of a **leaf** or **flower** before it opens, the unfolding bud was seen as a mystery, and symbol of purity. Poetically bud is anything premature requiring careful attention, or anything bud-like in appearance. It can suggest juvenile emotions including love, by extension a young child, the offshoot of a family, or someone immature, fragile, or of little merit. Buds were perceived as particularly susceptible to weather and disease. The **rose** bud was thought to be especially vulnerable. A bud was a sign of spring, of a progression in growth or life, something or someone of great potential beauty. Flower and vegetable buds featured in **salads** for taste and decoration.

(B) Delicate botanical images frequently enter the murky world of politics. Reacting to Somerset's report that all their French territories have been lost, York muses:

> Cold news for me; for I had hope of France
> As firmly as I hope for fertile England.
> Thus are my blossoms blasted in the bud,
> And caterpillars eat my leaves away;

> *(2H6 3.1.87–90)*

This is a singularly apt and concise application as the term '**caterpillars**' signifies political parasites. York's image conveys perfectly his restless eagerness to gain control of the kingdom. The capture of her son, young Arthur, leads Constance to lament: 'There was not such a gracious creature born./But now will canker-sorrow eat my bud,/And chase the native beauty from his cheek' (*JN* 3.4.81–3). Prince Edward reports his successful recruitment of soldiers, announcing, 'I have assembled my dear lord and father,/The choicest buds of all our English blood/For our affairs in France' (*E3* 2.2.83–5). This exuberant delight in the conscription of the finest young men both underwrites and undermines the enterprise. Vulnerable, 'buds' possess at least a latent capacity to register a negative aspect of the campaign. Buckingham, deploring the extravagant enterprise of The Field of the Cloth of Gold and the establishment of a treaty likely to be breached, precipitates Norfolk's confirmation: 'Which is budded out,/For France hath flaw'd the league, and hath attach'd/Our merchants' goods at Burdeaux' (*H8* 1.1.94–6). This single application of 'budded' is strategically placed in a discourse deeply engaged with political and economic considerations. Preparing for their decisive encounter, Hotspur's claim that Hal's 'name in arms' is inferior to his own is countered by the Prince with the prediction, 'I'll make it greater ere I part from thee,/And all the budding honors on thy crest/I'll crop to make a garland for my head' (*1H4* 5.4.70–3). The image of the bud appears frequently in the realm of love. Montague, endeavouring to discover the source of his son's loss of spirit, confides to Benvolio that Romeo is 'So far from sounding and discovery,/As is the bud bit with an envious worm,/Ere he can spread his sweet leaves to the air/Or dedicate his beauty to the sun' (*ROM* 1.1.150–3). This image of premature blighting, a persistent concept in the play, provides a poignant undercutting to Juliet's first-night parting from Romeo: 'Sweet, goodnight!/This bud of love, by summer's ripening breath,/May prove a beauteous flow'r when next we meet' (2.2.120–2). Kate, finally committing herself to Petruchio's game of perverse inversions, addresses an elderly wayfarer as, 'Young budding virgin, fair, and fresh, and sweet' (*SHR* 4.5.37). Adonis seeking to repel Venus' passionate assault protests his youthful un-readiness for such encounters: 'Who plucks the bud before one leaf put forth?' (*VEN* 416). Here the bud may be a leaf bud rather than the more frequently-used flower or blossom bud, because leaf was also used as a synonym for petal.

(C) Hoyles (1991: 249–50) notes that the word 'petal' did not enter the English language until 1682, commenting 'It is strange to think that the word petal, with all its connotations, was unknown to Shakespeare.' Contemporary writers often employ 'bud' metaphorically: Elyot (1565: 22) has children as 'the softe and tender buddes wherby the frute may growe wylde', and Spenser (ed. 1999, *The Shepheardes Calendar*) writes of budding hawthorn, buds of poetry and lust, of being cut down prematurely as 'my budding braunch thou wouldest crop'. See also **buttons**.

bulrush *Typha latifolia* L., is a native wetland or shallow-water **plant**. In Christian iconography the bulrush symbolized faithfulness and humility. As growing at the place where Moses was found, it became associated with Christ as the source of salvation.

Describing how the Jailer's Daughter yearns for Palamon's love, the forsaken wooer places the bulrush at the centre of his pathetic account: 'her careless tresses/A wreath of bulrush rounded; about her stuck/Thousand fresh water-flowers of several colors' (*TNK* 4.1.83–5). So at odds with the appeal of the unnamed water **flowers**, the forlorn bulrush is imbued with the symbolism of fidelity and humility. Heresbach (1596) sees the bulrush as an equal annoyance with **briers** and **brambles**; its only purpose is to provide fodder for foraging pigs. Spenser records a rustic use: 'To make fine cages for the Nightingale,/And Baskets of bulrushes was my wont' (ed. 1999, *The Shepheardes Calendar*, December: 79–80).

bur A general term for any plant which adheres to clothing, bur implies uselessness, idleness and tenacity. It is possibly burdock, *Arctium lappa* L., a native plant of wild and waste places, with ball-like **flowers**, actually long stiff scales with hooked tips or burs, which will cling to any passing animal for dispersal over a wide area. Burdock has a range of herbal and medicinal uses. Of value as fodder only for the donkey, it was symbolic of worthlessness. Taking pleasure in denigrating the Duke to the Friar (the Duke in disguise), Lucio adopts a manner of easy familiarity for another round of scurrilous abuse. Unwilling to accept the Friar's attempt to shake him off, he insists, 'By my troth, I'll go with thee to the lane's end. If bawdy talk offend you, we'll have very little of it. Nay, friar, I am a kind of bur, I shall stick' (*MM* 4.3.177–9). The outrageously entertaining Lucio insists on having the last word. His emblem is decidedly the bur. The difficulty of removing the bur is also in evidence when Lysander attempts to shake off his discarded sweetheart, Hermia: 'Hang off, thou cat, thou bur! Vile thing, let loose' (*MND* 3.2.260). Bartholomeus (1582) thinks the bur sticks to clothing for love of human beings, and recommends it medicinally. Ryden (1978: 55–7) compares the contemporary etymology and uses of bur and burdock. Mabey (2010) includes a chapter giving a broader approach to weeds including burdock. See **brier, dock, hardock**.

burnet *Poterium sanguisorba*, L., or **salad** burnet, is a **strewing herb**, the name deriving from its brownish **flowers**, which was often incorporated in salads for their fresh slightly cucumber-like taste. Its medicinal uses included dressing wounds. The name was also used for *Sanguisorba officinalis* L., or great burnet. Both are native plants and served some of the same medicinal purposes. Valued as a plant contributing to sustenance and beauty, the only reference to burnet belongs to Burgundy's description of the French countryside subsequent to Henry V's invasion: 'The even mead, that erst brought sweetly forth/The freckled cowslip, burnet, and green clover' (*H5* 5.2.48–9). Shakespeare effects a subtle balance to each line or grouping, with 'burnet' occupying a position between plants that are given appealing epithets. Contemporary sources agree on its medicinal uses. Drayton (1622) includes it as a strewing herb at the wedding of Thames and Isis, and Bacon (1625) recommends planting burnet where it will be trodden on to release its scent.

bush (A) A **shrub** particularly with low-growing **branches,** or several shrubs in a mass as a **thicket.** 'Bush' can be used metaphorically to indicate anything resembling it in shape, such as a mass of feathers or foliage, or it can signify a place of concealment. The vintner's sign with an **ivy**-bush, from the plant's association with Bacchus, was hung outside the premises to indicate good wine, hence its proverbial association with wine.

(B) Bush as a source of nourishment occurs in *TIM* where the eponymous hero berates the bandits for their greed: 'The oaks bear mast, the briers scarlet heps;/The bounteous housewife Nature on each bush/Lays her full mess before you. Want? why want?' (4.3.419–21). The conception of a desolate landscape affording neither sustenance nor shelter finds expression in *LR*. Gloucester attempts to dissuade Lear from leaving the protection of the castle: 'Alack, the night comes on, and the bleak winds/ Do sorely ruffle; for many miles about/There's scarce a bush' (2.4.300–2). The most sinister reference is metaphorical. In *2H6*, Suffolk informs Queen Margaret that he has set a trap for the Duchess of Gloucester: 'Madam, myself have lim'd a bush for her,/And plac'd a choir of such enticing birds/That she will light to listen to the lays' (1.3.88–90). The necromancer and his associates, seduced into a scheme to bring down the Duchess as a prelude to destroying her husband, are subsequently executed. This familiar figurative use also occurs in *SHR*. At her wedding feast Bianca attempts to avoid Petruchio's baiting: 'Am I your bird? I mean to shift my bush,/And then pursue me as you draw your bow' (5.2.46–7). The cosy domesticity of *WIV* may be slightly undermined when Page invites the party to his house for breakfast and sport: 'after, we'll a-birding together. I have a fine hawk for a bush' (3.3.230–1). The sport involved a sparrowhawk used to drive small birds out of a bush to be shot. Rosalind as Epilogue in *AYL* refers to the bush as a vintner's sign when playfully engaging the audience with a defence of her new role: 'If it be true that good wine needs no bush, 'tis true that a good play needs no epilogue. Yet to good wine they do use good bushes; and good plays prove the better by the help of good epilogues' (3–7). The fable that the Man in the Moon is accompanied by a bush arises in *TMP* and *MND* (twice). Stephano's assertion, 'I was the Man i'th'Moon, when time was', elicits Caliban's devotional commitment: 'I have seen thee in her, and I do adore thee. My mistress show'd me thee, and thy dog, and thy bush' (*TMP* 2.2.138–41). Having given due consideration to procuring moonshine for their play, the Mechanicals in *MND* alight on the idea that, 'one must come in with a bush of thorns and a lantern, and say he comes to disfigure, or to present, the person of Moonshine' (3.1.59–61). Peter Quince as Prologue duly introduces Moonshine complete with bush: 'This man, with lantern, dog, and bush of thorns' (5.1.135).

(C) The *OED* cites Brewer on the 'beggar's bush', a tree near Huntington, a noted rendezvous for itinerant beggars. Erasmus (1536: vol. 33) gives the proverbial 'good wine needs no bush' suggesting quality needs no advertisement. Poetically bushes were often uncomfortable or **thorny**, as Spenser's bramble bush, holly bush, bushes ranke, bushye brere (ed. 1999, *The Shepheardes Calendar*). The use of an ivy bush to indicate good wine was commonplace: Greene writes 'And that I have loved wine well, I would touch both the vintner and his bush' (1592, vol. 11, *The Defence of Conny-catching*: 69). Norden (1618) records bushes as signs of wasted, unproductive land.

buttons (A) The obvious meaning is fastenings for clothing, but buttons also indicated something of little value, or the **buds** of **flowers**, the last sometimes called bachelor's buttons, a popular name for **flowers** with button-like buds and flowers.

(B) There are two unambiguous mentions of buttons as buds and a further use which is questionable. Protective of his sister's virginity, Laertes cautions Ophelia to resist Hamlet's blandishments:

> The canker galls the infants of the spring
> Too oft before their buttons be disclos'd,
> And in the morn and liquid dew of youth
> Contagious blastments are most imminent.
>
> *(HAM 1.3.39–42)*

The idea of the **canker**-worm blighting the flower in the bud is not in itself remarkable, but it provides a telling image in a plea which is urgent and elaborate. For all the protective care embodied in this beautiful speech it has an oppressive dimension. Quite different in tone is Arcite's reverential soliloquy: 'O queen Emilia,/Fresher than May, sweeter/Than her gold buttons on the boughs, or all/Th'enamell'd knacks o'th'mead or garden!' (*TNK* 3.1.4–7). The natural world, moulded and cultivated by the gardener is both elevated as the ultimate standard of beauty and diminished when placed alongside the nonpareil of women. Its 'enamell'd knacks' are ornately showy, merely meretricious. An ambiguous case arises in *WIV*. The Host of the Garter speculates that Young Fenton will win Anne Page regardless of the manoeuvres designed to achieve a more suitable marriage (the favoured candidates in question being Slender and the eccentric French doctor): 'He capers, he dances, he has eyes of youth; he writes verses, he speaks holiday, he smells April and May – he will carry't, he will carry't – 'tis in his buttons – he will carry't' (3.2.67–70). Editors express uncertainty as to whether these are flower buds or clothes' buttons. References to the seasons particularly associated with budding makes the botanical meaning probable, though the doubtful origin of the phrase ''tis in his buttons', meaning 'it is a sure thing', leaves the door open to dispute. Arden 2 (78) tentatively proposes that 'the image is that of the flower that is yet to open but whose colour and character are already determined'. Arden 3 (212) admits uncertainty. Riverside (340) is unequivocal in settling for flower buds.

(C) The derivation of 'bachelors buttons' remains unclear: it seems likely that a wide range of flowers with tight button-like buds were called buttons, and modern writers give their individual identifications. Greene, writing of fragrant flowers, appears to suggest they were thought of as love charms: 'thereby I saw the Batchelers buttons whose virtue is to make wanton maidens weep when they have worn it forty weeks under their aprons for a favour' (1592, *A Quip,* 218). Lawson (1618) names **pansies,**

marjoram, strawberries, daffodils, leeks, onions and **daisies** as bachelors buttons, which he plants with small **herbs**. Amherst (1896) refers to bachelor's buttons as a suitable plant for **knot gardens**, but gives no identification. Thomas (1984) says that there were at least 20 species with the name of bachelor's buttons, to which Vickery (2010) adds another ten.

C

cabbage Any member of the *Brassica* L. family, often called coleworts or worts. The most common cultivated form was *Brassica oleracea var. capitata* L., a staple food, which was a constituent of **salads** for the rich, or cooked into a mush and eaten as pottage by the poor. The single mention of cabbage is the consequence of a verbal quibble. Despite Parson Evans' seemingly sympathetic comment on Falstaff's response to Justice Shallow's threats – '*Pauca verba;* Sir John, good worts' – his Welsh pronunciation 'worts' for 'words', becomes the butt of Falstaff's wit: 'Good worts? good cabbage' (*WIV* 1.1.120–1). Cabbage, usually as coleworts, features frequently in gardening and planting manuals. McLean (1981) categorizes it as the most important pot vegetable and comments on its use by different sections of society.

camomile Sometimes 'chamomile', *Chamaemelum nobile* L. is a low, quick-growing aromatic native **herb**, one of the seven Anglo-Saxon magic herbs. It symbolized energy, as it was early recognized that it grew more strongly if walked on; it was thought to restore health to weaker plants. Widely used for **strewing**, camomile was also valuable both in the kitchen and in early modern medical practice. The single mention, which is proverbial, is delivered by Falstaff in *1H4*. Caricaturing the King in a tavern diversion, his chastisement of Hal takes the form of neatly balanced antitheses: 'Harry, I do not only marvel where thou spendest thy time, but also how thou art accompanied; for though the camomile, the more it is trodden on, the faster it grows, yet youth, the more it is wasted, the sooner it wears' (2.4.398–402). Falstaff's catechistic address is both imitation and parody: a sly mockery of clichés that masquerade as profundities. Greene employs similar imagery: 'the camomile the more it is trodden, the sweeter smell it yieldeth, even so ought a good wife to be kinde to her husband midst his greatest discourtesies' (1592, vol. 11, *Philomela*: 199). Stuart and Sutherland (1987) give the use of camomile for **turf** seats; Sanecki (1994) notes its inclusion in the nine miraculous Anglo-Saxon herbs, recording its associations with magical intent, wealth, love and fragrance.

canker (A) a reddish-green moss-like substance which attacks **fruit trees** and wild **roses** producing rose-galls on stems resulting in the slow decay of **bark** and tissue. This term could apply to numerous other diseases affecting plants. Canker can also indicate a type of wild rose, or its fruit, canker **blossom** being the actual **flower**. Regional, now rare, usage of canker designated a variety of **plants** or fungi, including field **poppy**, dandelion and **toadstool**. Canker is an obsolete term for **caterpillar** or other insect larvae which attack plants. Figuratively it signified something internally destructive. In human beings it could be a literal or perceived spreading sore, particularly if it threatened beauty. Canker could be a corrosive, destructive agent, a cancer sore, a mouth ulcer, the (then) new disease of syphilis which was thought to eat the body away from the inside as canker did a rose. Poetically canker represented loss of love, virtue or destruction of beauty.

(B) A conception that the most beautiful plants in nature are those most susceptible to canker finds frequent expression in both plays and sonnets, exhibited, for instance, in such lines as, 'For canker vice the sweetest buds doth love' (*SON* 70.7); 'Yet writers say: as in the sweetest bud/The eating canker dwells' (*TGV* 1.1.42–3). In *SON* 35 the speaker rationalizes his loved one's transgression:

> No more be griev'd at that which thou hast done:
> Roses have thorns, and silver fountains mud,
> Clouds and eclipses stain both moon and sun,
> And loathsome canker lives in sweetest bud.

The canker worm occasionally features in a comic context. In *2H4* Poins produces a witty turn of phrase when referring to Falstaff's precocious Page: 'O that this blossom could be kept from cankers!' (2.2.94–5). In *MND*, Hermia rails against Helena for stealing Lysander's heart: 'O me, you juggler, you canker-blossom,/You thief of love! What, have you come by night/And stol'n my love's heart from him?' (3.2.282–4). There is room for uncertainty here as 'canker-blossom' might refer to the secret, stealthy, surreptitious nature of the canker-worm or to the wild rose, though elsewhere the wild rose is designated as 'canker' or 'canker-bloom'. A conflation may be present with Helena perceived to possess the beauty of the rose and the guile of the canker-worm. The sardonic Don John expresses contempt for his brother Don Pedro: 'I had rather be a canker in a hedge than a rose in his grace' (*ADO* 1.3.27–8). In the world of *ADO* social status is correlated with refinement and sophistication. Disdaining such niceties, the illegitimate Don John's preference for the hedge-rose might seem quite natural. Having emerged from a bruising interview with Henry IV, Hotspur denounces his father and his uncle for facilitating the dethronement of Richard II: 'To put down Richard, that sweet lovely rose,/And plant this thorn, this canker, Bullingbrook?' (*1H4* 1.3.175–6). This image, contrasting the refined domestic rose with its wild cousin, illustrates perfectly the potential of metaphor for influencing political perceptions. *SON* 54 also juxtaposes cultivated and wild roses:

> The rose looks fair, but fairer we it deem
> For that sweet odor which doth in it live.
> The canker-blooms have full as deep a dye
> As the perfumed tincture of the roses,
> Hang on such thorns, and play as wantonly,

> When summer's breath their masked buds discloses;
> But for their virtue only is their show,
> They live unwoo'd, and unrespected fade,
> Die to themselves. Sweet roses do not so,
> Of their sweet deaths are sweetest odors made:
>
> *(3.12)*

The cultivated rose is favoured because it is perfumed and distillation prolongs its life after its beauty has faded. Falstaff is brutally cynical when describing the bedraggled band that he has pressed into service: 'such as indeed were never soldiers, but discarded unjust servingmen, younger sons to younger brothers, revolted tapsters, and ostlers trade-fall'n, the cankers of a calm world and a long peace' (*1H4* 4.2.27–30). Arden 3 (291) quotes Nashe, *Piers Penniless* (1592), 'all the canker-womes that breed on the rust of piece'. 'Canker' as a sore or disease is articulated with clarity in *JN* (5.2.12–15).

(C) Callimachus contrasts canker and the rose: 'I see now that as the canker soonest enters into the white rose, so corruption doth easiliest creep into the white head' (Lyly, 1580, *Euphues*: 170). Spenser (1596: *Book IV, canto ii, 33.6 & Book V, canto vi, 33.9*) writes of the 'cursed Eld the cankerworme of writs', and 'cankred hate', while Parkinson (1629: 550) describes the effect on fruit trees: 'The canker is a shrewd disease when it happeneth to a tree; for it will eate the barke round, and so kill the very heart in a little space.' Drayton (1622) includes 'cank'red evil', and 'cank'ring lust', emphasizing its corrosiveness. Duncan-Jones (1995) points out that both Gerard and Parkinson identify the canker rose as the wild poppy, *Papaver rhoeas* L. She argues that the 'canker-blooms' in *SON* 54 refer to the wild poppy. Iyengar (2011) gives the full medical connotations of canker. See also **worm.**

caper This **bramble**-like **shrub**, *Capparis spinosa*, produces **flower buds** that can be pickled. 'Caper' is also a dance. Responding to Sir Andrew's assurance, 'Faith, I can cut a caper', Sir Toby Belch quibbles 'And I can cut the mutton to't' (*TN* 1.3.121–2). The word-play on the berry of this food-**plant**, used for mutton sauce, carries a sly allusion to 'mutton' as a prostitute. See Williams (2006: 212) and Arden 3 (178–9).

caraway *Carum carvi* L. is probably a naturalized escapee from cultivation rather than a native **plant**. Its **seeds** and oil had culinary and medicinal uses, including covering the **smell** of rotting teeth; it was often recommended to be eaten with **apples** to counteract their flatulent effect. Caraways provided flavouring to cakes and sweets. The Gloucestershire scenes in *2H4* are celebrated for capturing the atmosphere of a time and a place. Falstaff soliloquizes contemptuously on Shallow's little empire, but insinuates himself with his host as he scents a financial opportunity. Shallow, nurturing ambitions for titles, sees Falstaff as a vehicle for achieving these aspirations. His insistent hospitality is, therefore, both engaging and pitiable: 'Nay, you shall see my orchard, where, in an arbor, we will eat a last year's pippin of mine own graffing, with a dish of caraways, and so forth' (5.3.1–4). This scene of bucolic ease is soon disrupted by the interloper, Pistol, bringing news of Henry IV's death, thus propelling the hopes of Falstaff and Shallow into a fool's paradise. Cogan (1584: 48, 53) devotes a chapter to caraways saying the seeds were particularly to be 'used in making comfits and to be eaten with apples ... for all such things breede winde', a point he later emphasizes: 'howbeit we are wont to eate Carawayes or Biskettes, or some other kinde of Comfittes, or seedes together with Apples, thereby to breake wind engendered by them: and surely this is a verie good way for studentes'. Hall (Lane 1996) prescribes caraway for a range of problems. McLean (1981) gives the value of caraway oil and its use to cover the smell of rotting gums and teeth.

carduus benedictus, holy-thistle (A) *Carduus benedictus* now *Cnicus benedictus* L. is an annual **plant** of the **thistle** family, a native of waste places in Southern Europe, which flourished in England under cultivated conditions. Its colloquial name of 'holy thistle' reflects the belief that it was a direct gift from God, a universal panacea, and efficacious against the plague. An alternative explanation thought to account for its almost magical attributes, was its association with the Virgin Mary.

(B) The sole reference to this plant arises during the preparations for Hero's wedding in *ADO*. Beatrice complains of being 'sick': 'I am stuff'd cousin, I cannot smell'. The dialogue, already crackling with sexual innuendo, invites Margaret's recommended cure: 'Get you some of this distill'd *carduus benedictus,* and lay it to your heart; it is the only thing for a qualm'. Before Beatrice can respond, Hero picks up on the Benedick pun with the line, 'There thou prick'st her with a thistle'. At this point, the 'green sickness' or the virgin's complaint, anaemia, has been alluded to, also love-sickness, and the cure-all potential of this plant. Beatrice, reacting suspiciously to their apparent awareness of her romantic feelings towards Benedick, snaps '*Benedictus*! Why *benedictus*? You have some moral in *benedictus*'. Margaret, now scenting victory, completes the game: 'Moral? no, by my troth I have no moral meaning, I mean plain holy-thistle. You may think perchance that I think you are in love. Nay, by'r lady, I am not such a fool to think ... that you are in love, or that you will be in love, or that you can be in love. Yet Benedick was such another, and now is he become a man' (3.4.65–87). The female camaraderie, rivalry and release of sexual playfulness all contribute to human connectedness. While not all of the suggestiveness of this plant is apparent to the modern audience, it functions effectively as a pivot on which the exchanges are balanced.

(C) Heilmeyer's (2001: 26) comments have relevance for *ADO:* 'In Greek mythology ... a thistle can be seen as an allegory for being easily "ensnared" on prickles. However, in fairy tales thistles sometimes symbolize an enduring love.' Contemporary gardening books show that carduus benedictus was cultivated widely: Cogan (1584) says that it quickens all the senses, and recommends it against poison and the plague. Leith-Ross (2006) notes John Tradescant's account from Hatfield in May 1612 included carduus benedictus, and suggests it as an antidote to the plague. Iyengar (2011) includes the full medical applications of the plant.

carnation (A) *Dianthus caryophyllus* L. is an ornamental and medicinal introduction from southern Europe, probably in the sixteenth century. Iconographically the carnation was long associated with the Virgin Mary, the deep red **flower** given the meaning of pure love, whence it became a symbol of marriage. Carnation describes the colour of human flesh, or a deeper rose pink colour. The flower featured in needlework and other domestic decoration. The modern strongly coloured florists' carnation is a later American introduction.

(B) The word 'carnation' appears three times: twice to suggest colour. The single mention of the flower is pejorative, Perdita evincing a strong prejudice against a plant she deems to be artificial:

> the fairest flow'rs o'th'season
> Are our carnations and streak'd gillyvors
> (Which some call Nature's bastards). Of that kind
> Our rustic garden's barren, and I care not
> To get slips of them.
>
> *(WT 4.4. 81–5)*

Costard, having received a financial reward from Armado, asks Berowne, 'Pray you, sir, how much carnation ribbon may a man buy for a remuneration?' (*LLL* 3.1.145–6). 'Carnation' signifies rosy pink or 'flesh coloured'. Arden 2 (53) cites several plays of the period where this term is used. Mistress Quickly is the only other character to use carnation to convey colour. Defending Falstaff against the accusation that he referred to women as 'dev'ls incarnate', she claims, ''A could never abide carnation – 'twas a color he never lik'd' (*H5* 2.3.31–4). Launcelot Gobbo also succumbs to this malapropism, soliloquizing 'the Jew is the very devil incarnation' (*MV* 2.2.27).

(C) In Shakespeare's time, botanical definition was in its infancy, plant names were erratic. Modern carnation cultivars did not exist. 'Hybridization', while newly in the lexicon when applied to animals and people, did not come into general botanical currency until the nineteenth century, although the idea of **plant** sexuality was recognized about 1700. Bradford (1933) and others suggest that in *WT* Shakespeare is anticipating the idea of 'hybridization'. Writers appear to use carnation, **gillyvor**/ gillyflower and **pink** separately and interchangeably. Pink was a much older name, with carnation and gillyvor first used in the 1530s. Gerard (1597: 588–96) distinguishes between carnation and pink, but illustrates the former apparently as a double pink. Heilmeyer (2001: 64) observes that the carnation was 'associated with vanity and pride' – which may be an additional reason for Perdita's disdain for the flower. In Trevelyon's pattern book (1608) the only reference – an extensive one – is to carnation which in the context of needlework and decorative plasterwork would tend to suggest the larger flower which would be easier to detail than the smaller pink. Harvey (1978: 54) provides the most concentrated and detailed botanical analysis, concluding 'The garden forms of Carnation were known both in Turkey and the Middle East, and also in western Europe by 1500 but not a great deal earlier … the Carnation is not an ancient but a relatively modern addition to the garden flora.' Harvey (1976) also makes it clear that carnations are grown originally from seed and thereafter from cuttings or **slips**. Harvey (1978, 1989), Stuart and Sutherland (1987), Bushnell (2003: esp. 150–1), Watts (2007) and Stace (2010) all make perceptive observations. Leapman (2000) provides the details of Fairchild's early work on hybridization. See also **gillyvor, nature, pink, scion, stock.**

carrot, caret *Daucus carota,* L. a white-rooted native **plant** was eaten from prehistoric times; the sweeter, orange-coloured variety is a later medieval or early modern Middle Eastern introduction. Carrots were root pot-**herbs**, which were often cooked and eaten as part of a **salad**; the modern variety is far-removed from the original wild plant due to extensive breeding for size and flavour. It had a variety of medicinal uses, with gynaecological euphemisms suggesting its use to induce an abortion. The carrot is alluded to rather than named when Mistress Quickly mishears Parson Evans' reference to '*caret*' during William's Latin lesson. Her terse comment, 'And that's a good root' (*WIV* 4.1.53–4), possesses sexual significance. Given Mistress Quickly's expression of abhorrence when mistaking '*horum*' for 'whore', the root/penis association is probably inadvertent, but the relationship of the carrot with contraception would fall naturally within her purview. Holofernes also refers to '*caret*' ('it is wanting') but on this occasion there is no play on words – intended or unintended (*LLL* 4.2.123). The *OED* instances the varied spelling of the root which includes 'ca(r)et', 'carot', and 'carette', noting 'carret' was also used for the **locust**, the fruit of the carob tree. Boorde (1547), Hill (1577) and Dodoens (1578), all of whom may have sourced their information from Dioscorides, record the carrot as an aid to conception, a purpose for which it is still valued in India (Riddle 1992). See Willes (2011: 65) for a fascinating account of Richard Gardiner's treatise of 1599 and his work as proselytizer for vegetables.

caterpillar (A) The larva of a butterfly or moth, sometimes of other insects especially saw-flies, a caterpillar usually feeds on the **leaves** of plants, often maiming or destroying them. Figuratively it indicates a rapacious person or one who preys upon society.

  (B) Caterpillar is the most politically charged term in the lexicon of the **garden**. This creature – capable of denuding a plant of all its leaves overnight – was viewed as a natural shorthand for the political manoeuvrer and opportunist motivated by the desire for personal gain. Newly returned from exile and purposeful in his pursuit of the crown, Bolingbroke vows to remove some of Richard's adherents: 'Bushy, Bagot, and their complices,/The caterpillars of the commonwealth,/Which I have sworn to weed and pluck away' (*R2* 2.3.165–7). This is a key moment: Bolingbroke, about to cross the Rubicon, draws York into extra-judicial killing. It is significant that the term 'commonwealth', always associated with the public realm and signifying the welfare of the people as a whole, is strategically placed in this speech. Thus the caterpillar becomes an enemy of the people. Falstaff, a notorious parasite, has the temerity to indict the pilgrims he is about to rob at Gad's Hill: 'whorson caterpillars! bacon-fed knaves! they hate us youth. Down with them! fleece them!' (*1H4* 2.2.84–5). Regarding himself as the future King, the Duke of York agonizes over the loss of England's French territories: 'Thus are my blossoms blasted in the bud,/And caterpillars eat my leaves away' (*2H6* 3.1.89–90). A messenger announcing the arrival of Cade and his rebels in Southwark, reports, 'All scholars, lawyers, courtiers, gentlemen,/They call false caterpillars, and intend their death' (*2H6* 4.4.36–7). Interestingly, when confronting the rebels, Lord Say represents himself as a servant of the commonwealth. Caterpillars enter the realm of love in *VEN*. Protesting against Venus' physical demands, Adonis insists that she is driven by 'Lust' not 'Love': 'Which the hot tyrant stains, and soon bereaves,/As caterpillars do the tender leaves' (793–8). Even outside the political arena, then, the caterpillar's status is opprobrious.

(C) Gardening books and manuals include fanciful suggestions for destroying caterpillars. Lodge (1584: 4) uses the phrase, 'They bée the Caterpillers of a Common weale' which may suggest common parlance. Stubbes (1585: 127) personifies human caterpillars as the enemies of the poor: 'These, I saye, are the caterpillars and devouring locusts that massacre the poore.' This was the term applied to profiteering grocers by Richard Gardiner (see Willes (2011: 65)). Webster's Bosola draws the human analogy of parasites consuming their host: 'He and his brother are like plum-trees that grow crooked over standing-pools: they are rich and o'erladen with fruit, but none but crows, pies and caterpillars feed on them' (*Malfi* 1.1.49–52). Chute (1962) points out that the Puritans described actors as caterpillars of the commonwealth. See also **canker, worm**.

cedar (A) An evergreen conifer of the genus *Cedrus* especially *Cedrus libani* (more fully cedar of Lebanon) is native to Asia Minor. Familiar from classical, mythological and biblical sources, the suggested date of introduction is 1630–40, with specimens from **seed** still being scarce in the 1650s. The biblical cedar of Lebanon was regarded as sacred, the **tree** of the Cross. It was used emblematically and with reference to its biblically recorded qualities of height, strength and longevity. Gerard (1597: 1352–3) emphasizes its durability, resistance to disease and describes the **wood** as 'odoriferous'.

(B) Preparing to relinquish his 'rough magic', Prospero records the feats he has accomplished with his 'so potent art': 'the strong-bas'd promontory/Have I made shake, and by the spurs pluck'd up/The pine and cedar' (*TMP* 5.1.46–8). Before the battle at the end of *2H6,* Warwick compares himself to the immovable cedar: 'This day I'll wear aloft my burgonet,/As on a mountain top the cedar shows/That keeps his leaves in spite of any storm' (5.1.204–6). Dying on the battlefield he continues the analogy: 'Thus yields the cedar to the axe's edge,/Whose arms gave shelter to the princely eagle' (*3H6* 5.2.11–12). Significantly the cedar, choice of the mighty eagle, even towers above the oak, 'Jove's spreading tree' (14). Richard Gloucester uses the same image when contrasting his family with that of the upstarts – as he sees them – of Queen Elizabeth: 'but I was born so high,/Our aery buildeth in the cedar's top/And dallies with the wind and scorns the sun' (*R3* 1.3.262–4). This representation captures perfectly the cedar as the *nonpareil* of trees. Appalled at seeing his mother kneel before him – 'What's this?/Your knees to me? to your corrected son?' – Coriolanus alights on an image of perversity in nature: 'then let the mutinous winds/Strike the proud cedars 'gainst the fiery sun' (*COR* 5.3.56–60). Another mighty Roman warrior, Titus Andronicus, beaten down by the terrible events that have engulfed his family, says to his brother, 'Marcus, we are but shrubs, no cedars we,/No big-bon'd men fram'd of the Cyclops' size' (*TIT* 4.3.46–7). Lucrece, too, draws on the cedar/**shrub** antithesis when appealing to the lust-driven Tarquin: 'The cedar stoops not to the base shrub's foot,/But low shrubs wither at the cedar's root' (*LUC* 664–5). *CYM,* with four references to the cedar, more than any other work, includes the Soothsayer's reference to 'the majestic cedar' (5.5.457).

(C) Dekker emphasizes its emblematic importance when he writes that Queen Elizabeth's last sickness was marked by a storm that shook cedars, terrified the tallest **pines,** and cleft even the hardest hearts of **oak** (1603, *The Wonderful Year*). Greene also employs it emblematically: 'The tal Cedar that beareth only bare blossoms, is of more value than the apple tree that is laden with fruit' (1580–3, vol. 2, *Mamillia*: 48). Webster's Ferdinand records its stability: 'Distrust doth cause us seldome be deceiv'd;/You see, the oft shaking of the Cedar-tree/Fastens it more at roote' (1613, *Malfi,* 1.2.158–60). It does not feature in early plant-lore suggesting a later introduction, of which Campbell-Culver (2001: 124–6) gives the history and date of introduction. See Thomas (1984: 218) for an interesting historical reference.

centaury *Centaurium* Mill., a group of native **plants** includes several species used to treat eye problems. The description of Lear wearing a coronet of **weeds** and **flowers** leads to Cordelia's anxious instruction: 'A century send forth;/Search every acre in the high-grown field,/And bring him to our eye'(*LR* 4.4.6–8). There is common acceptance that 'century' means 100 soldiers but the suggestion in Arden 3 (322) that the word is triggered by association with the plant is interesting, especially as Gerard (1597: 545–6) comments on its healing properties – it is especially good for the eyes which is relevant to Lear – and on its favoured habitats such as 'the chalkie cliffs of Greenhith in Kent'. Colonna (1499: 22) refers to 'centaury and many other plants that grow among ruins'. Intriguingly, in the same scene, Gloucester describes Lear as, 'O ruin'd piece of nature' (134). At a subconscious level Cordelia may be influenced by Kent's rebuke to Lear in the opening scene: 'See better, Lear, and let me still remain/The true blank of thine eye'(1.1.158–9). Turner (1551: 267) likens its appearance to **marjoram**; the only use he gives that might benefit Lear is for the eyes, saying 'it purgeth away the darkness of the eyes'.

chaff (A) The process of winnowing the **harvest**, separating the useful **corn** from the **husks** or chaff is as old as man's cultivation of **crops**. Chaff was always useless, thrown away, burnt or carried away by the wind. By extension it indicated a worthless person, without function or place in society, the common people; chaff-less suggested something or someone uncontaminated or pure. To separate the chaff from the corn is proverbial.

(B) Chaff as inconsequential and worthless provides a valuable ingredient in the plays' imagery. Antonio's disquiet about Gratiano's volubility prompts Bassanio's observation, 'Gratiano speaks an infinite deal of nothing, more than any man in all Venice. His reasons are as two grains of wheat hid in two bushels of chaff; you shall seek all day ere you find them, and when you have them, they are not worth the search' (*MV* 1.1.114–18). Autolycus produces a witty phrase when soliloquizing on his purse-cutting at the sheep-shearing festivities: 'and had not the old man come in with a whoobub against his daughter and the King's son, and scar'd my choughs from the chaff, I had not left a purse alive in the whole army' (*WT* 4.4.615–18). The quicksilver wit offsets the cynical 'choughs from the chaff' – hopelessly gullible people beguiled by trash. A fascinating case arises in *2H4*. The rebels resolve to accept the terms and conditions of Prince John of Lancaster despite Mowbray's protestation, 'We shall be winnow'd with so rough a wind/That even our corn shall seem as light as chaff,/ And good from bad find no partition' (4.1.192–4). A masterpiece of clarity the chaff metaphor vitalizes the argument. An image that became part of the mental landscape of the period is also present in *H8*. Informed by the King that he is to be interrogated by the Council, Cranmer replies that he is 'right glad to catch this good occasion/Most throughly to be winnowed, where my chaff/And corn shall fly asunder' (5.1.109–11). Reporting to the Romans on his unsuccessful appeal to the exiled Coriolanus, Cominius says: 'I offered to awaken his regard/For's private friends. His answer to me was,/ He could not stay to pick them in a pile/Of noisome musty chaff'. Outraged that the tribunes engineered the hero's exile, Menenius addresses them indignantly: 'we are the grains,/You are the musty chaff, and you are smelt/Above the moon. We must be burnt for you' (*COR* 5.1.23–32). The image is particularly appropriate in a play that begins with a riot by hungry plebeians crying out for corn and Menenius's defence of the patricians with the fable of the belly. The voyeuristic Pandarus, identifying the returning heroes for Cressida, dismisses the common soldiers as, 'Asses, fools, dolts! chaff and bran, chaff and bran! porridge after meat!' (*TRO* 1.2.241–2). The single use of the word 'chaffless' is notable. Unsuccessful in his attempt to seduce Imogen, Iachimo claims to have been testing her virtue – which he sought to 'fan' or 'winnow' – on behalf of Posthumus: 'The love I bare him/Made me to fan you thus, but the gods made you/ (Unlike all others) chaffless' (*CYM* 1.6.176–8). Equally inventive is Palamon who berates Arcite for daring to love Emilia: 'A very thief in love, a chaffy lord,/Nor worth the name of villain!' (*TNK* 3.1.41–2). Here is a soft word with a hard edge.

(C) Bartholomeus (1582: 315) says chaff 'bee of no value to mans meate, but they bee meate to swine and fowles'. Asquith (2005) suggests a connection between burning chaff, *COR* and the Gunpowder plot. Biblical references to chaff are numerous.

chase (A) Chase can be the process of the **hunt,** the quarry in the hunt, as a verb to pursue for sport, a suitable territory for hunting, land carefully managed for the breeding of the animals to be hunted or an unenclosed tract of **land** in private or royal ownership which gives the maximum opportunity for hunting. It can be to persecute and harry the enemy; its literal meanings can be applied metaphorically. Laying a chase remains a technical term in real or royal **tennis** when the ball bounces for a second time without being hit, the point effectively being replayed.

(B) Both literal and figurative uses of 'pursuit in hunting' or the hunting ground itself are common. In a colourful hunting scene, complete with the cry of hounds and horns, Marcus comments, 'I have dogs, my lord,/Will rouse the proudest panther in the chase,/And climb the highest promontory top'. Titus responds with carefree vigour, 'And I have horse will follow where the game/Makes way, and runs like swallows o'er the plain' (*TIT* 2.2.20–4). Clearly, here, chase means the hunting ground. This moment is characterized by bleak irony. What seems to the Andronici a carnival hunt is, for their deadly enemies the Goths, an opportunity to begin the destruction of this Roman family. A place of entrapment described as 'Upon the north side of this pleasant chase' (2.3.255) is where Lavinia the 'dainty doe' (2.1.117) is raped and mutilated. The opening verse of *VEN* celebrates Adonis' passion for hunting: 'Rose-cheek'd Adonis hied him to the chase;/Hunting he lov'd, but love he laugh'd to scorn' (1.3–4). Another romantic pursuit takes place in *MND*. The determined Helena calls after Demetrius, 'Run when you will; the story shall be chang'd: Apollo flies, and Daphne holds the chase' (2.1.230–1). One of the most remarkable configurations arises in *AYL*. Jaques' anthropomorphic response to the languishing deer is recounted by the First Lord: 'the big round tears/Cours'd one another down his innocent nose/In piteous chase' (2.1.38–40). Not only does the hunting metaphor vitalize the conceit, one tear in pursuit of another emanating from the eye of a dying deer, but it draws on the Acteon myth, so that the light mockery of Jaques' sentimentality is embedded in well-established iconography. Interesting mirror images occur in *2H6* and *3H6*. Engaging Old Clifford on the battlefield the Duke of York exclaims: 'Hold, Warwick; seek thee out some other chase,/For I myself must hunt this deer to death' (*2H6* 5.2.14–15). When their sons meet in a subsequent battle Richard Gloucester, cornering Young Clifford, also rejects Warwick's assistance: 'Nay, Warwick, single out some other chase,/For I myself will hunt this wolf to death' (*3H6* 2.4.12–13). The image again enters political discourse in *R3*. Stanley's proposal that they escape to the north out of Richard's reach is dismissed by Hastings: 'To fly the boar before the boar pursues/Were to incense the boar to follow us,/And make pursuit where he did mean no chase' (3.2.28–30). Here the boar is the hunter not the quarry, the neat inversion imaging Richard's personal emblem. Prior to the famous stage direction (*Exit pursued by a bear*), Antigonus – the prey – cries, 'This is the chase' (*WT* 3.3.57).

(C) Harrison (1587) describes the operation of chases within royal **forests** while Manwood (1598) sets out the legal definition of a chase there. For a note on the mythology and iconography of deer see *AYL*, Arden 3, (193). Noel and Clark (1991) give the complicated definition of chase as a term in tennis. Berry (2001) provides a detailed study of the plays in relation to the culture of the hunt. See also Fletcher (2011).

cherry (A) *Prunus* L., probably *P. avium* L., the wild or bird cherry, and possibly *P.*

cerasus L., the dwarf cherry; some cultivated varieties may have been Roman introductions. This decorative, productive **tree** was grown for its **fruit**. The cherry, valued for its short, early season, also supplied timber. The iconography of the cherry was symbolic of heaven, particularly in connection with the Virgin and Child. Representing virginity, cherries were embroidered on Queen Elizabeth's clothing. Cherry-red is a descriptive colour, similar to rose-red, often symbolizing lips, and associated with kissing. As they frequently grew two to a stem, cherries were used poetically, in proverbs and as an emblem of closeness, or twin-ship. Cherry-pit was a child's game where cherry stones were thrown into a small hole.

(B) The tradition of the cherry symbolizing closeness or twinning, usually feminine, is best captured in *MND* where 'two in oneness' is the conceptual nucleus of the play. Believing Hermia to be part of a conspiracy to humiliate her, Helena alights on the ultimate emblem of unity to encapsulate their friendship:

> So we grew together,
> Like to a double cherry, seeming parted,
> But yet a union in partition,
> Two lovely berries moulded on one stem;
> So with two seeming bodies, but one heart,
>
> *(3.2.208–12)*

The association of cherries with kissing also finds expression in *MND*, though the romantic connection is parodied by Flute's playing of Thisbe. Complaining to the wall for obstructing access to her lover Pyramus, 'she' laments: 'My cherry lips have often kiss'd thy stones' (5.1.190). A different kind of undercutting occurs in this play when Demetrius is transformed by the love juice. Awaking, he praises Helena with a torrent of clichés: 'O, how ripe in show/Thy lips, those kissing cherries, tempting grow!' (3.2.139–40). In *TNK* the impending kiss of Hippolita and Theseus is anticipated by the First Queen: 'O, when/Her twinning cherries shall their sweetness fall/Upon thy tasteful lips' (*TNK* 1.1.177–9). The Wooer reports that the Jailer's Daughter, in her madness, sang of 'black-ey'd maids' with 'cherry lips and cheeks of damask roses' (4.1.72–4). Despite being subject to parody or cliché the descriptive 'cherry lips' continued to represent female beauty. Likewise, in its literal presentations, or representations, the cherry is perceived as both beautiful and delectable. Gower praises Marina who, 'with her needle composes/Nature's own shape of bud, bird, branch, or berry,/That even her art sisters the natural roses;/Her inkle, silk, twin with the rubied cherry' (*PER* 5.Cho. 5–8). Lamenting the death of Adonis, Venus describes how all of nature doted on him:

> When he was by, the birds such pleasure took,
> That some would sing, some other in their bills
> > Would bring him mulberries and ripe-red cherries:
> > He fed them with his sight, they him with berries.
>
> *(VEN 1101–4)*

The cherry, here draws on the iconography of virginity and purity. Richard Gloucester, intent on evading Brackenbury's injunction against speaking with Clarence, artfully alludes to the King's former mistress, now Hastings' lover: 'We say that Shore's wife hath a pretty foot,/A cherry lip, a bonny eye, a passing pleasing tongue' (*R3* 1.1.93–4). As part of a richly ironic speech, this observation reveals Richard's dangerously deft verbal touch – nominal praise that simultaneously deprecates her coming-on looseness. The game 'cherry-pit' achieves a single mention. Baiting the imprisoned Malvolio, Feste cries out to his victim, 'What, man, 'tis not for gravity to play at cherry-pit with Satan' (*TN* 3.4.115–16).

(C) Calderwood (1992: 23–71) is excellent on *MND*'s anamorphic doubling. Sidney (1580) writes of 'lips red and plum, as cherry's ruddy side', and 'those ruddy lips … rubies, cherries, and roses new', while Greene's includes, 'Face Rose hued, Cherry red, with a silver taint like a Lilly' (1616, vol. 9, *Greene's Mourning Garment*: 152). The cherry has been cultivated in Kent since the sixteenth century. The artificial prolongation of its fruiting season – the 'holy grail' of the gardener's skill – made such fruit a considerable luxury. Plat (1609) comments on the Carews' success in doing so for the visit of the Queen in August 1599. Arnold (1988) and Woodhouse (2008) suggest the fruit, a favourite of the Queen's, symbolized heaven and virginity, and that her partiality for it referenced acknowledged Marian iconography. Cherry trees, including a walk of one hundred black cherries, were planted at Lyveden New Bield by Tresham, probably for their Marian associations (Eburne 2008). Hobhouse (1992) provides details of its introduction, development and iconography. For brief descriptions of the game of cherry-pit, see Nares (1859), and Blake (2006: 159).

chestnut (A) The European sweet chestnut *Castanea sativa*, Mill. was a Roman introduction to England; the earliest date of the more familiar horse chestnut, *Aesculus hippocastanum* L., is 1616. The sweet chestnut was particularly valued for its **nuts** for dessert, which were dried to augment a meagre winter diet, and used medicinally. Its timber supplied chestnut paling or open fencing. The tree was not widely cultivated domestically as it required considerable space, but by the sixteenth century it was established in the wild, providing useful fodder for animals, especially deer. Chestnut is a reddish-brown colour.

(B) The chestnut is twice mentioned to signify colour and twice as the nut. Celia and Rosalind discoursing on the merits of Orlando alight on the colour of his hair. After Rosalind's apprehensive comment, 'His very hair is of the dissembling color', Celia rescues her with the playful riposte, 'Something browner than Judas's'. This encourages her friend to claim, 'I'faith, his hair is of a good color', inciting Celia to cap the matter with decisive equivocation: 'An excellent color. Your chestnut was ever the only color' (*AYL* 3.4.7–12). Clearly, chestnut is no more than a hair's breadth away from being as red as Judas's. The Jailer's Daughter, having lost her sanity, describes a clever horse that the Duke's 'chestnut mare' is 'horribly in love with' (*TNK* 5.2.61–2). These imaginary horses, of course, mirror her plight. The popularity of roasted chestnuts is suggested in *SHR*. Petruchio's speech of bravado, as he prepares for his first encounter with Kate, concludes: 'And do you tell me of a woman's tongue,/That gives not half so great a blow to hear/As will a chestnut in a farmer's fire?' (1.2.207–9). More seriously, one of the Witches in *MAC* is provoked by an act of selfishness: 'A sailor's wife had chestnuts in her lap,/And mounch'd, and mounch'd, and mounch'd. "Give me!", quoth I./"Aroint thee, witch!" the rump-fed ronyon cries' (1.3.4–6).

(C) Boorde (1542) includes chestnuts with **almonds**, suggesting that if eaten before a meal they could prevent drunkenness, and that they were nourishing, albeit carminative. Turner (1548: 198) comments on their general availability: 'chesnut which growe in divers places in the East (of England), the maniest that I have sene was in Kent'. Possibly, they were cultivated there with fruit trees. Cogan (1584) quotes Galen as his authority on the value of chestnuts as food, but comments that they were hurtful if eaten raw. Mabey (1996) details its place in the English countryside as an 'honorary' native tree. For probable dates of introduction of both types of chestnut see Campbell-Culver (2001).

chimney-sweeper (A) This is recorded as a vernacular Warwickshire name for ribwort or rib-grass, *Plantago lanceolata* L., which was found widely throughout the country. It may refer to the **bulrush**, *Typha* L., and is possibly another Warwickshire name for dandelion, *Taraxacum* F.H.Wigg, when it is ready to **seed**.

(B) Of the two references only one possibly relates to a plant. Baiting Berowne for loving a black-browed beauty, Dumaine says mockingly, 'To look like her are chimney-sweepers black' (*LLL*, 4.3.262). A line from the dirge in *CYM* is a source of contention: 'Golden lads and girls all must,/As chimney-sweepers, come to dust' (4.2.262–3). There is no meeting of minds about which plant is meant, if indeed, any botanical reference is implied. The dandelion with its passage from golden-headed flower to fluffy, dust-like seed heads is one of the most appealing candidates. But a case can be made for the bulrush which looks like a chimney-sweeper's brush. Of course, there is a natural antithesis inherent in 'golden lads and girls' and the blackened-faced chimney-sweeper, but it is possible that a plant is also implied here.

(C) The precise sources of regional and folk names can be difficult – even impossible – to verify. Britten and Holland (1886) give 'chimneysweeper' as a Warwickshire name for the heads of ribwort, and Grigson (1958) expands this usage. Mabey intimates that in Warwickshire a dandelion is a 'golden lad' when in flower and a 'chimney-sweeper' when ready to be blown to the wind – a suggestion picked up by Bryson (2008). *CYM* speaks of going to dust, but a dandelion floats away rather than disintegrating. The first recorded use of the job of chimney-sweeper is possibly 1518, the second being *LLL 4.3.264*. Professional websites suggest it only started later in the seventeenth century when the greatly increased use of coal left a potentially dangerous sticky deposit inside chimneys; modern brushes, which may have fuelled the dandelion analogy, were only invented in the eighteenth century, and early chimneys were swept by small boys with a hand-held brush and scraper, neither of which would suggest a dandelion.

www.ruchalachimney.com shows an undated business card, possibly c. 1600, for the combined jobs of chimney sweepers and nightmen, depicting a boy carrying a brush that might resemble a bulrush or **plantain**, but not remotely like a dandelion. Watts (2007) gives the folklore for *Plantago lanceolata* which includes its Cheshire rural name of chimney sweeper, citing Thistleton Dyer (1883), but no original source is traceable. We are indebted to Roy Vickery for his personal suggestion of, and extended reasoning for bulrush, which might reflect the chimney-sweeper's brush.

cicely *Myrrhis odorata* L. *Scop.* is a native **plant** whose **root**, aniseed-scented **leaves** and **seeds** were used for **salads**. It also had medicinal applications. While the **flower** is not mentioned, three characters are endowed with the name. Cicely is the name of a maid in *ERR*. Attempting to gain entry for his master and guests Dromio of Ephesus calls out, 'Maud, Bridget, Marion, Cic'ly, Gillian, Ginn!'. The names of the Ephesian domestics, surprisingly English, provide an example of Shakespeare's characteristic hybridization of his exotic locations. Cicely again belongs to the lower orders in *SHR*. Attempting to bewilder Christopher Sly, the First Servant tells him 'Sometimes you would call out for Cicely Hackett' (Ind. 2.89). In *TNK* Cicely is 'the sempster's daughter' (3.5.44). Tusser (1573) inveighs at length against the 'slut Cisley' who appears to be a dairymaid-cum-kitchen servant. Cicely was possibly a generic name for servant. Mabey (1996) includes a brief summary of the plant's uses and associations.

circummur'd (A) Shakespeare's is the first recorded use of the word, which suggests surrounded and enclosed by a wall. The *OED* has only two further examples, both meaning constrained. An association of ideas would probably have been made with medieval images of the Virgin Mary who was often depicted in a walled **garden** or *hortus conclusus*.

(B) The garden we are told about in *MM* is dark and secretive. The **garden-house**, the place intended for a secret assignation between Angelo and his intended victim Isabella, is at the centre of a series of concentric partitions. There are two gates and two keys. This inner sanctum which may be representative of the human soul is, perversely, the place of anticipated violation. The concentricity is articulated and authenticated by the secure walls: they enclose the garden and its segregated spaces, precipitating Shakespeare's coinage 'circummur'd'. Isabella's description conveys a picture that is both appealing and intimidating:

> He hath a garden circummur'd with brick,
> Whose western side is with a vineyard back'd;
> And to that vineyard is a planched gate,
> That makes his opening with this bigger key.
> This other doth command a little door,
> Which from the vineyard to the garden leads;
>
> *(4.1.28–33)*

(C) Harvey (1981) includes illustrations of medieval walled gardens, while McLeod (2008) gives details of Marian gardens and the *hortus conclusus*. Early modern gardens close to a great house were often protected by a wall providing privacy and a sheltered growing environment for more precious, tender plants. Such garden walls have survived, and can, for example, be seen at Thornbury in Gloucestershire, where a similar progression out into the wider landscape can still be traced; others are detailed in Henderson's gazetteer (2005). Tigner (2012: 116–31) provides telling commentary on gardens as 'erotic spaces' and the historical significance attaching to their enclosure.

clove The unopened **flower-buds** of *Eugenia aromatica,* also known as *Caryophyllus aromaticus,* cloves have been a commercially traded spice for at least two millennia. Imported from the East Indies, they are still widely used medicinally and to flavour food and drinks. Stuck into **lemons** and **oranges** they served both as a **pomander** and a preservative. The sole reference is in *LLL* where the young courtiers mock the theatrical performance of their social inferiors. Pouncing on Armado's line, 'Gave Hector's gift', Dumaine cries, 'A gilt nutmeg', encouraging Berowne's 'A lemon' (a pun on leman/lover), which invites Longeville's 'Stuck with cloves' opening the way for Dumaine's bawdy conclusion, 'No, cloven' a division implying female genitalia. The game does not stop there – the chain of food/drink/love/sex interplay continuing with 'mint' and 'columbine' (5.2.645–55). Hence Hector's gift of martial prowess, bestowed by Mars, is turned first into a lover's token conferred by a young man, before evolving into a woman's gift of sexual favours. Cogan (1584) gives their place of origin as the East Indies; he suggests that cloves will both help the digestion and act as an aphrodisiac. John Hall (Lane 1996) prescribes cloves medicinally. Tannahill (1988) includes brief details of trading in cloves, as well as giving an idea of the range of their culinary uses. Jardine (1996) notes the expansion of European trade in cloves, **ginger**, **pepper** and **nutmeg** in the sixteenth century.

clover, honey-stalk *Trifolium repens* L. the white clover is a widespread native **plant** of grassy and rough **ground**, with scented **flowers** attractive to **bees**, hence its local name of **honey-stalk**. It was grown widely as fodder, but could be fatal if animals were let loose on too luxuriant a **crop**. Burgundy celebrates the plant when describing the beauty and fertility of the French countryside prior to the English invasion: 'The even mead, that erst brought sweetly forth/The freckled cowslip, burnet and green clover' (*H5*, 5.2.48–9). Reassuring the Emperor Saturninus that she will bring down the Andronici family, Tamora promises:

> I will enchant the old Andronicus
> With words more sweet, and yet more dangerous,
> Than baits to fish, or honey-stalks to sheep,
> When as the one is wounded with the bait,
> The other rotted with delicious feed.

> *(TIT, 4.4.89–93)*

Drayton (1622) comments on its use as a fodder crop, and includes it with the flowers of the **meadow** strewn for the marriage of Thames and Isis. Grigson (1958) suggests honey-stalks and **honeysuckle** as local names for clover.

cockle (A) *Agrostemma githago* L. or sometimes *Lychnis githago* L., corn-cockle, is a flowering **weed** formerly found widely in **corn fields**. The reference is possibly to **darnel,** *Lolium temulentum* L., a weed of the **grass** family, the biblical tares which often designated any weeds found in corn. Both **plants** are poisonous. The presence of either reduced the value of the **crop** as the seedlings had to be removed by hand. Cockle had a range of medicinal uses. Metaphorically the plant suggested corruption, dissention or pollution. The cockle-shell was the emblem of St James of Compostella.

(B) Relinquishing their pledge to abjure the company of women for three years, the King and his coterie launch their campaign to win the hearts of the ladies with, '*Allons!, allons!* Sow'd cockle reap'd no corn' (*LLL* 4.3.380). This aphorism asserts the necessity of immediate and appropriate action. More pertinent is Coriolanus' outburst against the plebeians and their tribunes on discovering that they have revoked his election to the consulship:

> In soothing them we nourish 'gainst our Senate
> The cockle of rebellion, insolence, sedition,
> Which we ourselves have plough'd for, sow'd, and
>   scatter'd,
> By mingling them with us, the honor'd number,
>
>   (COR, 3.1.69–72)

Although he has never stooped to manual labour, the warrior is drawn to the imagery of agriculture to demonstrate the folly of allowing a political voice to the tillers of the soil.

(C) Spenser's 'weedye crop of care' included 'cockel for corne and chaffe for barley bare wynd' (ed. 1999, *The Shepheardes Calendar*, December: 122–4). According to Grattan and Singer (1952), cockle was used medicinally from Anglo-Saxon times. Ryden (1978: 39) suggests that Shakespeare was merely 'thinking of it as the opposite of good corn' because 'cockle and corn were often used as collocates as emblematic of "bad" and "good"'. Mabey (2010) describes its deleterious effects if harvested with the corn.

cod, codling A hard **apple**, which needed coddling or cooking before eating, as it was not suitable for eating raw. Codlings are now available as a discrete cultivar, for example Kentish codlin; it is an ancestor of the Bramley apple. The name was extended to immature or half-grown **fruit** of any variety, and the codling could be harvested before it was ripe. The word is present only in *TN* where it signifies not a hard apple but an immature one. Irritated by the persistence of Orsino's messenger, Malvolio informs Olivia that Cesario/Viola is 'Not yet old enough for a man, nor young enough for a boy; as a squash is before 'tis a peascod, or a codling when 'tis almost an apple' (1.5.156–8).

Markham (1615) mentions the making of codling tarts and pies. Jonson's Dol Common uses codling to describe a young man: 'A fine young quodling!' (1610, *The Alchemist* 1.1.189). Vaughan (1617) thinks that codlings with sugar and rose-water provide some of the best fruit for eating. See also **pease.**

coloquintida (A) Despite its colloquial name of 'bitter **apple**', coloquintida or colocynth is not an apple but a **gourd**, *Citrullus colocynthis* Schrad., which is found in the wild mountains of the Eastern Mediterranean. It was cultivated for medicinal purposes in Cyprus and Spain. Highly toxic and with a proverbially bitter taste, it is a drastic purgative.

(B) Preparatory to his departure for Cyprus, Iago convinces Roderigo that Othello's passion for Desdemona will be short-lived: 'These Moors are changeable in their wills – fill thy purse with money. The food that to him now is as luscious as locusts, shall be to him shortly as acerb as coloquintida' (*OTH*, 1.3.346–9). 'Locusts', the deliciously sweet fruit of the carob tree provides an extreme contrast to the bitterness of coloquintida. Moreover, they embody exoticism. Cyprus, famed for its carob trees, was also known for coloquintida which has Mediterranean provenance. Alliteration and assonance collude to create a proposition that is intensely persuasive. Sound is a critical collaborator in the process of manipulation: Shakespeare's botanical knowledge and linguistic sensibility combine to create compelling pressure.

(C) Turner (1548) records it 'in certeyne gardens in Germany' which suggests he had not seen it at home. A century later Parkinson (1640: 160–1) implies it was cultivated in England and 'nourished up' in the gardens of the 'curious'. Emphasizing its deadly qualities, particularly for pregnant women, he suggests the Northern constitution could tolerate only a quarter the dose recommended 'by the ancients'. He gives a wide range of complaints which coloquintida might treat. Contemporary writers focus on its bitterness: Greene writes, 'No, no, he knew all hearbes were not as bitter as *Coloquintida'* (1580–3, vol. 2, *Mamillia*: 17*)*, while Lyly's old gentleman thinks 'One drop of poison infecteth the whole tun of wine, one leaf of coloquintidia marreth and spoileth the whole pot of porridge' (1580, *Euphues*: 37).

columbine (A*) Aquilegia vulgaris* L. is an ornamental native **flower** found in the wild and in **gardens**; it has a variety of medicinal applications. As a member of the *Ranunculus* family which includes **aconitum**, it is poisonous and so fell out of the pharmacopoeia. Its name was suggested by the flower's apparent resemblance to the shape of a dove, *columba*, whence it was taken to symbolize the dove of the Holy Spirit, but it was also associated with sexuality and cuckoldry from the horned shape of the flowers; in proverbs it indicated thanklessness and worthlessness. An early heraldic flower, columbine featured frequently in embroidery.

(B) The first of the two references is precipitated by the overflow of mockery and mirth in *LLL* when the King and his fellows indulge their wit at the expense of the actors attempting the Pageant of the Nine Worthies. Armado, playing Hector says, 'I am that flower'. He is not allowed to finish his line as Dumaine cries, 'That mint', provoking Longaville's riposte, 'That columbine' (5.2.655). These comments imply the association of the columbine with thanklessness and worthlessness. The flower's link with the dove of peace could also be part of the mockery of the warrior. There may also be a sexual innuendo: a reference to cuckoldry. Intriguingly, the actors exhibit compassion. *LLL* Arden 2 (172) cites a *Twelfth Night Merriment* that includes the line 'thou marigold of mercye and columbine of compassion': it is possible that the connection between those flowers and their presumed attributes arises from the require-ments of alliteration. Nevertheless, compassion may well add another layer of meaning in *LLL*. More memorable are the columbines and **fennel** distributed by Ophelia in her madness: 'There's fennel for you, and columbines' (*HAM* 4.5.180–1). Editors presume that each plant contains a message and postulate their recipients. There is, however, nothing in the three available texts to resolve the uncertainty. That Ophelia conveys her ideas in code is acknowledged by Laertes: 'A document in madness, thoughts and remembrance fitted' (178–9). Arden 2 (359) states confidently that 'fennel and colum-bines, signifying marital infidelity' are given to Gertrude, (supporting this opinion in LN (538–9)). Though horns generally signify the cuckold himself, they can also refer to the woman who provides the horns. As past and present collide in this scene the suggestion of Gertrude's infidelity may be implied if she is the recipient. Heath (2003) identifies the columbine with ingratitude. This makes Claudius a potential recipient because of his treatment of Polonius who was buried in 'hugger-mugger' (4.5.84). However, the uncertainties are such that no authoritative judgement seems possible.

(C) No specific link has been found between columbine and **mint**. Its sexual associa-tions are well-documented: Langham (1597), Gerard (1597) and Culpeper (1653) say columbine speeds childbirth. Rowland (1981) records the medieval use of columbine as a male contraceptive: it 'extinguishes lust in the testicle'. Chapman dismisses it: 'A columbine? No; that thankless flower grows not in my garden' (1599, *All Fools*, 64–5). Freeman (1983) comments on its religious symbolism in relation to the Holy Spirit, its Marian attributions, and its association with love and fertility, citing its inclusion in Hieronymus Bosch's erotic *Garden of Delights* of c. 1500. Heilmeyer (2001: 20) notes that between 1430 and 1580 it 'appeared in many paintings as a sign of redemption and of the triumph of life over death' and adds, 'Its leaf divided into three parts represents the Christian trinity'. Trevelyon (1608) has patterns for embroidery, and Arnold (1988) distinguishes columbines embroidered on the Queen's clothing. Mabey (1996) explains the name, noting its use in church carvings. Heath (2003) considers at length the secondary meanings of the flower as including forsaken love, ingratitude and cuckoldry.

compost, composture (A) A poetical rather than practical word for a mixture of ingre-dients, a prepared **dung** or **manure** with connotations of excrement, contamination and dirt. The purpose of compost was to improve the **soil**. Compost also suggested a compound or a culinary stew usually of **fruit** and spices, where it carries the meaning more of enrichment.

(B) 'Compost' is used only once. After castigating his mother in the closet scene Hamlet becomes more temperate, prevailing on her to be penitent: 'Confess yourself to heaven,/Repent what's past, avoid what is to come,/And do not spread the compost on the weeds/To make them ranker' (*HAM,* 3.4.149–52). In a play replete with references to earth, worms and bodily decay this image vivifies the wilfulness that Hamlet sees in Gertrude's behaviour. Composture, too, appears only once. Admonishing the bandits Timon expatiates on theft as a universal phenomenon: 'the earth's a thief,/That feeds and breeds by a composture stol'n/From gen'ral excrement' (*TIM* 4.3.440–2). The word 'excrement' in all other cases applies to an outgrowth of hair and is not used in its modern sense. That Shakespeare in this play does, indeed, for the first time, use 'excrement' in its modern sense is intriguing, as is his coinage, 'composture'. It might seem strange, however, to conceive the gathering and blending of diverse waste materials as theft, but all Timon's examples in this speech are paradoxical.

(C) The *OED* gives only one possible early use of the word before 1587, confirming its less frequent use than dung or manure, and crediting Shakespeare with the first recorded use of 'composture'. Puttenham (1589) uses both compost and manure, while Drayton writes of the Northamptonshire earth which 'The Husbandman by Art, with Compost doth enrich' (1622, *Polyolbion*, 23.4). Nuttall (1989) provides a brief but insightful exploration of *TIM.* For a thorough exploration of **earth**, soil etc., in *HAM,* see de Grazia (2007).

corn (A) A generic term for **grain**, or any cereal **crop**, corn can also indicate **wheat, barley, rye** and **oats**. Maize, or turkey-corn, its contemporary name, was introduced from America to England during the sixteenth century. Initially regarded as a curiosity, it was not cultivated for food until later in the seventeenth century. The availability and price of corn and cereal crops was of crucial importance, particularly to the mass of the population for whom it was a staple food, so shortage of corn could have political repercussions.

(B) There does not seem to be any intention to identify different types of corn: it is generic, the basic sustenance of life. Almost one third of its uses are in *COR.* The opening exchanges involve a hungry populace craving bread and demanding the release of corn. Perceiving Caius Martius as the main obstacle, they clamour: 'Let us kill him, and we'll have corn at our own price. Is't a verdict?' (1.1.10–11). When Martius arrives at the scene to establish the source of their complaint – 'What's their seeking?' – Menenius informs him, 'For corn at their own rates, whereof they say/The city is well stor'd' (1.1.188–90). In this society corn is of strategic significance and exerts enormous pressure in the play. In very different circumstances Titania complains to Oberon of the hunger caused by crop failure due to unseasonal weather brought on by their quarrels: 'The ox hath therefore stretch'd his yoke in vain,/The ploughman lost his sweat, and the green corn/Hath rotted ere his youth attain'd a beard' (*MND* 2.1.93–5). It seems likely that this description mirrored the conditions of the time. The world of pastoral is never afflicted by bad weather, and it appears that the truant Fairy King has recently returned from a sojourn in that land: 'And in the shape of Corin sat all day,/Playing on pipes of corn, and versing love,/To amorous Phillida' (2.1.66–8). The 'pipes of corn' and the lovers' names place us firmly in the realms of pastoral poetry. The most shocking metaphorical application is in *TIT*. Attempting to emulate her sons' blood lust Tamora, about to stab Lavinia, is restrained by Demetrius who is intent on raping and mutilating her: 'First thrash the corn, and after burn the straw' (2.3.123). This most brutal of plays is richly endowed with the imagery of plants: sometimes sublime, at other times, as here, incongruity heightens the sense of revulsion. Marcus reverts to the corn image when endeavouring to reunite a society fragmented by murder and revenge: 'O, let me teach you how to knit again/This scattered corn into one mutual sheaf,/These broken limbs again into one body' (5.3.70–2). Cordelia provides a vivid account of the mad Lear wearing a crown of herbs and flowers, 'and all the idle weeds that grow/In our sustaining corn' (*LR,* 4.4.5–6). This literal example resonates powerfully in a play where there is a sharp division between characters who are like 'sustaining corn' and others who are wholly destructive. Corn as a physical presence that draws attention to itself as a deeply appreciated part of the landscape is well illustrated in *TNK*. Arcite receiving news of the games reflects on his past achievements: 'Well I could have wrestled,/The best men call'd it excellent; and run/Swifter than wind upon a field of corn,/Curling the wealthy ears' (2.3.75–8). The antithesis of this vision occurs in *E3* as a fleeing Frenchman describes the depredations wrought by the English invaders: 'I might perceive five cities all on fire,/Cornfields and vineyards burning like an oven' (3.2.56–7).

(C) Tusser (1557) gives corn as a generic term for all grains, but distinguishes the different types in his advice on sowing and cultivation. Harrison (1587) documents corn as a local trading commodity. Writing as early as 1587 he notes its abundance, but comments that it is largely available to the wealthy, forcing even their own households to make do with rye, barley and bread made of pease and beans. He notes that the profits made by landlords and in local markets bring about dearth of corn for the poor even in times of plenty (1587:133, 246–8). Stow considers that price rises are as much a matter of merchants' speculation as of bad weather (1604: 325). Overbury inveighs against the character of the 'ingrosser' of corn, a speculator or hoarder, calling them the vermin of the land and suggesting that speculation takes place even in times of plenty (1616: 89–90). Harrison (1938) includes examples of the politicization of corn, noting that in 1591 there was *A Proclamation against supplying the King of Spain with Corn.* He also documents the shortages and rising prices of 1595–6. Corn speculators continued to be a problem, and efforts to deal with them took one of them to the Star Chamber in 1597 where he was fined and imprisoned. Corn ships putting into English ports were impounded and their cargo seized. In 1601 corn was withheld from the Irish rebels to force their surrender. In 1610, 12 new granaries were completed at Bridewell to hold 6,000 quarters of corn for the poor. Several scholars, including most recently Nuttall (2007), suggest the 1607 Midland corn and enclosure riots may have informed the writing of *COR.* Tigner (2012: 14) notes that corn 'signifies civilization itself' and gives consideration to Lear's crown.

costard A large **apple**, from an equally large **tree**, the costard was available from the fourteenth to the seventeenth century. The stock is still available under compound names. The *OED* describes it as 'a large apple, distinctly five-sided, having five prominent ribs extending into the basin of the eye, and forming ridges round the crown'. It gave its name to costardmongers, later modified to costermongers, as sellers of **fruit**. Costard was a vernacular, often contemptuous name for the head. In three of the four plays where the word occurs it refers unequivocally to the head. *LLL,* however, has a character named Costard, and it is he who effects the first breach in Navarre's sex-free Eden: the apple that brings about the fall, he is probably responsible for Jaquenetta's fruitfulness (1.1.201–315). The single reference to costard-mongers is in *2H4* where Falstaff defends himself against the accusation of corrupting Prince Hal: 'Virtue is of so little regard in these costermongers' times that true valor is turn'd berrord' (1.2.168–9). The claim here is that in a world dominated by commerce, heroes are not valued. Amherst (1896), whose work is still authoritative, notes costard was listed separately from apples in general. McLean (1981) says it was one of the most popular medieval apples for eating and cider-making, suggesting the name derives from the French 'coste' for rib, the fruit being markedly ribbed. Harvey (1981) suggests that it was an expensive plant, costing four times as much as ordinary apple trees. Eburne (2008) records two types of costard among the seven varieties of apple planted at Lyveden New Bield in the 1590s.

coulter The iron blade fixed in front of the plough-share, the coulter makes a vertical slice in the **soil**, which is then cut horizontally by the share. The single mention occurs in Burgundy's description of the condition of French landscape and agriculture arising from Henry V's invasion: 'her fallow leas/The darnel, hemlock, and rank femetary/ Doth root upon, while that the coulter rusts/That should deracinate such savagery' (*H5* 5.2.44–7). The visually arresting representation of the rusting coulter discarded while rampant **weeds** take over valuable arable land is reinforced by the aural impact of the collision between 'coulter' and '**deracinate**'. The power of the coulter to rip out the invasive weeds is intensified by that rare word 'deracinate' (used only here and in *TRO* (1.3.99)). Markham (1613: 29) includes diagrammatic pictures of the component parts of the plough, including the 'coulture' which he describes as 'a long peece of Iron, made sharp at the neather end, and also sharp on one side and being for a stiffe clay it must be straighte without bending'. He also explains how to handle it. Drayton gives the same sense of violence in relation to the effects of enclosure: 'the share and coulter tear/The full corn-bearing glebe, where sometimes forests were' (1622, *Polyolbion* 19. 45–6).

covert, coverture (A) A shelter, or hiding-place, covert can suggest under cover, an overgrown and secretive place, or the provision of protection to wild animals or game as a **thicket** or **brake**. Metaphorically it indicates deceitfulness.

(B) Advising the young couple to disguise themselves for their escape from Bohemia, Camillo tells Perdita, 'Fortunate mistress (let my prophecy/Come home to ye!), you must retire yourself/Into some covert' (*WT,* 4.4.648–50). The First Keeper in

3H6 directs his associate to convenient cover as they stalk the deer: 'And in this covert will we make our stand,/Culling the principal of all the deer' (3.1.3–4). Benvolio, describing Romeo's desire for solitude to reflect on his unrequited love for Rosaline, says, 'Towards him I made, but he was ware of me,/And stole into the covert of the wood' (*ROM* 1.1.124–5). Here, the place of concealment is the wood itself and not a specific feature within the wood. Ursula, in *ADO*, who has spied Beatrice's hiding place, confides to Hero, 'So angle we for Beatrice, who even now/Is couched in the woodbine coverture' (3.1.29–30). The scented bower is, indeed, the pleasantest hiding place for eavesdropping. In the world of politics a hiding place becomes sinister and threatening. Warwick schemes to capture Edward IV under the cover of darkness: 'And now what rests but, in night's coverture,/.../We may surprise and take him at our pleasure?' A few lines later, even more menacingly, he refers to 'night's black mantle' (*3H6*, 4.2.13–22). The transition is telling: Warwick has secured the support of Clarence against his own brother and needs to lead the turncoat step by step like a nervous colt. In the Induction to *2H4*, Rumour enumerates the deceptions perpetrated against a gullible public: 'I speak of peace, while covert enmity/Under the smile of safety wounds the world' (9–10). On his return to Vienna the Duke ensnares Angelo by expressing admiration for his exemplary governance:

> O, your desert speaks loud, and I should wrong it
> To lock it in the wards of covert bosom,
> When it deserves with characters of brass
> A forted residence 'gainst the tooth of time
> And razure of oblivion.
>
> *(MM 5.1.9–13)*

At the close of the brutal proscription scene in *JC*, Antony invites Octavius to pursue remaining matters in secrecy: 'And let us presently go sit in council,/How covert matters may be best disclos'd,/And open perils surest answered' (4.1.45–7). The 'covert matters' are generally taken to mean the dangers that lurk for the triumvirate. Another possibility is that 'covert matters' are what Antony and Octavius 'fashion' for public presentation.

(C) Manwood (1598) records that the provision of coverts for game was a legal requirement in the royal forests, and details their management.

cowslip (A) *Primula veris* L. is a native spring **flower** of the same botanical genus and family as **primrose** and **oxlip**. The names of all three were often used interchangeably, and their uses frequently overlapped. The cowslip was a **strewing herb** and a constituent of cosmetics. It also had culinary and medicinal applications, and was an easily recognizable flower in embroidery for clothes and tapestry hangings.

(B) All references to the cowslip intimate responsiveness to the flower's delicacy. Burgundy's celebration of the French landscape includes a tender allusion to, 'The even mead, that erst brought sweetly forth/The freckled cowslip, burnet, and green clover' (*H5* 5.2.48–9). The epithet 'freckled', pertaining to the flower's reddish spots, conveys something of the reassuring nature of this familiar flower. It is this subtle detail that produces Iachimo's simile when gazing down in admiration at the sleeping Imogen: 'On her left breast/A mole cinque-spotted, like the crimson drops/I'th'bottom of a cowslip' (*CYM* 2.2.37–9). In the same play a distinction is made between cowslips and primroses. The Queen, an eager experimenter in poisons, commands, 'The violets, cowslips, and the primroses,/Bear to my closet' (1.5.83–4). Her interest is toxicological: her aim is to manipulate nature for her nefarious ends. The comforting appeal of the cowslip is apparent in *TMP* where Ariel sings, 'Where the bee sucks, there suck I,/In a cowslip's bell I lie' (5.1.88–9). This easy intimacy arises too in *MND*. The fairy, responding to Puck's questions, makes the cowslip central to her duties:

> And I serve the Fairy Queen,
> To dew her orbs upon the green.
> The cowslips tall her pensioners be,
> In their gold coats spots you see:
> Those be rubies, fairy favors,
> In those freckles live their savors.
> I must go seek some dewdrops here,
> And hang a pearl in every cowslip's ear.
>
> *(2.1.8–15)*

Here cowslips are elevated to the status of royal bodyguards, 'pensioners'. The modesty and stature afforded this flower is remarkable. It resists parody. Even Flute/Thisbe cannot undermine the status of the cowslip: 'These lily lips,/This cherry nose,/These yellow cowslip cheeks,/Are gone, are gone!' (5.1.330–3).

(C) Robinson's (1584) verse on the cowslip suggests its meaning as 'counsel' and 'secrets between lovers'. It is a strewing herb in Spenser (1596), and a **garland** flower in Drayton (1622). Greene makes a distinction between the different flowers: 'in pastures for sheep – there growes … the cowsloppe, the primrose, and the violet, which my flockes shall spare for flowers to make thee garlands' (1589, vol. 6, *Arcadia*: 58). Trevelyon (1608) includes patterns of cowslips for embroidery purposes. Sanecki (1994) gives the early superstitions, and Heath (2003) provides a botanical analysis; Iyengar (2011) details its medicinal applications.

crab (A) *Malus sylvestris* L. the native wild **apple** is the ancestor of all cultivated apple **trees**. It was the preferred **stock** on to which newer varieties, mainly French imports, were **grafted**. A small tree, its **wood** is renowned as being very tough; a common use was for staves, and walking sticks. It was also planted for its decorative **blossom** in spring. Although sweet food was less readily available, the **fruit** – crabs or crab-apples – were still a byword for acidity. They could only be eaten if cooked, served roasted or floated in beer with sweetener and spices. The raw fruit was also made into verjuice, a souring agent like vinegar. Because of its acidity and use for **grafting**, the crab carried figurative suggestions of something astringent, a sour or awkward person, or something that required art to be useful rather than relying on natural characteristics. Cancer, the crab, is a sign of the Zodiac.

(B) The sourness of the crab apple emerges during Petruchio's courtship of Katherine, the shrew. Responding to her obduracy he protests, 'Nay, come, Kate, come; you must not look so sour', provoking the riposte, 'It is my fashion when I see a crab' (*SHR* 2.1.228–9). Far from concluding even a phase of the verbal duel, this reply incites Petruchio's fertile wit. Lear, having found cold comfort with Goneril anticipates a warm welcome from Regan. The Fool, however, warns him, 'Shalt see thy other daughter will use thee kindly, for though she's as like this as a crab's like an apple, yet I can tell what I can tell'. When Lear asks for clarification the Fool affirms, 'She will taste as like this as a crab does to a crab' (*LR* 1.5.14–19). The hardness and acidity of the crab apple proves too generous a comparison. Only by registering crab as an apple rather than as a crustacean is the Fool's ironic barb understood.

The roasted crab apple receives two mentions. Boasting of his transformational antics, Puck exclaims: 'And sometime lurk I in a gossip's bowl,/In very likeness of a roasted crab' (*MND* 2.1.47–8). The song that closes *LLL* celebrates indoor warmth in the face of winter's discomforts, 'When roasted crabs hiss in the bowl'(5.2.925). In these instances the modern audience might mistakenly assume the crabs to be crustacea. There is genuine ambiguity in *TMP*. Caliban, eager to please his new-found master Stephano, pleads, 'I prithee let me bring thee where crabs grow'. Though 'grow' would suggest crab-apples, limpet-type shellfish might 'grow' on rocks. This is the opening line of a fascinating speech that includes 'scamels from the rock' (2.2.167–72) which feasibly are shellfish. One of Shakespeare's sources is Strachey's account of being shipwrecked in Bermuda. He relates how they had, 'taken from under the broken Rockes, Crevises oftentimes greater than any of our best *English* Lobsters; and likewise abundance of Crabbes, Oysters, and Wilkes' (cited in Arden 3 (296)). Armstrong (1946: 70) makes a succinct but persuasive case for the apple. 'Crab-tree' is mentioned three times. Its role as rootstock is alluded to by Suffolk in his vitriolic clash with Warwick: 'Thy mother took into her blameful bed/Some stern untutor'd churl; and noble stock/ Was graft with crab-tree slip, whose fruit thou art' (*2H6* 3.2.212–14). Traditionally it is the crab-tree which is exploited as valuable stock for grafting. Here the crab-tree is grafted onto worthier stock. The crab-tree suffers further disparagement in *COR* as Menenius lavishes praise on Caius Martius, his wife and mother, while recognizing that their popularity does not extend to the tribunes of the people: 'You are three/That Rome should dote on; yet, by the faith of men,/We have some old crab-trees here at home that will not/Be grafted to your relish' (2.1.186–9). Much esteemed as rootstock in horticulture the crab-tree is devalued in these plays. However, the crab-tree's value as a source for staves is revealed in *H8,* as the Porter attempts to control a crowd eager to catch a glimpse of the ceremony surrounding the birth of Elizabeth I: 'Fetch me a dozen crab-tree staves, and strong ones; these are but switches to 'em' (5.3.7–9). A neat and telling metaphor is provided by the discomforted Leontes when pressed to explain the other occasion when Hermione spoke 'to better purpose': 'Why, that was when/Three crabbed months had sour'd themselves to death,/Ere I could make thee open thy white hand,/And clap thyself my love' (*WT* 1.2.101–4). Interestingly, though accepting the possibility that the crustacean or the astrological sign might apply here, Arden 3 (158) favours 'sour-tasting', which would seem to be the more persuasive interpretation of the metaphor. The one unequivocal reference to the crustacean is in *HAM* where the eponymous hero baits Polonius, saying, 'for yourself, sir, shall grow old as I am, if like a crab you could go backward' (2.2.202–4). 'Crabbed', as a trait of character or demeanour, appears twice. Reflecting on his new-found love Miranda and her querulous father, Ferdinand muses, 'O she is/Ten times more gentle than her father's crabbed' (*TMP* 3.1.7–8). Irascible is perhaps the best fit, though 'harsh' might also capture its sense, which is probably the inference in *MM* when Lucio criticizes the Duke: 'A little more lenity to lechery would do no harm in him. Something too crabbed that way, friar' (3.2.97–8). It is likely that 'crabbed' owes something to crab-apple, which, when it is not boiled, is thought of as being hard and sour.

(C) Contemporary literature focuses on its proverbial acidity. Lyly's old gentleman writes: 'plant and translate the crab-tree where and whensoever it please you and it will never bear sweet apple' and 'no apple so sweet but a cunning grafter can change into a crab'(1580: 39, 245). Webster's Bosola deploys this practice as a sly insinuation: ''Tis a pretty art, this grafting'. The Duchess' defence of her marriage to her Steward is equally covert – ''Tis so: a bettring of nature' – provoking Bosola's offensive thrust, 'To make a pippin grow upon a crab,/A damson on a blackthorn' (1613, *Malfi*, 2.1.148–52). Christianson (2005) gives the staggering numbers of trees bought for planting at Hampton Court: 300 to nearly 13,000 of any one tree, including the crab, clearly highlighting its ornamental importance. McLeod (2008) explains the process by which 'hissing crabs' are obtained.

crop (A) Annual produce cultivated for food, especially cereal, a crop can be the **harvest**, the condition of bearing crops, **tillage**, cultivation, the yield or produce of some particular cereal or other **plant** in a single season or particular locality. Crop as a verb can mean to cut off or remove the 'crop' or head of a plant or **tree**, to lop off the **branches** of a tree, to cut off twigs or **leaves**; it is also used of animals biting off tops of plants or herbage in feeding. By extension it is to cut off, cut short or to indicate a punishment.

(B) There are literal references, but metaphorical applications are far more frequent. Lucrece inveighs against Time for failing, 'To cheer the ploughman with increaseful crops' (*LUC* 958). A fanciful example, where 'crop' is used as a verb, arises in *MND*. Titania instructs the fairies: 'The honey-bags steal from the humble-bees,/And for night-tapers crop their waxen thighs' (3.1.168–9). Iachimo, in his attempt to seduce Imogen, refers to the world and nature's bounty as 'this vaulted arch and the rich crop/ Of sea and land' (*CYM* 1.6.33–4). In the same play, Belarius muses how the young princes, brought up in the wilderness, display a royalty of nature: 'valor/That wildly grows in them but yields a crop/As if it had been sow'd' (4.2.179–81). Denouncing the Yorkist murderers of her son, Prince Edward, Queen Margaret cries, 'How sweet a plant have you untimely cropp'd' (*3H6,* 5.5.62). Richard Gloucester uses the same image when reflecting on this very action and his successful wooing of Anne: 'And will she yet abase her eyes on me,/That cropp'd the golden prime of this sweet prince/ And made her widow to a woeful bed?' (*R3* 1.2.246–8). In his vitriolic outpouring as he turns his back on Athens, Timon curses, 'Itches, blains,/Sow all th'Athenian bosoms, and their crop/Be general leprosy!' (*TIM* 4.1.28–30). The term is used in relation to giving birth in *ANT*. Agrippa, responding to Enobarbus' tales of Cleopatra, comments on her relationship with Julius Caesar: 'She made great Caesar lay his sword to bed;/ He ploughed her, and she cropp'd' (2.2.227–8).

(C) On the eve of his execution in 1586, Tichborne considers his life an unsuccessful crop: 'My crop of corn is but a field of tares' (Ault 1949, 120). Drayton applies it to the harvest: 'A rich and goodly crop from that unpleasant soil' (1622, *Polyolbion*, 14.122).

crow-flower (A) The most cited possibilities are common buttercup – *Ranunculus*, ssp., ragged robin – *Lychnis flos-cuculi* L., and bluebell, formerly *Endymion non-scriptus,* now *Hyacinthoides non-scripta* L. Chouard. Some authorities firmly proclaim the plant's precise identity, while others offer a range of suggestions.

(B) Shakespeare mentions the crow-flower only once. The first use of the word is usually attributed to the dramatist, but Gerard (1597) predates *HAM*. Gertrude's portrayal of Ophelia's drowning is precise in its focus on plants: 'Therewith fantastic garlands did she make/Of crow-flowers, nettles, daisies, and long purples' (*HAM* 4.7.168–9). The crow-flowers are clearly part of a garland that appears to be something of a galli-maufry. Each plant would 'speak' to Shakespeare's audience, but it is now impossible to determine what 'crow-flowers' represent given that their precise identity is uncertain. The term 'fantastic' merits consideration. It suggests something extravagant, strange, or even incongruous. Meanings cut across each other promoting ambiguity. Adorning herself with a garland may indicate Ophelia's thoughts of marriage or celebration. The flowers of the meadows and margins, so characteristic of country life, contrast sharply with the sophistication of the Court. This comparison itself constitutes a statement.

(C) The most comprehensive analysis of the identity of the crow-flower can be found in Heath (2003) who analyses the possible candidates, and the crow-flower's connection with 'crow-foot', a name given to several wild flowers. He considers the effect of the often cited buttercup as crow-flower, explaining that all varieties of common buttercup would have had a very unpleasant effect on Ophelia's skin. Gerard (1597: 599–600) discusses the ambiguities surrounding nomenclature, but fails to elicit clear identification. He notes crow-flowers were used in garlands: 'These are not used in medicine or nourishment: but they serve for garlands and crowns, and to decke up gardens'. Ryden (1978: 40–1) observes, 'Gerard's description of the habitat and efflorescence of the plant suggests *Lychnis flos-cuculi L.,* a common marsh-plant nowadays generally called ragged robin'. Mabey (1996) notes the local names current before the eighteenth century when the name 'buttercup' came into use. Tigner (2012: 101) suggests that crow-flowers were known as pinks, but all attempts at identification are speculative.

crown imperial *Fritillaria imperialis* L. is native to Persia and the southern Himalayas. A recent introduction into Europe via Constantinople it exemplified the developing commercial trade in **plants**. Thought at the time to be a **lily**, it is in fact a fritillary, and until the eighteenth century was available in only one colour. During the course of Perdita's disquisition on plants, she lists: 'bold oxlips, and/The crown imperial; lilies of all kinds/(The flow'r-de-luce being one)' (*WT* 4.4.125–7). No descriptive term is attached to 'The crown imperial'. Visually and aurally expressive, it needs none. This is one of the few occasions when Shakespeare mentions a newly arrived exotic. Gerard (1597: 203) says it came from Constantinople making 'denizons in our London gardens, whereof I have plenty'. Stuart and Sutherland (1987) have details of its introduction, while Watts (2007) notes its appearance provoked such a demand that prices rose rapidly. Pavord (2005: 297–300) gives the introduction date as the 1570s and reproduces a remarkable illustration of the crown imperial dating from the 1630s. It was a considerable novelty, even more so than the tulip which arrived in western Europe in 1559. Willes (2011: 257, 94) provides a succinct commentary on its introduction and reproduces the illustration represented on the title page of Clusius' (1601) *Rariorum plantarum historia*. Heilmeyer (2001: 40) recounts its symbolism which includes arrogance and crushed pride.

cuckoo-bud While it might refer to any **flower** in bud when the cuckoo sings, there is general agreement that cuckoo-bud indicates a variety of buttercup, possibly *Ranunculus acris* L., found in damp grassland, or *R. bulbosus* L., a plant of dry grassland. Both have an unpleasant effect on the skin, resulting in welts and other skin irritations; both are native **plants**. Shakespeare is the first recorded user of the name. The song of *Spring* at the close of *LLL* expresses the promise and threat of this season: the cuckoo is the herald of spring and is a symbol of infidelity. Cuckoo-buds play a central role in a delicate pictorial and musical composition: 'And cuckoo-buds of yellow hue/Do paint the meadows with delight,/The cuckoo then on every tree/Mocks married men' (5.2.896–9). Attempts to link cuckoo-buds with **cuckoo-flower** do not usually convince; most commentators pointedly say they represent two different plants. Beisly (1864) quotes Miller (1754) on *Ranunculus bulbosus* as cuckoo-buds; however Miller continuously uses crowfoot, not cuckoo-bud, for this ranunculus. This typifies the confusion and problems of tracing information in the nineteenth-century commentaries on Shakespeare's plants. Other suggestions are lesser celandine, cowslip or marsh marigold, but for a flower that 'paints the meadow', the meadow buttercup is the most likely candidate. See also **crow-flower.**

cuckoo-flower (A) Possibly any **plant** in **flower** when the cuckoo is calling, cuckoo-flower is a vernacular name for several wild flowers. However, as the other constituent parts of Lear's crown are specifically named, Shakespeare probably had a particular flower in mind, the most likely being a bitter-cress, **lady's smock**, *Cardamine pratensis* L. Other suggestions include cuckoo-pint, *Arum maculatum* L. (see **long purples**), ragged robin – *Lychnis flos-cuculi* L., largely for the similarities of name. Less certainly buttercup – *Ranunculus repens* L., or some other member of the campion genus *Lychnis* L. is included in the list of possible plants. Although flowers, all were common enough to be considered **weeds.**

(B) The description of the mad Lear, adorned with a crown of weeds masquerading as the golden one he gave away in the opening scene of the play, is expressive of simple, fractured humanity and representative of an ingrained attachment to the symbol of power. It is both assertive and an expression of humility. This is no traditional coronet of country festivities but a strange inversion – a fool's cap of kingship. Incongruity is at the heart of this image. Cordelia describes him, 'Crown'd with rank femiter and furrow-weeds,/With hardocks, hemlock, nettles, cuckoo-flow'rs' (*LR* 4.4.3–4). Lear's later references to sexual appetite and adultery (4.6.110–31) and the cuckoo's association with the cuckoo-flower may well symbolize infidelity and cuckoldry.

(C) Ryden (1978: 43–5) notes the '*Cuckoo-flower* is first attested in Lyte (1578), where it is used as a synonym both of "the wilde Gillofer" (probably *Lychnis flos-cuculi)* and of "the lesser Watercresse" (probably *Cardamine pratensis)*'. He adds that Gerard locates its flowering time as April or May, whereas the 'the high-grown field' (*LR* 4.4.7) suggests a later season. Armstrong (1946: 81) notes that buttercups were referred to as 'crazies' – this designation along with the association of the cuckoo with foolishness leads him to conclude that buttercups are the cuckoo-flowers in Lear's crown. Gerard (1597: 201–2) has a chapter 'Of wilde water-Cresses or cuckow-floures,' calling it 'Lady-smock', and noting 'These floure for the most parte in Aprill and May, when the Cuckow begins to sing her pleasant notes without stammering.' Parkinson (1629) appears to conflate **crow-flowers**, and cuckoo-flowers. Later possibilities become more fanciful: Nares (1859) says it must be the cowslip, as 'cocu'/'cucu' means cowslip in French; Mabey (1996) details its links with the cuckoo in folklore. While it is impossible to be certain, Stace (2010), who is very conservative in his use of vernacular names, gives *C. pratensis* as cuckoo-flower, and includes the defining characteristics of other candidates.

Cupid's flower This flower is commonly identified as 'Cupid's Dart', *Catananche caerulea* L., also known as Blue Cupidone, a late-sixteenth-century introduction from southern Europe. But it is unlikely that Shakespeare was referencing a very recent introduction which would not have had time to acquire the resonances that he employs. Later he calls it **love-in-idleness**, appearing to indicate the wild **pansy**, or heartsease, *Viola tricolor* L., which was thought to have aphrodisiac qualities, and which is sometimes identified as 'cupid's flower'. The numerous references to Cupid are connected directly with falling in love or being in love. In *MND* 'Cupid's flower', though named only once, plays a central part in the mischievous transformations which animate the play. Oberon relates how it acquired its other name, 'love-in-idleness', through Cupid's fallibility:

> Yet mark'd I where the bolt of Cupid fell.
> It fell upon a little western flower,
> Before milk-white, now purple with love's wound,
> And maidens call it love-in-idleness.

> *(2.1.165–8)*

Reconciliation with Titania leads Oberon to reverse the influence of 'love-in-idleness' by means of an antidote, 'Dian's bud'. The moon goddess, chaste Diana, is set against love-provoking Cupid: 'Dian's bud o'er Cupid's flower/Hath such force and blessed power' (4.1.73–4). Ellacombe (1896), Savage (1923) and Crystal and Crystal (2002) call it the pansy, saying the usage is unique to Shakespeare. Campbell-Culver (2001) identifies it as *C. caerulea* which was introduced in 1597; Watts (2007) suggests Cupid's flower as another name for love-in-idleness. See **love-in-idleness**.

cyme (A) The most usual identification of cyme is as a misreading for 'cynne' or 'senna', *Cassia angustifolia* or *acutifolia*, a purgative well-known from pre-classical times. While senna as a **plant** was not introduced until the mid-seventeenth century, it was already widely used, and well known for its purgative qualities. One writer suggests cyme could be a misspelling of apozem, a compound or concoction. Other candidates include **thyme**, cumin, **parsley** and basil.

(B) The single reference arises when Macbeth asks the Doctor whether he is able to cure Lady Macbeth, to 'Cleanse the stuff'd bosom of that perilous stuff/Which weighs upon the heart?'. The dispirited warrior continues with this idea of purgation: 'What rhubarb, cyme, or what purgative drug,/Would scour these English hence?' (*MAC*, 5.3.44–56). Here is a fascinating coalescing of the literal and metaphorical. These powerful purgatives work on the body but not on the mind and are impotent, too, in the political sphere.

(C) 'Senna' featured in the contemporary herbals, while 'cynne' does not. Rea (1920: 377) argues that 'As the reading *Cyme* of the First Folio is perfectly intelligible, there is no reason why it should not be restored to the text, and understood as meaning the tops and tendrils of the colewort.' An exchange of information in *Modern Language Notes* considers possible alternatives to senna: see Dunlap (1939), Sullivan (1941), Eliason (1942) and Smith (1945). Of their various suggestions, cumin seems unlikely, as it was not in the general repertoire of drugs at the time. The most plausible alternative is **thyme**, which served more as an emetic than a purgative, and had gynaecological applications. Hulme (1962) suggests that cyme is a shortened form of apozem, or aposeame, noting that a 1625 Stratford doctor's notes has senna spelt apozem. Hoeniger (1992) thinks 'senna' was sometimes spelt 'cynne', and sees 'cyme' as a misreading of this. Arden 2 (149) has an extensive note on this topic; updated in the Arden 3 footnote (283). Iyengar (2011) notes that senna would have been tempered with rhubarb to mitigate its powerful laxative effects.

cypress (A) *Cupressus sempervirens* L. is a partly tender **tree** recorded in England in the fourteenth century as an introduction from Italy and the Mediterranean, notably Cyprus, hence the name. It may have been planted in England by the Romans for hedging. Cypress had particular **garden** value as an evergreen. Its **wood** had notable anti-moth and preservative qualities which made it ideal for chests used to store linen. Medicinally it was an astringent. Cypress was a symbol of mourning, perhaps because it was **strewn** in time of plague. It was used figuratively to indicate a wide range of emotions and ideas from death, mourning and sadness to sanctity and uprightness. It may have given its name to 'cypress' as fine black cloth or gauze.

(B) One of the two references to cypress trees clearly draws on its association with death. Having been sentenced to exile by Henry VI, Suffolk curses his political adversaries with near hysterical venom. What appears to be his most temperate line is deceptive because the aural appeal is at odds with the deadly metaphor: 'Their sweetest shade a grove of cypress trees!' (*2H6* 3.2.323). The other example could hardly be more different. The calculating Tullus Aufidius, leader of the Volcians, once more humiliated in battle by Caius Martius, adopts a tone of suavity as he prepares to deliberate with the leadership: 'I am attended at the cypress grove. I pray you/('Tis south the city mills) bring me word thither/How the world goes, that to the pace of it/I may spur on my journey' (*COR* 1.10.30–3). Possessing no obvious symbolic significance the 'cypress grove' is perhaps only a source of local colour. Feste's plaintive song, 'Come away, come away, death,/And in sad cypress let me be laid' (*TN* 2.4.51–2) may allude to the black fabric associated with mourning (referred to earlier by Olivia (3.1.121)), a coffin made of cypress wood or one strewn with cypress boughs. This play, deriving its name from the last of the Christmas revels, constantly veers between a yearning for life in all its exuberant colours, and the pressures of death. It is not surprising therefore, that it is the only play with two references to this word. Olivia, overwhelmed by a passion for Cesario, confesses her anguish: 'To one of your receiving/Enough is shown; a cypress, not a bosom,/Hides my heart. So let me hear you speak' (3.1.120–2). Almost certainly she is referring to black gauze, the metaphor symbolizing her suffering of uncertainty and the fear of rejection. In *WT* juxtapositions of life and death are even more marked, a theme unexpectedly exemplified in Autolycus' jolly song: 'Lawn as white as driven snow,/Cypress black as e'er was crow' (4.4.218–9). After Baptista announces the auction of his daughter Bianca, Gremio opens the bidding with an inventory of his assets. The highly esteemed cypress chests accommodate luxurious fabrics:

> In cypress chests my arras counterpoints,
> Costly apparel, tents, and canopies,
> Fine linen, Turkey cushions boss'd with pearl,
> Valens of Venice gold in needlework;
>
> *(SHR 2.1.351–4)*

This play is singular in its extensive delineation of luxuries. From the England of the Lord in the opening scene to the wealthy elite of Italy these societies are replete with worldly goods.

(C) Colonna (1499) gives an idea of its extensive use in Italian **gardens**, and cypresses were planted at the centre of the **knots** in the great garden at Theobalds, suggesting their use as a rare specimen (Andrews 1993). Turner (1548) records 'plenty growing at Syon' where he was physician and gardener to Protector Somerset. Spenser (1596) describes the cypress as funeral, sad, and mournful, and Dekker writes that as the plague struck 'where all the pavement should instead of **green rushes** be strewed with blasted **rosemary**, withered hyacinths, fatal cypress and **yew**' (1603, *The Wonderful Year*: 104). Parkinson (1629) thinks cypress needs nourishing to grow in this country, and recommends its wood for chests because of its anti-moth and preservative qualities. Sidney (1580) suggests it represents death. For Peacham (1612) it indicates an undaunted spirit and for Hawkins (1633) scent and sanctity of life. Fleming and Gore (1988) note the Roman use of cypress at Fishbourne, while Harvey (1981, 1987) offers a date of introduction in the mid-fourteenth century, saying that Henry Daniel was already experimenting with its propagation.

D

daffodil (A) *Narcissus pseudo-narcissus* L. was a widespread wild woodland bulb, but is now rare. Although they were toxic to some degree, the roasted bulbs had a range of medical applications. New daffodil bulbs were introduced for planting in **knot** gardens as specimen plants. Featured symbolically and poetically as a harbinger of spring it could also signify foolishness. Modern references to the **narcissus** as a different flower from the daffodil represent a colloquial rather than a scientific distinction.

(B) Daffodils appear only in *WT* and *TNK*. Autolycus breathes new life into the action with his song, 'When daffadils begin to peer,/With heigh, the doxy over the dale!' (*WT* 4.3.1–2). One scene after Autolycus' anticipation of spring it has passed. Wishing she had 'some flow'rs o'th'spring' to bestow on her young friends, Perdita echoes the myth of Persephone:

> O Proserpina,
> For the flow'rs now, that, frighted, thou let'st fall
> From Dis's wagon! daffadils,
> That come before the swallow dares, and take
> The winds of March with beauty;
>
> *(4.4.116–20)*

'Daffadillies' appear in *TNK*. The Wooer reports to the Jailer the tenor of his daughter's song: 'I'll bring a bevy,/A hundred black-ey'd maids that love as I do,/With chaplets on their heads of daffadillies' (4.1.71–3). Sadness with the flickering awareness of folly may be implied here as the wretched girl struggles with heartbreak.

(C) Greene has the image of the 'yellow daffodil, a flowre fit for gelous Dottrels', implying foolishness (1592, vol. 11, *A Quip*: 213). In grief, Jonson enlists the daffodil as an emblem of sadness: 'Since nature's pride is now a withered daffodil' (1600, Ault 1949: 302). Wild daffodils were smaller, more delicate **flowers** than the cultivated varieties. Both Spenser (ed. 1999, *The Shepheardes Calendar*) and Drayton (1622) include them in **garlands** and for **strewing.** The confusion at the time between daffodil and asphodel is instanced by Dodoens (1578) who appears from the woodcut to show an asphodel under the title of daffodil. The *OED* gives asphodel as one meaning for daffodil, as do Britten and Holland (1886). Heilmeyer (2001: 62) notes that since carrying Persephone to the underworld 'Hades has worn a garland of narcissi on his brow' and that 'the daffodil has been viewed as a symbol of Christ's resurrection and promise of eternal life since the Middle ages'. Mabey (1996) has details of the rare survival of the wild daffodil. Knight (2009: 59) quotes Turner's comment that in some parts of England narcissi were referred to as the 'French gillyflower'.

daisy (A) *Bellis perennis* L., a native **flower**, the common daisy of grassland, **meadow** and **garden** flowers throughout spring and summer. The cultivated varieties are often double, with larger flowers and longer **stalks** than the wild ones. It was medicinally valuable. The daisy, an early flower, was a symbol of spring; it also suggested innocence, humility, purity and modesty, although it later came to be associated with dissembling and faithlessness. Because each flower lasts only a short time, it also represented grief, sadness and death. The daisy had long-standing mythological and religious associations and was a symbol of the Virgin Mary. It was an easy flower to replicate in embroidery.

(B) Varying symbolic meanings attaching to the daisy make for uncertainty. The song of spring in the closing moments of *LLL* is linked with artifice ('paint') and infidelity – the 'lady-smocks' and 'the cuckoo' both redolent of sexuality. Possessing both promise and threat the song touches on the daisy's piedness or duality:

> When daisies pied, and violets blue,
> And lady-smocks all silver white,
> And cuckoo-buds of yellow hue
> Do paint the meadow with delight,
> The cuckoo then on every tree
> Mocks married men;
>
> *(5.2.894–9)*

The wedding song at the opening of *TNK* casts no suspicious glance at the daisy: 'Maiden pinks, of odor faint,/Daisies smell-less, yet most quaint' (1.1.4–5). Fidelity and grief are the symbolic implications attaching to the situation in *CYM*. Finding Fidele/ Imogen attempting to bury a body, Lucius says, 'Let us/Find out the prettiest daisied plot we can,/And make him with our pikes and partisans/A grave' (4.2.397–400). In *LUC* innocence, purity, modesty and humility are implied by the description of Lucrece as she lies sleeping, her hand, 'On the green coverlet, whose perfect white/Show'd like an April daisy on the grass' (394–5).

Complications arise in *HAM*. Ophelia, allocating plants with deliberation, comments, 'There's a daisy. I would give you some violets, but they wither'd all when my father died' (4.5.184–5). Neither the recipients of Ophelia's flowers nor their meanings can be determined with certainty. Riverside (1222) identifies the daisy with dissembling without nominating the recipient. Arden 2 (LN 540–1) acknowledges the difficulties but proposes: 'The daisy has proved baffling … yet traditionally the daisy is the flower not of deceit but of love … As an emblem of love's victims the daisy has a latent ambivalence; the folly of being deceived, which is emphasized by Greene, may go with constant devotion.' Given this interpretation, it is puzzling that Claudius is assumed to be the recipient. Arden 3 (387) plausibly contends, 'daisies signify (unrequited) love and are appropriate to Ophelia herself'. Of the flowers distributed by Ophelia the daisy is the only one to reappear in Gertrude's description of Ophelia's drowning: 'Therewith fantastic garlands did she make/Of crow-flowers, nettles, daisies, and long purples' which takes place where 'a willow' – an unequivocal emblem of unrequited love – 'grows askaunt the brook' (5.1.166–9). The evident sexual associations of 'long purples' suggests a co-mingling of sex, faithless love and constancy. Contrary facets of the daisy might be activated: Hamlet's faithlessness and Ophelia's innocence.

(C) Both Hilliard's panel painting of Queen Elizabeth of 1583–4 and the 1585 Hever portrait show the royal association with the daisy (Arnold, 1988). Puttenham (1589), in considering art as modifier of **nature**, gives the example of the single wild daisy which when cultivated becomes double. Greene gives conflicting associations for the daisy, first as a source of love: 'her face is like a red and white Daisy growing in a green meddow, and thou like a bee, that commest and suckest honie from it…nay more' (1590, vol. 8, *Francescos* Fortunes: 197); later he suggests it has unpleasant associations: 'next grew the dissembling daisy to warn light of love wenches not to trust every fair promise that such amorous batchelers make them' (1592 *A Quip*, 218*)*. Trevelyon (1608) gives embroidery patterns for the daisy, and Amherst (1895) records its inclusion, presumably the cultivated double variety, in **knot gardens**. Heilmeyer (2001: 56) comments on the daisy's association with Aphrodite and its Christian identification with 'a love that conquers all things'. She adds that since the sixteenth century, daisies 'have symbolized contempt for worldly goods'. Heath (2003) has a table of commentators' views on its symbolic meanings from dissembling to innocence. Mabey (2010) notes the wider context of Shakespeare's daisy references.

damask (A) *Rosa damascena* Mill. is a hybrid of *R. gallica* L., a naturalized introduction from at least the beginning of the sixteenth century; possibly brought to England even earlier by returning Crusaders. It is better known as the red **rose** of Lancaster. Cultivated in the east for the very valuable attar of roses, the original rose oil was by weight more valuable than gold. 'Damask water' is an obsolete name for rose-water used in cooking and medicinal compounds. Damask could suggest the colour of the rose, with the pink or flushed cheeks from the usual colour of the **flower** providing a poetic reference for the colour of a woman's face. The damask **prune** (**plum**) was thought to be the best of its kind. 'Damask' was applied to substances originally produced in Damascus including damascene steel for swords; damask is a rich silk fabric woven with elaborate designs that can often only be seen when held up to the light.

(B) Most mentions of this rose focus on its co-mingling of red and white. In a witty engagement, the French courtier advises the Princess and her ladies (all of whom had been masked) to continue the baiting of Navarre and his fellows: 'Blow like sweet roses in this summer air'. Uncertain of his meaning the Princess inquires, 'How blow? how blow? speak to be understood'. Delighted by her perplexity, Boyet resolves the enigma: 'Fair ladies mask'd are roses in their bud;/Dismask'd, their damask sweet commixture shown,/Are angels veiling clouds, or roses blown' (*LLL* 5.2.293–7). 'Veiling, here, means 'lowering' or 'drawing aside'. A growing attraction for Ganymede/Rosalind prompts Phoebe to observe:

> There was a pretty redness in his lip,
> A little riper and more lusty red
> Than that mix'd in his cheek; 'twas just the difference
> Betwixt the constant red and mingled damask.
>
> *(AYL 3.5.120–3)*

One of the attributes ascribed to the fickle lover in *PP* is her perfect complexion: 'A lily pale, with damask dye to grace her' (7.5). *SON* 130 pivots on the contrast between an idealized woman and a real one: 'I have seen roses damask'd, red and white,/But no such roses see I in her cheeks' (5.6). Contemptuous of the plebeians' enthusiastic welcome for the victorious Caius Martius, Brutus the tribune is particularly scornful of the women who have prettified themselves for the occasion: 'our veil'd dames/Commit the war of white and damask in/Their nicely gawded cheeks to th'wanton spoil/Of Phoebus' burning kisses' (*COR* 2.1.215–8). The 'damask' is rouge, or its equivalent, which complements the white face paint. Scented gloves, advertised in his song, are part of Autolycus' pedlar's pack: 'Gloves as sweet as damask roses' (*WT* 4.4.220). A woman's cheeks are likened to damask roses in both *TN* (2.4.112) and *TNK* (4.1.74).

(C) The *Calendar of Letters and Papers Foreign and Domestic* gives the sheer quantities of imported plants, particularly roses, including one thousand **slips** of damask roses for a single occasion (Henry 8, 21ii, p. 402 19 December 1546–7). Maddison *et al.* (1977) note the debt to Thomas Linacre, Henry VIII's physician, who was thought to have introduced the damask rose to England; it is documented in Europe, however, from at least the thirteenth century. Singleton (1922) suggests that because of its sweet **smell,** damask was the favourite perfume for scenting gloves. Damask roses, **eglantine** and raspberries were planted in combination by Tresham where they 'may have been symbolic of Christ's passion' (Willes (2011: 41)). Thomas (1955) still offers one of the most comprehensive studies of the history and development of the rose. Potter's (2010) beautifully illustrated volume provides a wide-ranging exploration encompassing history, commerce and mythology. De Bray (1982) comments that most old red roses were in fact pink, lending more weight to their use in describing the complexion; she suggests that deep red is a modern rose colour. Palfrey (1997: 124–6) comments perceptively on Autolycus. See also **musk-rose.**

damson *Prunus domestica* L. ssp *insititia* L., the domesticated form of the wild **plum** or bullace **tree** bears small, sour, purple **fruit.** They were used extensively in medieval and early modern times. Plum and damson were often synonymous. The single mention arises in *2H6*. Simpcox feigning blindness claims he fell from a 'plum-tree' endeavouring to please his wife who 'desired some damsons' (2.1.95–100). The comment implies the names of these fruits were interchangeable. This scene has possible undertones, biblical and sexual. Arden 3 (204) suggests plums/damsons 'may connote testicles'. There may also be an allusion to Chaucer's 'The Merchant's Tale' where May engages in sexual congress with Damian up a **pear** tree as she attempts to outwit her blind and ancient husband, January. Contemporary information for plum and damson can overlap. Boorde (1547) says that damsons acted as a stimulant for the appetite, the opposite of **prunes** (dried plums) which were usually thought to work as a laxative. Drayton (1622) lists the damson with the dainty **apricock**, **pippin**, and varieties of **apple** growing in Kent. Parkinson (1629) suggests the tree's usefulness was limited because damson **stock** should not be used for **grafting**. Lawson (1618) recommends damsons as fruit particularly suited to a northern climate, thinking it especially valuable for decorative hedging. Andrews (1993) in his work on Theobalds shows that, unlike plums, damsons were not included among the 'choycest and rarest' fruit.

darnel (A) *Lolium temulentum* L., a **grass** commonly found in cornfields, darnel closely resembles **corn** until the latter is mature. It requires laborious hand-weeding to remove it from the growing **crop**. It was a **weed** both of cultivation and of neglect because if it survived to maturity it indicated poor **husbandry**. If darnel **seeds** were mixed with the **grain** and made into bread, they could be harmful, even dangerous, producing symptoms akin to drunkenness, and affecting the eyes, hence its metaphorical usage. As both a narcotic and an intoxicant, its effect was doubly potent when included in the **grain** made into beer. Darnel, even in small quantities, was poisonous to cattle. It is now known that the danger comes from the ergot fungus to which darnel is prone. Darnel, synonymous with any pernicious weed in the corn, was thought to have been the biblical tares, and was an alternative name for **corn-cockle**.

(B) Regaining Rouen for the French by her ploy of disguising soldiers as market traders, a truculent Joan Pucelle taunts her adversaries:

> Good morrow, gallants, want ye corn for bread?
> I think the Duke of Burgundy will fast
> Before he'll buy again at such a rate.
> 'Twas full of darnel; do you like the taste?

(1H6 3.2.41–4)

In addition to being unpalatable its adverse effect on eyesight is probably hinted at here as the French entered the town under the very eyes of the English. In *H5* Burgundy, making the case for peace, describes the laying waste of French agriculture: 'her fallow leas/The darnel, hemlock, and rank femetary/Doth root upon, while that the coulter rusts/That should deracinate such savagery' (5.2.44–7). The mad Lear is 'Crown'd' with 'rank femiter and furrow-weeds,/With hardocks, hemlock, nettles, cuckoo-flow'rs,/Darnel, and all the idle weeds that grow/In our sustaining corn' (*LR,* 4.4.3–6). The plant's damaging role is implicit in the catalogue, and in a play so deeply engaged with sight, insight and blindness (literal and figurative), there can be little doubt that it was intended to carry this additional resonance.

(C) Erasmus (1536: vol. 33) employed darnel metaphorically when writing 'they live on darnel', indicating lack of foresight. Turner (1548: 191) suggests 'lolium' would overwhelm the real crop: it 'groweth among corne, and the corne goeth out of kinde into darnel'. Harrison (1587: 248) shows how unscrupulous contemporary corn trading resulted in poor seed, and a predominance of darnel in the field. Parkinson (1640) lists the problems if it is mixed with wheat as causing a 'kinde of drunkennesse'; he quotes Virgil on the harm it does in fields and Pliny on its damage to sight. Hunt (1989) gives its effect on animals. Grieve (1978) details its continuing medicinal uses including as a narcotic. Mabey (2010) provides a wider context of weeds. Delineating the plants in Lear's crown, Tigner (2012: 109) comments on their individual attributes along with their collective influence.

dead men's fingers see **long purples**

deracinate Meaning the violent tearing up of **roots** the word is used both literally and metaphorically. This onomatopoeic word, a Shakespeare coinage, is deployed by Burgundy when portraying a forlorn agricultural landscape teeming with **weeds**: 'her fallow leas/The darnel, hemlock, and rank femetary/Doth root upon, while that the coulter rusts/That should deracinate such savagery' (*H5* 5.2.44–7). Its second mention, in *TRO,* is figurative. Having delineated the significance of hierarchy, Ulysses warns of the consequences of its violation: 'frights, changes, horrors/Divert and crack, rend and deracinate/The unity and married calm of states/Quite from their fixture!' (1.3.98–101). The ringing, dynamic nature of this word is strong enough to absorb into itself all the combustible words that precede it.

dew (A) The moisture deposited in minute drops on a cool surface by the condensation of the vapour in the atmosphere, dew forms in the evening or at night after a hot day. It is plentiful in the early morning, providing essential moisture for **plants** especially in summer. Figuratively dew can denote tears, moisture in the eyes; poetically it suggests moisture or gentle rain with the connotation of refreshment, and by extension it can be applied to the refreshing nature of sleep.

(B) Used in both literal and figurative senses, this word has a wide range of applications though few of them relate directly to plants. Dew is often used to signify tears; two alluring metaphorical examples relate to sleep; it encompasses blessings or generosity graciously bestowed; and is conceived as an infectious miasma. Preparing for his first encounter with Katherine the shrew, Petruchio rehearses his strategy: 'Say that she frown, I'll say she looks as clear/As morning roses newly wash'd with dew' (*SHR* 2.1.172–3). Reassuring Prospero of the safety of the King's ship, Ariel locates it 'in the deep nook, where once/Thou call'dst me up at midnight to fetch dew/From the still-vex'd Bermoothes' (*TMP* 1.2.227–9). In *MND* one of the Fairy's tasks is to bejewel Titania's fairy-rings: 'to dew her orbs upon the green' (2.1.9). The Fairy Queen's association with dew arises again when Oberon describes how, in 'her dotage', she garlanded Bottom:

> For she his hairy temples then had rounded
> With coronet of fresh and fragrant flowers;
> And that same dew which sometime on the buds
> Was wont to swell like round and orient pearls,
> Stood now within the pretty flouriets' eyes,
> Like tears that did their own disgrace bewail.
>
> *(4.1.51–6)*

Lennox affirms his commitment to the removal of Macbeth and the renewal of Scotland under its rightful monarch: 'To dew the sovereign flower and drown the weeds' (*MAC* 5.2.30). Laertes produces a beguiling metaphor when cautioning Ophelia to be wary of Hamlet: 'And in the morn and liquid dew of youth/Contagious blastments are most imminent' (*HAM* 1.3.41–2). The conception of 'dews' falling copiously is embedded in a striking utterance in *COR*. Aufidius, jealous of his co-commander Coriolanus, rationalizes the Roman's recent behaviour:

> He watered his new plants with dews of flattery,
> Seducing so my friends; and, to this end,
> He bow'd his nature, never known before
> But to be rough, unswayable, and free.
>
> *(5.6.22–5)*

The association of 'flattery' with Coriolanus is oxymoronic, but the image is wonderfully seductive, revealing how effective metaphor can be in the art of persuasion. Anne, narrating her suffering during her marriage to Richard Gloucester complains, 'For never yet one hour in his bed/Did I enjoy the golden dew of sleep,/But with his timorous dreams was still awak'd' (*R3* 4.1.82–4). A different note is struck by Brutus on discovering his boy Lucius fast asleep: 'It is no matter,/Enjoy the honey-heavy dew of slumber,/Thou hast no figures nor no fantasies,/Which busy care draws in the brains of men' (*JC* 2.1.229–32).

(C) Plat (1608) details gathering May dew in times of drought by using a sponge to capture the moisture from herbs, leaves, or grass. For Spenser dew was 'kindlye', and the lack of it bad both literally and metaphorically: 'Theyr rootes bene dryed up for lacke of dewe/Yet dewed with teares' (ed. 1999, *The Shepheardes Calendar* December: 111–12). Hawkins (1633) has a chapter on the symbolic virtues of dew, including an illustration of dew falling from the clouds like rain, describing it as 'the verie teares of Nature'. He moralizes on dew as representing the oil of grace, comparing the fertility of the earth after its watering by dew to the Virgin birth.

dewberry *Rubus caesius* L. The contemporary usage is not clear and probably covered a wide range of berry-bearing bushes including **gooseberry**, and **blackberry** with which most commentators identify it, although dewberries ripen earlier than blackberries. It was sometimes identified with the whinberry or **bilberry**, *Vaccinum myrtillus*

L. Its sole use is instructive given the uncertainty of the precise nature of the **fruit**. Titania directs her fairies to lavish attention on Bottom and to 'Feed him with apricocks and dewberries,/With purple grapes, green figs, and mulberries' (*MND* 3.1.166–7). There is no escaping the sensuous nature of these lines. The fruits are chosen not only for their refinement and delicacy, but also to fulfil poetic needs. Wholesome as they are, the probabilities seem against blackberries here, because elsewhere in the plays they are disparaged on account of their superabundance. Though there are dessert varieties, gooseberries are generally hard and seldom sweet. Perhaps 'whinberry', growing close to the 'dewy' ground, is the best candidate. Parkinson (1640) gives it as the 'winberry', but most contemporary references are to blackberry or gooseberry. Savage (1923) suggests that while the blackberry was common and worthless, the dewberry represents something more choice and special. Grieve (1978) includes it under blackberry, commenting that dewberries are distinguished by their large bloom-covered grains which are few in number.

Dian's bud There is a general consensus among earlier commentators that this is an *Artemesia,* probably *A. absinthum,* L., **wormwood,** also mugwort or mother-wort, the mother of **herbs,** named after Artemis, goddess of the hunt, hence its association with Diana. Wormwood is very bitter and would act as an antidote to something gentler or sweeter. It could help to wean a child from the breast. It was associated with sorcery and incantations, and used to counteract the evil eye. The imported Agnus castus, *Vitex agnus-castus*, the chaste **tree,** appears to have been overlooked by earlier writers, and is a possible candidate from its contemporary usage. Dian's bud is the antidote used by Oberon to reverse the love-inducing effects of '**love-in-idleness**': 'Dian's bud o'er Cupid's flower/Hath such force and blessed power' (*MND* 4.1.73–4). Diana, the goddess of chastity, is the appropriate counteragent to Cupid the mischievous promoter of promiscuity. Riverside (273) makes no mention of wormwood, identifying Dian's bud with the *agnus castus* or chaste tree, 'thought to preserve chastity'. Arden 2 (90) also advances this as a candidate. Judging by Langham's (1597) suggestions – he says agnus castus 'withstandeth all desire to filthie lechery, it frieth up the seed of generation' – it would be appropriate in the situation. Rowland (1981) records the extensive use of artemesia in medieval gynaecology.

dibble A tool still in the **gardener**'s repertoire, a dibble was used for making holes in which to **sow seeds, plant** bulbs or small seedlings. At its simplest it could be a pointed stick without a handle, or a more sophisticated tool with a cross-bar for the foot, forked or with several points to make a number of holes at any one time. The single use of 'dibble' is simple, yet it is part of the most interesting botanical dialogue in Shakespeare. Seeming to have accepted Polixenes' argument in favour of **pinks** – 'Then make your garden rich in gillyvors,/And do not call them nature's bastards' – Perdita resists growing them: 'I'll not put/The dibble in earth to set one slip of them' (*WT* 4.4.98–101). Opposed to any kind of artifice, this hybrid young woman – princess by birth but nurtured as a shepherd's daughter – rejects the prevailing enthusiasm for plant diversification. Polixenes' commitment to botanical cross-breeding, however, does not extend to societal intermarriage. The modern edition of Hill (1577) includes a wood-cut illustration of two **gardeners**, one planting seedlings with a dibble. Tusser (1573, ch. 33.22) includes the dibble as essential in **soil** preparation: 'Through cunning with dybble, rake, mattock, and spade,/By line and by leauell, trim garden is made'. Christianson (2005) records details of the use of dibbles, or 'debelles' in the gardens at Hampton Court.

dig The act of digging, by pushing a **spade** or another tool into the ground, represents the essential preparation of the **soil** before **sowing** or **planting**. It could suggest turning over the **ground**, making a hole, excavating or opening up the soil, removing a plant or disinterring something. Few mentions apply to agriculture or horticulture – and even they are tangential. Most are concerned with grave-digging – literal or figurative. Engaging in playful sophistry, the Gravedigger in *HAM* strives to aggrandize his profession by claiming, 'There is no ancient gentlemen but gard'ners, ditchers, and grave-makers; they hold up Adam's profession'. Asserting ''A was the first that ever bore arms', he concludes with the rhetorical question, 'The Scripture says Adam digg'd; could he dig without arms?' (5.1.29–37). Caliban, endeavouring to please his 'god' Stephano, promises, 'And I with my long nails will dig thee pig-nuts' (*TMP* 2.2.168). *SON* 2 anticipating the depredations of age provides the one figurative instance:

> When forty winters shall besiege thy brow,
> And dig deep trenches in thy beauty's field,
> Thy youth's proud livery, so gaz'd on now,
> Will be a totter'd weed of small worth held:
>
> *(1–4)*

Most writers take the process of digging for granted, though detailed instructions are given for **dunging,** which required digging. From Hill's illustrations (1577) it is clear that tools for digging have barely changed since early modern times. Markham (1613) includes digging as part of the **husbandman**'s work. Lawson (1618) gives specific advice against digging an **orchard** as it would disturb the tree roots. See also **twilled.**

distil (A) The extraction of the essence of a substance by vaporization through heat, the distillation process then uses condensation through exposure to cold. To distil is to infuse, figuratively to give forth or impart in minute quantities, to concentrate or purify. Specifically, in relation to **plants** and **flowers**, it is the extraction of their essence or a concentration of their properties for culinary, cosmetic or medicinal purposes. Distillation is the trickling down or falling in tiny drops as of rain or tears, or as in a vapour which condenses into drops.

(B) Distillation is used both literally and metaphorically. In its literal sense it can be a force for good or bad. Margaret in *ADO* refers to its medicinal application when she tells Beatrice: 'Get you some of this distill'd *carduus benedictus*' (3.4.73–4). The Friar advises Juliet to drink the potion he has distilled to induce a death-like sleep: 'And this distilling liquor drink thou off' (*ROM* 4.1.94). The malign Queen in *CYM* reminds her tutor, the doctor Cornelius, 'Hast thou not learn'd me how/To make perfumes? distill? preserve?' (1.5.12–13). The most vivid and chilling description of this process and its effects is made by the Ghost of Old Hamlet: 'Upon my secure hour thy uncle stole,/With juice of cursed hebona in a vial,/And in the porches of my ear did pour/ The leprous distillment ' (*HAM,* 1.5.62–4). Directing the deception of Christopher Sly, the Lord in *SHR* gives the instruction, 'Balm his foul head in warm distilled waters' (Ind.1.48). This world of luxury contrasts with the figurative use in *MND* where Theseus cautions Hermia against the 'barren' life of the cloister: 'But earthlier happy is the rose distill'd,/Than that which withering on the virgin thorn/Grows, lives, and dies in single blessedness' (1.1.76–8). The central idea of distillation as creating or abstracting an essence is given expression by Venus' delightful conceit when contemplating Adonis' panting breath:

> She feedeth on the steam, as on a prey,
> And calls it heavenly moisture, air of grace,
>> Wishing her cheeks were gardens full of flowers,
>> So they were dew'd with such distilling showers.
>
> *(VEN 63–6)*

The theme of distillation as a means of achieving continuity is present in three sonnets: in two of them the addressee is enjoined to procreate to ensure the perpetuation of his beauty: 'Then were not summer's distillation left/A liquid prisoner pent in walls of glass,/Beauty's effect with beauty were bereft' (*SON* 5.9–11); 'Then let not winter's ragged hand deface/In thee thy summer ere thou be distill'd' (6.1–2). The third proclaims the poet's pen as the preserver: 'And so of you, beauteous and lovely youth,/ When that shall vade, by verse distills your truth' (54.13–14).

(C) Contemporary writers on domestic economy include details of what, when and how to distil a wide range of plants. Hill (1577: 200) observes: 'A Necessarie table … briefly shewing the Physical operations of every hearb and plant therein contained, with the vertues of their distilled waters.' Tusser (1573) gives a list of summer plants for distillation which feature **carduus benedictus**, **fennel**, **fumitory**, **roses** and **strawberries**. Plat (1594) writes on the *Divers Chimicall Conclusions concerning the Art of Distillation* in which he gives the technicalities of the process and the wide variety of plants that could be used. See also **limbeck**.

dock Any one of several forms of docks, *Rumex* L., could be indicated, but here 'dock' is probably used generically. Docks are broad-leaved **plants** growing widely in a variety of habitats. They are a sign of neglected, uncultivated **land**, invasive deep-rooted **weeds** thriving on cultivated land, which can swamp **crops**, **seed** readily and are difficult to eradicate. Their **roots** are astringent. Their applications for skin problems followed from their well-known use in the alleviation of **nettle** stings. Describing how he would administer his utopian realm Gonzalo begins, 'Had I plantation of this isle, my lord'. He is interrupted by Antonio who deliberately misconstrues 'plantation' (denoting colonization) to mean cultivation – 'He'd sow't with nettle-seed'. The misinterpretation is taken up in spiteful mockery by Sebastian, 'Or docks, or mallows' (*TMP* 2.1.144–5). The intrusive and troublesome nature of this weed is made clear by Burgundy's epithet when recounting how Henry V's invasion has devastated French agriculture: 'and nothing teems/But hateful docks, rough thistles, kecksies, burs' (*H5* 5.2.51–2). Parkinson (1640) gives extensive detail on docks. Vickery (2010) suggests the seeds could be used to stimulate fertility, and that 'dock' was a local name given widely to a number of plants outside the *Rumex* genus. Mabey (2010) provides an overview, noting that they are persistent and difficult to eradicate. See **bur, hardock**.

dogberry There are several possible **plants** with the local name of dogberry including the dogwood, *Cornus sanguinea* L. The *OED* suggestions include dogwood, the **fruit** of the guelder **rose**, the dog rose, or bearberry, while other commentators propose the rowan. A character in *ADO*, Dogberry's comic status suggests his name is allusive. Soon after the entry of the Watch, Verges prompts his senior officer, 'Well, give them their charge, neighbor Dogberry' (3.3.7–8). Named only once, the endearingly pompous Dogberry noted for malapropisms, is given to inflated language to bolster his sense of consequence. He patronizes Verges who is certainly kept on the verge or the margin. Ryden (1978: 88) claims that the word had a derogatory meaning. De Bray (1982) says that *C. sanguinea* was used to wash mangy dogs, so providing a possible allusion for Shakespeare.

dove-house, dove-cote (A) Often a conical **garden** building with many tiers of nesting boxes, the purpose of a dove-house was to provide a constant supply of doves or pigeons for meat in winter.

(B) Besides providing local colour the dove-house forms part of the braid woven by Juliet's garrulous nurse to tell her tale of an earlier time: 'For then I had laid wormwood to my dug,/Sitting in the sun under the dove-house wall' (*ROM* 1.3.26–7). For all her meandering inconsequentiality the Nurse imparts critical information. Juliet's birthday, 'Lammas Eve', 31 July, is symbolic because the early **harvest** prefigures Juliet's short life. It also gives rise to her name. The only other reference occurs just before the death of the eponymous hero in *COR*. The machiavellian Aufidius, seeking a pretext for assassination, provokes the desired reaction to his insult 'boy of tears!'. Outraged, Coriolanus responds:

> 'Boy', false hound!
> If you have writ your annals true, 'tis there
> That, like an eagle in a dove-cote, I
> Flutter'd your Volscians in Corioles.
> Alone I did it. 'Boy'!

> *(5.6.100–15)*

Earlier, Aufidius had likened Caius Martius to a sea eagle or 'osprey' (4.7.34). The startling image 'eagle in a dove-cote' brings about the death of Coriolanus, but validates his status as the nonpareil of warriors and guarantees his place in history.

(C) Heresbach (1596) provides instructions for constructing a dove-house and enticing the doves into it to ensure a ready supply of meat for the table. Tusser (1573) comments that dove-**dung** was worth gold. Henderson (2005) in her comprehensive book includes many examples of such buildings, with a gazetteer of those still standing from Cornwall to Derbyshire.

draff See **husk**

dung, dunghill, ordure (A) Well-rotted animal faecal material for fertilizing **fields** and **gardens** to improve the **crop** or **plant** yield, the best dung came from doves, the worst being human excrement. Dung or ordure was used figuratively to suggest a heap of rubbish, the lowest and most degraded situation, or something tasting of **earth**. Applied to a human being it could designate an opprobrious person who led an evil existence or was of a very low station. 'Dungy' suggests something akin to the nature of dung, abounding in dung, foul, filthy, contaminating or defiling. Dung was thought to contribute to the spread of the plague.

(B) None of the mentions of dung show appreciation of its value as fertilizer. However, both references to ordure reflect acknowledgement of its vital function. *ANT* has the most colourful uses of 'dung' and 'dungy'. As Cleopatra prepares to commit suicide she elevates death over an earthly existence that derives its sustenance from animal excrement:

> and it is great
> To do that thing that ends all other deeds,
> Which shackles accidents and bolts up change,
> Which sleeps, and never palates more the dung,
> The beggar's nurse and Caesar's.

> *(5.2.4–8)*

The same sentiment is delivered in completely different circumstances in the opening scene when Antony, dismissing matters of state, affirms that love transcends all that is earthbound: 'our dungy earth alike/Feeds beast as man; the nobleness of life/Is to do thus [*embracing*]'(1.1.35–7). This seeming disdain for the thin layer of 'dungy earth' that makes life possible, even by characters who thrive on hyperbole, appears perverse as well as fanciful. Antigonus also uses Antony's term, but perhaps in a more neutral way. He avers that if Hermione is impure, 'We need no grave to bury honesty,/There's not a grain of it the face to sweeten/Of the whole dungy earth' (*WT* 2.1.155–7). The distinction seems to be between the insensate material world and the moral and ethical principles associated with the higher faculties of mankind. Arden 2 (38) and Arden 3 (198) suggest that this may derive from Psalms 83.10 'dung for the earth'. More prosaically, Lincoln takes up the cry of abuse against aliens in *STM* including their taste for root vegetables: 'Nay, it has infected it with the palsy, for these bastards of dung – as you know they grow in dung – have infected us'(1.1.12–15). Here, then, is the idea of dung being a source of infection – even by a second remove as a medium for growing the alien vegetable, the parsnip. This contempt for manure is indicated by Cornwall's instruction for the disposal of the body of the serving-man who stood out against his cruelty: 'throw this slave/Upon the dunghill' (*LR* 3.7.96–7). 'Dunghill' is a particularly opprobrious term, generally implying social inferiority. Confronted by a group of noblemen, Hubert has the temerity to defend himself. Outraged, the courtier Bigot cries 'Out, dunghill! dar'st thou brave a nobleman?' (*JN* 4.3.87). There is piquancy here as Hubert speaks with the courtesy and restraint belonging to a true gentleman. York, accused of treason, turns on the apprentice, Peter, denouncing him as 'Base dunghill villain and mechanical' (*2H6* 1.3.193) – every word of which is debasing. Frustrated by his failure to gain centre-stage to deliver the momentous news of Henry IV's death, Pistol complains of Shallow and Silence, 'Shall dunghill curs confront the Helicons?/And shall good news be baffled?' (*2H4* 5.3.104–5). Ordure, synonymous with dung appears twice. In *H5* the Constable of France cautions the Dauphin against underestimating the English King. He draws an analogy between the Prince's youthful excesses and gardeners who 'do with ordure hide those roots/That shall first spring and be most delicate' (2.4.39–40). Wishing to express appreciation for being rescued from the besieging Scots, the Countess of Salisbury endeavours to persuade King Edward III to enter her castle:

> For where the golden ore doth buried lie,
> The ground, undeck'd with nature's tapestry,
> Seems barren, sere, unfertile, fructless, dry;
> And where the upper turf of earth doth boast
> His pride, perfumes, and parti-color'd cost,
> Delve there, and find this issue and their pride
> To spring from ordure and corruption's side:
>
> *(E3 1.2.149–55)*

She uses this sequence of similes with such innocent grace that she beguiles the King, so becoming threatened by his sexual predation.

(C) Hill (1577) explores the subject extensively, recommending the best dung, from doves in descending order of usefulness through hens, cows, goats, cattle to horse dung and human excrement. Jonson's Tucca uses the smell to suggest someone of no importance: 'the slave smells ranker than some sixteen dunghills, and is seventeen times more rotten' (1612, *Poetaster,* 3.4.257). Webster's Duchess of Malfi hints that dunghills could be used for black magic when revealing her contempt for the indignities that might be inflicted on her: 'Then were't my picture, fashion'd out of wax,/Stucke with a magicall needle and then buried/In some fowle dung-hill'(1613 *Malfi* 4.1.62–4). Earlier Bosola suggests the **gardener** forced the **apricots** to **fruit** early by ripening them in horse-dung

(2.1.144). By tracing the productivity of the **vine** back to dung as the source of its fertility, Peacham (1612) moralizes that dung is the source of loathsome drunkenness. See also **compost**.

E

ear, earing, unear'd (A) An obsolete and archaic word for **ploughing**, earing is the breaking up of the **soil**, **tilling** and **sowing**; it is also an ear or head of **corn**.

(B) 'Earing' as ploughing, tilling or sowing appears figuratively in political, romantic and comic contexts; the 'ear of corn' is rarely mentioned. Receiving reports of desertions, Richard II gives way to despair and orders the dispersal of his army: 'That power I have, discharge, and let them go/To ear the land that hath some hope to grow,/For I have none' (*R2* 3.2.211–13). Richard knows instinctively that his process of decline has begun. Returning soldiers to the diurnal tasks of cultivating the land casts an oblique light on the world of power and politics: the trajectory in political life is parabolic; in agriculture circular. Equally apt, but more complex, is Antony's acknowledgement of dereliction of duty: 'O then we bring forth weeds/When our quick winds lie still, and our ills told us/Is as our earing' (*ANT* 1.2.109–11). Emendations of 'quick winds' are explored by Riverside (1397), but the substance remains the same: idleness promotes '**weeds**'. In *SON* 3.5–6 the addressee is encouraged to marry and procreate: 'For where is she so fair whose unear'd womb/Disdains the tillage of thy husbandry?'. Lavatch, the clown in *AWW*, argues the virtue of making his wife accessible to his friend: 'He that ears my land spares my team, and gives me leave to inn [harvest] the crop. If I be his cuckold, he's my drudge' (1.3.44–6). There are a few mentions of the 'ear of corn'. The spurned young shepherd, Silvius, abases himself before Phoebe:

> So holy and so perfect is my love,
> And I in such a poverty of grace,
> That I shall think it a most plenteous crop
> To glean the broken ears after the man
> That the main harvest reaps. Loose now and then
> A scatt'red smile, and that I'll live upon.
>
> *(AYL 3.5.99–104)*

Arcite recalls the days when he could run, 'Swifter than the wind upon a field of corn,/ Curling the wealthy ears' (*TNK* 2.3.77–8). Hamlet likens Claudius to 'a mildewed ear' (*HAM* 3.4.64).

(C) Markham (1613) uses 'ear' more extensively than any other contemporary source; it appears to be interchangeable with plough. Ear can also indicate further action in the sequence of plough, till, sow, with the suggestion of a series of operations in working the **land**. Greene writes of a rich farmer coveting a poor man's land, his pastures, good **grass**, his 'earable ground good corn' suggesting **fertile** land that is worth the taking (1592, vol. 11, *A Quip*: 284).

earth (A) The world, a pre-lapsarian state of **Eden**, **soil**, the medium for burying and place of burial, the hole or burrow of an animal; earth can also indicate one's native country, national identity, inheritance or **estate**. The adjective 'earthy' suggests ideas of being in touch with reality, covered by or made of earth, something or someone dirty, or contaminated; earth is the antithesis of the sea, and heaven. It can be elemental, or represent a mother figure.

(B) Many aspects of earth are expressed in the plays though there are few mentions of earth as a **growing** medium. The planet Earth is vividly represented in the Induction to *2H4* where Rumour, the choric voice, cautions the audience, 'I, from the orient to the drooping west/(Making the wind my post-horse), still unfold/The acts commenced on this ball of earth' (3–5). Puck promises to 'put a girdle round about the earth/In forty minutes' (*MND* 2.1.175–6). Hamlet uses the expression, 'this goodly frame, the earth' (*HAM* 2.2.298). Cleopatra tenderly refers to, 'The little O, th'earth' (*ANT* 5.2.80). Endeavouring to dissuade the King from his intended departure, the Countess of Salisbury pleads, 'Let not thy presence, like the April sun,/Flatter our earth, and suddenly be done' (*E3* 1.2.141–2). Earth as pliable, accommodating and palpable is apprehended in the Prologue to *H5* where the Chorus appeals to the audience, 'Think, when we talk of horses, that you see them/Printing their proud hoofs i'th'receiving earth' (26–7). At the heart of *R2* is the concept of the sanctity of the **soil** of England: it is the embodiment of the spirit of this island kingdom. John of Gaunt's paean to his country vibrates with a passion for the exclusiveness of this sacred space:

> This royal throne of kings, this sceptred isle,
> This earth of majesty, this seat of Mars,
> This other Eden, demi-paradise
>
> ...
>
> This blessed plot, this earth, this realm, this England,
>
> *(2.1.40–50)*

The play is animated by a notion of earth as the repository of national identity, of native being. On his return from Ireland Richard kneels in homage: 'Dear earth, I do salute thee with my hand,/Though rebels wound thee with their horses' hoofs' (3.2.6–7). Even so, those who celebrate the spiritual dimension of 'this earth' are prepared to violate it in pursuit of political advantage. Presciently, Carlisle warns Bolingbroke, 'The blood of English shall manure the ground,/And future ages groan for this foul act' (4.1.137–8). Delivering news of Norfolk's death in Italy, Carlisle reports, 'and there at Venice gave/ His body to that pleasant country's earth' (4.1.97–8). While Italy is perceived as a 'pleasant country' there is no sense of the special status that is accorded to England's earth.

The earth as an organism is represented by Bolingbroke when speaking of 'the tongueless caverns of the earth' (*R2* 1.1.105). Prospero energizes the planet when expressing incredulity at Ariel's reluctance to perform his duties:

> think'st it much to tread the ooze
> Of the salt deep,
> To run upon the sharp wind of the north,
> To do me business in the veins o'th'earth
> When it is bak'd with frost.

(TMP 1.2.252–6)

Prospero's rebuke to Caliban, 'Thou earth, thou! speak' (1.2.314), defines his slave's status. An apt riposte by the rustic Costard invites Holofernes' patronizing comment, 'a good lustre of conceit in a turf of earth' (*LLL* 4.2.87–8). When Leonato confides to Beatrice, 'Well, niece, I hope to see you one day fitted with a husband', her reaction is swift and dismissive: 'Not till God make men of some other mettle than earth' (*ADO* 2.1.57–60). Capulet, fearful that Juliet is too young, responds warily to Paris' marriage proposal: 'Earth hath swallowed all my hopes but she;/She's the hopeful lady of my earth' (*ROM* 1.2.14–15). A servant in *WT* announcing the arrival of an unknown princess describes her as 'the most peerless piece of earth, I think,/That e'er the sun shone bright on' (5.1.94–5). Leontes greets the young couple, Florizel and Perdita, using a metaphor that establishes earth as a life-sustaining, precious substance: 'Welcome hither,/As is the spring to th'earth' (5.1.151–2). This play, too, has a simple and direct reference to earth as the growing medium. Perdita, resisting Polixenes' encouragement to plant gillyvors, says, 'I'll not put/The dibble in earth to set one slip of them' (4.4.99–100). Earth as the antithesis of heaven is used by Julia when misguidedly placing her trust in Proteus: 'His heart as far from fraud as heaven from earth' (*TGV* 2.7.78). Isabella, reacting against Angelo's self-righteous interpretation of religious precepts, claims, ''Tis set down so in heaven, but not in earth' (*MM* 2.4.50). On the morning of his assassination Julius Caesar reflects on the turbulence and strange happenings of the night: 'Nor heaven nor earth have been at peace tonight' (*JC* 2.2.1).

The impending death of Antony causes Cleopatra to lament, 'The crown o'th'earth doth melt' (*ANT* 4.15.63). The dying hero is seen as the garland of the world. Octavius Caesar, dressing himself in the cloak of magnanimity, continues the process of elevation: 'She shall be buried by her Antony;/No grave upon the earth shall clip in it/A pair so famous' (5.2.359–60). *HAM* is the play which is most insistent on connecting the body to earth, a physical rotting and disintegration which returns the body to its element – 'this quintessence of dust' (2.2.308). Even Julius Caesar and Alexander the Great are subject to this process: 'Alexander returneth to dust, the dust is earth, of earth we make loam' (5.1.209–10). Hamlet inquires straightforwardly of the Gravedigger: 'How long will a man lie i'th'earth ere he rot?' (5.1.164). When Timon's request for help from the senators is rejected, he exclaims:

> These old fellows
> Have their ingratitude in them hereditary:
> Their blood is cak'd, 'tis cold, it seldom flows;
> 'Tis lack of kindly warmth they are not kind;
> And nature, as it grows again toward earth,
> Is fashion'd for the journey, dull and heavy.
>
> *(TIM 2.2.214–19)*

The phrase 'grows again toward earth' refers to impending death and return to the soil. The alienated Timon, digging for roots, is disgusted to discover gold: 'Come, damn'd earth,/Thou common whore of mankind, that puts odds/Among the rout of nations, I will make thee/Do thy right nature' (4.3.42–5). 'Earth' is sometimes used as a synonym for 'contemptible', but this 'damn'd earth' is gold which for Timon is the ultimate agent of destruction. The earth as actor in life's drama, threatening, strange, too palpable or frighteningly transmutive, is unique to *MAC*. Reflecting on the sudden disappearance of the Weird Sisters – 'that look not like th'inhabitants o'th'earth' (1.3.41) – Banquo exclaims, 'the earth hath bubbles, as the water has,/And these are of them. Whither are they vanish'd?' Macbeth responds, 'Into the air; and what seem'd corporal melted,/As breath into the wind' (1.3.79–82). On the night of Duncan's murder the earth's mutability is referred to by Lennox: 'Some say, the earth/Was feverous, and did shake' (2.3.60–1). Rosse adds to the choric or participatory role of earth: 'Is't night's predominance, or the day's shame,/That darkness does the face of earth entomb,/When living light should kiss it?' (2.4.8–10). Ironically, it is the all too solid quality of earth that disconcerts Macbeth as he moves to murder Duncan: 'Thou sure and firm-set earth,/Hear not my steps, which way they walk, for fear/The very stones prate of my whereabout' (2.1.56–8).

(C) Many contemporary books give considerable detail on how to improve the quality of the earth before planting. This was the **gardener**'s responsibility as Hill (1577: 25) makes clear: 'What care and diligence is required of every Gardener: to these, what increase and commoditie a well laboured earth yieldeth'. The night before his execution, Tichborne sees earth as both life and death: 'I trod the earth, and knew it was my tomb' (1586, Ault, 1949: 120). On the theory of humours, see Olsen (2007: 225–6). For an illuminating exploration of the significance of earth and land in *HAM* see de Grazia (2007).

ebony Any black hardwood of the family *Ebenaceae,* known in England from the fourteenth century, often with reference to its quality of intense blackness. Ebony is sometimes thought to be a candidate for **hebona**. This **Arabian tree** features in contemporary botanical literature as an exotic, renowned for its blackness. Of six mentions none relates to the growing tree. The blackness of its wood makes it analogous with hell. Arriving at the coronation of Henry V, Pistol adopts his familiar rhetorical style to inform Falstaff that Mistress Quickly and Doll are under arrest: 'Rouse up revenge from ebon den with fell Alecto's snake,/For Doll is in' (*2H4* 5.5.37–8). In keeping with his colourful bombast he weaves a tapestry from fragments gathered in the theatre, naming one of the furies and metamorphosing the prison cell to Hades. Baiting the imprisoned Malvolio who complains that his prison is as dark as 'hell', Feste counters, 'Why, it hath bay windows transparent as barricadoes, and the clerestories toward the south north are as lustrous as ebony' (*TN* 4.2.35–8). This wood, though proverbial for its blackness is luminous, which paradoxically, also makes it bright. Harrison (1933: 300) notes that when one ship was captured its manifest included over one thousand pieces of ebony, emphasizing its value as a traded commodity. Chancellor (1982: 32) observes that 'Pluto's throne was made of ebony and the statues of Egyptian gods and goddesses were carved from this uncompromisingly black wood'.

Eden (A) In Christian tradition a pre-lapsarian state, an idyllic existence before man started his destructive work. If the **garden** could be Eden, then the **gardener** could be Adam, and his work could represent an attempt to return uncultivated **nature** to a heavenly state. Eden can also continue the medieval idea of the enclosed space of the *hortus conclusus*, a place apart from the rigours of life, the *locus amoenus* of a landscape of delight. The garden is a defined space, as is an island; both garden and country could therefore be represented as places apart, other Edens. The idea of Eden invited illustration in the form of wood-cuts and even embroidery.

(B) The single evocation of Eden arises in John of Gaunt's famous 37-line speech celebrating England as 'This royal throne of kings, this sceptred isle,/This earth of majesty, this seat of Mars,/This other Eden, demi-paradise' (*R2* 2.1.40–2). This world is the epitome of all that can be conceived of as a chosen land, physically, spiritually and socially. It is, 'This blessed plot, this earth, this realm, this England' (50). Perhaps, too, the eulogy memorializes English heroes, especially those who prevailed against France. These legendary warriors –'Fear'd by their breed, and famous by their birth' (52) – who contributed to making England an Eden, had and will again lay waste France, 'this best garden of the world' (*H5* 5.2.36). Gaunt's heroes would not be universally admired. Although 'Eden' figures only once, there is the little Eden of Alexander Iden (pronounced, it seems, 'Eden') in Kent. Taking the air, Iden communes with himself on the comfort and tranquillity of his existence:

> Lord, who would live turmoiled in the court
> And may enjoy such quiet walks as these?
> This small inheritance my father left me
> Contenteth me, and worth a monarchy.

> *(2H6 4.10.16–19)*

After killing the interloper Jack Cade, Iden is knighted, and wins preferment at court – turning his back on the modest comfort of his little Eden. Here, as in the comedies and romances, the rural or pastoral existence affords many attractions, but these worlds are always abandoned in favour of sophisticated court life – the modern Eden.

(C) Greene sees England as a re-creation of Eden: 'Seeing then we are every way blest and favoured from above: that the Lorde our mercifulle God maketh England like Eden, a second Paradise' (1589, vol. 5, *The Spanish Masquerado*: 287). Parkinson (1629) invites his readers to step back into Eden, both by his title – *Paradisi in Sole Paradisus Terrestris* – and with the wood-cut of Eden as paradise which provides the frontispiece. Leslie and Raylor (1992) examine the links between Eden as paradise and the garden. Friedman (1976: 288) considers the exclusiveness of Gaunt's England, suggesting it 'anticipates Milton's characterization of Eden as a precarious repository of great treasure' with Satan appearing in the guise of the 'envy of less happier lands'. Tigner (2006) argues that *WT* represents the loss of innocence, the expulsion from Eden, with women once more accused of evil. She also (2012) examines the Edenic garden and its place in Shakespeare's plays.

eglantine (A) Sweet **brier** or eglantine, *Rosa rubiginosa* L., a native prickly **rose** with **fragrant** foliage and numerous small pink **flowers**. Originally wild, eglantine was cultivated for its **scent**, and as a covering for **arbours**. Queen Elizabeth adopted the eglantine as her personal emblem, as a representation of the Tudor rose, perhaps also adopting the Marian symbolism of virginity. Contemporary literature has many references to the eglantine as a compliment to the Queen; it regularly featured in embroidery.

(B) Celebrated for its beauty, its scent and its poetic name, the sweetbriar or eglantine receives two mentions. These attributes are implicit in Oberon's description of Titania's luxuriant bower, one of the most sensuous and visually arresting representations of plants anywhere in literature: 'Quite over-canopied with luscious woodbine,/ With sweet musk-roses and with eglantine'(*MND* 2.2.251–2). Arviragus, believing Fidele/Imogen is dead, prepares to bury the 'youth'. Again eglantine is set among flowers of the utmost delicacy:

> Thou shalt not lack
> The flower that's like thy face, pale primrose, nor
> The azur'd harebell, like thy veins; no, nor
> The leaf of eglantine, whom not to slander,
> Outsweet'ned not thy breath.

> *(CYM 4.2.220–24)*

Here it is the scented leaves that make the eglantine so admired. Indeed, it is Imogen's sweet breath that arrests Iachimo earlier in the play when he creeps out from his place of concealment: ''Tis her breathing that/Perfumes the chamber thus' (2.2.18–19).

(C) The eglantine was also the emblem of Bess of Hardwick: her 'Eglantine table' still stands in Hardwick. Although the imagery of the flower is lost in the considerable detail, it can be found round the collars of the stags which support her device: 'The redolent smele of Aeglantyne/We stagges exault to the devyne'. Strong (1998) cites Peele's record of the 1591 Theobalds entertainment, where, as a compliment to the Queen, the new garden for Burghley's son Robert Cecil included an arbour made entirely of eglantine. Spenser notes its moral: 'Sweet is the eglantine, but pricketh near' (ed. 1999, *Amoretti*: Sonnet xxvi). Arnold (1988) gives extensive details of the use of eglantine on the Queen's clothes and hangings. Jacques (1989) notes eglantine was planted in vast numbers, with 3,700 eglantines planted in the garden at Gray's Inn in the 1590s. See also **damask**, **musk-rose**.

elder (A) *Sambucus nigra* L. is a native small **tree** or **shrub** growing widely in **hedges**, woods, waste and rough **ground**, with honey-scented **flowers** and stinking **leaves**. **Buds**, flowers, **berries** and **roots** all had cosmetic, medicinal and culinary uses. In legend it was the tree of the Cross, or the tree on which Judas hung himself, but the superstitions relating to the tree are much older than Christianity. Proverbially 'elder' can suggest someone who was soft-hearted, or cowardly, but also someone old, to be respected for their age and wisdom, an older sibling; it can be pejorative and dismissive in regard to age.

(B) All uses draw on aspects traditionally ascribed to the tree. After defusing a quarrel the Host of the Garter light-heartedly alludes to the French doctor's cowardice: 'What says my Aesculapius? my Galien? my heart of elder? Ha? is he dead, bully stale?' (*WIV* 2.3.28–30). Mockery is also found in *LLL*. Presented with the Pageant of the Nine Worthies the young courtiers affect to mistake the famous warrior Judas Machabeus for Judas Iscariot: 'Judas was hang'd on an elder' (5.2.605–6). Falstaff is the butt of a joke when he is discovered in an amorous embrace with Doll. The disguised Hal comments to Poins, 'Look whe'er the wither'd elder hath not his pole claw'd like a parrot'. The implication of old age is accentuated by Hal's observation, 'Saturn and Venus this year in conjunction! What says th'almanac to that?' (*2H4* 2.4.258–64). A serious note is struck in *CYM* by the preservers of Fidele/Imogen. Guiderious perceives in the 'boy' a mixture of 'grief and patience', causing Arviragus to respond, 'Grow patience,/ And let the stinking elder, grief, untwine/His perishing root with the increasing vine' (4.2.57–60). The antithesis is between the 'stinking' elder's evil influence (grief) and the fruitful, life-enhancing vine (patience). The association of the elder with evil is all too clear in a scene of murder and deception. Inciting Saturninus to search 'Among the nettles at the elder-tree' (*TIT* 2.3.272) Tamora sets in motion a spiral of violence and suffering. The elder tree acts like a finger post to iniquity and anguish. The 'elder-gun', a pop-gun made by removing the pith from a branch of elder, is referred to in *H5*. Dismissing the suggestion that a monarch can be held to account by a soldier, Williams rebukes the disguised King: 'That's a perilous shot out of an elder-gun, that a poor and private displeasure can do against a monarch!' (4.1.197–9).

(C) Greene offers a proverbial view: 'wilt thou resemble the buddes of an Elder tree, which young are sweete and holesome, but blomd foorth are bitter and preudiciall' (1589, vol. 7, *Tullies Love*: 157). Marlowe's Ithamore includes some contemporary superstitions and perpetuates the Judas legend: ''Tis a strange thing of that Jew, he lives upon pickled grasshoppers and sauced mushrooms. ...The hat he wears, Judas left under the elder when he hanged himself' (1590, *The Jew of Malta*: 4.4.67–9).

Peacham (1612) suggests the elder growing out of ruins is emblematic of pride and a concomitant fall. Vickery (2010: 55) observes, 'elder is probably the most enigmatic plant in the folk-tradition of the British Isles', and gives country-wide examples of its use and superstition.

elm (A) A **tree** of the genus *Ulmus* L., the exact type is impossible to determine, but it may suggest the English elm *U. procera*, Salisb., which is probably a native tree; it is now very rare in southern England. Most parts of the tree were productive, the timber very hard and tough, and surviving well under water, so providing drainage pipes and bridge piles. Its **leaves**, **bark**, **branches** and **roots** had astringent, demulcent and diuretic properties. From biblical times elms were traditional props for **vines**, whence their proverbial use as a support, which survived even the death of the tree, a symbol of fidelity and the strength of love.

(B) *ERR* provides a classic example of the elm as support for the vine. The unhappy Adriana delivers a homily to her husband, beginning 'Thou art an elm, my husband, I a vine,/Whose weakness, married to thy stronger state,/Makes me with thy strength to communicate' (2.2.174–6). Titania, embracing Bottom, uses the same imagery but her tone is inviting: 'So doth the woodbine the sweet honeysuckle/Gently entwist; the female ivy so/Enrings the barky fingers of the elm' (*MND* 4.1.42–4). Unique usages, 'enrings' and 'barky' possess distinct physicality. The reference in *2H4* is terse. As Falstaff attempts to wriggle out of a tight corner Hal and Poins determine to cut off his retreat into prevarication. Poins demands, 'Answer, thou dead elm, answer' (2.4.331). In order to mollify them the disloyal Falstaff abuses both Doll and Mistress Quickly. This particular 'dead elm' is an unreliable support with respect to his friends. In the *H4* plays insults and banter usually involve copious wordplay, but this short, sharp thrust by Poins hits the mark with economy and precision.

(C) Calderwood (1992: 62) notes 'Beginning with Catullus (*Carmen* LXII), the marriage of feminine grapevine and masculine elm signifies the fruitful union of husband and wife'. Colonna (1499) probably draws on Ovid when he writes of the 'rough elms that suit the fruitful vines', and 'I am like … the climbing vine deprived of its pole and prop, lying prostrate without its supporting elm'. Jonson's Sejanus employs the same imagery of support:

> I, that did help
> To fell the lofty cedar of the world
> Germanicus; that at one stroke cut down
> Drusus, that upright elm; withered his vine;
>> *(1603,* Sejanus*: 5.4.71–4).*

Norden (1618) records the elm, **ash** and **oak**, as the most important timber trees, protected by statute under Henry VIII and Elizabeth. Arnold (1988) lists a jewel of a fruitful vine growing over dead elm in gold, diamonds and rubies. Mabey (1996) includes the tree's folklore, and provides a modern context.

eringo *Eryngium maritimum* L., sea-holly, was cultivated as a vegetable in **gardens**, and provided a sweetmeat when candied. Eringo had a range of medicinal applications from Anglo-Saxon times; it was widely thought to be a restorative of youth and an aphrodisiac. Demand grew in the sixteenth century with a flourishing trade centred on Colchester. Shakespeare is credited with the first mention of eringoes. Only Falstaff refers to them. During the assignation in the wood with the merry wives he calls for 'kissing comfits' to sweeten his breath and for aphrodisiacs to invigorate him: 'Let the sky rain potatoes; let it thunder to the tune of "Green-sleeves", hail kissing-comfits, and snow eringoes; let there come a tempest of provocation' (*WIV* 5.5.18–21). Falstaff's surrender to the power of language is as effective a stimulant as any that could be provided by **potatoes** or eringoes. The image he conjures up is visually absurd, extravagantly comic, and richly Falstaffian. Greene suggests its aphrodisiac qualities in recommending that 'to please the trug his mistress without he goes to the Apothecaries for Eringion' (1592, vol. 11, *A Quip*: 249). Gerard (1597: 1162–3) agrees, saying it is good given to the old and aged who 'want natural moisture, and good for younger who have no delight in venerie'. John Hall (Lane 1996: 237) includes eringo in one treatment for his wife Susanna, leading to speculation as to whether he was prescribing for menstrual or marital problems. Seager (1896) cites its restorative qualities; McLeod (2008) has details of the Colchester trade.

estate (A) **Landed** property, estate also signifies a state or condition, constitution or nature, personal financial standing, possessions, ability, status, position, property, future and capital. A physical estate, whether owned by the crown, a family or individual was usually cited by its place name: it was more common to talk of Theobalds or Burghley than of Cecil's estates. Ownership of an estate implies a considerable degree of wealth; such estates were often mapped for the first time in the sixteenth century.

(B) Most of the references relate to personal wealth or social standing. Surprisingly there is not one *unequivocal* reference to 'estate' as simply landed property. Unsurprisingly, *TIM* is the play where the term figures most strongly. Timon, reckless in his generosity, reduces himself to penury. Exasperated, the steward makes plain to his master the parlous condition of his finances: 'I did endure/Not seldom, nor no slight checks, when I have/Prompted you in the ebb of your estate/And your great flow of debts' (2.2.139–42). Clearly estate means total enterprise or accumulated assets: houses, lands, bonds, outstanding loans, precious metals and cash. Attempting to rescue his position, Timon recalls that a beneficiary of his largesse has recently received a substantial bequest: 'Ventidius lately/Buried his father, by whose death he's stepp'd/Into a great estate' (3.1.222–4). Once more it is not only land that pertains here but an aggregation of assets. The First Stranger, confiding in Lucius, cautions, 'Lord Timon's happy hours are done and past, and his estate shrinks from him' (3.2.6–7). This is a fascinating metaphor as it probably applies to Timon's total financial condition, but 'shrinks' gives a sense of the landed estate dwindling as it is being sold off piecemeal. Although it is evident that Timon's land-holding was extensive – 'To Lacedaemon did my land extend' (2.2.151) – what is not clear is whether all or any of the wealthy Athenians owned land. But in this society of conspicuous consumption 'estate' relates to overall financial position, including productive assets and valuables. Iachimo twice refers to his estate when enticing Posthumus to wager on Imogen's fidelity – 'I dare thereupon pawn a moi'ty of my estate to your ring'; 'Would I had put my estate and my neighbor's on th'approbation of what I have spoke!' (*CYM* 1.4.108–9; 123–4). Whilst this could relate to his landed property it is more likely that he is referring to his total wealth. Even Pander when contemplating retirement from brothel-keeping – 'if in our youths we could pick up some pretty estate, 'twere not amiss to keep our door hatch'd' (*PER* 4.2.32–3) – is probably referring to some little enterprise rather than landed property. At the other end of the social spectrum, Lord Aburgavenny reveals the enormous outlays required of his kinsmen for attendance at The Field of the Cloth of Gold: 'this so sicken'd their estates, that never/They shall abound as formerly' (*H8* 1.1.82–3). There can be no doubt that their manors and lands are included, but the term is almost certainly taking in all their productive assets and valuables. Thus while estate in the sense of lands and productive assets associated with them underpinned the financial strength of a highly important social stratum, it seems that the word is never used exclusively in this sense by Shakespeare. However, the physical representation of estate in terms of land and its various facets is alluded to by Warwick – although he does not use the term 'estate' – when he lies dying on the battlefield: 'My parks, my walks, my manors that I had,/Even now forsake me; and of all my lands/Is nothing left me but my body's length' (*3H6* 5.2.24–6).

(C) McRae (1996) writes of the **manorial** estates which were the target of many of the contemporary books on **husbandry**; he comments on the importance of the late sixteenth-century development of the estate map which showed both possessions and use of **land**. Henderson (2005) has details of several sixteenth-century estate maps, including the surviving ones by Ralph Agas, Ralph Treswell and William Senior. For further exploration of the term and additional examples see Thomas (2008: 111–12).

F

femetary, femiter, fumitory (A) *Fumaria officionalis* L., or fumitory, a common **weed** of waste **ground**. An early colonizer of neglected **land**, it was a considerable nuisance in **corn**, as it could smother an entire **crop**. Thought to have acquired its name 'smoke of the earth' from its sprawling growth habit, fumitory's acrid smoke was inhaled for medical purposes. Other uses included the treatment of eye and skin problems, a range of sexual diseases and as a purgative. As a self-fertile plant it was thought to self-generate spontaneously – it is rarely attractive to insects – leading to its association with witchcraft.

(B) Burgundy's description of the disordered state of the French countryside includes 'femetary' which takes hold when the normal tasks of agricultural **husbandry** are disrupted: 'her fallow leas/The darnel, hemlock, and rank femetary/Doth root upon, while that the coulter rusts/That should deracinate such savagery' (*H5* 5.2.44–7). Femetary is also described as 'rank' in *LR* where again the focus is on the threat it, and other weeds, pose to the very staff of life. Cordelia finds Lear, 'Crown'd with rank femiter and furrow-weeds,/With hardocks, hemlock, nettles, cuckoo-flow'rs,/Darnel, and all the idle weeds that grow/In our sustaining corn' (*LR* 4.4.3–6). The adulterated field of 'sustaining' corn invites comparison with Lear's description of Goneril as 'a disease that's in my flesh…/A plague-sore, or embossed carbuncle,/In my corrupted blood' (2.4.222–5). Having acknowledged the folly of his ill-treatment of Cordelia, Lear's inclusion of 'femiter' may be perceived as an attempt to improve his 'eyesight'. It may also be intended to purge his feelings of guilt and the rampant sexuality that seems to haunt him. Almost certainly Shakespeare is exploring the human subconscious and how guilt, anxiety and a quest for healing are expressed through plants.

(C) Turner (1538) recommends fumitory for eyes and 'sundry humours' suggesting it as a general panacea; Bright (1586) prescribes it in compounds for melancholy. Gerard (1597) includes its use for 'the French disease' or syphilis, while Parkinson (1640) thinks it effective against the plague, poison and putrid sores. Coats (1968) details the superstitions attached to the plant. Heath (2003) considers fumitory in relation to the other weeds in Lear's crown, and the properties of sight-giving that they have in common. Mabey (2010: 113) observes, 'The weed is named for its wispy, grey-green leaves, fancifully thought to resemble mist: *fumus terrae,* smoke of the earth.'

fennel (A) *Foeniculum vulgare* Mill., a hardy perennial **herb** smelling strongly of aniseed. Fennel was possibly a naturalized Roman introduction; it was served with fish, and as an aid to digestion. The seeds of fennel were chewed to stave off hunger, its young **leaves**, **roots** and **seeds** were used medicinally and in cooking. Given the ordinary diet dominated by **beans** and pulses, its carminative properties were particularly valued. Fennel was credited with magical properties, perhaps from the wide range of complaints that it could treat. A common contemporary use was for the eyes.

(B) Two of the three mentions give rise to interpretative or textual problems. Attempting to satisfy Doll's curiosity about Hal's affection for Poins, Falstaff answers, ''a plays at quoits well, and eats cunger and fennel' (*2H4* 2.4.244–5). This is more than a culinary affinity for both foods were classified as 'hot'. The comment may suggest a propensity for excessive indulgence. Fennel's association with flattery and with sex would be perceived as derogatory by the disguised auditors, Hal and Poins, and by the audience. One of the most interesting moments concerning **plants** arises in *HAM* where the distracted Ophelia, speaking a language which is both coded and clear, very deliberately bestows herbs and **flowers** on three principal characters. Her offer, 'There's fennel for you and columbines' (4.5.180), poses two problems: who are the recipients and what do the plants symbolize? Editors have failed to reach agreement in their efforts to resolve these questions. Riverside (1222) proposes that Claudius is given fennel (flattery) and **columbines** (ingratitude). Greene's *A Quip* makes a clear connection between fennel and women, which along with other references persuades Arden 2 (359) that fennel, signifying marital infidelity, is presented to Gertrude (see also LN 536–8). Arden 3 (388) accepting fennel as a symbol of flattery allots it 'to any courtier (or to the King)'. Other variations have been proposed. Although a plant does not always have the same symbolic meaning, the association of fennel with flattery is both strong and consistent. There is a textual problem in *ROM* where Old Capulet invites Paris to the evening festivities, promising, 'such delight/Among fresh fennel buds shall you this night/Inherit at my house' (1.2.28–30). Uncertainty attaches to the phrase 'fennel buds'/'female buds'. Following Q2, Riverside accepts 'fennel' as opposed to the 'female' of Q1 and F1. Arden 2 (96) puts a convincing case for Q2's 'fennel' being a misreading of Q1's and F1's 'female', but giving the other side of the argument cites Lyly's *Sapho and Phao* (2.4.61): 'fancie is a worm, that feedeth first upon fennel'. Arden 3 (143) adopts 'fennel', commenting, 'The image of young women as *fennel buds* may have been inspired by the fragrancy of fennel, and the vernal colour of its yellow flowers suits the "well apparelled April"…; Durham (120) notes that "Fennel was thrown in the path of brides, and it was especially the flower of newly married couples"'. This last observation opens the door to reading Ophelia's gift as mockery of Gertrude and Claudius.

(C) Boorde (1547) recommends fennel for sight, against poison and as a carminative; in his discursion on the properties of **simples**, Bullein (1564) suggests it can improve sight and might help fertility. Greene invites a knowing response from his audience when he combines fennel's associations of sex and flattery: 'Uppon a banke bordring by, grewe women's weedes, Fenell I meane for flatterers, fit generally for that Sexe while they are maidens' (1592, vol. 11, *A Quip*: 14). Heath's (2003) analysis of Ophelia's flowers documents its use to suggest flattery, and to a lesser extent wantonness. He argues that Shakespeare was playing on the certain knowledge of his audience that Ophelia's flowers were linked by their use as an antidote to poison, to treat the sight and for their sexual connotations. Knight (2009: 99) cites Gerard's view that both fennel and rue 'preserveth the eyesight'.

fern-seed Possible identifications include *Polypodium vulgare* L., *Dryopteris dilatata* Hoffm., and *Pteris* L. Although the idea of seeds may originate in the black spores on the back of fern fronds, ferns do not bear seed. It is the folklore and mythology that are relevant. The Doctrine of Signatures, which prescribed like to treat like, probably gave rise to the idea that if the fern could reproduce invisibly, it could be expected to make a person invisible, though this was limited to Midsummer Eve. The myth that fern-seed induces invisibility is both invoked and debunked in a dialogue between minor characters as they prepare to rob pilgrims. Gadshill, boasting that their high-ranking associates are able to flout or corrupt the law, says, 'We steal as in a castle, cock-sure; we have the receipt of fern-seed, we walk invisible'. The Chamberlain, showing scant regard for 'fern-seed' (whether literal of figurative), replies, 'Nay, by my faith, I think you are more beholding to the night than to fern-seed for your walking invisible' (*1H4* 2.1.88–90). Jonson's Ferret employs the same image of invisibility:

> Because, indeed I had
> No med'cine, sir, to go invisible;
> No fern-seed in my pocket; nor an opal,
> Wrapped in a bayleaf i' my left fist
> To charm their eyes with.
>
> *(1603, The New Inn, 1.6.18–22)*

fertile (A) Bearing or producing in plenty, fertile could refer both to **land** and people, its antithesis suggesting failure, **barrenness** and lack of productivity. Fertile often carries connotations of richness and abundance as a result of hard work while lack of fertility indicates failure to reproduce or sterility. Many **plants** and **trees** were thought to induce or encourage human fertility, including **birch, hazel, mistletoe** and **rosemary**.

(B) The numerous literal uses are straightforward; the figurative applications are diverse. The character most knowledgeable and responsive to the island's topography in *TMP* is Caliban. Reacting to ill-treatment he reminds Prospero of their early relationship: 'then I lov'd thee/And show'd thee all the qualities o'th'isle,/The fresh springs, brine-pits, barren place and fertile' (1.2.336–8). This is a gesture he repeats when he adopts a new master, Stephano: 'I'll show thee every fertile inch o'th'island' (2.2.148). In her successful bid to win Burgundy to the French cause Joan Pucelle begins her oration, 'Look on thy country, look on fertile France' (*1H6* 3.3.44). The Duke of York, lamenting the loss of French territories, muses, 'for I had hope of France,/Even as I have of fertile England's soil' (*2H6* 1.1.237–8). Hamlet, in his contemptuous dismissal of Osric, confides to Horatio, 'He hath much land, and fertile' (*HAM* 5.2.85). The Countess of Salisbury includes in her elaborate conceit a vision of bare ground seeming 'barren, sere, unfertile, fructless, dry' (*E3* 1.2.151). A paradoxical case is found in *TIM*. The disillusioned Timon acknowledges nature's bounty only after his heart has become frozen. He then pleads with nature to *curtail* its fertility: 'Ensear thy fertile and conceptious womb,/Let it no more bring out ingrateful man!' (4.3.187–8). Iago possesses an unsurpassed ability to combine the beautiful with the ugly and to do so with rhythmic movements of compelling force. Inciting Roderigo to undermine Othello's relationship with Desdemona, he urges: 'poison his delight,/Proclaim him in the streets; incense her kinsmen,/And though he in a fertile climate dwell,/Plague him with flies' (*OTH* 1.1.68–71). Commending the character-forming benefits of sack, Falstaff cites Hal as proof: 'Hereof comes it that Prince Harry is valiant, for the cold blood he did naturally inherit of his father, he hath, like lean, sterile, and bare land, manur'd, husbanded, and till'd with excellent endeavour of drinking good and good store of fertile sherris, that he is become very hot and valiant' (*2H4* 4.3.117–22). Fertile here is life enhancing, invigorating. Cesario/Viola, as ambassador to Olivia, affirms that Orsino loves her, 'With adorations, fertile tears,/With groans that thunder love, with sighs of fire' (*TN* 1.5.255–6).

(C) Aske's 1588 entertainment for the Queen, *Elizabetha Triumphans,* suggests the mystical relationship between the Queen and her country is entwined with the fertility of the land, with fertility seen as sacred and productive (Archer 2007). Hackett (1995) considers the Queen combined the complementary rather than contradictory qualities of virginity and fertility. Young (1972) comments on the connections in *TMP* between fertility and hospitality, barrenness and hostility. See also **Flora**.

fescue *Festuca* L., a large genus of native **grasses**. A tall variety may have given its name to the stick used in the schoolroom for pointing out letters. In *TNK* the plant and stick coalesce for the purpose of sexual innuendo. Four countrymen determine to go Maying despite fear of domestic disharmony. The most apprehensive is counselled on how to mollify his wife: 'Ay, do but put/A fescue in her fist, and you shall see her/Take a new lesson out, and be a good wench' (2.3.33–5). The length and caressive quality of the plant is married to the pointer's stiffness.

fetch Fetches or vetches are plants of the *Vicia* L., genus. Some are native wild **plants**; others such as *V. faba*, the broad **bean,** or *V. sativa* are cultivated for human or animal consumption. *V. cracca*, the common tufted vetch, a fodder **crop** at the time, is now a wild **flower** of hedgerows and **grassy** places. 'Fetch' appears only in *TMP*. During the masque Iris greets the goddess of fertility, 'Ceres, most bounteous lady, thy rich leas/Of wheat, rye, barley, fetches, oats, and pease' (4.1.60–1). Here is entertainment, a blessing, and a promise of fertility. Markham (1631) regards fetch as an invasive weed comparing it to tares. He claims it spoilt the quality of the beer if harvested with barley, but recommends its use with **straw** to light the fire for the malting process. De Bray

(1982: 124) notes that the Wilmcote farm records of 1490–1 include fetch, which she suggests was *V. cracca.*

field (A) Open **country** rather than woodland, fields were usually agricultural, and demarcated or divided by an artificial barrier such as a **hedge, wall** or fence. Field can indicate **land** reclaimed from common use or from the wild by enclosure thus becoming part of the constructed landscape. Militarily it is a place of battle, an area of military operations, or an actual battle; field was also a place for sport. It appears more often poetically than in practical manuals of **husbandry** which usually employ **ground** or **land**.

(B) Both in its literal and figurative applications the field provides an arena for social observation and engagement. Boyet announces to the French Princess and her attendants that they will not receive accommodation appropriate for a royal party. Navarre, he informs them, 'means to lodge you in the field,/Like one that comes here to besiege his court' (*LLL* 2.1.85–6). Boyet responds to the slight with suavity; the Princess with hauteur: '"welcome" I have not yet. The roof of this court is too high to be yours, and welcome to the wide fields too base to be mine' (2.1.91–4). The 'field', however, is carefully maintained **parkland**. 'Field' as **hunting** ground, rendering aesthetic pleasures, is apparent when Titus addresses his sons on a day deceptively rich with promise: 'The hunt is up, the morn is bright and grey,/The fields are fragrant and the woods are green' (*TIT* 2.2.1–2). The open field available for public pleasure, as opposed to being part of a private **estate**, is referred to by Shallow as he reminisces with Falstaff: 'O Sir John, do you remember since we lay all night in the Windmill in Saint George's Field?' (*2H4* 3.2.194–5). A map of 1600 locates a windmill there, though the 'Windmill' in question may have been a brothel. Arden 2 (105–6) provides geographical and social details. Its convenience and accessibility as a meeting place is confirmed in *2H6* when the Duke of York dismisses his soldiers with the injunction, 'Meet me to-morrow in Saint George's Field,/You shall have pay and every thing you wish' (5.1.46–7). Recounting his military achievements to his father, the Black Prince records cities overcome 'And others wasted, leaving at our heels,/A wide apparent field and beaten path,/For solitariness to progress in'(*E3* 3.3.21–3). A Frenchman has confirmed that this is no idle boast, reporting, 'Cornfields and vineyards burning like an oven' (3.2.57). As Capulet gazes down on the apparently dead Juliet, he momentarily acquires a tenderness and refinement of sensibility that finds expression in a simple but beautiful image: 'Death lies upon her like an untimely frost/Upon the sweetest flower of all the field' (*ROM* 4.5.28–9).

(C) In *The Mirror for Magistrates* (1559) field carries a sense of ownership, control and subsequent loss in adverse circumstances. Drayton (1622) revels in rich or fertile fields, fields of grain, and fields of stubble. In the context of the Forest of Arden, he notes the destruction of the untamed landscape of England by fields full of villages, writing of coursing and hawking as 'these brave sports of field'. Markham (1631) generally uses land or ground to designate the area for ploughing and tilling, although he makes the occasional reference to the tilth- or fallow-field, land set aside for those specific purposes. Spier and Anderson (1985: 457) note that open fields are twice referred to by Shakespeare as 'champion' lands (*LUC* 1247; *LR* 1.1.64).

fig, fico, figo (A) *Ficus carica* L. was **planted** widely in England in the sixteenth century, although its **fruit** was imported green from Mediterranean countries. Fig had extensive medicinal applications; particularly nourishing it was thought to be good for **fertility**; its sexually suggestive shape gave rise to bawdy humour. In figurative usage almost all its references were rude, crude, indecent or uncomplimentary, the gesture of 'making a fig' by putting the thumb between the first two fingers being intentionally sexual. This was believed to have originated in Spain, so to add 'Spanish' to fig was to emphasize the insult; as the Spanish were thought to administer poison in a fig, it carried sinister overtones. The idea of the fig leaf as an inadequate covering originated in the Garden of **Eden**.

(B) Three of the four references to the fruit are in *ANT*. For all four uses of the expression 'figo', or 'fico' we are indebted to Pistol; Iago has his own expletive, 'figs-end'. Charmian, in high spirits as she twits the Soothsayer about his enigmatic prediction that she will 'outlive the lady whom you serve', replies, 'O, excellent, I love long life better than figs' (*ANT* 1.2.31–2). There can be little doubt that this is a reference to male genitals, especially as her banter with Iras has been about getting husbands and children. Moreover, the subsequent dialogue is permeated with sexual innuendo. The tone is quite different in the closing scene as the guard announces to Cleopatra that 'a rural fellow…brings you figs' (5.2.233–5). The figs are camouflage for the asp which kills the Egyptian Queen. Symbols of sexuality and new life, they are also heralds of death. Cleopatra visualizes death as transformative: 'I am fire and air; my other elements/I give to baser life' (5.2.289–90). Sexual suggestion is also present in *MND*. Settling down for the night with Bottom, Titania enjoins her fairies to, 'Feed him with apricocks and dewberries,/With purple grapes, green figs, and mulberries' (3.1.166–7). Certainly the presence of 'apricocks' begins a sexual agitation, while the next line is richly sensual. Roderigo's reluctance to accept that Desdemona is ready to give herself to Cassio – 'I cannot believe that in her, she's full of most bless'd condition'– prompts Iago's masterly imprecation, 'Bless'd figs-end! The wine she drinks is made of grapes. If she had been bless'd, she would never have lov'd the Moor. Bless'd pudding!' (*OTH* 2.1.249–53). 'Grapes' lend a salacious air to the discourse; 'pudding' is a sausage, implying penis. The term 'bless'd figs-end' probably means 'bless'd vagina'. Iago has a facility for picking up a speaker's word to undermine him. In this short space he has transformed Desdemona from a virtuous woman to a 'strumpet' – the term applied to Bianca by Emilia (5.1.121) and to Desdemona by Othello (5.2.77). Pistol's quarrel with Fluellen is a result of the Welshman's unwillingness to lend support to the condemned Bardolph: 'Die and be damn'd! and *figo* for thy friendship!'. Failing to unsettle Fluellen, Pistol intensifies his verbal assault, 'The fig of Spain' (*H5* 3.6.57–9). Heightening the imprecation by making the Spanish connection is apparent in *2H4*.

Announcing the death of Henry IV to the disbelieving Falstaff, Pistol invites retribution if his veracity can be called into question: 'I speak truth./When Pistol lies, do this, and fig me like/The bragging Spaniard' (5.3.117–9). The accompanying gesture reinforces the obscenity. On the eve of Agincourt the disguised Henry V claims kinship with Fluellen thereby provoking another Pistol outburst: 'The *figo* for thee then!' (*H5* 4.1.59). Deeply attached to this dismissive term Pistol pounces on Nym for using the word 'steal': '"Convey", the wise it call. "Steal"? foh! a *fico* for the phrase!' (*WIV* 1.3.29–30). No matter what the play, Pistol finds opportunity to employ this expletive.

(C) Early modern literature makes extensive use of its association. Jonson's Face comments, 'Sirrah, I'll strip you'. Subtle's riposte – 'What to do? Lick figs?' – combines obscenity with an allusion to piles, known as *ficus morbus* from their shape (1612 *The Alchemist*, 1.1.3). Flamineo suggests he was daily expecting to be poisoned: 'I looke now for a Spanish fig, or an Italian sallat daily' (Webster 1612, *The White Devil*, 4.2.60). Palter (2002) has a chapter on the fig showing that in the ancient world it occupied the place of the modern apple. He includes the biblical and classical references, and uses Dante's *Inferno* to explain the fig gesture. Chancellor (1982: 34) explores its biblical import citing Micah 4.4: 'But they shall sit every man under his vine and under his fig tree' and notes, 'The fig, the vine, and the olive are the most important fruit trees in the Holy Land.' Dent (1981: F210, 211, 213).

filbert *Corylus maxima* Mill. is an alternative name for the **hazel tree** *C. avellana* L. on which the **nuts** grow in clusters. Modern identification makes a slight difference between the two **plants**, based on the size and shape of the nuts. The name is supposed to have come from the usual time of the nuts ripening, about 22 August, St Philbert's Day. Only Caliban mentions the filbert. His knowledge of the island's **flora** and fauna allows him to be of service to his new master, Stephano: 'I'll bring thee/To clust'ring filberts' (*TMP* 2.2.170–1). Here 'clust'ring' is a precise description of the way in which filberts grow, but the word also possesses poetic vigour. Boorde (1547) claims that filberts are better than hazels, and more nutritious, but that all nuts are best avoided even though they may act as an antidote to poisons. Bacon (1625) included the filbert in his list of plants in his 'purest of human pleasures', his perfect garden. Stace (2010) provides the precise modern identification of both hazel and filbert.

flag There are several candidates including *Iris pseudacorus* L., the native yellow **iris**, common in wet places, and *I. germanica* L., the bearded iris, a **garden plant** occasionally found in the wild, both of which are also candidates for **fleur-de-luce**. Flag might be *I. foetisissima* L., the Florentine or stinking iris, a native plant of dry woods and shady **banks**, or *Acorus calamus* L., the sweet flag, introduced into Britain during the second half of the sixteenth century and subsequently naturalized. Flag could also denote any floating **reed** or **rush**. All had some medicinal applications. The sole use of 'flag' in the botanical sense, whether it is the iris, **bulrush** or reed, is the source of an acute simile in *ANT*. The wavering nature of the common people – so much in conflict with the Roman ethos of constancy – is given clear expression by Octavius Caesar in response to the news that Pompey's popularity is in the ascendant: 'This common body,/Like to a vagabond flag upon the stream,/Goes to and back, lackeying the varying tide,/To rot itself with motion' (1.4.44–7). Norden (1618) classifies flags on an **estate** with **sedges**, and rushes as 'noisome' and symptomatic of boggy ground. Drayton (1622) includes flags with bulrushes and reeds, suggesting them as flowers for **garlands** which probably indicates *I. pseudacorus* but precludes *Acorus* which has relatively insignificant flowers. Mabey (1996) includes details of the varieties of wild native flags. For the precise modern botanical identification of the several possibilities, see Stace (2010).

flax, flaxen (A) *Linum* L., a genus of native **plants**, includes the blue-flowered annual *L. usitatissimum* L., one of the oldest **crops** in cultivation, grown for its fibre and as a source of linseed oil. Flax was spun for line or linen, cord, sail-cloth, and tow for candle-wicks; the cloth was also used for poultices and bandages. As tow, it caught fire easily, and its proverbial use suggested an inflammable situation: putting fire to flax meant the same as pouring oil on flames. It also indicated pale or white colouring as in hair in old age.

(B) Alluded to twice, the combustibility of flax is on one occasion associated with 'dew' which was supposed to intensify fire. Grieving over the body of his father, Young Clifford vows revenge that will admit no qualification: 'Tears virginal/Shall be to me even as the dew to fire,/And beauty, that the tyrant oft reclaims,/Shall to my flaming wrath be oil and flax' (*2H6* 5.2.52–5). As good as his word he becomes infamous for the cruel murder of the Yorkist child, Rutland, and his participation in the humiliation and decapitation of the Duke of York. On hearing the cry of triumph, 'Arcite', from the offstage combat, Emilia reflects on the presumed loser Palamon: 'God's lid, his richness/And costliness of spirit look'd through him, it could/No more be hid in him than fire in flax' (*TNK* 5.3.96–8). Deriding Falstaff's aspiration to seduce the merry wives, Ford cries, 'What, a hodge-pudding? A bag of flax?' to which Mistress Page adds, 'A puff'd man?' (*WIV* 5.5.151–2). Spinning flax for cloth gains a mention in *TN*. Sir Toby provides mocking reassurance to Sir Andrew that his hair is appealing: 'Excellent, it hangs like flax on a distaff; and I hope to see a huswife take thee between her legs, and spin it off' (1.3.102–4). Leontes is as distastefully ugly in his comment as Sir Toby is wittily cruel. Insisting on Hermione's infidelity he presses Camillo to concede, 'My wife's a hobby-horse, deserves a name/As rank as any flax-wench that puts to/Before her troth-plight: say't and justify't' (*WT* 1.2.276–8). The assumption here is that a working girl has easy morals. This contempt for common people is shared by Polixenes who dismisses Perdita as 'a sheep-hook' (4.4.420). Flaxen as 'white-haired' finds expression in Ophelia's lament for her dead father: 'His beard was as white as snow./All flaxen was his pole' (*HAM* 4.5.195–6). Its use as a bandage or poultice is revealed in *LR*. Coming to the aid of the blinded Gloucester a servant says, 'I'll fetch some flax and whites of eggs/To apply to his bleeding face. Now heaven help him!' (3.7.106–7).

(C) Markham (1631) writes of the duties of the good housewife which included particular skill in spinning and weaving wool, flax and **hemp**; he has a chapter on the complete process from preparing the soil for the seed through to the production of the finished fabric. Grieve (1978) gives the historical and biblical details of the preparation of the flax for spinning, and includes its early modern medicinal uses.

Flora A Roman goddess, Flora was often employed poetically to represent spring, **flowers** and **fertility**. The myth of Flora, as the goddess of spring, is alluded to by Florizel when addressing Perdita in her festival costume: 'These your unusual weeds to each part of you/Does give a life; no shepherdess, but Flora/Peering in April's front' (*WT* 4.4.1–3). In this memorable scene Perdita's comments and gestures make her synonymous with flowers. The main source of the story, Ovid's *Fastii,* was a ready subject in Renaissance art as in Botticelli's *Primavera* of 1482. Spenser (1579) depicts Elizabeth as Flora invoking her identification with the fertility of England and perpetual spring. Lyons (1977), who examines the extended myth and the tension in the narrative, suggests the Renaissance paintings of Flora represent a courtesan rather than the innocent goddess of spring. Heilmeyer (2001: 9–12) points out that 'During the Renaissance Virgil's pastorals and Ovid's *Metamorphoses* gained new significance' and observes, 'The goddess Flora, the protectress of gardens, is one of the oldest figures in the Roman pantheon.' She draws attention to the abduction of Chloris by Zephyrus, god of the west wind, and her transformation into Flora in Botticelli's painting. Perdita's 'winds of March' (*WT* 4.4.120) may allude to the god of the west wind.

flower (A) A complex organ in **plants**, usually coloured, not green, a flower consists of the reproductive organs of a plant. It can also indicate a flowering plant cultivated especially for its **blossoms**, or the blossom independently of the plant, with particular reference to its **smell** or beauty. Flower implies freshness and innocence; figuratively it can suggest a person in the prime of life, a treasured child, the flowering of youth, the height of beauty or fame, a state of energy or prosperity; 'deflowered' represents loss of virginity. Flowers had individual identities, characteristics, meanings, superstitions and associations; their symbolic and proverbial uses might draw on biblical and classical parallels, including luxury, purity, transience and impermanence.

(B) Flowers abound in the plays and poems, their literal presence notable not only for beauty and scent but also as cordials or drugs; figurative uses encompass innocence, sensibility, tenderness, virginity and transcendence. Friar Laurence sets out at first light to collect plants for medicinal purposes: 'I must up-fill this osier cage of ours/With baleful weeds and precious-juiced flowers' (*ROM* 2.3.7–8). The **roses** in the Temple Garden scene become emblems of allegiance and antagonism. Richard Plantagenet, later Duke of York, thanks one of the company for taking his side: 'Good Master Vernon, I am bound to you/That you on my behalf would pluck a flower' (*1H6* 2.4.128–9). A different kind of mischief is afoot when Oberon describes how the wild **pansy** or **love-in-idleness** acquired its purple colour and magical powers: 'Yet mark'd

I where the bolt of Cupid fell./It fell upon a little western flower,/Before milk-white, now purple with love's wound' (*MND* 2.1.165–7). Here is the source of the love-juice which causes turmoil and confusion in the Athenian wood. On some occasions flowers are used for **strewing** graves. Arviragus, speaking over the apparently dead body of Imogen/Fidele promises, 'Thou shalt not lack/The flower that's like thy face, pale primrose, nor/The azur'd harebell, like thy veins' (*CYM* 4.2.220–2). Queen Katherine instructs her companion, 'When I am dead, good wench,/Let me be us'd with honor;/strew me over/With maiden flowers, that all the world may know/I was a chaste wife to my grave' (*H8* 4.2.167–70). Titania accords sensibility to flowers when intimating their responsiveness to the moon: 'And when she weeps, weeps every little flower,/Lamenting some enforced chastity' (*MND* 3.1.199–200). In *TRO,* a play full of seers, even flowers are prescient. Hector's eagerness to get to the battlefield is recounted by Alexander: 'And to the field goes he; where every flower/Did as a prophet weep what it foresaw/In Hector's wrath' (1.2.9–11). Cominius addresses another martial hero, Caius Martius, as 'Flower of warriors' (*COR* 1.6.32). Paris is a different kind of flower: the ideal gentleman and potential husband. As Lady Capulet puts it, 'Verona's summer hath not such a flower'; an opinion confirmed by the Nurse, 'Nay, he's a flower, in faith, a very flower' (*ROM* 1.3.77–8). A French mariner expresses wonderment at the grandeur of the English fleet: 'Their streaming ensigns wrought of color'd silk,/Like to a meadow full of sundry flowers,/Adorns the naked bosom of the earth' (*E3* 3.1.68–70).

A 'flower-like' female generally implies gentleness and virginity. At the close of *AWW* the King tells Diana, 'If thou beest yet a fresh uncropped flower,/Choose thou thy husband, and I'll pay thy dower' (5.3.327–8). The young maiden who steers Cleopatra's barge, makes 'the silken tackle/Swell with the touches of those flower-soft hands' (*ANT* 2.2.209–10). Childhood and youth are expressed as flowering. Seeking to enter Harfleur, Henry V presents an image of his soldiers 'mowing like grass/Your fresh fair virgins and your flow'ring infants' (*H5* 3.3.13–14). Queen Elizabeth refers to the young princes murdered in the Tower as, 'My unblown flow'rs, new-appearing sweets!' (*R3* 4.4.10). Complaining of years of incarceration, Mortimer asserts that it was his legitimate claim to the throne, 'that imprison'd me/And hath detain'd me all my flow'ring youth' (*1H6* 2.5.55–6). Life itself is represented as a flower in *PER* when Cerimon observes consciousness flowing back into the seemingly dead Thiasa: 'See how she gins/To blow into life's flower again!' (3.2.94–5).

With typical dash and little thought, Hotspur responds to doubts about the wisdom of his rebellion with the metaphor, 'out of this nettle, danger, we pluck this flower, safety' (*1H4* 2.3.9–10). Fearing her husband's lack of guile, Lady Macbeth advises him, 'look like th'innocent flower,/But be the serpent under't' (*MAC* 1.5.62–6). When Mistress Quickly describes Falstaff's final moments, she says, 'For after I saw him fumble with the sheets, and play with flowers…I knew there was but one way' (*H5* 2.3.13–16). Arden 3 (182) suggests that these are flowers scattered on the bedclothes to ensure a sweet-smelling sick-room. Whether they are real or imaginary flowers, they companion him out of this world. Antony's vision of the after-life is certainly a flower-laden arena where he and Cleopatra will retain their celebrity: 'Where souls do couch on flowers, we'll hand in hand,/And with our sprightly port make the ghosts gaze' (*ANT* 4.14.51–2). Responding to Isabella's consolatory comments on his impending execution, Claudio protests, 'Think you I can a resolution fetch/From flow'ry tenderness?' (*MM* 3.1.81–2). Flowers as the epitome of the natural world are an invitation to artistic emulation in *TNK*. Emilia asks her lady's maid, 'Canst not thou work such flowers in silk, wench?'. Reassured, Emilia collects flowers as specimens: 'Keep these flowers,/We'll see how near art can come near their colors' (2.2.127–49). Capulet informs the newly-arrived groom, Paris, 'O son, the night before thy wedding-day/Hath Death lain with thy wife. There she lies,/Flower as she was, deflowered by him' (*ROM* 4.5.35–7). Adonis transcends death by becoming a flower: 'in his blood that on the ground lay spill'd,/A purple flow'r sprung up, check'red with white'(*VEN* 1167–68). The only mention of 'flow'rets' is visually arresting. The recently crowned King opens *1H4* by setting out a vision of domestic peace: 'No more shall trenching war channel her fields,/Nor bruise her flow'rets with the armed hoofs/ Of hostile paces' (1.1.7–9). Arden 3 (141) has a brief but interesting note on these lines.

(C) There was a new enjoyment in flowers grown for their beauty rather than for the purely functional purposes of food, medicine, cosmetics and hygiene (strewing). Decoratively flowers were visible on clothing and needlework, in portraits, plasterwork and furniture, as well as in the **garden**. Flowers were the subject of books and illustrations, making them available out of season and spreading knowledge of new introductions. Colonna (1499) writes of fruits and flowers round an erotic **fountain**, whose waters were channelled into a flowery place, using flowers to suggest both innocence and sexuality. Callimachus sees flowering as representative of youth: 'would you have me spend the flower of my youth as you do the withered race of your age?' (Lyly 1580 *Euphues*: 178). Spenser (1596) gathers, spreads, and strews flowers, recording them as fresh, fair and painted, and has them flourishing, fading, and falling untimely. Dekker emphasizes their commercial value in the context of the plague (1603, *The Wonderful Year*). Arnold (1988) gives extensive detail of the many flowers embroidered on the Queen's clothing, where they could convey messages emphasizing the English claim to the throne of France, suggest purity, or personal power. Many designs were taken from the new herbals, including Gerard's *Herball* of 1597, or from design books as for example Trevelyon (1608). Such designs could be applied to needlework or any household decoration. Heilmeyer (2001: 10–18) provides a summary of contrasting attitudes to flowers in art. Bushnell (2003) considers the place of flowers within the nature-culture debate of the time; Knight (2009) examines the literary context of flowers. Nicolson (2009) gives a sense of the novelty and excitement to be found in London gardens. Early modern understanding of floral metaphors should not be confused with the later romantic and sentimental 'language of flowers' of the nineteenth century. Dent (1981: F388.1). See also **pomander.**

flower-de-luce, fleur-de-lys (A) Possibly the originally blue introduction *Iris germanica* L., generally known as the bearded **iris**, or, a likely candidate for its golden **flowers**,

I. pseudacorus L; both might also indicate **flag**. Less likely it could be *I. foetidissima* L., the Florentine iris. The **roots** of all these **plants** had medicinal applications. The flower-de-luce was also a heraldic device of the arms of France, whence it was employed by kings of England to assert their claim to the French throne. It was called a **lily** from the French lys for lily, or iris. A floral symbol of the Virgin Mary, the flower-de-luce was emblematic of faith, valour and wisdom; as a heraldic symbol it has ceased to be identified with a particular plant.

(B) In all cases, except one, the 'flower-de-luce' appears as the emblem of France. In *E3* the imagery of flowers, banners and emblems lend vivid colouration to the conflict. The English fleet is portrayed majestically by the Mariner: 'The arms of England and of France unite/Are quart'red equally by herald's art' which provokes King John of France to exclaim, 'Dare he already crop the flower-de-luce?' (3.1.75–9). At the close of *H5,* the triumphant Henry V takes the French Princess as part of the settlement. Advancing his ambitions for their yet-to-be-born son, he asks, 'What say'st thou, my fair flower-de-luce?' (5.2.210). Here a young woman is likened to the flower, but Katherine is more – the emblem of her country and the possession of the English King. The tide has taken a dramatic turn by the opening scene of *1H6*. The messenger reports to the English King, 'Cropp'd are the flower-de-luces in your arms,/Of England's coat one half is cut away' (1.1.80–1). When Joan la Pucelle – the nemesis of the English – arrives on the scene she does so with a 'keen-edg'd sword,/Deck'd with five flower-de-luces on each side' (1.2.98–9). The only occasion when the flower is not the emblem of France is in *WT*. Perdita's list of desirable flowers includes, 'bold oxlips, and/The crown imperial; lilies of all kinds/(The flow'r-de-luce being one)' (4.4.125–7). This juxtaposition of '**crown imperial**' and 'flow'r-de-luce' could not fail to engender awareness of royalty – a theme highly relevant to the scene as the 'shepherdess' addressing a prince will be admonished by the King for her presumption. This moment of floral celebration resonates with matters regal, and of birthright.

(C) Trevelyon (1608) includes the 'fleur-de-lys' in several patterns for needlework or plasterwork. Arnold (1988) identifies it as *I. foetidissima* in her index of terms, where she gives details of the embroidery on the Queen's clothing, including her coronation robes which featured the flower-de-luce on the mantle; the Hardwick portrait of 1599 also shows the flower on her robes. Heath (2003) analyses it in the context of *WT* with particular reference to its skin-clearing properties and sexual connotations.

fluellen *Kickxia* Dumort, the *Fluellen* group of **plants** was said at the time to include *Fluellen*, speedwell; another possible contemporary identification is Paul's betony. All are members of the *Veronicacaea* family, in which modern designation betony is not included. This **flower** is present only as the name of a character. Pistol challenges the disguised King, 'Know'st thou Fluellen?' (*H5* 4.1.52). Plant names are generally allocated to the lower orders. Captain Fluellen stands a little higher. Although the plant most closely associated with the patriotic Welshman is the **leek**, which is referred to several times in the play, the delicate flower 'fluellen' may exert a playfully ironic pressure. Gerard (1597: 629) includes speedwell and Paul's betony under the name of Fluellen, and gives details of male and female Fluellen: 'These plants are comprehended under this generall name *Veronica*, with their additions, which distinguish the one from the other: we do call them in English Paules Betonie, or Speedwell. In Welch it is called Fluellen, and the Welch people do attribute great vertues unto the same.' Grigson (1974: 80) in *A Dictionary of English Plant Names,* drawing on Turner (1548) and Lyte (1578), confirms the Welsh association and notes that fluellen indicated 'herbs of St Llywelyn' – otherwise Fluellen – and referred to herbs in flower around 7 April, the saint's feast day.

forest, forester (A) Usually an extensive tract of **land** covered with **trees,** which themselves can also designate a **forest**. At the time forest often included pasture, **heath,** common and waste land. In some cases this was because an area formerly covered with trees had been brought into cultivation. Historically and legally forest was partly wooded land usually belonging to the crown, set apart for **hunting,** with its own laws and law officers; the only vestigial remains of this system is the New Forest. Poetically the forest could be a threatening place, while wooded hills were seen as pleasant and sheltering, a shady green space. Forest and **wood** could also be used interchangeably.

(B) For the most part forests are singularly unthreatening. Only a small number of cases are figurative. In *MND*, the main action is set in a magical wood; in *WIV* Windsor is blessed with a forest complete with an ancient **oak**. Half the uses of the word are to be found in *AYL,* a play where the forest appears at its most enigmatic. For Orlando it is initially an 'uncouth forest' (2.6.6); later he reminds Rosalind, 'there's no clock in the forest' (3.2.301). Rosalind, having made herself at home prettifies and domesticates it, describing their abode as situated 'in the skirts of the forest, like fringe upon a petticoat' (3.2.335–7). Oliver poeticizes the forest when asking, 'Where in the purlieus of this forest stands/A sheep-cote fenc'd about with olive-trees?' (4.3.76–7) – provoking Celia to parody his mode of speech. This flirtatious mythologizing of the forest as pastoral idyll is a source of recurrent engagement. The map containing and articulating the physical world is emblematic in *LR*. As Lear relinquishes power and distributes his land between his daughters, he creates a vision of a landscape affording aesthetic, recreational and productive potential: 'With shadowy forests and with champains rich'd,/With plenteous rivers and wide-skirted meads' (1.1.64–5). There is no felt presence of a rich landscape thereafter until we encounter the fields of Dover towards the end of the play. Palamon, imprisoned with his cousin Arcite, reflects on past adventures:

> To our Theban hounds,
> That shook the aged forest with their echoes,
> No more now must we hallow; no more shake
> Our pointed javelins, whilst the angry swine
> Flies like a Parthian quiver from our rages,
> Struck with our well-steel'd darts.

(TNK 2.2.46–51)

The real danger in these forests is posed by human beings. A forest where bestial deeds take place is perceived as a hunting ground and leisure **park**. Aaron the Moor, advising the brutal sons of Tamora, captures this atmosphere while preparing to violate the space: 'The forest walks are wide and spacious,/And many unfrequented plots there are,/Fitted by kind for rape and villainy' (*TIT* 2.1.114–16). Bolingbroke complains of another kind of violation. Before executing Bushy and Green he chastises them, 'you have fed upon my signories,/Dispark'd my parks and fell'd my forest woods,/ From my own windows torn my household coat' (*R2* 3.1.22–4). Here is an image of despoliation designed to eradicate identity and to demonstrate power of possession. Occasionally the forest is just a physical landmark. In *2H4* the rebel party is led by the Archbishop of York who inquires, 'What is this forest call'd?' Hastings replies, ''Tis Gaultree forest, and't shall please your Grace' (4.1.1–2). At the other extreme it is a medium for transformation. That unlikely 'forester', Falstaff, proposes to Hal, 'Let us be Diana's foresters, gentlemen of the shade, minions of the moon' (*1H4* 1.2.25–6). In the city setting of Rome, Antony draws on imagery of the forest as he stands over the body of Caesar:

> Here wast thou bay'd, brave heart,
> Here didst thou fall, and here thy hunters stand,
> Sign'd in thy spoil, and crimson'd in thy lethe.
> O world! thou wast the forest to this hart,
> And this indeed, O world, the heart of thee.
>
> *(JC 3.1.204–8)*

Again in the urban world of *TIM* a paradoxical image is employed by Apemantus when addressing the disillusioned Timon: 'The commonwealth of Athens is become a forest of beasts' (4.3.347–8).

(C) Manwood (1598) gives the history and legal status of forests. Drayton uses forests as natural features bearing testimony to the antiquity of the land when 'this whole Country's face was foresty' (1622 *Polyolbion*, 22.47). Daley (1983: esp. 174–80) analyses the contrasting meanings attaching to the word 'forest' observing that 'The notion of a leaf-smothered Arden is a romantic invention.' Cirillo (1971) emphasizes the reversal of roles in *AYL*, where the usually forbidding forest becomes a place of retreat and safety, the world of Robin Hood and his outlaws, the world of old England. Young (1972) has the most extensive examination of the forest in *AYL*. He sees Arden as mythic, transforming the threatening to a place of security, a mirror for the characters. Harrison (1992) notes the same inversion in *AYL* when as the city becomes threatening, the forest becomes the sanctuary. He comments on the personification of the forest/wood of Dunsinane, arguing that its 'impressing' or conscripting represents an inversion of the traditional savagery of forests. In the play savagery has been found instead in men, the forest coming as a rescuing and civilizing influence. Fletcher (2011) suggests that the forest was not dense woodland, but shot through with **glades** and **groves**. Nardizzi (eds Bruckner and Brayton 2011: 123–38) provides a helpful analysis of Manwood. Thomas (1983) analyses the changing functions of woods and forests between 1500 and 1800, and details shifting attitudes towards woodland.

forthright Forthright appears to have been a straight course or path in a grand garden. It could be used both literally and figuratively. As the King's party endeavour to make sense of the topography of the island, Gonzalo expresses their confusion and weariness: 'Here's a maze trod indeed/Through forth-rights and meanders!' (*TMP* 3.3.2–3). In a speech of almost 100 lines Ulysses attempts to persuade Achilles to rejoin the fight against the Trojans. He maintains that fame and honour must be constantly renewed by achievement: 'If you give way,/Or hedge aside from the direct forthright,/Like to an ent'red tide, they all rush by/And leave you hindmost'(*TRO* 3.3.157–60). 'Direct' qualifying 'forthright' is visually and aurally compelling. The *OED* records *TMP* as the earliest example, though *TRO* predates it by more than a decade. They cite Amherst's (1896) definition of forthrights as straight **garden** paths which corresponded to the plan of the house, the patterns in the enclosed beds harmonizing with the details of the architecture. Singleton (1922) gives the lengthiest description of forthrights, as the principal **walks** in straight lines at right angles to the terrace, intersected by other walks parallel to the terrace, which could be open or covered; a hard surface path or **turf**. Both possibly sourced the information from Nares (1859) who gives it as a straight path, but without including any evidence of the source for his information. No further reference has been traced. There is a similar definition in Crystal and Crystal (2002).

fountain, fount (A) A natural spring of water, its head or source, a well, an artificial stream of water; a fountain can also indicate a permanent supply of drinking water, a natural jet of water. By transference it can suggest the flow of blood in or from the veins. Fountains could also suggest the source of life or grace. They were generally elaborate features of trophy **gardens**.

(B) There are numerous allusions in the plays and poems to natural fountains; fewer to those man-made. The governing antithesis, whether literal or figurative, is between water that is sparkling or muddy; smoothly flowing or turbulent. All three cases in *MND* apply to natural fountains: two of them are meeting places for the quarrelling Oberon and Titania: 'By fountain clear, or spangled starlight sheen'; 'By paved fountain or by rushy brook' (2.1.29; 84). The other recalls harmony as Hippolyta reminisces to Theseus:

> I was with Hercules and Cadmus once,
> When in a wood of Crete they bay'd the bear
> With hounds of Sparta. Never did I hear
> Such gallant chiding; for besides the groves,
> The skies, the fountains, every region near
> Seem all one mutual cry. I never heard
> So musical a discord, such sweet thunder.

(4.1.112–18).

In the world of this play, fountains are integral to the landscape. The fount is a geographical marker in *MM*. The Duke soliloquizes on his course of action with respect to Angelo: 'Him I'll desire/To meet me at the consecrated fount,/A league below the city' (4.3.97–9). This could be the source of a stream or an artificial fountain. *TRO* has three interesting figurative examples. When the eponymous lovers finally come together, Cressida's hesitation causes Troilus to ask, 'What makes this pretty abruption? What too curious dreg espies my sweet lady in the fountain of our love?'. In a play where quest for purity is invariably thwarted her reply is telling: 'More dregs than water, if my fears have eyes' (3.2.64–8). Prophecy is also pervasive in the play. This antithesis between clear and muddy water arises later when Achilles muses, 'My mind is troubled, like a fountain stirr'd,/And I myself see not the bottom of it'. Thersites, ever ready to deflate, continues the metaphor: 'Would the fountain of your mind were clear again, that I might water an ass at it!' (3.3.308–11). In *H8* Buckingham claims that Wolsey's treason is confirmed 'by intelligence,/And proofs as clear as founts in July when/We see each grain of gravel' (1.1.153–5).

When Rosalind/Ganymede cautions Orlando, 'I will weep for nothing, like Diana in the fountain, and I will do that when you are dispos'd to be merry' (*AYL* 4.1.153–5) it seems likely that she is making some topical allusion. Montemayor's Diana weeps disingenuous tears into the fountain when pledging eternal love to her faithful shepherd. Female figures from classical mythology adorning sculpted fountains may also be alluded to. Venus, inviting Adonis to explore her, likens herself to an estate:

> I'll be a park, and thou shalt be my deer:
> Feed where thou wilt, on mountain, or in dale;
> Graze on my lips, and if those hills be dry,
> Stray lower, where the pleasant fountains lie.
>
> *(VEN 231–4)*

Venus' natural fountains were, indeed, emulated by the sculptors of the time who fashioned female mythological figures projecting jets of water from their breasts. The fountain is used figuratively to great effect in both comic and tragic contexts. Overwhelmed by jealousy, Othello acclaims Desdemona as the very well-spring of his being: 'The fountain from which my current runs/Or else dries up' (*OTH* 4.2.59–60). Julius Caesar narrates Calphurnia's dream to Decius Brutus: 'She dreamt to-night she saw my statue,/Which, like a fountain with a hundred spouts,/Did run pure blood'. Decius' interpretation – 'Your statue spouting blood in many pipes,/In which so many smiling Romans bathed' (*JC* 2.2.76–90) – invokes the conception of sanctified blood, spiritually reviving, something also promoted by Antony in the Forum. That even bloodier Roman play *TIT* has an image of terrible beauty. Encountering his mutilated niece Lavinia, Marcus conflates the violation with her radiance:

> Alas, a crimson river of warm blood,
> Like to a bubbling fountain stirr'd with wind,

Doth rise and fall between thy rosed lips,
Coming and going with thy honey breath.

(2.4.22–5)

The image is again foregrounded when Henry IV responds to York's revelation of Aumerle's treason:

O loyal father of a treacherous son!
Thou sheer, immaculate, and silver fountain,
From whence this stream through muddy passages
Hath held his current and defil'd himself!

(R2 5.3.60–3)

(C) Water has been associated with gardens since the river ran out of Eden. Fountains provided freshness and the sound of water. Dramatic, often multi-layered ones became an integral part of the Italian renaissance gardens the fame of which spread to northern Europe by engravings (Tchikine 2010). Fountains combined the symbolism of ancient gardens with a demonstration of their owner's considerable wealth, as both the engineering and stonework were very costly. Sometimes they contained trick mechanisms which would trigger a flow of water on the unsuspecting passer-by. Shakespeare includes nothing of the great water gardens such as Francis Bacon's at Gorhambury from 1608, or the more ephemeral, still extensive ones for the 1591 Queen's entertainment at Elvetham. Verbal images survive in contemporary descriptions particularly those of continental visitors like Hentzner (1598) and Waldstein (1600). Fountain imagery was pervasive, and features in the Preface of the *King James Bible*: 'the word of God is...a fountain of most pure water springing up unto eternal life'. Webster underlines its importance when he uses the fountain as a metaphor for political life in an opening scene of *The Duchess of Malfi* (1.1.12). A good modern source of information on Tudor fountains is Henderson's 'Medievalism in the English "Renaissance" Gardens' (Samson 2012).

fragrance See **smell**

frost (A) Freezing, the act of becoming frozen due to temperature falling below the freezing point of water; frost occurs when **dew** or vapour or the white hoar that appears on matter are subject to such a fall in temperature. Frost symbolizes winter; metaphorically it can suggest old age and infirmity.

(B) This natural phenomenon, a source of anxiety for horticulturists, exerts a strong and colourful influence, particularly in its figurative applications. Prospero, juxtaposing the intense physicality of the world with the sprite's intangible, penetrative **nature** complains of Ariel's reluctance, 'To run upon the sharp wind of the north,/To do me business in the veins o'th'earth/When it is bak'd with frost' (*TMP* 1.2.254–6). Titania protests to Oberon that the perverse weather experienced by mortals arises from conflict in the fairy world: 'hoary-headed frosts/Fall in the fresh lap of the crimson rose' (*MND* 2.1.107–8). Despite the disturbing nature of this topsy-turvy world the visual representation is one of extreme beauty. Acknowledging the association of frost with age, but emphasizing his temperance, Old Adam assures Orlando, 'Therefore my age is as a lusty winter,/Frosty, but kindly' (*AYL* 2.3.52–3). Condemned to exile, Bolingbroke refuses to be consoled: 'O, who can hold a fire in his hand/By thinking on the frosty Caucasus?' (*R2* 1.3.294–5). The configuration 'frosty Caucasus' gives these snow-covered mountains an irresistible physicality. *1H4* is a play littered with expectations. Hotspur, receiving a negative response from a potential supporter of his rebellion, exclaims, 'What a frosty-spirited rogue is this!' (2.3.20). Later, on the battlefield, news of Glendower's fatal delay provokes Worcester's comment, 'Ay, by my faith, that bears a frosty sound' (4.1.128). Contemplating his fall from power, Cardinal Wolsey provides a vivid analogy in which 'frost' is a decisive influence:

> This is the state of man: to-day he puts forth
> The tender leaves of hopes, to-morrow blossoms,
> And bears his blushing honors thick upon him;
> The third day comes a frost, a killing frost,
> And when he thinks, good easy man, full surely
> His greatness is a-ripening, nips his root,
> And then he falls as I do.
>
> *(H8 3.2.352–8)*

While this expansive but uncomplicated image invites immediate appreciation, Coriolanus' compressed expression catches the breath. Welcoming Rome's ultimate suppliants he addresses Valeria: 'The moon of Rome, chaste as the icicle/That's curdied by the frost from purest snow' (*COR* 5.3.65–6).

(C) Most horticultural writers on **plants** and **gardens** include suggestions on protecting plants from the frost. Tichborne (1586) in his elegy, written the night before his execution, sees his youth destroyed by 'a frost of cares' (both Ault 1949: 78, 120). Hill (1577) provides practical advice in time of frost, noting that **blossom** is particularly vulnerable to frost in spring, because of the sun's burning effect before the frost has worn off. Frost is a sign of age for Euphues: 'Would you have me spend the flower of my youth as you do the withered race of your age? Can the fair blood of my youth creep into the ground as it were frost-bitten?' (Lyly 1580, *Euphues*: 178). Greene also suggests that age is not an experience to be anticipated with any relish: 'intemperate in the frostie winter of their age;' (1591, vol. 9, *Farewell to Folly*: 323).

fruit, fruitful (A) Specifically fruit is the edible product of a **plant** or **tree**. Particularly when juicy or pulpy, fruit can imply **fertility**. Children can be described as the fruit of one's loins. It can suggest an outcome or issue of work, signifying productivity, generosity and liberality. Metaphorically fruit can signify a stage of life with youth as fruitful, when age is generally fruitless. Fruit can provide an indication of pregnancy in contrast to infertility and **barrenness**.

(B) Fruit, fruitfulness and fruitlessness permeate the plays. The literal sense of fertility and luxuriance is communicated by Lucentio on his entry to Padua: 'I am arriv'd for fruitful Lombardy,/The pleasant garden of great Italy' (*SHR* 1.1.3–4). In very different circumstances, Richmond endeavours to inspire his soldiers by vilifying Richard III: 'The wretched, bloody, and usurping boar,/That spoil'd your summer fields and fruitful vines' (*R3* 5.2.7–8). *TNK* has an engaging example when Palamon, in love with the very space that has been graced by Emilia's presence, begins his homage, 'Blessed garden,/And fruit and flowers more blessed' (2.2.232–3). This idealized representation of woman and garden is, nevertheless, saturated with sexual implications: '**Apricock**' and 'wanton' most obviously, but 'spread' possibly, and the twice mentioned 'fruit' may also carry sexual freight. Feigning unwillingness to accept the crown, Richard Gloucester objects, 'The royal tree hath left us royal fruit,/ Which mellow'd by the stealing hours of time,/Will well become the seat of majesty' (*R3* 3.7.167–9). Bishop Gardiner is straightforwardly brutal when discoursing on the pregnant Anne Boleyn: 'The fruit she goes with/I pray for heartily, that it may find/ Good time, and live; but for the stock, Sir Thomas,/I wish it grubb'd up now' (*H8* 5.1.20–3). Receiving news of Gaunt's death, Richard II flippantly responds, 'The ripest fruit first falls, and so doth he;/His time is spent, our pilgrimage must be./So much for that' (*R2* 2.1.153–5). Richard becomes more reflective when contemplating his own life and impending death (5.5.1–66). Returning from his first battle the Black Prince addresses the King with solemnity and pride: 'This sacrifice, the first-fruit of my sword,/Cropp'd and cut down even at the gate of death,/The King of Boheme, father, whom I slew' (*E3* 3.5.71–3). Cleopatra's welcome to the messenger from Antony is characteristically hyperbolic: 'Ram thou thy fruitful tidings in mine ears,/ That long time have been barren' (*ANT* 2.5.24–5). Fruit as dessert is used figuratively by Polonius who proposes the King and Queen receive news from Norway before he reveals the source of Hamlet's 'lunacy': 'Give first admittance to th'ambassadors;/My news shall be the fruit to that great feast' (*HAM* 2.2.51–2). The sense of fruitfulness as bountiful is intimated by two very different examples. Iago, manipulating Cassio, says of Desdemona, 'she's fram'd as fruitful/As the free elements' (*OTH* 2.3.341–2). Appealing to Timon for aid while acknowledging their past ingratitude, the senators promise, 'a recompense more fruitful' (*TIM* 5.1.150).

Theseus cautions Hermia that if she fails to comply with her father's choice of husband she risks, 'to be in shady cloister mew'd,/To live a barren sister all your life,/Chaunting faint hymns to the cold fruitless moon' (*MND* 1.1.71–3). As Oberon determines to draw the young lovers' confusions to an end, he informs Puck, 'When they next wake, all this derision/Shall seem a dream and fruitless vision' (3.2.370–1). 'Insubstantial' is probably the best equivalent of 'fruitless' here. Fruits meaning 'outcome' or 'upshot' is what Maria means in *TN* when encouraging her associates to view Malvolio's approach to Olivia in his yellow stockings: 'If you will then see the fruits of the sport, mark his first approach before my lady' (2.5.197–8). Iago has the same meaning when referring to the wounded Cassio: 'This is the fruits of whoring' (*OTH* 5.1.115). Othello anticipates the fulfilment of marriage when taking Desdemona to his bed for the first time: 'Come, my dear love,/The purchase made, the fruits are to ensue;/That profit's yet to come 'tween me and you' (2.3.8–10). Despite the diverse uses of these terms the only perplexing case arises in *AWW*. Lavatch, always eager to introduce a bawdy implication, responds to the Countess's question, 'You understand me?' with the sally, 'Most fruitfully, I am there before my legs' (2.2.69–70). Williams (1997: 135) claims that fruit can mean 'sexual parts'. As 'stand' can mean 'erection', the two parts fit together nicely. He does not mention this incident, but refers to *PER* when Antiochus says of his daughter, being wooed by Pericles, 'this fair Hesperides,/With golden fruit, but dangerous to be touch'd' (1.1.27–8).

(C) There was an ambivalent attitude towards eating fruit: Elyot (1541) and Boorde (1547) say it should be avoided in all illness, their advice reinforced by the contemporary belief in fruit as a source of plague infection. Markham (1631) appears to recognize the symptoms of a diet short of fruit when he writes of consequences of loose teeth and bad breath, both later understood to be indicative of scurvy. The compelling imagery of fruit appears in the Preface to the *King James Bible*: 'the word of God is.... not a herb but a tree, or rather a whole paradise of trees of life, that bring forth fruit every month, and the fruit thereof is for meat, and the leaves for medicine'. Fruit recurs throughout Drayton (1622), where entire counties, river banks and valleys are said to be fruitful. He sees fruitfulness as a characteristic both of the English race and the whole country, writing of a county's 'fruitful womb', of **orchards** great with fruit as if they were pregnant; he also applies fruitful to woods, **tillage**, **meads**, **earth**, pastures, store and **banks**. Sim (1997) records fruit which had a short growing and ripening season such as garden-grown **strawberries** and **cherries**, as a luxury for the very wealthy, and the newly available **peaches** and apricots as a considerable novelty. Palter (2002) gives extensive details of the literary background of many fruits; Knight (2009) considers the early modern literary context of fruit. See also **berry, damson, fig, gooseberry, grape, medlar, pear, plum, pomegranate, quince.**

furrow (A) A narrow trench made in the **earth** by the **plough**, more generally arable or ploughed **land**, a furrow can also be the land representing the length and breadth that a team could plough. By extension it may suggest a trench or drain, the track of a ship at sea, or anything resembling a furrow from a rut, indentation or groove to a deep wrinkle on the face. Furrow-weeds are any **weeds** growing in arable land that might be turned over by the plough, or that grow in the furrow after ploughing.

(B) There are only two literal references; figurative uses are diverse. In Prospero's masque Iris summons the reapers to join the celebration of blessing in honour of Miranda and Ferdinand: 'You sunburn'd sicklemen, of August weary,/Come hither from the furrow and be merry' (*TMP* 4.1.134–5). Cordelia describes Lear 'Crown'd with rank femiter and furrow-weeds' (*LR* 4.4.3). The Chorus in *H5,* having returned a triumphant Henry to England, sets in motion his return for France, inviting the audience to visualize the fleet: 'behold the threaden sails,/Borne with th'invisible and creeping wind,/Draw the huge bottoms through the furrowed sea,/Breasting the lofty surge' (3 Cho. 10–13). The metaphorical furrow possesses magnitude; Lear's very real 'furrow weeds' are flimsy reminders of nature's encroachment on soil and mind. The image of Henry's ships, fully engaged with the elements, is palpable and impressive, whereas Lear's turbulent mind is pitiful, his new crown mainly an assemblage of weeds. Bolingbroke is impressed by the 'breath of kings' when Richard reduces his term of exile from ten to six years. His father, John of Gaunt, though having acceded to the banishment, expresses resentment: 'Thou canst help time to furrow me with age,/But stop no wrinkle in his pilgrimage' (*R2* 1.3.215, 229–30). *SON* 22 also alludes to 'time's furrows' (3).

(C) Markham (1613) gives extensive instructions on how to achieve the best furrow, the needs of particular **soils** and **crops**, and other ploughing technicalities. Drayton writes of the sheep and pigs feeding on corn left in furrows after the **harvest**. He uses the image of ploughing to bemoan the incursion of man into what was formerly untamed **forest**, the furrow being a symbol of man's impact on the natural world: 'The Ridge and Furrow shewes, that once the crooked plow/Turn'd up the grassy turfe'(1622 *Polyolbion*, 19.43–4). Writing of the 1141 battle of Lincoln, Drayton emphasizes the slaughter that 'filled the furrows with sweltering blood' (22.127). Tigner (2012: 110) observes in a footnote that 'Both Byrd and Butler write that furrow-weeds are simply generic names for **weeds** that grow in furrows, but Gerard classifies Dog's grass and Dew as furrow grass, which "groweth in the well dunged grounds and fertill fields".' See also **ear.**

furze, gorse, goss Alternative names for the same **plant**, gorse is the standard name in southern England for the native, densely spiny, spreading **shrub**, *Ulex europaeus* L., which grows on uncultivated acidic **soil** and heathland; it can be a considerable nuisance if established in cultivated **land**. Used as bedding for cattle under a layer of **straw**, more importantly it provided fuel, both domestically and for small industry such as baking, brick-making or lime-burning. The only references to 'gorse' and 'furze' occur in *TMP*. The undesirable, infertile ground that is the natural soil for furze becomes appealing to Gonzalo as he contemplates the prospect of drowning in the sea-storm: 'Now would I give a thousand furlongs of sea for an acre of barren ground, long heath, brown furze, anything' (1.1.65–7). While Gonzalo refers only to furze, Ariel uses both names to describe the physical discomfort inflicted on the three would-be assassins as they are led through, 'Tooth'd briers, sharp furzes, pricking goss, and thorns' (4.1.180). The double mention 'furze' and 'goss' might imply some fine distinction between two similar plants. In most contemporary sources gorse and furze are synonymous. Markham, however, gives furze as fuel for the kiln, but recommends furze, gorse or whins for the maltster's use (1631). Norden (1618) in his land survey appears to suggest that they are two separate plants; he argues that furze on an estate should be recorded, that it was good for fuel, but with other weeds, including broom and gorse, its presence is a sign of idleness and lack of cultivation. Mabey (2010: 130–2) provides helpful commentary.

G

gallery (A) Possibly a development of the monastic cloister, a feature of the Italian renaissance **garden** which was less suited to the northern climate, a gallery was a roofed walk, open to the elements on one side, for walking in the fresh air without braving the weather. It could be an intermediate space between the house and garden for viewing the latter from the house, for displaying **statuary**, watching plays, **tennis** and other garden games, and listening to **music**. It provided a private space for love, intrigue and politics. Increasingly galleries were incorporated into the house as a long gallery for exercise and to display works of art.

(B) Of the four galleries that appear in the plays, two are possibly located in gardens or overlooking them; two form part of a house or castle. In *WT*, Leontes, eager to see Hermione's statue, comments to Paulina:

> Your gallery
> Have we pass'd through, not without much content
> In many singularities; but we saw not
> That which my daughter came to look upon,
> The statue of her mother.
>
> *(5.3.10–14)*

In performance there is seldom any hint of where the statue is located; the focus is on the statue itself – which Paulina says, she keeps, 'Lonely, apart' (18). The imminent arrival of the knights in *PER* prompts King Simonides to say, 'But stay, the knights are coming, we will withdraw/Into the gallery' (2.2.58–9). A structure overlooking an outdoor arena seems likely. The Countess of Auvergne, setting a trap for the English hero, Talbot, invites him to her castle. In the mistaken belief that she has captured him she boasts: 'Long time thy shadow hath been thrall to me,/For in my gallery thy picture hangs;/But now the substance shall endure the like' (*1H6* 2.3.36–8). Summoned to attend the King at midnight, Cranmer is granted the privilege of private conference when Lovell and Denny are instructed to 'Avoid the gallery'. Henry, assured that they will not be overheard, confides to Cranmer, 'Come, you and I must walk a turn together;/I have news to tell you' (*H8* 5.1.86–94). This is almost certainly an indoor long gallery.

(C) It is still possible to see where the gallery was at the Duke of Buckingham's Thornbury Castle, Gloucestershire; built against the **wall** of the house at first floor level it was open on one side overlooking the garden. Cloake (1995) gives some of the varied uses of the galleries at Richmond Palace under Elizabeth. Husselby and Henderson (2002) provide details of the galleries at Burghley and Theobalds. They also reference the Cecil house on the Strand where at a state banquet in 1581 guests ate in the great chamber, the garden gallery and the garden, suggesting the gallery was integral to the working of the house. Henderson (2005) has the most comprehensive study of galleries. Tigner (2006) argues that Hermione's statue was displayed in a garden gallery. Knight (2009) considers the contemporary literary context of galleries and their importance in viewing the garden.

garden (A) Enclosed **land** devoted to the cultivation of **trees**, **flowers**, **fruit** and vegetables, a garden suggests man's triumph over **nature**; a garden is a defined space with boundaries, in contrast with the unbounded landscape. Its size could vary considerably, from the immediate privy garden, extending to include the entire constructed landscape, encompassing **orchard**, **woodland** and **wilderness.** A garden could indicate a region of particular **fertility** and productivity – Kent was described as the Garden of England – and by extension England or another country could be a garden. The sixteenth century saw the birth of gardening as leisure and a status symbol. Gardens were controlled private spaces for informal eating, exercise and entertainment where encounters could be philosophical, sexual, musical or sporting. The garden provided proverbial, religious and metaphorical comparisons with the state of the country, of an individual, their soul or the church. A perfect garden was the re-creation of **Eden** before the fall of man, while the post-Edenic garden could represent forbidden love. **Weeds** and pests in the garden were a result of carelessness, ignorance, laziness or neglect by the **gardener**, representing corruption and the fall. If human beings are the gardeners then the gardening metaphor can be extended to their care of themselves, as evidenced by their wills and actions. As visual creations gardens lend themselves to reproduction in different media, particularly in needlework and painting.

(B) The word 'garden' is applied to diverse physical spaces fulfilling a wide range of dramatic functions. It is sometimes emblematic. England and France are both described as gardens. A gardener in *R2* describes England as 'our sea-walled garden' (3.4.43); Burgundy claims France to be 'this best garden of the world' (*H5* 5.2.36), a sentiment echoed by the Epilogue when referring to Henry's conquests: 'Fortune made his sword;/By which the world's best garden he achieved' (6–7). Lucentio, entering **Padua** for a course of study, confides to Tranio, 'I am arriv'd for fruitful Lombardy,/The pleasant garden of great Italy' (*SHR* 1.1.3–4). Arden 2 (171) points out, 'Padua is not and never was in Lombardy'. Nevertheless Shakespeare highlights the region's horticultural status. In *R2* the garden is emblematic of the body politic. At the opening of his extended analogy the Gardener reflects on Richard's governance, 'O, what a pity is it/That he had not so trimm'd and dress'd his land/As we this garden!' (3.4.55–7). In *1H6* the quarrel that breaks out in the Temple Garden (2.4.104–31) gains emblematic significance when the white and red **roses** growing there are plucked by the antagonists, York and Somerset, and their supporters. A productive garden provides a backdrop for the masterly political manoeuvring of Richard Gloucester whose first request on entering a critical meeting disconcerts the participants: 'My Lord of Ely, when I was last in Holborn,/I saw good strawberries in your garden there./I do beseech you send for some of them' (*R3* 3.4.31–3). Climbing into a garden in search of a 'sallet' the fugitive Jack Cade is confronted by the indignant owner Alexander Iden: 'Is't not enough to break into my garden,/And like a thief to come and rob my grounds' (*2H6* 4.10.15–34). The work-a-day function of the garden is deployed as a metaphor for the body by Iago when manipulating Roderigo: 'Our bodies are our gardens, to the which our wills are gardeners; so that if we plant nettles or sow lettuce, set hyssop and weed up tine, supply it with one gender of herbs or distract it with many, either to have it sterile with idleness or manur'd with industry – why, the power and corrigible authority of this lies in our wills' (*OTH* 1.3.320–6). Isabella, advising Marianna, provides a detailed description of the lay-out of Angelo's garden:

> He hath a garden circummur'd with brick,
> Whose western side is with a vineyard back'd;
> And to that vineyard is a planched gate,
> That makes his opening with this bigger key.
> The other doth command a little door,
> Which from the vineyard to the garden leads;
>
> *(MM 4.1.28–33)*

The precise location of the Costard-Jaquenetta sexual encounter is in the corner of the 'park' close to the 'curious-knotted garden' (*LLL* 1.1.206–46). The presence of partitions of various kinds, including doors, is intimated by Olivia's impatient dismissal of Sir Andrew and Sir Toby so that she can have private conference with Cesario/Viola: 'Let the garden door be shut, and leave me to my hearing' (*TN* 3.1.92–3).

The garden as a place of recreation or diversion possesses many facets. Hermione, perhaps taking Polixenes' arm, says to her husband, 'If you would seek us,/We are yours i'th'garden' (*WT* 1.2.177–8). Anxiously awaiting news of her husband, Richard II, the Queen asks her ladies, 'What sport shall we devise here in this garden/To drive away the heavy thought of care?' (*R2* 3.4.1–2). Antony, too, retreats to the garden to contemplate his situation or to vent his frustration. As Eros informs Enobarbus, 'He's walking in the garden –/…cries "fool Lepidus!"/And threats the throat of that his officer/That murd'red Pompey' (*ANT* 3.5.16–19). The garden is the emotional and dramatic fulcrum of *TNK*. Engaging her waiting-lady, Emilia reflects, 'This garden has a world of pleasures in't. What flow'r is this?'. Informed, ''Tis call'd narcissus, madam' she proceeds to discuss love and embroidery, designating the rose as her favourite flower (2.2.118–36). This delightfully discursive conversation takes place under the gaze of the imprisoned Arcite and Palamon, dear friends who become locked in bitter rivalry for the love of Emilia. Palamon exclaims, 'Blessed garden,/And fruit and flowers more blessed, that still blossom/As her bright eyes shine on ye' (2.2.232–4). The murder of Old Hamlet is shocking on several accounts, and not least because it was effected in a place of sanctuary: 'Sleeping within my orchard,/My custom always of the afternoon,/ Upon my secure hour thy uncle stole' (*HAM* 1.5.59–61). When Hamlet produces the play-within-a-play he describes how the murderer 'poisons' his victim 'i'th'garden for his estate' (3.2.261). The garden is used metaphorically to express Hamlet's heart-ache and loss of spirit: ''tis an unweeded garden/That grows to seed, things rank and gross in nature/Possess it merely' (1.2.135–7). Artois legitimizes English entitlement to the French throne via Edward's mother Isabel: 'And from the fragrant garden of her womb/ Your gracious self, the flower of Europe's hope,/Derived is inheritor to France' (*E3* 1.1.14–16).

(C) Arden 3 (419) comments briefly on the Parish or Paris Garden of *H8* (5.3.2). This disreputable area of modern Southwark boasted bear-baiting pits, **bowling alleys** and, after 1575 when the Corporation of London expelled the players, theatres (www.british-history.ac.uk, 18). Kyd dramatizes the perversion of the garden as a place of enjoyment and as a sanctuary with a murder scene, resulting in the permanent destruction of its fertility (1592, *The Spanish Tragedie)*. The Catholic priest Southwell (ed. 1967) inverts the garden as a place of safety, productivity and beauty by admitting grief, envy, jealousy and iniquity. John Stow (1604: 191) commenting on contemporary London gardens records how Cromwell, dissatisfied with the size of his new garden near the Augustine Friars church, took unilateral action to extend it into the Stows' garden. Bacon (1625) sets out the intellectually ideal garden of the time in his seminal essay 'Of Gardens'. Woodhouse (1999) demonstrates the theatricality of the Elizabethan garden. Bushnell (2003) points out that early modern humanist education often compared gardening with teaching, emphasizing the need to master **nature**, whether in the garden or in a child. In any study of the early modern garden, Henderson (2005) is invaluable. She includes records of designers of gardens and the gardeners themselves; her gazetteer of surviving structures is extensive. Knight (2009) analyses gardens both of plants and verse. Harrison (2008) explores the cultural history of gardens as a reflection of the human condition. Walsham (2011) sets the expansion of architecture and gardening in the context of the Reformation in England. Tigner (2012: 2, 113–31; 216) proposes that garden development under Elizabeth and the early Stuart kings mirrored the country's move from an inward-looking, self-sufficient paradise to an expansionist country seeking paradise in the New World. She argues for a symbiotic relationship between 'physical gardens and their literary representations' and analyzes garden enclosures and etymology. Maintaining that the garden cannot be divorced from the sexualized female body, she suggests that this theme appears throughout *WT* and that it is Hermione's use of 'garden' with its associations of forbidden love that triggers Leontes' jealousy. See also **bowls, tennis, music**.

gardener (A) Usually a male employee working in or overseeing the **garden**; women in the garden can often be distinguished by their work title of, for example, 'weeding women'. A gardener's job was to control and improve on **nature**. The change in Shakespeare's lifetime from the purely utilitarian to the experimental and ostentatious is reflected in many of the new books, which range from luxury publications for the owner, to instruction manuals for both owner/employer and employee/gardener. Figuratively, gardening encompassed a wide range of concepts including self-care, education, and spiritual growth.

(B) Gardeners have a physical presence only in *R2*. They do, however, dominate a celebrated scene. Richard's anxious Queen wanting to eavesdrop tells her waiting-lady, 'But stay, here come the gardeners./Let's step into the shadow of these trees' (3.4.24–5). The gardeners do indeed 'talk of state', juxtaposing methods of good gardening with good government. What surprises and antagonizes the Queen is their judicious résumé of Richard's reign and his impending fall. The distressed Queen responds with a curse: 'Gard'ner, for telling me these news of woe,/Pray God the plants thou graft'st may never grow'(100–1). Cautioning the Dauphin that Henry V is a formidable adversary, the Constable of France employs a remarkable metaphor to expose youthful antics as calculation: 'As gardeners do with ordure hide those roots/That shall first spring and be most delicate' (*H5* 2.4.39–40). Confronting the rebels, Sir Humphrey Stafford scorns Cade's audacious claim to the throne: 'Villain, thy father was a plasterer,/And thou thyself a shearman, art thou not?'. Unabashed, Cade's riposte is: 'And Adam was a gardener' (*2H6* 4.2.132–4). Iago, by means of analogy, contends that the human mind is as predisposed to cultivation as is the natural world: 'Our bodies are our gardens, to the which our wills are gardeners' (*OTH* 1.3.320–1).

(C) Some books assume a considerable degree of literacy on the part of the gardener; others advise the owner to monitor his employee carefully as there is a presumption of ignorance. Hill (1577) refers to the **husbandman** or gardener, and gives extensive details of his remit. Puttenham (1589) suggests the gardener is integral to the debate between art and **nature**; that as he **manures**, waters, **weeds** and **prunes**, he is helping nature to achieve her full potential. Christiansen (2005) includes the most comprehensive contemporary list of gardeners – at Hampton Court under Henry VII and Henry VIII. Willes (2011; 2014) offers a wealth of information including a survey of gardening manuals, tools and wage-rates.

garden-house (A) Alternatively banqueting-house, both were a byword as places of assignation. They are among the likely garden structures to have survived, although some were purely temporary, fragile single occasion constructions. As banqueting-houses, they provided a place of adjournment at the end of a long meal for a leisurely elaborate dessert and enjoyment of the garden. Such garden rooms could also be quite small, places for retreat, solitude or sexual encounters.

(B) It is clear that the garden-house provided a space for lovers' meetings, licit or illicit. In *MM* there are three mentions of the 'garden-house' that is central to Angelo's deception and eventual humiliation. In the closing scene he is confronted by Marianna with the truth of the bed trick: 'this is the body/That took away the match from Isabel,/And did supply thee at thy garden-house/In her imagin'd person' (5.1.210–13). Earlier, Isabella described how Angelo had given precise details how to gain access to this garden-house (4.1.28–35). A peculiar case arises in *TNK* when the Jailer's Daughter, afflicted by 'a most thick and profound melancholy', imagines wayward wives deceiving their husbands by surreptitious couplings: 'One cries, "O, that ever I did it behind the arras!" and then howls; th'other curses a suing fellow and her garden-house' (4.3.49–56). Although not designated as such, the description of the sexual encounter between Costard and Jaquenetta implies a 'garden-house' (*LLL* 1.1.244–6).

(C) Stow (1598: 390) writes of Goswell Street in London, 'replenished with small tenements, cottages, alleys, gardens, banqueting houses and bowling places', suggesting they were built in quite modest properties. Many surviving banqueting or garden houses are very accessible: at Montacute there are small pavilions in the garden; Longleat has turrets built on the roof. Holdenby, where they are long gone, had a banqueting-house three storeys high with six rooms to each floor, 100 yards from the main house. As with other garden buildings of the period, those that survive are best documented in Henderson (2005). Willes (2011: 129) provides a description of garden houses and their associated culinary delights.

garland (A) Also a **wreath**, made of **flowers** and **leaves** to be worn round the head or neck for decoration, celebration or protection from the plague; a garland suggested an abundance of flowers, their fragility representing life's uncertainties. Evergreen garlands implied a longer life, invoking a sense of eternity. Metaphorically a garland can imply respect for excellence or attainment in sport, referencing the **oak, laurel** or **olive** crown at the Greek and Roman games, and suggesting the adornment of garlanded sacrificial animals. It could also represent a physical crown of state.

(B) In the plays and poems 'garland' can signify: a crown – the 'golden round'; a wreath to honour heroic deeds; a 'wheaten' form representing virginity or peace; a coronet fashioned from a single plant – the **willow**, for instance, suggesting forsaken love; a gallimaufry of flowers, **herbs** and weeds woven into a garland, that may encompass tensions between celebration and anguish, authority and humility. The word 'garland', when applied to a character symbolizes the hero himself or a woman given him as a trophy, and is also the personification of Peace. The most celebrated garland belongs to the prolific and enigmatic botanical 'speaker' Ophelia. Stepping over the threshold into madness her chosen mode of articulacy is plants. The coronet she is wearing when she drowns is vividly described by Gertrude. Acquiring a new-found voice, the Queen frames the scene:

> There is a willow grows askaunt the brook,
> That shows his hoary leaves in the glassy stream,
> Therewith fantastic garlands did she make
> Of crow-flowers, nettles, daisies, and long purples
>
> *(HAM 4.7.166–9)*

The willow as the emblem of forsaken love sets the tone and establishes a singular presence, visually and thematically. While Shakespeare's audience would have been better able to respond to the symbolism involved, it is apparent that sex, death, suffering and betrayal all find expression in this garland. No doubt many of the meanings cut across each other – which should not be surprising given Ophelia's fractured mind. The garland's celebratory and sacrificial manifestations collide and collude in this melancholy scene. The willow garland as the symbol of forsaken love is equally poignant in *OTH*. Shortly before she is murdered Desdemona is haunted by the song 'Willow': '"Sing all a green willow must be my garland./Let nobody blame him, his scorn I approve"' (4.3.51–2). The tone of anguish is replaced by petulance in *ADO*. Believing Don Pedro has broken his word by wooing Hero for himself, the agitated Claudio is teased by Benedick: 'What fashion will you wear your garland of?' (2.1.188–9). Later he tells Don Pedro, 'I off'red him my company to a willow-tree, either to make him a garland, as being forsaken, or to bind him up a rod, as being worthy to be whipped' (217–20). Benedick makes two more mentions of the garland before the misunderstanding is resolved.

As Hal and Hotspur prepare for their fateful encounter at the Battle of Shrewsbury, Harry Percy expressing his sense of superiority – 'and would to God/Thy name in arms were now as great as mine!'– provokes the Prince's riposte, 'I'll make it greater ere I part from thee,/And all the budding honors on thy crest/I'll crop to make a garland for my head' (*1H4* 5.4.69–73). This is an apt response to the young firebrand earlier described as, 'Mars in swathling clothes,/This infant warrior' (3.2.112–13). Henry IV, close to death, bequeaths to Hal another kind of garland, the crown itself: 'So thou the garland wear'st successively' (*2H4* 4.5.201). The most celebrated warrior to receive the symbol of courage is Coriolanus. Following the battle of Corioli, Caius Martius not only 'Wears this war's garland' (*COR* 1.9.60) but is given the name Coriolanus. Commending him for Consul, Cominius rehearses his martial attainments beginning with his first battle from which he emerged 'brow-bound with the oak' through to his subsequent achievements: 'And in the brunt of seventeen battles since/He lurch'd all swords of the garland' (2.2.98–101). In *ANT*, Silius incites Ventidius to press home his advantage by pursuing the Parthians, 'so thy grand captain, Antony,/Shall set thee on triumphant chariots, and/Put garlands on thy head' (3.1.9–11) – advice that is declined for fear of eclipsing and thereby offending Antony. As Mark Antony dies, Cleopatra pronounces tenderly, 'O, wither'd is the garland of the war' (4.15.64). This conception of the hero as garland is also present in *COR*. In a vitriolic speech the scornful Caius Martius berates the plebeians for inconstancy: 'With every minute you do change a mind,/And call him noble, that was now your hate;/Him vild, that was your garland' (1.1.182–4).

Garland as celebratory ornament appears in the last line of the song 'Who is Silvia?': 'To her let us garlands bring' (*TGV* 4.2.53). Perdita provides a long list of flowers that she would like to bestow on her companions, especially Florizel, and concludes, 'O, these I lack,/To make you garlands of, and my sweet friend,/To strew him o'er and o'er!' (*WT* 4.4.127–9). The idea of sacrificial garlands arises in *ANT*. Charmian excitedly anticipating the promise of a husband, playfully suggests he will be adorned like a sacrificial animal because she is bound to make him a cuckold: 'where's the soothsayer that you prais'd so to th'Queen? O that I knew this husband, which, you say, must change his horns with garlands!' (1.2.2–5). Whether it should be 'change' (as in F) or 'charge' (a proposed emendation) makes little difference to the general point. See Arden 3 (95) and Riverside (1396). The garland as the emblem of peace finds expression in *HAM*. The Prince rehearses to Horatio the tenor of his substituted letter to the King of England: 'As love between them like the palm might flourish,/As peace should still her wheaten garland wear/And stand a comma 'tween their amities' (5.2.40–2). A 'wheaten garland' as the representation of virginity occurs in *TNK*. Emilia, '*in white...wearing a wheaten wreath...her hair stuck with flowers*' enters Diana's temple prior to the duel between the contenders for her love, and prays: 'He of the two pretenders that best loves me/ And has the truest title in't, let him/Take off my wheaten garland' (5.1.158–60). The emotional current of this speech may imply that she favours retaining the 'wheaten garland'. Earlier, representing Emilia as a wreath of victory, Arcite invoked Mars: 'You know my prize/Must be dragg'd out of blood; force and great feat/Must put my garland on, where she sticks/The queen of flowers' (5.1.42–5). This oxymoronic vision captures exactly the breathtaking folly of these 'noble kinsmen'. A curious case belongs to *H8*. Shortly before her death Queen Katherine experiences a vision, the stage direction for which includes, '*six personages, clad in white robes, wearing on their heads garlands of bays...branches of bays or palm in their hands*'. Katherine says, 'They promis'd me eternal happiness,/And brought me garlands, Griffith, which I feel/I am not worthy yet to wear' (4.2.90–2). These garlands seem to be hybrid, the bays representing victory and heroic achievement; the palm, the emblem of the pilgrim, appears to sanctify, preparing to welcome Katherine over the threshold into heaven.

(C) Heywood (1545) mourns his love with garlands of willow (Ault 1949, 14–15). Spenser (ed. 1999, *The Shepheardes Calendar*) reminds his readers that the fairest flowers in garlands will fade and become dust, a metaphor for the fragility of human life; he also writes of garlands as a sign of love and celebration. Davies' (1599) garlands for spring are eternal, green and unfading, representative of the virtues, the gifts of Astraea, herself symbolic of Elizabeth. Cornelia thinks her garland plants have protective powers: 'Reach the bayes,/Ile tie a garland here about his head;/Twill keepe my boy from lightning' (Webster 1612, *The White Devil*, 5.4.60). Heath (2003) provides a detailed analysis of Ophelia's garland (see under the individual flowers) and their associated meanings. He considers other garlands in Shakespeare, noting that in several plays garland is a metaphor for sacrifice. Willes (2011: 137) cites Spenser's detailed description of an Elizabethan coronet.

garlic (A) *Allium sativum* L., a pungent member of the **onion** family, garlic was of particular value in the rather flavourless pottage on which many depended, hence the association of its **smell** with poverty. Its wide range of medicinal purposes included counteracting poisons, as an aphrodisiac, a contraceptive and an abortifacient. While notorious for its strong smell, garlic could mask the unpleasant effects of rotting teeth and bad breath. It has attracted superstitions particularly in connection with witchcraft.

(B) There are five mentions of garlic, all of which are negative: it functions as a masking agent for bad breath, and it is an indicator of low social status. Bottom advises his fellow actors, 'eat no onions nor garlic, for we are to utter sweet breath; and I do not doubt but to hear them say, it is a sweet comedy' (*MND* 4.2.42–4). This prejudice is confirmed by Hotspur who has become so irritated by Glendower that he waspishly protests: 'I had rather live/With cheese and garlic in a windmill, far,/Than feed on cates and have him talk to me/In any summer house in Christendom' (*1H4* 3.1.159–63). Not knowing he is addressing the Duke in disguise, Lucio confides, 'The Duke... would eat mutton on Fridays...he would mouth with a beggar, though she smelt brown bread and garlic' (*MM* 3.2.181–4). Accusing him of having relations with prostitutes (mutton is slang for 'whore'), Lucio compounds his slander by suggesting the Duke would not be deterred even by bad breath. This might arise from a gross diet or by eating garlic to mask bad breath. Arden 2 (90) observes that 'coarse rye, or rye and wheat bread, the food of the poor, rapidly turned musty and affected the breath'. In *WT*, Dorcas indicates that eating garlic is necessary to disguise her rival's bad breath: 'Mopsa must be your mistress; marry, garlic,/To mend her kissing with!' (4.4.162–3). News that the exiled Roman hero has joined forces with the enemy and is marching on Rome leads Menenius to denounce the tribunes and plebeians who are responsible for Caius Martius' banishment: 'You have made good work,/You, and your apron men; you that stood so much/Upon the voice of occupation and/The breath of garlic-eaters!' (*COR* 4.6.95–8). This contempt for common people echoes Cleopatra's perception of 'Mechanic slaves' when she contemplates life as a prisoner in Rome: 'In their thick breaths,/Rank of gross diet, shall we be enclouded,/And forc'd to drink their vapor' (*ANT* 5.2.209–13).

(C) Many early writers comment on its power as a contraceptive and abortifacient. Stow (1598: 247) points out that St James Church, Garlick Hithe was so-called because 'of old time' garlic was sold on the river bank close by. Mabey notes the wide-spread growth of garlic in the wild and its influence on English place-names, confirming its ready availability to all sections of the population (1996: 417). Simoons (1998) devotes a complete chapter to garlic and associated plants: he records it as ritually impure from the smell, which also reflected social embarrassment. He notes its classical links to the underworld, and evil in general, whence its use as a charm, and its association with exorcism. Its ability to counteract poison led to its use to prevent and treat the plague.

germain More usually germens in the plural, germain is the rudiment of an organism, a germ, from which **seeds**, particularly very small ones, originate; it could also suggest a shoot or sprout, a young **branch** or sucker. The two magnificent speeches which incorporate this word have tempests and widespread devastation at their heart. Lear's storm-saturated invocation to nature seeks the annihilation of mankind: 'And thou, all-shaking thunder,/Strike flat the thick rotundity o'th'world!/Crack nature's moulds, all germains spill at once/That makes ingrateful man!' (*LR* 3.2.6–9). This anguished outburst is precipitated by the ultimate form of treachery in the Shakespearean universe:

ingratitude. Wary of equivocation, Macbeth demands of the Weird Sisters: 'though the treasure/Of nature's germains tumble all together,/Even till destruction sicken; answer me/To what I ask you' (*MAC* 4.1.58–61). Bartholomaeus (1582) suggests budding or a budding **graft** is called 'germen'. Nares (1859) says 'german' means related to, with 'germin' or 'germen' from the Latin 'germen' being a seed or **bud**. The *OED* gives *LR* and *MAC* as the earliest records of the word, with no further example until 1691.

gillyvor (A) Probably derived from the Arabic or Sanskrit for **clove**, gillyvor was a name for clove-scented native plants, and by extension for **plants** with a similar **smell**. It was also used at the time to denote varieties of **pink**, wallflower, sweet william, sweet rocket and stock. The **carnation** and gillyvor are members of the pink family, *Caryophyllaceae*. The names were used interchangeably, and all had medicinal and culinary applications. Given the reference to taking cuttings or '**slips**', gillyvor probably indicates the pink or carnation as other candidates for the name are grown from **seed** not propagated by cuttings, but in this instance the symbolism is more important than precise botanical identification.

(B) Gillyvors are found only in *WT* where they feature prominently among the desirable, but for Perdita, unacceptable flowers:

> the fairest flow'rs o'th'season
> Are our carnations and streak'd gillyvors
> (Which some call Nature's bastards). Of that kind
> Our rustic garden's barren, and I care not
> To get slips of them.
>
> *(4.4.81–5)*

Although both flowers are here viewed as aberrant, their artifice differs in that the gillyvors are 'streak'd'. The precise nature of Perdita's objection to these flowers is unclear, but making the case for cross-breeding and grafting, Polixenes concludes, 'Then make your garden rich in gillyvors,/And do not call them bastards' (98–9). The process of hybridization was not understood at the time but the delight taken in new forms and varieties led to vigorous though ineffectual efforts to enhance this process through human intervention.

(C) Tigner (2012: 123) notes, 'Though Perdita despises gillyflowers for their mutability and artificiality, the oxlips and lilies that she so craves for her lover are no less changeable. Lilies, like gillyflowers and later tulips, were valued for their ability to produce variations.' Bradford (1933) and others suggest that in *WT* Shakespeare is anticipating the idea of 'hybridization'. However, while just in the lexicon when applied to animals, the *term* 'hybridization' – as opposed to the concept – did not come into general botanical currency until the nineteenth century, although the idea of plant sexuality was recognized about 1700. Shakespeare is possibly demonstrating the contemporary interest in any plant that produced peculiar or monstrous variations. Bushnell (2003: 141–3) notes that 'From the end of the sixteenth century on, long before the biological process of plant hybridization was understood, stunning experiments filled the horticultural manuals, where we find recipes – some of them preposterous – for changing the scent, taste, and shape, and the very nature of all sorts of fruits and flowers.' She cites Della Porta's *Natural Magic* (1558 trans. 1658) as an example of the belief that variations were indeed achieved by deliberate manipulation: 'the clove gillyflower was once ordinary "that the gardeners art has made so dainty and sweet scented"'. The identification of gillyvor/gillyflower has long been the subject of debate. Harvey (1978) provides the most detailed botanical analysis, commenting that the identification problem is only present in English. Ault (1949) includes the pre-1576 poem *A Nosegay ever sweet*, with stanzas on gillyflowers for gentleness, and carnations for graciousness. Spenser (1579, *The Shepheardes Calendar*) and Lyly (1580, *Euphues*) use gillyflower, carnation and pink in one sentence demonstrating a recognition of different flowers (see *carnation* for quotes). Gerard (1597: 588–97) applies gillyflower to stocks, wallflowers and sweet rocket, with separate entries for pinks, which he says are different from carnations. Puttenham (1589) sees the gillyflower as artificial, an example of art as the 'alterer of nature'. For him, Tigner (2012: 123) observes, 'the poet, like the gardener, "by his arte" is commended for his ability to modify form'. She concludes, 'the gillyflower, along with the other hybrid plants is the positive emblem of artificiality'. The controversy centres on Perdita taking slips or cuttings; Plat (1654) gives instructions for **grafting** carnations by splicing cuttings on to other woody material, which is at variance with other commentators of the time. Dolan (1993) sees Perdita's rejection of the 'bastard' flower as a rejection of the conflation of art and nature. Mabey (1996) gives *Dianthus caryophyllus,* the native clove pink, as the Tudor gillyflower. See also **carnation, nature, scion, slip, stock**.

ginger (A) The rhizome of the tropical **plant** *Zingiber officinale,* was known from Anglo-Saxon times, but was not grown in England. Ginger was imported as a spice from the East Indies; it was traded as a commodity, bought for use and valued for its ability to spice up food and ale. Often associated with old age, ginger was extensively incorporated into medical compounds to treat a wide range of problems.

(B) The role of ginger as an everyday commodity is glanced at in *1H4*. The Second Carrier announces, 'I have a gammon of bacon and two razes of ginger, to be deliver'd as far as Charing-cross' (2.1.24–5). 'Razes' are **roots**. During the altercation arising from their late-night revels, Sir Toby challenges Malvolio, 'Dost thou think because thou art virtuous there shall be no more cakes and ale?'. Wanting to contribute to the steward's discomfiture, Feste adds, 'and ginger shall be hot i'th'mouth too' (*TN* 2.3.114–18). The shopping list provided by Perdita for the sheep-shearing festivities includes, 'saffron to color the warden pies; mace; dates…nutmegs, seven; a race or two of ginger' (*WT* 4.3.45–7). On the eve of the battle of Agincourt the Dauphin bestows lavish praise on his horse. Orleance's observation, 'He's of the color of the nutmeg', provokes the response, 'And of the heat of the ginger' (*H5* 3.7.19–20). Fearful of the news concerning the loss of one of Antonio's ships, Solanio responds to 'gossip Report' with the phrase, 'I would she were as lying a gossip in that as ever knapp'd ginger' (*MV* 3.1.7–9). Here is a reference to the predilection of old women for 'knapping' or eating ginger. Pompey Bum's disquisition on his fellow prisoners reveals one of the devices employed to evade the restriction limiting the allowable rate of interest to ten per cent. In order to secure a loan the borrower would be obliged to purchase unwanted goods at a price well above their market value: 'here's young Master Rash, he's in for a commodity of brown paper and old ginger, ninescore and seventeen pounds, of which he made five marks ready money. Marry then ginger was not much in request, for the old women were all dead' (*MM* 4.3.4–8). High mortality brought about by the plague (particularly severe in 1603) removed a substantial part of that market. Gingerbread is used twice. When Hotspur chides Kate for delivering an oath more suited to the citizen class than to an aristocrat, his metaphor relates to the staple, bread, rather than to confectionery:

> Swear me, Kate, like a lady as thou art,
> A good mouth-filling oath, and leave 'in sooth',
> And such protest of pepper-gingerbread,
> To velvet-guards and Sunday-citizens.
>
> *(1H4 3.1.253–6)*

In an illuminating note Arden 3 (256) suggests that 'pepper was added for some of the required ginger in the usual recipe producing a coarser and somewhat milder tasting bread'. Fitzpatrick (2011: 190) provides a different description of this bread claiming it is a spicier version of gingerbread, which might have contained spices such as cinnamon, nutmeg and cloves. This interpretation, however, does not accord so well with the implication of Hotspur's comment. Costard, expressing his admiration for the quick wit of Moth, makes the only reference to that treat for children, 'gingerbread': 'And I had but one penny in the world, thou shouldst have it to buy gingerbread' (*LLL* 5.1.71–2).

(C) The *OED* gives 'race', not 'raze', citing *1H4* (2.1.24–5). Boorde (1547) lists ginger's medical applications, while Parkinson (1640) makes it clear that ginger is an import. Hannett (1863) records the Warwickshire use of ginger for paying rents under Henry IV suggesting value and ready availability. Jardine (1996) notes the expansion of European trade in the sixteenth century in **cloves,** ginger, **pepper** and **nutmeg**. Thomas (2008: 297) elucidates financial manipulation and usury alluded to by Pompey Bum.

glade A small opening in woodland, whether natural or created by felling **trees**. Though there are numerous mentions of woodland and its various aspects there is but one reference to 'glade'. In a richly descriptive scene, the Wooer informs the Jailer how he observed his daughter singing: 'I laid me down/And list'ned to the words she sung, for then/Through a small glade cut by the fishermen,/I saw your daughter' (*TNK* 4.1.62–5). This is an unusual but finely delineated intimation of a glade as man-made space cut between **reeds** on a river **bank**. Fletcher (2011) notes that **forests** were not composed of endless trees, but were shot through with **groves** and glades giving much needed light for **saplings** to **grow**. See also **laund**.

gooseberry *Ribes uva-crispa*, L., a spiny **shrub** of the currant family, was cultivated to produce larger, slightly sweeter **berries** than were available in the wild. Its origin is uncertain, but probably it was a naturalized introduction at an unknown early date. The **gooseberry** was planted as a decorative shrub, both with **flowers** and in **hedging**. The **fruit** was baked into tarts, used as verjuice or fruit vinegar, and served as a relish with meat. It had medicinal properties, and proverbial meanings. Falstaff's posture during his verbal duel with the Lord Chief Justice involves the protestation that in a commercial age 'all other gifts appertinent to a man, as the malice of this age shapes them, are not worth a gooseberry' (*2H4* 1.2.171–3). Clearly a gooseberry, like the **blackberry**, being plentiful and therefore cheap was not highly valued. Hill (1577) lists six varieties which differ little from modern cultivars; he recommends incorporating gooseberries in a quick-set **hedge** as a barrier and defence for the **garden**. Andrews (1993) confirms its ornamental role at Theobalds, where they were planted with **roses** along a main route through the garden.

gorse see **furze**

gourd Plants of the family *Cucurbitaceæ*, gourd can refer to the whole **plant**, its fleshy **fruit**, or as dried fruit hollowed out and used as a container; a secondary meaning indicated a type of false dice. As a wild **vine**, **coloquintida** is a member of the gourd family, as is the cucumber. It is just possible that this vegetable family is alluded to on three occasions. However, in all three cases the general opinion is against it. When Pistol is dismissed from service by Falstaff he responds with pistolian rhetoric, shaping his abuse with alliteration, assonance and antithesis: 'Let vultures gripe thy guts! For gourd and fullam holds,/And high and low beguiles the rich and poor' (*WIV* 1.3.85–6). There seems to be no consciousness of the plant here. Editors appear to be unanimous in reading Pistol's reference in terms of the game of dice. *AWW* provides a more promising case. Parolles endeavours to persuade Helena that her return home will ultimately create a future 'strew'd with sweets,/Which they distill now in the curbed time,/To make the coming hour o'erflow with joy,/And pleasure drown the brim' (2.4.44–7). 'The curbed time' signifying a period of restraint may also allude to the flask or *curbita*, fashioned from the vegetable and used for distillation. Attempting to explain the friendship between Hal and Poins, Falstaff claims that they share a taste for 'cunger and fennel' (*2H4* 2.4.245). It has been suggested that 'conger' is a dialect word for cucumber, though it is generally taken to refer to the eel. Fitzpatrick (2011: 101) cites Gurr's view that in the Midlands 'conger' was 'a common term for "cucumber"'.

graft, graff (A) The insertion of a small piece of one **plant**, an off-shoot or **scion**, into a cut in the **bark** or stem of a second plant or **stock**, the purpose of **grafting** is to join two separate **root** systems to propagate a plant which did not grow true to form, to increase yield, or to produce a greater diversity of plants. The technique is as old as cultivation; it is especially suitable for propagation where plants grown from **seed**, such as fruit stones or pips, grow too slowly, and for the introduction of new stock from the wild. The process of grafting lent itself to extensive metaphor in contemporary literature. In the context of human generation grafting was seen as potentially dangerous as it could create a degree of inappropriate social mobility through the joining of unequal partners.

(B) There are a few literal examples of grafted plants but the majority of uses are figurative and relate to insemination and offspring. Acceding to Helicanus' request to purchase provisions, Lysimachus graciously replies, 'O Sir, a courtesy/Which if we should deny, the most just God/For every graff would send a caterpillar,/And so inflict our province'. He continues the imagery when expressing his admiration for Marina: 'She's such a one that were I well assur'd/Came of a gentle kind and noble stock,/I'd wish no better choice, and think me rarely to wed' (*PER* 5.1.58–69). Justice Shallow, proud of his hands-on approach to his estate, tells Falstaff, 'Nay, you shall see my orchard, where, in an arbor, we will eat a last year's pippin of mine own graffing' (*2H4* 5.3.1–3). Expressing her resentment towards the Gardener for speaking of Richard's failings, the Queen says, 'Pray God the plants thou graft'st may never grow' (*R2* 3.4.101). Responding to Henry V's steady march through French territory, the Dauphin urges action against the feeble offspring of their Norman progenitors:

> *O Dieu vivant!* shall a few sprays of us,
> The emptying of our fathers' luxury,
> Our scions, put in wild and savage stock,
> Spirit up so suddenly into the clouds
> And overlook their grafters?

The Duke of Britain drives home the point: 'Normans, but bastard Normans, Norman bastards!' (*H5* 3.5.5–10). Horticultural practice aims to achieve what the Dauphin sees as perverse; fine, productive plants are the product of grafting less vigorous 'scions' onto sturdy rootstock. Playing his part in Richard Gloucester's scheme to gain the crown, Buckingham rehearses the illegitimacy of Edward IV and his offspring, feigning that the 'royal house' will be subject to 'the corruption of a blemish'd stock/.../Her royal stock graft with ignoble plants' (*R3* 3.7.122–7). The ravished Lucrece determines to commit suicide rather than risk her husband's humiliation by nurturing Tarquin's offspring: 'This bastard graff shall never come to growth./He shall not boast who did thy stock pollute,/That thou art doting father of his fruit'(*LUC* 1062–4). In *2H6* this is precisely the accusation directed at York by Suffolk: 'Thy mother took into her blameful bed/Some stern untutor'd churl; and noble stock/Was graft with crab-tree slip, whose fruit thou art' (3.2.212–14). Figurative uses are occasionally oblique. The discreet articulacy of Bertram's father is praised by The King of France: 'his plausive words/He scatter'd not in ears, but grafted them,/To grow there and to bear' (*AWW* 1.2.53–5). Dissatisfied that Camillo refuses to confirm his suspicions, Leontes declares that his servant is dishonest, cowardly, 'or else thou must be counted/A servant grafted in my serious trust/And therein negligent' (*WT* 1.2.245–7). The implication is that if Camillo is loyal to his master he has been remiss. Testing Macduff's integrity, Malcolm affects to be more iniquitous than Macbeth: 'in whom I know/All the particulars of vice so grafted/That, when they shall be open'd, black Macbeth/Will seem as pure as snow' (*MAC* 4.3.50–3).

'Ingrafted' as a deeply ingrained feature of character or personality is propounded by Regan – 'he hath ever but slenderly known himself' – and Goneril when they collude to keep Lear in check: 'The best and soundest of his time hath been but rash; then must we look from his age to receive not alone the imperfections of long-ingraff'd condition, but therewithal the unruly waywardness that infirm and choleric years bring with them' (*LR* 1.1.293–9). Accepting Iago's misrepresentation of Cassio as a confirmed drunkard, Montano observes, 'And 'tis great pity that the noble Moor/Should hazard such a place as his own second/With one of an ingraft infirmity' (*OTH* 2.3.138–40). What is 'ingrafted' is irremovable. Opposing Brutus' decision to allow Antony to survive the assassination of Caesar, Cassius says, 'Yet I fear him,/For in the ingrafted love he bears to Caesar' (*JC* 2.1.183–4). The choice of word is instructive: the worldly Cassius is emotionally attuned – as his love of Brutus is later to prove (4.3.85–162). Poins confirms Hal's suspicion that a display of sorrow respecting his father's illness would be perceived as hypocrisy: 'because you have been so lewd and so much engraff'd to Falstaff' (*2H4* 2.2.62–3). It is an accusation made earlier by his father who interprets Hal's behaviour as retribution for the usurpation:

> Tell me else,
> Could such inordinate and low desires,
> Such poor, such bare, such lewd, such mean attempts,
> Such barren pleasures, rude society,
> As thou art match'd withal and grafted to,
> Accompany the greatness of thy blood,
> And hold their level with thy princely heart?
>
> *(1H4 3.2.11–17)*

The copious diction indicates incredulity at the behaviour of the heir apparent, his commitment to vice driven home by the phrase 'match'd withal and grafted to'. The Doctor, evaluating the strange imaginings of the Jailer's Daughter, ponders, 'How she continues this fancy! 'Tis not an engraff'd madness, but a most thick and profound melancholy' (*TNK* 4.3.48–50). This may be a fine distinction, but his diagnosis seems to be that her obsession has manifested itself in depression and is not a mental fracture which is irredeemable. Arden 3 (284) sees the distinction as one 'between psychosis (madness)' and 'obsessive neurosis sometimes called *melancholy*'.

(C) The old gentleman draws a comparison between the **husbandman**'s care in grafting and the importance of good parenting, while Euphues sees grafting as unnatural: 'you graft by art, which nothing touches nature' (Lyly 1580: 36, 39). Greene introduces the sexual language of grafting when he compares a girl's readiness for marriage to the making of a graft (1580–3, vol. 2, *Mamillia*: 36). Bosola makes a sly sexual insinuation that grafting is morally dubious; the Duchess demurs, claiming it is 'the bettering of nature'. Bosola's horticultural knowledge is flawed as he suggests that a pippin could be grafted when it was usually grown from seed (Webster 1613, *Malfi*, 2.1.149–52). The new books on gardening include many pages on grafting tools and techniques: Mascall's *Book of the Art and Maner, How to Plante and Graffe All Sortes of Trees* ran into 13 editions between 1569 and 1656. Sim (1997) records that Henry VIII's fruiterer, Richard Harris, introduced new grafts from the continent in 1533 to improve the existing range of fruit. See Ellerbeck (2011) for a historic and thematic exploration of grafting.

grain (A) Singly, grain is the **seed** of a **plant**; collectively it refers to cereal plants. It is also another word for **grape**. The politics of grain were particularly important in times of **crop** failure and food shortage. Grain is the detritus left after the malting process; figuratively it suggests any small particle as in a grain of sand. In the dyeing process, from the old French *graine* for kermes, grains were the dried bodies of scale insects found on Mediterranean kermes **oaks** (*Quercus coccifera* L.). They were used in early modern medical practice and as a source of red dye, whence 'in grain' which was short for 'dyed in grain', indicated a scarlet colour for cloth. Grain can also mean an uneven surface, with the natural arrangement of a hard material such as wood having rough parallel lines which makes any division or cutting along the line of the grain an easier process than cutting across it. Going against the grain suggests contrariness or a deliberate refusal to accept the more natural, easier way. Grain is used in proverbs to suggest both food and of minute size.

(B) 'Grain' as the embryo of life, seed, fruition, insignificantly small yet vital, gains abundant expression both literally and metaphorically. The grain of timber acquires imaginative significance. Grain as a basic requirement receives considerable attention; as seed-corn it is referred to by Antony during his seminar on Egyptian agriculture delivered to his fellow triumvirs: 'The higher Nilus swells,/The more it promises; as it ebbs, the seedsman/Upon the slime and ooze scatters his grain,/And shortly comes to harvest' (*ANT* 2.7.20–3). The word 'grain' in its socio-political role in society reverberates throughout *COR*. The plebeians' grievances dominate the opening of the play. The First Citizen protests that the patricians 'Suffer us to famish, and their store-houses cramm'd with grain' (1.1.80–1). In *MAC* its metaphorical use animates a play continually engaged with the process of growth and fruition. Turning to the Weird Sisters, who have promised so much to Macbeth, Banquo demands, 'If you can look into the seeds of time,/And say which grain will grow, and which will not,/Speak then to me' (1.3.58–60). The grain in timber receives remarkable expression on two occasions. In *TRO* Agamemnon, by way of analogy, rationalizes the Greeks' failure to make progress in the war:

> Checks and disasters
> Grow in the veins of actions highest rear'd,
> As knots, by the conflux of meeting sap,
> Infects the sound pine, and diverts his grain
> Tortive and errant from his course of growth.

(1.3.5–9)

Less elaborate but more dramatic is Aufidius' welcome to his old enemy, Caius Martius: 'Let me twine/Mine arms about that body, where against/My grained ash an hundred times hath broke/And scarr'd the moon with splinters' (*COR* 4.5.106–9). The same play gives rise to the first recorded use of a telling commonplace, 'against the grain', that continues to play a role in everyday discourse. Sicinius, a conniving tribune, advises the plebeians to prevaricate when revoking their support for Coriolanus' elevation to consulship: 'Say...that your minds,/Preoccupied with what you rather must do/Than what you should, made you against the grain/To voice him consul' (2.3.229–34). At the close of *ERR* Egeon addresses the wrong son when attempting to confirm his identity: 'Though now this grained face of mine be hid/In sap-consuming winter's drizzled snow' (5.1.312–13). Arden 2 (102) suggests, 'furrowed, lined like the grain of wood'.

Grain as something insignificantly small arises several times. Attempting to dissuade Hubert from putting out his eyes, Young Arthur pleads: 'O heaven! that there were but a mote in yours,/A grain, a dust, a gnat, a wandering hair,/Any annoyance in that precious sense!' (*JN* 4.1.91–3). Political concerns are foremost when Exeter warns the French that Henry V is transformed from his 'greener days': 'Now he weighs time/Even to the utmost grain' (*H5* 2.4.136–8). The Duke in *MM*, attempting to prepare Claudio for death, enters on a philosophical appraisal of mortality: 'Thou art not thyself,/For thou exists on many a thousand grains/That issue out of dust' (3.1.19–21). The least straightforward case arises in *WT* where Antigonus defends Hermione against Leontes' accusation of infidelity: 'If it be so,/We need no grave to bury honesty,/There's not a grain of it the face to sweeten/Of the whole dungy earth' (2.1.154–7). Both proverbial examples intimating 'deep-dyed' pertain to comic moments. Viola/Cesario responding to the removal of Olivia's veil comments tartly, 'Excellently done, if God did all', provoking the response, ''Tis in grain, sir, 'twill endure wind and weather' (*TN* 1.5.236–8). Dromio, pursued by the greasy kitchen maid, rebuffs his master's consolatory comment – 'that's a fault that water will mend' – with the riposte, 'No, sir, 'tis in grain, Noah's flood could not do it' (*ERR* 3.2.105–7).

(C) Stow (1604: 405) includes the Queen's 1586 proclamation for relief of the poor after a bad harvest and shortage of grain exacerbated by hoarding. Exports were prohibited. For Drayton (1622) grain represents crops and wealth, and symbolizes the **fertility** of the **land**. Spier and Anderson (1985) observe that Shakespeare's references to farming 'are frequent, knowledgeable and often vivid'.

grape (A) The **fruit** of the **vine**, *Vitis vinifera,* grape was a synonym for wine, an alternative name for a **berry**, and metaphorically indicated fruit in general. It was probably a Roman introduction into England, and its cultivation may have survived within the warmth of monastery **walls**. **Vineyards** are also recorded in early modern times. Iconographically, the grape referenced Dionysus/Bacchus, the god of wine, the celebrations associated with his cult being at best wild, sometimes orgiastic. As the Greek word for grape also meant unripe or sexually immature, there were possibilities for a play on words. Metaphorically grape could indicate sourness, deception, temptation, as well as refer to Aesop's fable of the fox and the grapes. The grape later acquired a wide range of Christian associations. Drinking wine was seen as good for the health, vine **leaves** were eaten, and wine was used in medical compounds. Dried grapes or **raisins** were a relatively new import.

(B) The grape as wine is a notable manifestation of pleasure in *ANT* where luxury, indulgence and sensuality are ubiquitous. The song accompanying the dance on Pompey's galley – a scene not found in Plutarch or other known sources – celebrates this potent contributor to festivity, fellowship and forgetfulness:

> Come, thou monarch of the vine,
> Plumpy Bacchus with pink eyne!
> In thy fats our cares be drown'd,
> With thy grapes our hairs be crown'd,
> Cup us till the world go round,
>
> *(2.7.113–17)*

Significantly, these carousers have to cajole the ultimate winner of this enmity, Octavius Caesar, 'The universal landlord' (3.13.72), to take a second cup of wine. More sombre, but retaining the sensation of luxuriating, is Cleopatra's declaration as she prepares for suicide: 'Now no more/The juice of Egypt's grape shall moist this lip' (5.2.281–2). The antithesis of this perspective is articulated by Timon as he curses the parasitic bandits: 'Go, suck the subtle blood o'th'grape./Till the high fever seethe your blood to froth' (*TIM* 4.3.429–30). In *MND* this fruit is among the luxuries provided to pamper Bottom: 'Feed him with apricocks and dewberries,/With purple grapes, green figs, and mulberries' (3.1.166–7). This is the only occasion when the colour of the grape is indicated, though in *TNK* the complexion of one of the tournament heroes is described as, 'a ripe grape, ruddy' (4.2.96). Having failed in his endeavour to placate the exiled Coriolanus, Menenius describes his intransigence. He portrays the former Roman hero as impervious to pleas or sentiment: 'The tartness of his face sours ripe grapes' (*COR* 5.4.17–18). Very different in feeling and circumstance is Lafew's teasing rebuke to the King for declining a remedy for his apparently incurable illness: 'O, will you eat/ No grapes, my royal fox? Yes, but you will/My noble grapes, and if my royal fox/ Could reach them' (*AWW* 2.1.69–72). In the belief that at last one of the young men chosen by Helena appears to want her, a relieved Lafew exclaims, 'There's one grape yet; I am sure thy father drunk wine' (2.3.99–100). Riverside (551) points out, '"Good wine makes good blood" was proverbial'. Responding to Roderigo's assessment of Desdemona, 'she's full of most bless'd condition', Iago demurs: 'Bless'd fig's-end! The wine she drinks is made of grapes' (*OTH* 2.1.249–52). Tarquin, contemplating the rape of Lucrece, evaluates his intended action and poses the rhetorical question, 'For one sweet grape who will the vine destroy?' (*LUC* 215). The description of Venus having Adonis in her grasp but failing to stir his passions is likened to 'poor birds, deceiv'd with painted grapes' (*VEN* 601). Typical of the tendency to give names to rooms in taverns is the reference in *MM* to the 'Bunch of Grapes' (2.1.129).

(C) Contemporary writers including Erasmus (1536) and Cogan (1584) give details of viticulture, which was largely sourced from classical writers. Buckingham's great palace at Thornbury Castle, Gloucestershire, demonstrates the existence of domestic vineyards in the sixteenth century. Their survival is confirmed by Bullein (1595) who says that while most grapes grow in the 'south parts of the world', he has seen them at Blaxhall, Suffolk, where he was vicar. Lyly's old gentleman reflects their biblical imagery: 'Is it possible to gather grapes of thorns, or figs of thistles, or to cause anything to strive against Nature?' (1580, *Euphues*: 39). Parkinson (1629) recognizes the problems of grape cultivation in England, claiming that vines were formerly grown much more widely, He gives new ways of preserving them for use during the winter, noting that John Tradescant grows 20 varieties. They were an easy visual image to reproduce in needlework and embroidery, and Trevelyon (1608) includes a number of vine patterns. For commentary on English viticulture see Tigner (2012: 84). Chancellor (1982: 36) notes 'The vine, its fruit and the wine made from it are mentioned constantly in the Bible ... The grape vine is the first cultivated plant to be recorded in the Bible'.

grass (A) A seasonal summer **crop,** grass indicates herbage in general for fodder or pasture; botanically it is any **plant** belonging to the family *Poaceae*. Grass can designate **land** on which grass is the permanent crop; it is a **garden** plant in its own right. As a generic, grass grows quickly and can recover from excessive treading or drought, so it symbolizes strength and regeneration; as a summer crop it represents seasonal sufficiency. Figuratively it can suggest extremes from luxuriant growth to poverty: it served as human sustenance in times of famine. To be mown down like grass carries the sub-text of extreme brutality, and man's life as grass suggests impermanence. Iconographically a grassy, **flower**-covered **meadow** can imply paradise.

(B) Grass is an indicator of the condition of an environment. Gonzalo attempts to encourage the survivors of the tempest by pointing out, 'How lush and lusty the grass looks! How green!' (*TMP* 2.1.53–4). Here is a place full of promise. The opposite extreme is visualized by Suffolk when railing against his exile: 'Well could I curse away a winter's night,/Though standing naked on a mountain top,/Where biting cold would never let grass grow' (*2H6* 3.2.335–7). The word is used to signify herbage when the famished Jack Cade enters Iden's garden: 'Wherefore, on a brick wall have I climb'd into this garden, to see if I can eat grass, or pick a sallet' (4.10.6–8). Rebuked for failing to distinguish between different kinds of herbs, Lavatch responds 'I am no great Nebuchadnezzar, sir, I have not much skill in grass' (*AWW* 4.5.20–1). This verbal engagement centres on the contrast between plants used for **salads** and those grown for **scent**. Nebuchadnezzar reputedly 'did eat grass as the oxen' (*Luke*). There is also a play on homonyms, 'grass' and 'grace'. The King of Navarre, disguised as a Russian, endeavours to secure a dance with the Princess of France: 'Say to her we have measur'd many miles,/To tread a measure with her on the grass' (*LLL* 5.2.184–5). The parkland where the ladies have been billeted is sufficiently manicured to afford comfortable dancing.

Pastureland is threatened with desecration in *R2*. Richard, resisting Bolingbroke's intended usurpation, warns Northumberland that the inevitable bloodshed will, 'Change the complexion of her maid-pale peace/To scarlet indignation, and bedew/Her pasters' grass with faithful English blood' (3.3.98–100). Richard is responding to the green/ red contrast employed earlier by his adversary who affects apprehension that 'such a crimson tempest should bedrench/The fresh green lap of fair King Richard's land' (3.3.46–7). England's land/earth/soil is venerated throughout this play, its green grass assimilating and expressing this spiritual dimension. In *H5* the Bishop of Ely uses grass as an analogy to explain the sudden transformation of the wayward Prince to the formidable King:

> And so the Prince obscur'd his contemplation
> Under the veil of wildness, which (no doubt)
> Grew like the summer grass, fastest by night,
> Unseen, yet crescive in his faculty.
>
> *(1.1.63–6)*

The hero himself resorts to the grass metaphor, though with brutal inversion, when he warns the governor of Harfleur what awaits his citizens if he does not surrender immediately:

> And the flesh'd soldier, rough and hard of heart,
> In liberty of bloody hand, shall range,
> With conscience wide as hell, mowing like grass
> Your fresh fair virgins and you flow'ring infants.
>
> *(3.3.11–14)*

In *TIT,* a play that continually draws on representations and images of landscape, Saturninus expresses his fears in a rare moment of sensibility: 'These tidings nip me, and I hang the head/As flowers with frost, or grass beat down with storms' (4.4.70–1). A lighter note is struck in *VEN*. Inviting Adonis to explore her, Venus describes her body in terms of parkland: 'Sweet bottom grass and high delightful plain,/Round rising hillocks, brakes obscure and rough' (236–7).

(C) Colonna (1499) pictures a world full of beauty with flowery grass, including the innocence of the flowers, people tumbling on **fragrant** flowers and rolling on grassy **ground**, and a level meadow of fragrant grass in a potent mixture of Edenic purity and considerable sexual suggestiveness. Stubbes (1585: 127) expressed indignation when the poor were reduced to eating grass as a result of the policy of enclosure: 'For these inclosures bee the causes why riche men eate upp poore men, as beastes dooe eate grasse. These, I saye, are the caterpillars and devouring locusts that massacre the poore.' Greene suggests good grass might be a source of envy and possible appropriation, writing of a rich farmer coveting the poor man's grass-bearing pasture (1592, vol. 11, *A Quip*: 284). For Drayton (1622) grass is symbolic of luxuriant growth and **fertile land**, providing banquets for animals, and clothing the river **bank**. Christianson (2005) includes a later map of Whitehall Palace, which suggests that there were a series of grass squares or 'plats' in the garden. Dent (1981: G422, 423).

green (A) The colour was associated with spring and pasture, and it could suggest vitality, love and cleanliness. Green also indicated ill-health, fear and contempt, and was a metaphor for youth, immaturity, rawness and indiscipline. It had an extensive range of literal and metaphorical uses. 'Green-eyed' indicated jealousy, and 'green-sickness' was thought to be due to sexual frustration, the cure for which was marriage. Green carried connotations of Englishness; the wild man who welcomed the Queen to entertainments was often dressed in green as the colour of **nature**, **woods** and the wild, recalling legends of the Green Man and Robin Hood.

(B) The vitalizing relationship between greenness and spring is exhibited on several occasions. One of the most invigorating is Titus' early morning summons: 'The hunt is up, the morn is bright and grey,/The fields are fragrant and the woods are green' (*TIT* 2.2.1–2). In the very next scene Tamora, too, celebrates the morning: 'The green leaves quiver with the cooling wind/And make a checker'd shadow on the ground' (2.3.14–15). *SON* 33 opens with a similar thrill at the morning's prospect: 'Kissing with golden face the meadows green,/Gilding pale streams with heavenly alcumy' (3–4). Green as greensward is alluded to in *MND*. The seasonal chaos caused by conflict in the fairy kingdom impinges even on the mortals' games: 'The nine men's morris is fill'd up with mud,/And the quaint mazes in the wanton green,/For lack of tread, are undistinguishable' (2.1.98–100). Riverside (261) points out 'the nine men's morris' is 'the turf marked with squares on which the rustic game of this name was played' and explains 'quaint mazes' as a 'complicated pattern of paths to be traced rapidly by a line of boys as sport'. Arden 2 (33) defines 'quaint' as 'ingeniously elaborated' and 'wanton' as 'luxuriant, rank, (*OED*'s earliest instance of this sense)'. The connection between green as the colour of love and 'Green-sleeves' is apparent in Falstaff's invocation as he prepares for his assignation with the merry wives: 'Let the sky rain potatoes; let it thunder to the tune of "Green-sleeves", hail kissing-comfits, and snow eringoes' (*WIV* 5.5.18–20). There is comic irony in a situation where Falstaff portrays himself as a young lover while summoning the aid of 'kissing-comfits' to sweeten his breath and much needed aphrodisiacs ('potatoes' and 'eringoes'). A more youthful suitor, Henry V, disavows the ability to undertake courtship like a moonstruck young lover: 'before God, Kate, I cannot look greenly, nor gasp out my eloquence' (*H5* 5.2.142–3).

Edward III, intent on seducing the Countess of Salisbury, confides to Lodowick: 'Then in the summer arbor sit by me,/Make it our council house, our cabinet:/Since green our thoughts, green be the conventicle' (*E3* 2.1.61–3). 'Green indeed is the color of lovers' says the lovesick Don Armado in response to Moth's assurance that Delilah's complexion (skin or temperament) was 'Of the sea-water green' (*LLL* 1.2.82–6). One of Moth's allusions is probably to the 'green-sickness', a form of anaemia ascribed at the time to a debility afflicting young women and curable by marriage. Juliet's father is impatient with what he perceives as the foolish intransigence of a young virgin: 'Out, you green-sickness carrion!' (*ROM* 3.5.156). Timon damns all forms of order, natural and social, with the plea, 'To general filths/Convert o'th'instant, green virginity!/Do't in your parents' eyes!' (*TIM* 4.1.6–8).

The connection between green and immaturity is captured succinctly by Exeter when responding to the Dauphin's assessment of Henry V: 'be assur'd, you'll find a difference,/As we his subjects have in wonder found,/Between the promise of his greener days/And these he masters now'(*H5* 2.4.134–7). Endowed with the formalities and accoutrements of chivalry the Black Prince responds, 'This honor you have done me animates/And cheers my green yet-scarce-appearing strength/With comfortable good-presaging signs' (*E3* 3.3.207–9). Having proposed that a 'little train' be sent for the young princes, Buckingham's justification is, 'lest by a multitude/The new-heal'd wound of malice should break out,/Which would be so much the more dangerous,/By how much the estate is green and yet ungovern'd' (*R3* 2.2.120–7). As there is an interregnum, both the accord and the state are green. Moreover, in accepting this argument Rivers refers to the 'compact': 'Yet since it is but green, it should be put/To no apparent likelihood of breach' (133–6). Queen Elinor advises her son John to come to an arrangement with the French so that they withdraw their support for young Arthur: 'That yon green boy shall have no sun to ripe/The bloom that promiseth a mighty fruit' (*JN* 2.1.472–3). Green as naïve, unworldly, is particularly significant in the political sphere. Pandulph, the Pope's legate, inducting Lewis of France into the arts of intrigue, mocks his fears: 'How green you are and fresh in this old world!' (3.4.144–5). As shrewd and ruthless a political figure as Claudius indicts himself for being inept and naïve with respect to handling Polonius' death and funeral: 'and we have done but greenly/In hugger-mugger to inter him' (*HAM* 4.5.83–4). This play also provides a non-political example when Polonius chides Ophelia for taking Hamlet's protestations of love at face value: 'You speak like a green girl,/Unsifted in such perilous circumstance' (1.3.101–2). The sense of 'fresh' is present when a cynical Claudius refers to the dead King. He begins his masterpiece of political rhetoric with: 'Though yet of Hamlet our dear brother's death/The memory be green' (1.2.1–2). Juliet contemplates the terror of waking up in the family tomb, 'Where bloody Tybalt, yet but green in earth,/Lies fest'ring in his shroud' (*ROM* 4.3.42–3). The biblical implication is present in Mistress Quickly's description of Falstaff's dying moments: ''a babbl'd of green fields' (*H5* 2.3.16–17). There are two references to 'green-eyed'. Reacting to Bassanio's choice of casket Portia voices relief: 'How all the other passions fleet to air,/As doubtful thoughts,

and rash-embrac'd despair,/And shudd'ring fear, and green-eyed jealousy!' (*MV* 3.2.
108–10). Even as he is inciting Othello's jealousy the calculating Iago cautions, 'O,
beware, my lord, of jealousy!/It is the green-ey'd monster which doth mock/The meat
it feeds on' (*OTH* 3.3.165–7).

(C) Greene offers the standard remedy of marriage and sex for green-sickness
(1580–3, vol. 2, *Mamillia*: 46). Stubbes (1585) sees green as the colour of licentiousness
and debauchery associated with May Day. Puttenham (1589) includes the metaphor of
a child as a green **twig** in contrast to an old man as a decayed **oak**. The Elvetham entertainment for the Queen in 1591 featured an extensive green iconography: it included
a temporary green **bower** strewn with fresh green **rushes**, eight hundred square feet
of snail mount with four circles of green **hedges**, and an address by a poet dressed in
green (Nichols 1788). Drayton (1622) uses green as the colour of summer, fertility and
growth. Parkinson (1629) recommends planting green **herbs** in **knot gardens,** and
includes a chapter on the care of evergreen trees, suggesting that many of them are
tender and require protection in winter. Chlorosis or green-sickness was actually linked
to iron deficiency; for a detailed exposition of green-sickness see Iyengar (2011: 152–4).

ground (A) The **earth,** as opposed to heaven, sea or air, personal space, ground
can also be **land** attached to a building, lands and **fields** in general, and **soil.** It can
indicate the possessor or occupier of that ground or the portion of land under tenanted
occupation. A sense of loss or waste accompanies **fruit** falling to the ground. It could
also be used metaphorically.

(B) Given the frequency with which the word appears, its horticultural applications
are surprisingly few. Going into exile, Bolingbroke's reverence is for something more
abstract than the medium for nurturing **plants**: 'Then England's ground, farewell, sweet
soil, adieu,/My mother, and my nurse, that bears me yet!' (*R2* 1.3.306–7). 'Ground' as
territory is signified by the Captain who describes the Norwegian assault on Poland
as a misadventure: 'We go to gain a little patch of ground/That hath in it no profit but
the name./To pay five ducats, five, I would not farm it' (*HAM* 4.4.18–20). 'Ground' as
country is implied by the First Lord in *PER*. Eager to secure the return of Pericles, he
urges Helicanus: 'if the Prince do live, let us salute him,/Or know the ground's made
happy by his breath./If in the world he live, we'll seek him out' (2.4.27–9). A difference
of opinion with Brutus, likely to escalate and to further demoralize the soldiers, leads
Cassius to direct Pindarus, 'Bid our commanders lead their charges off/A little from this
ground' (*JC* 4.2.47–9). This is a holding ground, not an arena of military conflict. Iago
is referring to battlegrounds when complaining of Cassio's preferment by Othello: 'And
I, of whom his eyes had seen the proof/At Rhodes, at Cyprus, and on other grounds/
Christen'd and heathen, must be belee'd and calm'd' (*OTH* 1.1.28–30). 'Ground' as
property arises in *WIV*. Ford, disguised as Brook, tells how his love for a married
woman has been thwarted: 'Like a fair house built on another man's ground, so that
I have lost my edifice by mistaking the place where I erected it' (2.2.215–7). Burial
ground, which figures with considerable frequency, is depicted vividly and simply by

Ophelia: 'I cannot choose but weep to think they would lay him i'th'cold ground' (*HAM* 4.5.69–70). Ophelia's own burial is a source of contention. The priest is intransigent when justifying her 'maimed rites': 'Her death was doubtful,/And but that the great command o'ersways the order,/She should in ground unsanctified been lodg'd/Till the last trumpet' (5.1.219–30).

The word offers a rich source for metaphor. Antony, addressing the conspirators in *JC*, expresses awareness of his predicament: 'alas, what shall I say?/My credit now stands on such slippery ground/That one of two bad ways you must conceit me,/Either a coward or a flatterer' (3.1.190–3). Ground as military advantage is implied by Iachimo's metaphor when boasting to Posthumus: 'With five times so much conversation, I should get ground of your fair mistress; make her go back, even to the yielding' (*CYM* 1.4.103–5). Boult, the brothel keeper in *PER*, confidently asserts that Marina's resolve will be broken: 'And if she were a thornier piece of ground than she is, she shall be plough'd' (4.6.144–5). Mowbray is dismayed when informed that Northumberland will not be joining the rebel forces: 'Thus do the hopes we have in him touch ground/And dash themselves to pieces' (*2H4* 4.1.17–18). Later in the play Henry IV advises his sons how to contend with Hal when he becomes king: 'being moody, give him time and scope,/Till that his passions, like a whale on ground,/Confound themselves with working' (4.4.39–41). Buckingham employs an interesting use when priming Richard Gloucester in the art of accepting the crown with reluctance: 'And look you get a prayer-book in your hand,/And stand between two churchmen, good my lord –/For on that ground I'll make a holy descant' (*R3* 3.7.47–9). Arden 3 (294) explains 'ground' here as 'melody upon which the descant or melodious variation is raised'. Foundation is the sense in *LLL* when Berowne invokes women as the source of enlightenment: 'From women's eyes this doctrine I derive:/They are the ground, the books, the academes,/From whence doth spring the true Promethean fire' (4.3.298–300). Cleon, Governor of Tharsus, is presiding over a desperate famine when he receives news of an approaching fleet, which he suspects is hostile. His dejected response is: 'What need we fear?/Our ground's the lowest, and we are half way there' (*PER* 1.4.77–8).

(C) Early modern gardening manuals use ground as a synonym for earth, soil and land when giving instructions on how to manage and improve private ground. Plat (1654) makes extensive reference to preparing the ground, earth or soil for **sowing** and planting by **digging**, **weeding** and **manuring**. Drayton (1622) uses ground variously, as earth, a sea or river as in 'watery ground', an individually named county, the basis of an idea, a foreign land, an estate, an uncultivated piece of land, hallowed-ground, solid ground. He writes of **tilling** the ground, and suggests the possibility of diving through the ground to end up in hell. His ground is usually qualified, as mossy, raised, watery, stony, well-watered, worthy, and he sees Eden as 'th'imparadized ground', a return to the original perfect **garden**.

grove (A) A small **wood**, a clump of **trees** affording **shade**, a grove could be planted to form an avenue or to screen a **walk**; it could be a natural feature, or deliberately planted and a sign of cultivation. Groves were originally planted to honour a deity, with many of **cypresses** or **myrtles** for Diana as goddess of the hunt. A grove might be welcoming or threatening, offering both cover to hunted animals, and to the hunter to surprise his prey. In a **garden** it could provide a shady, secluded place for a variety of purposes including political scheming, assignations and sexual liaisons.

(B) *MND* has the most references. Puck explains that as a result of the quarrel over the Indian boy, Oberon and Titania 'never meet in grove or green,/By fountain clear, or spangled starlight sheen,/But they do square' (2.1.28–30). Alighting on the fractious young lovers, Oberon determines that the disdainful Demetrius will soon dote on Helena: 'Fare thee well, nymph. Ere he do leave this grove,/Thou shalt fly him, and he shall seek thy love' (2.1.245–6). Engaging in his first verbal duel with Kate, Petruchio draws on the grove's connection with Diana: 'Did ever Dian so become a grove/As Kate this chamber with her princely gait?' (*SHR* 2.1.258–9). Accepting Gloucester's challenge to a duel the Cardinal designates a venue: 'And if thou dar'st,/This evening, on the east side of the grove' (*2H6* 2.1.41–2). In *COR* Aufidius gives instructions where he is to be found: 'I am attended at the cypress grove' (1.10.30). When the 'grove' is qualified it usually takes on a specific meaning. The 'cypress' is usually associated with death though in this case it is probably just a geographical marker. The melancholic Romeo is observed by Benvolio, 'underneath a grove of sycamore' (*ROM* 1.1.121). This location takes on significance because the sycamore symbolizes love-sickness. Quite different, but equally portentous is its role in *VEN*. The Goddess bids good-morrow to the sun, and then 'she hasteth to a myrtle grove' (865) justly fearing Adonis will fall victim to the boar. The myrtle's symbolic identification with love and joy is fused with its other role in mythology as the death tree. The opening lines from the final stanza of *PP* celebrate the myrtle grove as a natural venue for festive release: 'As it fell upon a day,/In the merry month of May,/Sitting in a pleasant shade,/Which a grove of myrtles made' (20.1–4). A French mariner perceives the English fleet seen at a distance as resembling 'a grove of wither'd pines' (*E3* 3.1.66). Acknowledging Westmorland's account of Hotspur's achievements, the King's response, though acquiescent, is ambivalent:

> Yea, there thou mak'st me sad, and mak'st me sin
> In envy that my Lord Northumberland
> Should be the father to so blest a son –
> A son who is the theme of honor's tongue,
> Amongst a grove the very straightest plant,
> Who is sweet Fortune's minion and her pride,
>
> *(1H4 1.1.78–83)*

(C) Groves were a recurring feature of Renaissance **gardens**, sometimes retaining their dedication to Diana and planted with the same varieties of trees. Hentzner (1598) comments on the groves ornamented with trellis work at Nonsuch, which Waldstein (1600) describes as beautified by topiary work. He specifies one particular grove, dedicated to Diana, with a temple and **fountain**. Peacham (1612) suggests groves should be impenetrable to the eyes of those outside. According to Drayton (1622), groves could be delicious places where the birds sang, dark homes for Druids, meeting places for King Arthur's knights, provide cover for huntsmen emulating Diana, or a playground for nymphs.

grow (A) To demonstrate life by natural vegetative processes, put out **leaves** and **flowers**. In both animals and immaterial things, to grow is to come into existence, or to increase in size by natural development. To grow can be to increase in numbers, degree, or size, or in a specific quality, or to presume upon or take liberties in a relationship. Growth is an indicator of life in a human or **plant**, suggesting the start of life, the germinating of **seed**, or the emergence of a plant from the **ground**.

(B) Metaphors based on growing, flowering and **weeding** are abundant, and there are several literal references to plant growth. Fluellen reminds Henry V how the **leek** became a national emblem during the campaign of the Black Prince: 'the Welshmen did good service in a garden where leeks did grow' (*H5* 4.7.98–9). *MAC* is the source of numerous metaphorical applications. Banquo challenges the Weird Sisters: 'If you can look into the seeds of time,/And say which grain will grow, and which will not,/Speak then to me' (1.3.58–60). Thanking the returning heroes, Duncan exclaims, 'I have begun to plant thee, and will labor/To make thee full of growing'. Banquo's elegant response continues the metaphor: 'There if I grow,/The harvest is your own' (1.4.28–33). Equally refined is Edward III's gratitude for the support he receives for his impending French campaign: 'This counsel, Artois, like to fruitful showers,/Hath added growth unto my dignity' (*E3* 1.1.42–3). The song in the opening scene in *TNK* has the couplet, 'Oxlips, in their cradles growing,/Marigolds on death-beds blowing' (10–11). Arcite, mindful of the deprivation imprisonment will bring, complains, 'The vine shall grow, but we shall never see it' (2.2.43). Emilia, the blameless cause of the deadly strife between Arcite and Palamon, proclaims at Diana's altar, 'If well inspir'd, this battle shall confound/Both these brave knights, and I, a virgin flow'r,/Must grow alone, unpluck'd' (5.1.166–8). A picturesque example occurs in *CYM*. Complaining of intrusion during her farewell to Posthumus, Imogen says:

> ere I could
> Give him that parting kiss which I had set
> Betwixt two charming words, comes in my father,
> And like the tyrannous breathing of the north
> Shakes all our buds from growing.
>
> *(1.3.33–7)*

Hamlet, reviling the burgeoning corruption of his world, reflects ''tis an unweeded garden/That grows to seed, things rank and gross in nature/Possess it merely' (*HAM* 1.2.135–7). Attempting to explain the long years of failure to overcome the Trojans, Agamemnon employs a rarefied analogy:

> Checks and disasters
> Grow in the veins of actions highest rear'd,
> As knots, by the conflux of meeting sap,
> Infects the sound pine, and diverts his grain
> Tortive and errant from his course of growth.
>
> *(TRO 1.3.5–9)*

(C) In gardening books 'grow' is employed literally. Hill (1577) provides details of the best growing conditions for many domestic plants as well as including their growth habits. Markham (1613) performs a similar analysis for **field crops**. Spurgeon (1935) comments on Shakespeare's use of grow and growth, noting his tendency to think of human affairs in terms of growing plants and **trees**, which is especially marked in times of stress and emotion, and the recurrent imagery of growth and destruction of trees in the historical plays.

H

hade Hade, hadeland, or sometimes the still current headland: an obsolete term for the strip of **land** left unploughed as a boundary line, or as means of access between two **ploughed** areas of a **field**. It can also signify a **grassy** margin giving space for the plough to turn, or land that has been left fallow. As workaday matters and preparations for the entertainment of Falstaff commingle in Shallow's Gloucestershire orchard, Davy inquires of his master, 'and again, sir, shall we sow the hade land with red wheat?' (*2H4* 5.1.14–15). The implication is that they have already ploughed the hade land – almost certainly a piece previously left fallow – and a decision is awaited for choice of **sowing**. This scene of bucolic bustle embraces the minutiae of verbal and physical traffic. Davy even manages to achieve a piece of petty corruption by securing a promise from Shallow that his friend, the 'arrant knave' Visor, will 'have no wrong' (41–52). Tusser (1573) uses 'hedlond' for mowing the grass. Drayton appears to suggest the hade is more pasture than an unused strip of land: 'And on the lower Leas, as on the higher Hades/The daintie Clover growes (of grasse the onely silke)' (1622, *Polyolbion* 12, 400–1). Perhaps drawing on Drayton, Nares (1859) argues that it is a Saxon word for high pasture.

hardock Sometimes 'hoardock', this is the only recorded use of what appears to be a coarse **weed**. Possible botanical identifications include great burdock, *Arctium lappa* L., a member of *Rumex* L. the **dock** family, and charlock or wild mustard, *Sinapis arvensis* L. Its single appearance and first recorded use is in *LR*. Cordelia describes the mad Lear, 'Crown'd with rank femiter and furrow-weeds,/With hardocks, hemlock, nettles, cuckoo-flow'rs' (4.4.3–4). The 'crown' is perhaps an emblem of humility. Ryden (1978: 56) suggests Shakespeare invented the word 'hordock', using 'hor' or 'hoar' meaning hoary, grey or white to qualify dock. Sprinkle-Jackson (1989) and Bate (2009) consider that Shakespeare meant charlock, wild mustard, *Sinapis arvensis* L. which would be a more suitable component of a coronet. But as Heath points out in his analysis of the weeds in Lear's crown, this would be unlikely because there is no suggestion of hardock as an alternative name at the time. Heath (2003: 108–9) notes the double meaning of all Lear's weeds, suggesting the function of hardock/burdock was to protect against bites and stings which would make sense in the context. Mabey (2010: 155–8) observes 'From the mid-seventeenth century, Shakespeare's despised "hardocks", the expansive, floppy-leaved, adhesive-fruited burdock, began to feature in landscape paintings … It was the first weed to be credited with some kind of artistic – or architectural – beauty.' He also notes that 'burdock has no specific symbolism'.

harebell The consensus suggests Shakespeare was not referring to the harebell, *Campanula rotundifolia* L., but to the wild bluebell, *Hyacinthoides non-scripta* L. Chouard ex Rothm, at the time known as 'wild hyacinth' whose vernacular name was 'harebell'. Having discovered the seemingly dead Fidele/Imogen, Arviragus announces his intention to **strew** the grave with **flowers**: 'Thou shalt not lack/The flower that's like thy face, pale primrose, nor/The azur'd harebell, like thy veins' (*CYM* 4.2.220–2). The 'azur'd harebell' is a vital agent: visually and aurally its influence is accentuated by the rhythmic movement of the passage. The harebell flowers in mid-late summer, which adds weight to the identification as bluebell which would be in flower with the **primrose.** Barnfield (1593, Ault 1949) has the 'harebell' (presumably 'bluebell') growing with primrose, **cowslip** and **daffodil.** Drayton (1622) records harebells growing extensively in the Oxfordshire countryside. He includes them in his **wreath** of flowers. Gerard (1597: 111) has an illustration of the bluebell which he calls 'the blew Hare-bels or English Iacinth'. Ryden (1978: 51) notes 'in Shakespeare's time *harebell* was applied to the wild hyacinth, *Endymion non-scriptus* L., Garcke, nowadays usually named *bluebell*'. He suggests that 'In his description of the flower-colour of the plant Shakespeare may possibly have been influenced by Lyte' (1578), who refers to 'Hyacinthes' as 'of colour most commonly blew lyke azure'.

harrow A heavy frame of timber or iron, a harrow is drawn over **ploughed land** to break it up, loosen **weeds** and prepare the **ground** for **sowing seed**. To harrow is to break up, crush or pulverize, to cover the seed with **earth**. By extension it is to wound someone's feelings or greatly distress them. The harrowing of hell was frequently depicted in paintings of the Last Judgement. Anticipating the appeals of his mother, wife and son on behalf of the Romans, Coriolanus, poised with the Volscian army and aching for revenge, muses: 'Let the Volsces/Plough Rome and harrow Italy, I'll never/ Be such a gosling to obey instinct' (*COR* 5.3.33–5). He does, however, surrender to instinct, but his twin-vision of agriculture and warfare is illuminating. The warrior, who reveres the battlefield while disdaining menial labour, regards these agricultural imple-ments as physically coercive rather than as instruments of production. The Ghost warns Hamlet, 'I could a tale unfold whose lightest word/Would harrow up thy soul, freeze thy young blood' (*HAM* 1.5.15–16). By its mere appearance the spectre has already created an emotional tension. In the opening scene Horatio confesses to Barnardo, 'it harrows me with fear and wonder' (1.1.44–5). Although the *OED* makes no connection between the use of harrow in farming, and the medieval religious concept of the harrowing of hell, it seems unlikely the two ideas were completely separated. Markham (1613) includes considerable detail on harrows and the process of harrowing the land, illus-trating the tool's components and design with precise measurements.

harvest (A) The reaping and gathering in of ripened **grain**, or other products for human or animal consumption whether directly for the producer or as a saleable commodity. The harvest was an integral part of early modern rural life, its quality affecting the lives of all. It can also indicate harvest-time, autumn, or the process of ageing before the onset of old age. Harvest-home celebrated the final gathering of the **crop**, while a metaphorical early harvest can suggest premature death. A harvestman was a labourer, particularly one who left home to bring in the harvest. Figuratively, harvest can be the fruit or product of an action or effort.

(B) An extensive and elaborate celebration of harvest forms part of the nuptial blessing given by Ceres: 'Spring come to you at the farthest/In the very end of harvest!' (*TMP* 4.1.114–15). In a very different kind of celebration on board Pompey's galley, Antony delivers a commentary on Egyptian agriculture: 'The higher Nilus swells,/The more it promises; as it ebbs, the seedsman/Upon the slime and ooze scatters his grain,/And shortly comes to harvest' (*ANT* 2.7.20–3). Figurative uses are numerous. Having regained Rouen for the French by disguising her soldiers as peasants carrying **corn**, Joan Pucelle, mocking her English adversaries, provokes Burgundy's riposte: 'Scoff on, vile fiend and shameless courtezan!/I trust ere long to choke thee with thine own,/And make thee curse the harvest of that corn' (*1H6* 3.2.45–7). York anticipates that on his return from Ireland he will capitalize on the confusion created by the Kentish rebel, Jack Cade: 'And reap the harvest which that rascal sow'd' (*2H6* 3.1.381). Buckingham, even as he conspires to secure the throne for Richard Gloucester, cynically commiserates with the family and friends of the deceased Edward IV: 'Though we have spent our harvest of this king,/We are to reap the harvest of his son' (*R3* 2.2.115–16). The wounded Audley anticipates his imminent demise when asking to be taken to Edward III: 'I'll smile and tell him that this open scar/Doth end the harvest of his Audley's war' (*E3* 4.8.9–10). Harvest-home is used twice. In his colourful account of why he refused to hand over prisoners to the King's representative, Hotspur describes a pristine dandy who accosted him at the end of the battle: 'neat and trimly dress'd,/Fresh as a bridegroom, and his chin new reap'd/Show'd like a stubble-land at harvest-home' (*1H4* 1.3.33–5). This image is a piquant element in a flamboyant narration. Outlining his plan to seduce Mistress Ford, Falstaff confides to her disguised husband, 'I will use her as the key of the cuckoldly rogue's coffer, and there's my harvest-home' (*WIV* 2.2.273–5). The hard-earned reward for a season's endeavour is devalued to ill-gotten gain by the parasitic old knight – though this 'harvest-home' reaps no reward. The harvest-man figures in an unexpected context. The mother of Caius Martius reassures her daughter-on-law, Virgilia, that her husband will overcome Rome's arch enemy: 'His bloody brow/With his mail'd hand then wiping, forth he goes,/Like to a harvest-man that's task'd to mow/Or all or lose his hire' (*COR* 1.3.34–7). That the formidable Volumnia should draw on imagery of a piece-worker in agriculture is surprising given the patrician contempt shown by both mother and son towards manual labour.

(C) Tusser (1573) emphasizes the importance of preparation for the harvest in August, detailing the particulars of each crop, saying the 'harvest lord' should be paid more than the other workmen, and the harvest should end in a good feast. Spier and Anderson (1985) observe that Shakespeare's references to farming 'are frequent, knowledgeable and often vivid'. On his English travels, Hentzner (1598: 79) witnessed such a harvest-home between Windsor and Staines, noting the last load was crowned with **flowers**, with a richly dressed figure which he supposed might represent Ceres. Hoskins (1964) emphasizes the economic effects of bad harvests particularly in the 1590s.

hawthorn (A) *Crataegus monogyna* Jacq. is a small, widely-distributed native **tree** or **shrub** with sharp **thorns**, which often served as a **hedging plant**. For country people the emergence of its **buds** heralded spring, its **flowers** the may-flower, because they were out for the May Day celebrations, hence the vernacular name of 'may'. The abundant thorns gave rise to the country name of thorn or white-thorn. Hawthorn still has a range of medical uses. It was considered a magic tree attracting many country superstitions, possibly because it was long-living and often stood on its own, sometimes being the only tree in grassland. As a result it was closely associated with shepherds for whom it could provide shelter; by extension the hawthorn was associated with a pastoral life.

(B) The celebratory nature of the plant through its association with springtime and love is evident in *MND*. Helena, feeling eclipsed by Hermia, complains: 'Your eyes are lodestars, and your tongue's sweet air/More tuneable than lark to shepherd's ear/When wheat is green, when hawthorn buds appear' (1.1.183–5). The disguised Rosalind teases Orlando, 'There is a man haunts the forest, that abuses our young plants with carving "Rosalind" on their barks; hangs odes upon hawthorns, and elegies on brambles' (*AYL* 3.2.359–62). Justifying his forthright approach to courtship the autumnal Falstaff declares to Mistress Ford, 'Come, I cannot cog and say thou art this and that, like a many of these lisping hawthorn buds, that come like women in men's apparel, and smell like Bucklersbury in simple time – I cannot' (*WIV* 3.3.70–3). The pastoral dimension is expressed by Henry VI as he compares the life of the shepherd with that of a king:

> Gives not the hawthorn bush a sweeter shade
> To shepherds looking on their silly sheep
> Than doth a rich embroider'd canopy
> To kings that fear their subjects' treachery?
>
> *(3H6 2.5.42–5)*

This plant in its wintry aspect finds expression in Edgar's anguished cry: 'Through the sharp hawthorn blow the cold winds' (*LR* 3.4.46–7) – a line repeated later (98).

(C) The hawthorn's association with magic since antiquity makes its presence in *MND* particularly apposite. Sackville (1563) gives its loss of leaves as a marker of winter. For Braithwaite its thorns symbolized the rape of Philomel, when he writes of the nightingale with hawthorn pressed to her breast (c. 1619, both Ault 1949). As the holy thorn of Glastonbury, it was thought to offer protection against witchcraft, lightning and disease. Walsham (2011) records the Puritan attacks on the Glastonbury thorn, suggesting the survival of belief in its magico-religious powers. Mabey (1996) provides details of its historical and continuing folklore associations.

hay The primary meaning is dried **grass** used for animal fodder or bedding. 'Hay' or 'hey' also refers to a country dance and to 'home thrust' in fencing. As the Witches in *MAC* respond to a slight by heaping curses on a sailor, one vows, 'I'll drain him dry as hay' (1.3.18). The Fool in *LR* alludes to a man who 'in pure kindness to his horse butter'd his hay' (2.4.125–6). Equally bizarre is the report of the Jailer's Daughter in *TNK* of a clever horse possessing 'A very fair hand, and casts himself th'accounts/Of all his hay and provender' (5.2.58–9). Autolycus sings of engaging in sexual frolics or 'tumbling in the hay' (*WT* 4.3.12). The transformed Bottom discovers new culinary tastes: 'Methinks I have a great desire for a bottle of hay. Good hay, sweet hay hath no fellow' (*MND* 4.1.32–4). There is a metaphorical use in *3H6*. Edward IV sensing a critical moment in the conflict with the resurgent Queen Margaret and Warwick cries out, 'The sun shines hot, and, if we use delay,/Cold biting winter mars our hop'd for hay' (4.8.60–1). In *E3* Warwick reluctantly fulfilling his promise to importune his daughter on behalf of the King argues, 'The sun that withers hay doth nourish grass;/The King that would disdain thee will advance thee' (2.1.390–1). 'Disdain' means to defile or dishonour. Aaron the Moor makes the only reference to 'haystalks', including it in the list of iniquities he has not managed to accomplish: 'Set fire on barns and haystalks in the night/And bid the owners quench them with their tears' (*TIT* 5.1.133–4). Constable Dull makes the sole mention of the dance (*LLL* 5.1.154). Mercutio has the distinction of making the only allusion to the 'home thrust' in fencing (*ROM* 2.4.26).

hazel (A) *Corylus avellana* L. a wild native **shrub** of hedgerows, scrub and woodland. It was cultivated for **hedging**, wattle fencing and **nuts.** The **coppiced** stems were used for charcoal. Their particularly flexible quality made them suitable to be used in dowsing for water, giving rise to the idea that hazel had magic powers. Its nuts, known as **filberts** when cultivated, were food for both man and foraging animals. Hazel had some medical and cosmetic applications.

(B) Mercutio's fantasy of Queen Mab celebrates the fairy's carriage: 'Her chariot is an empty hazel-nut,/Made by the joiner squirrel or old grub,/Time out a'mind the fairies' coachmakers' (*ROM* 1.4.59–61). The same character wittily upbraids the peace-maker Benvolio for being quarrelsome: 'Thou wilt quarrel with a man for cracking nuts, having no other reason but because thou hast hazel eyes' (3.1.18–20). Another madcap is responsible for the remaining jocular reference. Petruchio, in the famous courtship scene, elevates the plant when praising Katherine: 'Kate like the hazel-twig/Is straight and slender, and as brown in hue/As hazel-nuts, and sweeter than the kernels' (*SHR* 2.1.253–5). Salisbury recounts the situation of the Black Prince surrounded by the French forces as 'A hazel wand amidst a wood of pines' (*E3* 5.1.142).

(C) Cogan (1584) advises students not to eat hazels as they cause wind and vomiting; Heresbach (1596) regards them only as forage for animals. Mabey (1996) details its cultivation, use and folk-lore. Christianson (2005) includes the very considerable numbers – from hundreds to tens of thousands – of plants including hazel **slips** ordered for Hampton Court to stabilize embankments in the Pond Garden and moat edges.

heath Open, uncultivated **land,** or wasteland naturally covered with low growing **plants** and **shrubs,** including the **heath,** heather or ling plant, *Calluna vulgaris* L. and bell heather *Erica cinera* L. Heath also indicated a cultivated area of the **garden** carefully contrived to look wild and untamed. All three references relate to **barren ground.** The Second Witch confirms that their next meeting will be 'Upon the heath' (*MAC* 1.1.6), but when the encounter occurs Macbeth refers to 'this blasted heath' (1.3.77). Fearful of drowning, Gonzalo cries, 'Now would I give a thousand furlongs of sea for an acre of barren ground, long heath, brown furze, anything' (*TMP* 1.1.65–7). The heather or ling plant is almost certainly intimated here. The juxta-position of heath and **furze** is particularly apposite as they have similar ecological requirements. Turner (1551) notes the plant was used to treat snake-bite, possibly by association of ideas as some native snakes live on heath-land. Peacham (1612) writes of humility as an unproductive world overgrown with heath and **moss,** both of which symbolize the wild and uncultivated. Drayton's (1622) heaths are natural wild places, but Bacon (1625) includes a cultivated heath as the central part of his ideal garden.

hebona (A) A poisonous **plant,** hebona is variously glossed as **ebony,** family *Ebenaceae,* **yew,** *Taxus baccata* L., or most likely henbane, *Hyoscyamus niger* L. The last was also called 'insane', and so was possibly identical with '**insane root'.** Other suggestions include deadly nightshade, *Atropa belladonna* L., from its old English name of enoron, and **hemlock,** *Conium maculatum* L. Compelling arguments point to henbane, but both **yew** and deadly nightshade, known for their toxicity and ready avail-ability, are possible candidates. Ebony was not native, was less available, and generally was used as a resin thereby making **distillation** most unlikely.

(B) Used only once the lethal nature of this insidious plant is described in detail by the Ghost of Old Hamlet:

> Upon my secure hour thy uncle stole,
> With juice of cursed hebona in a vial,
> And in the porches of my ears did pour
> The leprous distillment, whose effect
> Holds such an enmity with blood of man
> That swift as quicksilver it courses through
> The natural gates and alleys of the body,
> And with a sudden vigor it doth posset
> And curd, like eager droppings into milk,
> The thin and wholesome blood. So did it mine,
> And a most instant tetter bark'd about,
> Most lazar-like, with vile and loathsome crust
> All my smooth body.

(HAM 1.5.61–73)

The remarkable feature of this clinical exposition is the image of a deadly substance corrupting the blood and skin. No other poison receives such vivid consideration. The poisoning, perpetrated in a virtually sanctified space, the orchard, is emblematic of the body politic.

(C) Bartholomeus calls hebona 'insane', suggesting the epithet would have been recognized at the time (1582: 99). Parkinson (1640) gives the medicinal properties of henbane, including the use of oil pressed from its **seeds** for earache, so its aural application was not peculiar and would not have excited interest. Administration of drugs either by ear or via another bodily orifice was not uncommon: Sir Thomas Overbury was poisoned by an enema in 1615. A pharmacologist, Macht (1918; 1949) argues cogently in favour of henbane. He gives the main possibilities as yew, henbane, ebony, hemlock and deadly nightshade, reasoning that the serious contenders are yew and henbane, and noting there is no evidence that yew was ever administered aurally. Ryden (1978: 53) believes 'In selecting this plant word Shakespeare followed a literary tradition; his "juice of cursed hebenon/hebona" reflects Marlowe's "jouyce of Hebon" in *The Jew of Malta* (3.4.)'. Writing from a medical perspective, Kail (1986) thinks hebona is probably henbane. Heath (2003) points out that later in the play Ophelia incorporates **nettles** into her garland, which could refer back to henbane as hebona, as nettles provided a rare antidote to the toxicity of henbane. For extensive discussion on this topic see Tigner (2012: 92–7).

hedge (A) A row of **bushes, shrubs** or small **trees,** a hedge could be planted as a barrier or boundary, or to provide a decorative and productive feature in formal **gardens**. Extensive, well-clipped hedging could form a **maze**, divide different parts of the garden, or form the knots for a **knot** garden. 'Hedge' features in many vernacular phrases. Hedge can be used metaphorically in relation not only to land, but to an island hedged or fenced by the sea. A hedge can exclude as well as enclose.

(B) The importance of well-maintained hedges is evidenced in two significant situations in the history plays. The condition of the French countryside subsequent to the invasion of Henry V is described by Burgundy: 'her hedges even-pleach'd,/Like prisoners wildly overgrown with hair,/Put forth disorder'd twigs'; the neglect, a consequence of the disruption of economic life, is ubiquitous: 'all our vineyards, fallows, meads, and hedges,/Defective in their natures, grow to wildness' (*H5* 5.2.42–55). A gardener in *R2,* required to be scrupulous in his horticultural practices, is exasperated by the monarch's failure to follow these principles: 'the whole land,/Is full of weeds, her fairest flowers chok'd up,/Her fruit-trees all unprun'd, her hedges ruin'd' (3.4.43–5). The countryside hedgerow is alluded to by Don John who expresses distaste for courting his brother's approval: 'I had rather be a canker in a hedge than a rose in his grace' (*ADO* 1.2.27–8). The hedge as useful for drying laundry is implied by Falstaff when reflecting that his ragged recruits will 'find linen enough on every hedge' (*1H4* 4.2.47–8). Autolycus refers to 'The white sheet bleaching on the hedge' (*WT* 4.3.5); later the hedge provides a convenient screen for him to urinate. He tells the shepherds,

'I will but look upon the hedge, and follow you' (4.4.825–6). The hedgerow affording sustenance in extremity is illustrated by Antony's response to hunger as he crossed the Alps with his defeated army. Octavius Caesar recalls Antony's endurance as a model of Roman fortitude: 'thy palate then did deign/The roughest berry on the rudest hedge;/Yea, like the stag, when snow the pasture sheets,/The barks of trees thou brows'd' (*ANT* 1.4.63–6).

Austria, extravagant in his pledge of support for young Arthur against King John, celebrates England's natural defence: 'Even till that England, hedg'd in with the main,/That water-walled bulwark, still secure/And confident from foreign purposes' (*JN* 2.1.26–8). To be hedged-in, however, is not always beneficial. During the famous quarrel scene in *JC* the defensive Cassius cautions his angry brother-in-arms, 'Brutus, bait not me,/I'll not endure it. You forget yourself/To hedge me in' (4.3.28–30). In this context the term implies constraint. For Falstaff 'to hedge' is to manoeuvre disreputably or dishonestly. Vociferating against Pistol's unwillingness to act as go-between, he exclaims, 'You stand upon your honor!… I myself sometimes, leaving the fear of God on the left hand, and hiding mine honor in mine necessity, am fain to shuffle, to hedge, and to lurch' (*WIV* 2.2.20–5). The copious diction of the last line draws this indignation to a richly comic conclusion, as 'shuffle' means to engage in underhand dealing, while 'lurch' signifies stealing or pilfering. Falstaff's modern-day counterpart, minimizing his disreputable actions, would admit to having to 'duck and dive'. When Helen insists that the reluctant Pandarus sing a song in lieu of the entertainment he has disrupted, she is blocking his attempt at prevarication: 'Nay, this shall not hedge us out, we'll hear you sing, certainly' (*TRO* 3.1.60–1). The association of a hedge with poverty is found in *2H6*. Dick responds to Cade's assertion that he is 'of an honorable house', with the comment, 'Ay, by my faith, the field is honorable, and there he was born, under a hedge; for his father had never a house but the cage' (4.2.49–52). Talbot, indicting Sir John Fastolfe for cowardice, proposes that he be stripped of his honours: 'And should (if I were worthy to be judge)/Be quite degraded, like a hedge-born swain/That doth presume to boast of gentle blood' (*1H6* 4.1.42–4). There are two references to 'hedge-corner' as a marker to designate a locale (*SHR* Ind.1.20 and *AWW* 4.1.2).

(C) Andrews (1993) cites the 1650 Parliamentary Survey of Theobalds, recording the details of the great garden as being double the size of Hampton Court, the knot gardens comprising nine large gardens or knots all laid out with low hedges, the whole surrounded by another hedge. The survey shows that the entire garden was surrounded by thorn hedges which were inter-planted with several hundred **sycamore**, **lime** and **elm** trees, giving an idea of the scale and length of the hedging. Mabey (1996) provides a historical background. Dent (1981: H361.1).

hemlock (A) *Conium maculatum* L. is found on damp, waste ground. It is of the same family as **carrot**, **fennel**, **parsnip** and cow **parsley**, and possibly identical with keck, kex or **kecksies**. Hemlock was long known to be extremely toxic, and thought to act more quickly if taken in wine: it may have been the poison self-administered by Socrates. Its spotted stem, suggesting its poisonous nature, marks it out from other plants in the same family. If administered in minute doses it is a sedative, and can dry up breast milk. It can counteract other poisons, but the smallest overdose may result in paralysis, or death. Attracting a number of superstitions and traditions in folklore, like many poisons it was associated with the devil and witchcraft. It was credited with power over aspects of sexuality. Hemlock was not cultivated in **gardens**, but always gathered from the wild, being considered more powerful if dug up at night.

(B) The sinister associations of the plant come to the fore during the incantation of the Third Witch in *MAC*. Among the human and animal fragments thrown into the cauldron is 'Root of hemlock digg'd i'th'dark' (4.1.25). The crown worn by the mad Lear includes, 'hardocks, hemlock, nettles, cuckoo-flow'rs' (*LR* 4.4.4). This crown represents an inversion of majesty. The inclusion of hemlock may be a quest to improve 'eyesight', an acknowledgement of poor judgement emanating from an island of awareness in a sea of madness. The varying and contradictory possibilities may well reflect Lear's fractured mind. The third reference to hemlock arises in Burgundy's description of the weed-infested and disordered state of French agriculture in the wake of Henry V's invasion: 'her fallow leas/The darnel, hemlock, and rank femetary/Doth root upon' (*H5* 5.2.44–6).

(C) Chancellor (1982: 38) describing the plant as 'about five feet tall, with fine, fern-like leaves and tiny white flowers on top of branching stems' notes that the biblical references to hemlock, wormwood or gall symbolized 'bitter calamity and misfortune' which would seem to be apposite to Lear. Riddle (1992) suggests hemlock was used in England in the sixteenth century as an abortifacient. Tusser (1573) combines hemlock with some of the other **weeds** which appear in Lear's crown by suggesting that **grass**, **thistle**, **bur**, **mustard seed**, **mallow** and **nettles** are 'very ill neighbours' and inimical to farmers. Contemporary literature reflects the dangers of hemlock. Heath (2003) links the weeds in Lear's crown, and notes that they all have uses to treat sight and sexual problems. Tigner (2012: 110) quotes Turner's opinion that hemlock 'is good to put unto eye medicines to quenche the ache withal' and observes that even though hemlock is poisonous Lear's crown also contains an antidote to its toxicity, for nettles, according to Gerard, 'remedie against the venmous qualitie of hemlock'.

hemp (A) *Cannabis sativa* L. is a widely distributed introduction from west and central Asia, cultivated for its fibre; it is remarkable in that the female **plant** is much longer-lived than the male. With the expansion of the navy it was much in demand and so grown widely as a **crop**. Hemp fibre was made into sailcloth, sacks, cords and ropes, notably the hangman's rope. It was woven into coarse fabric which was generally despised by those who could afford better material, with 'hempen' suggesting rusticity. Hemp has a long history of medical use.

(B) Making a plea for clemency on behalf of Bardolph, Pistol exclaims, 'Let gallows gape for dog, let man go free,/And let not hemp his windpipe suffocate' (*H5* 3.6.42–3). The less lethal use of the plant also occurs in this play. The Chorus directs the audience back again to France after Henry's triumphant return to England: 'Play with your fancies: and in them behold/Upon the hempen tackle ship-boys climbing' (3 Cho. 7–8). The rustic signification is encountered in *MND* with Puck's amused disparagement of the mechanicals: 'What hempen home-spuns have we swagg'ring here,/So near the cradle of the Fairy Queen?' (3.1.77–8). The single use of 'hempseed' is attributable to the Hostess in *2H4* who, in the midst of a fracas, denounces Falstaff as 'thou hempseed!' (2.1.58). She means 'gallows-bird', someone destined for hanging.

(C) In an extensive chapter on the use of wool, hemp, flax and cloth, Markham (1631) emphasizes that working with hemp was for women. Drayton suggests hemp drained the soil of nutrients: 'for hemp most hugely rank,/Doth bear away the best', but he cites it as an important crop in the rich earth of Lincolnshire (1622, *Polyolbion*: 2.27–8, 25.3). Mabey (1996) notes its modern revival as a crop. Mcleod (2008) observes that it was a valuable medieval crop providing rope, sailcloth and the very hard-wearing hempen homespun cloth.

hep More commonly 'hips', heps are the **fruit** of the native wild or dog **rose**, *Rosa canina* L., and by extension the fruit of all roses; they symbolized fruitfulness and abundance. The dog rose is widely distributed in most hedgerows, scrub-land and woodland borders. The only mention is in *TIM*. Justifying their rapacity in terms of 'want', the thieves are admonished by Timon who extols **nature's** prodigality: 'The oaks bear mast, the briers scarlet heps;/The bounteous huswife Nature on each bush/ Lays her full mess before you. Want? why want?' (4.3.419–21). During this phase of living in the wild, Timon's misanthropic rage is countered by a refined appreciation of the natural world in all its beauty and abundance. Gerard (1597) says children eat heps or **berries** and make them into chains for decoration; he adds that they can be cooked in tarts. They were easy to reproduce in needlework and so featured in embroidery patterns including Trevelyon's 1608 pattern book.

herb, herb-woman (A) A generic term for any useful **plant**, more specifically herbs are those whose **leaves**, stems or **flowers** have culinary or medicinal attributes, or which were valued for their **smell**. Distinctions were not made between herb, vegetable and flower. Raw green food was regarded with suspicion, so many of the herbs now used uncooked were added in the cooking process. They were seen as nourishing in themselves rather than simply adding flavour. The proficient housewife and cook had an encyclopaedic knowledge of which herbs provided the best flavouring for, or accompaniment to, any dish; they also added colour and flavour to a bland diet, especially in winter. The new **knot** gardens were filled with **fragrant** herbs; 'nose-herbs' provided an all important sweet-smelling environment, whether as freshly-**strewn** herbs and **rushes** on the floor, or in a **pomander**, particularly when negotiating the stinking streets of London. Herbs were supplied to **apothecaries** by the herb-women who might also fulfil a secondary role of brothel keeper. A 'herbal' was a sixteenth-century word, now obsolete, for a book containing the names and descriptions of herbs, or of plants in general, with their properties and virtues; a treatise on plants. A book containing a collection of botanical specimens was known as a 'herbarium'.

(B) The generic use of the term to cover a range of plants including flowers is apparent in *MND* when Oberon instructs Puck to seek out the flower whose juice has magical powers: 'Fetch me that flow'r; the herb I showed thee once' (2.1.169). Oberon uses the word 'herb' three more times when referring to a flower. Distinctions are made by the narrator in *VEN* when portraying the response of the natural world to Adonis' deadly wound: 'No flow'r was nigh, no grass, herb, leaf, or weed,/But stole his blood, and seem'd with him to bleed' (1055–6). The difference between salad herbs and 'nose herbs', valued for their scent, emerges during a dialogue between Lafew and Lavatch in *AWW*. The former, bewailing the loss of the apparently dead Helena, observes, 'We may pick a thousand sallets ere we light on such another herb', drawing the response, 'Indeed, sir, she was the sweet marjorom of the sallet, or rather the herb of grace'. Lafew then chides the household fool: 'They are not herbs, you knave, they are nose-herbs' (4.5.13–19). The Gardener in *R2* responds to the sorrowful Queen's rebuke with compassion: 'Here did she fall a tear, here in this place/I'll set a bank of rue, sour herb of grace' (3.4.104–5). The young Duke of York expresses anxiety at his spurt of growth because of his uncle Gloucester's maxim, 'Small herbs have grace, great weeds do grow apace' (*R3* 2.4.13). Asserting that human passions are subject to self-control, Iago also deploys analogy during his dialogue with Roderigo: 'Our bodies are our gardens, to the which our wills are gardeners'; to 'supply it with one gender of herbs or distract it with many' (*OTH* 1.3.320–4). Given the wholesome nature of herbs it is curious that 'herb-woman' came to mean bawd or brothel-keeper. The sole use arises in *PER* when Lysimachus, mistaking Marina for a prostitute, explains that her 'principal' is 'your herb-woman, she that sets seeds and roots of shame and iniquity' (4.6.84–6). Titus' response to Saturninus' cynical offer to release his sons in exchange for a severed hand, is 'such with'red herbs as these/Are meet for plucking up' (*TIT* 3.1.177–8). To lose a hand at his age, Titus rationalizes, is of little consequence. The play's imagery is deeply engaged with plants, especially in association with human limbs.

(C) Herbs were everywhere: Colonna (1499) strews them about **meadow**s, and carpets the ground with herbs. He describes fragrant and magic herbs, and details sweet-smelling herbs for the knot garden. Hill (1577) includes sections on the cultivation of 'physick' and 'fragrant hearbs', while Greene acknowledges the contribution of new publications by commenting on an infinite variety of flowers 'that to know their names and operations I needed some curious herbal' (1592, vol. 11, *A Quip*: 219). Dekker comments on the commercial value of herbs saying that 'only herb-wives and gardeners' did well out of the plague when the price of flowers and herbs rose exponentially (1603, *The Wonderful Year*). Turner places considerable value on the knowledge of women domestically and as gatherers of herbs (cited by Knight (2009)), but Johnson, (1629; 1632: 101) an apothecary himself, is scathing about herb-women and their capabilities. He writes of careless druggists of supreme ignorance who 'to the great peril of their patients, lays himself open to the mockery of the women who deal in roots', calling herb-women greedy, dirty, ignorant and crafty. The proliferation of books on domestic and gardening matters underline the extensive knowledge and use of herbs in early modern times, but much of the information in the herbals came directly from classical sources, reducing their usefulness as many of the plants did not grow in England. Herbals, essentially horticultural and medical treatises about plants, flourished from about 1530 to the mid-seventeenth century, and were among the earliest books on plants published in English. A succinct summary of the place and role of herbals can be found in Elliot, 'The World of the Renaissance Herbal' in Samson (2012: 24–41).

hermit (A) One who from religious motives has retired to a solitary life, a hermit is particularly associated with Christian recluses. The idea is sourced from classical **gardens**; a hermitage in a garden might be a grotto, or gloomy cave, which could be decorated with exotic shells, and include **statues**, or feature water devices to startle the unwary visitor. The hermit in a masque or entertainment represents the untamed world, or **wilderness**, suggesting one who inhabits it from choice rather than necessity or banishment.

(B) Witnessing the death of his uncle Mortimer, after long years of incarceration, Richard Plantagenet compassions: 'In prison hast thou spent a pilgrimage,/And like a hermit overpass'd thy days' (*1H6* 2.5.116–7). Championing Rosaline's beauty, Berowne avows, 'A wither'd hermit, fivescore winters worn,/Might shake off fifty, looking in her eye' (*LLL* 4.3.238–9). At the close of the same play the French Princess postpones acceptance of a marriage proposal from the King of Navarre, declaring, 'Your oath I will not trust, but go with speed/To some forlorn and naked hermitage,/Remote from all the pleasures of the world' (5.2.794–6). *TRO* has a remarkable metaphorical example. Chiding Hector for being recklessly magnanimous on the battlefield Troilus pleads: 'For th'love of all the gods,/Let's leave the hermit pity with our mother'. His plea that for the warrior, pity should be isolated, distanced, and remote is disregarded by Hector whose 'Fool's play' (5.3.43–5) costs him his life. Duke Frederick and Jaques embrace a hermit's life but these 'convertites' (*AYL* 5.4.184) do not use the word 'hermit'.

(C) Drayton writes of the solitary life of the hermit as an escape from society as if it were a regular occurrence: 'Whereas the Hermit leades a sweet retyred life,/From Villages repleate with ragg'd and sweating Clownes,/And from the lothsome ayres of smoky cittied Townes' (1622, *Polyolbion*, 13.164–6). He implies that the hermit is a noble former soldier who has exchanged physical battles for spiritual ones, and suggests such an existence was part of a golden, holy, but mythical, past. In her comprehensive study of the Tudor house and garden, Henderson (2005) gives details of grottos, hermits and hermitages.

hew (A) To cut off, cut down or cut away, to sever, or to bring to the ground. To hew is also to cut off at the **root,** to cut or fell **trees** for use or destruction, to trim to size, to hack at or to strike blows. The term appears in the context of a fight or battle, in the severing of **limbs** of trees and people, and in cutting down trees.

(B) *TIT* and *3H6* have the most references, which is unsurprising given their violent nature and the way in which the human body is perceived as tree-like with limbs that can be cut off. The only literal use occurs in *MAC*. Approaching Birnam Wood, Malcolm instructs his soldiers to adopt camouflage: 'Let every soldier hew him down a bough,/And bear't before him' (5.4.4–5). Describing how York was hacked to death the Messenger informs his sons: 'And many strokes, though with a little axe,/Hews down and fells the hardest-timber'd oak./By many hands your father was subdu'd' (*3H6* 2.1.54–6). Caius Martius also employs an incisive image. Expressing contempt for the inconstant plebeians he rails: 'He that depends/Upon your favors swims with fins of lead,/And hews down oaks with rushes' (*COR* 1.1.179–81). Despite the praises heaped upon Talbot and his son by Burgundy and Joan Pucelle, the Bastard of Orleans responds to the heroes' deaths with the demand, 'Hew them to pieces, hack their bones asunder' (*1H6* 4.7.47) – an action then vetoed by Charles. Preparing to assault the forces of Henry VI and Queen Margaret, George, Duke of Clarence warns, 'We'll never leave till we have hewn thee down' (*3H6* 2.2.168). Later in the same play Richard Gloucester soliloquizes how he will satisfy his craving for the crown by destroying his own family. Visualizing his predicament as someone 'lost in a thorny wood' he is determined to liberate himself: 'And from that torment I will free myself,/Or hew my way out with a bloody axe' (3.2.174–81). In the opening scene of *TIT*, Lucius, son of the eponymous hero, requests permission to perform a Roman ritual: 'Give us the proudest prisoner of the Goths,/That we may hew his limbs and on a pile/*Ad manes fratrum* sacrifice his flesh' (96–8). A little later he adds, 'Let's hew his limbs till they be clean consum'd' (129). This action provokes terrible retribution including the rape and mutilation of Lavinia. Her uncle Marcus, using imagery of compassionate beauty when faced with the sight of his mutilated niece, asks 'what stern ungentle hands/Hath lopp'd and hew'd, and made thy body bare/Of her two branches, those sweet ornaments' (2.4.16–18). Representing the impending assassination of Julius Caesar as an act of noble sacrifice, Brutus deploys imagery of solicitude in an unconscious attempt to sanitize a bloody deed: 'Let's carve him as a dish fit for the gods,/Not hew him as a carcass fit for hounds' (*JC* 2.1.173–4).

(C) Hew appears infrequently: Philautus comments on the effect of time: 'great oaks hewn down with many blows' (1580 Lyly: *Euphues,* 251). Spenser (1596) uses hew to describe blows traded in a fight. For the Roman plays see Thomas (1989) and Chernaik (2011); Foakes (2003) and Leggatt (2005) explore violence.

holly *Ilex aquifolium* L. is a slow-growing, native, evergreen **tree** with spiny **leaves** and red **berries**. Easily trimmed, it is a good **hedging** plant, the spines repelling man and beast. A hard **wood**, holly had only limited practical use, although its leaves, **bark** and berries all had medical applications. The leaves and berries of the holly feature frequently in song, in folklore, in superstition and religious symbolism, especially in relation to Christmas. References to this plant are confined to Amiens' celebratory song performed for the entertainment of the exiled Duke and his companions. The refrain is: 'Heigh-ho, sing heigh-ho! unto the green holly,/Most friendship is feigning, most loving mere folly./Then heigh-ho, the holly!' (*AYL* 2.7.180–2). Evidently the holly embodies a feeling of festive release, and seems also to be associated with fidelity in a world characterized by inconstancy. Moore (1947) details the emergence and significance of the holly and ivy carols in the sixteenth century. Mabey (1996) includes extensive detail of its local use and associations.

honey-stalk See **clover**

honeysuckle (A) *Lonicera periclymenum* L. is a native climbing **plant** of **woods** and **hedges**, with intensely **scented** flowers. It was sometimes called **woodbine,** but woodbine might indicate any climbing plant, whereas honeysuckle described a scented flower. The name was also given to **clover**, trefoil and **eglantine**. Honeysuckle served a wide range of medical purposes. Its growth habit and sensuous scent both became associated with intense love and steadfastness.

(B) A literal reference is to be found in *ADO* when Hero instructs Margaret to lure Beatrice 'into the pleached bower,/Where honeysuckles, ripened by the sun,/Forbid the sun to enter' (3.1.7–9). Here is the perfect place for concealment, eavesdropping and noting. Inviting Bottom to enjoy her embraces, Titania coos reassuringly, 'Sleep thou, and I will wind thee in my arms/.../So doth the woodbine the sweet honeysuckle/ Gently entwist' (*MND* 4.1.40–3). Whatever plant is designated as 'woodbine' it is evidently a natural complement to the sensuous honeysuckle. Acceptance of alternative punctuation (commas after woodbine and honeysuckle) would mean that woodbine *is* the honeysuckle. The cradling of a gross creature like the ass-headed Bottom by the Fairy Queen is discordant enough, but the lyricism and sensuality of the language intensifies the incongruity. A delectable malapropism is forged by Mistress Quickly when she denigrates Falstaff as he attempts to defend himself against the arresting officers: 'Ah, thou honeysuckle villain! wilt thou kill God's officers and the King's?' (*2H4* 2.1.50–1). It is assumed that she means 'homicidal', but the oxymoronic 'honeysuckle villain' captures perfectly his ability to allure and deceive the hostess of the tavern who is soon to forgive him yet again and to sell more of her property to provide him with a further 'loan'.

(C) Turner (1538) conflates 'wod bynde and honysuccles', by giving *periclymenum* for both, as does Le Moyne (1586, ed. Hulton 1977) in his book of botanical illustrations, where the woodcut clearly shows the honeysuckle, although he names it as woodbine. Trevelyon (1608) includes a large number of honeysuckle patterns, confirming its extensive employment in the decorative arts. Markham (1631) appears to indicate two separate plants by including woodbine and honeysuckle in one remedy. Ryden (1978: 81–3) proposes that in *ADO*, 'honeysuckles' might indicate the scented flower and 'woodbine' the woody structure of the plant. He comments perceptively on the ambiguous situation in *MND*. Willes (2011: 86) reproduces the iconic portrait of William Cecil, Lord Burghley, riding on his mule carrying a nosegay of **pinks** and honeysuckle. Heilmeyer (2001: 36) observes that from the Middle Ages 'the honey-suckle was a symbol not only of lasting pleasure, but of permanence and steadfastness'.

hunt (A) The act of hunting or chasing a wild animal is to kill for sport or for food. To hunt is to pursue a wild animal or a person. Hunting was a privileged sport with royal hunting **forests** or **parks** expanding through the middle ages, covering vast swathes of the country, and greatly restricting access for the majority of people. By the early modern period hunting was increasingly recreational. It reflected the greater availability of other food supplies and the growth of leisure activities; it was particularly enjoyed by both Elizabeth and James.

(B) References to the hunt are numerous, both literal and figurative. An elaborate hunting scene that reveals the pleasures and trappings of the sport enjoyed by a wealthy gentleman is found in *SHR*. The Lord's enthusiasm and gratification are intimated by his instruction to his servant:

> Huntsman, I charge thee, tender well my hounds
> (Brach, Merriman, the poor cur, is emboss'd),
> And couple Clouder with the deep-mouth'd brach,
> Saw'st thou not, boy, how Silver made it good
> At the hedge-corner, in the coldest fault?
> I would not lose the dog for twenty pound.
>
> *(Ind.1.16–21)*

In the opening stanza of *VEN* the narrator says of Adonis, 'Rose-cheek'd Adonis hied him to the chase;/Hunting he lov'd, but love he laugh'd to scorn' (3–4). Berowne announces in *LLL*, 'The Princess comes to hunt here in the park' (3.1.164). Everything about this play from the landscape to the language exhibits control, order and elegance. After Theseus and Hippolyta converse enthusiastically about their hunting experiences and the ancestry of Theseus' dogs, the Duke finally decides, 'Our purpos'd hunting shall be set aside' (*MND* 4.1.183). Their conversation, rich in sound and colour, creates a compelling picture of the diverse elements associated with hunting parks. The Duke's proposal – 'We will, fair queen, up to the mountain's top,/ And mark the musical confusion/Of hounds and echo in conjunction' – is accepted with alacrity:

> I was with Hercules and Cadmus once,
> When in a wood of Crete they bay'd the bear
> With hounds of Sparta. Never did I hear
> Such gallant chiding; for besides the groves,
> The skies, the fountains, every region near
> Seem all one mutual cry. I never heard
> So musical a discord, such sweet thunder.
>
> *(4.1.106–18)*

Here is a sense of an integrated landscape satisfying physical and aesthetic aspirations, the repeated use of oxymoron embodying a major theme of the play: harmony arising out of conflict. Oblivious to the guile and malice of Saturninus and Tamora, Titus invites them 'To hunt the panther and the hart with me' (*TIT* 1.1.493). As they set out, Titus paints a scene of expectation and beauty: 'The hunt is up, the morn is bright and grey,/The fields are fragrant and the woods are green' (2.2.1–2). Demetrius, anticipating rape and murder, mocks such enthusiasm: 'Chiron we hunt not, we, with horse nor hound,/But hope to pluck a dainty doe to ground' (2.2.25–6). With ten separate mentions, this is the play with the highest number of references to hunting. This activity also figures prominently in *CYM*. Belarius, referring to the carcass, says, 'Boys, we'll go dress our hunt' (3.6.89). The supreme warrior, Caius Martius, preparing for battle against the Volscian hero Aufidius, expresses his readiness in terms of the hunt: 'He is a lion/That I am proud to hunt' (*COR* 1.1.235–6). Edgar is the quarry in *LR*: 'I heard myself proclaim'd,/And by the happy hollow of a tree/Escap'd the hunt' (2.3.1–3).

(C) Hunting both for food and entertainment are occupations as old as man. Raven (1947) says the medieval world revolved round the activities of hunting and hawking, both of which had arcane languages, rules and ceremonies, colouring the world-view of those who participated, and those who were excluded. Hentzner (1598: 76) shows that hunting was both a spectator sport and integrated into the garden. He describes the 380 paces long viewing walk at Windsor 'whence the nobility and persons of distinction can take the pleasure of seeing hunting and hawking in a lawn of sufficient space'. Waldstein (1600: 159) includes the arrangements at Nonsuch for the Queen to participate in the hunt when she was no longer able to ride to hounds: a platform was built where she could sit or stand to shoot at the deer as they were driven past. Henderson (2005) provides details of contemporary and surviving hunting stands, including the elaborate tower built at Chatsworth in 1570. She explains that hunting often provided the impetus for enclosure of land into a park, stimulating the production of many of the early **estate** maps. Vaughan (1617) includes hunting in his list of exercises good for the health. Drayton delivers a lyrical exposition of a stag hunt in the Forest of Arden, employing imagery from the classical and mythological worlds while focusing in detail on the Arden landscape (1622, *Polyolbion*, 13.87–161). The *OED* notes that the Franchise of Park Act, which gave the right to keep and hunt animals on a particular piece of land, was only removed from the statute book in 1971. Fletcher (2011) provides an account of deer parks.

husbandry (A) The administration of a house and **land**, food production and the materials concerned in all these operations were covered by the concept of husbandry. It included responsibility for land under cultivation, and management of both house and outside space. Husbandry was seen as a masculine occupation, the female counterpart being housewifery. Many new gardening books detailed the skills of husbandry, providing a job description for work previously carried out without formalization, and incorporating the new leisure activities in the **garden**. The breadth of skills required in husbandry provided considerable opportunity for analogy and use in emblem books.

(B) The sense of overall management of household affairs is apparent in *MV*. Portia leaving Belmont appoints a deputy for the administration of her household: 'Lorenzo, I commit into your hands/The husbandry and manage of my house/Until my lord's return' (3.5.24–6). This domestic scene contrasts with the wide sweep of French landscape in *H5*. Describing the neglected condition of agriculture consequent upon Henry V's invasion, Burgundy complains, 'And all her husbandry doth lie on heaps,/Corrupting in its own fertility' (5.2.39–40). Inciting Henry VI to discard Humphrey, Duke of Gloucester, Queen Margaret resorts to horticultural metaphor: 'Now 'tis the spring, and weeds are shallow-rooted;/Suffer them now, and they'll o'ergrow the garden,/And choke the herbs for want of husbandry' (*2H6* 3.1.31–3). Husbandry as responsible horticultural activity is so fundamental to the sensibility of the age that it slips easily into political discourse. A complex comparison between war and industrious agricultural activity arises when Alexander describes Hector leaving at daybreak for the battlefield: 'And like as there were husbandry in war,/Before the sun rose he was harness'd light,/And to the field goes he' (*TRO* 1.2.7–9). In this compressed economic/military juxtaposition of the early-rising farmer with the eager warrior, the harness as armour doubles for the accoutrement of the plough horse; 'field' signifies both **tillage** and battlefield. A particularly fine figurative example appears in *MM*. Lucio informs Isabella that Juliet has been made pregnant by her brother:

> Your brother and his lover have embrac'd.
> As those that feed grow full, as blossoming time
> That from the seedness the bare fallow brings
> To teeming foison, even so her plenteous womb
> Expresseth his full tilth and husbandry.

(1.4.40–4)

The same image recurs in *SON* 3 when the speaker prevails upon the young man to marry and procreate: 'For where is she so fair whose unear'd womb/Disdains the tillage of thy husbandry?' (5–6). Husbandry signifying careful nurturing of resources finds expression in Banquo's beautiful conceit to his son Fleance when accounting for the starless night: 'There's husbandry in heaven,/Their candles are all out' (*MAC* 2.1.4–5).

(C) Fitzherbert (1533) is clear that husbandry is biblically ordained, being concerned with land management, rather than partnership in marriage. In Lyly (1580: 102) Euphues compares good husbandry to the hard work needed to make one's way in the world; he draws an analogy between the schoolmaster and the husbandman, giving parallels between teaching, and tilling and **grafting**. Harrison (1938) shows the breadth of meaning of husbandry, referencing an Act of Parliament of 1598 concerning the decay of towns and of husbandry, and another for maintenance of tillage and husbandry. Peacham (1612) instances the husbandman's skills to demonstrate the need for discipline:

> The Husband good, that by experience knows,
> With cunning skill, to prune, and when to plant,
> Must lop the Tree where ranck aboundance growes,
> As well as helpe the barren in her want:

(192–5)

McRae (1996) emphasises the role of the new agricultural literature, particularly Fitzherbert (1533) and Tusser (1570), in improving husbandry, suggesting that they saw good husbandry as a justification for property ownership.

As he lived as a husbandman, it is appropriate that Markham (1613) provides the most comprehensive overview of the work of husbandry. Leslie and Raylor (1992) consider the culture of the contemporary husbandry manuals. Bushnell (2003) sets husbandry in the context of the nature-culture debate of the time.

husk, draff The dried outside covering of certain **fruits** and **seeds**, collectively **chaff**. By extension and figuratively husk and draff could suggest the outside or external part of anything, generally with a sense of worthlessness and roughness, in contrast to the value contained therein. The husk is what is left by the pigs when foraging; draff is also the dregs or lees fed to pigs. During the opening collision with his oppressive brother, Orlando complains, 'Shall I keep your hogs and eat husks with them? What prodigal portion have I spent, that I should come to such penury?' (*AYL* 1.1.37–9). Falstaff's recruits are even more impoverished. These conscripts lack the means to buy out their service: 'you would think that I had a hundred and fifty totter'd prodigals lately come from swine-keeping, from eating draff and husks' (*1H4* 4.2.33–5). The same contempt is expressed by the Constable of France when contemplating the English soldiers before the battle of Agincourt: 'Do but behold yond poor and starved band,/And your fair show shall suck away their souls,/Leaving them but the shales and husks of men' (*H5* 4.2.16–18). The movement from the literal to the metaphorical lends peculiar force to this representation. Even more remarkable is Agamemnon's welcome to Hector on his visit to the Greek camp. Exhibiting a rare flight of imagination he seeks to isolate the present moment from the contamination of the past and the future: 'What's past and what's to come is strew'd with husks/And formless ruin of oblivion' (*TRO* 4.5.166–7). The landscape that resides outside the present is made visually bleak by this image. The disparaged 'husk' has proved to be of significant worth to the dramatist.

hyssop (A) *Hyssopus officinalis* L., an aromatic evergreen native of southern Europe was introduced into England, and by the mid-fifteenth century featured in lists of cultivated **plants**. It served medicinal and culinary purposes, and is a bitter-tasting **herb** which added flavouring to soups and stews. Hyssop was often planted with **thyme,** particularly in **knot gardens**, as they were thought to stimulate each other's growth. It symbolized penitence and humility.

(B) Reference to this plant is unique to *OTH*. Responding to Roderigo's admission that he is not able to subdue his infatuation with Desdemona, Iago insists, by way of analogy, that all human beings posses such control: 'Our bodies are our gardens, to the which our wills are gardeners; so that if we will plant nettles or sow lettuce, set hyssop and weed up tine, supply it with one gender of herbs or distract it with many, either to have it sterile with idleness or manur'd with industry – why, the power and corrigible authority of this lies in our wills' (1.3.320–6). Ever the improviser, Iago delivers a homily he knows to be spurious as he is a victim of a jealousy that 'Doth (like a poisonous mineral) gnaw my inwards' (2.1.297). The cleansing property of hyssop may well be alluded to in this example thereby intensifying the gap between Iago's moralizing and his own unalterable nature. See **thyme** for consideration of **'tine'**.

(C) Chancellor (1982: 38) cites the psalmist's prayer (Ps. 51.7), 'Purge me with hyssop' as indicative of the 'purificatory use of the plant'. Early medical records of hyssop included its use as a purgative, and for gynaecological conditions (Rowland 1981). Drayton partners hyssop with thyme as **strewing** herbs: 'Cleere Isop, and therewith the comfortable Thyme' (1622, *Polyolbion*, 15.199). Dendle and Touwaide (2008) suggest that with parsley and sage, hyssop was one of the most commonly used herbs to treat the sick. McLeod (2008) includes its culinary uses; she says that it was used as an abortifacient, but that such use was very dangerous.

I

imp (A) A young shoot, **sapling**, sucker, a **scion** or **slip** of a **plant** or **tree**, an imp was used for **grafting**; it could also indicate the graft itself. Figuratively imp can suggest offspring, child of a noble house, boy, young man, or in a derogatory sense fellow; archaically 'to imp' can be to implant or engraft by marriage into a family. Imp can imply a child of the devil, an evil spirit. To imp in falconry means to mend a bird's feathers.

(B) Imp as young shoot translates naturally to a child. Armado refers affectionately to Moth as 'dear imp' (*LLL* 1.2.5). During the play performed for the King's party, Moth as Hercules 'in minority' (5.1.134) is introduced by Holofernes: 'Great Hercules is presented by this imp' (5.2.588). Pistol twice employs imp as scion. At the coronation of Henry V he calls out, 'The heavens thee guard and keep, most royal imp of fame!' (*2H4* 5.5.42). On the eve of the battle of Agincourt, he confides to the disguised monarch: 'The King's a bawcock, and a heart of gold,/A lad of life, an imp of fame' (*H5* 4.1.44–5). Offshoot of noble stock exercises peculiar pressure in the history plays. In *R2*, however, the word is used metaphorically with respect to its separate ornithological significance. Northumberland anticipates that Bolingbroke's impending return from exile will, 'Imp out our country's broken wing,/Redeem from broking pawn the blemish'd crown' (2.1.292–3).

(C) Spenser (1596) uses imp regularly to suggest a child or youth. Heresbach (1596) writes of the ordering of an imp **garden**, so the young trees can be nourished before planting out when they are some two years old. McLean (1981) points out nurseries of young plants were called 'impyards' or 'impgarths'. Thomas (1983: 219) observes that 'Woodmen employed a terminology which was anthropomorphic ... A fruitful cross was called "a wife"; one without seed was a "maiden" or "widow". A young shoot of felled coppice was an "imp" and a tree too old to yield useful timber a "dotard".'

insane root Probably **henbane**: commentators generally choose henbane or **hemlock**, both of which have long been known as highly toxic. Other suggestions include the equally poisonous deadly nightshade, and **mandrake**. Baffled by the mysterious disappearance of the Weird Sisters, Macbeth says, 'What seem'd corporal melted,/As breath into the wind'; eliciting Banquo's uneasy response, 'Were such things here as we do speak about?/Or have we eaten on the insane root/That takes the reason prisoner?' (*MAC* 1.3.81–5). The only *OED* reference for 'insane root' causing insanity is *MAC*. Bartholomeus's description of henbane as 'insana' was rendered 'insane' in the translation of the work into English by Batman, so it is likely that Shakespeare's contemporaries would have understood henbane on hearing 'insane root' (1582: 299). Ryden (1978) cites earlier commentators in support of henbane. Iyengar (2011) considers hemlock the most likely **plant** because it treated epilepsy, which might resonate with the suggestion in *MAC* 3.4.53 that Macbeth was subject to seizures. Arden 2 (17) summarizes the literary and historical commentary on the possible identity of this plant.

iris (A) References are most commonly to *Iris pseudacorus* L., native yellow iris common in wet places or *I. germanica* L., the bearded iris, a **garden plant** occasionally found in the wild. These along with *I. foetisissima* L., the Florentine or stinking iris, a native plant of dry woods and shady **banks** are candidates for **fleur-de-luce** and **flag**. 'Iris' can refer to the Greek goddess, messenger of the gods, to a rainbow-like or iridescent halo of colours, and to the anatomical iris of the membrane of the eye. In Christian iconography and symbolism the rainbow represents pardon and reconciliation.

(B) Both the flower and the rainbow are probably intimated when Ulysses, scheming to curb the arrogance of Achilles, argues, 'that will physic the great Myrmidon,/Who broils in loud applause, and make him fall/His crest that prouder than blue Iris bends' (*TRO* 1.3.377–9). Arden 3 (181) concurs with this likelihood of a double meaning; Riverside (493) and Arden 2 (150) argue that the reference is exclusively to the rainbow. Although not designated 'iris' there is almost certainly a mention of the flower when Octavius Caesar decries the inconstancy of the people: 'This common body,/Like to a vagabond flag upon the stream,/Goes to and back, lackying the varying tide,/To rot itself with motion' (*ANT* 1.4.44–7). Iris appears in *TMP* where she is addressed by Ceres as 'many-colored messenger' and 'heavenly bow' (4.1.76–86). In *2H6* she is invoked by Queen Margaret in her parting words to the exiled Suffolk: 'Let me hear from thee;/For whereso'er thou art in this world's globe,/I'll have an Iris that shall find thee out' (3.2.405–7). This delicate expression emanates from a character anathematized as having a 'tiger's heart wrapp'd in a woman's hide!' (*3H6* 1.4.137). An appealing reference to the goddess is to be found in *TNK* when the Wooer describes the distracted Jailer's Daughter:

> about her stuck
> Thousand fresh water-flowers of several colors,
> That methought she appear'd like the fair nymph
> That feeds the lake with waters, or as Iris
> Newly dropp'd down from heaven.

> *(4.1.84–8)*

Hoping that Helena will reveal her love for Bertram, the Countess deploys Iris in such a way that three of the ideas may be present – goddess, rainbow and membrane of the eye: 'What's the matter,/That this distempered messenger of wet,/The many-color'd Iris rounds thine eye?' (*AWW* 1.3.150–2).

(C) In his emblem book of Marian iconography Hawkins (1633: 92–102) gives the iris as the rainbow, the tiara or the fairest dress of Nature, and a mirror for human ignorance. He analyses the meaning of the colours and its reflection of the nature of the Virgin Mary. Graves (2000) gives the full story of the Greek myth of Iris. Mabey (1996) has details of the varieties of wild native iris.

ivy (A) *Hedera helix* L., common native ivy, is an evergreen climbing **plant** which grows over fences, on old buildings, and up **trees**. Its **leaves** and **berries** had considerable medicinal use. Ivy could also signify **honeysuckle,** bindweed and other climbing plants. Human parallels could be drawn from its unchecked growth and smothering habits. Ivy was sacred to Bacchus/Dionysus, the classical god of wine; an ivy **bush** hung outside a shop indicated that it sold wine. As an evergreen, ivy symbolized immortality and was used as decoration in winter festivities. Its growing habit suggested ruins, decay and the **wilderness**. Ivy was thought of as a feminine plant from its twining habit, in contrast to the **prickly** male **holly**.

(B) The romantic aspect of ivy, symbolizing mutual embrace, physical and emotional, finds expression only in *MND*. As Titania prepares to settle down for the night with Bottom she enjoins her paramour, 'Sleep thou, and I will wind thee in my arms' before using the plant analogy: 'So doth the woodbine the sweet honeysuckle/Gently entwist; the female ivy so/Enrings the barky fingers of the elm' (4.1.40–4). Prospero represents ivy as parasitical when recounting to Miranda the culmination of Antonio's usurpation: 'now he was/The ivy which had hid my princely trunk,/And suck'd my verdure out on't' (*TMP* 1.2.85–7). A fascinating use arises in *ERR* where the jealous wife, Adriana, contrasts positive affinity – 'Thou art an elm, my husband, I a vine' – with destructive cohering or promiscuity: 'If aught possess thee from me, it is dross,/Usurping ivy, brier, or idle moss' (2.2.174–8). There is a problem of nomenclature in *WT*. The old shepherd, searching for lost sheep, muses, 'If anywhere I have them, 'tis by the sea-side, browsing of ivy' (3.3.67–8). Arden 3 (240) proposes the 'ivy' is really seaweed or sea-holly growing in sand dunes and refers to *Pandosto* where the sheep feed on 'sea-ivy'. Ivy is again associated with shepherds in *PP* when the suitor promises his sweetheart, 'A belt of straw and ivy buds,/With coral clasps and amber studs' (19.13–14). Reference to 'ivy-tods' or bushes is to be found in *TNK* when Pirithous describes a knight: 'His head's yellow,/Hard-hair'd, and curl'd, thick twin'd like ivy-tods,/Not to undo with thunder' (4.2.103–5).

(C) The climbing habit of ivy caused Gascoigne to associate it with ambition (Merridew, 1825). Spenser (ed. 1999, *The Shepheardes Calendar)* describes it as wanton; in his dedication, Lyly links ivy and wine: 'Where the wine is neat there needeth no ivy-bush' (1580, *Euphues*: 29). Moore (1947) examines the symbolism of early modern carols of the holly and ivy, while Barber (1959) comments on the importance of Shakespeare's seasonal songs and the relationship between the male holly and the female ivy. Mabey (1996) gives its myths and associations. Lees-Jeffries (2007) suggests ivy might be a remedy for drunkenness, and also, from its twining habit, a symbol of lasciviousness.

K

kecksies Keck or kex is an alternative name for any wild **plant** of the Apiaceae or **carrot** family, noted for their hollow stems. The particular reference might be to cow parsley, *Anthriscus sylvestris* L., a plant of uncultivated **ground**, wild **angelica**, *Angelica sylvestris* L., or **hemlock**, *Conium maculatum* L. Precise identification is not possible. Most commentators agree on hemlock. First recorded in Shakespeare, kecksies listed with **docks**, **thistles** and **burrs** are suggestive of neglect and decay. Its only appearance is in a catalogue of **weeds** which paints a woeful picture of the French landscape following the English invasion: 'and nothing teems/But hateful docks, rough thistles, kecksies, burs' (*H5* 5.2.51–2). As hemlock has been cited a few lines earlier by Burgundy, a different plant seems likely here. Mabey (1996) points out that when dry hemlock loses its poisonous qualities.

kernel (A) Botanically an individual **seed**, an **apple** or **grape** pip; the kernel is generally the softer edible part of a seed within a **nut**, a **grain** of **wheat** or any cereal **plant**. It can also be a granule of salt, and an enlarged gland or swelling. Figuratively, a kernel is the core of something immaterial, the essence of an argument, the central part of any system.

(B) Excoriating Parolles for feigning social and military stature, Lafew dismisses him with the insult, 'Go to, sir, you were beaten in Italy for picking a kernel out of a pomegranate' (*AWW* 2.3.258–9). This implies that people strike him on the slightest pretext. Returning to his theme, Lafew cautions Bertram against his extravagantly dressed associate: 'believe this of me: there can be no kernel in this light nut; the soul of this man is his clothes' (2.5.42–4). Reviling Achilles and Ajax, Thersites quips, 'Hector shall have a great catch, and 'a knock out either of your brains; 'a were as good crack a fusty nut with no kernel' (*TRO* 2.1.99–102). Excusing his strange demeanour Leontes claims that observation of his small son made him reflect: 'How like (methought) I then was to this kernel,/This squash, this gentleman' (*WT* 1.2.159–60). During his opening engagement with Kate, Petruchio affects to find everything about her delectable: 'Kate like the hazel-twig/Is straight and slender, and as brown in hue/As hazel-nuts, and sweeter than the kernels' (*SHR* 2.1.253–5). Much less playful is Sebastian's ridicule of Gonzalo: 'I think he will carry this island home in his pocket, and give it to his son for an apple'. This draws a response from his fellow mocker, Antonio: 'And sowing the kernels of it in the sea, bring forth more islands' (*TMP* 2.1.91–4).

(C) Greene comments proverbially: 'the purest pome-granates may have one rotten kernel, and the perfectest man is not without some blemish' (1616, vol. 9, *Greene's Mourning Garment*: 129). Drayton (1622) remarks on the skills of the **gardeners** of Kent which include setting kernels to provide future stock. Parkinson (1629) writes of sowing the kernels in the tree nursery as an alternative to **grafting**.

knot (A) A **garden** laid out in intricate geometric designs, where the **flower** beds are edged with low **hedging** or bricks. A knot could also be any designed flower bed, a **labyrinth** or **maze**. In plants 'to knot' is to form a **bud** or hard node which in **wood** will go against the **grain** or spoil the pattern. Knotty wood signifies venerability and age.

(B) There are only two references to knot-gardens, one literal and one figurative. Knots as distortions in the grain of the wood feature prominently. Other meanings in the plays – ties, love-knots, the marriage vow, virgin-knot, twisting into knots, and political or social groupings – are abundant. The sole literal use occurs in *LLL* where the elaborate knot-garden is also emblematic. Though it serves only as a pleasing backdrop for a frolic, it is representative of the intricate verbal dance of the courtiers and the patterned formality of the play. Armado's letter identifies the place where Costard and Jaquenetta have been discovered *in flagrante delicto*: 'from the west corner of thy curious-knotted garden' (1.1.246). The picture conjured up by the letter contrasts the free-spirited rustics with the chafing, self-imposed restraint of the court. Drawing a detailed analogy between the garden and the body politic, one of the diligent gardeners in *R2* includes in his catalogue of neglect the complaint: 'Her fruit-trees all unprun'd, her hedges ruin'd,/Her knots disordered, and her wholesome herbs/Swarming with caterpillars?' (3.4.45–7). The 'knot garden' is integral to the total garden design. The 'knotted oak' is the source of a vivid image. Elaborating on Agamemnon's argument that true merit is achieved only through severe trial, Nestor instances, 'when the splitting wind/Makes flexible the knees of knotted oaks' (*TRO* 1.3.49–50). Awed by the strange and violent happenings on the eve of Caesar's assassination the frightened Casca recalls marvels that have now been transcended: 'I have seen tempests when the scolding winds/Have riv'd the knotty oaks, and I have seen/Th'ambitious oceans swell, and rage, and foam' (*JC* 1.3.5–7).

(C) Knot gardens were labour intensive, often architectural in concept, reflecting the design of the house, or the coat of arms of the family. Newly available printed books provided designs, many of which were too complicated to translate into reality. Colonna (1499) has the earliest known representations of knot gardens; some of his plants, including **thyme, marjoram, lavender** and **hyssop**, are repeated in English knot gardens. Hill (1568) includes the first written instructions on constructing a knot garden. Peacham (1612) anachronistically presents Eden as a knot garden with specimen plants in pots inside the knots. The same patterns served for embroidery, for plasterwork ceilings and for the knot garden, and can also be seen on clothing, and in interiors and paintings of the period. Whalley and Jennings (1998) give the most comprehensive exposition and history of the knot garden. Jacques (1989) also comments on the knot garden as part of 'The Compartiment System'. Henderson (2005) includes some designs from Serlio which could be used for ceilings, or for knot gardens, and summarizes the development of knots. Knots began to go out of fashion after 1600.

knot-grass *Polygonum aviculare* L. is not a **grass** but a common native **weed** of waste **ground** with a prostrate, creeping habit. It strangles other **plants** and is difficult to eradicate; the name could be applied to other plants of similar habit. Knot-grass was widely thought to stunt growth if drunk in an infusion. The only use of knot-grass arises from Lysander's disparagement of Hermia: 'Get you gone, you dwarf;/You minimus, of hind'ring knot-grass made;/You bead, you acorn' (*MND* 3.2.328–30). The inclusion of knot-grass is singularly pertinent as she is proving so difficult to throw off. Her erstwhile lover growing increasingly impatient persistently minifies her. In Beaumont's *The Knight of the Burning Pestle,* the citizen's wife gives currency to the idea of knot-grass stunting growth: 'the child's a fatherless child, and say they should put him in a straight pair of gaskins, 'twere worse than knot-grass; he would never grow after it' (1613, II.1).

L

labyrinth (A) In early modern times a **garden** labyrinth was generally a structure made of **hedges** with a series of interconnecting paths or passages designed to perplex. It could also suggest a **maze** or a **knot-garden**. The best known labyrinth is that on Crete where the Minotaur lived, through which Ariadne guided Theseus. By transference a labyrinth can be an intricate or complicated arrangement of physical features, ideas or events.

(B) The labyrinth, a popular garden feature of the period, is used only figuratively. It is, however, the darker image of its Cretan precursor that occupies Suffolk towards the close of *1H6*. Enamoured of Margaret of Anjou he is torn between thoughts of promoting a dynastic marriage and personal desire: 'O, wert thou for myself! but, Suffolk, stay,/Thou mayest not wander in that labyrinth,/There Minotaurs and ugly treasons lurk' (5.3.187–9). Delivering the closing lines of the play, his machiavellian solution assuages his romantic disappointment: 'Margaret shall now be Queen, and rule the King;/But I will rule both her, the King, and realm'. Thersites, seething with rage against the systematic abuse he suffers at the hands of the blockish Greek heroes, begins his soliloquy, 'How now, Thersites? What, lost in the labyrinth of thy fury?' (*TRO* 2.3.1–2). His subsequent evaluation of the political and military elite suggests that they, too, are lost in a labyrinth (5.4.9–17). Venus' simile comes closest to a physical representation of the labyrinth when advising Adonis how to evade the dreaded boar by emulating the strategy of the hare: 'He cranks and crosses with a thousand doubles:/The many musits through the which he goes/Are like a labyrinth to amaze his foes.' (*VEN* 682–4). The 'musits' are gaps in hedges. Arden 3 (191) notes that 'A muset or musit … is also the "form" or lair of a hare (*OED* muset), which was also called a meaze, mace, muise, or muse' and adds that the spelling 'maze', 'prepares for the puns *labyrinth* and *amaze*'.

(C) Hill's *The Gardener's Labyrinth* (1577), thought to be the first English book on gardening, suggests that finding one's way through unfamiliar situations was central to understanding the techniques of gardening. His material was not original, and the title may reflect Hill's experience in tracking a path through herbals, classical works, astrological, culinary and medical books to produce his own digest. Greene sees labyrinths as places of loss of innocence and even debauchery; he writes of dealings with courtesans, recommending his reader 'lye not here in a consuming labyrinth'. He warns of 'Beauty that leadeth youth captive into the labyrinth' (1616, vol. 9, *Greene's Mourning Garment*: 178, 189).

lady-smock (A) *Cardamine pratensis*, L. is a native **flower** of damp **meadows** with very pale lilac flowers, varying from almost white to a deeper purple; the name is said to have been suggested by clothes **strewn** in the **fields** to dry. It may also represent the Christianization of a pagan association with the ill-luck thought to accompany the return of the cuckoo. The flower was associated with Mary as it flowered about Lady-tide, 25 March.

(B) The only appearance of this flower is in the song of 'spring' set in opposition to 'winter' at the close of *LLL*: 'When daisies pied, and violets blue,/And lady-smocks all silver-white,/And cuckoo-buds of yellow hue/Do paint the meadows with delight' (5.2.894–7). This verse celebrates spring with its promise, tempered by anxieties associated with sexual release. Symbolizing maidens' petticoats, the lady-smocks are playfully alluring, innocent contributors to the artifice of painting. At the same time the herald of cuckoldry, the cuckoo, is a mocking presence. Williams (2006: 279) defines 'smock' as a 'woman's chemise or linen undergarment, hence a woman in her sexual capacity', so these delicate flowers are as flirtatious as they are seemingly coy.

(C) There has been some controversy about the precise identification, but the authoritative Magazine of the *Royal Botanic Gardens, Kew* (autumn 2011) provides an illustration entitled 'the **cuckoo flower**, or lady's smock, *Cardamine pratensis,* L.' A contemporary example of the complicated early categorization of flowers is shown by the Latin name given to lady-smock by Johnson on his botanizing expeditions; he found it on Hampstead Heath and called it *Cardamine altera Lob. Flos Cuculi, Dod. Sisymbrium aquaticum alterum, Matth. Tab.* (1629; 1632: 68, 130). Grindon (1883) says it was associated with loose women, and Hatfield (2007), perhaps drawing on Grindon, suggests that smock was the equivalent to the modern 'piece of skirt'. This idea possibly comes from an inversion of the Marian association, or from the promiscuous way in which *C. pratensis* **seeds**. Mabey (2010: 117) quotes John Clare's famous letter on this subject in which he relates that the wood anemone is called 'lady smock' by children, and that 'cuckoo' is a term 'common people' use for a species of 'orchis'. See McLay (1967) for a close reading of the songs in *LLL*.

land, landlord (A) The solid **earth** in contrast to sea or water, land also designates a tract or stretch of country, part of the **earth** marked out by boundaries as in a country, kingdom or territory. It refers to military matters in contrast to naval ones: 'land-service' is military service on the land rather than at sea. 'Land-fish' suggests dumb, out of its element, as in 'a fish out of water'. Land can designate **ground** or **soil** with a particular use, such as arable land, or it can be an undefined expanse of country. It could provide a sense of identity whether for a monarch or the holder of a landed **estate**; it might suggest loss of identity and status as in landless. Originally a landlord was a lord or owner of land, the person who let land to a tenant. Possibly by the sixteenth century 'landlord' was employed in a wider sense as a person from whom a third party held any tenement, whether a piece of land, a building or part of a building.

(B) All these aspects of land find colourful expression in the plays. The chief unifying feature is the awareness of land as generative: its productivity can be valued so that assessment in terms of a capital sum or as an annual flow of income can be measured. Matters of inheritance from plots to kingdoms are appraised and calculated. The trade-off between land as a capital asset which generates a stream of income is juxtaposed with liquid assets in *H5*. The Archbishop of Canterbury confides to Ely the advantage of providing ready money for Henry V's French campaign as means of thwarting an impending parliamentary bill intended to expropriate church lands: 'For all the temporal lands, which men devout/By testament have given to the Church,/ Would they strip from us' (1.1.9–11). Notwithstanding Canterbury's vested interest he is invited by the King to give an unbiased opinion on the justice of invading France (1.2.9–31). The generative capacity of land is central to *TIM*. The eponymous hero finances an extravagant lifestyle of entertaining and gift-giving by exhausting the very asset that supports this flow of largesse. His land acts as collateral or as Flavius puts it when referring to his creditors, 'his land's put to their books' (1.2.200). Informed by his steward that he is ruined, the incredulous Timon exclaims: 'To Lacedaemon did my land extend'. His mistaken belief that such land-holding could support any level of expenditure is refuted by Flavius' telling response: 'O my good lord, the world is but a word;/Were it all yours to give it in a breath,/How quickly were it gone!' (2.2.151–4). *SHR* is a play in which the transactional nature of land is foregrounded. Making his bid for Kate, Petruchio informs Baptista that with the demise of his father he is, 'Left soly heir to all his lands and goods' and is assured in return by his future father-in-law, 'After my death, the one half of my lands' (2.1.117–21). The auctioning of Bianca is less terse but equally businesslike. Gremio's houses, movables and livestock are capped by Tranio's offer of 'two thousand ducats by the year/Of fruitful land, all which shall be her jointure' (369–70).

The whole of England and parts of France are contested and negotiated in *JN*. However, before hostilities can begin in earnest, the opening scene is interrupted by a domestic inheritance dispute. The Bastard Falconbridge relinquishes his property rights to his younger brother in order to follow his uncle John: 'Brother, take you my land, I'll take my chance./Your face hath got five hundred pound a year' (1.1.151–2). *R2* is the play in which land acquires a spiritual dimension. Not merely procreative substance or indicator of wealth, the land is, as John of Gaunt eulogizes, 'This other Eden, demi-paradise'. Indeed, not only does it have a biblical correlation but worldly approbation: 'This land of such dear souls, this dear dear land,/Dear for her reputation through the world' (2.1.42–58). Even so, 'The fresh green lap of fair King Richard's land' (3.3.47) has been mortgaged to finance the monarch's extravagance. This 'other Eden', 'this dear dear land', is a marketable commodity. Registering the menace posed by the threat of rebellion, Falstaff informs Hal: 'You may buy land now as cheap as stinking mack'rel' (*1H4* 2.4.359–60). Apportioning the kingdom – before gaining possession of it – the rebels consider the value and extent of land. Mortimer allocates territory to his Welsh and Northumbrian allies:

> All westward, Wales beyond the Severn shore,
> And all the fertile land within that bound,
> To Owen Glendower; and, dear coz, to you
> The remnant northward lying off from Trent.
>
> *(3.1.75–8)*

Hotspur, however, is dissatisfied with his share: 'Methinks my moi'ty, north from Burton here,/In quantity equals not one of yours' (95–6). Here is the new age of map-making, an overview of land facilitating careful evaluation and stimulating contention. Now land is truly bounded and parcelled. *HAM* explores many dimensions of land from the petty acquisition of Polish territory by Fortinbras (4.4.18–19) to the global ambitions of Julius Caesar and Alexander the Great (5.1.209–10). At a more local level the skull of a supposed lawyer 'might be in's time a great buyer of land, with his statutes, his recognizances, his fines, his double vouchers, his recoveries' (5.1.103–6). Land is commodified, wrapped up in documents yet scarce enough for bones to be disinterred to make room for new tenants. It is everything but fruitful in this play. When fertility is encountered it is eclipsed by the context. Osric, who has achieved political status under the new regime, is dismissed contemptuously by Hamlet as one who 'hath much land and fertile;...'Tis a chough, but, as I say, spacious in the possession of dirt' (5.2.85–8).

Only occasionally is agricultural land mentioned in such a simple, direct way as Davey's question to Shallow: 'sir, shall we sow the hade land with wheat?' (*2H4* 5.1.14–15). One of the few comments on land as elemental arises in a simile in *H8* when Lovell comments on Cardinal Wolsey's largesse: 'That churchman bears a bounteous mind indeed,/A hand as fruitful as the land that feeds us' (1.3.55–6). Iachimo, giving expression to the world's magnitude and fruitfulness, refers to 'this vaulted arch and the rich crop/Of sea and land' (*CYM* 1.6.33–4). A very different metaphorical example is to be found in *OTH* when Iago comments salaciously on Othello's marriage to Desdemona: 'Faith, he to-night hath boarded a land carract./If it prove lawful prize, he's made forever' (1.2.50–1). The implication is that not only has he made a sexual conquest but also a commercial one. The carrack was a large trading ship; 'prize' is booty. In this play rich in nautical imagery, equivalence is made between a ship and productive land. Two of the three references to 'landlord' are informative. Gaunt dismisses Richard II as 'Landlord of England art thou now, not king' (*R2* 2.1.113) because he has mortgaged so much of his land. Thidias recommends Cleopatra trust the all-conquering Octavius Caesar: 'put yourself under his shroud,/The universal landlord' (*ANT* 3.13.71–2). Here is the character who owns the world.

(C) Land ownership was a major sixteenth-century issue. Quest-Ritson (2001) notes that in the 1520s one-sixth of the land in England was held by the church; of this three-quarters had been sold by 1558 mainly to the gentry, to reward the supporters of the new Tudor dynasty. Their exploitation of the resources of their new lands whether for minerals or through enclosure for sheep were major causes of social unrest later in the century. Norden's *Surveyors Dialogue* of 1618, replete with biblical references, presents the changing attitude to land. He sets out for the first time how to assess and measure land, the relationship of lord and tenant, how to keep copies and deeds, measure acreages and improve the land. Drayton (1622) employs a wide range of meanings for land: as the country, the countryside, a particular county, an extent of countryside under particular control, an estate, the earth in contrast to water and sea. It was an alternative to **field**, and designated land as a valuable commodity: 'our rich land'. For a summary of the significance of maps with particular reference to Shakespeare see Kinney (2004: 101–50). Tigner (2012) suggests that in the entertainments for Elizabeth at Kenilworth and Elvetham the physical land provided an image of her body, an intimate association of monarch and country. Particularly relevant to *R2* is Clarke (2006). For a thorough exploration of land in *HAM* see de Grazia (2007).

larks'-heels Possible candidates include *Tropaeolum minus* L., nasturtium or Indian cress, *Consolida ajacis* L., larkspur, and **aconitum** *Aconitum napellus* L.; the flowers all have similar spur-like features on their lower petals. This **flower** is present only in the song celebrating a marriage at the start of *TNK*. Signalling the peculiar virtues of a wide range of flowers the opening stanzas conclude with 'Larks'-heels trim' (1.1.12). Both Riverside (1693) and Arden 3 (141) state, albeit without discussion, that the **plant** in question is larkspur. As there does not appear to be any strong symbolic significance involved – and the subsequent two verses relate to birds – larkspur would seem to be a reasonable choice. The *OED* gives nasturtium, but the examples lack precision. Gerard (1597) likens the spur on Indian cress to that on larks-heel, indicating he saw them as different plants, but elsewhere he appears to conflate larkspur, lark's heel, lark's claw and aconitum. Harvey (1972) clearly identifies larks' heels as larkspur.

laund (A) Sometimes **lawn**, a **laund** was an open space in woodland, a **glade**; by extension it could suggest untilled **ground** or pasture.

(B) A reasonable inference from the comment of the deer-stalking keeper in *3H6* is that a laund is an opening or glade in the woodland: 'Under this thick-grown brake we'll shroud ourselves,/For through this laund anon the deer will come' (3.1.1–2). This same sense, though with an augmented implication of a long clear stretch of ground, rather like a track through the woods **hedged** by **trees** and **shrubs**, is implied by Adonis' rapid retreat from Venus' passionate kissing: 'And homeward through the dark laund runs apace' (*VEN* 813). In *ERR* the excitable Dromio of Syracuse describes the constable as 'one that countermands/The passages of alleys, creeks, and narrow lands' (4.2.37–8). Riverside (128) implies that in an urban context 'lanes' might be the intended word as 'creeks' are 'narrow winding passages'. *ERR*, Arden 2 (70) favours 'launds', citing Onions' argument that 'land' should read 'laund' in both *LLL* and *TMP*. Riverside (239) plausibly interprets the Princess' injunction to make a rapid retreat – 'Whip to our tents, as roes [run] o'er land' (*LLL* 5.2.309) – as signifying 'laund' an 'open space in a woodland area'. However, Iris' call to the water nymphs to 'Leave your crisp channels, and on this green land/Answer your summons' (*TMP* 4.1.130–1) is less likely to mean 'laund'.

(C) Manwood (1598) in his detailed history of English **forests** notes that those under royal law for **hunting** should have feeding places and 'lawnds' for the king's deer. Drayton (1622) uses laund to designate open spaces in forests, suggesting places for the deer to feed, making them easy prey for the hunter. Landsberg (1998: 23) describes launds as 'grassy treeless rides, which radiated out in all directions from a lodge' giving unrestricted opportunities for hunting and unlimited views. Fletcher (2011) thinks they were created in front of hunting **lodges** to provide a good view of the chase; he notes that the variant of deer 'lawns' was also used.

laurel (A) Now obsolete for **bay-tree** or bay-laurel, *Laurus nobilis* L., the classical laurel, is a naturalized introduction valued for its aromatic **leaves**, which have culinary and medicinal uses. Laurel can also indicate the tree's foliage as an emblem of victory, or as conferring literary distinction. Figuratively, 'to rest on one's laurels' is to retire from a contest or to rely on past victories. 'To look to one's laurels' is to take care not to lose pre-eminence; a laurel crown or **wreath** represented power or victory, and by extension fame or renown. Laurel suggested the story of Daphne's metamorphosis into the laurel tree. Some contemporary writers applied laurel to the native spurge-laurel, *Daphne laureola* L., or the native *Daphne mezereum* L. The laurel, or cherry-laurel, *Prunus laurocerasus* L., found extensively in modern **gardens**, is a larger evergreen **shrub**, and a later introduction.

(B) Declining to accept the position of Protector under Henry VI, Clarence protests:

> No, Warwick, thou art worthy of the sway,
> To whom the heav'ns in thy nativity
> Adjudg'd an olive branch and laurel crown,
> As likely to be blest in peace and war;

> *(3H6 4.6.32–5)*

Warwick's achievements have merited this acclaim though his fortunes are about to wane. Another formidable warrior, Titus Andronicus, is 'bound with laurel boughs' (*TIT* 1.1.74) following his triumph over the Goths. A more colourful and enigmatic general associated with this emblem is Antony. As he departs from Egypt for a military encounter with Pompey, Cleopatra blesses his enterprise: 'Upon your sword/Sit laurel victory, and smooth success/Be strew'd before your feet!' (*ANT* 1.3.99–101). The Black Prince is a virgin warrior when Derby ceremoniously places a helmet on his head with the words 'Wherewith the chamber of thy brain is fenc'd,/So may thy temples with Bellona's hand/Be still adorn'd with laurel victory' (*E3* 3.3.188–90). Laurel as part of the fabric that binds society finds expression in Ulysses' famous speech on hierarchy:

> How could communities,
> Degrees in schools, and brotherhoods in cities,

Peaceful commerce from dividable shores,
The primogenity and due of birth,
Prerogative of age, crowns, sceptres, laurels,
But by degree stand in authentic place?

(TRO 1.3.103–8)

(C) Grove, comparing his love's faithfulness to the tree's evergreen qualities, writes of laurel as the bay: 'Like as the Bay, that bears on branches sweet/The Laurel leaf that lasteth always green' (1587, Ault 1949, 122). Greene suggests a superstitious use of laurel: 'he which weareth Laurell cannot be hurt with lightning' (1585, vol. 5, *Planetomachia*: 75). At the 1591 Elvetham pageant for the Queen, a poet **garlanded** with laurel signalled classical allusions of peace and victory (Nichols 1788). Spenser (1596) also uses laurel as a sign of peace and victory, and the mark of wise poets. Peacham (1612: 23) echoes the classical association of laurel as bay, and appears to invoke Colonna (1499) when he writes to the Earl of Southampton 'three garlands Colonna did devize' of **olive**, laurel and **oak**.

lavender (A) A **plant** of the *Lavandula* L. genus, commonly *Lavandula angustifolia* Mill., a Mediterranean native; widely cultivated throughout Europe, it was probably a Roman introduction. Lavender was extensively planted in **knot-gardens**, grown for **strewing herbs** and to mask unpleasant **smells**. It was thought to preserve linen and clothes from moths. The **flowers** had culinary and cosmetic uses; its oil was widely used medicinally as a general panacea, with calming and sedative effects; it also served as a contraceptive and abortifacient.

(B) Following her disputation with Polixenes over the merits of **gillyflowers**, Perdita bestows flowers and herbs on both the King and Camillo:

Here's flow'rs for you:
Hot lavender, mints, savory, marjorum,
The marigold, that goes to bed wi'th'sun,
And with him rises weeping. These are flow'rs
Of middle summer, and I think they are given
To men of middle age.

(WT 4.4.103–8)

The sound values and rhythm of Perdita's commentary create a sensation of delicacy and grace. There are two points of interest here. The possible symbolic association with affection – Perdita is both kindly and playful – and the 'hot' lavender. All the plants listed by her were termed 'hot' by the herbalists of the day. Extensive footnotes in Arden 2 (95) include Bacon's distinction: earlier **blooming** plants are 'cold' because they 'have a quicker perception of heat … than the hot herbs have'. Arden 3 (265) connects this question to the theory of humours – the four elements of hot, cold, dry and moist – observing that Perdita's herbs being **fragrant** and aromatic fall into the Elizabethan category of 'hot'and also notes that lavender was emblematic of affection.

(C) Gerard (1597: 469) gives its medicinal values, warning that as a 'hot' herb there are dangers in careless use, that 'divers rash & overbold Apothecaries, and other foolish women do by and by give such compositions, and others of the like kind' to their patients 'to whom they can give nothing worse, seeing those things do very much hurt, and oftentimes bring death itself'. Hackett (1995) notes lavender was one of the **scented** plants used for decoration and strewing at the 1559 banquet at Greenwich to celebrate the Queen's coronation.

lawn An alternative spelling for the more usual **laund**, an open space in woodland. Lawn as a **grassy** area in the **garden** is at the earliest a later seventeenth-century usage. There is no reference to 'lawn' meaning cultivated grass. There are, however, six mentions of 'lawn' as a delicate fabric. Autolycus, advertising his wares, includes 'Lawn as white as driven snow' (*WT* 4.4.218). The material is not so prized as to persuade Emilia to succumb to infidelity: 'Marry I would not do such a thing for a joint-ring, nor for measures of lawn, nor for gowns, petticoats, nor caps, nor any petty exhibition' (*OTH* 4.3.72–4). Hentzner (1598: 76) suggests either a large area of grass or open space for the hunt when he describes the three hundred and eighty paces long viewing walk at Windsor 'whence the nobility and persons of distinction can take the pleasure of seeing hunting and hawking in a lawn of sufficient space'.

leaf (A) The green organ of a **plant** produced from a stem or **branch**, a **leaf** is part of the plant which collectively constitutes its foliage. Technically leaf indicates the whole structure including a **stalk**; popularly it designates the blade alone. Leaves can provide covering for people, including the proverbial **fig**-leaf of Eden, or a shelter in a **wood**. By extension leaf suggests spring, and youth, and also means a page in a book.

(B) There are a few mentions of the leaf of a book, but more numerous are the botanical examples, all of which are interesting. Antony's schoolteacher, acting as his ambassador to Octavius Caesar, gives expression to a singularly delicate image: 'I was of late as petty to his ends/As is the morn-dew on the myrtle leaf/To his grand sea' (*ANT* 3.12.8–10). Arviragus' paean to the seemingly dead Fidele/Imogen refers to 'The leaf of eglantine, whom not to slander,/Outsweet'ned not thy breath' (*CYM* 4.2.223–4). Riverside (1595) proposes honeysuckle for **eglantine**; Arden 2 (130) the sweet briar (which has scented leaves). Given the reference to 'leaf' the latter is more likely albeit 'leaf' can signify a petal. Adonis is succinct in his rejection of Venus' amorous advances claiming his immaturity as defence: 'Who plucks the bud before one leaf put forth?' (*VEN* 416). Because of its propensity to quiver in the breeze the aspen leaf has a distinguished literary heritage. This poetic association is drawn on by Mistress Quickly – to unintended comic effect. Expressing her distress at the impending entry of the noisome, swaggering Pistol, she frets, 'Feel, masters, how I shake, look you, I warrant you...and 'twere an aspen leaf' (*2H4* 2.4.105–9). The other reference to aspen is remarkable for its marriage of tender lyricism with anguish. Marcus, encountering his mutilated niece, Lavinia, laments:

> O, had the monster seen those lily hands
> Tremble like aspen leaves upon a lute,
> And make the silken strings delight to kiss them,
> He would not then have touch'd them for his life!
>
> *(TIT 2.4.44–7)*

In the same play Tamora considers the effect of leaves in motion: 'The green leaves quiver with the cooling wind/And make a checker'd shadow on the ground' (2.3.14–15). What might be described as a painterly representation arises in *HAM*. Gertrude's description of Ophelia's death begins, 'There is a willow grows askaunt the brook,/That shows his hoary leaves in the glassy stream' (4.7.166–7). Timon uses the analogy of seasons to express his bitterness towards the hangers-on who have deserted him: 'That numberless upon me stuck as leaves/Do on the oak, have with one winter's brush/Fell from their boughs, and left me open, bare/For every storm that blows' (*TIM* 4.3.263–6). Similarly, Belarius narrates his fall from favour at court:

> Then I was a tree
> Whose boughs did bend with fruit; but in one night,
> A storm or robbery (call it what you will)
> Shook down my mellow hangings, nay, my leaves,
> And left me bare to weather.
>
> *(CYM 3.3.60–4)*

The leaf exercises considerable poetic power in moments of failure and defeat. The **Gardener** in *R2* reproves one of his helpers for condemning Richard's neglect of the realm: 'He that hath suffered this disordered spring/Hath now himself met with the fall of leaf' (3.4.48–9). The third Citizen in *R3* cautions of imminent political change following the death of Edward IV: 'When great leaves fall, then winter is at hand' (2.3.33). A poetically dense image is embodied in Macbeth's reflection on the course his life has taken: 'I have liv'd long enough: my way of life/Is fall'n into the sear, the yellow leaf' (*MAC* 5.3.22–3). The rest of the speech is explicit, detailed and uncomplicated, yet it is 'the yellow leaf' with its suggestion of sapless, autumnal dryness that captures his despair. The conception of leaves yellowing or falling as images of age, decay or loss is frequent in the sonnets: 'Sap check'd with frost and lusty leaves quite gone' (*SON* 5.7); 'When lofty trees I see barren of leaves,/Which erst from heat did canopy the herd' (12.5–6); 'That time of year thou mayst in me behold/When yellow leaves, or none, or few, do hang/Upon those boughs which shake against the cold' (73.1–3). Adonis, resisting Venus' advances, likens **caterpillars** to Lust's assault on beauty: 'Which the hot tyrant stains, and soon bereaves,/As caterpillars do the tender leaves' (*VEN* 797–8). This forceful image is also articulated by York. Receiving tidings of further English losses in France he bewails the prospect of a shrinking kingdom: 'Thus are my blossoms blasted in the bud,/And caterpillars eat my leaves away' (*2H6* 3.1.89–90). Delicacy characterizes the imagery in *PP* (16.5) and *LLL* (4.3.103–4): 'Through the velvet leaves the wind/All unseen can passage find'. The poems are identical but for an additional couplet in Dumaine's composition. That 'leaves' can mean petals is indicated by Basset who complains that Vernon, 'Upbraided me about the rose I wear,/Saying the sanguine color of the leaves/Did represent my master's blushing cheeks' (*1H6* 4.1.91–3). 'Leavy' is employed three times, most delightfully in the song in *ADO* that asserts, 'The fraud of men was ever so,/Since summer first was leavy' (2.3.72–3). As Malcolm's army approaches Macbeth's castle he instructs them to discard their camouflage: 'your leavy screens throw down,/And show like those you are' (*MAC* 5.6.1–2). In *PER* Lysimachus refers to a 'leavy shelter that abuts against/The island's side' (5.1.51–2). Whatever the context the word exercises a softening effect.

(C) Greene writes of the Queen as a flower surrounded by leaves: 'And peace from heaven shall harbour in these leaves/That gorgeous beautifies this matchless flower' (1594, vol. 13, *Frier Bacon*: 102). Leaves attract particular recurring adjectives. Spenser (1596) gives **shady**, **withered**, unmoving, stirring leaves; he also uses leaf to represent one part of the normal growth cycle which includes **bud** and **flower**. For Grove (1587) evergreen leaves of **bay** or **laurel** represent permanence and constancy. Arnold (1988) includes lists of the Queen's wardrobe with leaves of silver, gold and mother-of-pearl; she includes a reproduction of the Hever portrait of c. 1585 where her dress is covered with **acorns**, leaves, **honeysuckle**, **roses** and **daisies**. Knight (2009) provides a fascinating exploration of the relationship between plants and print culture. Hoyles (1991: 244–50) notes the adoption of the word 'petal' by John Ray in 1682, observing 'It is strange to think that the word petal, with all its connotations, was unknown to Shakespeare.'

leathercoat A russet **apple** with a rough skin which does not change colour as it ripens, the name was possibly overtaken by 'russet' which is still in use. Its only appearance is in Justice Shallow's orchard. The entertainment having reached the stage where even Silence has begun to sing, Davy, following Shallow's instructions to indulge his guests, presents Bardolph with a culinary treat: 'There's a dish of leathercoats for you' (*2H4* 5.3.41–2).

leek (A) *Allium porrum* L. is a member of the **onion** family, possibly a Roman introduction, widely grown for culinary purposes. A staple part of the diet, particularly for the poor, it provided flavouring and colour for pottage. Because the leek is easy to cultivate it came to represent something of little value, but it had medical applications. It is the national emblem of Wales.

(B) The dietary and emblematic aspects of the leek are brought out in 18 references, two-thirds of them arising in *H5*. The disguised monarch is instructed by Pistol to convey a message to **Fluellen**: 'Tell him I'll knock his leek about his pate/Upon

Saint Davy's day' (4.1.54–5). Retribution follows. During the quarrel the loquacious Welshman inflicts punishment on the all too provocative Pistol who protests, 'I am qualmish at the smell of leek', contending that he would not eat one 'for Cadwallader and all his goats'. Resorting to physical force Fluellen retorts, 'if you can mock a leek, you can eat a leek'. Compelling him to comply, the Welshman adds tauntingly, 'Bite, I pray you, it is good for your green wound and your ploody coxcomb'. Emphasizing its medicinal property he insists: 'Nay, pray you throw none away, the skin is good for your broken coxcomb'. Pistol receives a final chastisement from Gower who acknowledges the emblematic significance of the leek: 'Will you mock at an ancient tradition, begun upon an honorable respect, and worn as a memorable trophy of predeceas'd valor, and dare not avouch in your deeds any of your words?' (5.1.21–73). This historical event, a remarkable victory by the Black Prince, is recalled by Fluellen in his dialogue with the King: 'the Welshman did good service in a garden where leeks did grow, wearing leeks in their Monmouth caps, which, your Majesty know, to this hour is an honorable badge of the service; and I do believe your Majesty takes no scorn to wear the leek upon Saint Tavy's day'. The Monmouth-born monarch rewards Fluellen's enthusiastic narrative with a declaration of kinship: 'I wear it for a memorable honor;/For I am Welsh, you know, good countryman' (4.7.98–105). Flute/Thisbe provides the only figurative use when grieving over the body of Pyramus. Referring to her dead lover's 'lily lips', 'cherry nose' and 'yellow cowslip cheeks' she completes the infelicities: 'His eyes were green as leeks' (*MND* 5.1.330–5).

(C) That every **gardening** book of the time advises on the cultivation of leeks demonstrates their ready availability. Tusser (1573) writes that leeks were particularly important during Lenten fasting, while Hill (1577) devotes a chapter to their cultivation, **manuring** and **sowing**. Bullein (1595) says they are evil, hinder sleep, but if eaten with honey can act as a purgative for the blood, noting in addition that they are particularly bad if eaten raw. Lehner (1960) relates the sixth-century Welsh legend of St David ordering the Britons to wear leeks in their caps to distinguish them from enemies, whence it came to represent Wales. McLean (1981) notes the historical importance of the leek in medieval cookery, and suggests they also served to bleach hair, as toothpaste, and as a stock medicine to treat the plague.

lemon (A) Contemporary sources refer to both the 'lemon' and the 'citron', sometimes interchangeably. It is not clear whether Shakespeare means the citron, *Citrus medica* L., an ovate **fruit** with a thick greeny-yellow rind and acid juice, which was imported almost entirely for medicinal use, or the lemon, *Citrus x limon* L. Also an ovate fruit with a yellow rind, which gave its name to the colour lemon-yellow, the lemon was widely used in cooking, and as an oil both in cookery and perfumery. Stuck with **cloves**, lemons could be used instead of the more usual **orange** as a **pomander**. Lemon lent itself to a play on words with the use of 'leman' as lover.

(B) The single reference to this fruit arises out of a competitive exercise of wit by young courtiers intent on mocking the theatrical performance of their social inferiors in *LLL*. Armado's allusion to Hector's 'gift' provokes Dumaine's interjection, 'A gilt nutmeg', which, as Arden 3 (280) points out, was 'a nutmeg glazed with the yolk of an egg: a common gift of lovers' and 'used for spicing drinks'. This opens the way for the lemon/leman (lover) pun by Berowne: 'A lemon'. Longeville pursues the theme with sexual innuendo, 'Stuck with cloves', thereby facilitating Dumaine's riposte, 'No, cloven', a division implying female genitalia. The game does not stop there, the chain of food/drink/love/sex interplay continues with 'mint' and 'columbine' (5.2.645–55). What this exchange reveals is the propensity of these wits to expose all the possibilities and associations of words. The sophistication nullifies any potential disquiet about its unsavoury sexual nature. The victims of this mockery are presumed to be of no more significance than the lemon, an evaluation countered by Holofernes' incisive rebuke: 'This is not generous, not gentle, not humble' (629).

(C) Heilmeyer (2001: 88) observes: 'fragrant lemons would be carried by mourners on their way to a graveyard. They were spiked with cloves or decorated with **rosemary** sprigs as a sign of eternal life.' This may be pertinent to *LLL* where Armado alludes to Hector's death and burial (5.2.660–1). Though lemons were not grown in England before the sixteenth century, they had an extensive range of uses. Henderson (2005) records a letter from Burghley in 1561 asking a contact in Paris to help him acquire lemon, **pomegranate** and **myrtle trees**, commenting that he already has an **orange** tree. Hill (1577) recommends trying to grow lemons in the kitchen garden with sufficient protection from inclement weather. In his medical practice, Hall used citrons and lemons for their juice and in syrup for a wide range of complaints, which suggests a ready availability of both (Lane 1996). Bacon (1625) writes of oranges and lemons being 'stoved', or overwintered in some permanent or temporary heated building. Madelaine (1982) provides the lemon/leman link in the context of the rotten oranges of *ADO* 4.1.31. Campbell-Culver (2001) distinguishes between the citrus species.

lettuce (A) A **plant** of the genus *Lactuca*, particularly *L. sativa* L., the cultivated or **garden** lettuce, a plant of every **herb** garden. The name is often used in the singular to denote lettuce **leaves** in the plural, which are used for **salad**, and it can refer to other green plants that are included in salads. Lettuce could stimulate the appetite, help digestion, ameliorate a hangover, act as both an aphrodisiac and anaphrodisiac, and as a soporific.

(B) This plant is mentioned only once. Responding to Roderigo's confession of his continuing infatuation with Desdemona, Iago's reprimand takes the form of an analogy: 'Our bodies are our gardens, to the which our wills are gardeners; so that if we will plant nettles or sow lettuce, set hyssop and weed up tine…why, the power and corrigible authority of this lies in our wills' (*OTH* 1.3.320–6). There may be a play on 'will' as sexual desire and as self-control (see for instance *SON* 135). 'Tine' was used to refer to 'thyme'. However, in the context of 'weed up', Riverside (1258) proposes that 'tine' here intimates 'tares or wild grasses' (but see entry for **thyme**). Arden 3 (156) points out the allusion to Galatians 6.7, 'whatsoever a man soweth, that shall he also reap'. It may be a mistake to probe more deeply for the significance of Iago's examples because he has the facility to dazzle his auditor with seeming profundity whilst uttering a commonplace.

(C) Greene uses lettuce metaphorically: 'but in faith my lippes are too coarse for such Lettice' (1578, vol. 5, *Penelope's Web*: 233), and 'lips like lettice, as the man is so is his manners' (1587, vol. 3, *The Tritameron*: 60*)*. Markham (1631) recommends lettuce for thirst in fevers, with ale for a frenzy, as a soporific. He includes it in his list of plants to have as part of **simple** or compound salads.

lily (A) *Lilium* L., a bulbous **plant**, a native of the northern hemisphere, has strongly **scented**, large, showy white **flowers** on a tall stem. It can indicate any plant of the genus, including *Lilium candidum* L., the white or Madonna lily which until the early sixteenth century was the only lily in English gardens. An exemplar of whiteness and purity in all cultures, it regularly describes a person or substance of exceptional whiteness, fairness or purity. These characteristics were common to classical and Christian mythology. In Christian teaching its long association with the Virgin Mary and symbolism of the Annunciation is particularly notable. The lily was thought to combine the qualities of an ancient **fertility** symbol, and spiritual healing. It was a ready metaphor and symbol in poetry, frequently contrasted with the red **rose**. Included with reference to its scent, and for its association with purity and virginity, the lily was incorporated into the iconography and symbolism attached to the Queen. Offset by a reputedly foul **smell**, the beauty of the flower was in notable contrast to the common medicinal uses of the bulb. Its colour and purity were thought to be transferable, hence its widespread use as a cosmetic. Varieties of wild native lilies, including the fritillary, grew extensively in the countryside.

(B) With over 20 references, the various attributes of this plant are well represented. At the simplest level Launce describes his sister's complexion and delicate figure: 'she is as white as a lily and as small as a wand' (*TGV* 2.3.20–1). Declining to collude with the King of Navarre's oath-breaking, the Princess of France vows: 'Now by my maiden honor, yet as pure/As the unsallied lily' (*LLL* 5.2.351–2). At the close of *H8* Archbishop Cranmer predicts that the newly baptized baby, the future Elizabeth I, 'yet a virgin,/A most unspotted lily shall she pass/To th'ground, and all the world shall mourn her' (5.4.60–2). Interestingly, in the play's other lily allusion the desolate Queen Katherine creates an image of a fall from favour: 'Like the lily,/That once was mistress of the field, and flourish'd,/I'll hang my head and perish' (3.1.151–3). The lily as the epitome of grace and beauty is evidenced too, in *JN*. Prosecuting the right of her son Arthur to the throne of England, Constance extols his attributes: 'Of Nature's gifts thou mayst with lilies boast,/And with the half-blown rose' (3.1.53–4). The combination of red and white, lily and rose, is applied with singular force to the beautiful and modest Lucrece. Interweaving like a bicoloured ribbon through three stanzas, the red of blushes and the white of purity culminate in 'The silent war of lilies and of roses' (*LUC* 71). The lily is particularly effective as an image because it brings together the ideas of delicacy, whiteness and purity. Iachimo, entranced by the sleeping Imogen, marvels: 'fresh lily,/And whiter than the sheets!' (*CYM* 2.2.15–16). Guiderius, alighting on the seemingly dead Imogen/Fidele resorts to the same image: 'O sweetest, fairest lily!' (4.2.201). Lavinia is also referred to twice in terms of the lily. Sighting his mutilated niece, Marcus exclaims:

> O, had the monster seen those lily hands
> Tremble like aspen leaves upon a lute,
> And make the silken strings delight to kiss them,
> He would not then have touch'd them for his life!
>
> *(TIT 2.4.44–7)*

A little later, Titus, reading Lavinia's response to his narration, says, 'When I did name her brothers, then fresh tears/Stood on her cheeks, as doth the honey-dew/Upon a gath'red lily almost withered' (3.1.111–13).

The lily is transcended by the loved-one in *SON* 98: 'Nor did I wonder at the lily's white' (9); and again in *SON* 99: 'The lily I condemned for thy hand' (6). When a fine character succumbs to duplicity the fall from grace is truly damnable: 'For sweetest things turn sourest by their deeds;/Lilies that fester smell far worse than weeds' (94.13–14). This powerful warning recurs in *E3* when Warwick praises his daughter, the Countess of Salisbury, for rejecting the King's proposal of double adultery: 'Dark night seems darker by the lightning flash;/Lilies that fester smell far worse than weeds' (2.1.450–1). The perfection of the lily is evoked in *JN*. Salisbury pours scorn on King John's determination to have a second coronation: 'To gild refined gold, to paint the lily' is 'wasteful and ridiculous excess' (4.2.11–16). No character is more lavish in the praise and distribution of flowers than Perdita whose catalogue includes, 'lilies of all kinds/(The flow'r-de-luce being one)' (*WT* 4.4.126–7). In *TRO* lilies are emblematic of sensual delight. On the verge of achieving his longed-for consummation with Cressida, Troilus addresses the go-between Pandarus: 'O, be thou my Charon,/And give me swift transportance to these fields/Where I may wallow in the lily-beds' (3.2.10–12). While the Virgilian connection is evident, the presence of the Song of Solomon is equally strong: 2.16, 4.5, 6.1–2, 7.2. Reaching beyond the realm of purity into sensuality the lily is also susceptible to parody. During rehearsal Thisbe praises her lover as 'Most radiant Pyramus, most lily-white of hue,/Of color like the red rose on triumphant brier' (*MND* 3.1.93–4). During the performance, however, the anatomical comparisons have been transformed – like so much else in this play – to 'These lily lips,/This cherry nose,/These yellow cowslip cheeks' (5.1.330–2). As whiteness is associated with cowardice (cheeks becoming pale with fear), Shakespeare is inspired to produce the first recorded example of the term 'lily-livered'. Responding to the unwelcome news of the size of the English army, Macbeth berates the nervous servant, 'Go prick thy face, and over-red thy fear,/Thou lily-liver'd boy' (*MAC* 5.3.14–15). More deserving of such contempt is Oswald in *LR*. Kent's torrent of vituperation includes such epithets as 'a lily-liver'd, action-taking, whoreson, glass-gazing, superserviceable, finical rogue' (2.2.17–19).

(C) Gerard (1597) lists seventeen and Parkinson (1629) 22 varieties of lily, all possible candidates for Perdita's 'lilies of all kinds'. As Tigner (2012: 123) points out, 'Lilies, like gillyflowers and later tulips were valued for their ability to produce variations', citing Parkinson's recognition of the augmentation of varieties 'in these daies'. Spenser (1596) includes the full range of the flower's possible uses: 'arrayed in lily white', a bed of sweet lilies as a precursor to betrayal, 'lily paps', lily juice squeezed for bruises and wounds, a 'lily complexion' and a 'lily hand'. In his contemplation of the lily's significance, Peacham (1612) says the lily is clothed by power divine, is religion's weed, a badge of chastity, and surpasses the glory of a king. Hawkins (1633) combines Catholic iconography, folk-lore and classical mythology in the chapter on the lily in his emblem book. He suggests that it symbolizes the Virgin's immaculate chastity, as well as being the sceptre of Diana, and the **flower-de-luce**, the symbol of France. He uses it to signify the spilt milk of nature, an extension of the idea which originated with the Eve/Hera/Mary myths. Mabey (1996) details the varieties of wild native lilies. Dent (1981: 295.1–295.4, 296, 296.1, 297).

limb (A) A main **branch** of a **tree**, a **limb** can represent a part of the human or animal body including leg, arm, wing, as distinct from the head or trunk; an obsolete use also indicates any organ or part of the human body.

(B) The few arboreal uses are figurative. Most of the numerous mentions are to body parts rather than to the branch of a tree. Leonato, for instance, refers to 'Both strength of limb, and policy of mind' (*ADO* 4.1.198), while Brutus dismisses the political significance of Mark Antony with the comment, 'Antony is but a limb of Caesar' (*JC* 2.1.165). An ambiguous metaphorical use is to be found in *2H6* where Queen Margaret celebrates the removal of the Duke of Gloucester from his position as Lord Protector (having already engineered the disgrace of his foolish wife Eleanor): 'two pulls at once –/His lady banish'd, and a limb lopp'd off./This staff of honor raught, there let it stand,/Where it best fits to be, in Henry's hand' (2.3.41–4). 'Pulls' is a horticultural image, signifying to draw up by the roots ('especially a food plant' *SOD*). As attention is directed towards the wooden staff of office, the 'limb' in question is as likely to be arboreal as anatomical. *TIT* presents an interesting case as the hacking off of hands/ arms is suggestive of the cutting of branches. Titus' sons call for the exercise of the Roman rite of mutilating and burning the chief of the prisoners: 'upon a pile of wood,/ Let's hew his limbs'; 'Alarbus' limbs are lopp'd' (1.1.128–143). This barbarous act is later perpetrated on Lavinia. Discovered by her uncle, Marcus, he cries, 'what stern ungentle hands/Hath lopp'd and hew'd, and made thy body bare/Of her two branches' (2.4.16–18). The persistence of this image is illustrated by Marcus' hope for renewal in the final scene: 'O, let me teach you how to knit again/This scattered corn into one mutual sheaf,/These broken limbs again into one body' (5.3.70–2). The limbs here are scattered **corn**, but in a play that has more dismemberment than any other, human limbs inhabit the imagination.

(C) Drayton refers to the battle of Hexham in 1464, and says of the slaughter:

'Then limbs like boughs were lop'd, from shoulders armes do flie' (1622, *Polyolbion* 22.1067).

limbeck A limbeck, or alembic, is a **gourd**-shaped vessel used in household prepara-tions which contained the substance to be **distilled**. It carried connotations of alchemical distillation. A vivid representation is provided by Lady Macbeth when explaining to her reluctant husband how the murder of Duncan will be effected:

> his two chamberlains
> Will I with wine and wassail so convince,
> That memory, the warder of the brain,
> Shall be a fume, and the receipt of reason
> A limbeck only.
>
> *(MAC 1.7.63–7)*

The conception here is that of the wine rising from the stomach to the brain: fumes rise to the upper part of the body acting as an alembic. The only other case occurs in the self-critical opening lines of *SON* 119: 'What potions have I drunk of Siren tears/ Distill'd from limbecks foul as hell within'. Its usual positive association, distillation of flowers for perfume, is perverted in both these uses. Brunschwig (1525) includes illustrations of the distilling processes, while Plat (1594: 3) says that 'A Copper body, or brasse pot, with a pewter Limbecke, and a glasse receiver, are all the necessarie Instruments' for the distilling process. Vaughan (1617) provides a recipe for the widely used preventative and cure-all known as Dr Stevens' water, and details the processes in its distillation, which included the use of limbeck. Iyengar (2011) expands on the limbeck as a model for the brain.

lime, line-grove (A) Bird-lime, a viscous preparation from the **bark** of **holly** or the **berries** of **mistletoe**, was spread on the **branch** of a **tree** to catch small birds. That meaning is now only found poetically, but the idea of liming as entrapment can also apply to human beings. The lime tree is the native *Tilia cordata* L., also line or linden tree. **Line-** or **lime-groves** were very long-living from the **plant's** habit of regeneration from broken **roots** and fallen trees, while **coppicing** can prolong its life almost indefi-nitely. A tree with highly **scented flowers**, it had some medicinal uses, and the **leaves** served to fill pillows. Lime is the mineral, calcium oxide, or slaked lime, calcium hydroxide; the lime **fruit** is a later introduction. Line is also an alternative name for **flax**.

(B) The diverse uses of 'lime' are all found in the plays. *TMP* has the one possible mention of a lime tree. Informing Prospero of the whereabouts of the King's party Ariel reassures him: 'In the same fashion as you gave in charge,/Just as you left them; all prisoners, sir,/In the line-grove which weather-fends your cell' (5.1.8–10). This is likely to be a grove or a group of trees affording protection against the weather. Arden 3 (263) avers, 'a grove of trees of the linden genus *Tilia*, sometimes referred to as the European lime. Though these trees are ornamental and do not bear fruit, editions from Dryden and Davenant to Oxford have emended to "lime grove". Others retain F's original'. Arden 2 (107) traces the main outlines of the ebb and flow of editors' opinions. The suggestion that 'line-grove' refers to a clothes line seems somewhat improbable. Agreeing to employ Bardolph as a tapster, the Host of the Garter demands: 'Let me see thee froth and lime' (*WIV* 1.3.14). It is 'slaked lime' that is referred to here, not lime juice. Riverside (328) points out, 'Serving beer with a heavy froth allowed short measure; adding lime to cheap wine masked its sour taste.' The disconsolate Falstaff, returned from his misadventure at Gad's Hill, complains: 'You rogue, here's lime in this sack too' (*1H4* 2.4.124). Responding to her precocious child, Lady Macduff draws upon the image of trapping birds with lime: 'Poor bird, thou'dst never fear the net nor lime' (*MAC* 4.2.34). Delighting in the success of their scheme to persuade Beatrice that Benedick is in love with her, Ursula assures Hero: 'She's limed, I warrant you. We have caught her, madam' (*ADO* 3.1.104–5).

(C) Gerard (1597) believes mistletoe berries provide the best bird-lime, rather than that from holm **oak** or holly bark, but notes it is poisonous if eaten by man. Euphues comments on the contrast between appearance and actuality: 'the box-tree is always green, but the seed is poison; tilia (lime) hath a sweet rind and a pleasant leaf, but the fruit so bitter that no beast will bite it' (1580 Lyly, *Euphues*: 286). Bacon (1625) particularly notes the value of the scented flowers in the garden. Spurgeon (1935) observes that the process of liming birds was a cruel sport and suggests that Shakespeare's liming images reflect this. Mabey (1996) details native use and folklore. Arden 3 (263) suggests that the reference could be to the European lime, *T. europaea* L., but that is a later hybrid of *T. platyphyllos* Scop., and *T. cordata* Mill.

locust The **fruit** of the Mediterranean carob **tree**, *Ceratonia siliqua* L., the locust **bean** was used as a sweetener before sugar became readily available. Carob syrup was an important export from Cyprus where the tree grew extensively. While some trees were grown as exotics in England, the climate did not permit their **flowering** or fruiting. Carob is a chocolate substitute. It is widely suggested that carat as a measure of gold comes from the carob, as the **seeds** were used by **apothecaries** and jewellers for their uniformity of weight. The *OED* gives the alternative of '**carret**' for locust. The one mention of this plant is highly significant. As the Venetians prepare to set sail for Cyprus, Iago persuades Roderigo to sell his land and join the expedition in order to gain access to Desdemona: 'These Moors are changeable in their wills…The food that to him now is as luscious as locusts, shall be to him shortly as acerb as the coloquintida' (*OTH* 1.3.346–9). Iago appears to have imbibed some of Othello's exoticisms. Alliteration and assonance collude to dazzling effect while also drawing on a botanical source linked closely to Cyprus. In his idealized **garden** Colonna (1499: 96) describes a 'grove of carob trees such as Cyprus could not produce' emphasizing the high reputation of the carobs from the island. Turner (1548) mentions it in his list of **herbs** as a carob, while Gerard (1597) records the seeds he has **sown**, and notes that 'they have prospered'. He says it was thought to be the same as John the Baptist's locusts in **wilderness**. Parkinson (1640) emphasizes its exoticism by noting that it grows in hotter countries of the east, calls it the sweet-bean tree, and records it as a sugar substitute.

lodge (A) A small house, a purpose-built permanent structure, sometimes a temporary hut, tent or **arbour**. A lodge could feature in a **park**, or **woods**, for use while **hunting**, for rest, entertainment, contemplation, or as a temporary place to stay. Lodge could be used interchangeably with loggia or **gallery** to indicate part of the main house. It could suggest a house or cottage at the entrance to an **estate** or park occupied by an employee, possibly as gate-keeper, warrener, or **gardener**. To lodge is to stay in tents or other temporary accommodation, or to provide someone with such accommodation, to house or harbour them. 'To lodge' can also mean to beat down **crops**. It can suggest the entertaining or harbouring of thoughts.

(B) Lodge as integral to an estate is revealed in the opening scene of *WIV* when Justice Shallow confronts Falstaff with his misdemeanours: 'Knight, you have beaten my men, kill'd my deer, and broke open my lodge' (111–12). Costard is punished for his dalliance with Jaquenetta, but she is allowed to remain to fulfil her duties. Armado, her enamoured keeper, informs her, 'I will visit thee at the lodge' (*LLL* 1.2.135). The best indication of the lodge as a place for rest during a hunt is in *TIT*. Saturninus refuses to believe the report of his brother's death: 'He and his lady both are at the lodge,/Upon the north side of this pleasant chase' (2.3.254–5). Benedick uses the term figuratively when describing the love-sick Claudio: 'I found him here as melancholy as a lodge in a warren' (*ADO* 2.1.214–15). Hares and rabbits were proverbially associated with melancholy. An isolated place in a busy warren is a possible meaning. Arden 2 (121) admits uncertainty with respect to the full import of the comment, but cites Isaiah 1.7–8 to trace the origin of a lodge as a lonely place of retreat: 'and the daughter of Zion is left as a cottage in a vineyard, as a lodge in a garden of cucumbers'. Arden 3 (191) suggests an 'isolated hunting lodge in a game park'. Lodge in the sense of to 'beat down' is used to striking effect. Acknowledging Bolingbroke's impending usurpation, Richard II tells the weeping Aumerle, 'We'll make foul weather with despised tears;/Our sighs and they shall lodge the summer corn,/And make a dearth in this revolting land' (*R2* 3.3.161–3). Determined to prove Gloucester's death was not natural, Warwick describes the victim's appearance: 'His well-proportion'd beard made rough and rugged,/Like to the summer's corn by tempest lodged' (*2H6* 3.2.175–6). Macbeth demands that the 'secret, black, and midnight hags?' be unsparing in their predictions: 'Though bladed corn be lodg'd, and trees blown down' (*MAC* 4.1.48–55). A fine example of lodge meaning to 'lie down' arises in the Dauphin's assertion that his horse merits unlimited praise: 'Nay the man hath no wit that cannot, from the rising of the lark to the lodging of the lamb, vary deserv'd praise on my palfrey' (*H5* 3.7.31–3). Lodge as place of temporary residence occurs with great frequency but is never used more disdainfully than by Boyet when informing the French Princess of the hospitality her party is to receive from the King of Navarre: 'He rather means to lodge you in the field,/Like one that comes here to besiege his court' (*LLL* 2.1.85–6). At the other end of the social spectrum Mistress Quickly complains, 'for we cannot lodge and board a dozen or fourteen gentlewomen that live honestly by the prick of their needles but it will be thought we keep a bawdy-house straight' (*H5* 2.1.32–5). 'Lodged' is occasionally used figuratively in the sense of 'harboured' or 'entertained', as in Richard Gloucester's apparent plea for reconciliation and universal amity: 'If ever any grudge were lodg'd between us' (*R3* 2.1.66).

(C) While the initial impetus for building lodges came from the use of parks for hunting, they could also function on social occasions, or even for assignations. They could be purely functional buildings or extremely elaborate; close to the main house or distant from it. The Triangular Lodge that Thomas Tresham built at Rushton as a warrener's lodge in 1593–5 is entirely constructed round the number three, reflecting his Catholicism and personal symbolism. This extraordinary tiny structure must have been even more eye-catching when surrounded by the rough open **ground** of a large-scale rabbit warren. Tresham's hunting lodge at Lyveden New Bield is even more elaborate, and is the best place for the modern visitor to glimpse the complicated thinking behind such constructions (Eburne 2008). Henderson (2005) explores the lodge as 'loggia' or gallery, an important renaissance architectural form and includes details of their extensive incorporation into sixteenth-century English building forms (Gent 1995). She gives the use of lodges as buildings removed from the house with a gazetteer of surviving structures. See also **garden-house**.

long heath *Calluna vulgaris* is found on moorland or **land** deemed unproductive. Gonzalo, fearing the ship is about to be overwhelmed in the tempest, exclaims: 'Now would I give a thousand furlongs of sea for an acre of barren ground, long heath, brown furze, any thing' (*TMP* 1.1.65–7). Both Arden 2 (8–9) and Arden 3 (148–9) discuss at length various attempts to identify 'long heath'. They cite Hanmer's emendation of 'ling' ('heather') for 'long'. However, they advance the case for a particular **plant** by reference to Lyte's translation of Dodoens' *Niewe Herbal* (1578) who writes of 'long heath' that 'beareth his flowers amongst the stemmes' and 'small heath' which produces **flowers** 'in turfs at the toppes of branches'. Ryden (1978: 31, 69) lists long heath as one of the 15 plants named by Shakespeare that resists attempts at definitive identification. He observes, 'The spinous furze grows together with "long heath", a name used by Lyte in a distinct sense (Calluna as against "Erica")', adding, 'Shakespeare's intention here was not to particularize but to accumulate'.

long purples (A) A precise identification of long purples is elusive: the most realistic possibilities are two native wild **plants**, early purple orchid, *O. mascula* L., and lords-and-ladies or cuckoo-pint, *Arum maculatum* L. The *OED* gives long purples as 'a local name for *Orchis mascula, Lythrum salicaria*, and other plants', citing *HAM*, with two examples from John Clare in 1821, who, however, was writing about purple loose-strife, *L. salicaria*.

(B) Describing Ophelia's drowning, Gertrude details her 'fantastic garlands' made 'Of crow-flowers, nettles, daisies, and long purples/That liberal shepherd's give a grosser name,/But our cull-cold maids do dead men's fingers call them' (*HAM* 4.7.168–71). There can be little doubt that the long purples possess sexual significance given that they are also known by a 'grosser name'. From the onset of her madness, Ophelia's discourse, replete with sexual implications, draws on the symbolic associations of **herbs** and **flowers**. As this is Shakespeare's only reference to the plant it is difficult to extract specific meanings. Ophelia's demise generates a descriptive power surpassing anything the Queen has exhibited during the course of the action. The symbolism attaching to the plants, their physical presence in the mind's eye, allied to the rhythmic flow of a line culminating in the tingling 'long purples', is the embodiment of delicacy. The 'fantastic garlands', 'crownet weeds' and 'weedy trophies' (168–74) all imply incongruity; a gallimaufry of plants, redolent with meaning but, to use the words Ophelia employs when speaking of Hamlet, 'Like sweet bells jangled out of time and harsh' (3.1.158).

(C) Identifications rely heavily on the inexact science of folklore: both possible plants have sexually explicit local names and spotted **leaves**; both could be difficult to work into a crown, which perhaps was of less import than their symbolism. The arum likes a damp habitat, is more finger-like, is a larger, showier plant and has a wider distribution. It has a more sexually explicit appearance, its vernacular name of cuckoo-pint, from pintel or penis, is derived from the clearly phallic upright purple or buff coloured spadix within the sheath-like spathe, making it an obvious candidate. The reputation of the orchid as an aphrodisiac dates from classical times; 'orchis' as Greek for testicle or stone, derived from its stone-like **roots**, was used to treat genital problems. However, it is not a plant of damp places though growth habit may not have played a part in Shakespeare's use. The alternative name of dead men's fingers, possibly derived from finger being used as a euphemism for penis, could refer to either plant. Heath (2003) considers the sources since Lightfoot (1777). He gives the botanical characteristics of both plants, and concludes that Shakespeare wrote of the arum. He picks up on Ophelia's song of bonny sweet Robin (4.5.187), noting that wake-robin served as an alternative name for the arum. Wentersdorf (1978: 416–17) who settles on the 'Wild Arum or Cuckoo-pint' provides an interesting discussion of Ophelia's **garland** and of Lear's coronet focusing on their incongruity or grotesqueness. Otten (1979) in a fascinating article makes a persuasive case for *Serapia's stones,* Gerard's *Satyrion Royall.* She points out that in death Ophelia is 'garlanded with floral genitalia'. Mabey (1996) lists separately the details and associations of the possible candidates. See also Laroche in Bruckner and Brayton (eds) (2011).

lop (A) As a noun the smaller **branches** and **twigs** of a **tree**; as a verb to trim, shorten or cut off. Lopping is the action of such trimming, and figuratively could be applied to the cutting off of the head or **limbs** of a person.

(B) An incisive figurative use is to be found in *H8*. The King dismayed by the report of a new burdensome tax, exposes its folly by means of analogy:

> Sixt part of each?
> A trembling contribution! Why, we take
> From every tree, lop, bark, and part o'th'timber;
> And, though we leave it with a root, thus hack'd,
> The air will drink the sap.
>
> (1.2.94–8)

The imagery is highly effective, revealing the danger of imposing a *rate* of tax that will diminish the productive base of the society and therefore future tax revenues. Assessing the reign of Richard II, the Gardener applies the principles of horticulture to government: 'Superfluous branches/We lop away, that bearing boughs may live;/Had he done so, himself had borne the crown,/Which waste of idle hours hath quite thrown down' (*R2* 3.4.63–6). At the close of the battle of Towton Richard vetoes Edward's intended magnanimity:

> Revoke that doom of mercy, for 'tis Clifford,
> Who, not contented that he lopp'd the branch
> In hewing Rutland when his leaves put forth,
> But set his murth'ring knife unto the root
> From whence the tender spray did sweetly spring,
> I mean our princely father, Duke of York.
>
> (3H6 2.6.46–51)

(C) *Mirror for Magistrates* (1559) notes that lopping encouraged the growth in trees, and suggests its application to people. This is echoed by Southwell when he was facing his own arrest and martyrdom: 'The lopped tree in time may grow againe' (ed. 1967: 57). Drayton (1622) uses lop figuratively in comparing human limbs chopped off in battle to the **boughs** of trees.

love-in-idleness (A) This **plant** is usually, probably correctly, glossed as a native wild **flower**, the heartsease, or wild **pansy**, *Viola tricolor* L., a member of the **violet** family. Some contemporary writers identify it as a violet, while others extend the name to introduced plants of the genus wallflower, *Cheiranthus* L. It is now a rare regional name for the *V. tricolour*. The modern cultivated pansy, a mid-nineteenth century development, is *V. x wittrockiana* Gams ex Kappert. The heartsease or wild pansy is varicoloured; a single flower can include crimson, yellow and purple, hence its identification with the Trinity.

(B) This flower has four names, three of which appear in the plays: in *MND* it is designated both as 'love-in-idleness' and as 'Cupid's flower'; it is found in *HAM* under its more familiar name, 'pansy' where Ophelia says 'And there is pansies, that's for thoughts' (4.5.176–7); its other name 'heartsease' is not present in Shakespeare. It is the subject of a delightful conceit in *MND*. Titania's refusal to surrender the Indian boy to Oberon leads him to retaliate by infusing her eyes with love juice extracted from the flower. The circumstance of its magical potency and its colour transformation is both lyrical and fanciful in a way that brings together images that animate the play. Cupid's misdirected arrow has a profound botanical outcome: 'It fell upon a little western flower,/Before milk-white, now purple with love's wound,/And maidens call it love-in-idleness' (2.1.166–8). Later in the play it is referred to as 'Cupid's flower' (4.1.73). The associations of the flower permeate the play: love, marital disharmony, wantonness, betrayal. Its aphrodisiac effects are manifest. The only other naming of love-in-idleness is probably inadvertent. Lucentio newly arrived in Padua, catches sight of Bianca and immediately falls in love: 'I never thought it possible or likely./But see, while idly I stood looking on,/I found the effect of love-in-idleness' (*SHR* 1.1.149–51). It is unlikely that Henry V is consciously referring to the plant during his long complaint about the burdens of kingship: 'What infinite heart's ease/Must kings neglect, that private men enjoy!' (*H5* 4.1.236–7).

(C) Greene confirms contemporary identification of it as the wild pansy: 'the checkered paunsie or partly coloured hartes ease, an herbe sildome seene' because of lack of agreement between spouses (1592, vol. 11, *A Quip*: 214). Wilson (2004) suggests its use is a clue to Shakespeare's Catholic sympathies, reflecting Catholic practice in anointing the marriage bed. Mabey comments that 'Shakespeare here is mixing classical myth, Midlands vernacular and sheer comic invention' and notes that he 'transforms his own knowledge of plant lore into a fantastical dramatic device' (2010: 107–115).

M

mace see nutmeg

mallow The common, or wild mallow, *Malva sylvestris* L., originally a native **plant** of wasteland it is also cultivated. It has a range of medicinal uses. The single mention of this plant alludes to its intrusive nature as a **weed**. Gonzalo's meditation, 'Had I the plantation of this isle', is mischievously misinterpreted by Antonio to mean 'cultivation' rather than 'colonization'. Antonio gibes, 'He'd sow't with nettle-seed'; inviting Sebastian's quip, 'Or docks, or mallows' (*TMP* 2.1.144–5). Jonson's Mosca refers to it with bitter **herbs** as a plant of no value (1610, *Volpone* 1.1.56). In his land survey Norden (1618) lists mallow with **nettles** and **thistles** as unprofitable symbols of neglected **land**. Heilmeyer (2001: 54) notes 'Mallows are among the oldest cultivated plants known to humans'.

mandrake, mandragora (A) A poisonous, narcotic Mediterranean **plant**, *Mandragora officinarum* has a forked **root**. In cultivation it was probably a sixteenth-century introduction; it was certainly in regular use considerably earlier. Mandrake is difficult to **grow** in northern climes as it requires warmth. Commonly, 'mandrake' indicated the plant and 'mandragora' the drug, although the terms could be interchangeable. Mandrake had anaesthetic, emetic, purgative, soporific, analgesic and aphrodisiac properties; administered with **poppy** – both powerful substances in their own right – mandrake was particularly potent. It was reputed to shriek when pulled up.

(B) Observing the approach of Othello, Iago exults at the sight of his distraught victim: 'Look where he comes! Not poppy, nor mandragora,/Nor all the drowsy syrups of the world/Shall ever medicine thee to that sweet sleep/Which thou ow'dst yesterday' (*OTH* 3.3.330–3). Luxuriating in words that are highly seductive Iago savours the moment – the jealousy he has instigated has worked its magic. Here sublime expression is used to celebrate intense anguish. Sleep, 'Balm of hurt minds' (*MAC* 2.2.36), is revered by the dramatist as the agency of renewal and as one of **nature's** great psychic needs. This speech derives its somniferous effect from subtly articulated assonance. The phrase, 'poppy nor mandragora' is pivotal, the narcotic alliance mirrored in a verbal configuration: 'poppy' is easeful; 'mandragora' possesses a peculiar duality, its repeated 'r' sounds colliding with soft syllables hints at turbulence. Antony's departure for Rome leads Cleopatra to exclaim, 'Give me to drink mandragora', eliciting Charmian's question, 'Why, madam?'. The Egyptian Queen replies with languid hyperbole: 'That I might sleep out this great gap of time/My Antony is away' (*ANT* 1.5.4–6). Belief in the power of the mandrake's scream to kill is indicated by Suffolk: 'Would curses kill, as doth the mandrake's groan...every joint should seem to curse and ban' (*2H6* 3.2.310–19). The conviction that the scream of the mandrake promotes insanity is illustrated by Juliet. She expresses horror at the prospect of waking up in the family vault: 'What with loathsome smells,/And shrieks like mandrakes' torn out of the earth,/That living mortals, hearing them, run mad' (*ROM* 4.3.46–8). The thinness of the mandrake gives rise to Falstaff's jokes in *2H4*. He compares his Page unfavourably with his own bulk: 'Thou whoreson mandrake, thou art fitter to be worn in my cap than to wait at my heels' (1.2.14–16). He is much more expansive when mocking Justice Shallow: ''A was so forlorn, that his dimensions to my thick sight were invisible. 'A was the very genius of famine, yet lecherous as a monkey, and the whores call'd him mandrake' (3.2.313–15).

(C) Accredited with magical powers from the perceived human appearance of its forked root, the mandrake has been recorded as stimulating conception since Genesis. Given its association with lust, fertility and power to bring about downfall and death, it was linked with the **apple** of **Eden**. Lyly (1580, *Euphues*: 286) and Greene (1584, vol. 2, *Anatomie of Fortune*: 224) both refer to the potentially deadly effects of its soporific qualities in identical terms: 'which may cast thee into a dead sleep'. Jonson's Sejanus employs the same combination of mandrake and poppy as *OTH*:

> Well, read my charms,
> And may they lay that hold upon thy senses,
> As thou hast snuffed up hemlock, or ta'en down
> The juice of poppy and of mandrakes.
>
> *(1603 Sejanus, 3.2.107–10).*

Simoons (1998) provides an extensive historical analysis of the mandrake, noting its semi-human attributes from classical times, and the considerable demand which often resulted in substitution of the readily available and much cheaper native white briony, *Bryonia dioica* Jacq. He records its use to stimulate sexual passion and conception, as a medical cure-all, as the cause of and treatment for madness and as a powerful narcotic, often associated with the world of evil spirits and witches. The mythology is perpetuated in chapter six of *Harry Potter and the Chamber of Secrets*. Knight (2009: 107) recounts Gerard's disdain for the superstitions associated with this plant.

manor (A) From Anglo-Saxon times a manor was a unit of English territorial organization in feudal law consisting of the **lands** belonging to or under the jurisdiction of a feudal lord. It came to designate a landed possession, the **estate** of a lord, including both land and manor house; it could indicate the house alone. Manors represented ownership, social status and wealth; as originally understood they were not abolished in English law until the Law of Property Act of 1925. By the sixteenth century manors – as house and land – could be readily bought by a social aspirant to confer status, or provide a dowry to attract a noble but impoverished husband.

(B) The centrality of the manor in terms of status, power and pride in possession is perfectly captured by Warwick as he lies dying on the battlefield: 'My parks, my walks, my manors that I had,/Even now forsake me; and of all my lands/Is nothing left me but my body's length' (*3H6* 5.2.24–6). Critical of the Field of the Cloth of Gold celebrations because of the financial burdens imposed on the participants, Lord Aburgavenny confides: 'I do know/Kinsmen of mine, three at the least, that have/By this so sicken'd their estates, that never/They shall abound as formerly'. Buckingham responds: 'O, many/Have broke their backs with laying manors on 'em/For this great journey' (*H8* 1.1.80–5). The manors on their backs, of course, are the finery essential for themselves and their entourage. Vast capital assets are dissipated to participate in a grand pageant of conspicuous consumption and display. Relinquishing power to Bolingbroke, Richard II lists everything he is surrendering: 'All pomp and majesty I do forswear;/My manors, rents, revenues I forgo' (*R2* 4.1.211–12). At the very moment of dethronement the financial foundation of his position is specified.

(C) In his land survey Norden (1618) records the manor as pivotal in land ownership, where it continued the medieval system of estate management. Massinger's Goldwire summarizes a contemporary meaning of manor as a dowry for the daughters of a social climbing merchant: 'For besides a payment on the nail for a manor/Late purchas'd by my master, his young daughters/Are ripe for marriage'(1632 *The City Madam* 1.1.6–8). McRae (1996: 137–43) notes that contemporary books on **husbandry** were aimed primarily at the owners of manorial estates for whom husbandry was both a gentlemanly and godly pursuit. He suggests that the manorial system of self-sufficiency developed into a seemingly unending process of accumulation of land.

manure (A) Synonymous with **dung**, excrement and **compost**, particularly when spread over or mixed with **soil** as a fertilizer, 'manure' gained general linguistic currency in the sixteenth century. The verb, to manure, came to suggest **tilling** or cultivating the **land**. The concept of land improvement by spreading manure was used figuratively when applied to the blood of those killed on the battle field.

(B) All the uses are figurative. As Bolingbroke is about to ascend the throne Carlisle warns of the inevitable consequences of usurpation. His lengthy and colourful discourse to the assembly is prescient: 'And if you crown him, let me prophesy,/The blood of English shall manure the ground,/And future ages groan for this foul act' (*R2* 4.1.136–8). Commending Hal's temperament over that of his brother John, Falstaff attributes the difference to sack: 'Hereof comes it that Prince Harry is valiant, for the cold blood he did naturally inherit of his father, he hath, like lean, sterile, and bare land, manur'd, husbanded, and till'd with excellent endeavour of drinking good and good store of fertile sherris, that he is become very hot and valiant' (*2H4* 4.3.117–22). Iago's homily on the parallel between the cultivation of the mind and of the **garden** – 'either to have it sterile with idleness or manur'd with industry' – concludes that it is a matter of choice: 'why, the power and corrigible authority of this lies in our wills' (*OTH* 1.3.324–6).

(C) Fitzherbert (1533) and Tusser (1557) are among the earliest writers on manure, but the subject was not developed until Hill (1577) and Heresbach (1596). Spenser (1596) describes the savage wilderness as unpeopled and unmanured. Plat (1609) complains there was a general neglect of manuring, a lack of knowledge of how it should be done, with a consequent shortage of winter fodder. Thirsk (1967) comments on the circular effect of a growing population, with the concomitant increase in the demand for food, leading to increasing requirements for manure to improve the **fertility** of the land, and then to the keeping of larger numbers of animals resulting in pressure on land use and distribution. Woodward (Chartres and Hey 1990) notes the growing awareness from 1500 of inadequate manuring. He details various materials that might be used, suggesting that increasing recognition of the significance of manuring came from the rediscovery of classical texts which focused on the importance of improving the soil. See Geisweidt in Bruckner and Brayton (eds), (2011) for a perceptive essay focusing on *ANT.*

marigold (A) *Calendula officinalis* L. is a naturalized introduction, the **flowers** of which have the frequently noted characteristic of responding to the sun's path in opening and closing; the name was also given to other **plants** of similar habit. It was widely used medicinally, as a hair colourant, and to colour and flavour food as a cheap substitute for **saffron**. Its association with the heavens was possibly transferred from Greek myth to the Virgin Mary, whence derives the etymology of the flower's name. In a now obsolete meaning, a marigold suggested a follower or supporter of Queen Mary; several modern sources give alternative names of **mary-bud** and marygold, suggesting an ongoing connection. The flower was associated figuratively with death, funerals, resurrection and hope.

(B) The Romances are deeply engaged with death and resurrection so it is unsurprising that this flower appears in three out of these five plays. In the earliest, *PER*, Marina **strews** the grave of her nurse Lychorida with 'purple violets, and marigolds' (4.1.15). *WT* is the play where the sense of resurrection is strongest. Among the flowers Perdita presents to Polixenes and Camillo is 'The marigold, that goes to bed wi'th'sun,/And with him rises weeping' (4.4.105–6). *TNK* opens with a song as part of the wedding ceremony. Despite its celebratory nature the song refers to 'Marigolds on death-beds blowing' (1.1.11). Though the association of the flower with graves is apparent the song is full of hope; morbidity is absent. *SON* 25 maintains the connection between hope and death with the image of the marigold:

> Great princes' favourites their fair leaves spread
> But as the marigold at the sun's eye,
> And in themselves their pride lies buried,
> For at a frown they in their glory die.
>
> (5.8.)

As the marigold's display of beauty is contingent on the sun, so too is a courtier's magnificence dependent on the continuing favour of the monarch. 'Marigold', 'buried' and 'die' are packed closely together. Prior to the rape of Lucrece, which precipitates her suicide, she is described lying in bed: 'Her eyes like marigolds had sheath'd their light,/And canopied in darkness sweetly lay,/Till they might open to adorn the day' (*LUC* 397–9). The symbolism of death and resurrection is again in evidence. Celebrated by poets Lucrece finds enduring life in her reputation for purity.

(C) Greene uses the flower's characteristic of following the sun to represent fidelity, saying it could teach a wife duty and submission to her husband; however he also asserts that it represented the inconstancy of women (1589, vol. 9, *Alcida*: 84). Fisher (2011) says the flower was associated with death, and that its link to resurrection and hope came from its habit of daily closing only to reopen in response to the sun the following day. Heilmeyer (2001: 72) observes of the marigold 'Its Latin name is *calendula* or small calendar, derived from the Roman word *calendae*, meaning the first day of the month' and adds 'On account of its bright yellow colour it was also used as a food dye in the Middle Ages instead of expensive saffron.'

marjoram, marjorum *Origanum vulgare*, the native wild marjoram, and the less pungent variety *O. majorana*, sweet or knotted marjoram, had extensive medical uses: for melancholy, to comfort the brain, for urinary retention and as an antidote to poison. Marjoram was also a staple culinary and **strewing herb**. Lafew's commendation of the seemingly dead Helena – 'We may pick a thousand sallets ere we light on such another herb' – elicits Lavatch's riposte, 'Indeed, sir, she was the sweet marjorom of the sallet, or rather the herb of grace' (*AWW* 4.5.16–17). Alluding to repentance Lavatch moves naturally to **rue**, the 'herb of grace'. Addressing what he imagines are soldiers, Lear demands a password from Edgar/Mad Tom and is satisfied with the reply, 'Sweet marjorum' (*LR* 4.6.93). As the **plant** was used to treat mental illness Edgar's response may be a spontaneous exclamation. It seems to serve merely for variety when Perdita includes it among the 'flow'rs' given to Polixenes and Camillo: 'Hot lavender, mints, savory, marjorum' (*WT* 4.4.104). In a playfully witty or conceited sonnet, various flowers are accused of stealing their virtues from the loved one, including 'buds of marjerom had stol'n thy hair' (*SON* 99.7). Wild marjoram was a feature of **knot-gardens** for its **scent** and attractiveness to **bees**. Dodoens (1578) gives its use to treat urinary retention. Bright (1586) includes marjoram in the herbs which he recommends both for alleviating melancholia and to cheer from its **smell**.

marrow As a vegetable, marrow is an eighteenth-century introduction. Bone marrow, the material in bone cavities, was originally thought to constitute the inner substance of the brain and by extension the tissue or substance of both bone and other parts that were particularly sensitive to strong emotions, such as fear, heat and pain. Marrow came to signify an inner core, the seat of strength and vitality with specific sexual connotations.

Figuratively and often with a biblical reference, it suggested nourishing richness, with marrow as fatness, and succulence. Though the word is used ten times, only one of the uses could relate to some kind of **plant**. The misanthropic Timon having exiled himself to the wilderness inverts the usual appeal for plenitude. He pleads with **Nature**, 'Dry up thy marrows, vines, and plough-torn leas,/Whereof ingrateful man, with liquorish draughts/And morsels unctious, greases his pure mind' (*TIM* 4.3.193–5). Editors have been much exercised by this critical line. Some kind of plant could be intended because 'marrows' are linked with 'vines' and cultivated ground. The consensus, however, is that 'marrows' signifies the inner power of **growth** or 'nourishing richness'. Timon is the only character to use the word twice. Castigating the citizens of Athens he calls for a blight to diminish the innermost vitality of the young: 'Lust, and liberty,/Creep in the minds and marrows of our youth' (4.1.25–6). When Hamlet refers to 'The pith and marrow of our attribute' (*HAM* 1.4.22) he means the very core and essence of Danish reputation. This concept of a vital inner force is also articulated by Venus: 'My flesh is soft and plump, my marrow burning' (*VEN* 142).

mary-buds (A) The *OED*, citing Shakespeare as the sole source, identifies mary-bud as either **marigold**, *Calendula officinalis* L., or the marsh-marigold, *Caltha palustris* L. Most commentators favour the marigold.

(B) Its only appearance is in a song. The clownish Cloten employs musicians to herald Imogen:

> Hark, hark, the lark at heaven's gate sings,
>   And Phoebus gins arise,
> His steeds to water at those springs
>   On chalic'd flow'rs that lies;
> And winking Mary-buds begin to ope their golden eyes;
>   *(CYM 2.3.20–4)*

The proximity of 'chalic'd' to 'Mary-buds' promotes awareness of the marigold's association with the Virgin Mary. However, the innocence of this song is framed by Cloten's coarse sexual puns and his contempt for music. Before the performance begins he comments, 'Come on, tune. If you can penetrate her with your fingering, so; we'll try with tongue too' (14–15). At its conclusion – impervious to beauty or purity – he continues the sexual innuendo and musical disparagement. Celebrating the natural world's life-enhancing diurnal rhythms, the song interweaves aesthetic delight with spiritual awareness and like Imogen resists violation or contamination.

(C) Rootsey (1832), a botanist, is the sole dissident in the general identification of Mary-buds as the marigold; he thinks it to be a common rural name for the marsh-marigold, probably identical with the **crow-flower**. See **marigold**.

mast The fallen **fruit** of **beech**, **oak**, **chestnut** and other woodland **trees**, mast was valuable as forage, an essential supply of autumn and winter food for farm and wild animals; this supply was threatened by the enclosure of common land. Mast served as human food from classical times; it has been used to make a drink resembling coffee. 'To mast' is to fatten animals on mast. Mast is also the support for sails on a ship. Only one of the ten uses of mast is arboreal. Subsisting on wild **plants**, Timon challenges the bandits' claim that they are 'not thieves, but men that much do want': 'The oaks bear mast, the briers scarlet heps;/The bounteous huswife Nature on each bush/Lays her full mess before you. Want? why want?' (*TIM* 4.3.419–21). Timon is unsurpassed in expressing the bounty of the **natural** world and its ability to satisfy genuine need. The humble mast plays a strategic role in this richly resonant speech. Elyot (1565) records the use of mast as human food by the Greek philosophers including Socrates, suggesting a simple diet without meat and fish. Plat (1594) says the best oil for lamps comes from beech mast. Heresbach (1596) discusses the relative merits of mast from different trees for a variety of domestic animals, noting that oak is best, followed by beech for cattle and pigs, saying that mast from different trees flavours the meat differently.

mattock A tool resembling a pick at one end, a mattock had an adze-like blade at the other, set at right-angles to the handle and curving inwards towards it. It was used to break up hard **ground**, uproot **bushes** and small **trees**; metaphorically it could imply probing, or **digging** for information. Used three times, and then only in the first two tragedies, the implement is not employed in horticulture. Titus, in his deranged state, instructs Publius and Sempronius to probe the depths and to plead 'for justice and for aid':

> 'Tis you must dig with mattock and with spade,
> And pierce the inmost centre of the earth;
> Then when you come to Pluto's region,
> I pray you deliver him this petition.

> *(TIT 4.3.11–15)*

In *ROM* the implement is used on two occasions to gain access to the Capulet monument. First, Romeo calls out, 'Give me that mattock and the wrenching iron' (5.3.22); later, detaining Friar Lawrence, the Watch report: 'We took this mattock and this spade from him' (5.3.185). Tusser (1573) says the **dibble, rake**, mattock and **spade** are the most essential tools in the **garden**. Heresbach (1596) recommends breaking up the **soil** round trees in the **orchard** with a mattock, before **dunging** them. The modern edition of Hill (1577) has an elegant picture of a **gardener** using a mattock to transplant **seedlings** into a raised bed, which is not representative of the usual more strenuous and less careful use of the tool. Norden (1618) recommends using mattocks to break up ground after **ploughing**, and to clear **furrows** for **grain**. Christianson (2005) has details of contemporary tools used at Hampton Court, including a mattock.

maze (A) Designed as puzzles, mazes had interconnecting paths or passages only one of which provided the correct way through. Earlier mazes often reflected a spiritual aim but in the sixteenth century they mainly provided amusement. Mazed or maz(e)y means in a state of mental confusion, delirium, bewilderment, or having confused, muddled thoughts.

(B) Both literal and figurative uses are represented. Accounting for his arrival in Padua, Petruchio explains: 'Antonio, my father, is deceas'd,/And I have thrust myself into this maze,/Happily to wive and thrive as best I may' (*SHR* 1.2.54–6). He acknowledges that finding the right wife and negotiating the inevitable financial transactions is fraught with hazards and uncertainties. As Alonso attempts to come to terms with the dizzying denouement in *TMP*, he exclaims, 'This is as strange a maze as e'er men trod' (5.1.242). A singular usage arises in *MND* when Titania describes the disruption in the **natural** world caused by disharmony in the fairy kingdom. The mortals have been deprived of their rustic entertainment because the complicated patterns etched on the **grass** have become obscured: 'The nine men's morris is fill'd up with mud,/And the quaint mazes in the wanton green,/For lack of tread, are undistinguishable'. As Titania continues with her complaint she refers to the bewilderment of humankind when confronted by these strange upheavals: 'The chiding autumn, angry winter, change/ Their wonted liveries; and the mazed world,/By their increase, now knows not which is which' (2.1.98–114).

(C) The earliest pleasure-mazes are described by Colonna (1499). When visiting England in 1599, Platter (ed. 1937: 197) described two including that at Nonsuch: 'From here we came to a maze or labyrinth surrounded by high shrubberies to prevent one passing over or through them.' Raleigh uses a maze as a metaphor for false love: 'A maze wherein affection finds no end' (1588, Ault 1949: 127). Amherst (1895: 322) records the 1649 Parliamentary survey for the Cecil house at Wimbledon where there were extensive **knot-gardens**, a maze and a **wilderness**, the maze 'cut out into several meanders, circles, semi-circles, windings and intricate turnings'.

mead, meadow (A) A **field**, rich cultivated **land**, a mead or meadow provided a marked contrast to uncultivated or **untilled** fields. Often depicted as the **flower-strewn** fields of poetry or the flowery background in tapestries, meads and meadows appeared to be the prerogative of the wealthy and leisured, but they could also be enjoyed by working country people who took advantage of their surroundings. They could be threatened by flood, **frost** or neglect. Mead is also an alcoholic drink made by fermenting honey and water.

(B) References are pervasive: they can be colourful and life-enhancing or monochrome and emotionally sombre. Titania provides a topographical essay on the landscape she has traversed with her entourage: 'on hill, in dale, forest, or mead,/ By paved fountain or by rushy brook,/Or in the beached margent of the sea' (*MND* 2.1.83–5). Burgundy's description of the mead is as a flower meadow: 'The even mead, that erst brought sweetly forth/The freckled cowslip, burnet, and green clover' (*H5* 5.2.48–9). The association of the mead with flowers, highly decorative and poetically suggestive, is again present in Arcite's comparison: 'O queen Emilia,/Fresher than May, sweeter/Than her gold buttons on the boughs, or all/Th'enamell'd knacks o'th'mead or garden!' (*TNK* 3.1.4–7). The song of spring at the close of *LLL* describes the flowers that 'Do paint the meadows with delight' (5.2.897). *SON* 33 employs the caressing image of the sun, 'Kissing with golden face the meadows green' (3). A French mariner provides a vivid picture of the English fleet with 'Their streaming ensigns wrought of color'd silk,/Like to a meadow full of sundry flowers' (*E3* 3.1.68–9). In *TMP,* Ceres emphasizes the fecundity of the meadow: 'flat meads thatch'd with stover' (4.1.63). As he apportions his kingdom Lear conveys its beauty and fertility: 'With shadowy forests and with champains rich'd,/With plenteous rivers and wide-skirted meads' (*LR* 1.1.64–5). The epitome of loveliness in the natural landscape, the mead's susceptibility to blighting gives it particular weight as a simile. The transformed Katherine tells the resentful widow in the closing scene of *SHR,* 'Fie, fie, unknit that threat'ning unkind brow,/.../It blots thy beauty, as frosts do bite the meads' (5.2.136–9). The conception of scarred meads as the image of desolation is apparent in *LUC*: 'Poor Lucrece' cheeks unto her maid seem so/As winter meads when sun doth melt the snow' (1217–18). More stark is Titus' image of his grieving family's faces: 'How they are stain'd like meadows not yet dry,/With miry slime left on them by the flood?' (*TIT* 3.1.125–6). Preparing to take the mutilated Lavinia to her father, Marcus laments, 'For such a sight will blind a father's eye./One hour's storm will drown the fragrant meads,/What will whole months of tears thy father's eyes?' (2.4.53–5).

(C) While technically interchangeable with meadow, the term mead is more poetic as evidenced when Heresbach (1596) writing of practicalities, gives pasture and meadows, rather than meads. Drayton (1622) uses meads throughout *Polyolbion*: they are **fruitful**, **grassy**, goodly, flowery, silent, replenished, delicious, pleasant, embroidered, verdant, dainty and rich. But they could also be under threat: if submerged they are **rank**, and they can be despoiled in war. Spenser's mead resembles a rich piece of embroidery: 'And all the meades adorned with daintie gemmes,/Fit to decke maydens bowres,/And crowne their Paramours' (ed. 1999, *Prothalamion*, 14–16). Thirsk (1967) has details of agricultural meadows of the time. Mabey (1996) defines a meadow technically as grassland cut for **hay**, where animals are excluded in the growing time of March to June or July, but suggests that this is now an anachronism; he argues that the sense of what has been lost with intensive agriculture has led to the modern re-creation of wild-flower meadows.

medlar (A) *Mespilus germanica* L. is related to the **hawthorn.** It is noted for its **fruit** which resembles a small, brown-skinned or russet **apple**, and is still propagated by **grafting** on to the hawthorn. Medlar is both the **tree** and its fruit, which in colder countries is hard when **ripe**. It has to be stored to decay or 'blet' before it can be eaten raw or made into jam or jelly. The fruit's appearance led to the nickname of 'open-arse', whence it became a slang word for female genitalia, extended to indicate a prostitute or disreputable woman. It could also provide a play on words with meddle/meddler.

(B) Its literary use is linked to the fruit's reputation as being fit to eat only when it is almost **rotten** and for the word's potential for punning: 'meddle' can mean both sexual intercourse and 'to interfere'. Responding to Touchstone's mockery of Orlando's verses Rosalind disowns them: 'I found them on a tree'. Touchstone keeping up the pressure wittily replies, 'Truly, the tree yields bad fruit'. Administering the *coup de grace* Rosalind puns: 'I'll graff it with you, and then I shall graff it with a medlar. Then it will be the earliest fruit i'th'country; for you'll be rotten ere you be half ripe, and that's the right virtue of the medlar' (*AYL* 3.2.115–20). Turning from the playful to the acerbic, a similar dialogue takes place in *TIM*. Apemantus baits the destitute Timon: 'There's a medlar for thee, eat it'. Expressing disdain for his uninvited visitor Timon retorts, 'On what I hate I feed not'. Persisting, the cynic philosopher asks, 'Dost hate a medlar?' attracting the surly pun: 'Ay, though it look like thee'. Undeterred, Apemantus drives home the lesson he came to deliver to the bankrupt: 'And th'hadst hated meddlers sooner, thou shouldst have lov'd thyself better now' (4.3.304–10). The peculiar quality of the medlar, not being fit to eat until it is almost rotten, translates to a prostitute. Lucio confides to the disguised Duke that he lied in a paternity case because, 'They would else have married me to the rotten medlar' (*MM* 4.3.173–4). The other sexual aspect is intimated by Mercutio as he visualizes Romeo's unprofitable longing for Rosaline:

> Now will he sit under a medlar tree,
> And wish his mistress were that kind of fruit
> As maids call medlars, when they laugh alone.
> O, Romeo, that she were, O that she were
> An open-arse, thou a pop'rin pear!
>
> *(ROM 2.1.34–8)*

The **pear** in question, from Poperinghe near Ypres, is a play on penis and coupling.

(C) Overbury associates the bawd, who is as much procuress as prostitute, with the medlar: 'Here yeeres are sixty and odde: that she accounts her best time of trading; for a Bawde is like a medlar, shee's not ripe, till she be rotten. Her envie is like that of the Devil; To have all faire women like her; and because it is impossible they should catch it being so young, she hurries it to them by diseases'(1616: 62). Quest-Ritson (2001) points out that all levels of society had access to the medlar as fruit. Palter (2002) has details of the bletting process, and the fruit's uses; he includes literary references from Chaucer, notes the repeated play on words of ripe and rotten that accompanied it, and draws on Freeman (1983) for the symbolic link to fertility.

mildew Honey-dew, a **growth** or disease on the surface of a **plant**, is most notable after exposure to damp conditions. 'To mildew' is to contaminate with the disease, whence metaphorically it can apply to human disease and contamination. During Hamlet's confrontation with Gertrude in the closet scene he compares the portrait of his father with that of Claudius: 'This was your husband. Look you now what follows:/Here is your husband, like a mildewed ear,/Blasting his wholesome brother' (*HAM* 3.4.63–5). Not only is there the antithesis between 'mildewed' (diseased and contaminating) and 'wholesome', but 'blasting', meaning 'infecting', captures precisely the action of the murder, the 'leprous distillment' poured into the ear. The word 'blasting' arises three times in Genesis 41 where Joseph, interpreting Pharaoh's dream, predicts that seven years of plenty will be followed by seven years of famine. Edgar, as Mad Tom, uses the verb to intimate the blighting of **ripe crops** when enumerating the afflictions perpetrated by Flibbertigibbet who, 'mildews the white wheat' (*LR* 3.4.118).

mint (A) Any **plant** of the aromatic genus *Mentha* L., some mints are native plants, others naturalized. A staple kitchen and **strewing herb**, discerning cooks and medical practitioners would know which variety would serve their purpose. Mint has a very wide range of medicinal uses, often as **distilled** oil, and has well-documented applications as a contraceptive and abortifacient. Mint is coinage or money, the apparatus or an establishment for such coining; to mint is to coin money, and can indicate the place of origin, the source of invention or fabrication.

(B) The word appears five times: three are numismatic; two relate to the plant. The herbs and flowers distributed by Perdita include, 'Hot lavender, mints, savory, marjorum' (*WT* 4.4.104). All that can be gleaned from this line is that there may be several kinds of mint. Perdita's speech and those that follow reveal her heightened aesthetic sensibility with respect to plants. Just as brief, but rather more puzzling, is Dumaine's contribution to the mockery of Armado during the performance put on for the royal party. Playing Hector of Troy, Armado begins a line, 'I am that flower', provoking Dumaine's interjection, 'That mint', which in turn precipitates Longaville's addition, 'That columbine' (*LLL* 5.2.655). Editors tend to be silent on the import of these comments. Arden 3 (280–1) admits defeat: 'Some insult is implied, but remains obscure'. Presumably, the concept of 'the flower of chivalry' is being undercut by the commonplace mint. The **columbine** has its own derogatory associations including cuckoldry. That there is some link between these plants is the only certainty.

(C) No particular link or shared meaning has been found with columbine. The use of mint to induce abortion or to bring out a still-born foetus is documented from Macer's Herbal of the eleventh century (Riddle 1992). All the contemporary writers devote a considerable amount of space to varieties of mint and its very wide range of medicinal uses. Typical is Gerard (1597: 553) who writes that mint is 'marvellous wholesome' for the stomach among many other uses, also noting that it can work as a contraceptive.

mistletoe *Viscum album* L. is an evergreen, parasitic **plant** growing on the upper **branches** of a variety of usually broad-**leaved trees** including **apple**, **oak**, poplar and **lime**. From pre-historic times it was regarded as sacred and evil, magical and healing. Although its **berries** are poisonous, mistletoe had a number of medicinal uses; the sticky berries provided a reliable source of **lime** for entrapping birds. Its association with paganism, Roman and Norse mythology, and the druidic and Celtic religions caused it to be banned from churches. The single reference is to be found in *TIT* where it is perceived as malign. After describing the woodland's shimmering delicacy Tamora changes the mood. She affects to have been lured to a particularly forbidding spot: 'A barren detested vale you see it is;/The trees, though summer, yet forlorn and lean,/ Overcome with moss and baleful mistletoe' (2.3.93–5). The Queen of the Goths has a singular gift for describing landscape, but this representation appears to be a fiction: the epithet 'baleful' attaching to mistletoe is an effective contrivance. Parkinson (1640) notes disapprovingly that the most superstitious would hang pieces of mistletoe round a child's neck for protection against witchcraft and evil; he thought that if a woman wore a piece on her arm it would help her conceive. Singleton (1922) gives its Norse and classical associations, and Lehner (1960) explains its banning from churches on account of its pagan associations. Mabey (1996) provides extensive details of its folklore.

moss (A) True mosses, *Bryopsida*, grow in large quantities in damp places, on stones or **trees**; moss could also possibly indicate the Fructicose Lichens, prevalent mosses of ancient, particularly **oak, woodland**. Moss could fill or line roofs, and was collected for fodder and bedding for cattle. Moss could signify age and venerability, wildness and lack of the influence of civilization, or the grave.

(B) All five references to moss are of interest. A compassionate representation arises in *CYM*. Contemplating winter Arviragus imagines, 'The raddock would,/ With charitable bill' place 'furr'd moss' on Imogen/Fidele's grave 'When flow'rs are none' (4.2.224–8). Adriana strikes a very different note when accusing her husband of infidelity: 'If aught possess thee from me, it is dross,/Usurping ivy, brier or idle moss' (*ERR* 2.2.177–8). Glendower's claim that his birth was heralded by remarkable events in the **natural** world is ridiculed by Hotspur. He ascribes the phenomena to trapped wind in the earth's womb, 'which, for enlargement striving,/Shakes the old beldame earth, and topples down/Steeples and moss-grown towers' (*1H4* 3.1.30–2). Moss representing longevity is used, too, in *AYL*. Oliver describes the place where Orlando discovered him sleeping in the **forest**: 'Under an old oak, whose boughs were moss'd with age/And high top bald with dry antiquity' (4.3.104–5). The entire narrative, set in a peculiar idiom, is not naturalistic scene painting but pastiche. What Tamora achieves when pretending to have been lured to a forbidding part of the **hunting park** is a lurid fiction: 'A barren detested vale you see it is;/The trees, though summer, yet forlorn and lean,/Overcome with moss and baleful mistletoe' (*TIT* 2.3.93–5). Moss plays its part in authenticating this all too plausible narrative.

(C) Tusser (1573) thinks moss a nuisance if it grows on thatched roofs, and recommends its removal. Gascoigne (1575) records that the Queen was greeted at Kenilworth by a **green** man covered in moss, suggestive of the wild. Spenser (ed. 1999, *The Shepheardes Calendar*) uses moss to represent age. He writes of being overcast with grey moss, mossy **branches** of old oak, green moss to cover nakedness, and bare ground covered with hoary moss. Peacham (1612) says that emblematically moss represents humility.

mulberry (A) *Morus nigra* L. the black mulberry belongs to the same botanical family as the **fig**; both are thought to be Roman introductions into England. It is a slow-growing, slow-**fruiting tree**. The fruit is so soft to the touch that the slightest pressure stains both hands and clothing when **harvested**. In Ovid's *Metamorphoses* the fruit was originally white but acquired its dark-red colour by virtue of being stained with the blood of Pyramus. It could be confused with the biblical **sycamore** fig, also *Morus*, and the sycamore, *Acer pseudoplatanus* L., an entirely different tree. Eaten as a fruit it was sometimes called a **blackberry** or included under the general heading of **berries**. Mulberry had a wide range of medicinal uses, and symbolically from its slow-growing habit it signified patience.

(B) Four of the five uses are literal. The single figurative application occurs in *COR*, where Volumnia instructs Coriolanus how to re-engage the plebeians with a display of humility. At the very centre of this master-class in political manoeuvring is an unexpected image:

> Thy knee bussing the stones (for in such business
> Action is eloquence, and the eyes of th'ignorant
> More learned than the ears), waving thy head,
> Which often thus correcting thy stout heart,
> Now humble as the ripest mulberry
> That will not hold the handling:

(3.2.75–80)

Titania instructs her fairies to pamper Bottom: 'Feed him with apricocks and dewberries,/ With purple grapes, green figs, and mulberries' (*MND* 3.1.166–7). These rhythmic lines celebrate the colour and fleshy sensuality of the fruits. The implication that mulberries grow freely in the woods recurs in *TNK* where the Jailer's Daughter is reported repeating 'Palamon is gone,/Is gone to th'wood to gather mulberries./I'll find him out to-morrow' (4.1.67–9). The Mechanicals' play of 'very tragical mirth' (*MND* 5.1.57) describes a double suicide: 'And Thisby, tarrying in mulberry shade,/His dagger drew, and died' (5.1.148–9). In Golding's Ovid the tragic lovers arrange to 'tarie underneath a tree', bearing the 'faire high Mulberie with fruit as white as snow'. Once 'besprickled' with Pyramus' blood, 'A deep darke purple colour straight upon the Berries cast' (Bk 4, 89–90). Mulberries are also associated with tragedy in *VEN*. The goddess, grieving over the dead Adonis, laments:

> When he was by, the birds such pleasure took,
> That some would sing, some other in their bills
> Would bring him mulberries and ripe-red cherries:
> He fed them with his sight, they him with berries.

(1101–4)

(C) Parkinson comments on its growth habit and medicinal qualities; he lists it with sycamore, which he calls the mulberry fig, and the true fig tree (1640: 1491–3).

Andrews (1993) writes of the extensive **planting** of fruit trees at Theobalds, where there was a Green or Mulberry Walk, with 72 mulberry trees planted against a brick **wall** for warmth. Campbell-Culver (2001) details James I's planned silk-industry.

mushrumps, mushroom A fleshy fungal **fruiting** body with a **stalk** and dome-shaped cap lined underneath with gills; a mushroom is also the macroscopic fruiting body of a fungus, especially a basidiomycete. The most common culinary mushroom is *Agaricus bisporus*. Although they are all part of the same biological kingdom, in popular language 'mushroom' represents the edible species, while 'toadstool' applies to the inedible or poisonous ones, associated with fairies as in fairy rings, and the world of magic. The mushroom is proverbial for its rapid **growth**, hence its secondary meaning of something that has suddenly sprung up, or an upstart. The solitary *naming* of this fruiting body is part of Prospero's incantatory rehearsal of his achievements: 'you demi-puppets that/By moonshine do the green sour ringlets make,/Whereof the ewe not bites; and you whose pastime/Is to make midnight mushrumps' (*TMP* 5.1.36–9). The curfew is the time when spirits are free to engage in activities which include the making of fairy rings. These are also alluded to by the disguised Mistress Quickly when encouraging her fellow 'fairies': 'And nightly, meadow-fairies, look you sing,/Like to the Garter's compass, in a ring'(*WIV* 5.5.65–6). Here again mushrooms are associated with magic and fairy circles. Marlowe's Ithamore suggests their association with an underclass: ''Tis a strange thing of that Jew, he lives upon pickled grasshoppers and sauced mushrooms' (1590, *The Jew of Malta*: 4.4.67–8), while Flamineo suggests the meaning of an upstart: 'and if gentlemen enough, so many earlie mushromes, whose best growth sprang from a dunghill, should not aspire to gentilitie' (Webster 1612, *The White Devil:* 3.3.41).

music (A) A frequent leisure activity in the early modern **garden**, music was played in open **galleries** round courtyard gardens which provided elegant settings where the sounds would not be lost, as well as in the gardens themselves. Musicians would provide entertainment and distraction on long journeys on the Thames between palaces and great houses.

(B) Music is a significant feature in many of the plays. Engendering delight, sadness, anguish and consolation it can be crucial for restoring health to the body or the mind, and is a critical ingredient in magical events. There are well over 200 references to music in the canon – with an abundance of open air performances, many of them taking place in gardens. The outdoor music initiated by Lorenzo in *MV* suffuses the scene, exerting an influence on atmosphere and discourse. Having instructed the musicians, 'bring your music forth into the air', Lorenzo reflects on the night-sky and human responsiveness:

> How sweet the moonlight sleeps upon this bank!
> Here will we sit, and let the sound of music
> Creep in our ears. Soft stillness and the night
> Become the touches of sweet harmony.

Following his lyrical contemplation of the music of the spheres, Lorenzo bids the musicians, 'Come ho, and wake Diana with a hymn,/With sweetest touches pierce your mistress' ear'. Jessica, however, darkens the tone with her reflection, 'I am never merry when I hear sweet music'. Turning this avowal into a commendation – 'the reason is your spirits are attentive' – her lover declares, 'The man that hath no music in himself,/ Nor is not moved with concord of sweet sounds,/Is fit for treasons, stratagems and spoils'. The arrival of Portia and Nerissa introduces another strand into this discourse. Nerissa's observation, 'It is your music, madam, of the house', prompts Portia's thoughtful response, 'Nothing is good, I see, without respect;/Methinks it sounds much sweeter than by day' (5.1.53–100). The blending of music with the **natural** world, pervasive in the plays and in the culture of the day, finds memorable expression in Caliban's reverie (*TMP* 3.2.135–43).

A particularly playful scene with garden music occurs in *ADO*. As the teasing conspirators Don Pedro and Claudio draw the musicians into the garden, the young man points to the intimate relationship between sound and setting: 'How still the evening is,/ As hush'd on purpose to grace harmony!'. Benedick, however, overhearing the music from his place of concealment, muses, 'Now, divine air! now is his soul ravish'd!/Is it not strange that sheep's guts should hale souls out of men's bodies?'. This scene in the garden engages the variegated strands of the play. The song itself glances at male inconstancy: 'Sigh no more, ladies, sigh no more,/Men were deceivers ever' (2.3.38–63). The serenading of women by musicians beneath their windows happens several times: pivotally in *ADO* (3.3.144–63); sordidly in *CYM* (2.3.11–31); and movingly in *TGV* where Proteus' direction to the musicians to render the song 'Who is Silvia?' (4.2.39–53) is overheard by his betrayed lover Julia. The consolatory aspect of music outdoors finds expression in *MM*. The disguised Duke encounters Mariana listening to a melancholy love song: 'Take, O, take those lips away,/That so sweetly were forsworn'. She explains, 'My mirth it much displeas'd, but pleas'd my woe' (4.1.1–13). In a play dominated by darkness, it is one of the few daylight scenes. It usually follows the interval as the beginning of the process of renewal – though more uncertainly than is the entrance of the singing wayfarer Autolycus at a similar stage of *WT* (4.3.1–12). Feste is the chief agency of music in *TN*. His songs give eloquent expression to life's travails. From the warning that 'Youth's a stuff will not endure' (2.3.51) through the melancholy 'come away death' (2.4.51) to the refrain of the song that closes the play, 'For the rain it raineth every day' his music weaves a rainbow ribbon through the action. However, it is Cesario/Viola in the guise of Orsino's ambassador of love who exerts the greatest influence. Responding to Olivia's challenge, 'Why, what would you do?' the young messenger replies,

> Make me a willow cabin at your gate,
> And call upon my soul within the house;
> Write loyal cantons of condemned love,
> And sing them loud even in the dead of night;
>
> *(1.5.267–71)*

The impassioned reaction to rejected love which captures Olivia's heart, images a garden complete with a 'willow cabin', the retreat of the spurned lover. Duke Senior in *AYL* takes the accomplished Amiens with him to the Forest of Arden where he provides the antidote to harsh conditions with the song 'Blow, blow, thou winter wind' (2.7.174–90). This play, which has more songs than any other, concludes with a dance. Likewise, in *LLL,* a play where most of the action takes place in the **park**, Rosaline appears to accept an invitation to dance – 'Play, music, then!' – only to dash the hopes of the young men with the abrupt, 'Not yet; no dance: thus change I like the moon' (5.2.210–12). The even more capricious Cleopatra informs her entourage, 'Give me my angle, we'll to th'river; there,/My music playing far off, I will betray/Tawny-finn'd fishes' (*ANT* 2.5.10–12). These examples convey enthusiasm for out-of-doors music and affinity between this versatile entertainment and gardens or landscape.

(C) The modern edition of Hill (1577) includes a picture of musicians entertaining those sitting in an **arbour** and two outside who appear to be dancing. Woodhouse (1999) gives Laneham's comment that the 1575 Kenilworth entertainment included music 'for rejoysing the mynd'. She quotes Nichols on Kenilworth, as saying music was played under the Queen's window, and that musicians, hidden in a **bower,** were playing as she passed out of the park. Henderson (2005) marks the correlation between the intersecting forms of the Elizabethan dance and the designs of the gardens, where they were sometimes performed. She documents the use of music in gardens and notes that Bacon's water gardens at Gorhambury included a banqueting house with a dedicated music room. Dent (1981: M1319.1).

musk-rose (A) Contextually a wild **plant**, musk-rose presents identification problems because *Rosa moschata* Mill, the musk-rose, is cultivated rather than wild. *R. arvensis* Huds. the field-rose seems a possible candidate if Shakespeare is assumed to be botanically correct. It seems more likely, however, that he included the musk-rose for its **scent** rather than being concerned with botanical exactitude. The musk rose is important as the parent of a group of roses, including the **damask** rose, much valued for their scent and long-**blooming** season.

(B) The musk-rose appears only in *MND,* a play imbued with the scent, colour and texture of plants. The first mention is in Oberon's celebrated paean to the delicate, sensuous, luxurious space of Titania's repose, 'Quite over-canopied with luscious woodbine,/With sweet musk-roses and with eglantine' (2.1.251–2). This **perfumed bower** is a theatre of dreams. Mabey (2010: 112) observes that the diverse plants included in this speech, 'grow in different habitats, and flower at different times of the year'. This may be true – but not in the fairy kingdom. On such occasions Shakespeare's extravagant imagination and verbal virtuosity transcends botanical constraints. The second mention is more prosaic. Allocating tasks to her fairy entourage Titania commands: 'Some to kill cankers in the musk-rose buds' (2.2.3). These roses are to be protected from the invasive grub. The Fairy Queen's affection for this flower is again apparent when she **garlands** Bottom: 'Come sit thee down upon this flow'ry bed,/

While I thy amiable cheeks do coy,/And stick musk-roses in thy sleek smooth head' (4.1.1–3). This moment, intensified by Oberon's elaborate description a few lines later (51–6), has inspired many painters to recreate the scene.

(C) The *OED* summarizes the identification problems. Parkinson (1629) says the musk-rose is autumn-flowering, and found only in gardens; he particularly recommends it grown over an **arbour** for its powerful sweet **smell**. Reasoning from the **canker** in *MND* 2.2.4, Singleton (1922) suggests that Shakespeare meant the dog- or canker-rose, *R. canina* L., quoting Hakluyt as saying that the musk rose was introduced c. 1532 from North Africa or Spain, that it was a tall rose, used for arbours, clearly not a wild plant. Thomas (1955), a notable rose authority, gives the *R. moschata* or musk-rose as a c. 1590 introduction from western Asia into European gardens, and says that its scent can travel up to one hundred yards, so making it a distinct candidate for the 'sweet musk-rose', but most unlikely to be growing in the wild. For Shakespeare's plants Potter (2010) in her extensive history of the rose draws on Gerard for the musk-rose as a wild plant.

mustard, Mustardseed (A) Members of the *Brassicacaea* or **cabbage** family, mustard includes *Brassica nigra* L., the native black mustard; other plants belong to the genus *Sinapis* L., several of which have been domesticated or are still used from the wild, including *S. arvensis* or charlock. Mustard can refer to any **plant** of the family used to make the condiment of mustard to add pungency to food. As a paste, mustard was applied to plasters for external application for specific conditions. Mustard with a prefix of a place name denotes its association with a particular source of manufacture as in Tewkesbury mustard.

(B) On all three occasions when mustard is referred to as a condiment it is the source of comic banter. Touchstone makes repeated use of the word before resolving his conundrum to demonstrate that the knight was not forsworn: 'swearing by his honor, for he never had any; or if he had, he had sworn it away before ever he saw those pancakes or that mustard' (*AYL* 1.2.77–80). Darker is Grumio baiting the hungry Katherine in *SHR*. Starting with the question, 'What say you to a piece of beef and mustard?' his verbal 'game' ends with the taunt, 'Why then the mustard without the beef' (4.3.23–30). More pithy is Falstaff's reply to Doll's observation, 'They say Poins has a good wit': 'He a good wit? Hang him, baboon! his wit's as thick as Tewkesbury mustard' (*2H4* 2.4.239–41). Mustardseed, described in the Bible as the smallest of all **seeds**, appears only in *MND* as the name of one of the fairies. Bottom alludes to its role as fodder, its association with forbearance and as being hot: 'Good Master Mustardseed, I know your patience well. That same cowardly, giant-like ox-beef hath devour'd many a gentleman of your house. I promise you your kindred hath made my eyes water ere now' (3.1.191–5).

(C) Cogan (1584: 167) notes 'The best mustard that I knowe in all England is made at Tewkesbery in Glocestershyre.' Thirsk (1967) gives mustard as a specialist **crop** in Norfolk and around Tewkesbury. McLean (1981) includes its value in disguising **rotten** food, because the oil first irritates then anaesthetizes the digestive system; she notes that taken after a large meal it would act as an emetic. Mason (2006) has a separate entry in her book of local foods for Tewkesbury mustard, notes its dull ochre colour, saying it was made from coarsely ground crushed mustard seed, and had a sharp taste, with sweet, horseradish-like aftertaste. Karim-Cooper (2006) gives mustard seed as a major ingredient of Elizabethan cosmetics, including those used on the stage. The biblical mustard seed refers to black mustard *Brassica nigra*: 'The kingdom of heaven is like a grain of mustard seed…which is indeed the least of all seeds: but when it is grown, it is the greatest among herbs, and becometh a tree' (Mt. 13.31–2)

myrtle (A) A small **tree** of the Mediterranean family, *Myrtus*, notably *M. communis*, has dark, shiny, evergreen aromatic **leaves** and **fragrant** white **flowers**, its **wood** soft, offering no resistance. Even though rare it supplied some medicinal remedies. There appears to be no clear evidence on the date of the myrtle's introduction; it was possibly a Roman survival, or a much later arrival. It can be **grown** in the south of England, and has traditionally been associated with weddings, an extension perhaps of its association with Venus, in whose honour myrtle **groves** were **planted**.

(B) All six references to this plant are interesting. They arise in political, social and romantic contexts. *ANT* has a particularly delicate image. Antony's envoy introduces himself to Octavius Caesar with due humility: 'I was of late as petty to his ends/As is the morn-dew on the myrtle leaf/To his grand sea' (3.12.8–10). The symbolism of mortification may be present here as it is a moment of degradation for Antony. Contrasting heavenly justice with the harshness of human judgement, Isabella denounces Angelo's condemnation of her brother: 'Merciful heaven,/Thou rather with thy sharp and sulphurous bolt/Splits the unwedgeable and gnarled oak/Than the soft myrtle' (*MM* 2.2.114–17). The natural antithesis of the oak and the myrtle is a potent element in a wide-ranging debate about justice, social values and human frailty. All four romantic uses, three of them in *PP*, encompass the delicate nature of a myrtle grove and celebrate its leaves. The emotional colouration attaching to this plant is demonstrated in *VEN*. The anxious Venus, fearful for Adonis' safety, hurries away in the hope of finding him: 'she hasteth to a myrtle grove,/Musing the morning is so much o'er worn,/And yet she hears no tidings of her love' (865–7). The myrtle's symbolic identification with love and joy may be overlaid in this case with its other place in mythology as the death tree. The association of Venus and Adonis with the plant is also present in *PP*: 'Venus, with Adonis sitting by her,/Under a myrtle shade began to woo him' (xi, 1–2). The grove again presents itself as the ideal shaded place at the opening of xx: 'In the merry Month of May,/Sitting in a pleasant shade,/Which a grove of myrtles made' (2–4). The beauty of the natural world represented in embroidery is revealed in *PP* when the lover promises his sweetheart 'A cap of flowers, and a kirtle/Embroidered all with leaves of myrtle' (19.11–12). Clearly this plant is extolled for its natural beauty and for its romantic associations.

(C) The extensive use of myrtle that Colonna (1499) notes is testimony to its Mediterranean origins: he includes groves of myrtles, dried myrtle burnt for its aromatic smell, and uses it for **arbours**, **knots** and **strewing**. Greene knew the tree's reputation for soft wood: 'As the sappy Myrtle tree wil quickly rotte: so the hard Oake will never be eaten with wormes' (1580–3, vol. 2, Mamillia: 61). Bacon (1625) includes it in his ideal garden. In Catholic iconography it symbolized mortification (Hawkins 1633). Lehner (1960) says it was sacred to Hebrews who covered the tent of Tabernacle with myrtle, to Egyptians as a symbol of love and joy, and in Greece and Rome where it was dedicated to Aphrodite and Venus respectively. Heilmeyer (2001: 60) notes 'In Ancient Greece members of the Athenian municipal authorities wore wreaths of myrtle as a symbol of their power and willingness to reach a mutual agreement.' She also observes that 'whoever suffered the pain of unrequited love … would be turned into a myrtle grove in the underworld'.

N

narcissus (A) The genus *Narcissus* L. covers a large number of spring-**flowering** bulbs, including **daffodils**, natives of Europe and the Mediterranean. Modern botany has daffodil and narcissus in one genus *Narcissus* L., the sub-divisions of which now number thousands. In Greek mythology Narcissus was a beautiful youth who fell in love with his own reflection in water and subsequently pined to death, hence its allusive use to suggest someone characterized by extreme self-admiration and vanity, a narcissist.

(B) All five references allude to the youth of mythology though one also applies to the **plant**. Emilia wandering in the **garden** with her lady asks, 'What flow'r is this?'. Informed ''Tis call'd narcissus, madam', Emilia sighs, 'That was a fair boy certain, but a fool,/To love himself. Were there not maids enough?'. Reflecting on the custom of embroidering clothes, bed linen and hangings with illustrations of the **natural** world she enquires, 'Canst not thou work such flowers in silk, wench?' (*TNK* 2.2.119–30).

(C) Turner (1548) appears to be feeling his way towards a botanical distinction between narcissus and daffodil, writing of the white daffodil as *Narcissus heabacus*, and separately of the yellow daffodil. In company with his contemporaries he sees the asphodel as an 'affodil or daffodil', a type of narcissus, although it is now known to belong to a different botanical family. Coats (1968) summarizes classical mythology and plant identification. Stuart and Sutherland (1987) give sixteenth-century dates for the introduction of some varieties.

nature (A) For early modern man the **garden** could represent nature untamed and uncontrolled; it was the work of the **gardener** to discipline and control it. 'Disnatured' suggests the forcible removal of a person's nature or identity, while 'unnatural' has connotations of going against particular aspects of nature. Nature can be the power perceived as energizing the material world, sometimes personified as Mother Nature.

(B) The word is ubiquitous and has many implications: in *LR* where the word is used more frequently than in any other play there are at least seven distinct meanings. This discussion focuses on plants and their hinterland: the natural world both as a creative force and as an ecological system amenable to empirical scrutiny. Two remarkable phrases capture the intricacy of the natural world and its resistance to scientific analysis. Having asked Aeneas not to divulge his assignation with Cressida, Troilus is assured, 'the secrets of nature/Have not more gift in taciturnity' (*TRO* 4.2.72–3). Though current at the time in the discourse of the natural world the term 'secrets of nature' when juxtaposed with 'taciturnity' is revelatory. The compact phrase opens a window to the challenges faced by the most rigorous scientific enquiry. Nature is subjected to constant interrogation but strenuously resists explication. Challenged by Charmian, 'Is't you, sir, that know things?' the Soothsayer responds, 'In nature's infinite book of secrecy/A little I can read' (*ANT* 1.2.8–11). Despite rapid scientific progress, the dramatist is acutely aware of the enormous gap between the store of human understanding and the infinite and yet to be probed complexities of the natural world.

The Romances' engagement with human genetics in terms of the transmission of physical characteristics spills over into the sphere of botany in *WT*. Though there was no genuine understanding of the process of cross-fertilization there was a fervent desire to find ways of augmenting plant diversity. Perdita resists **growing** 'carnations and streak'd gillivors (Which some call Nature's bastards)' because as she expresses it 'There is an art which in their piedness shares/With great creating Nature'. This is countered by Polixenes who maintains that enhancement of **plant** variety does not undermine the integrity of Nature:

> Yet Nature is made better by no mean
> But Nature makes that mean; so over that art
> Which you say adds to Nature, is an art
> That Nature makes. You see, sweet maid, we marry
> A gentler scion to the wildest stock,
> And make conceive a bark of baser kind
> By bud of nobler race. This is an art
> Which does mend Nature – change it rather; but
> The art itself is Nature.

As far as Polixenes and the plant collectors of the day were concerned Nature is an active agent – intervention is complementary; the relationship collaborative. Perdita and the princes in *CYM* are hybrids, of royal birth but brought up in a rustic environment. All exhibit a refinement of nature. Extolling the dignity of his adopted sons Belarius draws instinctively on plants for his imagery:

> O thou goddess,
> Thou divine Nature, thou thyself thou blazon'st
> In these two princely boys! They are as gentle
> As zephyrs blowing below the violet,
> Not wagging his sweet head; and yet as rough,
> Their royal blood enchaf'd, as the rud'st wind
> That by the top doth take the mountain pine
> And make him stoop to th'vale.

> *(4.2.169–76)*

An aspect of this refinement of human nature is the tendency to appreciate, represent and elevate Nature in diverse ways. Capturing or reconfiguring nature is exhibited by Marina who, 'with her needle composes/Nature's own shape of bud, bird, branch, or berry,/That even her art sisters the natural roses;/Her inkle, silk, twin with the rubied cherry' (*PER* Cho.5.5–8). Enumerating the largesse that 'Nature and Fortune' have bestowed on her son, Constance concludes, 'Of Nature's gifts thou mayst with lilies boast,/And with the half-blown rose'(*JN*3.1.52–4). Nature's fecundity is highlighted by Timon who scornfully dismisses the thieves' assertion that their theft arises from 'want': 'The bounteous huswife Nature on each bush/Lays her full mess before you' (*TIM* 4.3.420–1). Gonzalo's discourse on utopia anticipates a creative force that is boundless: 'All things in common nature should produce/Without sweat or endeavour' (*TMP* 2.1.160–1).

Burgundy's description of the despoliation of French agriculture caused by the English invasion is a frequently cited passage in this volume, but two lines demand attention here: 'And all our vineyards, fallows, meads, and hedges,/Defective in their natures, grow to wildness' (*H5* 5.2.54–5). Paradoxically, cultivation is perceived as natural; wildness as deviant. War violates the symbiotic collaboration between human agency and nature.

The conception of Nature holding together all the elements in equilibrium lies behind many of the anguished cries of desperate or despairing characters who either *dare* or *will* chaos or annihilation. Northumberland receiving news of Hotspur's death commits himself to renewed rebellion: 'Let heaven kiss earth! now let not Nature's hand/Keep the wild flood confin'd! let order die!'(*2H4* 1.1.153–4). Macbeth is even more forceful, demanding the Weird Sisters keep nothing back when foretelling the future: 'though the treasure/Of nature's germains tumble all together,/Even till destruction sicken' (*MAC* 4.1.58–60). The idea that **seeds** constitute the ultimate matter of nature is also ventilated by **Lear** as he challenges the elements on the **heath**. Conjuring up an image of universal destruction he concludes with the plea, 'Crack nature's moulds, all germains spill at once/That makes ingrateful man!'(*LR* 3.2.8–9).

(C) Bradford (1933) and others suggest that in *WT* Shakespeare is anticipating the idea of 'hybridization'. The key to a genuine understanding of this process, plant sexuality, was not achieved for at least another century. Dolan (1993) and Munroe in Bruckner and Brayton (eds) (2011), focus on art and nature in *WT*. Significant in the context of art and nature is Montaigne's essay 'Of Cannibals' (published in 1580 reprinted *TMP* Arden 3 (303–14)). Writing of the Wilton garden, Taylor (1623) sums up the relationship between art and nature in the garden, with Nature as the gardener's tutor and the gardener as a modern Adam. Bushnell (2003) links teaching and gardening, and explores the extensive early modern debate around nature and the garden. Henderson (2005) comments on the wild man who represented the natural world, while civilized man had control over nature; she notes that this was reflected in the ideas of the pageant for the Queen at Kenilworth in 1575 and gives details of the **green** room at Theobalds which was said to be so natural a garden that the birds flew in to nest in its artificial **trees**. Tigner (2012: 10) in her extensive consideration of literature and the Renaissance garden argues that the garden 'functions uniquely as the crossroad between culture and nature'. See Dent (1981:N42, 43, 47). See also **gillyvor, scion, stock**.

nettle (A) *Urtica dioica* L., the native common stinging nettle, is a **weed** of waste, uncultivated or neglected **ground**, with stinging hairs which can cause considerable discomfort to human beings and to some animals. Nettle can suggest any similar **plant** with the same stinging properties; the name is also applied to other plants usually of the *Lamiaceae* or dead-nettle family, which lack the sting of the true nettle. It had a wide range of medical applications ranging from treatment of cancers to counteracting stings and poisons; it was thought to act as an aphrodisiac and contraceptive.

(B) Of its numerous uses the nettle carries symbolic potential only in the coronets of Ophelia and Lear. However, it plays a significant part in vitalizing expression. Gertrude describes Ophelia's 'fantastic garlands' consisting of 'crow-flowers, nettles, daisies, and long purples' (*HAM* 4.7.169–70). Nettles reputed to heal wounds and give comfort were seen as a remedy for a diseased mind. This symbolism may also apply to Lear's 'crown' of 'hardocks, hemlock, nettles, cuckoo-flow'rs' (*LR* 4.4.4). These plants suggest wide-ranging and possibly contradictory implications characteristic of a fractured mind searching for a mode of articulacy. Accounting for the transformation of the wayward Prince to a model King, The Bishop of Ely provides a succinct analogy: 'The strawberry grows underneath the nettle,/And wholesome berries thrive and ripen best/Neighbor'd by fruit of baser quality' (*H5* 1.1.60–2). Disdain for the plant is expressed in *TMP* when Antonio mockingly responds to Gonzalo's vision of colonizing the island: 'He'd sow't with nettle-seed' (2.1.145). The discomfort caused by nettles is illustrated by Richard II's plea to his kingdom's 'Dear earth': 'Yield stinging nettles to mine enemies' (*R2* 3.2.6–18). Leontes likens the condition of sexual betrayal to, 'thorns, nettles, tails of wasps' (*WT* 1.2.329).

The term 'nettled' has probably lost touch with its origins but its metaphorical use is very clear in *3H6* when the young Edward, Prince of Wales, observes approvingly, 'Nay, mark how Lewis stamps as he were nettled' (3.3.169). Hotspur's angry response to the King's treatment of the Northumberland family provokes Worcester's rebuke, 'Why, what a wasp-stung and impatient fool/Art thou to break into this woman's mood'. Unbowed the charismatic hero seizes upon the stinging image: 'Why, look you, I am whipt and scourg'd with rods,/Nettled and stung with pismires, when I hear/Of this vile politician Bullingbrook' (*1H4* 1.3.236–41). Later in the play he scorns the cautionary advice of a potential ally: ''Tis dangerous to take a cold, to sleep, to drink, but I tell you, my lord fool, out of this nettle, danger, we pluck this flower, safety' (2.3.8–10). A nettle as commonplace is present in Menenius' caustic comment on the tribunes: 'We call a nettle but a nettle, and/The faults of fools but folly' (*COR* 2.1.190–1). A 'countryman' or rustic dancer in *TNK* is provoked into using an aphorism when chastising a colleague for losing his temper: 'Now when the credit of our town lay on it,/Now to be frampal, now to piss o'th'nettle!' (3.5.56–7).

(C) Albertus Magnus (1565: 4) says that if a man holds both nettle, and yarrow, he is 'sure from all feare, & fantasye, or vysion' possibly suggesting nettle as a treatment for madness. In that case Lear (4.4.4) is wearing his own cure. Gerard (1597: 569–72) says that it 'stirs up lust'. He adds that it can be an antidote both for its own sting, and work as a counter-poison to **mushrooms, hemlock**, henbane and serpent stings. Mabey (1996) includes its folk-lore and details its British habitat. Heath (2003) suggests Victorian sensibilities preferred prettiness to sexual innuendo when they identified the nettles in Ophelia's **garland** with the dead nettle, *Lamium*. He analyses contemporary comment and subsequent identifications. If it could be used to treat madness, that would make nettle an appropriate plant for both Ophelia and Lear. Heath suggests Lear's weeds appear to have been chosen for their symbolism and medicinal properties rather than any reference to an ecologically correct habitat.

nosegay, posy (A) A bunch of fresh **flowers, herbs** or nose-herbs, a nosegay or posy was carried to provide a sweet **smell** to counter the stench of urban surroundings. It could be a decorative luxury, a small posy or bunch of flowers picked from a cottage **garden**, or a symbol of a holiday. Both nosegays and posies conjured up an idyllic rustic life. A collection of poems can still be known as a nosegay or posy, the latter from the archaic 'poesie'. A posy is also a short inscription on or inside a ring.

(B) There are no examples of 'posy' as a bunch of flowers though there are three mentions of the word signifying an inscription on a ring (*MV* 5.1.148–51; *HAM* 3.2.152). Nosegays, however, are present as love tokens. Disrupting the opening scene of *MND,* Egeus complains to Duke Theseus that Lysander has 'bewitch'd' his daughter Hermia, with 'Knacks, trifles, nosegays, sweetmeats' (1.1.27–34). The young Shepherd, designated 'Clown', complains that Perdita's lavish preparation for the sheep-shearing feast includes, 'four and twenty nosegays for the shearers' (*WT* 4.3.41–2). The distracted Jailer's Daughter intimates that young women make nosegays to capture a man's heart: 'We maids that have our livers perish'd, crack'd to pieces with love…do nothing all day long but pick flowers with Proserpine. Then will I make Palamon a nosegay' (*TNK* 4.3.23–6). The only reference to 'nose-herbs' is in *AWW*. Lavatch's praise of Helen as 'the sweet marjorom of the sallet, or rather the herb of grace' is fine-tuned by Lafew who makes the distinction between herbs for culinary purposes and those for **scent**: 'They are not herbs, you knave, they are nose-herbs' (4.5.16–19).

(C) Gascoigne's 1575 collection of poetry is entitled *The Posies.* Drayton's 'lusty jocund swains' wear the nosegays of their country-girls, and nymphs gather flowers for nosegays at the wedding of Thames and Isis (1622). Knight (2009) suggests posies bridged the gap between the botanical and the printed representations of the **garden**, and elaborates on the garden of verse. Willes (2011: 86) includes the picture of Burghley, riding in his gardens on a mule with a posy of **pinks** and **honeysuckles** in his hand, both probably chosen for their scent, the latter also a symbol of love and steadfastness. See also **pomander**.

nut, nut-hook (A) Botanically a nut is a **fruit**, but more usually it indicates the hard edible kernel of a fruit or seed; many 'nuts' are actually seeds. Nut-bearing trees such as the **hazel** could be cultivated; wild nuts were available to all, and in good years provided ready, free food. A rare usage, nut-hook is a hooked stick used to pull down **branches** of **trees** so the nuts can be picked; its slang meaning as a beadle or constable is obsolete. A nut can suggest something trifling, or of little value. In proverbial and allusive uses a nut can indicate dealing with a difficult problem.

(B) 'Nut' figures in the plays as material for jest. Contemptuous of Parolles' pretensions Lafew tells Bertram, 'there can be no kernel in this light nut; the soul of this man is his clothes' (*AWW* 2.5.43–4). Thersites dismisses the Greek warriors, Achilles and Ajax, with the comment, 'Hector shall have a great catch, and 'a knock out either of your brains; 'a were as good crack a fusty nut with no kernel' (*TRO* 2.1.99–102). Touchstone's ditty parodies Orlando's verses: 'Sweetest nut hath sourest rind,/Such a nut is Rosalind' (*AYL* 3.2.109–10). Unfamiliar with the culinary tastes of an ass, Titania proposes a treat for Bottom: 'I have a venturous fairy that shall seek/The squirrel's hoard, and fetch thee new nuts'. He, however, expresses a preference for 'a handful or two of dried peas'(*MND* 4.1.35–8). The significance of a nutshell as a small, constricted space is present in *HAM*. Rejecting Rosencrantz's claim that his problem is ambition the Prince retorts: 'O God, I could be bounded in a nutshell, and count myself a king of infinite space – were it not that I have bad dreams' (2.2.254–6). As Mistress Quickly and Doll are arrested in the closing phase of *2H4,* the latter begins her invective against the officers by adopting the slang term for them: 'Nuthook, nuthook, you lie' (5.4.7). Threatening Slender for accusing him of theft, Nym is the only other character to employ the term: 'Be advis'd, sir, and pass good humors. I will say "marry trap" with you, if you run the nuthook's humor on me – that is the very note of it' (*WIV* 1.1.166–9).

(C) Lyly's Lucilla uses a nut to represent something of little value when she reproaches herself: 'he must needs think thee inconstant; if he perceive thee to be won with a nut, he will imagine that thou wilt be lost with an apple' (1580, *Euphues*: 53). Stylized nuts were used in needlework and other decorative forms: Trevelyon (1608) includes patterns for them and Arnold (1988) lists flower-work and nuts embroidered on the Queen's clothes. Thirsk (1967) comments on the value of nuts as a wild food source, noting that they were not gathered before 1 September, Nut Day. See also **pig-nut**.

nutmeg, mace The hard aromatic **kernel**, and aromatic **seed** of *Myristica fragrans* which was native to the East Indies. Nutmeg and mace were valued and traded both as spices and for **herbal** medicine. There is no mention of the nutmeg **tree** but the **fruits** are required by Perdita for the sheep-shearing feast. The Young Shepherd rehearsing the required ingredients includes, 'mace; dates, none – that's out of my note; nutmegs, seven' (*WT* 4.3.46–7). The other reference arises out of the competitive exercise of wit by the young men intent on mocking the theatrical performance of their social inferiors in *LLL*. Armado's allusion to Hector's 'gift' provokes Dumaine's interjection, 'a gilt nutmeg' which Arden 3 (280) points out was 'a nutmeg glazed with the yolk of an egg: a common gift of lovers' and 'used for spicing drinks'. This opens the way for the lemon/leman (lover) pun by Berowne – 'A lemon'. Longeville pursues the theme with sexual innuendo, 'Stuck with cloves', thereby facilitating Dumains's riposte, 'No, cloven' (5.2.645–9), a division implying female genitalia. Nutmeg can sometimes be found as *nux moschata*. Cogan (1584) says that nutmegs are particularly good for students, and with Langham (1597) gives the medicinal virtues of mace and nutmeg. Grieve (1978) gives both as a tonic and stimulant, but warns that if taken in excess they may cause over-excitement. Jardine (1996) notes the expansion of European trade in **cloves**, **ginger**, **pepper** and nutmeg in the sixteenth century.

O

oak (A) Any **tree** of the genus *Quercus* L., also of the **beech** family Fagaceae, including sweet **chestnut**. Oak was renowned for its size, its long life and for the strength of its **wood**. It was of particular value in ship building and for house timbers. It was frequently used metaphorically to suggest durability, solidity, toughness, strength and reliability. **Planting** oaks represented an investment in the future: their commercial value would not be realized for several generations. Oak **wreaths** suggested victory; the tree's symbolism and easily recognizable shape made it a repeated pattern in house decoration and needlework. Its **fruit** or **acorns** were autumn fodder for grazing animals. In times of famine they were ground to make flour; they provided a coffee-like drink into the twentieth century. Oak **bark** was used for tanning; the tree also supplied medicinal remedies from its **leaves**, bark, inner pith and acorns.

(B) Many aspects of the oak are represented in the plays. *WIV* has most mentions and is notable for an oak which marks the meeting place of Falstaff and the wives, and is the location for the jest that completes his humiliation. Mistress Page recounts how 'there want not many that do fear/In deep of night to walk by this Herne's oak' (4.4.39–40). It is unsurprising that two of the three situations in which a wreath of oak leaves figures as the emblem of military triumph pertain to the warrior Caius Martius Coriolanus. His mother Volumnia confides to Virgilia how she was 'pleas'd to let him seek danger where he was like to find fame. To cruel war I sent him, from whence he return'd, his brows bound with oak' (*COR* 1.3.12–15). Later she reports to Menenius, 'he comes the third time home with the oaken garland' (2.1.124–5). Supporting his nomination for consul, Cominius catalogues his astonishing triumphs, beginning with his very first battle: 'He prov'd best man i'th'field, and for his meed/Was brow-bound with the oak' (2.2.97–8). The other reference is found in *TNK*. Describing a prisoner the Messenger reveals, 'About his head he wears the winner's oak' (4.2.137). The immense strength of the oak is intimated by the soldier's description of Coriolanus as, 'the rock, the oak not to be wind-shaken' (*COR* 5.2.111). The eponymous hero exhibits his contempt for the plebeians by asserting; 'He that depends/Upon your favors swims with fins of lead,/And hews down oaks with rushes' (1.1.179–81). The oak tree is prominent in images of power and destruction. Challenging the elements, the defenceless Lear cries, 'You sulph'rous and thought-executing fires,/Vaunt-couriers of oak-cleaving thunder-bolts,/Singe my white head!' (*LR* 3.2.4–6). Nestor alights on the image to illustrate circumstances that would overwhelm all but the most courageous: 'when the splitting wind/Makes flexible the knees of knotted oaks' (*TRO* 1.3.49–50). Casca claims to have witnessed, 'tempests when the scolding winds/Have riv'd the knotty oaks' (*JC* 1.3.5–6). Prospero threatens Ariel, 'If thou murmur'st, I will rend an oak/And peg thee in his knotty entrails' (*TMP* 1.2.294–5). That this is no idle threat is confirmed by Prospero's account of his dominance: 'to the dread rattling thunder/Have I given fire, and rifted Jove's stout oak/With his own bolt' (5.1.44–6). Defending the prowess of his aging warrior Audley against the mockery of the French, King Edward asserts, 'Know that these grave scholars of experience,/Like stiff-grown oaks, will stand immovable/When whirlwind quickly turns up younger trees' (*E3* 3.3.128–30). The oak's solidity constitutes a natural antithesis to things flawed or decaying. Paulina says of Leontes' irrational jealousy, 'The root of his opinion, which is rotten/As ever oak was sound' (*WT* 2.3.90–1). Isabella sets a 'Merciful heaven' against the heartless indifference of man: 'Thou rather with thy sharp and sulphurous bolt/Splits the unwedgeable and gnarled oak/Than the soft myrtle' (*MM* 2.2.114–17). A key line in the dirge in *CYM* is, 'To thee the reed is as the oak' (4.2.267). *OTH* is a play rich in nautical imagery. Visualizing the tempest raging off the coast of Cyprus, Montano fears for the plight of the Venetian fleet: 'What ribs of oak, when mountains melt on them,/Can hold the mortise?' (2.1.8–9). Oak is the ultimate test of durability. The tightness of its **grain** is deployed by Iago when attempting to convince Othello that Desdemona is naturally duplicitous: 'She that so young could give out such a seeming/To seel her father's eyes up, close as oak,/He thought 'twas witchcraft' (3.3.209–11).

(C) Colonna (1499: 295) naming eight different kinds of oak in one sentence, writes of 'ancient furrowed oaks', and 'pleasant groves of friendly oaks'. Norden (1618) records the oak, **ash** and **elm** as the main timber trees, protected by statute under both Henry VIII and Elizabeth. Levin (1970) suggests that Falstaff is purified by the mock-ceremonial under the Windsor oak. Mabey (1996) examines the place of the oak in English history. Baker (2008: 111) records the oak as a lightning tree of great magical powers and notes that Herne's oak stood in Windsor Little Park until 1796. Walsham (2011: 524) has the continuing use of oak trees as assembly points, with the 'Reformation Oak' in Norfolk being the place where Kett raised his rebellion in 1549. See Dent (1981: 01, 03).

oat (A) *Avena* L. is a cereal **grain** of the **grass** family, the cultivated form being *A. sativa* L., which was **grown** for human food and animal fodder. Oats were easier to grow than other cereals, and therefore cheaper; consequently oat bread was less valued than that made from **wheat**. In times of shortage oats were used to adulterate other cereals; in particular they were a staple constituent of pottage. Oats had many medical applications. 'Oaten' was a derogatory term suggesting a countryman rather than a city sophisticate; oat **straw** provided reeds for rustic pipes.

(B) Oats infiltrate the plays in subtle and surprising ways. The Captain in *LR* justifies his role as would-be assassin: 'I cannot draw a cart, nor eat dried oats' (5.3.38). The Second Carrier in *1H4* perturbed by the state of affairs at the inn since the demise of Robin ostler, elicits the response, 'Poor fellow never joy'd since the price of oats rose, it was the death of him' (2.1.12–13). This little cameo adds pathos and comedy to social engagement that occupies the play's hinterland. The Jailer's Daughter expresses pity for the chestnut mare who is scorned by a fine stallion despite having a dowry: 'Some two hundred bottles,/And twenty strike of oats' (*TNK* 5.2.64–5). Bales of hay and bushels of oats are indicated here. The situation is, of course, a projection of her own plight. Given a choice of delicacies by Titania, the transformed Bottom responds: 'Truly, a peck of provender; I could munch your good dry oats' (*MND* 4.1.32–3). His proviso that the oats be dry echoes the Carrier's anxiety in *1H4* (2.1.8–10). Delivering her blessing on the impending marriage of Ferdinand and Miranda, Iris invokes the goddess of agriculture: 'Ceres, most bounteous lady, thy rich leas/Of wheat, rye, barley, fetches, oats, and peas' (*TMP* 4.1.60–1). The Song of Spring at the close of *LLL* celebrates a season 'When shepherds pipe on oaten straws' (5.2.903).

(C) Dodoens (1578) regards it as a poor food, suitable only for animals. Cogan (1584) claims that oats replace meat in the North and in Cornwall. Markham (1631) rejects the French view that oats were only suitable for animal fodder; he includes a complete chapter on the value of oats and their dietary virtues. Vaughan (1617: 33) says that oaten bread is baked in Wales, where he records it was thought to be 'of a binding property but greatly strengthening'. Oat pipes were widely used, and Spenser's Cuddie has 'pyped erst so long with payne/That all mine Oten reedes bene rent and wore' (ed. 1999, *The Shepheardes Calendar*: 7–8). Dent (1981: O1, 3).

olive (A) A Mediterranean native, *Olea europaea* L. has a very long history in cultivation, providing oil and **fruit** as dietary staples. In Greek mythology it was emblematic of peace: 'to hold out the olive branch' is to sue for peace; someone 'bearing an olive branch' comes in peace. After the Flood, an olive branch was seen as God's offering of peace to Noah and his family, a symbol that the **earth** would never be inundated again. In Christian iconography an olive **branch** is shown at the Annunciation and Christ's entry into Jerusalem. While the olive could be grown in carefully controlled, protected **garden** conditions in England it was most unlikely to be found growing wild, or to produce fruit. However, olive oil appears to have been readily available and to have had a wide range of culinary and medicinal applications.

(B) Six of the eight references are to the olive as symbol of peace; there are two literal mentions of olive trees. The Forest of Arden is fantastical. Home to lions it has a curious blend of flora and fauna that includes **palm** trees and olive trees. Ganymede/Rosalind advises the infatuated Phoebe, 'If you will know my house,/'Tis at the tuft of olives here hard by' (*AYL* 3.5.74–5). The unusual 'tuft' meaning 'small group' is not unique to this play: *R2* has 'yon tuft of trees' (2.3.53) and *WT* 'the tuft of pines' (2.1.34). Looking for their cottage Oliver asks Celia and Rosalind, 'Where in the purlieus of this forest stands/A sheep-cote fenc'd about with olive-trees?' (4.3.76–7). *SON* 107 refers to olive trees as symbols of perpetual peace: 'And peace proclaims olives of endless age' (8). Desire for lasting peace is expressed by Alcibiades at the close of *TIM*: 'Bring me into your city,/And I will use the olive with my sword:/Make war breed peace, make

olive

peace stint war' (5.4.81–3). Preparing for what he believes will be the final battle with Antony, Octavius Caesar announces: 'The time of universal peace is near./Prove this a prosp'rous day, the three-nook'd world/Shall bear the olive freely' (*ANT* 4.6.4–6). Declining the Protectorship Clarence extols the kingmaker:

> No, Warwick, thou art worthy of the sway,
>
> To whom the heav'ns in thy nativity
>
> Adjudg'd an olive branch and laurel crown,
>
> As likely to be blest in peace and war;
>
> *(3H6 4.6.32–5).*

On his death-bed in *2H4,* the King is reassured by Westmorland that Prince John has completed the rout of the rebels: 'There is not now a rebel's sword unsheath'd,/But Peace puts forth her olive every where' (4.4.86–7). In a lighter context Orsino's ambassador, Cesario/Viola, assures Olivia, 'I bring no overture of war, no taxation of homage; I hold the olive in my hand; my words are as full of peace as matter' (*TN* 1.5.208–11).

(C) Harrison (1587) has heard of wild olive trees growing in England; however, he thinks them unlikely to bear fruit. Hawkins (1633) devotes a chapter to the device of the olive, as a representation of mercy, with the oil as the blood of the tree, and a source of income for the **husbandman**. He notes its figurative presence in the Annunciation as a symbol of mercy and peace, saying both the olive and Mary are evergreen and eternal. Yates (1975) comments on the depictions of Elizabeth with an olive branch in her hand that symbolizes peace – as shown in the c. 1580 Welbeck portrait (Arnold 1988).

onion (A) The *Allium* genus includes **leek**, **garlic** and onion, *Allium cepa* L. All were used both raw and cooked, the onion being less pungent than garlic. Onion is well-known for its effect to make a handler cry; it also provides a yellow dye. Possibly a Roman introduction, it was widely grown, but it was generally associated with poorer sections of society where it was used to flavour bland food such as pottage. Onion had a considerable range of medical uses.

(B) The onion's impact on breath receives only one mention. There are several allusions to its tendency to produce tears. Bottom famously cautions his fellow thespians, 'And, most dear actors, eat no onions nor garlic, for we are to utter sweet breath; and I do not doubt but to hear them say, it is a sweet comedy' (*MND* 4.2.42–4). Close to tears at the seemingly happy denouement of *AWW,* Lafew turns to Parolles for a handkerchief: 'Mine eyes smell onions, I shall weep anon' (5.3.320). More usually, onions are associated with false tears. Playing the part of Christopher Sly's wife, Bartholomew is required to shed tears: 'And if the boy have not a woman's gift/ To rain a shower of commanded tears,/An onion will do well for such a shift' (*SHR* Ind.1.124–6). Enobarbus responds to news of the death of Antony's wife Fulvia, with the cynical comment, 'This grief is crown'd with consolation: your old smock brings forth a new petticoat, and indeed the tears live in an onion that should water this sorrow' (*ANT* 1.2.167–70). Later in the play, however, Antony's farewell to his soldiers on the eve of battle moves Enobarbus to plead, 'What mean you, sir,/To give them this discomfort? Look, they weep,/And I, an ass, am onion ey'd. For shame,/Transform us not to women' (4.2.33–6).

(C) Markham (1615) gives a recipe for pottage made from the most basic ingredients of **oatmeal** and onions, without even **herbs**. Parkinson (1640) comments on its pungency; he includes its medical uses saying that it could induce menstruation, a euphemism for its potential as an abortifacient. Riddle (1992) documents the same use from classical times. Coles (1656) demonstrates the uneven understanding of plant classification by categorizing onions with turnips and **potatoes** rather than with garlic.

orange (A) One of a variety of citrus **fruits**, the reference is to the Seville orange, *Citrus aurantium*, with bitter pulp, or *C. sinensis*, the sweeter China orange which was eaten as both flesh and pulped juice. Initially oranges were a considerable rarity in England and valued as a luxurious fruit; they were the first of the citrus **trees** to be cultivated in the country. They were prescribed medicinally for a variety of conditions including colds, and might form the basis of **pomanders**. Orange water was **distilled** and prized for its **scent**; the oil was used to add fragrance to clothes, notably gloves. By the later sixteenth century large quantities of oranges were imported from Spain for sale in theatres for refreshment, the women who carried on the trade being regarded as little more than prostitutes, hence 'orange-woman' carried a derogatory connotation.

(B) This fruit figures only in *ADO*. Believing he has been duped by Don Pedro, Claudio shows all the signs of a man disappointed in love. Beatrice interprets his monosyllabic replies with a pun on the famous Seville oranges: 'The Count is neither sad, nor sick, nor merry, nor well; but civil count, civil as an orange, and something of that jealous complexion' (2.1.293–5). Believing Hero is unchaste, Claudio hands her back to her father with the contemptuous words, 'Give not this rotten orange to your friend' (4.1.32), pointing to an association between oranges and prostitution. Even without awareness of that connotation a modern audience would still feel the force of the 'rotten' orange. The dismissive attitude towards an 'orange-wife' is apparent in *COR*, though it does not carry any necessary association with prostitution. Hurling abuse at the tribunes, Menenius claims, 'You wear out a good wholesome forenoon in hearing a cause between an orange-wife and a forset-seller, and then rejourn the controversy of threepence to a second day of audience' (2.1.69–72).

(C) Bacon (1625) sees no problem in suggesting oranges were important in the garden; he includes them with his winter **plants**, but notes they have to be stoved, or over-wintered, in specially constructed **garden** buildings. Parkinson (1629) also gives clear directions on over-wintering oranges, indicating an expensive, but not uncommon process he knows about, even if he has not practised it. Bacon (1981) credits Burghley with the first orangery in England; Henderson (2005) says that Burghley already had orange trees by 1561, when he wrote to Paris for the procurement of **lemons** and **pomegranates**, perhaps an indication that oranges were not as difficult to cultivate as other rarities. Black (1983) gives a detailed history of oranges in western Europe, noting Sir Francis Carew at Beddington as an early recipient; he grew a group of trees, or orangery, protected from the worst of the weather by wooden houses with fires in them. These were so successful that by the later seventeenth century John Evelyn recorded that they produced thousands of fruit; if so this would make it the most successful orangery ever in England. Madelaine (1982: 491) suggests there was a powerful contrast in *ADO* 4.1.31 between the orange as the **apple** of **Eden**, and its association with venereal disease. Palter (2002) charts the spread of the cultivation of the orange and discusses its role in art and literature.

orchard (A) A **garden** enclosed with fencing or a **wall** for the cultivation of **fruit trees**, an orchard could also be a pleasure garden. Productive **trees** and **bushes** including **nuts**, and **herbs** were protected from theft by the walls or fences; these also created a micro-climate where plants would fruit or **flower** earlier and for a longer period than outside. It was a place of much experimentation, where **grafting** techniques were honed and new varieties of common and rare fruit grown. Orchards could be laid out formally, with **walks** or **allies**, and **arbours** between the rows of trees. Aesthetics and leisure overlapped with productivity, and they were places to rest, or even sleep, and offered space for exercise; orchards could provide privacy for meditation, conversation, love affairs and sexual encounters. They could bridge the gap between the formality of the garden surrounding the house and the wider **park**. Sometimes described as **wilder-nesses**, they carried undertones of an **Edenic** existence, of fruitfulness and perfection, a place of both delight and reward.

(B) The orchard as a place of leisure designed for play, courtship, conversation and intrigue is found in *ADO*. The botanical and social nature of this carefully constructed and embellished space is revealed by Antonio who confides to Leonato, 'The Prince and Count Claudio, walking in a thick-pleach'd alley in mine orchard, were thus much over-heard by a man of mine' (1.2.8–11). This sense of a place of leisure is again brought out when Benedick says to the boy, 'In my chamber-window lies a book, bring it hither to me in the orchard' (2.3.3–4). As part of the conspiracy to gull Beatrice, Hero tells Margaret, 'Whisper her ear, and tell her I and Ursley/Walk in the orchard, and our whole discourse/Is all of her'. Enlightening Ursula, Hero refers to a another feature of the orchard: 'As we do trace this alley up and down,/ Our talk must only be of Benedick' (3.1.4–17). Borachio is overheard by the Watch giving an account of the deception effected to defame Hero: 'I should first tell thee how the Prince, Claudio, and my master, planted and plac'd and possess'd by my master Don John, saw afar off in the orchard this amiable encounter' (3.3.148–52). In this play the orchard affords a physical and emotional centre for pleasure and conspiracy. Responding to the sight of Olivia engaging Cesario/Viola in conver-sation, Sir Andrew Aguecheek complains, 'I saw't i'th'orchard' (*TN* 3.2.7). He is again a participant in a comic scene choreographed by Sir Toby Belch when directed to confront Cesario/Viola to provoke a duel: 'Go, Sir Andrew, scout me for him at the corner of the orchard like a bum-baily' (3.4.176–7). A place of frequent encounters in this play, Sir Toby warns Viola that Sir Andrew, 'bloody as the hunter, attends thee at the orchard-end' (3.4.223).

The orchard is a natural place for courtship. As Troilus anticipates his first meeting with Cressida, Pandarus advises, 'Walk here i'th'orchard, I'll bring her straight' (*TRO* 3.2.16–17). That it is protected is apparent in the most famous of love scenes. Juliet, expressing her delight and apprehension to Romeo, wonders, 'How camest thou hither, tell me, and wherefore?/The orchard walls are high and hard to climb' (*ROM* 2.2.62–3). The Porter informs Lord Bardolph, 'His lordship is walk'd forth into the orchard./Please it your honor knock but at the gate' (*2H4* 1.1.4–5). Both here and in *JC* where Brutus delivers his decisive soliloquy (2.1.10–34), the orchard is a private place conducive to meditation. The orchard as a place for conversation and dining is evidenced in *2H4*. In a companionable moment Justice Shallow exhibits great pride in his orchard, insisting to Falstaff, 'Nay, you shall see my orchard, where, in an arbor, we will eat a last year's pippin of mine own graffing, with a dish of caraways, and so forth. Come, cousin Silence – and then to bed' (5.3.1–4). Its potential as a source of solace and recuperation is suggested in *JN*. Pembroke reports that the King, 'holds belief,/That being brought into the open air,/It would allay the burning quality/Of that fell poison which assaileth him'. This leads Prince Henry to advise 'Let him be brought into the orchard here' (5.7.6–10). In *HAM* the orchard represents a sanctified space that is violated. The Ghost of Old Hamlet begins the account of his murder, crucially, with reference to time and place: 'Sleeping within my orchard,/My custom always of the afternoon,/Upon my secure hour thy uncle stole' (1.5.59–61). The orchard as a place of enjoyment and leisure in the public consciousness is highlighted in *JC*. The reading of Caesar's will is the climactic moment in Antony's forum speech:

> Moreover, he hath left you all his walks,
> His private arbors and new-planted orchards,
> On this side Tiber; he hath left them you,
> And to your heirs for ever – common pleasures,
> To walk abroad and recreate yourselves.
> Here was a Caesar! When comes such another?
>
> *(3.2.247–52)*

Here is genuine benefaction: normally the preserve of personal privilege, these beautiful spaces for recreation and re-creation are validated as the endowment of every citizen. A figurative use occurs in *LC* where the betrayed young woman reflects:

> For further I could say this man's untrue,
> And knew the patterns of his foul beguiling,
> Heard where his plants in others' orchards grew,
> Saw how deceits were gilded in his smiling,
>
> *(169–72)*

A remarkable image is provided by Audley when describing a segment of the encircling French army:

> gilded upright pikes do seem
> Straight trees of gold, the pendants, leaves,
> And their device of antique heraldry,
> Quart'red in colors, seeming sundry fruits
> Makes it the orchard of the Hesperides.
>
> *(E3 4.4.25–9)*

(C) Tusser (1573) prefaces his comments on the orchard saying it should be cherished, because it produces great reward and great pleasure. Lyly's (1580: 206) Fidus sees orchards as aesthetically desirable and apparently restricted to the wealthy: 'It is this only [beauty] that princes desire in their houses, gardens, orchards, and beds.' Palter (2002) gives the literary background of the orchard. Henderson (2005) says the orchard and wilderness at Nonsuch provided a link from the formality of the gardens to the **grove** of Diana and the wilderness beyond. Among the best-documented contemporary orchards are those of Sir Thomas Tresham at Lyveden New Bield where Eburne's (2008) research shows that Tresham's planting ideas were probably influenced by his extensive book collection. Willes (2011: 39–49, 63) quotes Robert Cecil's comment on Lyveden as 'one of the fairest orchards that is in England', noting that his **gardener** travelled throughout England to acquire the desired trees. She comments 'Audiences watching a performance of *Richard II* would have made the connection between a fruitful orchard and an ordered family.' The same author cites William Lambarde's *Perambulation of Kent* (written 1570; published 1576) who gives an account of the emergence of the Kentish orchards as a conscious act of import substitution and notes 'within half a century orchards were flourishing all over the country'.

osier (A) Any of several varieties of *Salix* or **willow**, osier usually suggested *S. viminalis* L., a native **tree** with sufficiently tough and pliable **branches** for making baskets, wattle fencing and **arbours**; the name also identified the product. Osiers were grown and **coppiced** on a vast scale to meet the extensive demand. All willows are plants of damp or wet places, and so symbolize grief and mourning. Osiers and willow at the time did not refer to the now well-established weeping willow which was a later seventeenth-century introduction at the earliest.

(B) The osier is a vivid physical feature and a symbol of unrequited love in *PP* where landscape intertwines with feeling: 'When Cytherea (all in love forlorn)/A longing tarriance for Adonis made/Under an osier growing by a brook' (vi.3–5). Oliver's poeticized, 'Where in the purlieus of this forest stands/A sheep-cote fenc'd about with olive-trees?' affords Celia the opportunity to respond playfully when directing him: 'The rank of osiers by the murmuring stream/Left on your right hand brings you to the place' (*AYL* 4.3.76–80). The plant's flexibility makes for a natural contrast to the fixity of the **oak**, something illustrated by Berowne's letter of surrender to Rosaline: 'Though to myself forsworn, to thee I'll faithful prove;/Those thoughts to me were oaks, to thee like osiers bow'd' (*LLL* 4.2.107–8). The entire letter is replicated in *PP* 5. Collecting medicinal plants at first light, Friar Lawrence gathers them in an osier basket: 'I must up-fill this osier cage of ours/With baleful weeds and precious-juiced flowers' (*ROM* 2.3.7–8). Viola's imagined 'willow cabin', like the Friar's basket, would also be fashioned from osiers (*TN* 1.5.268).

(C) Norden (1618) considers osiers the only **crop** to be **harvested** from wet **ground**. Parkinson (1640) writes of osier and willow together, giving a list of the considerable uses of woven osiers, including baskets, chairs, cradles; he adds that they can be used to tie up **vines**, trees and **hedges**, and to make stakes and hoops to support other plants. Young (1945) suggests willow might provide the **palms** for Palm Sunday; separately he notes that growing osiers in **reed** beds can strengthen the river **bank** and help to prevent flooding. Mabey (1996) details and images its modern use. Willes (2011) writes of the several generations of the Banbury family of the parish of St Margaret's Westminster in the sixteenth century, who were basket-makers and appear to have **grown** their own osiers in Westminster.

oxlip *Primula elatior* (L.) Hill, was not truly identified until the nineteenth century. The oxlip that appears in Shakespeare's plays is a cross between the cowslip and primrose. Now generally known as the 'false oxlip', it is a botanically complex hybrid, about which there are considerable differences of opinion. The oxlip first makes its appearance growing on Oberon's celebrated bank in *MND:* 'I know a bank where the wild thyme blows,/Where oxlips and the nodding violet grows' (2.2.249–50). The flower is used once again in an equally beguiling passage in *WT.* Perdita's description of the **flowers** she would like to give to her friends include the natural neighbours, 'violets, dim', 'pale primroses' and, 'bold oxlips' (4.4.120–5). The first scene in *TNK*, a play suffused with flowers, has a song which includes, 'Oxlips in their cradles growing'. Interestingly, this verse begins, 'Primrose, first-born child of Ver,/Merry spring-time's harbinger' (1.1.7–10). Again these near cousins are found in close proximity. Stace (2010) gives the precise botanical differences. Grindon (1883) comments enigmatically that the oxlip is botanically uncertain but more interesting than the cowslip. Mabey (1996: 168–70) provides a history of the plant's botanical identification noting 'Oxlips hybridize with both the cowslip and the primrose, producing an almost complete range of intermediate types.'

P

Padua Its famous university was founded in the thirteenth century. In 1533 the Venetian senate confirmed the appointment of its first professor of *Simplicia medicamenti*, 'plants for medicine' the modern equivalent of professor of botany. Its botanical **garden** established in 1545 – the first in Renaissance Europe was founded a year earlier in Pisa (1544) – remains the world's oldest academic botanical garden still in its original location. The Oxford botanical garden, the first in England, was not set up until 1621. In the opening scene of *SHR* Lucentio, having left his home town of Pisa, announces:

> Tranio, since for the great desire I had
> To see fair Padua, nursery of arts,
> I am arriv'd for fruitful Lombardy,
> The pleasant garden of great Italy,

(1.1.1–4)

Willes (2011: 78–9) elaborates on the relationship between botanical studies and the Venetian dominance of the eastern trade in spices. She also notes (fn 279) that the earliest botanical gardens in Europe were those established in the ninth century in the palace of Madinat al-Zahra outside Cordoba. Terwen-Dionisius (1994) remarks on the survival of the original concept and circular geometric design at Padua's botanical garden. Knight (2009) sets Padua in a literary context. Arden 2 (171) points out that Padua 'never was in Lombardy' but adds, 'Ortelius' map of Europe has Lombardy written right across northern Italy from the French Alps to Trieste'. See **fertile**.

palm (A) One of a large number of **trees** and **shrubs** of the *Arecaceae* (*Palmae*) family growing in warm or tropical regions, it commonly indicated the **date** palm. A **leaf**, **branch** or frond from such a tree, or such leaves collectively, was worn by pilgrims returning from the Holy Land. Palm leaves were carried to mark Palm Sunday, but **willow** could be a more readily available substitute. In classical times palm was a symbol of peace and victory; figuratively it still suggests victory, pre-eminence, the first prize, or honour when used in such phrases as 'to bear the palm', 'to yield the palm'. The palm tree was frequently used to suggest victory, praise, honour, interdependence, and regenerative powers. It also indicates the anatomical palm of the hand.

(B) The only mention of the tree is in the unlikely setting of the Forest of Arden. One of Orlando's poems is 'found on a palm tree' (*AYL* 3.2.175–6). All other references are to the branch as a symbol of triumph, prestige or peace. Perceiving an erosion of the collegiate system, Cassius is exasperated by the homage paid to Julius Caesar: 'Ye gods, it doth amaze me/A man of such a feeble temper should/So get the start of the majestic world/And bear the palm alone' (*JC* 1.2.128–31). Financial standing is present in *TIM*. Hearing that the misanthrope has discovered gold, the avaricious Painter predicts, 'You shall see him a palm in Athens again, and flourish/With the highest' (5.1.10–11). In times of conflict it is the warrior who receives celebrity status. Responding to Paris' request that she help unarm Hector, Helen enthuses, 'Yea, what he shall receive of us in duty/Gives us more palm in beauty than we have,/Yea, overshines ourself' (*TRO* 3.1.156–8). Recounting to Horatio the political pressure contained in Claudius' letter to the King of England, Hamlet reveals how he echoed the use of the Danish/English accord in his substitute letter: 'As love between them like the palm might flourish,/As peace should still her wheaten garland wear' (*HAM* 5.2.40–1). Compliance with Claudius' request – 'He should those bearers put to sudden death,/Not shriving time allow'd' (46–7) – is a prerequisite for the continuance of peaceful relations. Shakespeare coins the word 'palmy' in *HAM* where Horatio alludes to Rome's peace and prosperity prior to the assassination of Caesar: 'In the most high and palmy state of Rome,/A little ere the mightiest Julius fell' (1.1.113–14). Of the numerous references to the palm of the hand only one is germane to the plant. The first exchange of words between Romeo and Juliet takes the form of a sonnet. The wordplay that animates the sonnet has at its centre Juliet's lines, 'For saints have hands that pilgrims' hands do touch,/And palm to palm is holy palmer's kiss' (*ROM* 1.5.99–100).

(C) Watts (1991: 64) points out, 'The Italian noun *romeo* means "pilgrim"; in 1598 John Florio's dictionary translated it as "palmer" (a pilgrim whose palm leaf shows that he has visited the Holy Land)'. Erasmus (1536, vol. 31) writes that to bear the palm is proverbial rather than a direct reference to an actual victory; he also suggests it was a symbol of virility. Hawkins' (1633) book of emblems includes a chapter on the palm, describing it as a representation of victory, and the emblem of faithfulness, fortitude and patience. In his concern for vernacular names and precise identification, Turner provides early evidence of the substitution of willow for palm, and argues that the mis-naming of willow as palm was effectively idolatry (Knight 2009: 63). Young (1945) is one of several writers to note that willow replaced the palm on Palm Sunday, and contemporary anecdotal evidence bears this out. Yates (1975) notes the depictions of Elizabeth with a crown of palm as an emblem of victory. See also Dent (1981: P37.1).

pansy (A) Originally the native heartsease, the wild pansy *Viola tricolor* L. was probably Shakespeare's **love-in-idleness**, but pansy now denotes the cultivated form of the **flower**, *Viola x wittrockiana* Gams ex Kappert. Some early modern writers also identify it as a **plant** of the wallflower genus, *Cheiranthus* L. The name was said to derive from the French *pensée*, meaning thought, thus generating word-play. Pansies had a range of medical uses, including the treatment of heart problems, hence the name of heartsease; this led to their association with thoughts and love.

(B) The flower appears under this name only in *HAM,* though it is present in *MND* as 'love-in-idleness' and as 'Cupid's flower'. Its other name, 'heartsease', is not used by Shakespeare. Ophelia chooses to distribute plants to key figures in *HAM,* presumably as a mode of expression suited to her mental state, and possibly out of a need to communicate her feelings obliquely rather than directly. There is a good deal of conjecture surrounding the meanings attaching to some of these plants, but for others their meaning is explicit: 'There's rosemary, that's for remembrance; pray you, love, remember. And there is pansies, that's for thoughts' (4.5.175–7). Both Arden 2 (359) and Arden 3 (387–8) propose that Laertes is the person to whom these plants are given.

(C) Arnold (1988) and Osborne (1989) detail pansies in the embroidered flowers on the Queen's dresses, as in the c. 1580 Welbeck and 1599 Hardwick portraits. Strong (1998) describes the **garden** at Theobalds which was laid out for the Queen's visit in 1591, where the **knot-garden** was planted not with the traditional **herbs** but with emblematic flowers, including pansies to represent the three Graces. Heath (2003) provides a table of the proverbial and associated meanings attributed to the pansy which include thoughts, love, courtship, and in one instance, troubles. Mabey (2010: 111–12) provides helpful commentary on the differing names attaching to this flower and to its habitat. Martindale and Taylor (2004: 54–62) consider 'love-in-idleness' in its classical context.

park, dispark'd (A) Park can designate any large enclosed piece of **land**, usually **woodland** and pasture, attached to or surrounding a **manor**, house, castle or other large domestic building, which was used for recreation as in **hunting** or for keeping cattle, sheep or deer. In law, originally, a park was an enclosed tract of land held by royal grant, reserved for keeping and hunting deer and other game. Parks were a symbol of social status. 'To park' was to lodge troops in an encampment, to fence animals in, to enclose land as pasture, or to make into a park; 'dispark' represented loss of land and the tearing down of fences.

(B) The park as a valued possession is indicated by Bolingbroke using the expro-priation of his inheritance to justify his return from exile : 'you have fed upon my signories,/Dispark'd my parks and fell'd my forest woods,/From my own windows torn my household coat' (*R2* 3.1.22–4). Here is an accusation of despoliation, something more than theft: a violation of property and identity. Park as integral to landowning is evidenced also by Warwick as he lies dying on the battlefield. Fundamental to his identity is the landed property he is leaving behind: 'My parks, my walks, my manors that I had,/Even now forsake me; and of all my lands/Is nothing left me but my body's length' (*3H6* 5.2.24–6). On a diplomatic mission to Navarre, the French Princess and her ladies are initially dismayed to discover that they are to be lodged in the park. The park, however, proves to be highly congenial providing every kind of convenience and entertainment. Even the hunting seems refined, confined and easeful – almost bloodless. Berowne, instructing Costard to deliver a letter, says 'The Princess comes to hunt here in the park' (*LLL* 3.1.164). Hunting gives rise to a witty discourse on 'brow', 'horns', 'bow-hand', 'shot' 'prick', 'mark', 'hit', 'clout', 'cleaving the pin', so rich in sexual innuendo that Maria calls a halt: 'Come, come, you talk greasily, your lips grow foul' (4.1.111–37). In the next scene, the lower orders, too, become engaged with the deer hunt though their disputation is more pedantic than lubricious. The park here is not just a setting for the hunt, it is the engine of social and linguistic engagement; another theatre easing constraints, releasing and vitalizing the propensity for play. In *3H6,* Richard Gloucester, contriving the escape of his brother Edward, confides to his associates, 'Leave off to wonder why I drew you hither/Into this chiefest thicket of the park'. It emerges that the prisoner is allowed to hunt in the park 'to disport himself' (4.5.2–8). In *TIT* the park is an enigmatic place. A natural world of delicacy and beauty it becomes an arena for the unnatural – murder, mutilation and rape. Marcus tells how he discovered his dismembered niece: 'O, thus I found her straying in the park,/Seeking to hide herself, as doth the deer/ That hath receiv'd some unrecuring wound' (3.1.88–90). A feature of Windsor Park is that it affords access to all the citizens of the neighbourhood. Though a suitable venue for the final humiliation of Falstaff, Page doubts that the fat knight will take the bait: 'How? To send him word they'll meet him in the park at midnight? Fie, fie, he'll never come' (*WIV* 4.4.17–19). This play has the only mention of the Petty or Little Park which Simple, attempting to give directions, distinguishes from Windsor Great Park: 'Marry, sir, the pittie-ward, the park-ward – every way; Old Windsor way, and every way but the Town way' (3.1.5–7). Leaving Belmont, Portia conveys a sense of its scale and grandeur when instructing Nerissa: 'But come, I'll tell thee all my whole device/When I am in my coach, which stays for us/At the park-gate' (*MV* 3.4.81–3). On only three occasions is park used figuratively. Endeavouring to persuade Cymbeline to forswear his allegiance to Rome, the Queen emphasizes, 'The natural bravery of your isle, which stands/As Neptune's park, ribb'd and pal'd in/ With oaks unscalable and roaring waters' (*CYM* 3.1.18–20). Unlike Riverside who follow F, most editors accept Theobald's emendation of 'rocks' for 'oaks'. The park as a place bounded and encircled is central to Venus' self-representation as she offers herself to Adonis: 'since I have hemm'd thee here/Within the circuit of this ivory pale,/I'll be a park, and thou shalt be my deer' (*VEN* 229–31). The rest of this playful enticement provides a detailed description of an Elizabethan park, including **fountains** which were sometimes adorned with female statues, their breasts spouting water. The situation in *1H6* is one of war, but the association of deer with the park is again present. Taken by surprise the English hero Talbot exclaims: 'How are we park'd and bounded in a pale,/A little herd of England's timorous deer,/Maz'd with a yelping kennel of French curs!' (4.2.45–7). The rest of the speech develops this empathy with the deer, a tendency found elsewhere in Shakespeare, e.g. *AYL* (2.1.21–65); *TIT* (3.1.88–90); *JC* (3.1.204–10); *LUC* (1149–53).

(C) Holinshed (1577) includes a chapter on parks and warrens, seeing parks in negative terms of servitude imposed by the Normans and unproductive because they are concerned with hunting for pleasure rather than **husbandry**. Hentzner (1598: 53) appears impressed by the parks that he saw on his travels in England: 'such parks are common throughout England, belonging to those that are distinguished either for their rank or riches'. Stow (1598) records that land, formerly belonging to the hospital of St James was annexed by Henry VIII who built a manor there, and then enclosed the land with a brick **wall**, so creating St James's Park. Henderson (2005) shows some early estate maps of later sixteenth-century parks, noting their importance for hunting, and gives a sense of the wider use of parkland. Fletcher's (2011) history of deer parks provides a wealth of detail.

parsley *Petroselinum crispum* Hill, a Mediterranean native, is an early, probably Roman, introduction. This staple culinary **herb** provided flavour, colour and garnish for a wide variety of foods. Parsley served as a contraceptive and was the source of a number of superstitions. Impatient with his master Lucentio for his slow response to the arrangements made for his secret marriage to Bianca, Biondello provides the only mention of parsley: 'I knew a wench married in an afternoon as she went to the garden for parsley to stuff a rabbit, and so may you, sir' (*SHR* 4.4.99–101). Parsley features in every book on cooking, usually in conjunction with other culinary herbs; medicinally it was often part of a compound preparation. Vaughan (1617: 91) writes that 'there is no garden hearb comes neere unto Parsley, as well for toothsomenesse as for health' which sums up the universality of its use. Riddle (1992) and Fraser (2002) both comment on its use as a contraceptive.

parsnip (A) *Pastinaca sativa* L. is a naturalized possibly Roman introduction, widely grown for its fleshy **root**. Initially used as animal fodder, it became part of the human diet through improved **plant** breeding.

(B) The parsnip and other root vegetables newly imported from the Continent were thought by some to be unhygienic, giving xenophobes an excuse to denigrate immigrants. In *STM*, the vegetable receives two brief mentions in a scene generally ascribed to Shakespeare. A chauvinistic Englishman claims, 'They bring in strange roots, which is merely to the undoing of poor prentices, for what's a sorry parsnip to a good heart?'. The implication is that the vegetable is not sustaining enough for a lusty Englishman. Williamson supports Lincoln with the negative comment: 'Trash, trash; they breed sore eyes and 'tis enough to infect the city with the palsy'. Lincoln rounds off the subject: 'Nay, it has infected it with the palsy, for these bastards of dung – as you know they grow in dung – have infected us, and it is our infection will make the city shake, which partly comes through the eating of parsnips' (II.c. 8–15). In the light of the horticultural practices of the day and increasing awareness of the importance of **dung** for **soil fertility**, this objection is a demonstration of ignorance. However, in *Malfi* (2.1.143–5), Bosola, too, hopes to provoke disgust by making a similar observation. Arden *Sir Thomas More* (181) comments that, 'Disdain for vegetables was part of English self-characterisation' and that '*Sorry parsnip* probably relates to market **gardening** techniques newly imported from the Low Countries'.

(C) Instructions on cultivating parsnips appear in most gardening books of the time, suggesting their importance. Tusser (1557) says that in Lent the parsnip was a great boon to the housewife, perhaps as a replacement for meat, while Cogan (1584) underlines their value saying parsnips could replace grain in time of famine. Parkinson (1629) believes the parsnip to be very nourishing with the particular virtue that it will keep all winter, providing an essential food for man and beast until spring. Willes (2011: 64–70) gives a detailed account of the promotion of parsnips and other root vegetables by Hugh Platt and Richard Gardiner, along with the contributions of the immigrant Dutch and Flemish gardeners.

peach *Prunus persica* (L) Batsch, the peach **tree** is an introduction from China, via Persia or Spain. It probably arrived with the Romans, and it was a later re-introduction c. 1200. 'Peach' also refers to the **fruit** and its colour; 'to peach' is to accuse, or impeach. It is only the colour of the fruit that is mentioned. Pompey Bum provides a lively account of his fellow prisoners and their misdemeanours including, 'Master Caper', arrested 'at the suit of Master Three-pile the mercer, for some four suits of peach-color'd satin' (*MM* 4.3.9–11). Hal refers to Poins' 'silk stockings…that were peach-color'd once' (*2H4* 2.2.15–16). The slang term for 'impeach' is used by Falstaff when he threatens Hal, 'If I be ta'en, I'll peach for this' (*1H4* 2.2.44). There are few contemporary references, but Estienne (1616) observes that the peach tree flourishes when planted against a **wall**. Campbell-Culver (2001) gives details of its introduction. Willes (2011: 41) notes that Tresham had a parterre of peach trees under-planted with **strawberries**. Palter (2002: 228, 241–52) points out that early Italian still-life paintings often included peaches and provides an exploration of the fruit in literature.

pear (A) *Pyrus* L., the most common cultivated variety being *P. communis* L., the pear was probably native to Europe and western Asia, and included varieties which are not now commonly available. Shakespeare mentions two: **warden** and **poperin**, both of which were regarded as **fruits** in their own right. Pears were valued above **apples**, and thought more of a luxury because of their tenderness and vulnerability to bruising. They were readily available to all levels of society, and found in every **orchard**; the ordinary cultivated variety differed little from its wild counterpart. Pears were cooked or served as dessert fruit, and made into perry as an alcoholic drink. In an extended, obsolete meaning, pear could imply something of little value, as in 'not worth a pear'. The shape of the fruit was a source of male sexual imagery.

(B) Its culinary import receives short shrift but the pear does lend itself to lively verbal engagement. Attempting to puncture Romeo's idealization of Rosaline, Mercutio calls out in the night, 'O, Romeo, that she were, O that she were/An open-arse, thou a pop'rin pear!' (*ROM* 2.1.37–8). The wordplay on **medlar** ('open-arse') and '**poperin**' is in keeping with Mercutio's humour. This deflation, however, is misplaced because Romeo, already in pursuit of Juliet, has acquired an authentic language of love. Leaving aside the obvious possibilities associated with 'poperin', the pear itself imparts sexual suggestion. Affecting worldliness, Parolles advises Helena to relinquish her virginity while it is of value: 'your virginity, your old virginity, is like one of our French wither'd pears, it looks ill, it eats dryly, marry, 'tis a wither'd pear; it was formerly better, marry, yet 'tis a wither'd pear' (*AWW* 1.1. 160–3). In *WIV* Falstaff soliloquizes on his beating following his second failed attempt on the virtue and purse of Mistress Ford. He fears that if his humiliation became known at Court, the courtiers 'would whip me with their fine wits till I were as crestfall'n as a dried pear' (4.5.99–100). The dried pear as the epitome of ignominy is strong enough without additional layers, but the link between 'crestfall'n' and 'cocks' makes it likely that Falstaff's phrase carries sexual freight.

(C) Heresbach regards the pear **tree** as 'the chiefest beauty of the orchard' (1596, book II). Vaughan warns particularly 'nice Maydes' to beware of eating **green** fruit, especially **apples** and pears, in October, as it can 'tempt wanton bodies' and lead to the green-sickness (1617: 268). Knight (2009: 91) quotes Gerard's observation of one **gardener growing** 'three score sundrie sorts of Peares'. Palter (2002) provides the literary background to the fruit, suggesting that the sexual imagery of the male pear and female apple date from at least the fourteenth century.

pease, **peasecod**, **Peaseblossom** (A) *Pisum sativum* L. has been staple fodder and food for millennia; they would last through the winter because they could easily be dried and rehydrated, and were eaten more by ordinary people than served at feasts, although fresh young pease were a delicacy. They were preferred by all to the more notoriously 'windy' **bean**. The peapod or peas(e)cod is the pod which contains the individual pease; young peapods were referred to as **squash**. Pea is a later seventeenth-century variation of pease; pease and peascod-time are both archaic terms. Allusively a pea can represent something very small and insignificant, or of little value. Peasecod provided obvious opportunities for sexual innuendo: for example, when associated with codpiece.

(B) Invoking the goddess of agriculture, Iris begins her welcome, 'Ceres, most bounteous lady, thy rich leas/Of wheat, rye, barley, fetches, oats, and pease' (*TMP* 4.1.60–1). The transformed Bottom declines the nuts proffered by Titania: 'I had rather have a handful or two of dried peas' (*MND* 4.1.37–8). The Second Carrier in *1H4* expresses dismay at the decline in the standard of housekeeping since the demise of Robin: 'Peas and beans are as dank here as a dog, and that is the next way to give poor jades the bots. This house is turn'd upside down since Robin ostler died' (2.1.8–11). 'Bots', or intestinal worms were believed to arise from inappropriate storage of animal feed. As Arden 3 (185) explains, these parasitical worms resulted 'from eating feed on which the worms' eggs have been laid'. At a more elevated social level, Berowne draws on pease for similitude: 'This fellow pecks up wit as pigeons pease' (*LLL* 5.2.315). Comparing his experience with the love-sick young shepherd, Touchstone recalls his courtship of Jane Smile: 'I remember the wooing of a peascod instead of her, from whom I took two cods, and giving her them again, said with weeping tears, "Wear these for my sake"' (*AYL* 2.4.51–4). Mavolio describes the tenacious messenger from Orsino as 'Not yet old enough for a man, nor young enough for a boy; as a squash is before 'tis a peascod' (*TN* 1.5.156–7). The heedless relinquishing of power by **Lear** provokes the Fool to liken his master to an empty peascod: 'That's a sheal'd peascod' (*LR* 1.4.200). Bottom, referring to the fairy Peaseblossom, says, 'I pray you commend me to Mistress Squash, your mother, and to Master Peascod, your father' (*MND* 3.2.186–7). The badly used yet sentimental Mistress Quickly bids farewell to Falstaff with the words, 'I have known thee these twenty-nine years, come peascod-time, but an honester and truer-hearted man – well, fare thee well' (*2H4* 2.4.383–4).

(C) Tusser (1573) suggests peas are a dual-purpose food: the ripe peascods would be ready to eat in July, while dried they could be made with **leeks** into porridge in Lent. Stow (1598: 408) comments on the vagaries of the food supply, noting that in the summer of 1598 peas were expensive because of a late spring and cold summer, selling for eight pence a peck, which looks an extraordinary price when set against the one penny a peck for **cherries** later in the summer. Peas and peapods provided an easy and recognizable pattern for decorative work; their designs can be found in Trevelyon (1608).

peony see **pioned**

pepper, peppercorn, peppered (A) *Piper nigrum* L. is a climbing **shrub** native to south Asia. Pepper designates both the **plant** and its spicy prepared **seeds**. It was valuable as a traded commodity, and is used allusively to denote pungency or spiciness. A peppercorn rent was a nominal amount; peppercorn later came to indicate something trifling or of no importance. Peppered is to be pelted, to be hit repeatedly, provoked, ruined or sexually assaulted.

(B) 'Pepper', 'peppercorn' and 'pepper-gingerbread' are mentioned once each, the first two in a comic context. Falstaff muses on his loss of physical bulk: 'I shall be out of heart shortly, and then I shall have no strength to repent. And I have not forgotten what the inside of a church is made of, I am a peppercorn, a brewer's horse' (*1H4* 3.3.6–9). The prospect of 'plump Jack' resembling the small, shrunken **berry** of the pepper plant is a test of the imagination. Brewer's horses were proverbially worn-out or decrepit. Andrew Aguecheek, incited to write an insolent challenge to Cesario/Viola, shows it to Sir Toby and Fabian, saying: 'I warrant there's vinegar and pepper in't' (*TN* 3.4.143–4). The ingredient that adds bite to Sir Andrew's letter is, in a different context, a source of blandness for Hotspur. Upbraiding Kate for resorting to an oath used by the citizen class, Hotspur likens 'in good sooth' to bread that had pepper added to give it a milder taste – the verbal equivalent of lacking vigour:

> Swear me, Kate, like a lady as thou art,
> A good mouth-filling oath, and leave 'in sooth',
> And such protest of pepper-gingerbread,
> To velvet-guards and Sunday-citizens.

> *(1H4 3.1.253–6)*

Arden3 (256) explains, 'mealy-mouthed phrases (*pepper gingerbread* was a bread in which pepper was added for some of the required ginger in the usual recipe, producing a coarser and somewhat milder-tasting bread)'. Ford makes the only reference to a pepper-box when searching his house for Falstaff: 'he cannot creep into a halfpenny purse, nor into a pepper-box' (*WIV* 3.5.146–7). Falstaff makes two of the three references to 'pepper'd' (*1H4* 2.4.191; 5.3.36); Mercutio the other (*ROM* 3.1.99).

(C) Dodoens (1578) considers the culinary and medicinal virtues of pepper. Parkinson (1640: 1603–5) includes several varieties of pepper; he suggests that it was valued as a carminative and an antidote to poisons. Hannett (1863: 147) shows that pepper was a traded commodity under Henry IV, detailing payment for **land** rents in the Forest of Arden which included one pound of pepper, a large amount of an expensive item. Trease and Evans (1983) note its availability in England since at least A.D.1000 suggesting an early use was to treat venereal diseases and chronic bronchitis. Jardine (1996) comments on the expansion of European trade in cloves, **ginger**, **pepper** and **nutmeg** in the sixteenth century.

perfume see **smell**

pig-nut *Conopodium majus* (Gouan) Loret, also called **earth**-nut, is a native **plant** of grasslands, hedgerows and woods found throughout England. It has sweetish edible tubers. This plant appears only on Prospero's island where it has a localized habitat and significant status. Enticing Stephano and Trinculo with promise of culinary variety, Caliban begins, 'I prithee let me bring thee where crabs grow;/And I with my long nails will dig thee pig-nuts' (*TMP* 2.2.167–8). Arden 3 (217) identifies it as *Bunium flexuosum,* a name that does not feature in Stace (2010), who defines it as *C. majus*; he also includes the great pig-nut, *B. bulbocastanum.* McLean (1981) points out that pig-nuts were valuable as a plentiful wild food. Mabey (1996) notes their modern use, suggesting a taste like **hazel** nuts, saying that they are now no longer common due to loss of habitat. Both he and Vickery (2010) record that as late as the end of the twentieth century children were known to dig them up as a snack.

Pimpernel Any one of several herbaceous **plants** either of the genus *Pimpinella* L., the burnet-saxifrages, or *Sanguisorba* L., the **burnets**; the two plants could readily be confused. Pimpernel is also the name of *Anagallis arvensis* L., the scarlet pimpernel. The three are now known to belong to different plant families. All were associated with folklore, and had a few medicinal applications. Pimpernel was also represented in needlework. This plant appears only as the name of a character. The serving men in *SHR* endeavour to persuade Christopher Sly that he is a great lord. They echo the names he has mentioned but dismiss them as pure fantasy: 'Stephen Sly, and old John Naps of Greece,/And Peter Turph, and Henry Pimpernell' (Ind.2 93–4). Two are given botanical names: 'Turph' or **turf**, and 'Pimpernell'. It matters little what precise flower is represented here. The whole Sly episode is imbued with local colour. Greece is possibly a misreading of Greet, a village 20 miles from Stratford-upon-Avon.

pine (A) Numerous evergreen coniferous **trees** and **shrubs** of northern temperate regions constitute the genus *Pinus* L. in England. Shakespeare is probably referring to the tall, common, native *P. sylvestris* L., or Scots **pine**. The long needle-like **leaves** in clusters on the side shoots provide valuable turpentine and tar. Several varieties have edible **seeds** and some kinds were used medicinally. The pine was also valued for its resinous **smell**. The long, straight trunks provided masts for sailing ships. Figuratively the pine tree signified height and vantage point.

(B) References to this tree assert its prominence and strength. Prospero's 'rough magic' enables him to uproot the mightiest trees: 'the strong-bas'd promontory/Have I made shake, and by the spurs pluck'd up/The pine and cedar' (*TMP* 5.1.46–50). The pine was also Ariel's prison (1.2.277–93). Several powerful characters are identified with this tree. Celebrating the removal of the Duke of Gloucester from the position of Lord Protector, Suffolk gloats, 'Thus droops this lofty pine and hangs his sprays' (*2H6* 2.3.45). More intimate is Antony's rueful and self-pitying remark as he acknowledges defeat at the hands of Octavius Caesar: 'and this pine is bark'd,/That overtopp'd them all' (*ANT* 4.12.23–4). The majesty of the pine is visualized by Richard II at a moment when the sun – the 'searching eye of heaven' – rises and 'fires the proud tops of the eastern pines' (*R2* 3.2.37–42). The image of the pine standing proud, supreme and defiant is afforded singular force in *CYM*. Belarius, approving the gentleness of the 'princely boys', emphasizes their manliness: 'and yet as rough,/Their royal blood enchaf'd, as the rud'st wind/That by the top doth take the mountain pine/And make him stoop to th'vale' (4.2.171–6). Nothing in the world of *TRO* is without blemish. Agamemnon uses an idiosyncratic image to rationalize the continuing failure of the Greeks to defeat the Trojans:

> Checks and disasters
> Grow in the veins of actions highest rear'd,
> As knots, by the conflux of meeting sap,
> Infects the sound pine, and diverts his grain
> Tortive and errant from his course of growth.
>
> *(1.3.5–9)*

Shylock's intransigence is imaged by Antonio as elemental, the pines and wind in contention creating a compelling aural effect: 'You may as well forbid the mountain pines/To wag their high tops, and to make no noise/When they are fretten with the gusts of heaven' (*MV* 4.1.75–7).

(C) Peacham (1612) writes of the 'lofty pine' using its height metaphorically to suggest support for the state. Parkinson (1629) recommends planting specimen pines in the **orchard**. Apart from the culinary value of pine-nuts, he suggests there is little use for it other than as a decorative tree.

pink (A) Probably *D. plumarius* L., but the pink can be one of various **plants** of the genus *Dianthus* (family *Caryophyllaceae*), all of which have **fragrant** white or pink **flowers**, often with a dark centre or dark stripes or markings on the petals. It is a native of central Europe, although some local species, including the cheddar and maiden pinks, are native English flowers. While any distinction between pinks and **carnations** or gillyflowers/**gillyvors** was unclear, pinks were generally smaller, less intensively cultivated and strongly **scented**, often of **clove**. However, gillyvor could indicate either pink or carnation. Pinks had medicinal and culinary uses: they were added to wine for flavouring and as a sweetener, hence their colloquial name of sops-in-wine; they also carried symbolic meanings. Pink refers to a half-shut eye, and to pink is to cut material in a decorative way. Its use as a colour in the red spectrum is probably of a later date.

(B) References to this flower are few. The single direct allusion to the flower's scent is in the opening song of *TNK* which has the line, 'Maiden pinks, of odor faint' (1.1.4). The 'odor faint' probably means delicate scent. Arden 3 (141) notes, 'Maiden pinks i.e., fresh pinks, also used for **strewing** upon the grave of a maiden or faithful wife'. Engaged in a battle of wits, Mercutio teases Romeo, 'Nay, I am the very pink of courtesy', eliciting the riposte, 'Pink for flower'; followed by Mercutio's 'Right', Romeo adds, 'Why then my pump is well flower'd' (*ROM* 2.4.57–60). The word-play relates to the flower, 'pink' as the epitome of courtesy and to the decoration on footwear produced by pinking shears. Hats, too, are decorated in this way. One of the attendants controlling the crowd at the christening of Elizabeth comments derisively on a 'haberdasher's wife' whose 'pink'd porringer fell off her head' (*H8* 5.3.47–8). The song in *ANT* describes 'Plumpy Bacchus with pink eyne!' (2.7.114). Arden 3 (170) accepts the *OED* interpretation: 'having small, narrow, or half-closed eyes; also squint-eyed'.

(C) There is no consensus about the discrete identities of the plants. Lyly (1580, *Euphues*) writes of gill-flowers, pinks and sops-in-wine in a single sentence, while Drayton's (1622) version is carnations, pinks, and sops-in-wine. Unlike many of their contemporaries, both record three separate flowers. Gerard (1597: 472–80) writes of clove 'gilloflowers', but appears to conflate them with carnations. Harvey (1978: 46–57) in the most concentrated botanical analysis available, concludes that from Elizabethan times 'pink' was used to designate the whole genus *Dianthus*, and that it may refer to plants in the wild rather than those in cultivation, a designation originally proposed by Gerard. Mabey (1996) lists the native pinks, giving D. *caryophyllus* as the Tudor gillyflower.

pioned, peony (A) Some commentators include 'peony' as the true meaning of 'pioned', but a more likely meaning, now obsolete, is 'dug' or 'excavated', with the concomitant **twilled** suggesting a woven or plaited **hedge** to reinforce a **bank** created with the excavated **soil**.

(B) Praising Ceres' creation and governance of the **natural** world, Iris images a landscape that has been thoughtfully managed. Her description alights on something peculiarly picturesque: 'Thy banks with pioned and twilled brims,/Which spongy April at thy hest betrims,/To make cold nymphs chaste crowns' (*TMP* 4.1.64–6). The 'pioned' or carefully tended banks buttressed and trimmed, provide a backdrop for the spring **flowers** that will decorate 'chaste crowns'. Perhaps more concerned with rhythm and association than with botanical accuracy, Shakespeare is willing to strain seasonal precision. It is appealing therefore to picture peonies swaying in the breeze. However, careful reading of this passage makes the prospect of peonies flaunting themselves with early spring flowers seem unlikely.

(C) Nineteenth-century commentators have led many astray: Beisley (1864) suggests peony and **lily** for pioned and twilled, while Grindon (1883) gives a practical analysis of the passage, and decides Shakespeare meant **mattock** and **spade**. Ellacombe (1896) recognizes Shakespeare's use of 'pioner' for a miner or digger (*H5* 3.2.87; *HAM* 1.5.163; *OTH* 3.3.346; *LUC* 1380), but says that this reading seems tame: 'I shall assume, therefore, that the flower is meant, spelt in the form piony'. This is represent-ative of his idiosyncratic identification of flowers. The most convincing contribution to the debate comes from Fox (1957: 515–16) who argues from the context that the banks need not be those of a river, but could be defining **meadow** boundaries which require delineation and reinforcement, the brim being the top or edge not the brimming or over-flowing water. He quotes Spenser (1596: II.x.63) for a contemporary use of pioned as dug or excavated, notes that twilled means ridged, and suggests that a Warwickshire usage, so far untraced, included the use of plaited **osiers** to form a **hedge** and prevent erosion. Consadine (2003) argues in favour of the idea of **digging**: he says pioned was used at the time as excavated or sloping, and less persuasively that twilled represents twigged, the use of small **branches** to support the slope. Personal research has confirmed that pioned continues to be used for dug or trimmed in Warwickshire into the twenty-first century. 'Peonies' would be of no use on a boundary and could not be interwoven or plaited. Knight (2009: 108) cites Gerard's discussion of peonies and the myths surrounding them which reveals that these were well-known plants in horti-cultural circles. The peony is attractive for its rich symbolism, especially in relation to *TMP*. As Heilmeyer (2001: 68) observes 'Throughout antiquity, it was associated with Apollo, the god of light, who passed it on to Paeon, the physician of the gods – after whom the flower takes its scientific name ... with its luminous flowers and healing **roots** it unites the forces of dark and light.'

pippin Originally a late-ripening sweet **apple** which kept well, the pippin is the ancestor of many modern bright-coloured eating apples which still retain the name. Pippin came to designate an apple **tree**, later any **fruit** tree that was grown from **seed** rather than propagated by **grafting**. The pairing of apples and cheese as a congenial way of rounding off a meal is suggested by Parson Evans' hasty despatch of Simple with a letter for Mistress Quickly: 'I pray you be gone. I will make an end of my dinner; there's pippins and cheese to come' (*WIV* 1.2.11–13). Similarly, Justice Shallow takes pride in providing a treat to be enjoyed after supper: 'Nay, you shall see my orchard, where, in an arbor, we will eat a last year's pippin of mine own graffing, with a dish of caraways, and so forth' (*2H4* 5.3.1–3). Here is the more usual combination – apples and caraway seeds. Drayton appears to suggest that contrary to accepted practice, the pippin was grafted (1622, *Polyolbion* 18: 677–9).

planched A boarded, planked structure, Shakespeare's planched gate is a rare use of the word to describe a rustic gate in a **wall**. Found only in *MM,* its context is significant. Isabella explains to Marianna how she is to find her way to the place designated by Angelo for what he anticipates will be the achievement of his sexual blackmail, but will instead result in the bed-trick. Gates, doors and keys are visually and conceptually expressive: 'He hath a garden circummur'd with brick,/Whose western side is with a vineyard back'd;/And to that vineyard is a planched gate' (4.1.28–30). Both Nares (1859) and the *OED* quote the only other example of the word which comes in Gorges' translation of Lucan: 'Yet with his hoofes doth beat and rent/The planched floore'. The garden at Thornbury Castle in Gloucestershire still demonstrates the progression from the **garden** through a planked gate, in this case formerly leading to the **orchard**, where both wall and gate are the early sixteenth-century survivals.

plane *Platanus* L. is the oriental plane, *P. orientalis* L. being a medieval introduction from south-east Europe and south-west Asia. A large, spreading **tree**, the name was given to any tree of the genus *Platanus,* its **leaves** and **wood**. Its large leaves, smooth **bark** and spiky **fruit** were all used in early modern medicine; it also carried emblematic meanings. It is not the familiar 'London' plane of many English cities which is a later seventeenth-century cross. Confusingly the name of plane was also given to the **sycamore**, *Acer pseudoplatanus* L. because of a similarity between the leaves. A play abounding in references to plants, *TNK* contains the single mention of 'plane'. Having freed Palamon, the Jailer's Daughter then directs him to safety: 'I have sent him where a cedar,/Higher than all the rest, spreads like a plane/Fast by a brook' (2.6.4–6). She seems peculiarly attached to the natural world. Perhaps there is a hint of the emblematic in her idolatrous love for Palamon which is destined to be fruitless. Even more significance attaches to the tree's association with virtue and fidelity. The plane tree has long been thought sterile. Peacham (1612) writes that it is known for its shade. Hawkins (1633) uses it as an emblem of faith. Mabey (1996) provides its modern context.

plant (A) A young, newly-planted **tree, shrub**, vegetable or **flower**, or one intended for planting. More generally a plant is a living organism capable of photosynthesis. Figuratively it can be something planted, a young person or a novice; **withered** plants can suggest old age. 'To plant' is to set a plant, seed or bulb in the **soil** to take **root** and **grow**, or to establish a **garden** or **orchard**. It can suggest founding or establishing a community, society, colony or church, and can also be a synonym for 'to place' or 'to put'.

   (B) Plants have interesting literal and figurative applications. Remarkably the process of planting is rarely used in a strictly literal sense. Most frequently the term relates to planting a king; occasionally to conferring a dignity or honour; abstractions of all kinds are planted. The dethroned Richard II warns Northumberland that Bolingbroke as King, 'shall think that thou, which knowest the way/To plant unrightful kings, wilt know again,/Being ne'er so little urg'd, another way/To pluck him headlong from the usurped throne' (*R2* 5.1.62–5). The prediction is verified in *1H4*. Expressing admiration for Hotspur, Bolingbroke describes him as, 'A son who is the theme of honor's tongue,/Amongst a grove the very straightest plant,/Who is sweet Fortune's minion and her pride' (*1H4* 1.1.81–3). This regard is not reciprocated. Hotspur denounces his father Northumberland and his uncle Worcester for their role in supplanting Richard: 'To put down Richard, that sweet lovely rose,/And plant this thorn, this canker, Bullingbrook?'(1.3.175–6). Queen Margaret vilifies the Yorkists for killing her son Prince Edward: 'How sweet a plant have you untimely cropp'd!' (*3H6* 5.5.62). Earlier in the play Warwick, demanding the deposition of Henry VI, boasts, 'I'll plant Plantagenet, root him up who dares' (1.1.48). King Duncan, welcoming the victorious Macbeth and Banquo, promises, 'I have begun to plant thee, and will labor/To make thee full of growing'. Banquo's response is in perfect harmony with the theme of reciprocity: 'There if I grow,/The harvest is your own' (*MAC* 1.4.28–33). Abstractions such as friendship and courage are also planted. At the close of *H5* the French King, accepting English demands, gives his daughter to Henry V in the hope that these kingdoms, 'May cease their hatred; and this dear conjunction/Plant neighborhood and Christian-like accord' (5.2.352–3). During the Battle of Towton, George, Duke of Clarence, recommends that his comrades in arms encourage their troops with promises of rich rewards: 'This may plant courage in their quailing breasts' (*3H6* 2.3.54).

Iago comes closest to a literal use of 'planting' when he draws on the analogy between gardening and the cultivation of self-control. Deriding Roderigo's obsession with Desdemona, he argues, 'Our bodies are our gardens, to the which our wills are gardeners; so that if we will plant nettles or sow lettuce, set hyssop and weed up tine, supply it with one gender of herbs or distract it with many, either to have it sterile with idleness or manur'd with industry – why, the power and corrigible authority of this lies in our wills' (*OTH* 1.3.320–6).

Armado is referred to by Navarre as 'A man in all the world's new fashion planted' (*LLL* 1.1.164). Commenting on the likelihood of Coriolanus gaining the support of the plebeians, the Second Officer maintains he has 'planted his honors in their eyes and his actions in their hearts' (*COR* 2.2.29–30). Tamora threatens Bassianus, 'Had I the pow'r that some say Dian had,/Thy temples should be planted presently/With horns, as was Actaeon's' (*TIT* 2.3.61–3). Fearful that Antony's departure for Rome will lead him to desert her, Cleopatra maintains, 'yet at the first/I saw the treasons planted' (*ANT* 1.3.25–6). Malcolm, in the closing speech of *MAC,* acknowledges his obligations and the need for renewal: 'What's more to do,/Which would be planted newly with the time,/As calling home our exil'd friends abroad/…We will perform in measure, time, and place' (5.9.30–9). This play so deeply engaged with planting and time, captures in the syntax a *tabula rasa*: 'planted *newly*'. An extended image is provided by Warwick when presenting King Edward's proposal of marriage to the Lady Bona:

> Myself have often heard him say, and swear,
> That this his love was an eternal plant,
> Whereof the root was fix'd in virtue's ground,
> The leaves and fruit maintain'd with beauty's sun,
>
> *(3H6 3.3.123–6)*

Rosaline teases Orlando about a man 'that abuses our young plants with carving "Rosaline" on their barks' (*AYL* 3.2.360–1). More seriously the Queen berates the Gardener in *R2* for his appraisal of Richard's fall: 'Gard'ner, for telling me these news of woe,/Pray God the plants thou graft'st may never grow'(3.4.100–1). The Friar undertaking his early morning task says, 'O, mickle is the powerful grace that lies/In plants, herbs, stones, and their true qualities' (*ROM* 2.3.15–16). Making his prognostications at Elizabeth's christening, Cranmer identifies her with peace and security: 'In her days every man shall eat in safety/Under his own vine what he plants' (*H8* 5.4.33–4). Observing the drunkenness aboard Pompey's galley the First Servant comments wryly: 'Some o'their plants are ill rooted already, the least wind i'th'world will blow them down' (*ANT* 2.7.1–3). Accounting for the popularity of the Roman exile with the Volsces, Aufidius rationalizes that Coriolanus, 'watered his new plants with dews of flattery' (*COR* 5.6.22). This metaphor is so persuasive that it lends a ring of truth to a fabrication.

(C) Because they need individual treatment, plants are usually referred to in gardening books by name or function, so 'plant' does not often feature. The few books with an index which includes 'plant' have unenlightening entries.

plantain, plantan More usually 'plantain', this is any one of various low-growing **plants** of the genus *Plantago* L., most commonly the widely distributed native plants *P. major* L. the greater or common plantain, and *P. lanceolata* L., the ribwort plantain. Plantain is used of any plant resembling the true plantain, which had a considerable range of medicinal uses, including as a dressing on wounds, and for bruises. Both mentions refer to the plant's efficacy. In *LLL*, Moth quibbles on the word **costard**, the **apple** of that name, a word used for 'head' and the character Costard. He informs Armado, 'Here's a costard broken in a shin'. Untangling the ensuing confusion Costard exclaims, 'O sir, plantan, a plain plantan; no l'envoy, no l'envoy, no salve, sir, but a plantan!' (3.1.69–74). The linguistic engagement relates to 'l'envoy' a form of footnote to a literary work, 'salve' or salute and 'salve' as ointment or healing **balm**. After listening to Benvolio's lesson on how to cure the pain of unrequited love, Romeo invokes the efficacy of the plant: 'Your plantan leaf is excellent for that'. Responding, Benvolio asks, 'For what, I pray thee?', only to receive a kick and the answer, 'For your broken shin' (*ROM* 1.2.51–2). Bartholomeus (1582) recommends plantain for wounds; while Hall (Lane 1996) uses plantain extensively, it appears only three times in the index. Culpeper expands on the many recommendations of his predecessors, giving its use for lunatic and frenetic persons adding 'briefly, the plantains are singularly good wound-herbs' (1653: 297). Le Strange (1977) notes that the fresh **leaves** of plantain are still prescribed for wounds, burns and stings.

plantation In horticultural terms a plantation is the action of planting **seeds** or **plants** in the **ground**; it also indicates a cultivated **flower**-bed or a group of growing plants. Its use to designate a clump or group of **trees** is a later word. Plantation also signifies a colony or settlement. The word appears only in *TMP* where, in a brief exchange, two meanings collide. Gonzalo beginning to outline his idea for the creation of a utopian world uses the word in the sense of a 'colony': 'Had I plantation of this isle, my lord'. Before he can continue, his hostile auditors pervert his meaning: Antonio jokes, 'He'd sow't with nettle-seed', leading to Sebastian's mocking, 'Or docks, or mallows' (2.1.144–5).

pleached (A) A **pruning** operation popular at the time, pleaching is carried out on **trees** to produce a regular, flat pattern of **branches** which are tied or entwined to form a border, boundary or **hedge**. It can suggest fenced, bordered, interlaced, intertwined or entangled or overarched with branches which could also be trained to create a **bower** or **arbour**.

(B) Both meanings of 'pleached' appear in the plays: one is descriptive, the other figurative. In *ADO* Hero charges Margaret to draw Beatrice to a spot convenient for eavesdropping:

> And bid her steal into the pleached bower,
> Where honeysuckles, ripened by the sun,
> Forbid the sun to enter, like favourites
> Made proud by princes that advance their pride
> Against the power that bred it.

> *(3.1.7–11)*

Beginning with a simple description, Hero cannot resist engaging in similitude: play, botany and politics are comfortably interwoven. Antony employs the image when prevailing upon Eros to assist his suicide: 'Wouldst thou be window'd in great Rome, and see/Thy master thus with pleach'd arms, bending down/His corrigible neck, his face subdu'd/To penetrative shame' (*ANT* 4.14.72–5).

(C) While there are contemporary illustrations of pleached hedges and trees, the word is seldom used at the time. The *OED* records Shakespeare as the only user until Scott in 1822. For illustrations of pleached trees forming arbours and bowers see Hill (ed. 1988). Modern pleached hedges and arbours can be seen in the **gardens** at Hampton Court Palace, Surrey.

plough, plow (A) An agricultural implement with fixed blades in a frame, a plough is used to break up and turn over the **soil** before sowing **seed**. In a rare usage it can suggest the unit of **land** that one team can plough in a year; 'the plough' can also be the team of oxen or horses used for ploughing. It features as a symbol of agricultural life, by extension indicating any instrument resembling a plough. To plough is to make furrows in the **earth,** to prepare for sowing and planting, to work as a ploughman, create a line as if by ploughing, and figuratively to score or scratch as if by ploughing, to furrow the face with wrinkles, or cause wrinkles to appear.

(B) Plough is used twice in a literal sense. The numerous metaphorical cases relate to war, and male sexual conquest. The sexual meaning may be original to Shakespeare. The Spanish soldier Armado is so taken with the country-wench Jaquenetta that he expresses his willingness to become a farmer for her sake: 'I have vow'd to Jaquenetta to hold the plough for her sweet love three year' (*LLL* 5.2.883–4). The Fourth Countryman in *TNK* is persuaded to sacrifice a day's work for merriment: 'Let the plough play to-day, I'll tickle't out/Of the jades' tails to-morrow' (2.3.28–9). Thersites pours scorn on Achilles and Ajax, claiming they are manipulated by Ulysses and Nestor who 'yoke you like draught-oxen, and make you plough up the wars' (*TRO* 2.1.106–7). Incensed by the concessions made to the plebeians, Coriolanus vociferates, 'In soothing them we nourish 'gainst our Senate/The cockle of rebellion, insolence, sedition,/Which we ourselves have plough'd for, sow'd, and scatter'd' (*COR* 3.1.69–71). Anticipating appeals from his mother and wife to spare Rome, he is defiant: 'Let the Volsces/Plough Rome and harrow Italy, I'll never/Be such a gosling to obey instinct' (5.3.33–5). It is a curious image for a man who glorifies war and for whom manual work is alien to his experience and anathema to his ethos. The image of ploughing the sea occurs twice. The Mariner's colourful description of the invading English fleet concludes, 'Thus tightly carried with a merry gale,/They plough the ocean hitherward amain' (*E3* 3.1.77–8). Responding to the greed of the Poet and the Painter, Timon reflects on the power of gold: ''Tis thou that rig'st the bark and plough'st the foam' (*TIM* 5.1.50). The meaning would seem to be that the pursuit of gold initiates all ventures. Antony angrily taunts Cleopatra, 'let/Patient Octavia plough thy visage up/With her prepared nails' (*ANT* 4.12.37–9). Agrippa casting a backward glance at Cleopatra's affair with Julius Caesar uses the word in a sexual way: 'She made great Caesar lay his sword to bed;/He ploughed her, and she cropp'd' (2.2.227–8). According to Plutarch the 'crop', Caesarion, was later murdered at the behest of Octavius Caesar. Boult, responding enthusiastically to Bawd's injunction to rape the newly acquired but recalcitrant recruit to the brothel, says of Marina, 'And if were she a thornier piece of ground than she is, she shall be plough'd' (*PER* 4.6.144–5). Timon vents his spleen on 'ingrateful man' by inciting nature to 'Dry up thy marrows, vines, and plough-torn leas' (*TIM* 4.3.188–92). Here nature is violated by the plough; its productive affinity denied. The ploughman gains several mentions. A sympathetic Titania complains that contention in the fairy world has spilled over into the realm of human beings. Because of unseasonal weather, 'The ox hath therefore stretch'd his yoke in vain,/The ploughman lost his sweat, and the green corn/Hath rotted ere his youth attain'd a beard'(*MND* 2.1.93–5). Troilus draws on the ploughman's rough hands when attempting to give perfect expression to Cressida's refined beauty: 'to whose soft seizure/The cygnet's down is harsh, and spirit of sense/ Hard as the palm of ploughman' (*TRO* 1.1.57–9).

(C) Shakespeare's usage predates the *OED*'s earliest example of 1660 for the slang meaning of having sexual intercourse with a woman. Using both spellings, Markham (1613) includes several chapters on the plough or plow, providing detailed illustrations of its constituent parts. He writes of the different types of plough and ploughing techniques required for various kinds of soil, using 'plough' to indicate other agricultural processes such as **earing, tilling** and **manuring**. Spier and Anderson (1985: 448–61) argue that Shakespeare's farming credentials are linked to his intimate knowledge of Tusser (1573). McRae (1996: 8) sees the plough as 'a central symbol of agricultural activity and rural life' and 'an emblem of traditional structures of rural society' in the early modern period. He cites Robert Cecil's Commons speech of 1601: 'I do not dwell in the country, I am not acquainted with the plough: But I think that whosoever doth not maintain the Plough, destroys this Kingdom.' See also **coulter**.

plum, prune, pruin (A) *Prunus domestica* L., a cultivated form of the wild plum, is closely related to the **damson**, *Prunus domestica* L. ssp *insititia* L. An early, possibly Roman, introduction, it was found in the wild and in **orchard**s, and was readily available to all sections of society. **Green** or unripe plums are notoriously sour. Plum can suggest plump, or swelling up, becoming light as dough rising, fattening. Plum-pottage or pudding was a thick sweet stew which included plums and other fruit eaten in the winter as a treat, particularly at Christmas. Both **leaves** and gum from the **bark** had medicinal uses. Prune or pruin is the dried fruit preserved for eating through the winter, which from classical times served as a laxative. Prunes – often associated with brothels – gradually fell out of favour in the sixteenth century as **raisins** became more readily available.

(B) It is the contexts in which this fruit is found that gives it piquancy. Constance cautions her son Arthur against the blandishments of Elinor: 'Give grandame kingdom, and it grandame will/Give it a plum, a cherry, and a fig' (*JN* 2.1.161–2). A rustic in *TNK* dismisses the threat that might be posed by Arcite in the wrestling match: 'Hang him, plum porridge!' (2.3.72). Arden 3 (204) explains, 'the sort of person who would eat this thick sweet broth "made of beef, dried fruits, white bread, spices, wine and sugar; eaten at Christmas" (Proudfoot). "Milksop" derives from the same idea'. In contrast to such disparagement, the Schoolmaster in the same play despairs at the inability of his charges to benefit from his best endeavours: 'Have my rudiments/Been labor'd so long with ye, milk'd unto ye,/And by a figure, even the very plum-broth/And marrow of my understanding laid upon ye' (3.5.3–6). Arden 3 (230) comments 'the very best. Plum-broth was much like plum-porridge. Bone-marrow was considered the choicest part of the meat.' Intriguingly, of these almost identical dishes one is used to deprecate, the other to commend. Attempting to escape Venus' amorous persuasion, Adonis resorts to a common simile: 'The mellow plum doth fall, the green sticks fast,/Or being early pluck'd, is sour to taste' (*VEN* 527–8). *PP* bemoans premature losses: 'Like a green plum that hangs upon a tree,/And falls (through wind) before the fall should be' (10.5–6).

The close and sometimes confused relationship between plums and damsons emerges from an incident in *2H6*. Buckingham exposes the fraudulent Simpcox who claims to have been blind from birth and crippled after falling from a 'plum-tree' while gathering 'damsons' for his wife (2.1.94–100). Hamlet uses a curious phrase when describing the eyes of old men, 'purging thick amber and plum-tree gum' (*HAM* 2.2.198–9). Arden 2 (247) points out, 'Gerard's *Herbal* speaks of "the gum which cometh out of the plum-tree"'. The association of prunes with prostitution is revealed in *MM*. Pompey Bum, the bawd in Mistress Overdone's establishment, begins his prevarication by explaining how Constable Elbow's wife entered the premises: 'Sir, she came in great with child; and longing (saving your honor's reverence) for stew'd pruins. Sir, we had but two in the house'. Given that a dish of prunes placed in a window was the sign for a brothel, Pompey's attempt at obfuscation seems ill conceived, but it leads to a digression on the quality of dishes. Checked by Escalus, he tells of Master Froth's 'cracking the stones of the foresaid pruins' (2.1.89–107). Arden 2 (32) explains Pompey's multiple sexual innuendos. Doll is magnificently direct when she undermines the swaggering Pistol, claiming he lives off the brothel's culinary scraps: 'You a captain! you slave, for what? for tearing a poor whore's ruff in a bawdy-house? He a captain! hang him, rogue! he lives upon mouldy stew'd pruins and dried cakes' (*2H4* 2.4.144–7). Arden 2 (72) points out that prunes were one of the ingredients in a boiled broth used as a cure for venereal disease. The parasitical Falstaff denounces the Hostess of the Tavern as a bawd: 'There's no more faith in thee than in a stew'd prune' (*1H4* 3.3.112–13). Slender narrates how he sustained an injury 'with playing at sword and dagger with a master of fence (three veneys for a dish of stew'd prunes)' (*WIV* 1.1.283–5). Access to prostitutes is the prize for the winner of the 'veneys' or 'bouts'. Arden 2 (18) indicates that prunes 'seem to have been served inside the house as an aphrodisiac' adding that they became 'a synonym for prostitute – as did "hot meat"'. Prunes are not exclusively associated with prostitution. In the wholesome atmosphere of the sheep-shearing feast the young shepherd, designated 'Clown', rehearses the shopping list provided by Perdita. He concludes with, 'four pounds of pruins, and as many raisins o'th'sun' (*WT* 4.3.48–9).

(C) Cogan (1584) thinks the best plums for prunes come from the Damascene plum, but notes that as it fails to thrive in England, prunes have to be imported from France. He suggests they should be eaten with wine or water before meals to ameliorate constipation. Dismissing their nutritional value, he says they are more meet for swine than men. Vaughan (1617) recommends a combination of senna (see **cyme**) and prunes to act as a purgative. Palter (2002) calls plums a modest kind of fruit, a marker of lower social status.

pomander Both a mixture of dried **flowers** and aromatic substances and the hollow ball, box or container in which the mixture was carried, a pomander could be hung round the neck or waist to protect against noxious **smells** and the plague. Figuratively a pomander was something **scented** or with a particularly sweet smell, a book of prayers, poems and secrets. A cheap pomander container would have featured in a pedlar's wares. Autolycus is the only bearer of a pomander. Boasting of his profitable visit to the country festival he reveals that his are of poor quality: 'I have sold all my trompery; not a counterfeit stone, not a ribbon, glass, pomander, brooch, table-book, ballad, knife, tape, glove, shoe-tie, bracelet, horn-ring, to keep my pack from fasting' (*WT* 4.4.596–600). A different kind of pomander may be alluded to in *LLL*. It has been suggested that Berowne's 'A lemon' followed by Longeville's 'Stuck with cloves' (5.2.647–8) was used as defence against the pestilence in addition to its primary function of flavouring drinks. Arden 2 (171) notes: 'Halliwell quotes from Bradwell, 1636, that a lemon stuck with cloves was a good thing to smell occasionally against the pestilence'. Many contemporary writers give instructions for the making of pomanders. Plat (1594) recommends they should include **roses**, while Vaughan (1617) considers pomanders make the heart merry. McLean (1981) notes the value of the scent of roses and gives their inclusion in pomanders, washballs, cosmetics and ointments. See Knight (2009: 129–32) for instructive observations on the relationship between the floral and literary kinds. Palfrey (1997: 124–6) provides a clear-eyed assessment of Autolycus.

pomegranate (A) *Punica granatum*, a **shrub** or small **tree**, is widely cultivated in warm countries, and may have grown in England from the sixteenth century, but without **fruiting**. The pomegranate was the emblem of Persephone; it was supposed to have sprung from the blood of the dead Adonis, like the **Adonis flower**, or from that of the dead Dionysus. It was later thought by some to be the **apple** of **Eden**. The pomegranate has been used for millennia in carving, needlework and other ornamental work to symbolize bounty, sexuality and **fertility** because of its abundant number of **seeds**; but it was used as a contraceptive, and had a wide range of medicinal applications.

(B) Juliet, wanting to prolong her night with Romeo, delivers a speech fraught with symbolism:

> Wilt thou begone? it is not yet near day.
> It was the nightingale, and not the lark,
> That pierc'd the fearful hollow of thine ear;
> Nightly she sings on yond pomegranate tree.
> Believe me, love, it was the nightingale.

(ROM 3.5.1–5)

This plea is both highly allusive and elusive. Lyrical and visual, it evokes a moment of beauty and desperate hope. The symbolism of the pomegranate resides in the light/dark dichotomy critical to the Persephone myth. Kidnapped by Hades she is released once a year to be reunited with her loving mother, Demeter, and so becomes the harbinger of spring. Her return to the underworld is assured when she eats the pomegranate seed which symbolizes marriage. Romeo insists that the threshold light is the faint light of morning and the bird song is that of the lark and not the nightingale: 'It was the lark, the herald of the morn,/No nightingale. Look, love, what envious streaks/Do lace the severing clouds in yonder east' (6–8). The three mentions of the nightingale point to the story of Philomena's rape and her ultimate transformation to a nightingale (though in the Greek version she becomes a swallow; it is her sister Procne who becomes the nightingale). Other images also impregnate this scene especially those associated with bounty, sacrifice and thwarted sexual fertility. Becoming emblematic of young love, Romeo and Juliet generate their own mythological power. Another pomegranate reference is elusive in a different way. Stripping Parolles of his pretensions, Lafew says, 'Go to, sir, you were beaten in Italy for picking a kernel out of a pomegranate. You are a vagabond and no true traveller' (*AWW* 2.3.258–60). Editors have failed to find anything more revealing in this case than to suggest that people were eager to beat him on the most trivial pretext. Francis the drawer in *1H4* makes the only other reference when designating the name of a room in the tavern: 'Look down into the Pomgarnet, Ralph' (2.4.37–8).

(C) Pomegranates were used if not grown in England by at least the thirteenth century: Labarge (1982) details the surprisingly large quantities of medicines that Edward I took on his travels round the country in 1286, including pomegranate wine. Harvey (1987) has shown that in the middle of the fourteenth century Henry Daniel experimented with **growing** the pomegranate in his Stepney **garden**, but could not get it to fruit. It was the chosen device of Catherine of Aragon, and survives in carvings and paintings of the time. It was well enough known to feature proverbially in literary works: Greene writes 'the purest pomegranates may have one rotten **kernel**, and the perfectest man is not without some blemish' (1616, vol. 9, *Greene's Mourning Garment*: 129). Heilmeyer (2001: 30) notes that the pomegranate was 'a symbol of diversity in unity, of immortality and lasting fertility. But above all else Aphrodite's favourite tree, first planted by her in Cyprus, is a symbol of sensual love and passion.' Palter (2002) provides a wide range of literary references. Henderson (2005) records Burghley writing to a friend in Paris in 1561 to say that he already had an **orange** tree, but asking for a pomegranate and a **lemon** to be sent to him. Riddle (2010) gives the history of its use from pre-historic times and includes the Persephone myth and its Christian symbolism. The Bible abounds in references to the pomegranate.

pomewater A large, juicy, sharp-tasting variety of **apple**, its first recorded use figures uniquely in Holofernes' disquisition on deer: 'The deer was (as you know) *sanguis*, in blood, ripe as the pomewater, who now hangeth like a jewel in the ear of *caelo*, the sky, the welkin, the heaven, and anon falleth like a crab on the face of *terra*, the soil, the land, the earth' (*LLL* 4.2.3–7). The fleshy, juicy **pomewater** is juxtaposed with the small, hard, sour **crab**-apple. Despite the prolixity of the schoolmaster, his differentiation between the living and the dead deer is appropriately paralleled by the contrasting apples. Although not recorded before *LLL* (c. 1595) pomewater seems to have quickly gained favour as Drayton (1622) calls it well-known, and Parkinson (1640) includes it as a juicy apple. Markham (1615) recommends its use for the 'flux' or diarrhoea.

pond, pool (A) The two words for a body of water largely overlap: both are small, usually man-made water features, created by excavating a hollow or damming an existing watercourse. Both can also suggest a natural feature, a lake, mere or tarn, a **pool** or **pond** in a river or **stream**. They were often distinguished by their purpose as for example 'fish-pond'.

(B) These features of **gardens, fields** and **meadows** are the source of several vivid images. His intense jealousy leads Leontes to image female susceptibility to male predation:

> And many a man there is (even at this present,
> Now, while I speak this) holds his wife by th'arm,
> That little thinks she has been sluic'd in's absence,
> And his pond fish'd by his next neighbor – by
> Sir Smile, his neighbor.
>
> *(WT 1.2.192–6)*

Attempting to explain the defeat of Hotspur and his army at Shrewsbury, Lord Bardolph alights on this image of the fish-pond: 'their weapons only/Seem'd on our side; but for their spirits and souls,/This word, rebellion, it had froze them up,/As fish are in a pond' (*2H4* 1.1.197–200). Isabella's disclosure to Claudio of Angelo's proposed sexual blackmail images unfathomable wickedness: 'His filth within being cast, he would appear/A pond as deep as hell' (*MM* 3.1.92–3). 'Cast' can be interpreted in several ways but in the light of the pond allusion Riverside (600) suggests 'cleared out', as in dredging. Familiar, too, and distasteful, is stagnant water and its accretions. The garrulous Gratiano advises Antonio not to adopt an excessively serious demeanour:

> There are a sort of men whose visages
> Do cream and mantle like a standing pond,
> And do a willful stillness entertain,
> With purpose to be dress'd in an opinion
> Of wisdom, gravity, profound conceit,
>
> *(MV 1.1.88–92)*

We learn from Ariel that there are reservoirs of unwholesome water on Prospero's island which hamper and defile the would-be assassins, Caliban, Stephano and Trinculo: 'At last I left them/I'th'filthy-mantled pool beyond your cell,/There dancing up to th'chins' (*TMP* 4.1.181–3). Describing the indignities he suffers as a social outcast in his role as Mad Tom, Edgar reveals that he 'drinks the green mantle of the standing pool' (*LR* 3.4.133). There are several examples of 'puddle' representing filthy water. A compelling use is that provided by Octavius Caesar when recalling the Antony of old during his retreat over the Alps: 'Thou didst drink/The stale of horses and the gilded puddle/Which beasts would cough at' (*ANT* 1.4.61–3). That a pool can be appreciated as being clear and appealing is affirmed by a remarkable image in *CYM.* Imogen reflects, 'I'th'world's volume/Our Britain seems as of it, but not in't;/In a great pool a swan's nest' (3.4.137–9).

(C) Heresbach (1596) points out that ponds or pools are essential for the supply of water close to the house, at the same time noting their importance for cattle and other livestock. Ponds and pools are frequently indexed together as fish-ponds; Landsberg (1996: 70) records their value in the medieval economy and has a picture of 'a storage-type fishpond' which illuminates Leontes' imagery (*WT* 1.2.194–8). The excavations required to make such bodies of water may survive when the garden has long gone: the extensive contemporary ponds can still be seen in aerial photographs of Sir Christopher Hatton's Holdenby, and of Harrington, both in Northamptonshire (Steane 1977; Samson 2012). Ponds could contain **fountains** as part of decorative water features. Earlier functional ponds were often developed in the late Tudor garden into entire water gardens and then into canals and bodies of water like those at Gorhambury and Lyveden New Bield. Henderson (2005) provides the most comprehensive overview of ponds and water features.

poperin, pop'rin Now rare, the poperin or poppering **pear** described both the **tree** and its **fruit**. There is some doubt over its date of introduction and its source of origin, but it probably came from Flanders, and may have been first cultivated by John Leland under Henry VIII. Because of their shape all types of pears lent themselves to sexual imagery. Deriving its name from Poperinghe, near Ypres, this celebrated fruit is mentioned only once and in a sexual context. Mercutio says of Rosaline: 'O, Romeo, that she were, O that she were/An open-arse, thou a pop'rin pear!' (*ROM* 2.1.37–8). This bawdy joke alludes to the **medlar** along with the pear. Parkinson (1629) provides detailed descriptions of three types of 'popperin' as he spells it. Nares (1859) writes that Henry VIII, his chaplain or possibly Cardinal Wolsey, gave the living of Poperingues in Flanders, later renamed Popering, sometimes Peuplingues or Pepeling, to John Leland the antiquarian, though there is no record that he ever went there. Blake (2006) says Poperinghe was taken to be a euphemism for penis thus extending the pear's sexual metaphor.

poppy (A) The genus *Papaver* L. includes both the **field** or common poppy, *P. rhoeas* L., which is very slightly narcotic, and soporific, and the far-Eastern introduction, the highly toxic and narcotic, opium poppy, *P. somniferum* L. The two plants were often conflated, allowing room for confusion; poppy also designated the end product of opium extract. Figuratively it could suggest anything narcotic; medicinally it was an analgesic, and a soporific. It could have serious if not fatal side-effects, being particularly toxic if used in conjunction with **mandrake**. The poppy was associated with Demeter and with her daughter Persephone's time in the underworld.

(B) Iago makes the only mention of this **flower**, citing it for its narcotic potential. He delivers lines of extreme beauty while celebrating a monstrous achievement – Othello's collapse into jealousy: 'Not poppy, nor mandragora,/Nor all the drowsy syrups of the world/Shall ever medicine thee to that sweet sleep/Which thou ow'dst yesterday' (*OTH* 3.3.330–3). A notable poetic feature is the poppy's contribution to the sound values: it colludes and collides with its sister drug **mandragora**; it also possesses a singular life at odds with its status as a soporific.

(C) Heilmeyer (2001: 58) notes, 'Demeter, the goddess of fertility and agriculture, wore poppy flowers and seeds as did Morpheus, the god of sleep and dreams, and Hypnos, the god of sleep', adding, 'The poppy has always been seen as a magical flower suspended between good and evil, light and darkness, healing and annihilation.' Barabas 'drank of poppy and cold mandrake juice;/And being asleep, belike they thought me dead' (1590, Marlowe, *The Jew of Malta*, V.i.82–3). Middleton's waiting woman Diaphanta uses poppy as a synonym for opium: 'A little poppy, sir, were good to cause you sleep' (*The Changeling*, 1.1.148). Duncan-Jones (1995: 521–5) notes that Gerard and Parkinson identify the **canker rose** as the wild poppy: she argues that the canker **blooms** in *SON* 54 refer to the wild poppy, *Papaver rhoeas* L. rather than the rose. Mabey (1996) provides extensive detail of its folklore and symbolism from Egyptian times. Mabey (2010: 205) contrasts the symbolic associations of the poppy in Christian culture where it is linked to transience and death, with other traditions where it represents fertility and new life. Pollard (2005) provides an overview of the role of opiate drugs in the early modern theatre, and Karim-Cooper (2006) records poppy-oil as an important ingredient in theatrical cosmetics at the time.

postern (A) A side or back entrance, a postern was commonly a gate away from the main door, particularly one that is private or unobtrusive, an escape, refuge; it can also suggest a less than honourable exit. Postern gates were usually sited at the back or side of a house, or if in a wall, away from the main gates.

(B) Meeting her protector, Silvia advises, 'Go on, good Eglamour,/Out at the postern by the abbey wall;/I fear I am attended by some spies' (*TGV* 5.1.8–10). A much more dangerous escape is that negotiated by Camillo for Polixenes: 'Your followers I will whisper to the business,/And will by twos and threes at several posterns/Clear them o'th'city'. Camillo then affirms: 'It is mine authority to command/The keys of all the posterns' (*WT* 1.2.437–64). The special status attaching to the posterns is emphasized by Leontes: 'How came the posterns/So easily open?' (2.1.52–3). Its role in defining the threshold is apparent in *MM* where the Duke responds to urgent knocking: 'How now? what noise? That spirit's possess'd with haste/That wounds th'unsisting postern with these strokes' (4.2.88–9). Meditating on the complexities of life the imprisoned Richard II calls to mind passages from Luke 18.25 and Matthew 19.24: 'It is as hard to come as for a camel/To thread the postern of a small needle's eye' (*R2* 5.5.16–17). Arden 3 (462) has a useful footnote on this subject accepting that Shakespeare was probably aware of 'needle' signifying a 'small pedestrian entrance in a city gate'. This gate, in a garden or city **wall**, had consequences disproportionate to its size.

(C) De Flores uses postern as a gate by which to effect a surreptitious entry: 'Yes, here are all the keys; I was afraid, my lord,/I'd wanted for the postern, this is it' (*The Changeling*, 3.1.1–2).

potato (A) It is difficult to be certain whether Shakespeare meant the sweet potato, *Ipomoea batatas*, or the staple food **crop**, *Solanum tuberosum,* as the two were often not differentiated in Elizabethan times. The sweet potato was an import from South America and Florida via Spain and Portugal. 'Potato' refers to both the **plant** and the tuber.

(B) The potato figures only twice, but on both occasions its potential as an aphrodisiac is implicit – though the significance might well be lost on a modern audience. Indeed, in *WIV* there is a potential incongruity unless there is an appreciation of what was thought to be the sexually vitalizing attribute of this exotic vegetable. As Falstaff prepares for his encounter with the merry wives he calls forth aids to sweeten his breath ('kissing comfits'), and to renew his enfeebled masculine prowess: 'Let the sky rain potatoes; let it thunder to the tune of "Green-sleeves", hail kissing-comfits, and snow eringoes; let there come a tempest of provocation' (5.5.18–21). **Eringoes,** another supposed aphrodisiac, are candied **roots** of sea-holly. The related scene in *TRO* is sordid. Thersites watches in the shadows as Diomed engages in his unceremonious seduction of Cressida. As the game proceeds this cynical voyeur observes, 'How the devil Luxury, with his fat rump and potato finger, tickles these together! Fry, lechery, fry!' (5.2.55–7). Contamination continually leeches into this play despite the frequency with which high ideals and aspirations – such as the pledge of love between Troilus and Cressida – are expressed.

(C) Gerard (1597: 780–2) demonstrates that the two plants were known to be different by describing and accurately illustrating their contrasting **growth** habits. He notes the virtue of the sweet potato to 'comfort, nourish, and strengthen the bodie, procure bodily lust, and that with greedinesse'. Middleton's Touchwood mentions eringoes, artichokes and potatoes as suitable food for a wedding feast, underlining their erotic connotations (1613, *A Chaste Maid in Cheapside,* 3.3.16–18). Reader (2009) provides an extensive history of the potato, the familiar *Solanum tuberosum,* which became a staple crop in northern Europe. Willes (2011) describes the uncertainty surrounding dates of introduction and places of origin. It is noteworthy that the plant Gerard is holding in the portrait that adorns his *Herbal* is the potato, *Solanum tuberosum*; there is also a separate illustration of the plant. Both are conveniently reproduced by Willes (90–1).

primrose (A) *Primula vulgaris* Huds. is an early flowering native spring **plant** with generally pale yellow **flowers**, growing in **woods, hedge-banks** and damp grassland. Primroses, **cowslips** and **oxlips** are all members of the same botanical genus and family. The primrose is a symbol of the countryside, and a sign of spring; by extension it can suggest the first or the best of something, the first flowering, or first **fruits**. It had both culinary and medicinal applications. The 'primrose path' means an appealing course of action but one that may lead to disaster.

(B) The flower's association with youthfulness is present when Hermia confides to Helena the location of her assignation with Lysander: 'And in the wood, where often you and I/Upon faint primrose beds were won't to lie,/Emptying our bosoms of their counsel sweet' (*MND* 1.1.214–16). This allusion is celebrated in the song that opens *TNK*: 'Primrose, first-born child of Ver,/Merry spring-time's harbinger,/With her bells dim' (1.1.7–9). The 'bells' have provoked emendations, but their buds are bell-like. No such ambiguity is present in Perdita's celebrated flower-speech: 'pale primroses,/That die unmarried, ere they can behold/Bright Phoebus in his strength (a malady/Most incident to maids)' (*WT* 4.4.122–5). Arviragus **strewing** flowers on the seemingly dead Fidele/Imogen promises: 'Thou shalt not lack/The flower that's like thy face, pale primrose' (*CYM* 4.2.220–1). In this, the only play with two mentions of the flower, the Queen requires 'violets, cowslips, and the primroses' (1.5.83) for nefarious purposes. Significantly, none of the usual epithets are attached to the flowers here. The image of the primrose path arises twice. Having listened to Laertes' caution to safeguard her virginity, Ophelia accepts the moral lesson but registers a caveat:

> Do not, as some ungracious pastors do,
> Show me the steep and thorny way to heaven,
> Whiles, like a puff'd and reckless libertine,
> Himself the primrose path of dalliance treads,
>
> *(HAM 1.3.47–50)*

The Porter in *MAC* temporarily suspends his game of allocating diverse professions to places in hell because he feels the cold: 'I'll devil-porter it no further. I had thought to have let in some of all professions that go the primrose way to th'everlasting bonfire' (2.3.17–21).

(C) The *OED* cites *HAM* as the earliest recorded use of the 'primrose path'. In contemporary literature the primrose was frequently symbolic. Greene's several instances include 'That I with the primrose of my fresh wit,/May tumble her tyrannie under my feete' (1590, vol. 8, *Francesco's Fortune*: 217). Markham (1631) advocates the flower and **roots** to clear the eyes; he recommends primrose flowers in **salads**. Lawson (1618) thinks it is essential to have primroses in the **orchard**. Amherst (1895) writes that primroses might be used to fill up the beds in **knot-gardens**, but Coats (1968) suggests that the flower is never happy in cultivated **soil**. Armstrong (1946: 80) comments on the association of the primrose with death. Mabey (1996) includes details of its modern use and associations.

prune (A) To prune is to trim or cut back a **tree**, **shrub** or large **plant** to control **growth** and stimulate **flowering** or **fruit** production. Neglected pruning of plants can lead to diminished productivity, infertility or death. The act of pruning could represent human control over unruly **nature**. Figuratively prune can indicate cutting back or trimming something superfluous or undesirable, removing unnecessary or unwanted elements. 'Pole-clipt' refers either to pruning or to **vines** being trained on poles. Prune meaning 'preening', a term derived from falconry, can be used metaphorically for 'to smarten up'. The dried fruit is discussed under **plum (prune, pruin)**.

(B) The only certain literal mention stresses the importance of pruning. The condition of French agriculture consequent on the English invasion causes Burgundy to lament, 'Her vine, the merry cheerer of the heart,/Unpruned dies' (*H5* 5.2.41–2). A second literal example may be present in *TMP*. Delineating the activities over which Ceres, the goddess of fertility presides, Iris refers to 'thy pole-clipt vineyard' (4.1.68). This could imply either the action of pruning or the entwining of vines around poles. An under-**gardener** in *R2* expresses resentment that their **garden**, which is emblematic of the body politic, should be so carefully maintained when the commonwealth is neglected: 'the whole land,/Is full of weeds, her fairest flowers chok'd up,/Her fruit-trees all unprun'd, her hedges ruin'd' (3.4.43–5). The tree-pruning metaphor is used by Adriana when berating her neglectful husband:

> If aught possess thee from me, it is dross,
>
> Usurping ivy, brier, or idle moss,
>
> Who, all for want of pruning, with intrusion
>
> Infect thy sap, and live on thy confusion.
>
> *(ERR 2.2.177–80)*

Forced to flee his home to avoid his brother's malice, Orlando reluctantly accepts Adam's offer of allegiance and his life's savings: 'But, poor old man, thou prun'st a rotten tree,/That cannot so much as a blossom yield/In lieu of all thy pains and husbandry' (*AYL* 2.3.63–5). Prune signifying preening arises a few times. Pretending to be immune to romantic impulses, Berowne chides the King, 'When shall you see me write a thing in rhyme,/Or groan for Joan, or spend a minute's time/In pruning me?' (*LLL* 4.3.179–81). Its origin as a term from falconry is apparent when Westmorland warns Henry IV that Hotspur's recalcitrance arises from Worcester's incitement: 'Which makes him prune himself, and bristle up/The crest of youth against your dignity' (*1H4* 1.1.98–9). Responding to Jove's apparition, Sicinius comments on the god's holy eagle: 'His royal bird/Prunes the immortal wing, and cloys his beak,/As when his god is pleas'd' (*CYM* 5.4.117–19).

(C) Puttenham (1589) writes of art as an assistant to nature, seeing the gardener's work as **manuring** the **soil**, watering, weeding **herbs** and flowers, and pruning **branches** to let the sun in to bring forth flowers and fruits. Markham (1613) devotes a chapter to 'the Dressing, Dungging, Proyning, and Preserving of Trees', detailing the tools to be used, and how to prune a tree. Spurgeon (1935: 86–8, 216–23) writes that Shakespeare's most constant running metaphor of growth as seen in garden and **orchard**, includes deterioration, decay, and destruction brought about by the carelessness and ignorance of the gardener as shown by untended **weeds**, the presence of pests including **caterpillars**, a lack of pruning and manuring, and the untimely cutting of trees. Samson (2012: 12) suggests that pruning controlled the excess growth of nature, paralleling the need to control or prune human desire.

pumpion, pumpkin (A) Originally any edible **gourd** of the genus *Cucurbita* L., or *Cucumis* L., now classified as cucumbers. At the time pumpion was used, sometimes interchangeably, for any edible gourd including melon. By association with the size and shape of the **plant**, pumpion or pumpkin was readily employed in a derogatory sense to describe a fat man.

(B) In retaliation for Falstaff's assault on the wives' honour, Mistress Ford alights on the pumpkin as an appropriate epithet for the fat knight: 'We'll use this unwholesome humidity, this gross wat'ry pumpion. We'll teach him to know turtles from jays' (*WIV* 3.3.40–2). The turtle-dove was an emblem of fidelity; the jay symbolized all that is meretricious. A feature of this play is its abundance of popular sayings and biblical expressions: there is a common-sense practicality embedded in this everyday discourse which is averse to pretention. Throughout his appearances in the plays Falstaff's bulk is a target for mockery: the 'pumpion' or 'pumpkin' contains a fine balance between mockery and indignation. A harsher tone and blunter wit emanates from the common people who disparage the immigrants in *STM*. Lincoln bases his contempt on their supposed enjoyment of **parsnips**, goading the 'Clown' to respond, 'True, and pumpions together' (II.c 16). These xenophobes reinforce their prejudices on the flimsiest of arguments. The only other mention of this vegetable is as a malapropism delivered by **Costard**. Playing Pompey the Great in The Pageant of the Nine Worthies, he introduces himself as 'Pompion the Great' (*LLL* 5.2.502).

(C) Pompion or pumpion are earlier variants: the earliest *OED* reference to pumpkin is in 1647, while melon designates any of various edible gourds. Hill (1577) has a chapter on 'Of the rare helps of the Pompons, Mellons and Musk Mellions' but he refers more widely to 'gourds'. Gerard (1597: 772–5, 918) includes melons or pompions, as well as wild pompions and gourds, suggesting that the pompion might be a food of last resort because if baked 'it doth fill the bodie full of flatuous or windie belchings, and its food utterly unwholesome for such as live idly; but unto robustious and rusticke people, nothing hurteth that filleth the belly'. Drayton records them **growing** in Norfolk, describing them as 'The great moist Pumpion' (1622, *Polyolbion* 20.53).

Q

quince (A) *Cydonia oblonga* Mill. is possibly a Roman introduction; it is of the same botanical family as the **pear**, on which quince stock was often used for **grafting**. The **fruit** is hard and astringent when raw, but aromatic and deep orange coloured when cooked. It was eaten as a delicacy as a paste or made into tarts, with many contemporary writers including recipes for marmalade made with quinces. The fruit provided some medicinal remedies; it was thought to improve the intelligence of children in the womb and also to be effective against poison. Sacred to Venus, quince fruits came to be associated with weddings; as with the **orange** and the **pomegranate**, it has been identified with the golden **apple** of the Hesperides.

(B) Occupied with the wedding preparations, Lady Capulet demands, 'fetch more spices, nurse', only to be rebuffed by the servant who has other business: 'They call for dates and quinces in the pastry' (*ROM* 4.4.1–2). The symbolic role of the quince as a wedding food is present in a scene with a lively sense of the bustle and anxiety that accompanies such occasions. The association of quince with marriage appears, too, in *MND* although the **fruit** itself is absent. The leader of the Mechanicals, the character who directs and introduces the entertainment for the newlyweds, is Peter Quince. His name is mentioned eight times. Although everyone in the group has a name connected to his trade – 'quines' or 'quoines' are wooden wedges used by carpenters like Peter Quince – in a play replete with doubling the symbolism of the fruit is even more significant.

(C) Parker (2003) provides an exhaustive analysis of the quince as integral to marriage ceremonies, noting 'it was part of a rich network of associations with marriage, sexuality, and fruitful "issue" in the period, as well as of multi-lingual connections and metamorphic spellings that conflated it with coigns, quoyns, sexual corners or coining, and the *cunnus* or "queynte" its sounds suggests'. She adds, 'the connection between the "Quince" and weddings was also a visual commonplace by the time of Shakespeare's play', and concludes, '"Quince" thus came with a rich set of associations in the period – with aphrodisiacs or love portions, with fruitfulness and sexuality, with exotic locations (as well as the homelier qualities of the breath-freshener and digestive for the "stomach"), and with overcoming the Amazon-like resistance of Atalanta, who is conflated with Hippolyta in Shakespeare's marriage play as well as in *Two Noble Kinsmen*'. Its applications were varied. Boorde (1547) and Bullein (1564) recommend quince to counteract drunkenness, so it was an appropriate food for a wedding. Dodoens (1578) and Gerard (1597) suggest eating quinces when pregnant to aid the child's intelligence, while according to Parkinson (1640) quince juice was particularly effective against poison. Palter (2002) provides literary and artistic references for the quince.

R

radish, redish *Raphanus sativus* L. is a naturalized, probably Roman, introduction, which was eaten both cooked and raw as a vegetable and in **salads**. Other **plants** of the same genus have in the past been grown for fodder. Radishes were prescribed for a number of medical conditions; eating radishes was thought to make one thin. Falstaff is the only character to allude to this plant. Describing his fictional fight at Gad's Hill, he responds to Hal's feigned incredulity: 'if I fought not with fifty of them, I am a bunch of radish' (*1H4* 2.4.185–6). The association of radish with thinness is apparent in *2H4*. Exposing a falsehood rather than delivering one, Falstaff soliloquizes on Shallow's fanciful disquisition on his youthful adventures. The fat knight protests, 'When 'a was naked, he was for all the world like a fork'd redish, with a head fantastically carv'd upon it with a knife. 'A was so forlorn, that his dimensions to any thick sight were invisible' (3.2. 310–13). For 'plump Jack' a thin man could never be anything other than pitiable. Elyot (1541) notes radishes have the virtue to 'extenuate or make thin'. Vaughan (1617: 93, 136) recommends young radishes should be served with mutton or that they should be cooked and eaten with oil, vinegar and honey or sugar. He adds that it 'stirreth up lust'. Parkinson (1629) writes that while they are a stimulant if eaten before a meal, eating them with bread alone is poor man's food.

raisin, flapdragon (A) Raisins or dried **grapes** became more readily available in the sixteenth century, often supplanting **prunes**. They were particularly valuable for their high sugar content, and could be eaten raw or added to both savoury dishes and desserts. Flapdragon was another name for the more commonly known 'snapdragon', a game in which raisins were snatched out of burning brandy and eaten while still flaming.

(B) Perdita's shopping list for the sheep-shearing feast gives rise to the only *direct* mention of raisins. The young shepherd, designated 'Clown', rehearsing his instructions includes, 'four pounds of pruins, and as many raisins o'th'sun' (*WT* 4.3.48–9). However, raisin and reason inspired homonymic puns which may be the source of an indirect reference to raisons. Resisting the interrogation of Hal and Poins, Falstaff retorts, 'Give you a reason on compulsion? if reasons were as plentiful as blackberries, I would give no man reason upon compulsion, I' (*1H4* 2.4.238–40). The sun-dried grapes make three further appearances without being named, thanks to the game 'flapdragon'. This entertainment involved extracting an object, usually a raisin, from lighted liquor and swallowing it. Enumerating the attributes which secures Poins' favour with Hal, Falstaff claims he 'drinks off candles' ends for flap-dragons' (*2H4* 2.4.246). Responding to a display of verbal extravagance, **Costard** teases Moth, 'I marvel thy master hath not eaten thee for a word, for thou art not so long by the head as *honorificabilitudinitatibus*: thou art easier swallow'd than a flap-dragon' (*LLL* 5.1.39–42). Besides producing the longest word in the canon, the rustic provides a neat representation of the raisin game. The swallowing action is imaged by the young shepherd narrating the sinking of the ship that brings Perdita to Bohemia: 'to see how the sea flap-dragon'd it' (*WT* 3.3.98).

(C) Spier and Anderson (1985: 455fn) in an interesting article note that raison and reason gave rise to homonymic puns. *2H4* Arden 2 (80) provides contemporary commentary on the game. Palter (2002) explains the traditional process where the grapes are laid out in the sun to dry naturally. Raisins are now known to contain trace minerals which would have supplemented the limited winter diet.

rake (A) A **gardening** or farming implement for drawing together **leaves**, a rake can also serve to smooth the surface of the **soil**. It can describe a very thin person. Metaphorically, raking something up suggests uncovering something, often unsavoury, from the past; raking in money indicates acquiring a considerable amount of money possibly in a dishonest way.

(B) All six mentions of this implement are metaphorical. They are diverse and colourful. As the hungry plebeians take to the streets in *COR* the First Citizen urges: 'Let us revenge this with our pikes, ere we become rakes; for the gods know I speak this in hunger for bread, not in thirst for revenge' (1.1.22–5). The neat antithesis reflects rational anger. Exeter presents an elaborate document to the King of France setting out Henry V's lineage as proof of the legitimacy of his claim to the French throne: ''Tis no sinister nor awkward claim,/Pick'd from the worm-holes of long-vanished days,/Nor from the dust of old oblivion rak'd' (*H5* 2.4.85–7). Failure to render up the crown, he warns, will result in 'Bloody constraint; for if you hide the crown/Even in your hearts, there will he rake for it' (97–8). The violence of the metaphor is an apt prologue to the horrors that follow. Having gained access to Wolsey's inventory of personal wealth, Henry VIII gasps: 'How, i'th'name of thrift,/Does he rake this together?' (*H8* 3.2.109–10). Having several meanings, 'thrift' here signifies 'economic activity' or 'financial management'. A difficult construction occurs in *LR*. Goneril's letter revealing her scheme to murder Albany is read by a horrified Edgar: 'Here, in the sands,/Thee I'll rake up, the post unsanctified/Of murtherous lechers' (4.6.273–5). The 'post unsanctified' relates to its cynical contents, or to the despicable carrier, Oswald; 'rake up' probably means to bring to the surface. Alternative interpretations can be found in Arden 3 (348). In his attempt to win Silvia, Proteus claims that Valentine is dead. She responds, 'And so suppose am I; for in his grave/Assure thyself my love is buried', prompting the ugly riposte, 'Sweet lady, let me rake it from the earth' (*TGV* 4.2.113–15). This simple implement lends itself to telling insights into character and situation.

(C) Contemporary illustrations in Hill (1577) show a range of **garden** tools including a rake, with several raking operations including raking in **manure** and preparing a **seed** bed. Christiansen (2005) has details of the tools, including rakes, used at Hampton

Court under Henry VIII. The design of the modern garden rake is unchanged and its function remains the same.

rank see **smell**

reed (A) **Grasses** of the genus *Phragmites* Adans, reeds grow in large stands or groups in water or marshy **ground**. Collectively, reed suggests a mass or bed of reeds; the cut **stems** of the **plants** were used mainly for thatching, or unthreshed **wheat straw**, 'to reed' being to thatch. Reed can refer to anything made from reeds, as a reed pen, dart or arrow. It can be a simple musical pipe made from a reed or a hollow stem of another plant, usually as **oaten** reed; a reed or reedy voice suggests either an unbroken boy's voice or the piping tone of old age. The reed is often linked to the **rush** and the **flag**. Because of its slender stem, reed is used to suggest something fragile, flexible or unreliable: it can be a symbol of weakness, humility and submission. The contrast between the powerful **oak** and the submissive reed dates back at least to Aesop and myths of Pan.

(B) As features of landscape reeds figure prominently in *TNK*. The country Wooer of the Jailer's Daughter delivers a sensitive account of how while fishing he hears singing, 'From the far shore, thick set with reeds and sedges'. Curious, he is guided to the location by her voice, 'but yet perceiv'd not/Who made the sound, the rushes and the reeds/Had so encompass'd it' (4.1.54–62). His extensive description – fluid, mobile, naturalistic – provides a fascinating contrast to Gertrude's painterly account of Ophelia's death (*HAM* 4.7.166–83). Hotspur, a master of colourful if not plausible narrative, describes the fierce battle between Mortimer and Owen Glendower, 'on the gentle Severn's sedgy bank'. The river, 'affrighted with their bloody looks,/Ran fearfully among the trembling reeds,/And hid his crisp head in the hollow bank' (*1H4* 1.3.98–106). The 'trembling reeds' are highly visual and a vital ingredient in Hotspur's hyperbolic account. The natural antithesis between the reed and the oak is sensitively expressed in the dirge in *CYM*: 'Care no more to clothe and eat,/To thee the reed is as the oak' (4.2.266–7). The fragility of the reed is intimated by the Second Servant's observation on Lepidus' drunkenness: 'Why, this it is to have a name in great men's fellowship. I had as live have a reed that will do me no service as a partisan I could not heave' (*ANT* 2.7.11–13). *TMP* has an interesting example of reeds as thatch. Describing the condition of Alonso and his entourage, Ariel says of Gonzalo: 'His tears run down his beard like winter's drops/From eaves of reeds' (5.1.16–17).

(C) Turner (1551) gives the various uses of the reed as well as its medicinal applications. Holinshed (1577, vol. 1: 358) suggests the destruction of woodland has led to the predominance in some places of less useful plants including flags, reed and rush. Most of Drayton's (1622) reeds are located in Norfolk; he writes of bristling reeds on river **banks**, quivering reeds, of a reedy bed, and has reed, rush and flag **growing** together on the same river banks, as well as suggesting their use for winter fodder as **stover**. Ovid's *Metamorphoses* (trans. 1567, book XI) gives the story of Pan; Smith (1932) outlines the story of Syrinx, an Arcadian nymph, who was chased by Pan and at her own request metamorphosed into a reed from which Pan made his flute. Mabey (1996) includes details of local usage.

reek see **smell**

rhubarb (A) The genus *Rheum* L. is a naturalized introduction from China. Rhubarb was not eaten at the time, being administered medicinally only in a dried form, as both an astringent and a purgative. It could also designate *Rumex patientia* L., the patience **dock**, said to have been used in monasteries in place of rhubarb, thus giving its common name of monk's rhubarb, *Rhabarbarum monachorum* L. Rhubarb could indicate any **plant** resembling rhubarb with its large **leaves**, or any bitter purgative.

(B) The function of the plant is made plain in its one appearance. The dejected Macbeth deplores the Doctor's impotence:

> If thou couldst, doctor, cast
> The water of my land, find her disease,
> And purge it to a sound and pristine health,
> I would applaud thee to the very echo,
> That should applaud again. – Pull't off, I say. –
> What rhubarb, cyme, or what purgative drug,
> Would scour these English hence?

(MAC 5.3.50–6)

Macbeth's obsession with purgation is ironic as he is perceived by his antagonists as the disease that must be purged.

(C) Tusser (1573) includes 'rubarb' among the necessary plants for the medicinal **herb garden**, while Bright (1586) and Bullein (1595) remark on its purgative qualities. Ferdinand calls for rhubarb as a purgative: 'Rubarbe, oh, for rubarbe/To purge this choler' (Webster 1613, *Malfi* 2.5.12–13). Karim-Cooper (2006) records rhubarb as a common constituent of early modern cosmetics. Mason (2006) suggests the plant is of Siberian origin, imported to England before the fifteenth century, and that the first recipe for its culinary use is only found in 1783. Stace (2010) gives *R. rhabarbarum* L. as the widely cultivated modern vegetable, and *R. palmatum* L. as the ornamental rhubarb which was formerly used medicinally.

ripe (A) Of **fruit** ripe indicates a readiness to be **harvested**; it can also mean at the full extent of useful, natural **growth**, ready to be cut or mown. Figuratively, ripe suggests a state of readiness, maturity, something resembling ripe fruit such as the complexion, or full red lips; it could describe a death, suggesting coming at a perceived fitting time, or after a long life. Ripe of a person or of the mind suggests mature judgement or knowledge, well-qualified by study or in one's prime. Ripe can indicate readiness, timeliness, fitness for a purpose, ready for curative treatment, brought to a state of maturity, carefully considered. Over-ripe can imply excess, **rottenness**, decay. With so many meanings, ripe lends itself readily to metaphorical uses.

(B) Remarkably, of the 70 uses of 'ripe' and its adjuncts, only a few are literal. Ripening and ripeness is a concept that pervades every aspect of life: feasting, favour, physical or mental preparedness, bodily injuries, sins, needs, seasons, colours, drunkenness, judgement, play, thoughts, moods, human development, learning, passion, people, life and time itself all manifest a progression towards ripening – and beyond. Venus refers to the birds that pandering to Adonis 'Would bring him mulberries and ripe-red cherries' (*VEN* 1103). Hero tells Margaret to lure Beatrice, 'into the pleached bower,/Where honeysuckles, ripened by the sun,/Forbid the sun to enter' (*ADO* 3.1.7–9). As the newly reconciled antagonists celebrate their agreement aboard his galley, Pompey jests, 'This is not yet an Alexandrian feast', to which Antony replies, 'It ripens towards it' (*ANT* 2.7.96–7). Undermining the rebel Archbishop at the battlefield conference the coldly calculating Prince John challenges him: 'That man that sits within a monarch's heart/And ripens in the sunshine of his favor/Would he abuse the countenance of the King' (*2H4* 4.2.11–13). The image conveys an accusation of ingratitude, while simultaneously emphasizing the status of the monarch. Physical and mental preparedness is intimated by Ely during his championing of war with France: 'and my thrice-puissant liege/Is in the very May-morn of his youth,/Ripe for exploits and mighty enterprises' (*H5* 1.2.119–21). Announcing his King's defiance, Mountjoy claims the French could have responded earlier to Henry's invasion, 'but that we thought not good to bruise an injury till it were full ripe' (3.6.121–3). Queen Margaret, excoriating Richard Gloucester swears, 'If heaven have any grievous plague in store/.../O, let them keep it till thy sins be ripe' (*R3* 1.3.216–18).

This word inevitably enters the sphere of romance. Demetrius' clichéd praise of Helena has one almost sober and affecting image: 'O, how ripe in show/Thy lips, those kissing cherries, tempting grow!' (*MND* 3.2.139–40). Love, like a flower, can ripen as Juliet tells Romeo: 'This bud of love, by summer's ripening breath,/May prove a beauteous flow'r when next we meet' (*ROM* 2.2.121–2). Time *per se* is often an ingredient in love. Salerio reports Antonio's parting words to Bassanio: 'stay the very riping of the time'(*MV* 2.8.40). Likewise, Antonio uses the term to mean urgency or fullness of need when seeking funding for Bassanio's enterprise: 'Shylock, albeit I neither lend nor borrow/By taking nor by giving of excess,/Yet to supply the ripe wants of my friend,/I'll break a custom' (1.3.61–4). Observing the entry of the drunken miscreants, Alonso jeers, 'And Trinculo is reeling ripe' (*TMP* 5.1.279). Commending his friend Proteus to the Duke, Valentine deploys glib antithesis: 'His head unmellowed, but his judgement ripe' (*TGV* 2.4.70). Offering a list of plays ready for performance Philostrate announces to Theseus, 'There is a brief how many sports are ripe' (*MND* 5.1.42). Believing he has been betrayed, Orsino threatens Cesario/Viola: 'Come, boy, with me, my thoughts are ripe in mischief' (*TN* 5.1.129). In *R2*, the Queen fears 'Some unborn sorrow, ripe in fortune's womb' (2.2.10). Elinor, to thwart the claims of young Arthur, persuades her son to seek accommodation with the French King: 'That yon green boy shall have no sun to ripe/The bloom that promiseth a mighty fruit' (*JN* 2.1.472–3). Reading the growing anger of King John, Salisbury observes: 'His passion is so ripe, it needs must break' (4.2.79). Impatient for rebellion to begin, Hotspur is assured by Worcester they will proceed, 'When time is ripe, which will be suddenly' (*1H4* 1.3.294). Griffith eulogizing Cardinal Wolsey records, 'From his cradle/He was a scholar, and a ripe and good one' (*H8* 4.2.50–1). Hector's ubiquitous presence on his final day of battle gives rise to Nestor's disturbing image: 'then is he yonder,/And there the strawy Greeks, ripe for his edge,/Fall down before him like a mower's swath' (*TRO* 5.5.23–5). The Chorus in *PER* announces that Marina is now 'a full-grown wench,/Even ripe for marriage rite' (4.16–17). Colour is also gauged by ripeness as Phoebe, having fallen in love with Ganymede/Rosalind, makes clear: 'There was a pretty redness in his lip,/A little riper and more lusty red/Than that mix'd in his cheek' (*AYL* 3.5.120–2). Describing a knight participating in the bloody martial contest, Pirithous says, 'his complexion/Is, as a ripe grape, ruddy' (*TNK* 4.2.95–6). Explaining by analogy how the formerly dissolute Prince has become a monarch of such stature, Ely says, 'The strawberry grows underneath the nettle,/And wholesome berries thrive and ripen best/Neighbor'd by fruit of baser quality' (*H5* 1.1.60–2). The melancholy Jaques philosophizes: 'And so from hour to hour, we ripe and ripe,/And then from hour to hour, we rot and rot' (*AYL* 2.7.26–7). Edgar, however, provides another perspective on life and time: 'Men must endure/Their going hence even as their coming hither,/Ripeness is all' (*LR* 5.2.9–11).

(C) The *Mirror for Magistrates* (1559) sees the early death of a king as unripe, and the young prince coming to the throne prematurely is described as 'not ripe to govern'. Stubbes (1585: 8) sees ripeness as excess and rottenness: 'The greatest abuse which, in my judgement, both offendeth God most, and is there not a little advanced, is the execrable sin of pride, and excesse in apparel, which is there so stinckyng ripe, as the filthie fruits, and lothsome dregges thereof.' Middleton alludes to the **medlar** which was eaten when bletted or rotten, suggesting ripeness and rottenness are very close: 'for he that marries a whore looks like a fellow bound all his life time to a medlar-tree; and that's good stuff; 'tis no sooner ripe but it looks rotten' (1621, *Women Beware Women* 4.2.99–100). Palter (2002) explores ripeness in the context of the medlar.

root (A) Botanically a root is the underground part of a **plant** conveying water and nutrients to the rest of the organism, anchoring it, making it less vulnerable to casual damage or uprooting. It is the permanent **stock** of the plant from which it can be regenerated. To uproot or pull up by the roots can be both literal, as to remove a plant by pulling the entire root system up, and figurative, as in to eradicate, remove or destroy. Literally 'to take root' is to put a plant in the **ground** under favourable conditions for it to make a root system to sustain it; figuratively of a person it is to settle into a place or situation. The roots of plants provided medicines, and some were cultivated as food, including **carrots**, **turnips** and **parsnips**. Collectively known as 'roots', these were generally dismissed as the food of the poor, and only eaten by the better off when included as decoration in **salads**, or in time of famine. Root is used as an anatomical reference to many structures in the human body. In the abstract it represents the source, origin or cause of something. It can also be the essence, innate or fundamental centre or heart of a subject, the core support for a person or an idea.

(B) There are several literal references to roots. Often they relate to a basic form of sustenance. A majority of these cases are in *TIM* where they are the inverse of luxury. The figurative examples relate most frequently to the family **tree**, especially to royal lineage. But friendships, antagonisms and feelings are also measured by their rootedness. Responding to Arviragus' observation that Fidele/Imogen 'yokes/A smiling with a sigh' Guiderius elaborates 'I do note/That grief and patience, rooted in them both,/Mingle their spurs together' (*CYM* 4.2.51–8). The roots of **trees** constitute the ultimate anchor in life just as the root of the heart reflects the deepest point of feeling. The literal references provide colour and atmosphere. Benvolio identifies the place where he spied the melancholic Romeo: 'underneath the grove of sycamore/That westward rooteth from the city side' (*ROM* 1.1.121–2). Jaques is described as lying, 'Under an oak, whose antique root peeps out/Upon the brook that brawls along this wood' (*AYL* 2.1.31–2). A persistent critic of indulgence, Apemantus concludes grace at Timon's banquet with the declaration: 'Rich men sin, and I eat root'. When the dancers enter he adds, 'Like madness is the glory of this life,/As this pomp shows to a little oil and root' (*TIM* 1.2.71; 134–5). Unexpectedly, it is Timon who becomes more closely associated with roots as diet. Retreating to the wilderness he prays, 'Yield him whom all the human sons do hate,/From forth thy plenteous bosom, one poor root!' (4.3.185–6). Thereafter, Timon the misanthropist is identified with roots. He is also responsible for a singularly disturbing image when excoriating mankind. He petitions the sun, 'For each true word, a blister, and each false/Be as a cantherizing to the root o'th'tongue,/Consuming it with speaking!' (5.1.132–4). Commending their new friend Fidele/Imogen, Guiderius reveals a favourable opinion of this staple when prepared with delicacy: 'But his neat cookery! he cut our roots in characters' (*CYM* 4.2.49). Aaron promises his infant child nourishment befitting a warrior: 'I'll make you feed on berries and on roots,/And feed on curds and whey, and suck the goat' (*TIT* 4.2.177–8).

A Frenchman fleeing English invaders cries: 'Sweet-flow'ring peace, the root of happy life,/Is quite abandon'd and expuls'd the land' (*E3* 3.2.47–8). The Duchess of Gloucester images the heritage of her deceased husband as the offspring of Edward III: 'One flourishing branch of his most royal root'. Attempting to persuade York to avenge the murder of his brother, she reminds him of his ancestry and obligation: 'Edward's seven sons, where of thyself art one,/Were as seven vials of his sacred blood,/Or seven fair branches springing from one root' (*R2* 1.2.11–18). This act of vengeance is undertaken by her nephew who, as reported by the **Gardener**, deals first with Richard's favourites: 'The weeds which his broad-spreading leaves did shelter,/That seem'd in eating him to hold him up,/Are pluck'd up root and all by Bullingbrook' (3.4.50–2). Bolingbroke's usurpation inevitably perpetuates this consideration of genealogical roots. In *1H6*, Warwick defends York from Suffolk's disparagement by specifying his lineage, concluding, 'Spring crestless yeomen from so deep a root?' (2.4.85). In

3H6 he swears, 'I'll plant Plantagenet, root him up who dares' (1.1.48). During a critical confrontation with Queen Margaret, Edward of York claims, 'Hadst thou been meek, our title still had slept', to which his brother George adds, 'But when we saw our sunshine made thy spring,/And that thy summer bred us no increase,/We set the axe to thy usurping root' (2.2.160–5). So stricken is the grieving widow of Edward IV that not even her children are a consolation: 'Why grow the branches when the root is gone?' (*R3* 2.2.41). Discovering her father has been suborned to persuade her to sacrifice herself to the King's lust, the Countess of Salisbury demands: 'Hath he no means to stain my honest blood/But to corrupt the author of my blood/To be his scandalous and vile solicitor?' and concludes 'No marvel though the branches be then infected,/When poison hath encompassed the root' (*E3* 2.1.415–19). Root as 'source' is a conceptually vitalizing image. Paulina censures Leontes for the wilfulness of his jealous behaviour: 'The root of his opinion, which is rotten/As ever oak or stone was sound' (*WT* 2.3.90–1). Indicting Proteus for betraying her, Julia asks, 'How oft hast thou with perjury cleft the root?' (*TGV* 5.4.103). Perceiving Cleopatra's anguish at the death of Antony, Dolabella professes, 'but I do feel,/By the rebound of yours, a grief that smites/My very heart at root' (*ANT* 5.2.103–5). To questions about Posthumus' origins, the Second Gentleman replies, 'I cannot delve him to the root' (*CYM* 1.1.28) but then proceeds to deliver a substantial history. Henry VIII is responsible for an interesting configuration when addressing Cranmer: 'Stand up, good Canterbury!/Thy truth and thy integrity is rooted/In us, thy friend' (*H8* 5.1.113–15). Reminding Archidamus of the duration of the friendship between Leontes and Polixenes, Camillo avers: 'They were train'd together in their childhoods; and there rooted betwixt them then such an affection, which cannot choose but branch now' (*WT* 1.1.22–4). Expressing her love for Helena, the Countess says, 'If she had partaken of my flesh, and cost me the dearest groans of a mother, I could not have ow'd her a more rooted love' (*AWW* 4.5.10–12). Hatred can be as deeply rooted as love. Caliban asserts that Prospero's spirits, 'all do hate him/As rootedly as I' (*TMP* 3.2.94–5).

The idea of having to dig deeply to pull up the root instigates diverse imagistic uses. Macbeth asks the Doctor, 'Canst thou not minister to a mind diseas'd,/Pluck from the memory a rooted sorrow,/Raze out the written troubles of the brain' (*MAC* 5.3.40–2). Iago claims to have heard Cassio talk in his sleep and 'Cry, "O sweet creature!" then kiss me hard,/As if he pluck'd up kisses by the roots/That grew upon my lips' (*OTH* 3.3.422–4). Valentine alights on an extravagant conceit when extolling the unparalleled beauty of Silvia. He fears that if the earth touched his 'lady's train', it might, out of pride, 'Disdain to root the summer-swelling flow'r,/And make rough winter everlastingly' (*TGV* 2.4.159–63). More sober is Cardinal Wolsey's introspection on his loss of office:

> This is the state of man: to-day he puts forth
> The tender leaves of hopes, to-morrow blossoms,
> And bears his blushing honors thick upon him;

> The third day comes a frost, a killing frost,
> And when he thinks, good easy man, full surely
> His greatness is a-ripening, nips his root,
> And then he falls as I do.
>
> *(H8 3.2.352–8)*

There are two interesting mentions in *PER*. The eponymous hero subordinates self-interest to the welfare of his citizens, acknowledging princes are 'no more but as the tops of trees,/Which fence the roots they grow by and defend them' (1.2.30–1). A contrasting sense of civic values is revealed by Lysimachus the governor of Mytilene. On entering the brothel he responds to Marina's perplexity about the identity of her 'principal' with the explanation, 'Why, your herb-woman, she that sets seeds and roots of shame and iniquity' (4.6.84–6). The single reference to 'rooting' relates appropriately to Richard Gloucester whose emblem was the wild boar. Queen Margaret's torrent of curses includes the appellation, 'Thou elvish-mark'd, abortive, rooting hog!' (*R3* 1.3.227).

(C) Erasmus (1536, vol. 32) writes of destroying something root and **branch**, indicating complete annihilation. Cassander sees the child as the metaphorical root, requiring nurture: 'And if thou have any care either of the green bud which springeth out of the tender stalk, or the timely fruit which is to grow of so good a root, seek not to kill the one or hasten the other;' (Lyly *Euphues*, 1580: 177). Willes (2011: 64–5) records the effects of the 1590s famines when **grains**, **peas** and **beans** were expensive and in short supply, noting that this was contemporaneous with the writing and staging of Richard II. She comments on the importance of roots and the advocates of root cultivation, including Sir Hugh Plat, and Richard Gardiner, a Shropshire linen draper-turned-horticulturalist, who supplied the poor with discounted **seeds** and vegetables. She also discusses the social snobbery attached to eating roots.

rose (A) A **flower** or **plant** of the genus *Rosa* L., rose includes both wild and cultivated varieties, including *R. gallica* L., the red **damask** rose, **eglantine** and **musk** rose; at the time only a few colours and varieties were available. Rose could be synonymous with **brier**, but this usually suggested a wild plant, possibly also the **blackberry** or **bramble**. Historically, red and white roses were adopted by the houses of Lancaster and York; they were amalgamated by Henry VII to form the Tudor rose. A source of **scent**, flavouring and oil, sometimes designated a **herb**, the rose had extensive cosmetic, culinary and medicinal uses; rose could describe other plants with a rose-like appearance or **smell**. Rose suggested a delicate red or pink colour, a fresh or ruddy-hued complexion, as in roses in someone's cheeks. It was an indication of health or vitality, and was frequently contrasted with the **lily**. Figuratively the rose suggested surpassing beauty, fragrance, purity or depth of colour. There was often the implication of transience, and vulnerability to disease or pests. The flower of the rose was frequently contrasted with the prickles or **thorns** which spoil perfection. In the ancient world the rose was sacred to

Venus/Aphrodite; it was associated with sexuality, love and marriage; it could apply to a woman of great beauty, excellence or virtue, a paragon, which could include the Virgin Mary. The same iconography was adopted by Queen Elizabeth to suggest her virginity and sacred marriage to the country. An easily depicted flower which carried layers of meaning, the rose featured regularly in needlework, carving or other representational work; it also suggested any design which resembled that of a rose, such as a mariner's compass.

(B) Direct references to roses – not qualified by variants such as eglantine and damask – number 122 if 'rosed' and the few compound words 'rose-water', 'rose-cheek'd' and 'rose-lipp'd' are included. The Temple Garden scene (*1H6* 2.4) has most mentions (17). In addition to becoming family emblems the flower represents perfection, scent, colour, complexion, youth, virginity, vulnerability and the ephemeral. There is a single case of 'cakes of roses': compressed rose petals which serve as perfume (*ROM* 5.1.47). The most famous reference must be Juliet's rhetorical question, 'What's in a name?' and her contention, 'That which we call a rose/By any other word would smell as sweet' (2.2.43–4). This seemingly uncomplicated proposition raises complex philosophical and linguistic questions. The rose's status as the most admired flower is supported by Emilia in *TNK*. She tells her waiting gentlewoman, 'Of all flow'rs/Methinks a rose is best' (2.2.135–6). Her reason for this preference is fascinating and unorthodox (see **brier rose**). The rose as the epitome of beauty is celebrated in the opening lines of *SON* 1: 'From fairest creatures we desire increase,/That thereby beauty's rose might never die' (1–2). *SON* 95 begins with the rose as the model of perfection and susceptibility: 'How sweet and lovely doth thou make the shame/Which, like a canker in the fragrant rose,/Doth spot the beauty of thy budding name!'. *SON* 54 is dedicated in its entirety to scent: 'The rose looks fair, but fairer we it deem/For that sweet odor which doth in it live' (3–4). Petruchio commandeers a singularly appealing phrase when preparing a strategy for his first encounter with Kate: 'Say that she frown, I'll say she looks as clear/As morning roses newly wash'd with dew' (*SHR* 2.1.172–3).

The rose is defined by its colour in Titania's reflections on the perversity of the seasons: 'hoary-headed frosts/Fall in the fresh lap of the crimson rose' (*MND* 2.1.107–8). Only in *SON* 98 is the red rose described as 'vermillion'. Recounting his pain at the absence of his friend, the speaker says,

> Nor did I wonder at the lily's white,
> Nor praise the deep vermillion in the rose,
> They were but sweet, but figures of delight,
> Drawn after you, you pattern of all those.

> *(9–12)*

The flower's redness inspires Mistress Quickly when comforting the deathly pale Doll: 'and your color, I warrant you, is as red as any rose' (*2H4* 2.4.24–5). This is one of the few occasions when the rose is associated with the lower orders. The disguised Julia provides an elaborate reply to Silvia's question, 'Is she not passing fair?':

> She, in my judgement, was as fair as you;
> But since she did neglect her looking-glass,
> And threw her sun-expelling mask away,
> The air hath starv'd the roses in her cheeks,

(TGV 4.4.148–54)

Observing Hermia's reaction to Theseus' judgement, Lysander asks, 'why is your cheek so pale?/How chance the roses there do fade so fast?' (*MND* 1.1.128–9). An especially delicate simile emerges in *VEN* as the goddess reacts to Adonis' plan to hunt: '"The boar!" Quoth she, whereat a sudden pale,/Like lawn being spread upon the blushing rose,/Usurps her cheek; she trembles at his tale' (589–91). The juxtaposition of her cheek as a rose overspread with a delicate white fabric and the imagined presence of the brutish boar create an intensely realized moment.

Cautioning Hermia, Theseus elevates marriage and the **distilled** rose over celibacy and the fleeting beauty of an unharvested rose: 'earthlier happy is the rose distill'd,/Than that which withering on the virgin thorn/Grows, lives, and dies in single blessedness' (*MND* 1.1.76–8). Orsino draws on the rose to acknowledge the transience of female beauty, 'For women are as roses, whose fair flow'r/Being once display'd, doth fall that very hour', eliciting the poignant response from Cesario/Viola: 'And so they are; alas, that they are so!/To die, even when they to perfection grow!' (*TN* 2.4.38–41). *SON* 109 closes with renewal of friendship confirmed by unbounded devotion: 'For nothing this wide universe I call,/Save thou, my rose, in it thou art my all' (13–14). Catching sight of her husband as she approaches the tower, the Queen communes with herself or murmurs as an aside, 'But soft, but see, or rather do not see,/My fair rose wither' (*R2* 5.1.7–8). Richard II is again identified with the rose in *1H4*. Hotspur berates his father and his uncle for aiding Bolingbroke's usurpation of Richard's throne: 'To put down Richard, that sweet lovely rose,/And plant this thorn, this canker, Bullingbrook?' (1.3.175–6). The primary antithesis is between the cultivated rose and the wild rose, but 'canker' also refers to the grub that destroys the flower so that the word almost certainly carries a double meaning.

The association of the rose with virginity emerges during Burgundy's description of the French Princess as 'a maid yet ros'd over with the virgin crimson of modesty' (*H5* 5.2.295–6). Discovering Helena's attachment to Bertram, the solicitous Countess muses, 'This thorn/Doth to our rose of youth rightly belong' (*AWW* 1.3.129–30). Challenging Octavius Caesar to single combat Antony resentfully instructs the ambassador: 'To him again, tell him he wears the rose/Of youth upon him' (*ANT* 3.13.20–1). In the same scene Cleopatra draws on the rose image when addressing the messenger, but here it is to mark an important contrast: 'What, no more ceremony? See, my women,/Against the blown rose may they stop their nose/That kneel'd unto the buds' (38–40). The rose as life-force or essence is voiced by Othello when preparing to murder Desdemona: 'When I have pluck'd thy rose,/I cannot give it vital growth again,/It needs must wither. I'll smell thee on the tree' (*OTH* 5.2.13–15). '*Thy* rose' intensifies the beauty and meaning of Othello's utterance, endowing the rose with unique status. Interestingly, Arden 2 and Arden 3 accept Q's '*the* rose' rather than F's '*thy*'. Q provides a simple analogy; F adds a powerful dimension by means of transmutation: the astonishing spiritual and physical loveliness of this woman is conceptualized *as* a rose. The phrase occupies the same line as 'thy light' making it easy for inadvertent repetition by the typesetter. However, 'thy light relume' is a startling phrase in itself, and is the first recorded use of 'relume'; 'thy light' and 'thy rose' are parallel phrases that capture the radiance and beauty of the life-force. The entire passage with 'chaste stars' and 'whiter skin of hers than snow,/And smooth as monumental alabaster' (2–5) sanctifies and reverences this resplendent woman. The symbolizing of hope and nobility is captured by the rhetorical figure hendiadys in *HAM*. Reflecting on the Hamlet of yesterday, Ophelia remembers him as 'Th'expectation and rose of the fair state' (3.1.152). Hamlet having fallen from grace accuses his mother of a greater fall; her conduct he claims 'takes off the rose/From the fair forehead of an innocent love/And sets a blister there' (3.4.42–4). Faced with Ophelia's insanity Laertes addresses her as 'O rose of May!' (4.5.158). Here is recognition of purity and innocence.

Throughout the first tetralogy commentary on roses as emblems of the contending houses of York and Lancaster is marked by awareness of incongruity. This lovely flower represents antagonism, strife and blood-letting from the moment the Duke of York invites his potential supporters, 'From off this brier pluck a white rose with me' (*1H6* 2.4.30), through to Richmond's declaration at the close of *R3*, 'We will unite the White Rose and the Red'. Having witnessed a son kill his father and a father kill his son Henry VI laments:

> O that my death would stay these ruthful deeds!
> O, pity, pity, gentle heaven, pity!
> The red rose and the white are on his face,
> The fatal colors of our striving houses;
> The one his purple blood right well resembles,
> The other his pale cheeks, methinks, presenteth.
> Wither one rose, and let the other flourish;
> If you contend, a thousand lives must wither.
>
> *(3H6 2.5.95–102)*

The whiteness of the rose is given peculiar force in *2H6*. Musing on the political situation the Duke of York determines to bide his time before striking: 'Then will I raise aloft the milk-white rose,/With whose sweet smell the air shall be perfum'd' (1.1.254–5). Richard Gloucester desecrates the rose when provoking his father to break the accord with Henry VI: 'I cannot rest/Until the white rose that I wear be dy'd/Even in the lukewarm blood of Henry's heart' (*3H6* 1.2.32–4).

Hamlet makes a unique reference when, in high spirits following the success of the play-within-a-play, he asks, 'Would not this...with two Provincial roses on my raz'd shoes, get me a fellowship in a cry of players?' (*HAM* 3.2.275–8). These are rosettes worn by actors on their shoes. 'Rosed' (as opposed to 'ros'd over' of *H5* (5.2.295)) appears only in *TIT.* This delightful epithet belongs to an improbably bleak situation. Encountering his mutilated niece, Marcus sees blood rippling from her mouth: 'Alas, a crimson river of warm blood,/Like to a bubbling fountain stirr'd with wind,/Doth rise and fall between thy rosed lips' (2.4.22–4). Embarking on his scheme to delude Christopher Sly, the Lord advises, 'Let one attend him with a silver basin/ Full of rose-water and bestrew'd with flowers' (*SHR* Ind.1.55–6). 'Rose-cheek'd' appears twice. The opening verse of *VEN* encompasses the tension at the heart of the narrative: 'Rose-cheek'd Adonis hied him to the chase/Hunting he lov'd, but love he laugh'd to scorn' (1.3–4). *TIM,* in stark contrast, has the eponymous hero inciting the prostitute Timandra to use her trade to destroy the Athenians: 'Give them diseases, leaving with thee their lust./Make use of thy salt hours, season the slaves/For tubs and baths, bring down rose-cheek'd youth/To the tub-fast and the diet' (4.3.85–8). The 'tub-fast' was the recommended treatment for syphilis. 'Rose-lipp'd' appears once. Overwhelmed by jealousy and perplexity, Othello delivers a complex speech addressed partly to Desdemona and partly to some imaginary influence. He concludes, 'Turn thy complexion there,/Patience, thou young and rose-lipp'd cherubin –/Ay, here look grim as hell!' (*OTH* 4.2.62–4). Arden 2 (153–4) laments, 'This is a most tiresome crux' before devoting much effort to clarification. Arden 3 (277) citing Bevington, proposes: 'Even Patience, that rose-lipp'd cherub, will look grim and pale at this spectacle', adding, '"rose-lipp'd" is a coinage (with sexual overtones?)'.

(C) Roses were everywhere in early modern England, serving a wide range of culinary and medicinal purposes. They are ubiquitous in literature and horticulture. Gerard (1597: 1077) summarizes the flower's iconic importance: 'for the rose doth deserve the chiefest and most principall place among all flowers whatsoever, being not onely esteemed for his beautie, vertues, and his fragrant and odoriferous smell; but also bicause it is the honor and ornament of our English Scepter, as by the conjunction appeereth in the uniting of those two most royall houses of Lancaster and Yorke'. In his medical notebook, Hall (Lane 1996) includes in the index one reference each to rose, rose-water and rosewood; however it includes over 60 uses of the plant in individual remedies with an extensive range of ailments treated using rose water, rose honey, powder from seeds, a syrup and conserve of roses, oil and distilled water. Thomas (1955) remains an authoritative, approachable authority on the history and development of the flower. McLean (1981) traces the rose's symbolism over nearly three millennia, giving the history of its classical and Marian associations and meanings. She suggests red roses represented cultivation while in medieval literature white ones were wild. Duncan-Jones (1995) notes that Gerard and Parkinson identify the **canker** rose as the wild **poppy.** She argues that the canker blooms of *SON* 54 indicate the wild poppy, *Papaver rhoeas* L. The rose provides Trevelyon (1609) with the largest number of designs of any pattern or flower; Arnold (1988) includes illustrations of portraits of the Queen, noting the importance of both the Tudor rose and French fleur-de-lis (**flower-de-luce**) as symbols of power. Mabey (1996) provides details of the varieties of wild, native roses. Potter (2010) in a wide-ranging history of the flower includes fine illustrations. Dent (R177, 178, 182).

rosemary (A) *Rosmarinus officinalis* L. is an introduction from southern Europe. Particularly valued in the **garden** as an evergreen, it was used in cooking, **perfumery** and medicine. Emblematically it signified remembrance, hence its association with both weddings and funerals. Rosemary was widely thought to prevent infection by the plague, and to be an effective abortifacient. It was also considered hopeful and associated with renewal and revival.

(B) Because of its symbolic significance rosemary exerts a strong emotional pressure when appearing in both playful and sombre contexts. Perdita graciously welcomes the disguised Polixenes and Camillo: 'For you there's rosemary and rue; these keep/Seeming and savor all the winter long./Grace and remembrance be to you both' (*WT* 4.4.74–6). 'Seeming and savor' relate to colour and scent. Although she has spelt out the meanings attaching to the **plants**, Polixenes teases, 'well you fit our ages/ With flow'rs of winter' (78–9). It is noteworthy that he refers to these **herbs** as 'flow'rs' revealing the interchangeability of these terms. The scene also indicates the assimilation of plants into the mental landscape of country folk. Most memorable is Ophelia who distributes plants with sadness and deliberation so that they speak in a very different way: 'There's rosemary, that's for remembrance; pray you, love, remember. And there is pansies, that's for thoughts'. The likely recipient is Laertes who responds: 'A document in madness, thoughts and remembrance fitted' (*HAM* 4.5.175–9).

In *ROM* the herb appears in two dialogues that are entirely different in texture. The significance is somewhat opaque in the exchange between Romeo and the Nurse, who asks rhetorically, 'Doth not rosemary and Romeo begin both with a letter?'. Having mystified Romeo, she continues to ramble before concluding that Juliet 'hath the prettiest sententious of it, of you and rosemary, that it would do you good to hear it' (2.4.206–12). Arden 2 (153) suggests 'the possible quibble on U and R, *yew* and *rosemary*'. This conjunction of **yew** and rosemary, casting a shadow, looks in two directions: yew is associated with death; rosemary a common component of the marriage bouquet is also placed on the deceased. The Friar consoles Juliet's parents as they grieve over their seemingly dead daughter: 'Dry up your tears, and stick your rosemary/On this fair corse, and as the custom is,/And in her best array, bear her to church' (4.5.79–81). This makes clear the funereal function of the plant and resonates with the Nurse's ambiguous expression. Bleak outer and inner landscapes are present in *LR* where Edgar derives inspiration for disguise from 'Bedlam beggars, who, with roaring voices,/Strike in their num'd and mortified arms/Pins, wooden pricks, nails, sprigs of rosemary' (2.3.14–16). The spikiness of the **woody** stems of rosemary justifies its inclusion but the plant's symbolic association with death and hope of reunion might apply. It is the herb's culinary role that is drawn on for its figurative application in *PER*. A dish garnished with rosemary was viewed as elaborate or 'fancy'. Bawd images this sentiment when scolding Marina for adopting a posture of superiority: 'Marry, come up, my dish of chastity with rosemary and bays!' (4.6.150–1).

(C) Dekker notes that as the plague struck, 'rosemary, which had wont to be sold for twelvepence an armful, now went for six shillings a handful' (1603, *The Wonderful Year*). Harvey (1972) provides extensive information on the early history of rosemary in England. In his study of Ophelia's flowers, Heath (2003) notes the earlier consensus that rosemary was known to stimulate the brain, used to celebrate marriages, associated with remembrance, and regarded as a valuable culinary herb. He comments that writers tended to gloss over the darker side of its association with the plague and death; he gives its alternative use to stimulate courage, improve the eyesight and guard against poisons. Christianson (2005) records Thomas More's love for rosemary, which he grew over his **garden walls**, both because it attracted **bees** and was sacred to remembrance. Karim-Cooper (2006) records rosemary as a regular ingredient in early modern cosmetics, including those used on the stage. Dendle and Touwaide (2008) include an informative chapter on its medicinal use.

rot (A) To decay, of **plants** and other natural material, to rot is also to undergo decomposition, grow **rank**, and of other materials to corrode, rust, deteriorate or disintegrate. Rotten is the state of **natural** things that have passed the stage of **ripeness**, an inevitable part of the process of **growth** and decay. The process of rotting has considerable application in the **garden**. It is often applied figuratively to suggest human degeneration and decay, sometimes in connection with venereal disease; it could also be used as an imprecation. Rot could indicate any wasting disease which resulted in the decay or festering of the human body, it could represent the effects of a long imprisonment, describe the state of a wound, or a corpse, and allude to both moral and social decay.

(B) The main literal uses of rotting relate to the human body. The botanical sense of rotting is confined to a few literal and figurative examples. As an expletive it is used with considerable ferocity. In *MND* Titania expresses her dismay at the consequences of unseasonable weather: 'and the green corn/Hath rotted ere his youth attained a beard' (2.1.94–5). Hatred motivates Timon's plea to bring contagion upon the Athenians: 'O blessed breeding sun, draw from the earth/Rotten humidity' (*TIM* 4.3.1–2). Agamemnon threatens that Achilles will be shunned if he fails to return to the battlefield: 'Yea, like fair fruit in an unwholesome dish,/Are like to rot untasted' (*TRO* 2.3.120–1). Agreeing with Gremio's evaluation of Katherine the shrew, Hortensio observes, 'Faith, as you say, there's small choice in rotten apples' (*SHR* 1.1.134–5). Branding Hero a harlot, Claudio rejects her with the dismissive phrase, 'Give not this rotten orange to your friend' (*ADO* 4.1.32). Boasting of his past misdeeds Lucio confesses that he lied when denying paternity: 'They would else have married me to the rotten medlar' (*MM* 4.3.173–4). The medlar was edible only when virtually rotten. Here the woman *is* a prostitute. The peculiar characteristic of the medlar is revealed by Rosaline in her punning rebuke to Touchstone, 'for you'll be rotten ere you be half ripe, and that's the right virtue of the medlar' (*AYL* 3.2.119–20). Orlando's response to Adam's generosity is self-deprecating: 'But, poor old man, thou prun'st a rotten tree,/That cannot so much as a blossom yield' (2.3.63–4).

The epithet is frequently deployed with incisiveness in the political sphere. Accusing Coriolanus of betraying the Volscians, Aufidius indicts him for 'Breaking his oath and resolution like/A twist of rotten silk' (*COR* 5.6.94–5). *HAM* provides a memorable phrase relating to the world of politics. Marcellus claims, 'Something is rotten in the state of Denmark' (1.4.90). In a play constantly engaged with land and soil in various forms, Hamlet inquires of the Gravedigger, 'How long will a man lie i'th'earth ere he rot?' (5.1.164). Claudio is horrified rather than curious in his contemplation of death: 'Ay, but to die, and go we know not where;/To lie in cold obstruction, and to rot' (*MM* 3.1.117–18). Camillo's attempt to defend Hermione from the accusation of infidelity provokes Leontes' angry interruption, 'Make that thy question, and go rot!' (*WT* 1.2.324). Angered by Imogen's praise of Posthumus, Cloten responds with a curse: 'The south-fog rot him' (*CYM* 2.3.131). Oxymoron is the presiding rhetorical figure in Constance's expression of despair in *JN*: 'O amiable lovely death!/Thou odoriferous stench! sound rottenness!' (3.4.25–6). Venus is responsible for a persuasive analogy as she endeavours to provoke Adonis' surrender: 'Fair flowers that are not gath'red in their prime/Rot, and consume themselves in little time' (*VEN* 131–2).

(C) Webster's Bosola speaks of the human body representing the process of rotting: 'And though continually we beare about us/A rotten and dead body, we delight/To hide it in rich tissew' (1613, *Malfi* 2.1.62–4). Leantio considers rot is the essential source of **fertility**. Even rotten **grounds** and **dunghills** promote growth (1621, Middleton, *Women Beware Women* 3.2.50–52*)*. Madelaine (1982) points out the contemporary association between rottenness and venereal disease. Palter (2002), in his consideration of the **medlar**, better eaten rotten than ripe, notes these ideas and associations in some literary contexts.

rue, herb grace (A) *Ruta graveolens* L. often known by its vernacular name herb grace, or herb of grace, is a naturalized Mediterranean introduction **grown** in England since Roman times. Its yellow **flowers** and bitter, strongly **scented leaves** can cause skin irritations. It was used extensively to treat sight problems, and also known as an abortifacient from classical times. It was associated with sorrow, repentance, distress and regret, pity and compassion; 'to rue' is to regret, grieve, to feel sorrow, to feel penitence or to cause someone else to do so.

(B) The **plant** appears in only four plays. In *AWW,* however, the word 'rue' is not used: Lavatch praises Helena as 'the herb of grace' (4.5.17). 'Rue' as something to regret is used frequently. The symbolic significance of rue is explicit in *R2*. In response to the Queen's distress the **Gardener** pledges: 'I'll set a bank of rue, sour herb of grace./Rue, even for ruth, here shortly shall be seen,/In the remembrance of a weeping queen' (3.4.105–7). 'Ruth' or pity is his motive for memorializing the Queen's anguish. It may also be an act of penitence because the Gardener has been the innocent source of her knowledge of Richard's plight. The situation in *HAM* is less clear. Riverside assumes that Ophelia's words and actions are directed towards Gertrude when she says, 'There's rue for you, and here's some for me; we may call it herb of grace a'Sundays. You may wear your rue with a difference' (4.5.181–3). 'Difference' is a term drawn from heraldry, variations in a coat-of-arms distinguishing between different branches of a family. The heraldry reference may be directed at the twice-married Gertrude. Here exists an entire web of connections relating to both Gertrude and Claudius, an indication of their past acts and an incitement to repentance and reform. Arden 2 (359) confidently makes Claudius the recipient; Arden 3, (387) nominates the King or the Queen. Either potential recipient has reason for regret and repentance. It is conceivable that these two characters are given rue in turn. The rue Ophelia retains for herself relates to her sorrow. Heath (2003: 61) cites rue's efficacy for the improvement of sight, invigorating memory, preserving chastity, and as protection against insect and snake bites. Perdita's greeting and gifts to the disguised visitors, Polixenes and Camillo, is uncomplicated: 'For you there's rosemary and rue; these keep/Seeming and savor all the winter long./Grace and remembrance be to you both' (*WT* 4.4.74–6). There is no hint of such meanings as compassion, sorrow or regret; the herb of grace is purely an emblem of chaste salutation. One of its assumed attributes, to improve eyesight, could well operate at a subterranean level for Polixenes who enthusiastically accepts cross-breeding in plants but deplores the notion of a prince marrying a peasant. The commonplace use 'rue' as 'regret' is present in King John's warning to the French King: 'France, thou shalt rue this hour within this hour' (*JN* 3.1.323).

(C) Webster's Cornelia echoes Ophelia: 'There's Rosemarie for you, and Rue for you,/Heartsease for you. I pray make much of it' (1612, *The White Devil* 5.4.71–2). Heath (2003) points out that the Victorian writers did not choose to analyse the dark side of rue's applications including its use to induce abortion; he notes the importance of its properties, whether literally or metaphorically, to improve sight, kill lust, possibly induce sterility and impotence, and counteract poison as in the context of *HAM* 4.5.181, 183. Dent (1981:R198).

rush (A) *Juncaceae* is a large family of marsh and waterside **plants** with stiff, often hollow **stems**; they had some medicinal applications. Its practical domestic functions included use as a rush-light or candle made from the pith of the stem, roofing material for thatching, and **strewing** material on floors to keep dirt and dust at bay, to welcome visitors and absorb mess. Rush can also refer to any similar plants in appearance or usage such as **dock**, **flag**, **sedge**, **bulrush** and **reed**. Rush rings were made with the stem or **stalk** of a rush as a token of marriage; there is some suggestion that they were used for unrecognized ceremonies.

(B) A poignant use of **'rush'** for a wedding ring is that made by the Jailer's Daughter. Hopelessly enamoured of the high-ranking Palamon, the young woman is described indulging her fantasies: 'Rings she made/Of rushes that grew by, and to 'em spoke/The prettiest posies – "Thus our true love's tied",/"This you may loose, not me", and many a one' (*TNK* 4.1.88–91). The rustic tradition is confirmed by Lavatch's list of matching or complementary elements: 'as Tib's rush for Tom's forefinger' (*AWW* 2.2.22–3). This simple plant is endowed with poetic vitality by Phoebe in *AYL*. Defending herself against the accusation of injuring the lovesick shepherd she challenges him, 'lean upon a rush,/The cicatrice and capable impressure/Thy palm some moment keeps; but now mine eyes,/Which I have darted at thee, hurt thee not' (3.5.22–5). In the same play Ganymede/Rosalind, toying with Orlando, says of her uncle: 'He taught me how to know a man in love; in which cage of rushes I am sure you are not prisoner' (3.2.370–1). More usually, examples of their fragility are found in social and martial milieus. Caius Martius expresses disdain for the plebeians' inconstancy: 'He that depends/Upon your favors swims with fins of lead,/And hews down oaks with rushes' (*COR* 1.1.179–81). Later, a Senator confronting this warrior from the **walls** of Corioles brags, 'our gates,/Which yet seem shut, we have but pinn'd with rushes,/They'll open of themselves' (1.4.17–19). Rushes as floor covering is revealed by Grumio in his anxious check on preparations for Petruchio's arrival: 'Is supper ready, the house trimm'd, rushes strew'd, cobwebs swept' (*SHR* 4.1.45–7). Their use in ceremonies is exhibited in *2H4* as the First Strewer cries out in readiness for the coronation procession, 'More rushes, more rushes' (5.5.1). Less urgent and more comely is Glendower's translation of his daughter's words to Mortimer: 'She bids you on the wanton rushes lay you down,/And rest your gentle head upon her lap,/And she will sing the song that pleaseth you' (*1H4* 3.1.211–13). Here 'wanton' implies comforting or luxurious. Titania employs the sole use of 'rushy' when rehearsing the various places where she and Oberon have quarrelled: 'By paved fountain or by rushy brook' (*MND* 2.1.84). There is only one mention of a rush-candle. Kate, submitting to Petruchio or realizing the nature of the game, says of the sun, 'be it moon, or sun, or what you please;/And if you please to call it a rush-candle,/Henceforth I vow it shall be so for me' (*SHR* 4.5.13–15).

(C) Boorde (1547) thinks that straw and rushes on the floor can carry the plague and recommends fumigating them with a patented powder of several **herbs**. Greene focuses on the idea of a knot in a rush as a symbol of marriage, writing of 'some women fretting they could not find a knot in a rush' (1592, vol. 11, *A Quip*: 219). Rohde considers it is impossible to differentiate between the various plants; she comments that the rich used rushes as carpet, while the poor used the pith for rush candles, and that it served both as a betrothal ring and as thatching material (1924, *Shakespeare's Wild Flowers*). Mabey (1996) has details of its modern cultivation.

rye *Secale cereale* L. originally from south-west Asia, it is a naturalized introduction of unknown date and was widely cultivated at the time. Rye **grains** were used for coarse bread, beer and spirits, and animal fodder. Rye often grew better than choicer grains in bad seasons: it matures earlier than other grain **crops**, and is tolerant of poor **soils** and low temperatures. The song of springtime celebration in *AYL* suggests that a field of rye was appreciated as a place for courtship: 'Between the acres of the rye,/With a hey, and a ho, and a hey nonino,/These pretty country folk would lie' (5.3.22–4). In Prospero's masque, Iris calls forth the goddess of agriculture: 'Ceres, most bounteous lady, thy rich leas/Of wheat, rye, barley, fetches, oats, and pease' (*TMP* 4.1.60–1). Iris refers to this plant again when inviting the 'sunburn'd sicklemen' to, 'Make holiday; your rye-straw hats put on,/And these fresh nymphs encounter every one/In country footing' (4.1.134–8). Boorde (1547) and Cogan (1584) agree that the best and most digestible bread is made of half rye and half **wheat** grains. Parkinson (1640: 1129) suggests that the **plant** is so well known that it needs little description; he notes its limited medicinal uses. Sim (1997) notes that in time of famine people would resort to the lesser grains including rye as a substitute for the more expensive wheat when this was in short supply.

S

saffron (A) *Crocus sativus* L. is a native **plant** of damp **meadows** and open woods. Its name was also given to other plants including **marigold** and meadow saffron or bastard saffron, *Colchicum autumnale* L. which were regularly used as colouring substitutes for the real product. Saffron is used in cooking, for medicinal purposes and as a dye. Although it was expensive, saffron provided a cheaper alternative to gold in manuscript illumination.

(B) Used four times, the only exclusively culinary use is in *WT*. Perdita instructs her 'brother' to purchase 'saffron to color the warden pies' (4.3.45–6). The **wardens** in question are **pears**. There is, however, a culinary component in Lafew's critique of Parolles' role in leading Bertram astray: 'your son was misled with a snipt-taffata fellow there, whose villainous saffron would have made all the unbak'd and doughy youth of a nation in his color' (*AWW* 4.5.1–4). This wonderfully compact dissection of Parolles exposes both his predilection for fancy clothes and the influence he has on those around him. As saffron was used to starch ruffs and to colour cakes, the image connects its sartorial and culinary uses. The 'snipt-taffata' was slashed silk that allowed another colour to show through. Antipholus of Ephesus refers to Dr Pinch as 'this companion with the saffron face' (*ERR* 4.4.61). The colour that may signify an unhealthy complexion can, nevertheless, be extolled for its bright beauty. Ceres responds to the welcome of Iris the 'many colored messenger', 'Who with thy saffron wings upon my flow'rs/Diffusest honey-drops, refreshing show'rs' (*TMP* 4.1.76–9).

(C) *AWW* Arden 2 (120) observes 'saffron was used to dye both starch (and so ruffs) and cakes'. Turner (1551) indicates that bastard saffron was used by **apothecaries**, suggesting the substitution was a well-known and common practice. As both plants **flower** in the autumn there could have been some potentially dangerous confusion, given the toxicity of *C. autumnale*. Harrison (1587) writes extensively on growing and dressing saffron, indicating its economic importance. McLean (1981) notes the use of saffron as a substitute for gold on illuminated manuscripts, and explains the difficulties in its cultivation. Campbell-Culver (2001) observes its name is a fusion of Greek and Arabic; it is one of the most ancient of named plants and one of the most valuable spices; it was part of trade carried out between the Phoenicians and Cornish tin mines. She provides the background to the western commerce in saffron and notes that it was responsible for the renaming of the Essex town of Chipping Walden to Saffron Walden in the fourteenth century.

salad, sallet (A) An edible mixture of **herbs, flowers** and cooked vegetables, raw ones being generally considered unhealthy. Sometimes very elaborate concoctions for presentation purposes, they would include carved **root** vegetables, and even be decorated with gold or other precious substances. Salads were usually served dressed with oil, vinegar and often sugar. Metaphorically, salad can suggest youth, immaturity, or an untried nature from the usual **green** colour of its constituents.

(B) Teased by Charmian for having used the language of love to Julius Caesar that she now reserves for Antony, Cleopatra brushes off the criticism: 'My salad days,/When I was green in judgement, cold in blood,/To say as I said then!' (*ANT* 1.5.73–5). The two literal references allow no flippancy. The desperate Jack Cade, punning on helmet, commends the virtues of the salad: 'I climb'd into this garden, to see if I can eat grass, or pick a sallet another while, which is not amiss to cool a man's stomach this hot weather. And I think this word 'sallet' was born to do me good; for many a time, but for a sallet, my brain-pan had been cleft with a brown bill; and many a time, when I have been dry and bravely marching, it hath serv'd me instead of a quart pot to drink in; and now the word 'sallet' must serve me to feed on' (*2H6* 4.10.7–15). The disguised Edgar describes how, as a social outcast, he 'eats cow-dung for sallets' (*LR* 3.4.132). During an interesting botanical exchange between Lafew and Lavatch, the old courtier says of Helena, 'We may pick a thousand sallets ere we light on such another herb'. The 'Clown' responds, 'Indeed, sir, she was the sweet marjorom of the sallet, or rather the herb of grace' (*AWW* 4.5.13–16). Choosing a speech to be performed by the visiting actors, Hamlet praises the play because it is not meretricious; integrity is prized above popularity: 'I remember one said there were no sallets in the lines to make the matter savory' (*HAM* 2.2.440–2). 'Sallets' is glossed as 'spicy jokes' in Riverside (1205). This is confusing to the modern ear as today the salad is hardly noteworthy for its spicy constituents.

(C) Markham (1631: 64–6) includes recipes for simple sallats which included **radish**, chives, boiled **carrots, turnips**, skirrets, various **lettuces** with oil, all seasoned with salt and sugar, suggesting that other ingredients such as **samphire** and **bean cods** could be added. His compound sallats were much more intricate, being composed of dozens of ingredients; his 'strange sallats' were expensive to produce and often only for show. Rohde (1925) lists the great variety of plants that could be included; she gives James I's preferences for at least 35 ingredients, saying that boiled salads, often including **garlic**, were useful additions to the winter diet. Munroe (eds Bruckner and Brayton 2011: 149) examines Markham's idea of the sallats purely for show considering them an indication of the contemporary interest in the artificial. Appelbaum (2006) provides an exploration of the culinary practices of the time.

samphire (A) Also called rock samphire, *Crithmum maritimum* L. is a native **plant** growing on cliffs, rocks and occasionally on sand and shingle. Samphire has fleshy, aromatic, salty leaves that can be eaten as a vegetable or pickled for **salads** or as a preserve, and has some medicinal uses. It has been suggested that its name is a corruption of 'herbe de St Pierre', or St Peter's herb, from petros, a rock, its usual habitat. Samphire was dangerous to **harvest** when growing on cliffs. The modern edible samphire found on marsh or marginal tidal land is usually common glasswort, *Salicornia europaea* L.

(B) The sole reference to this plant appears in the finest piece of perspective landscape in the canon. Having notionally steered Gloucester to the edge of Dover cliff, Edgar endeavours to persuade his father that he is poised on the cliff top: 'Half way down/Hangs one that gathers samphire, dreadful trade!' (*LR* 4.6.14–15). The phrase 'dreadful trade!' at the end of the line gives immediacy to the plight of the samphire gatherer. Clinging tenaciously to the rock face he risks his life every time he engages in his employment – and he adds a pulse-beat to this astonishing description.

(C) Turner (1548: 289) comments on the Dover trade: 'sampere growth much in rockes and cliffs beside Douer'. Langham (1597) gives the widest list of medicinal uses, saying it can preserve permanent youth. Middleton's Maud suggests samphire is a seasonal and sought-after product in London: 'What had us wives been good for? To make sallats,/Or else cried up and down for sampier' (ed. 1885, *A Chaste Maid in Cheapside* 1.1.8–9). Drayton includes its Kentish origin when writing of maritime products with healing properties: 'Rob *Dovers* neighbouring Cleeves of Sampyre, to excite/His dull and sickly taste, and stirre up appetite' (1622, *Polyolbion* 18. 763–4). De Bray (1982) records the danger of the samphire trade.

sap (A) The vital fluid circulating in **plants**. Figuratively it is the life force that sustains a person. Sap can occasionally mean juice or fluid of any kind. Sappy suggests full of sap, which particularly in the spring can render **wood** useless for the fire, or for working. It can suggest a youthful, vigorous person, with sapless indicating lifelessness, infirmity or weakness. A **sapling** is both a young **tree** and a young inexperienced person.

(B) A lively source of imagery, there is no strictly literal application. The **Gardener** in *R2* contrasts the casual ineptitude of Richard's rule with the rigorous endeavours of horticulturalists: 'We at time of year/Do wound the bark, the skin of our fruit-trees,/Lest being over-proud in sap and blood,/With too much riches it confound itself'(3.4.57–60). Warning of the depredations of time *SON* 5 likens the human condition to the natural world:

> For never-resting time leads summer on
> To hideous winter and confounds him there,
> Sap check'd with frost and lusty leaves quite gone,
> Beauty o'ersnow'd and bareness every where:

> *(5–8)*

Disconcerted that his son fails to recognize him, Egeon acknowledges the ravages of time:

> Though now this grained face of mine be hid
> In sap-consuming winter's drizzled snow,

> And all the conduits of my blood froze up,
> Yet hath my night of life some memory,

(ERR 5.1.312–15)

Preparing for his first battle, the Black Prince declares that should he falter, 'Wither my heart! that, like a sapless tree,/I may remain the map of infamy' (*E3* 3.3.217–18). Its metaphorical range is illustrated by Norfolk's caution to Gloucester in *H8*: 'there is no English soul/More stronger to direct you than yourself,/If with the sap of reason you would quench,/Or but allay, the fire of passion' (1.1.146–9). The advice comes too late: Buckingham, outmanoeuvred by Wolsey, is arrested and executed. Sap as blood is present in Queen Elizabeth's sardonic response to Richard's proposal to marry her daughter. She suggests he 'present her…/A handkerchief, which, say to her, did drain/The purple sap from her sweet brother's body,/And bid her wipe her weeping eyes withal' (*R3* 4.4.274–8). Accepting Camillo's advice to make his way to Sicilia, Florizel acknowledges the wisdom of the proposal: 'There is some sap in this' (*WT* 4.4.565). A similar sentiment is expressed by Antony, on the eve of battle, as he readies himself for Cleopatra's birthday party: 'Come on, my queen,/There's sap in't yet' (*ANT* 3.13.190–1).

(C) Drayton (1622) uses sap to suggest the renewal of life in the spring. Plat (1608) records checking sap in trees, avoiding sappiness in wood, and of gathering sap from plants and **herbs**. Ault (1949) includes several examples of the use of sap as the source of life, sap as moistening the **roots** of a tree, kindly sap killed by the **frost**, plants cheered by fresh sap, and trees consuming sap.

sapling A young **tree**; figuratively it indicates a young or inexperienced person, or someone vulnerable or in need of discipline. There are no literal examples and only three metaphorical uses. Responding to his grandson's plea to comfort Lavinia, Titus retorts, 'Peace, tender sapling, thou art made of tears,/And tears will quickly melt thy life away' (*TIT* 3.2.50–1). Very different in tone is Bawd in *PER* as he attempts to force Marina into prostitution: 'Come, you're a young foolish sapling, and must be bow'd as I would have you' (4.2.87–8). Pretending he has been afflicted by witchcraft, Richard Gloucester announces to the assembly, 'Look how I am bewitch'd; behold, mine arm/Is like a blasted sapling, wither'd up' (*R3* 3.4.68–9).

savory (A) Winter savory, *Satureja montana* L., a culinary **herb** and a perennial small **shrub**, is a naturalized introduction from southern Europe. It was used as a carminative; its former medicinal applications were mostly gynaecological. It is now primarily ornamental.

(B) Its appearance as part of Perdita's distribution of herbs and **flowers** to friends and guests owes more to fittingness than to symbolism: 'Here's flow'rs for you:/Hot lavender, mints, savory, marjorum' (*WT* 4.4.103–4). Of its two other mentions the word does not pertain to plants but signifies 'spiced-up' or 'tasty'. Hamlet uses culinary metaphors when praising a play which 'pleas'd not the million, 'twas caviar to the general...an excellent play, well digested in the scenes, set down with as much modesty as cunning. I remember one said there were no sallets in the lines to make the matter savory' (*HAM* 2.2.436–42). Elizabethan **salads** were spicy. Hamlet approves a refusal to compromise the integrity of the play by appealing to the undiscerning. This idea of 'pleasing the palate' finds literal expression in *CYM*. Belarius serving their common fare after a hard day's **hunting**, concludes, 'Come, our stomachs/Will make what's homely savory; weariness/Can snore upon the flint, when resty sloth/Finds the down pillow hard' (3.6.32–5).

(C) Elyot (1541: 30) believes savory will stimulate the digestion, sharpen sight, relieve phlegm and that it 'stirreth carnall appetite'. Bullein (1595) and Coles (1656) describe it as a hot herb. Gerard (1597: 462) recommends it as a carminative: 'it doth marvellously prevaile against winde'. There is no clear date for its introduction: Harvey (1992) records it being cultivated in the ecclesiastical **gardens** at Lambeth and Westminster in the fourteenth century. Rowland (1981) and Riddle (1992) detail its use in medieval gynaecology. Some commentators refer to the annual summer savory, as *S. hortensis*, but this is not listed in Stace (2010) as a modern plant identification.

scent see **smell**

scion (A) A shoot or **twig**, a scion can also be a sucker thrown up by a **plant** or **tree**. More specifically it designated either a **slip** for **grafting** or the graft itself. Figuratively scion served to suggest a member of a family, particularly a young person of marriageable age.

(B) The literal use appears in a critical botanical discourse. Perdita refuses to grow 'carnations and streak'd gillyvors' because 'There is an art which in their piedness shares/With great creating Nature'. Polixenes maintains:

> You see, sweet maid, we marry
> A gentler scion to the wildest stock,
> And make conceive a bark of baser kind
> By bud of nobler race. This is an art
> Which does mend Nature – change it rather; but
> The art itself is Nature.

> *(WT 4.4.82–97)*

The case for grafting and plant improvement could hardly be better expressed. Perdita gives grudging assent to the argument – 'So it is' (97) – but refuses to endorse the practice. Espousing the virtues of cross-fertilization in the natural world, Polixenes rejects cross-breeding in the social universe. It is precisely this biological phenomenon that provokes the fury of the Dauphin when reacting to the military successes of Henry V:

> *O Dieu vivant*! Shall a few sprays of us,
> The emptying of our father's luxury,
> Our scions, put in wild and savage stock,
> Spirit up so suddenly into the clouds
> And overlook their grafters?

The Duke of Britain, adds, 'Normans, but bastard Normans, Norman bastards!' (*H5* 3.5.5–10). Iago's chastisement of Roderigo for doting on Desdemona is decidedly horticultural. Advancing the proposition, 'Our bodies are our gardens, to the which our wills are gardeners', he concludes, 'we have reason to cool our raging motions, our carnal stings, our unbitted lusts; whereof I take this that you call love to be a sect or scion' (*OTH* 1.3.320–32). The irony embodied in this elaborate analogy – 'our wills are gardeners' – is that Iago can do nothing to tame his own jealous nature.

(C) Plat (1608) gives instructions on how to select suitable scions for grafting. Markham (1613) writes of cutting away the 'bastard cyons' that have grown too big for grafting, drawing strength away from the main tree, and suggesting that some can be planted on their own where they may take **root**. He notes that young scions which grow straight from the root of the parent tree should provide a tree as good as the original: human parallels were drawn when a son followed in his father's footsteps. Bradford (1933) and others suggest that in *WT* Shakespeare is anticipating the idea of 'hybridization' but as plant sexuality was not recognized for another 100 years and the word not generally used in a botanical sense until the nineteenth century, it is possible he is demonstrating the contemporary interest in monstrosities and peculiarities. Ellerbeck (2011) provides a historic and thematic exploration. See also **gillyvor, nature, slip, stock**.

scythe (A) An agricultural implement, a scythe has a long, sharp curving blade fixed at an angle to the handle. It is wielded with both hands to mow **grass** and **crops**, whence it became a symbol of cultivation. Figuratively and by transference it is an attribute of time, personified as Old Father Time, who carries a scythe.

(B) There is one literal use but several metaphorical examples – influenced primarily by the emblem of Old Father Time's scythe. Burgundy's disquisition on the condition of French agriculture in the wake of the English invasion tells of the land, 'Wanting the scythe withal, uncorrected, rank,/Conceives by idleness' (*H5* 5.2.50–1). At the opening of *LLL* dedication to three years of scholarship and abstinence is designed to achieve lasting fame: 'When spite of cormorant devouring Time,/Th'endeavor of this present breath may buy/That honor which shall bate his scythe's keen edge,/And make us heirs to all eternity' (1.1.4–7). *SON* 12 commends a surer way of outwitting death: 'And nothing 'gainst Time's scythe can make defense/Save breed, to brave him when he takes thee hence' (13–14). Contemplation of the woman's decline in *LC* reminds the reader that Time often diminishes life before ending it: 'Time had not scythed all that youth begun,/Nor youth all quit, but spite of heaven's fell rage,/Some beauty peep'd through lettice of sear'd age' (12–14).

(C) Heresbach (1596) writes of cutting swathes of corn with the scythe. Drayton also associates it with the **harvest**: 'The most aboundant swathe, whose Gleabe such goodly eares,/As to the weightie sheafe with sythe and sickle cut' (1622, *Polyolbion* 14.100–1). Markham (1613) writes of the corn being ready for the **sickle**, appearing to suggest that the long-handled scythe cuts crops to the **ground**, while the short sickle leaves the **stalks** behind. **Grass** in the garden cut using a scythe could produce a result as even as a modern lawnmower. See Spier and Anderson (1985: 451).

sedge (A) Coarse **grassy**, **rush**-like **plants**, sedges grow in water or wet places; botanically the name belongs to the *Carex* L. genus; in different regions sedge can indicate other plants. Sedge can be an individual plant or a mass of plants; it could be interchangeable with **flag**, **reed** and rush, although these had specific domestic applications which the true sedge did not. It is not possible to make a precise identification; Shakespeare probably uses sedge generically rather than specifically.

(B) The plant figures in a beguiling passage in *TGV*. Seeking to justify her pursuit of Proteus, Julia compares disruption to the course of love with obstruction of the natural flow of water:

> The current that with gentle murmur glides,
> Thou know'st, being stopp'd, impatiently doth rage;
> But when his fair course is not hindered,
> He makes sweet music with th'enamell'd stones,
> Giving a gentle kiss to every sedge
> He overtaketh in his pilgrimage.

> *(2.7.25–30)*

Commenting on Claudio, the disconsolate lover, Benedick muses, 'Alas, poor hurt fowl, now will he creep into sedges' (*ADO* 2.1.202–3). In Prospero's masque Iris calls forth the river nymphs to celebrate the impending marriage of Miranda and Ferdinand: 'You nymphs, call'd Naiades, of the windring brooks,/With your sedg'd crowns and ever-harmless looks,/Leave your crisp channels' (*TMP* 4.1.128–30). Imagination rather than veracity shapes Hotspur's version of the bloody encounter between his brother-in-law, Mortimer, and Owen Glendower 'on the gentle Severn's sedgy bank' (*1H4* 1.3.98). His artistry is remarkable given his contempt for 'mincing poetry' (3.1.132) – though he fails to convince a sceptical Henry IV.

(C) Holinshed (1577, vol. 1: 358) argues that the destruction of woodland has led to the predominance in some places of less useful plants including flags, sedge, reed and rush. Heresbach (1596) notes its economic value as the **roots** provide fodder for foraging swine. Drayton (1622) suggests sedges can provide both thatching materials and winter fodder. Mabey (1996) details the varieties and their modern uses.

seed (A) Something put in the **ground** or **sown** to reproduce the parent **plant, seed** can be used both singly and collectively as the seeds in **fruit**. It is often associated with

growth or development. Seed suggests fruitfulness and **fertility**; it can allude to such religious teaching as the Christian parable of the sower. To set seed is to sow embryonic plants; to go to seed suggests deterioration or neglect. Seed can also refer to human sperm, suggesting fertility and pregnancy.

(B) Most of the frequent mentions are figurative. The only use of 'seedsman' appears in Mark Antony's disquisition on Egyptian agriculture: 'The higher Nilus swells,/The more it promises; as it ebbs, the seedsman/Upon the slime and ooze scatters his grain,/And shortly comes to harvest' (*ANT* 2.7.20–3). This seemingly effortless fertility epitomizes a world of ease and plenitude. The melancholy Hamlet perceives seeding not as productive but as stultifying: ''tis an unweeded garden/That grows to seed, things rank and gross in nature/Possess it merely' (*HAM* 1.2.135–7). A deep-seated arrogance is the source of a vivid image in *TRO*. Pointing to the indiscipline shown by the aloof Achilles, Ulysses warns of contagion:

> the seeded pride
> That hath to this maturity blown up
> In rank Achilles must or now be cropp'd,
> Or shedding, breed a nursery of like evil,
> To overbulk us all.
>
> *(1.3.316–20)*

A positive attitude to the wild seed is given by the Countess in *AWW*. Wanting to be thought of as Helena's mother she maintains: ''Tis often seen/Adoption strives with nature, and choice breeds/A native slip to us from foreign seeds' (1.3.144–6). A wild **scion** or slip is grafted onto the native stock to produce something highly valued. The life of an underclass, not seen elsewhere in the play, is exposed by Romeo's description of the impoverished Apothecary: 'about his shelves/A beggarly account of empty boxes,/Green earthen pots, bladders, and musty seeds' (*ROM* 5.1.44–6). A gentler tribulation is experienced by Florizel who trusts to Camillo's strategy for facilitating his escape with Perdita: 'It cannot fail, but by/The violation of my faith, and then/Let nature crush the sides o'th'earth together,/And mar the seeds within!' (*WT* 4.4.476–9). Here is a conception of seeds as the most fundamental constituents of life – something found both in *LR* (3.2.8) and *MAC* (4.1.59) where the word used is '**germains**' or '**germans**'.

Attempting to modify the Dauphin's dismissive attitude towards Henry V, the French King reminds his son of the havoc caused by Edward III, who at Crecy, 'Saw his heroical seed, and smil'd to see him,/Mangle the work of nature, and deface/The patterns that by God and by French fathers/Had twenty years been made' (*H5* 2.4.59–62). The same image, with equal trepidation, is articulated by Macbeth: 'the seeds of Banquo kings!' (*MAC* 3.1.69). More abstract is Banquo's challenge to the Weird Sisters: 'If you can look into the seeds of time,/And say which grain will grow, and which will not,/Speak then to me' (1.3.58–60). An acute observation is made in *MM*. Communicating Angelo's ruthless policy of social reform to Mistress Overdone,

Pompey the bawd declares, 'All houses in the suburbs of Vienna must be pluck'd down'. When she inquires about the city houses he exposes speculative investment and corruption: 'They shall stand for seed. They had gone down too, but that a wise burgher put in for them' (1.2.95–100). This play also has a beguiling description of pregnancy. The scurrilous Lucio, informing Isabella that her brother is in prison accused of fornication, expresses himself with unaccustomed delicacy: 'as blossoming time/That from the seedness the bare fallow brings/To teeming foison, even so her plenteous womb/Expresseth his full tilth and husbandry' (1.4.41–4). The antithesis of this perception of pregnancy arises in *PER*. Lysimachus informs Marina that her 'principal', the brothel owner, is 'your herb-woman, she that sets seeds and roots of shame and iniquity' (4.6.84–6). This image of seeding is one of perversity: the 'herb-woman' is responsible for degradation, disease and disgrace.

(C) Gardeners had learnt since cultivation began when best to sow seeds, so the information given in books was often a formulization of established practice, although Hill (1577: chs. 1–3) includes such phrases as 'rare and secret helps', 'diligence and skill', 'worthy instructions to be conceived', 'skill, industry and secrets' suggesting arcane rather than accepted general knowledge. Holinshed (1577: 350) notes the introduction of new seeds: 'the nobilitie, who make their provision yearlie for new seeds out of strange countries, from whence they have them aboundantlie'. Stow (1598: 263) gives details of shops or sheds on the north side of Cheap ward, in one of which 'a woman sold seeds, roots, and herbs', bringing seeds and cultivation to the heart of the city. Willes (2011: 54–6, 116) discusses seed merchants in early modern England, detailing seed imports which were important for the propagation and distribution of new introductions. She comments on a rare 1600 pamphlet by Sir Hugh Plat which advocated methodical sowing of seeds thus challenging the time-honoured custom of random broadcasting which required greater quantities of seed.

shade (A) Shade is shelter from the sun's light and heat; also the provision of such protection. It can indicate the coming of darkness and night. Shade can represent protection, but equally it can act as a metaphor for impending death. Shade has always been important to **gardeners**: some **plants** are suitable for planting in the shade; some need full sun. For preservation of a fair complexion, women of higher social status resorted to shaded **arbours** and **bowers**.

(B) The necessity to make provision for shade in **gardens** is constantly stressed in the gardening books of the period. In both plays and poems, whether natural (clouds etc.) or manufactured (arbours, bowers), shade frequently contributes to sensory experience. Describing the morning, Tamora creates a scene remarkable for the marriage of its visual and aural elements: 'The green leaves quiver with the cooling wind/And make a checker'd shadow on the ground./Under their sweet shade, Aaron, let us sit' (*TIT* 2.3.14–16). Central to this evocation of the parkland or woodland is the 'checker'd shadow'. Henry VI's vision of bucolic innocence and ease is part of a tradition which elevates the blessings of a simple life over the burdens of kingship: 'Gives not the hawthorn bush a sweeter shade/To shepherds looking on their silly sheep/Than doth a rich embroider'd canopy' (*3H6* 2.5.42–4). This contemplation of an uncomplicated life is echoed both by Henry IV (*2H4* 3.1.4–31) and Henry V (*H5* 4.1.230–84). Thisbe is described as 'tarrying in mulberry shade' (*MND* 5.1.148). Orlando encounters the exiled Duke in the Forest of Arden, 'Under the shade of melancholy boughs' (*AYL* 2.7.111). This expression infuses the literal with the emotive. The shade of night is the natural ambiance for fairies. When Puck alerts his master to the sound of 'the morning lark', Oberon replies, 'Then, my queen, in silence sad,/Trip we after night's shade' (*MND* 4.1.94–6). Mistress Quickly is conversant with this tradition. In her unlikely disguise as Queen of the Fairies she recites to her entourage, 'Fairies, black, grey, green, and white,/You moonshine revellers, and shades of night' (*WIV* 5.5.37–8). The 'shades' here are 'spirits'. Cambridge, the would-be assassin, hypocritically tells the King, 'There's not, I think, a subject/That sits in heart-grief and uneasiness/Under the sweet shade of your government' (*H5* 2.2.26–8). 'Protection' is the primary meaning, though 'sweet shade' carries with it a wider sense of social integration. The antithesis of this kind of shade is embodied in Joan Pucelle's curse on York and Warwick as she is led to her execution: 'May never glorious sun reflex his beams/Upon the country where you make abode;/But darkness and the gloomy shade of death/Environ you' (*1H6* 5.4.87–90). Suffolk, too, curses his enemies: 'Their sweetest shade a grove of cypress trees!' (*2H6* 3.2.323). The **cypress** is, of course, associated with death. For Mowbray, the prospect of exile presages life bereft of meaning: 'Then thus I turn me from my country's light,/To dwell in solemn shades of endless night' (*R2* 1.3.176–7). The loved one in *SON* 18 will overcome death thanks to the life-giving power of the writer: 'Nor shall Death brag thou wand'rest in his shade,/When in eternal lines to time thou grow'st' (11–12).

(C) Browne (1613–16, Book 1, Song II) comments on the **plane** tree being extolled for providing shade: 'The heavie-headed plane-tree, by whose shade/The grasse growes thickest, men are fresher made'. Peacham (1612) suggests shade can be threatening, writing of a shady wood with uncouth paths and hidden ways. Drayton (1622) also sees shade as threatening, 'dark and sleepy', 'secret and gloomy'. Ault's anthology (1949) includes many examples of shade providing a place to rest or to escape from the sun and from work. Shady bowers and **groves** are places of ease, but can also be forlorn; they can foreshadow death as hell's eternal shade.

shrub (A) A **woody plant** with several **stems** growing from a single **root** or a low-growing woody plant with a single stem, a **shrub** provides shelter and protection. It might suggest an uncultivated space rather than a **garden**. Figuratively a shrub can indicate something or someone insignificant, mean or inferior. Shrubs might also denote a nuisance or threat if they hindered cultivation.

(B) A shrubless landscape is the epitome of desolation. Trinculo complains, 'Here's neither bush nor shrub to bear off any weather at all' (*TMP* 2.2.18–19). This brief comment – the only literal one – serves as a reminder of how people depended on natural features for protection from the elements. As he lies dying on the battlefield, Warwick reflects on his past glories:

> Thus yields the cedar to the axe's edge,
> Whose arms gave shelter to the princely eagle,
> Under whose shade the ramping lion slept,
> Whose top-branch overpeer'd Jove's spreading tree,
> And kept low shrubs from winter's pow'rful wind.
>
> *(3H6 5.2.11–15)*

A more modest perspective is provided by another warrior, Titus Andronicus. Beaten down by events he confides to his brother: 'Marcus, we are but shrubs, no cedars we' (*TIT* 4.3.46). The humble status of the shrub is also figured in *LUC*. Attempting to dissuade Tarquin from his intended rape, Lucrece endeavours to demonstrate that ugly thoughts are unworthy of a king: 'The lesser thing should not the greater hide:/The cedar stoops not to the base shrub's foot,/But low shrubs wither at the cedar's root' (663–5).

(C) Tusser (1573) recommends cutting down and destroying shrubs, **bushes** and **thorns.** Waldstein (1600: 159) provides a rare contemporary instance of shrubs in a cultivated context, albeit a constructed **wilderness** at Nonsuch, writing of a spacious enclosure with shrubs and bushes. He describes a platform constructed out of growing shrubs to facilitate the Queen's shooting at deer during the **hunt**. For Norden (1618) shrubs signify uncultivated, unproductive **land**.

sickle An agricultural implement, a sickle has a short handle, curved blade, and properly a serrated cutting edge which could cut **crops** and **grass**. The only literal sickles to appear in the plays are those borne by the sicklemen summoned by Ceres: 'You sunburn'd sicklemen, of August weary,/Come hither from the furrow and be merry'(*TMP* 4.1.134–5). Threatening that their incursion into French territory is but a harbinger of ruin, King Edward demands, 'Therefore, Valois, say, wilt thou yet resign,/ Before the sickle's thrust into the corn,/Or that enkindled fury turn to flame?' (*E3* 3.3.111–13). Father Time's sickle appears in *SON* 116 (10) and in *SON* 126 (2). The modern edition of Hill (1577) has contemporary illustrations of how to use a sickle in an **orchard**. Markham (1613) writes of the corn being fully **ripe** and ready for the sickle. He appears to suggest that when the sickle is used the crop is not cut to the **ground**, whereas the **scythe** leaves nothing standing. See Spier and Anderson (1985: 451).

simple(s) (A) Individual preparations usually for medicinal purposes. Simples were made from a single substance, unmixed and uncompounded. 'To simple' was to look for and collect the individual **plants** or **herbs**. There were professional collectors, often **herb-women**, who also might prescribe their use, and sell their herbs to physicians to be used as simples, or to **apothecaries** to be made into compound medicinal products. One centre of this operation was in **Bucklersbury**. There was no system of quality control, so that a good knowledge of plants was essential. Mistakes could be fatal. Herb-women were sometimes accused of adulterating the pure product.

(B) Simples are collected, sold, compounded and praised for their efficacy. While the most notable collector of simples is the Friar in *ROM,* he does not use the word. It is Romeo who employs the term during his vivid account of the starved and bedraggled Apothecary, 'In tatt'red weeds, with overwhelming brows,/Culling of simples' (5.1.39–40). Acknowledging simples are sometimes effective antidotes, Laertes confides to Claudius that there is no such remedy for the poison he has secured: 'no cataplasm so rare,/Collected from all simples that have virtue/Under the moon, can save the thing from death/That is but scratch'd withal' (*HAM* 4.7.143–6). The Doctor in *LR* advises Cordelia: 'Our foster-nurse of nature is repose,/The which he lacks; that to provoke in him/Are many simples operative, whose power/Will close the eye of anguish' (4.4.12–15). The eccentric Doctor Caius refuses to leave the house without his concoctions: 'Dere is some simples in my closet, dat I vill not for the varld I shall leave behind' (*WIV* 1.4.63–4). Another eccentric, Jaques, uses the word in the sense of 'ingredient' when analysing his highly individual melancholy, which is, 'compounded of many simples' (*AYL* 4.1.16). The only reference to London's famous herb district appears in *WIV.* Courting Mistress Ford, Falstaff cajoles: 'Come, I cannot cog and say thou art this and that, like a many of these lisping hawthorn buds, that come like women in men's apparel, and smell like Bucklersbury in simple time' (3.3.70–3).

(C) Knowledge of the appropriate plants was a collaborative process as Greene notes: 'yet the Phisition by reading oft knoweth the nature of the Simple as well as the Gardiner that planteth it' (1587, vol. 5, *Penelope's Web:* 151). He considers that the properties of the plants and the diseases they may cure can be indicated by the plants themselves, a concept known as the doctrine of signatures: 'there grew many simples whose virtues taught men to be subtle and to think nature by her weeds warned men to be wary and by their secret properties to check wanton and sensual imperfections' (1592, *A Quip* 213*).* Drayton (1622, *Polyolbion* 13. 231–4) writes of a choicest selection of simples, claiming that even such herbalists as Dodoens and Gerard fail to record them all. Iyengar (2011) says that physicians and wise women were allowed to dispense simples, while the apothecary supplied compound medicines. In practice the distinctions were probably blurred for convenience.

slip (A) A **twig**, shoot or **scion**, a **slip** could be taken from a **plant** or **tree** for **grafting** or planting to increase the **stock** of the plant; a tender slip was a shoot of a plant susceptible to **frost** or other damage. By extension, a slip was a descendant, or a young person, especially one of slender build.

(B) The various kinds of slips such as falling down, falling from grace, licence to evade punishment, or counterfeit coinage (*VEN* 515) all receive attention, though the ancestry-offspring use dominates. A problematic horticultural use arises in *WT* when Perdita explains her disinclination to **grow** 'carnations and streak'd gillyvors'. She reasons: 'For I have heard it said,/There is an art which in their piedness shares/With great creating Nature'. In response Polixenes sets out the case for grafting and the role of human intervention. Though accepting the argument, she says defiantly, 'I'll not put/The dibble in earth to set one slip of them' (4.4.82–100). Perdita seems to refer to cuttings, and indeed, **carnations** can be propagated by means of slips. Her dislike of these **flowers** appears to arise from the belief that they are subject to cross-breeding. Although plant variety was eagerly sought and the concept of 'hybridization' had captured the imagination the capacity to achieve it did not exist at the time – nor was the word itself used in this sphere. In *MAC* the Witches' cauldron contains a gruesome concoction of human and animal parts. Its vegetative contents are, 'Root of hemlock' and 'slips of yew/Sliver'd in the moon's eclipse' (4.1.25–8). The **yew's** connection with death and with graveyards explains why it is favoured by the Weird Sisters. The slips would not be cuttings, however, but slivers. **Hemlock** is a poison associated in folklore with witchcraft and the devil. Only bits of things go into this mixture. The Countess in *AWW* provides a vivid analogy when conveying her love for an adopted child: ''Tis often seen/Adoption strives with nature, and choice breeds/A native slip to us from foreign seeds' (1.3.144–6). Unlike the warm-hearted Countess, Suffolk employs the analogy to disparage Warwick: 'Thy mother took into her blameful bed/ Some stern untutor'd churl; and noble stock/Was graft with crab-tree slip, whose fruit thou art' (*2H6* 3.2.212–14). 'Offspring' is the meaning earlier in the play when Warwick confirms his adherence to York's cause as legitimate heir to the throne:

> Henry doth claim the crown from John of Gaunt,
> The fourth son, York claims it from the third;
> Till Lionel's issue fails, his should not reign.
> It fails not yet, but flourishes in thee,
> And in thy sons, fair slips of such a stock.

(2.2.54–8)

(C) Bradford (1933) and others suggest that in *WT* Shakespeare is anticipating the *idea* of 'hybridization'. The *word* is not used in the botanical context until much later. It is possible he is demonstrating the contemporary interest in monstrosities and peculiarities. Erasmus (1536, vol. 31) writes 'the slip of a noble tree bears fruit at once', suggesting that well-endowed minds come to fruition early. Elyot (1565, fol. 17) suggests slips of reason can begin to burgeon in children when they are still small, a contemporary meaning that has not been found elsewhere. Hill (1577) talks of slipping plants, in the sense of breaking off slips or small stems to be replanted straight away to form a new plant, which he thinks will produce a better plant. Parkinson (1629) writes of setting and planting slips, operations which would not include grafting. See Ellerbeck (2011) for a historic and thematic exploration with a focus on *AWW*. See also **gillyvor, nature, scion, stock**.

smell, fragrance, perfume, rank, reek, scent (A) All reflect an olfactory sense, the importance of which – when personal hygiene was of a relatively low standard – cannot be overemphasized. Foul smells were prevalent in towns and houses because of lack of drainage. Both they and polluted air were seen as causes of the plague, thereby promoting the use of **posies** and **pomanders, strewing herbs, reeds** and **rushes**, and such **knot-garden** plants as **balm, lavender, myrtle, roses** and **rosemary**. The term fragrance and scent reflect pleasant, sweet smells; rank was the term used to describe vegetation, a row of **trees**, or to indicate something unpleasantly **fertile**, overgrown, rampant and uncontrolled, highly offensive, foul or **rotting**. Rank used of a medical condition indicates something festering or swollen with disease. Applied to a person, rank suggests morally evil, lustful, licentious, festering. Scent is the animal trail followed in hunting.

(B) Even when confined to **flowers**, references to smell are so frequent that only a sample is given. Famously the anguished Juliet protests, 'What's in a name? That which we call a rose/By any other word would smell as sweet' (*ROM* 2.2.43–4). Othello, about to murder Desdemona cannot resist kissing her: 'When I have pluck'd thy rose,/I cannot give it vital growth again,/It needs must wither. I'll smell thee on the tree' (*OTH* 5.2.13–15). In an attempt to seduce Adonis, Venus blazons natural affinities: 'Torches are made to light, jewels to wear,/Dainties to taste, fresh beauty for the use,/Herbs for their smell, and sappy plants to bear' (*VEN* 163–5). Although this is the only time Shakespeare uses 'to bear' in this context, it is now a commonly used phrase for a fruit-bearing plant. Berating Death, Venus asks, 'what dost thou mean/To stifle beauty, and to steal his breath?/Who when he liv'd, his breath and beauty set/Gloss on the rose, smell to the violet' (933–6). Towards the close of the poem Venus caresses the flower into which Adonis has been metamorphosed: 'She bows her head, the new-sprung flow'r to smell,/Comparing it to her Adonis' breath' (1171–2). Responding to the denouement in *AWW* the lachrymose Lafew uses a delightful phrase: 'Mine eyes smell onions, I shall weep anon' (5.3.320). There is nothing metaphorical about Pistol's response when challenged by the **leek**-bearing Fluellen: 'Hence! I am qualmish at the smell of leek' (*H5* 5.1.21). Warming to his new-found luxury, Christopher Sly exults, 'I smell sweet savors, and I feel soft things' (*SHR* Ind. 2.71). Baiting the hook to catch Falstaff, Mistress Quickly revels in the fantasy of Mistress Ford's suitors: 'smelling so sweetly, all musk, and so rushling' (*WIV* 2.2.66–7).

Oberon is solicitous of Titania when recalling the sight of Bottom decorated with her floral **wreath**: 'For she his hairy temples then had rounded/With coronet of fresh and fragrant flowers' (*MND* 4.1.51–2). This representation of incongruity has inspired fine paintings. The alliteration ensures consciousness of sight and scent. *TIT* is the only play where 'fragrant' appears twice. Rousing his party for the early morning **hunt** Titus calls, 'The hunt is up, the morn is bright and grey,/The fields are fragrant and the woods are green' (2.2.1–2). Sound values once again work to enhance the sense of colour and scent. Seeing the mutilated Lavinia, Marcus shudders at the prospect of presenting this fearful sight to Titus: 'One hour's storm will drown the fragrant meads,/What will whole months of tears thy father's eyes?' (2.4.54–5). The poem in *PP* that begins 'Live with me and be my love' has a verse redolent with scent: 'There will I make thee a bed of roses,/With a thousand fragrant posies' (xix.9–10). The phrase 'a thousand fragrant posies' is also in *WIV* (3.1.20). While fragrance is mainly associated with **meadow** flowers, *SON* 95 refers to 'the fragrant rose' (2).

It is remarkable that with over 30 mentions of 'perfume', only two relate to flowers: the air, perfumed in diverse ways, is sometimes suffused by a woman's breath. Concealed in Imogen's bed-chamber, Iachimo is enthralled: ''Tis her breathing that/ Perfumes the chamber thus' (*CYM* 2.2.18–19). More prosaic is the 'Perfume for a lady's chamber' (*WT* 4.4.223) supplied by that 'snapper-up of unconsider'd trifles' (4.3.26), Autolycus. King John's decision to indulge himself with a second coronation is deplored by Salisbury who protests it is, 'To throw a perfume on the violet' (*JN* 4.2.12). Laertes cautions Ophelia that Hamlet's affections are fleeting: 'A violet in the youth of primy nature,/Forward, not permanent, sweet, not lasting,/The perfume and suppliance of a minute' (*HAM* 1.3.7–9). Exoticism comes to the fore in *ANT.* Enobarbus' mesmerising description of Cleopatra's barge deploys the word twice: 'Purple the sails, and so perfumed that/The winds were love-sick with them'; 'From the barge/A strange invisible perfume hits the sense/Of the adjacent wharfs' (2.2.193–213). An appalling example is present in *TIT.* Lucius reports the successful completion of the Roman rite: 'Alarbus' limbs are lopp'd,/And entrails feed the sacrificing fire,/Whose smoke like incense doth perfume the sky' (1.1.143–5). Apemantus attempts to demonstrate to Timon the futility of his withdrawal from Athenian life: 'Thy flatterers yet wear silk, drink wine, lie soft,/Hug their diseas'd perfumes, and have forgot/That ever Timon was' (*TIM* 4.3.206–8). This unique phrase 'diseas'd perfumes' relates to women of easy virtue. The very same scene has another use: Apemantus continuing to taunt Timon refers to the misanthrope's days of wealth and popularity: 'When thou wast in thy gilt and thy perfume, they mock'd thee for too much curiosity' (301–3). Though 'perfume' here may well be literal, the primary meaning embraces the idea of 'blessed condition'. 'Curiosity' intimates fastidiousness or 'over elaborate' entertainments.

Three of the four mentions of 'scent' pertain to the hunt, that much-loved sport of the **landed** gentry. The First Huntsman defending the superiority of his favoured dog, Belman, maintains, 'He cried upon it at the merest loss,/And twice to-day pick'd out the dullest scent' (*SHR* Ind.1.23–4). Malvolio's attempt to extract a favourable meaning from the cryptic component of the forged letter causes Sir Toby to observe, 'He is now at a cold scent' (*TN* 2.5.122). Venus pleads that if Adonis insists on hunting the boar he should emulate the hare's tactic of disguising his scent: 'For there his smell with others being mingled,/The hot scent-snuffing hounds are driven to doubt' (*VEN* 691–2). The fourth example occurs in *HAM.* 'Detect' is probably the meaning when the Ghost expresses awareness of imminent dawn: 'But soft, methinks I scent the morning air' (1.5.58).

'Rank' generally refers to rampant vegetative growth. Hamlet's vision is one of a world burgeoning with **weeds**: ''tis an unweeded garden/That grows to seed, things rank and gross in nature/Possess it merely' (*HAM* 1.2.135–7). On one occasion it means a grouping of trees (*AYL* 4.3.79). Its application as 'foul smelling' is extensive and varied.

An amusing case arises in *WIV* where Falstaff recounts the condition of the laundry basket that facilitated his escape: 'there was the rankest compound of villainous smell that ever offended nostril' (3.5.91–3). Cleopatra represents to Iras the humiliation they will endure if paraded before Rome's 'Mechanic slaves': 'In their thick breaths,/Rank of gross diet, shall we be enclouded,/And forc'd to drink their vapor' (*ANT* 5.2.209–13). The addressee in *SON* 69 is exposed to severe scrutiny: 'To thy fair flower add the rank smell of weeds:/But why thy odor matcheth not thy show,/The soil is this, that thou dost common grow' (12–14). The metaphor gathers even more force in Claudius' acknowledgement of his crime: 'O, my offense is rank, it smells to heaven,/It hath the primal eldest curse upon't,/A brother's murther' (*HAM* 3.3.36–8). There are several attributes incorporated in the words 'reek' and 'reeky' with different aspects dominating in varying contexts. Intrinsic to the concept, however, is the discharge into the air of foul-smelling moisture or fumes suffused with bloated or decaying vegetation. Responding to the plebeians' decision to exile him, Coriolanus is scathing: 'You common cry of curs, whose breath I hate/As reek a'th'rotten fens' (*COR* 3.3.120–1). See *SON* 130.8.

(C) The importance of creating sweet smells is well documented in the literature of the time. Bright (1586: 266) prescribes herbs for the melancholic: 'Neither is the braine and heart only cheered and conforted by the inward receiving of these simples, but whatsoever of them is of pleasant and fragraunt smell, that agreeth with ech, and giveth recreation and increase to the spirits of both.' In his comments on the year of the plague, Dekker notes that it started with wonders, as evidenced by 'dressed orchards and gardens', and 'sweet odours' from flowers, but ended in a 'rank and rotten grave' (1603, *The Wonderful Year*). Rawcliffe (2008: 3–21) argues gardens 'constituted a frontline defence in the battle against disease'. She comments that whereas fear of stench and bad air could be associated with the idea of purgatory and hell as characterized by foul smells of pitch and sulphur, so heaven was epitomized by floral sweetness. Rawcliffe also notes that while aromatherapy may be an alternative treatment now, in medieval and early modern times it was an important part of medicinal practice.

soil (A) A synonym for **earth** or **ground**, soil can suggest the place of one's birth, one's native country, ground in relation to its composition, a particular type of earth or mould, or the capacity to sustain **growing plants**. Soil can designate a muddy place used by wild animals for wallowing, or suggest moral stain or tarnish. To soil means to bring disgrace or discredit, to foul, pollute or defile.

(B) This sustaining substance embodies a spiritual dimension in *R2*. Bolingbroke's valediction proclaims its maternal nurturing: 'Then England's ground, farewell, sweet soil, adieu;/My mother, and my nurse, that bears me yet!' (1.3.306–7). Richard's stated reason for his cousin's exile is: 'For that our kingdom's earth should not be soil'd/ With that dear blood which it hath fostered' (1.3.125–6). The prosaic nature of soil occurs later in the play when the **Gardener**, who makes an extended analogy between management of the **garden** and of the state, tells his assistant, 'You thus employed, I will go root away/The noisome weeds which without profit suck/The soil's fertility from wholesome flowers' (3.4.37–9). The soil/earth linkage also occurs in *2H4*. Reviewing his reign the dying Henry IV reassures Hal that the stigma of usurpation will diminish with his death: 'For all the soil of the achievement goes/With me into the earth' (4.5.189–90). The wordplay is intriguing: Bolingbroke's 'soil' or stain echoes Richard's warning of England's 'earth' being 'soil'd'. In the opening scene of *1H4* the King announces the arrival of a traveller from the north: 'Sir Walter Blunt, new lighted from his horse,/Stain'd with the variation of each soil/Betwixt that Holmedon and this seat of ours' (63–5). This representation of the horse bearing the physical evidence of the diverse soils of England embodies the wholeness of the kingdom, soon to be threatened with dismemberment. Henry IV deploys 'soil' as analogy when questioning the company favoured by Prince Hal: 'Most subject is the fattest soil to weeds,/And he, the noble image of my youth,/Is overspread with them' (*2H4* 4.4.54–6). Discovering that the only way to survive in the Forest of Arden is to become a landowner, Celia appoints Corin as intermediary for the purchase of a farm: 'if you like upon report/The soil, the profit, and this kind of life,/I will your very faithful feeder be,/And buy it with your gold right suddenly' (*AYL* 2.4.97–100). Critical to the arrangement is assessment of the 'soil' and the rate of return it provides. The same economic principles apply in this pastoral world as elsewhere.

(C) Earth and soil were used interchangeably in Elizabethan times. Hill (1577) refers throughout to earth rather than soil, while Drayton (1622) says of *Polyolbion* that he will write of 'the sundry varying soils'. He later writes of the 'jealous soil', soil that is variously sweet, consecrated, swelling, unpleasant, healthful, dear, rich, the goodness and fatness of the soil, and talks of selling soil when land is enclosed. Plat (1654) has no entry in his index for soil, and for earth says 'see ground' under which heading he lists the improvements necessary to grow good plants. Archer (2007: 1) includes the acclaim of the Queen by James Aske in 1588 as 'Elizabetha Triumphans', 'renowned Queene of this renowned land, Renowned land, because a fruitfull soile' suggesting a mystical relationship between the Queen and the **fertile** soil of England.

sow (A) The act of scattering **seed** on prepared **ground**, to **sow** is to **grow** or produce a **crop**, by extension to cover a place thickly with a substance, or to distribute. Figuratively it indicates an action that brings results or rewards, as in biblical usage.

(B) All the uses except one are figurative. Davy provides the literal mention when he asks Justice Shallow, 'sir, shall we sow the hade land with wheat?' (*2H4* 5.1.14–15). Speaking on behalf of Cardinal Campeius and himself, Cardinal Wolsey tries to reassure Queen Katherine: 'We are to cure such sorrows, not to sow 'em' (*H8* 3.1.158). It is interesting that it is 'wild' Nature that Timon extols. He uses 'sow' only in a negative way. In a particularly perverse representation of this life-giving activity he prays, 'Itches, blains,/Sow all th'Athenian bosoms, and their crop/Be general leprosy! (*TIM* 4.1.28–30). Asked by prostitutes what they should do in return for his gold, Timon returns to this image: 'Consumptions sow/In hollow bones of man, strike their sharp shins,/And mar men's spurring' (4.3.151–3). The bones made hollow by syphilis will prevent the sowing of fertile seed. Belarius marvels at the princely virtues evinced by young men of royal stock who have grown up in rusticity: 'valor/That wildly grows in them but yields a crop/As if it had been sow'd' (*CYM* 4.2.179–81). Having cynically persuaded Cade to instigate rebellion during his absence, York anticipates his gains: 'Why then from Ireland come I with my strength,/And reap the harvest which that rascal sow'd' (*2H6* 3.1.380–1). Opposing political representation for the plebeians, Coriolanus employs imagery surprising for a patrician who despises manual labour: 'In soothing them we nourish 'gainst our Senate/The cockle of rebellion, insolence, sedition,/Which we ourselves have plough'd for, sow'd, and scatter'd' (*COR* 3.1.69–71).

(C) Great emphasis is placed on the need to prepare the ground properly before sowing seed. The *Mirror for Magistrates* (1559: 381) emphasizes the moral to be drawn from proper and improper preparation of the ground for sowing: 'What grayne proves wel that is so rashely sowen?'. With many still believing that it was crucial to sow according to the phases of the moon, Hill (1577, ch. 19) includes 'Certaine precepts of the skilful in our time, for the sowing of many delectable **flowers**, and the tender **hearbs**, with the observations of the Moone, in these and other matters necessary'. Markham (1613) provides detailed instructions on preparing the ground for sowing different crops including **ploughing** and **manuring**.

spade An essential **garden** tool for **digging** or cutting **ground**, a spade was used to prepare for **sowing** or **planting**, usually after the ground had been loosened or turned over with a **mattock**; it also served to prepare graves. The gravedigger scene in *HAM* has half the mentions. The first of the Gravedigger's contributions indicates the tenor of his lively banter: 'Come, my spade. There is no ancient gentlemen but gard'ners, ditchers, and grave-makers; they hold up Adam's profession' (5.1.29–31). Although this implement figures in three more plays it is not associated with gardening, though Timon, digging for roots, is asked by Apemantus, 'Why this spade? this place?' (*TIM* 4.3.204). Both in *TIT* and in *ROM* it is used in conjunction with a mattock. Titus persuades his kinsmen to 'dig with mattock and spade,/And pierce the inmost centre of the earth;/Then when you come to Pluto's region,/I pray you deliver him this petition' (*TIT* 4.3.11–14). The Friar uses a spade to gain access to the Capulet tomb. The watch report, 'We took this mattock and this spade from him' (*ROM* 5.3.185). The modern edition of Hill (1577) contains contemporary illustrations of garden tools and their uses, which include a spade. Drayton (1622) cites the spade as a tool to cut turves or peat. Dent (1981: S699). Christianson (2005) has details of contemporary tools used at Hampton Court.

speargrass One possible identification is lesser spearwort, *Ranunculus flammula* L., 'spear' referring to **leaf**-shape rather than nose-bleed inducing properties; like other members of the *Ranunculus* genus, it could raise blisters. Alternative candidates are couch **grass**, *Elytrigia repens* L., and yarrow or sneezewort, *Achillea ptarmica* L. All were believed to induce a nose-bleed. Bardolph is the only character to refer to this

plant, though the instigator is Falstaff. Having been robbed at Gad's Hill, the fat knight concocts a story of bravery, persuading his associates to collude in the fantasy. Once his back is turned, however, Peto confesses all, leading to Bardolph's revelation of how Falstaff induced their bloodstained condition: 'Yea, and to tickle our noses with spear-grass to make them bleed, and then to beslubber our garments with it and swear it was the blood of true men' (*1H4* 2.4.309–11). In a play replete with duplicity and misrepresentations this incident provides an engaging example of counterfeiting. Gerard (1597) calls the common yarrow *A. ptarmica* 'nose-bleed', as the result of putting the plant up one's nose. This is at variance with the other uses of the plant to stop bleeding. Ryden (1978: 64) notes, '*Speargrass* is used by Turner (1548) as a synonym of *spearwort, Rununculus flammula* L., lesser spearwort … Neither Lyte nor Gerard adduces the word in any sense (specific or generic) … Shakespeare may have been familiar with *speargrass* as a synonym of *spearwort*'. Many commentators leave the precise identification open. Iyengar (2011) notes that *R. flammula* was used by beggars to fake skin ulcers.

spray (A) A slender shoot or **twig**, collectively spray indicates such shoots whether still growing or cut for fuel. More specifically sprays can be **hazel** or **birch twigs** used in thatching. By extension, a spray can suggest a child, a dependant, or someone vulnerable.

(B) Only one of the four uses is literal, and even here the circumstance has a political dimension. The **Gardener** instructs one of his assistants: 'Go thou, and like an executioner/Cut off the heads of too fast growing sprays,/That look too lofty in our commonwealth' (*R2* 3.4.33–5). The focus of the scene is the use of a **garden** as an exemplar for good government. Sharing the pleasure of Queen Margaret in the removal of Gloucester from office, Suffolk boasts, 'Thus droops this lofty pine and hangs his sprays,/Thus Eleanor's pride dies in her youngest days' (*2H6* 2.3.45–6). The sprays are **branches**, signifying dependants. At the close of the battle of Towton Richard vetoes his brother's magnanimity:

> Revoke that doom of mercy, for 'tis Clifford,
> Who, not contented that he lopp'd the branch
> In hewing Rutland when his leaves put forth,
> But set his murth'ring knife unto the root
> From whence that tender spray did sweetly spring,
> I mean our princely father, Duke of York.
>
> *(3H6 2.6.46–51)*

In response to Henry V's steady march through French territory, the Dauphin urges action against the feeble offspring of their Norman progenitors:

> shall a few sprays of us,
> The emptying of our fathers' luxury,
> Our scions, put in wild and savage stock,

> Spirit up so suddenly into the clouds
> And overlook their grafters?

(H5 3.5.5–9)

Here, the usually vocal but unimaginative Dauphin displays surprising mental agility in disparaging his formidable adversaries.

squash The unripe pod of a **pea**, a squash can refer to a child, or be applied contemptuously to people. It is to squeeze, press or beat into a pulp. The word appears as an apt metaphor for a juvenile in *TN* and *WT*. Asked to describe the imperturbable messenger Cesario/Viola, Malvolio answers, 'Not yet old enough for a man, nor young enough for a boy; as a squash is before 'tis a peascod, or a codling when 'tis almost an apple' (*TN* 1.5.156–8). In an attempt to mask signs of his jealousy, Leontes claims that the sight of his son Mamillius evoked remembrance of his own childhood: 'How like (methought) I then was to this kernel,/This squash, this gentleman' (*WT* 1.2.159–60). A different perspective prevails in fairyland. The transformed Bottom addresses Peaseblossom: 'I pray you commend me to Mistress Squash, your mother, and to Master Peascod, your father' (*MND* 3.2.186–7). The *OED* gives no further example of the word's use until Ruskin (1886), noting that squash as **gourd** was first used in 1643.

stalk The main **stem** of a **plant** bearing **leaves** and **flowers**. Its only literal appearance is in *VEN* where it is the reincarnation of the dead Adonis:

> She bows her head, the new-sprung flow'r to smell,
> Comparing it to her Adonis' breath,
> And says within her bosom it shall dwell,
> Since he himself is reft from her by death.
>   She crops the stalk, and in the breach appears
>   Green-dropping sap, which she compares to tears.

(1171–6)

LC has a couplet in which the betrayed woman reflects how she sacrificed herself to a thankless lover: 'Threw my affections in his charmed power,/Reserv'd the stalk and gave him all my flower' (146–7). In the remarkable brothel scene in *PER,* Bawd advertises Marina's virginity to his high-ranking client, Lysimachus: 'Here comes that which grows to the stalk, never pluck'd yet, I can assure you' (4.6.41–2). In *R3* Tyrrel narrates Forrest's description of the princes in the tower before they were murdered: 'Their lips were four red roses on a stalk,/Which in their summer beauty kiss'd each other' (*R3* 4.3.12–13).

statue (A) A three-dimensional representation usually in stone or marble of a living being, allegorical person or deity, a statue was often of life-size proportions. Demand for classical sculptures and statues grew as the Italian renaissance influence reached

England, although they were still novelties in the later sixteenth century. They were housed in special **galleries**, arcades, **garden** buildings, and provided focal points in the **garden**, often featuring on **fountains**; in the seventeenth century statues were frequently sited in grottoes. Statue also suggests stillness, or a lack of feelings.

(B) Statues, frequently incorporating classical motifs, were important features of garden landscape. What at the time served to surprise and impress guests as they savoured the delights of these elaborately designed gardens acquires artistic, social and political focus in the plays. Although all but one of the statues is located in urban spaces they resonate with the classical images so familiar in the gardens of the day. The only statue situated in a garden proves not to be a statue at all. The Third Gentleman's description sets the scene: 'The princess hearing of her mother's statue, which is in the keeping of Paulina – a piece many years in doing and now newly perform'd by that rare Italian master, Julio Romano' (*WT* 5.2.94–7). The only named artist in the canon, Julio Romano died in 1546 and so was neither contemporary with the poet nor with the social universe of the play. He was not only a painter and sculptor but also a garden designer. Perdita's desire to kiss the 'statue' is thwarted by Paulina's caution, 'the color's/Not dry', indicating that these statues were generally painted. Reacting to the spectacle Leontes marvels, 'Would you not deem it breath'd? and that those veins/Did verily bear blood?' and later adds 'What fine chisel/Could ever yet cut breath?' (5.3.47–79). A scene profoundly engaged with statuary and artistic genius turns on the idea of illusion. Paulina's scheme beguiles the viewers just as art itself is a masterly deception. Moreover, at the moment Leontes discovers that Hermione is living he utters the words which elevate life above art: 'O, she's warm!' (109). Even so it is Shakespeare's dramatic art that intensifies awareness of the creative relationship between art and **nature**.

Montague and Capulet make a commitment to erect statues dedicated to the memory of the victims of family antagonism. The former proposes:

> For I will raise a statue in pure gold,
> That whiles Verona by that name is known,
> There shall no figure at such rate be set
> As that of true and faithful Juliet.

Capulet responds: 'As rich shall Romeo's by his lady's lie,/Poor sacrifices of our enmity!' (*ROM* 5.3.299–304). Statues embody and project history. Past heroes and their statues cast long shadows in *JC*. Brutus is in thrall to his great ancestor and it is at the site of his statue that one of Cassius' forged appeals to Brutus is placed: 'set this up with wax/Upon old Brutus' statue' (1.3.145–6). Disconcerted by Calphurnia's pleading, Caesar communicates the source of his anxieties to Decius: 'She dreamt to-night she saw my statue,/Which, like a fountain with an hundred spouts,/Did run pure blood'. Decius artfully reinterprets the dream so that the 'statue spouting blood in many pipes'(2.2.76–85) becomes a symbol of Caesar's greatness. The apogee of Brutus' aspirations is realized when the plebeians applaud his justification for the assassination and cry, 'Give him a statue with his ancestors' (3.2.50). Later in the forum scene Antony, dramatizing Caesar's death, elicits remembrance of another statue: 'Even at the base of Pompey's statue/(Which all the while ran blood) great Caesar fell' (3.2.188–9). These statues are not lifeless memorials but representations of values and conflicts. The praises heaped on the awe-inspiring Caius Martius are epitomized by the comment, 'the nobles bended,/As if to Jove's statue' (*COR* 2.1.265–6). Queen Margaret, angered by Henry VI's reaction to Gloucester's death, says bitterly, 'Erect his statue and worship it,/And make my image but an alehouse sign' (*2H6* 3.2.80–1). Responding to a setback, Alanson encourages Joan de Pucelle: 'We'll set thy statue in some holy place,/And have thee reverenc'd like a blessed saint' (*1H6* 3.3.14–15). Attempting to mollify Cleopatra, the messenger portrays Octavia's inertia: 'She creeps;/Her motion and her station are as one;/She shows a body rather than a life,/A statue, than a breather' (*ANT* 3.3.18–21). Buckingham, too, draws on this difference when describing the citizens' response to the proposal that Richard be crowned: 'No, so God help me, they spake not a word,/But like dumb statues, or breathing stones,/Star'd each on other, and look'd deadly pale' (*R3* 3.7.24–6).

(C) Henderson (2005) records the earliest English references being to the statues in Burghley's gardens. He was a pioneer in the inclusion of statuary in gardens, loggias or open garden galleries such as those at Cecil House in the Strand. In 1561 he was sent statues of twelve emperors; there were others at Theobalds, where Hentzner (1598) notes seeing them in a semicircle in the summerhouse. Drayton comments on statues in galleries and gardens:

> Large Galleries where piece with piece doth seeme to strive,
> Of Pictures done to life, Landskip, and Perspective;
> Thence goodly Gardens sees, where Antique Statues stand
> In Stone and Copper, cut by many a skilfull hand;
> *(1622, Polyolbion 26. 87–90).*

Bacon (1625) is ambivalent about the place of statues in his perfect garden: he surrounds the **fountain** with 'fine rails of low statues'. However, later comments suggest he would be happier without them, regarding them as ostentatious, 'adding nothing to the true pleasure of a garden'. Colonna (1499: 71) expresses his wonderment for a statue in similar terms to Leontes: 'I judged that there had never been an image of such perfection made by chisel or knife, and wondered not unreasonably whether a living being had been turned to stone in this place and thus petrified'. Tigner (2012: 125–31) provides a detailed analysis of the role of statuary in the Renaissance garden and notes that Julio Romano had designed a secret garden. Thorne (2000) and Meek (2009) both offer interesting perspectives on this topic.

stem The slender support of the fruit, flower or leaf attached to the twig or branch. It can indicate a line of ancestry. The only botanical mention arises during Helena's protestation against what she perceives to be Hermia's betrayal. Recalling their former intimacy she alights on a telling image: 'So we grew together,/Like to a double cherry, seeming parted,/But yet an union in partition,/Two lovely berries moulded on one stem' (*MND* 3.2.208–11). Its application to the sphere of family inheritance and bloodline is adduced twice. The dying Mortimer preparing to inform York that he is the true claimant to the English throne addresses him as, 'sweet stem from York's great stock' (*1H6* 2.5.41). The French King uses the same term in relation to Henry V when warning the Dauphin of the English invader's descent from Edward III: 'This is a stem/Of that victorious stock; and let us fear/The native mightiness and fate of him' (*H5* 2.4.62–4).

stock (A) *Matthiola* sp.W.T. Aiton, the stock **flower** was sometimes called stock **gillyvor**. Stock is also the **stem** or trunk of a **tree** as distinguished from its **branches**, the cleft in a stem into which a **scion** or **graft** is inserted. The stock in grafting was thought to represent the true source of life, with the concomitant suggestion that accidental or artificially created **plants** were inferior or meretricious. Stock might also indicate anything moribund or motionless, and figuratively a senseless or stupid person. Stock for grafting provided an analogy for the family, the founder of a race or family, a line of descent, a lineage, a family or descendants of a common ancestor.

(B) There is only one literal mention. It is the familial sense of the word that dominates. Justifying horticultural practices designed to vary and to improve plants, Polixenes replies to Perdita's scepticism: 'we marry/A gentler scion to the wildest stock,/And make conceive a bark of baser kind/By bud of nobler race' (*WT* 4.4.92–5). The histories make up a high proportion of familial applications with claim and counter claim, **land** rights and assertions of lineal superiority. Family antagonisms also spill over into other genres. That great disturber of the peace, Tybalt, disrupts Capulet's entertainment with, 'Now, by the stock and honor of my kin,/To strike him dead I hold it not a sin' (*ROM* 1.5.58–9). Having disparaged Posthumus as a libertine, Iachimo attempts to persuade Imogen that by virtue of her lineage she should exact retribution: 'Be reveng'd,/Or she that bore you was no queen, and you/Recoil from your great stock' (*CYM* 1.6.126–8). This less than compelling argument fails to deceive Imogen. Another machiavellian, Brutus the tribune, rehearses the plebeians' in their excuses for withdrawal of their earlier support for Caius Martius' election to consulship: 'Say we read lectures to you,/How youngly he began to serve his country,/How long continued, and what stock he springs of –/The noble house o'th'Martians' (*COR* 2.3.235–8). Griffith representing to Queen Katherine the finer qualities of the late Cardinal Wolsey, begins, 'This Cardinal,/Though from an humble stock, undoubtedly/Was fashion'd to much honor' (*H8* 4.2.48–50). In sharp contrast to this gracious account, Bishop Gardiner in the same play displays grossness of spirit when denouncing the pregnant Ann Bullen: 'The fruit she goes with/I pray for heartily, that it may find/Good time, and live; but for the stock, Sir Thomas,/I wish it grubb'd up now' (5.1.20–3).

(C) Contemporary writers emphasize the importance of choosing the correct stock for grafting. Some thought entirely new varieties of plant could be produced by the choice of stock and graft, as for example Parkinson (1629) who suggests grafting a white **rose** on a **broom** would create a yellow rose. This was a purely theoretical proposition and technically would not have worked. Jonson provides an early instance of 'hybrid' which did not appear in a botanical context until the late eighteenth century: the Nurse uses stock for family background and descent 'He is descended of a right good stock, sir', which contrasts a few lines later with the Host's comment, 'She's a wild Irish born, sir, and a hybrid' (1603, *The New Inn* 2.6.23, 26). Lawson (1618) gives precise detail on suitable stocks for grafting; Mascall (1640) includes three chapters on the particular stocks to choose for grafting specific plants. Drayton (1622) writes of English royal descent: 'the stock of Troy'; 'grafted in the stock of great Plantagenet'. See Dent for examples of stock as 'senseless' (1981: S866.1). See also **gillyvor**, **nature**, **scion**, **slip**.

stover Now obsolete, stover is thought to be derived from the French 'estover' or 'estouvier' meaning variously something necessary, winter forage, or nourishment. It is also the provision of food for both people and animals for a journey. The single appearance of this **crop** is in Prospero's colourful pre-nuptial masque where Iris praises the benevolence of the goddess of agriculture: 'Thy turfy mountains, where live nibbling sheep,/And flat meads thatch'd with stover, them to keep' (*TMP* 4.1.62–3). The implication here is of animal feed for sheep. Arden 2 (97) refers to stover as 'Winter food for cattle' and quotes Ovid, *Metamorphoses,* (v.116): 'Dame Ceres…made corne and stover soft to grow upon the ground'. Shakespeare's interesting choice of adjective 'thatch'd', images a matted layer, perhaps hinting at its function as thatch for roofing. Tusser (1570, November: 11) suggests stover was a troublesome crop that required careful attention: 'If houseroom will serve lay thy stoover up drye/And every sort by itselfe for to lie'. Drayton gives the same **plants** for thatching materials and winter fodder: 'To draw out **sedge** and **reed**, for thatch and stover fit' (1622, *Polyolbion* 24.145). Spier and Anderson (1985) enlists stover to support their argument that Shakespeare knew Tusser's work well, and that Shakespeare may have had a farming background.

straw (A) The usually dry **stalks** of cereal plants for litter and fodder for cattle, straw is also the unwanted parts of other **crops** including **peas** and **beans**. It had wide-ranging uses, as bedding, as fuel, for thatching, as a packing material; straw could also be woven or plaited to make a variety of domestic objects ranging from hats to beehives. As a single stalk, straw can suggest something worthless or feeble; alternatively it could indicate something highly inflammable. A man of straw suggests a counterfeit, an imaginary adversary, or an invented argument. 'To straw' is to feed animals straw, bed them down in straw; alternatively it is to **strew** as in to scatter or spread. An **oaten** pipe is made from oat straw; straw-coloured is the dun or neutral colour of straw.

  (B) Straw as synonymous with things weak and frail or worthless is used frequently, but so too is the material used as floor-covering or bedding. Its highly flammable nature is also significant. There are two cases of straw used for decorative rustic belts or hats. The lover's song in *PP* promises the young women clothes, flowers and appropriate accoutrements, including, 'A belt of straw and ivy buds,/With coral clasps and amber studs' (xix 13–14). The deserted young woman in *LC* is much less fortunate, or at a different stage in the relationship. She is described simply: 'Upon her head a platted hive of straw,/Which fortified her visage from the sun' (8–9). Straw as bedding is intimated when Parolles, disparaging Dumaine, says to his presumed captors, 'in his sleep he does little harm, save to his bed-clothes about him; but they know his conditions and lay him in straw' (*AWW* 4.3.256–8). Directed to draw Barnadine from his cell, Pompey, elevated to the status of assistant hangman, claims, 'he is coming. I hear his straw rustle' (*MM* 4.3.35–6). Reflecting on Lear's ordeal, Cordelia asks, 'wast thou fain, poor father,/To hovel thee with swine and rogues forlorn/In short and musty straw?' (*LR* 4.7.37–9). Falstaff's promise to Shallow that he will 'be the man yet that shall make you great', is met with scepticism: 'I cannot perceive how, unless you give me your doublet and stuff me out with straw' (*2H4* 5.5.79–82). The song that brings *LLL* to a close provides the only allusion to one of the traditional uses of straw: 'When shepherds pipe on oaten straws' (5.2.903).

The combustible nature of straw is exemplified both in love and politics. Prospero cautions Ferdinand, 'Look thou be true; do not give dalliance/Too much the rein. The strongest oaths are straw/To th'fire i'th'blood' (*TMP* 4.1.51–3). A young man denounces his lover's frailty, complaining, 'She burnt with love, as straw with fire flameth,/She burnt out love, as soon as straw out-burneth' (*PP* vii.13–14). Drawing Casca into the conspiracy, Cassius reasons, 'Those that with haste will make a mighty fire/Begin it with weak straws' (*JC* 1.3.107–8).

Straw as analogous to weakness or worthlessness is exhibited by the garrulous Pistol who, departing for war, cautions his new bride, 'the word is "Pitch and pay";/Trust none;/For oaths are straws, men's faiths are wafer-cakes' (*H5* 2.3.49–51). Straw as trivial or worthless is captured by Hermione during her trial: 'no life/(I prize it not a straw), but for mine honor,/Which I would free' (*WT* 3.2.109–11). Hamlet pressures the word when deriding the folly of Fortinbras' assault on Poland: 'Two thousand souls and twenty thousand ducats/Will not debate the question of this straw' (*HAM* 4.4.25–6). A few lines later, however, he maintains, 'Rightly to be great/Is not to stir without great argument,/But greatly to find quarrel in a straw/When honor's at the stake' (53–6). Only Bottom refers to the colour of straw. Contemplating his role in the play he says, 'I will discharge it in either your straw-color beard, your orange-tawny beard, your purple-in-grain beard, or your French-crown-color beard, your perfit yellow' (*MND* 1.2.93–6). 'Strawy' occurs only in *TRO*. The image occurs in Nestor's vivid description of the ubiquitous Hector annihilating the Greeks: 'then is he yonder,/And there the strawy Greeks, ripe for his edge,/Fall down before him like a mower's swath' (5.5.23–5).

(C) Boorde (1547) believes that straw and **rushes** can carry the plague; he recommends rooms be fumigated with his patent powder which included burnt juniper, **rosemary**, rushes, **laurel** and **marjoram**. Tusser (1570) says packing salt-fish in pease straw will prevent it **rotting**. He sets out straw as cattle fodder in order of quality, from **rye** as the best, through **wheat**, pease, to oat, **barley** and **hay**. Holinshed (1577, vol. 1:

358) suggests the destruction of woodland has led to the predominance in some places of less useful plants including **broom**, **turf**, **heath**, **furze**, ling, **brakes**, whins, **flags**, straw, **sedge**, **reed** and rush. Arnold (1988) in an inventory of the Queen's wardrobe notes a range of unusual colours including straw and **ash**, as well as **peach**, **orange**, **marigold**, **willow**, **chestnut**, citron as yellow, rush **green** and **carnation** red.

strawberry (A) *Fragaria* L. is a native **fruit**, long-used medicinally and as a food. Shakespeare's strawberry was the low-growing, small alpine *F. vesca* L., found in the wild, and cultivated in **gardens**; the modern large strawberry was not available until the nineteenth century. An easily recognizable pattern, the strawberry was replicated on clothing and wall-hangings, and had a range of contradictory symbolic associations including jealousy, rivalry and sexuality, purity and innocence; emblematically it was often shown with a serpent to suggest something both sweet, and threatening and hidden. Both **flower** and fruit were associated with the Virgin Mary.

(B) The paucity of mentions, there are only three, is in inverse proportion to its significance. The first allusion arises during the specially held meeting designed to effect Richard Gloucester's acquisition of the throne. Seeking to discompose those sitting around the table, Richard makes a seemingly harmless request: 'My Lord of Ely, when I was last in Holborn,/I saw good strawberries in your garden there./I do beseech you send for some of them' (*R3* 3.4.31–3). The Bishop, finding on his return that Richard and Buckingham have withdrawn, asks, 'Where is my lord the Duke of Gloucester? I have sent for these strawberries' (46–7). The innocuous strawberries acquire agency, contributing to a presentiment of terror. This scene is best described as Stalinesque. The significance attaching to this fruit in *H5* seems tame by comparison. Attempting to account for the sudden transformation of a dissolute prince into a peerless monarch, the Bishop of Ely uses a homely analogy:

> The strawberry grows underneath the nettle,
> And wholesome berries thrive and ripen best
> Neighbor'd by fruit of baser quality;
> And so the Prince obscur'd his contemplation
> Under the veil of wildness, which (no doubt)
> Grew like the summer grass, fastest by night,
> Unseen, yet crescive in his faculty.

(H5 1.1.60–6)

This delightful rationalization with its gentle pace and contemplative wisdom is a prelude to an agreement on the advantages to be gained from war with France. The Archbishop of Canterbury, espoused by Henry for his impartiality, will exert decisive influence in the decision-making process. Vested interests prevail as surely as strawberries 'grow best/Neighbor'd by fruit of grosser quality'. The handkerchief spotted with strawberries, Othello's first gift to Desdemona, plays a critical role in completing his descent into jealousy. Having obtained the handkerchief from Emilia,

Iago asks the Moor, 'Tell me but this,/Have you not sometimes seen a handkerchief/ Spotted with strawberries in your wive's hand?' (*OTH* 3.3.433–5). Later confronting Desdemona, Othello recounts its history and significance: 'there's magic in the web of it' (3.4.69). It is the contrariety of the symbolism that is most telling. Named by Pliny and Virgil *Fraga vesca*, the delicately **fragrant** ones, the positive associations apply to Desdemona: abundance, chastity, paradise, heaven; the negative aspects, sensuality and eroticism, are ascribed to Desdemona by Othello once he is in thrall to jealousy.

(C) Turner (1548: 180) suggests the general availability of the **plant**: 'Fragaria, the strawbery leafe whose fruit is called a strawbery. Every man knoweth wel inough where strawberies growe.' Hill (1577) says strawberries are easy to cultivate, preferring the shadow of other plants, and even though they grow low on the **earth**, they have a 'marvellous innocency' and are not affected by any crawling poisonous insects. Holinshed (1577, vol. 3: 380) includes the story of Richard III and the Bishop of Ely. Paradin (1591: 83) describes an emblem of a strawberry plant entwined by a snake with the motto: 'the adder lurketh privilie in the grasse'. Palter (2002) includes a chapter on the strawberry in art and literature. McLeod (2008) says the fruit represented temptation, but also symbolized purity, a chaste bride and the delights of the marriage bed; she gives the Marian symbolism of the strawberry as does Fisher (2011). Heilmeyer (2001: 28) notes, 'the poet Ovid describes wild strawberries in his *Metamorphoses* as the fruit of the Golden Age'. She also discusses its role in Christian iconography and its duality.

strew, strewments, strow (A) To strew or strow is to spread loosely, often deliberately. Strewments are **rushes**, **straw**, **herbs** or **flowers** spread over a floor or another surface for the purpose of decoration. They were comforting, a sign of hospitality and cleanliness, and served to deaden noise. Some plants were chosen for their **smell**: **mint** was thought to deter fleas; **rosemary** and **wormwood** to deter other insects. Plants such as rosemary and **rue** were thought to counter the spread of plague, while strewing **marigolds** was associated with death. Strew could be used figuratively.

(B) The importance of strewing in households is evidenced by Grumio when he questions his fellow servants about their preparedness for Petruchio's arrival: 'Is supper ready, the house trimm'd, rushes strew'd, cobwebs swept...?' (*SHR* 4.1.45–9). Addressing her companions, Perdita specifies the flowers she wishes she had, 'To make you garlands of, and my sweet friend,/To strew him o'er and o'er!' (*WT* 4.4.128–9). The welcome given to Julius Caesar by the Roman citizenry is abhorrent to his political opponents: 'And do you now strew flowers in his way,/That comes in triumph over Pompey's blood?' (*JC* 1.1.50–1). Flavius the tribune is here alluding to Caesar's victory over Pompey's sons. Volumnia is accorded universal acclaim for dissuading her son from destroying Rome: 'Behold our patroness, the life of Rome!/Call all your tribes together, praise the gods,/And make triumphant fires! Strew flowers before them' (*COR* 5.5.1–3). As Mark Antony leaves for Rome, Cleopatra bids him a gracious farewell: 'Upon your sword/Sit laurel victory, and smooth success/Be strew'd before your feet!'

(*ANT* 1.3.99–101). Responding to Laertes' protest at the truncated funeral obsequies for Ophelia, the priest retorts, 'Yet here she is allow'd her virgin crants,/Her maiden strewments, and the bringing home/Of bell and burial' (*HAM* 5.1.232–4). She receives rites in excess of those normally granted to one whose death was 'doubtful' (227). Gertrude conflates the marriage and funeral strewments: 'I hop'd thou shouldst have been my Hamlet's wife./I thought thy bride-bed to have deck'd, sweet maid,/And not have strew'd thy grave' (244–6). Earlier in the play Horatio says of Ophelia, ''Twere good she were spoken with, for she may strew/Dangerous conjectures in ill-breeding minds'(4.5.14–15). A deft political question is posed by the Duchess of York seeking to identify those who have gained positions of power under the new regime of Henry IV: 'Who are the violets now/That strew the green lap of the new-come spring?' (*R2* 5.2.46–7). An intriguing case arises in *TRO*. The Grecian commander, Agamemnon, extending a gracious welcome to Hector, endeavours to create a moment of tranquillity in the midst of a war of attrition: 'What's past and what's to come is strew'd with husks/And formless ruin of oblivion' (4.5.166–7). As the King of Navarre and his associates surrender to love, Berowne anticipates the celebratory entertainment: 'For revels, dances, masks, and merry hours/Forerun fair Love, strewing her way with flowers' (*LLL* 4.3.376–7).

(C) Amherst (1595) believes that the custom of strewing flowers with rushes to spread on floors began in the sixteenth century. Batey (1986) notes that the Queen took a personal strewing woman for her apartments with her on all her progresses round the country. Knight (2009: 115–16) cites contemporaries on the attention devoted to the use of such **plants**.

sycamore (A) *Acer pseudoplatanus* L. is a large **tree** of genus *Acer* L., the maples, a widely-growing naturalized introduction probably prior to 1000 A.D.; it was valued for its **wood** and as a **shady** ornamental tree. The same name – sycamore or sycomore – is confusingly given to a species of **fig**, *Ficus sycomorus* L. common in Egypt and Syria, which bears some resemblance to the **mulberry**. Some commentators suggest further confusion of identity with the **plane** tree, *Platanus* L., both because of the name and some similarity between the **leaves** of the two trees.

(B) The sycamore's symbolic association with love-sickness is clearly evidenced in two of its mentions – obliquely in the third. Benvolio recounts to Romeo's parents his observation of their love-sick son and his studied isolation: 'Where, underneath the grove of sycamore/That westward rooteth from this city side,/So early walking did I see your son' (*ROM* 1.1.121–3). The 'grove of sycamore' lends strong emotional pressure to the romantic idiom. The contrast between this picture of self-indulgence and Romeo's linguistic vitality when he falls in love with Juliet could hardly be more marked. In a scene imbued with genuine longing and intensity of feeling, Desdemona invokes unrequited love with her recollection of the 'willow song'. Another layer of tragic compression emerges when having recounted the sad story of Barbary whose lover went mad, she sings, 'The poor soul sat sighing by a sycamore tree,/Sing all a green willow' (*OTH* 4.3.40–1). The polished French courtier Boyet explains to the Princess how he overheard the plans of the King of Navarre: 'Under the cool shade of a sycamore/I thought to close mine eyes some half an hour' (*LLL* 5.2.89–90). While the witty Boyet could only be in love with himself, as Berowne implies (5.2.317–34), the young men in question are all desperately love-sick. Unlike the other comedies, these young men do not succeed in winning their loves within the time frame of the play. The sycamore does, therefore, cast a dark shadow as well as a playful one in this highly patterned and verbally versatile comedy.

(C) Parkinson (1629) lists it as the acer, noting its value in providing shade, but with nothing else to recommend it. In 1640 he writes of the sycomorus, as the true sycamore or mulberry fig. Culpeper (1653: 370–1) says the acer is 'vulgarly called sycamores in England' that they are a kind of maple, but the virtues he enumerates all belong to the fig. The sycamore was planted by the Cecils at both Theobalds and Wimbledon. Mabey (1996) analyses its place in the English countryside.

T

tennis (A) Now known as real tennis, the game possibly originated in Paris. Courts are open or covered; they include angled **walls** and a roofed penthouse. Such courts were a feature of sixteenth-century gardens. Tennis attracted people from a wide range of social backgrounds from royalty to apprentices; it fell into disrepute because of the associated betting. Its arcane rules include laying and beating **chases**, and hitting the ball into the hazard gallery or into hazard. Modern lawn tennis is a nineteenth-century development of real tennis.

(B) The wide-ranging references to the game in the plays suggest that awareness of it was not confined to the social elite. Wanting Reynaldo to gain knowledge of Laertes' behaviour in Paris, Polonius advises him to insinuate himself with strangers using such lines as, 'There falling out at tennis' (*HAM* 2.1.57). There is also a French connection in *H8*. Lovell derides courtiers who adopt French manners and 'The faith they have in tennis and tall stockings' (1.3.30). Humouring his deranged daughter who ascribes astonishing talents to an imaginary horse, the Jailer says, 'Having these virtues,/I think he might be brought to play at tennis' (*TNK* 5.2.55–6). Hal, patronizing Poins, points up the disparity between them: 'What a disgrace is it in me to remember thy name, or to know thy face to-morrow…or to bear the inventory of thy shirts, as one for superfluity, and another for use! But the tennis-court-keeper knows better than I, for it is a low ebb of linen with thee when thou keepest not racket there' (*2H4* 2.2.13–20). Curiously, 'tennis-court' is used only once and is employed figuratively. Having survived shipwreck, Pericles appeals to fishermen as 'A man whom both the waters and the wind,/In that vast tennis-court, hath made the ball/For them to play upon, entreats you pity him' (*PER* 2.1.59–61). Commenting on Benedick's recent removal of his beard, Claudio claims, 'the old ornament of his cheek hath already stuff'd tennis-balls' (*ADO* 3.2.46–7). The revelation that the 'tun of treasure' sent by the Dauphin consists of 'tennis balls' provokes a response replete with the technical terms of the game. Prefiguring a fearsome invasion, it is the moment when Henry V makes an unofficial declaration of war:

> When we have match'd our *rackets* to these *balls*,
> We will in France, by God's grace, play a *set*
> Shall strike his father's crown into the *hazard*.
> Tell him he hath made a *match* with such a *wrangler*

That all the *courts* of France will be disturb'd
With *chaces*.

(H5 1.2.255–66)

This display of verbal panache is only the beginning of a speech of almost 40 lines.

(C) Elizabethan literature suggests the game was widely known and played. Elyot (1541: 12–13) recommends it as 'swift exercise without violence' which 'do exercise the bodye commodiousely'. Stubbes (1585) inveighs against the evils of tennis and **bowls**, but acknowledges 'these be the only exercises used in every man's house al the yere through'. Massinger's Luke warns that the tennis court is an attraction that lures the apprentices from their work (1632, *The City Madam* 5.2.49). Husselby and Henderson (2002) give details of the 'sports complex' at Cecil House in the Strand, accessed by a separate street entrance, suggesting its use was not limited to members of the household. Henderson (2005) points out Henry VIII's devotion to sport, and includes the most comprehensive list of contemporary courts. Plate 31 in the Riverside Shakespeare illustrates real tennis; the modern court differs little, and such courts can be found in America and Australia, as well as across Europe. De Luze (1933, trans. 1979) and Noel and Clark (1991) give detailed histories of the game.

thicket, coppice, copse (A) A dense **growth** of **shrubs**, small **trees** and underwood, or a **brake**, a thicket was made up of low trees or **bushes** growing closely together. Thickets provided places of refuge both for man and hunted animals. Copse or coppice is a small wood or thicket, where the trees and shrubs are regularly cut or 'coppiced' for fuel and other practical purposes.

(B) 'Thicket' receives six mentions; 'coppice' and 'copse' one each. Plotting the escape of his brother Edward, Richard Gloucester reassures his associates, 'Leave off to wonder why I drew you hither/Into this chiefest thicket of the park' (*3H6* 4.5.2–3). The not unkindly outlaws in *TGV* express confidence that they will soon capture Silvia's guide, Sir Eglamour: 'the thicket is beset, he cannot scape' (5.3.11). This cover is the source of more innocent concealment in *TNK*. The Schoolmaster choreographs his fellow performers to add an element of surprise to the Duke's entertainment: 'For why, here stand I; here the Duke comes; there are you,/Close in the thicket' (3.5.12–13). The only metaphorical use is in *TRO*. Achilles' refusal to leave his tent for dialogue with the Greek leadership exasperates Ulysses: 'There is no tarrying here, the hart Achilles/ Keeps thicket' (2.3.258–9). Playfully undermining the entertainment provided for her party the Princess asks, 'where is the bush/That we must stand and play the murtherer in?'. The Forester, having found the ideal spot for the Princess's success in the hunt, advises, 'Hereby, upon the edge of yonder coppice,/A stand where you may make the fairest shoot' (*LLL* 4.1.7–10). In this play a simple comment generally provokes verbal elaboration; here the Princess exercises her wit by downgrading the 'coppice' to a 'bush' and transforming the elegantly devised hunt to slaughter. Adonis is about to make his escape from Venus' amorous embraces when his horse is distracted and bolts: 'But lo from forth a copse that neighbors by,/A breeding jennet, lusty, young, and proud,/Adonis' trampling courser doth espy' (*VEN* 259–61).

thistle (A) A plant of the *Carduus* L. genus and other related genera, thistle could refer to any prickly **plant**, including **eryngium**; they are invasive **weeds**, their globular, purple **flower**-heads making them very attractive to **bees**. Emblematically thistles can suggest prickles and **thorns;** thistles symbolize other irritations, including neglected **husbandry**. The donkey is the only animal to graze on thistles, otherwise generally regarded by horticulturalists as useless. A stylized thistle shape featured in needlework of the time.

(B) The first of the three mentions of this plant reveals that it is attractive to bees: Bottom instructs Cobweb, 'kill me a red-hipp'd humble-bee on the top of a thistle; and, good mounsieur, bring me the honeybag' (*MND* 4.1.11–13). The plant's association with neglect is present in Burgundy's description of French agriculture in the wake of the English invasion: 'and nothing teems/But hateful docks, rough thistles, kecksies, burs,/Losing both beauty and utility' (*H5* 5.2.51–3). The thistle's medicinal value is implied during the teasing of Beatrice in *ADO*. Marrying Beatrice's need for a cold-cure and her new-found love for Benedick, Margaret tells her, 'Get you some of this distill'd *carduus benedictus*, and lay it to your heart; it is the only thing for a qualm', precipitating Hero's barb, 'There thou prick'st her with a thistle' (3.4.73–6).

(C) Tusser (1573) says thistles should be weeded out in May before the **crop** is cut as they will damage the tools at **harvest**. Langham (1597) provides the most extensive list of ailments which the thistle could treat. Peacham (1612) sees the **rose** and thistle, which was already the emblem of Scotland, growing together as a symbol of unity. Mabey (1996) details the wide range of members of the thistle family and their place in the countryside. Heilmeyer (2001: 26) cites its classical and Christian associations. See also **carduus benedictus**.

thorn (A) A sharp, pointed, rigid growth in the **stem** of a **plant**, or elsewhere, a **thorn** is a spine or prickle. It can also indicate the **wood** or **branch** of a thorn **tree** or **bush**, or any plant that bears thorns or prickles, including **rose, bramble, brier, hawthorn** or whitethorn, and blackthorn. To thorn is to plant with thorn bushes or lay a quick-set **hedge**. A deliberately constructed thorn barrier is generally perceived as purposeful, while thorns individually are seen to be threatening, hurtful and damaging. Figuratively, a thorn can indicate anything causing grief or pain.

(B) The use of 'thorn' for a rosebush is intimated by Theseus when warning Hermia against the privations of a nunnery: 'But earthlier happy is the rose distill'd,/Than that which withering on the virgin thorn/Grows, lives, and dies in single blessedness' (*MND* 1.1.76–8). This is also the meaning indicated by Somerset in the Temple Garden when he invites potential supporters to 'Pluck a red rose off this thorn with me' (*1H6* 2.4.33). Later in the scene he alludes to the spiky stem: 'Hath not thy rose a thorn, Plantagenet?' calling forth the riposte, 'Ay sharp and piercing, to maintain his truth' (69–70). At the close of the Battle of Tewkesbury the victorious King Edward IV comments on the resistance of the Lancastrian Prince Edward: 'What? can so young a thorn begin to prick?' (*3H6* 5.5.13). Alluding to the pangs of love, the Countess contemplates Helena's longing for Bertram: 'this thorn/Doth to our rose of youth rightly belong' (*AWW* 1.3.129–30). Later in the play Diana draws on a related metaphorical use when resisting Bertram's blandishments: 'but when you have our roses,/You barely leave our thorns to prick ourselves,/And mock us with our bareness' (4.2.18–20). In its literal sense 'thorny' is used once. In *SHR* the Lord and his men attempt to interest Sly with descriptions of paintings: 'Or Daphne roaming through a thorny wood,/Scratching her legs that one shall swear she bleeds' (*Ind* 2.57–8). Metaphorically it is employed twice. Encountering Queen Margaret and her army, King Edward encourages his men, 'Brave followers, yonder stands the thorny wood,/Which by the heavens' assistance and your strength,/Must by the roots be hewn up yet ere night' (*3H6* 5.4.67–9). Ophelia responds to Laertes' moral injunction with the caution:

> Do not, as some ungracious pastors do,
> Show me the steep and thorny way to heaven,
> Whiles, like a puff'd and reckless libertine,
> Himself the primrose path of dalliance treads,

> *(HAM 1.3.47–50)*

The only use of 'thornier' occurs in *PER* when Boult reassures Bawd that the recalcitrant Marina will soon be made to accept her function in the brothel: 'And if she were a thornier piece of ground than she is, she shall be plough'd' (4.6.144–5).

(C) The symbolism of thorns was widespread, and included the Christian crown of thorns. Colonna (1499) demonstrates the universality of their iconography, including references to a tangle of thorns, rough places crammed with thorns, dense thorn bushes and love's thorny insults; he also uses them to suggest a threatening place. Tusser (1573) emphasizes the need for the good **husbandman** to remove thorns from his crops, while Hill (1577) gives detailed instructions for making a functional and decorative thorn hedge which included **gooseberries** and hawthorn. Early modern poets employ the thorn to suggest the myth of Philomela, the princess transformed into a nightingale which was thought to sing when pierced by a thorn (Ault 1949, Smith and Marindin 1932). Christianson (2005) gives details of the plants that were bought for Henry VIII in huge numbers, including hundreds of whitethorn plants, and thousands of other hedging plants. See also **hawthorn, thistle**.

thyme, time, tine (A) *Thymus* L. is a low-growing **shrubby plant** with aromatic **leaves**; the family includes *T. vulgaris* L., the **garden** thyme of Mediterranean origin now naturalized, and *T. serpyllum* L., a native plant of **heath** and breckland. Thyme featured frequently in **knot-gardens** for its **fragrant** leaves, and for its culinary uses; it was often combined with **hyssop**. It had a wide range of medicinal applications, and served as a **strewing herb**.

(B) The first of the three mentions of this plant occurs in the opening line of Oberon's lyrical description of Titania's bower: 'I know a bank where the wild thyme blows'(*MND* 2.1.249). The 'wild thyme' 'blows' or 'blooms', and perhaps casts its perfume into the air. With explicit reference to the plant's scent, thyme is present in the flower-song that forms part of the festivity in the opening scene of *TNK*: 'Maiden pinks, of odor faint,/Daisies smell-less, yet most quaint,/And sweet thyme true' (1.1.4–6). The third case has been the subject of much confusion as a result of different spellings and editorial interventions. Iago's chastisement of Roderigo for doting on Desdemona ('it is not in my virtue to amend it') takes the form of a horticultural analogy: 'Our bodies are our gardens, to the which our wills are gardeners; so that if we will plant nettles or sow lettuce, set hyssop and weed up tine...why, the power and corrigible authority of this lies in our wills' (*OTH* 1.3. 320–6). Riverside opts for 'tine', transposing the 'Time' of F1 to 'tine' meaning 'vetch' or 'tares' in preference to the 'thyme' of Q1. Given the traditional complementarity of hyssop and thyme in horticultural practice, Iago would seem to be referring to the herb thyme. A source of uncertainty arises from 'weed up', though it is conceivable that to 'weed up' thyme is to keep it in check. Incapable of subduing his own jealousy, Iago delights in a facile comparison to bemuse and control Roderigo. Iago's homily has layers of meaning, one of which Arden 3 (156) instances as a biblical allusion to Galatians 6.7: 'whatsoever a man soweth, that shall he also reap'. Moreover, his horticultural commonplace has unintended implications. Just as opposites are deemed to flourish best when placed together in a garden, so too the outwardly incompatible Othello and Desdemona discover mutuality.

(C) Langham (1597), Riddle (1992) and Rowland (1981) all suggest the use of thyme in gynaecology and as an abortifacient. Markham (1631) includes it in a patent medicine and as flavouring for meat; he notes its distillation in a **limbeck** with other herbs to make a compress. Parkinson (1629) details several varieties, noting that thyme, **marjoram** and **savory** are often planted to edge knots; he comments that as they do not keep a satisfactory shape for more than a year, they are not the best herbs for this purpose.

till, tillage, tilth (A) To work the **land**, tilling is essential preparation for **sowing** and **planting crops**; it can also be to raise the crop, cultivate the land and individual plants. Till also suggests human **fertility** and procreation. Figuratively, it can mean to cultivate the mind or a particular virtue.

(B) 'Till' is never used in a horticultural or agricultural sense. Both 'till'd' and 'tillage' appear once each; 'tilth' twice. *TMP* provides a literal example. Enumerating the principles of government for his imagined commonwealth Gonzalo maintains there will be 'no kind of traffic.../.../Bourn, bound of land, tilth, vineyard, none' (2.1.149–53). All productive resources are to be held in common. In *SON* 3 the speaker encourages the young man to marry and procreate, asserting he is not constrained by lack of opportunity: 'For where is she so fair whose unear'd womb/Disdains the tillage of thy husbandry?' (5–6). This image, with a pun on 'husband' and 'husbandman', operates too in Lucio's uncharacteristically beautiful description of Juliet's pregnancy – a consequence of Claudio's 'husbandry': 'even so her plenteous womb/Expresseth his full tilth and husbandry' (*MM* 1.4.43–4). Lucio appeals to Isabella to petition for her brother's reprieve because it is a capital offence for unmarried men like Claudio to father children in Angelo's Vienna. Falstaff is an improbable character to be associated with tilling, but like others detached from physical labour the metaphor comes naturally to him. Soliloquizing on Hal's superiority to his father and to his brother John he reasons: 'for the cold blood he did naturally inherit of his father, he hath, like lean, sterile, and bare land, manur'd, husbanded, and till'd with excellent endeavour of drinking good and good store of fertile sherris, that he is become very hot and valiant' (*2H4* 4.3.117–22). Only Falstaff could deploy the carefully managed process of **husbandry** to justify the consumption of 'sack'.

(C) Drayton writes of 'earth by nature made to till' suggesting good agricultural land or 'fruitful tillage', and refers to the wild boar 'whose tusks turn'd up our tilths'. He says that Albion's daughter Tenet 'doth only give herself to tillage of the ground' indicating the mythology behind the fertility of Kent (1622, *Polyolbion* 3.114, 9.18, 13.342, 18.723). Gardeners continue to create a fine tilth for **sowing** and planting.

toadstool A Basidiomycete fungus with a round disc-like top and slender **stalk**, a toadstool resembles and is sometimes called a **mushroom**. Toadstool is popularly used to refer to poisonous or inedible fungi, as distinct from edible 'mushrooms'. The sole use of the word occurs during a quarrel between Ajax and Thersites. The illiterate warrior demands, 'Toadstool! Learn me the proclamation' (*TRO* 2.1.21). Thersites is a poor physical specimen so this derogatory name-calling no doubt draws on all the unsavoury associations of this fungus including its noxious potential. Arden 3 (183) suggests that there is also the implication of 'the stool or excrement of a toad'. Early modern writers agree on the unpleasant associations of the toadstool: Spenser calls it 'the grieslie todestoole'(ed. 1999, *The Shepheardes Calendar,* December: 69). Cogan (1584: 263) believes the appearance of many toadstools is a sign that the plague is imminent, commenting 'many Wormes breede of putrefaction of the earth; Toade stooles and rotten herbes abound'. Gerard (1597: 1384–7) has toadstools and mushrooms under one entry, saying that most are venomous and few good for eating. At the time all fungi were associated with fairies, good or bad. See **mushroom**.

tree (A) A perennial **plant** with a self-supporting **woody** main **stem** or trunk, a tree usually develops offshoots or **branches** at some distance from the **ground**; it often grows to a considerable height. It is distinguished from **bushes** and **shrubs** by its **growth** habit, although tree can also designate tall bushes, shrubs and perennial plants. In literature, trees could be personified or given human characteristics. Figuratively, tree could suggest height and upright stance, stand for the head of a family or a lineage, with a decaying tree representing old age. From ancient times trees were worshipped as the home of the gods. They were planted to create sacred spaces, and seen as symbols of fertility and renewal. Depending on whether they flourished or withered they could symbolize life or death. 'Tree' was a frequent synonym for both the Christian Cross and the gallows.

(B) Trees appear with great frequency in the plays and poems. The Forest of Arden in *AYL* is a prolific source. The first line of Amiens' song, 'Under the greenwood tree' (2.5.1) provided the title for an early Hardy novel. Celebrating his love, Orlando announces: 'O, Rosalind, these trees shall be my books,/And in their barks my thoughts I'll character' (3.2.5–6). Celia laughingly says of Orlando, 'I found him under a tree, like a dropp'd acorn' (3.2.234–5). The tree's component parts as an ideal measure of fittingness is adopted by Maria when playfully claiming, 'Dumaine is mine, as sure as bark on tree' (*LLL* 5.2.285). Three imaginative applications are found in *ANT*. Octavius Caesar describes Antony's fortitude as he retreated over the Alps: 'Yea, like the stag, when snow the pasture sheets,/The barks of trees thou brows'd' (1.4.65–6). The same speaker provides a remarkably colourful and conceited image when chastising his sister for returning to Rome with so little ceremony: 'the trees by th'way/Should have borne men, and expectation fainted,/Longing for what it had not' (3.6.46–8). Antony also uses a conceit. He conveys his feeling of dissolution by describing how clouds image physical features:

> Sometime we see a cloud that's dragonish,
> A vapor sometime like a bear or lion,
> A tower'd citadel, a pendant rock,
> A forked mountain, or blue promontory
> With trees upon't that nod unto the world,
> And mock our eyes with air.
>
> *(4.14.2–7).*

Some of the figurative uses show trees suffusing a scene with delicacy. Communing with Jessica in the **garden**, Lorenzo creates a moment where past and present meld:

> The moon shines bright. In such a night as this,
> When the sweet wind did gently kiss the trees,
> And they did make no noise, in such a night
> Troilus methinks mounted the Trojan walls,
> And sigh'd his soul toward the Grecian tents,
> Where Cressid lay that night.
>
> *(MV 5.1.1–6)*

Othello asks to be remembered by the Venetians as 'one whose subdue'd eyes,/Albeit unused to the melting mood,/Drops tears as fast as the Arabian trees/Their medicinable gum' (*OTH* 5.2.348–51). Richard Gloucester employs a memorable image when describing the response to Warwick's portrayal of York's death: 'That all the standers-by had wet their cheeks/Like trees bedash'd with rain' (*R3* 1.2.162–3). Buckingham collusively importunes Richard Gloucester to accept the crown, but is cunningly rebuffed: 'The royal tree hath left us royal fruit,/Which mellow'd by the stealing hours of time,/Will well become the seat of majesty' (3.7.167–9). Audley likens 'the gilded upright pikes' of the French to 'Straight trees of gold' (*E3* 4.4.25–6). Appalling human or supernatural events are often epitomized by the up-rooting of trees. Moments before being murdered by Richard Gloucester, Henry VI vociferates, 'The owl shriek'd at thy birth, an evil sign;/The night-crow cried, aboding luckless time;/Dogs howl'd, and hideous tempest shook down trees' (*3H6* 5.6.44–6). The ominous nature of the **cypress** gives vitality to Suffolk's cursing of his enemies: 'Their sweetest shade a grove of cypress trees!' (*2H6* 3.2.323). Stephano's terse reminder to his associate that he is a subordinate is both comic and sinister: 'Trinculo, keep a good tongue in your head. If you prove a mutineer – the next tree!' (*TMP* 3.2.35–6). Henry VIII exposes the folly of Wolsey's imposition of excessive taxation by drawing on the analogy of the tree: 'Why, we take/From every tree, lop, bark, and part o'th'timber;/And, though we leave it with a root, thus hack'd,/The air will drink the sap' (*H8* 1.2.95–8).

(C) Tree management in **woodland**, **orchards** and gardens occupied considerable space in Elizabethan gardening manuals. Throughout *The Shepheardes Calendar* (1579) and *The Faerie Queene* (1596), Spenser has instances of aged and lofty trees, using 'tree' to suggest the human lineage. The Preface to the King James Bible (1611) describes the word of God as 'not a herb but a tree, or rather a whole paradise of trees of life', demonstrating how deeply entrenched was the tree metaphor in the language of Christianity. Walsham (2011) points out the role of trees in religious and cultural identity. Tigner (2012) examines the link between *R2* and the biblical concept of the Tree of Life.

trowel A hand tool with a flat or slightly rounded metal plate fixed to a short wooden handle, a trowel is still used by a range of craftsmen including masons, builders and plasterers for spreading, moulding and smoothing. A trowel as a **garden** tool for small-scale planting dates from the eighteenth century, although contemporary illustrations show something similar. Its use in *AYL* is proverbial. Celia responds to Touchstone's contribution to a verbal game with the riposte: 'Well said – that was laid on with a trowel' (1.2.106). The imputation is a lack of finesse or nicety, seeming to draw on the trowel's function for applying mortar: probably a reference to an implement useful for building a garden wall rather than to one for planting.

turf (A) A sod or piece of **grass**, a slab cut from the surface of the **soil** with grass and other **plants** growing on it, turf can symbolize possession of **land**. Turf is also the covering of grass and other plants which forms grassland. A turf is a slab or piece of peat **dug** as fuel. 'Turves' were used to create seats in medieval gardens.

(B) Four of the seven allusions pertain to turf as a pillow or seat; one relates to a fortification; one disparagingly to a rustic; in *E3* the Countess of Salisbury provides an elaborate contrast between substrata and surface, 'the upper turf of earth' (1.2.152). Prospero's masque, a rich source for plants and agricultural activities, includes the sole use of 'turfy' – grazing land. Identifying Ceres as the giver of nature's fecundity, Iris alludes to her 'turfy mountains, where live nibbling sheep,/And flat meads thatch'd with stover, them to keep' (*TMP* 4.1.62–3). Inviting Celia and Ganymede/Rosalind to observe the courtship of Silvius and Phoebe, Corin, the old shepherd offers: 'Mistress and master, you have oft inquired/After the shepherd that complain'd of love,/Who you saw sitting by me on the turf' (*AYL* 3.4.47–9). Lost in the Athenian wood with his lover Hermia, Lysander attempts to organize their sleeping arrangements: 'One turf shall serve as pillow for us both,/One heart, one bed, two bosoms, and one troth' (*MND* 2.2.41–2). Henry V is less enthusiastic about the adequacy of turf as a pillow, especially French turf. Encountering Erpingham in the early hours of the morning, before the battle of Agincourt, he observes, 'Good morrow, old Sir Thomas Erpingham./A good soft pillow for that good white head/Were better than a churlish turf of France' (*H5* 4.1.13–15). Ophelia in her torment sings of her dead father: 'He is dead and gone,/At his head a grass-green turf,/At his heels a stone' (*HAM* 4.5.30–2). Referring to the narrow lane where an old man and his two sons thwarted the Roman army, Posthumus describes it as 'ditch'd, and wall'd with turf' (*CYM* 5.3.14). Here turf forms part of a modest but critical fortification. Commending the response given by Costard, designated 'Clown', the 'Pedant' Holofernes condescends: 'a good lustre of conceit in a turf of earth; fire enough for a flint, pearl enough for a swine: 'tis pretty; it is well' (*LLL* 4.2.87–9). This, the only figurative example, reveals the estimation of the rustic and the magnitude of the distance between the educated and the uneducated – which is no more nor less than it is between the gentlemen aristocrats and Holofernes who, later in the play, censures their supercilious behaviour: 'This is not generous, not gentle, not humble' (5.2.629). One of Christopher Sly's cronies is named Peter Turph (*SHR* Ind.2.94).

(C) Dürer's painting in 1503 of *The Great Piece of Turf* is an early example of accurate botanical observation and includes a considerable variety of plants and grass. Pavord (2005: 141) provides a reproduction of this famous painting. Amherst (1895) instances a turf terrace walk at the Cecil house at Wimbledon.

turnip *Brassica oleracea* L., *ssp. rapa* is a **root** vegetable, the **leaves** of which provide greens and also serve as animal fodder. It has been cultivated since ancient times and was probably a Roman introduction. At the time, the leaves were more widely eaten than the roots, which were thought to be unpalatable and to have too carminative an effect. This root **crop** is mentioned in a comic moment in *WIV*. Anne Page, already in love with Fenton, expresses her disgust at her mother's choice, the French doctor, Caius: 'Alas, I had rather be set quick i'th'earth,/And bowl'd to death with turnips!' (3.4.86–7). Centred on a middle-class community the play has an abundance of colloquial sayings and the highest proportion of prose in the canon. The Arden 3 edition of *STM* contains a section of the play not included in *Riverside*. At the opening of sc. 4 Clown Betts, preparing with others to assail immigrants, cries out, 'Come, come, we'll tickle their turnips, we'll butter their boxes! Shall strangers rule the roast?'. This outpouring of xenophobia creates a scene of black comedy. Turnips were largely eaten by the poor in soups and pottages, although Markham (1631) suggests adding turnips to compound **salads**. Hill (1577: 211) gives extensive details on its cultivation and medicinal uses, noting 'it removeth the venereal act'. Chartres and Hey (eds), (1990) details how the Protestant immigration of the later sixteenth century from continental Europe was largely responsible for the introduction of root vegetables.

twig (A) A slender shoot from a **branch** or **stem**, a **twig** is also a metaphor for youth and inexperience. Twigs covered in '**lime**', a viscous substance usually extracted from the **berries** of **mistletoe**, were used to trap birds.

(B) Of its five mentions, two are directly horticultural, two relate to limed twigs to catch birds, and one to the birch rod for beating. The **Gardener** in *R2* observing the **apricot tree** laden with **fruit** instructs his assistant, 'Give some supportance to the bending twigs' (3.4.32). Citing the neglect of French agriculture following the English invasion, Burgundy laments, 'her hedges even-pleach'd,/Like prisoners wildly overgrown with hair,/Put forth disorder'd twigs' (*H5* 5.2.42–4). Both cases in *AWW* are figurative. Mariana cautions Diana against the blandishments of the French troops: 'Many a maid hath been seduc'd by them, and the misery is, example, that so terrible shows in the wrack of maidenhood, cannot for all that dissuade succession, but that they are lim'd with twigs that threatens them' (3.5.20–4). The First Lord, about to expose the boastful Parolles, prepares to close the trap: 'I must go look my twigs. He shall be caught' (3.6.107–8). To justify his departure the Duke maintains his governance has been too lax:

> Now, as fond fathers,
> Having bound up the threat'ning twigs of birch,
> Only to stick it in their children's sight
> For terror, not to use, in time the rod
> Becomes more mock'd than fear'd; so our decrees,
> Dead to infliction, to themselves are dead,
> And liberty plucks justice by the nose;
>
> *(MM 1.3.23–9)*

(C) Consadine's (2003: 160–6) complicated proposal of 'twigged' in place of 'twilled' in *TMP* (4.1.64) seems unlikely. Spenser includes baskets made of twigs (ed. 1999, *Prothalamion*, 24–5).

twilled (A) As the only recorded use of twilled as trimmed, earlier commentators either ignored the word, or turned it and **pioned** with which it is associated, into **plants** ranging from **willow** to **peony**. Modern vernacular Warwickshire use of 'twilled' meaning 'trimmed' has been reported to the authors.

(B) Iris acclaims the fertility-inducing powers of Ceres with the attractive but obscure description, 'Thy banks with pioned and twilled brims,/Which spongy April at thy hest betrims/To make cold nymphs chaste crowns' (*TMP* 4.1.64–6). Arden 3 (247) comments: 'The most persuasive explanation of this long-debated phrase seems to be that the meadow's banks are lacerated or trenched (*pioned*) by the currents of streams or drainage ditches and tangled with exposed roots, but whether the phrase describes natural erosion or human efforts to prevent further damage (i.e. *twilled* or woven with sticks) has no consensus.' The specific plants previously proposed by editors such as 'lilied' or 'willow'd' have not gained general acceptance. Arden 2 (97) provides a summary of the more interesting explanations including Massingham's contention that 'pionies' is a local name for a variety of wild orchis, but leans towards Harrison's interpretation of 'pioned' and 'twilled' as referring to 'dug' and 'woven'. There is no definitive answer but the picture implies a **bank** of interweaving materials creating an environment conducive to the proliferation of **flowers** ideal for fashioning into 'chaste crowns', **wreathes** or **garlands**.

(C) Harrison (1943) and Fox (1957) bear out the interpretation of twilled as meaning woven or layered **hedges** on top of or beside a river bank. Consadine's complicated proposal of 'twigged' in place of 'twilled' is unpersuasive (2003: 160–6). For excellent summaries of the debates and contributions on 'pioned and twilled brims' see Arden 2 (97–8); Arden 3 (247); Fox, 'A crux in "*The Tempest*"', N&Q, 202, n.s.4.; Thomas P. Harrison, 'A note on *The Tempest*: a sequel' (1957), 515–16 *MLN* 58, June (1943), 422–6. Christiansen gives details of banks at Hampton Court being strengthened in this way under Henry VIII (2005: 103). See **pioned**.

V

vegetive (A) Pertaining to or characteristic of vegetables or **plants**; vegetive was rarely used to indicate a particular vegetable.

(B) The word 'vegetives', unique to *PER*, represents plants as storehouses of curative properties requiring careful analysis to elicit their efficacious attributes. During an early morning encounter with servants and visitors, Cerimon, 'a lord of Ephesus' and a medical practitioner, reflects on his vocation:

> 'Tis known, I ever
> Have studied physic; through which secret art,
> By turning o'er authorities, I have,
> Together with my practice, made familiar
> To me and to my aid the blest infusions
> That dwells in vegetives, in metals, stones;
>
> *(PER 3.2.31–6)*

This discourse is reminiscent of the Friar in *ROM* (2.3.1–30) who at first light collects his medicinal plants. In both cases there is a reverence for nature's gifts and an acknowledgement that empirical observation is essential to scientific endeavour. Cerimon produces a near miracle by bringing the coffined Thaisa back to life. Intriguingly, despite his scientific approach he commands that 'rough and woeful music' be played as part of the remedy to revive the woman in the coffin. When Thaisa begins to show signs of life his use of imagery is striking: 'See how she gins/To blow into life's flower again!' (88–95). Human and plant life are interwoven.

(C) Tusser (1570, July) uses vegetive to suggest the life of a plant: 'Not rend of, but cut of, rype beane with a knife, for hinderinge stalk, of her vegetiue life'. Nares (1859), with reference to Middleton's *The Old Law*, suggests that 'vegetive' indicates something less than human: 'Yet in noble man reform it,/And make us better than those vegetives/Whose souls die with them' (1.1.327–9).

verdure (A) The fresh **green** colour of vegetation, verdure can describe any green, flourishing **plants** or **trees**, and by extension a fresh or flourishing condition. Verdure tapestries provided richly ornamental representations of trees and other plants, and were important in blurring the distinction between the **garden** and inside spaces.

(B) Reference to 'verdure' as a burgeoning life force that can be depleted is employed twice, on both occasions figuratively. Valentine uses an analogy to confirm the imprudence of premature commitment to love:

> And writers say: as the most forward bud
> Is eaten by the canker ere it blow,
> Even so by love the young and tender wit
> Is turn'd to folly, blasting in the bud,
> Losing his verdure, even in the prime,
> And all the fair effects of future hopes.

(TGV 1.1.45–50)

Verdure here is 'vitality'. Politics is the topic in *TMP*. Prospero, the deposed Duke of Milan, tells Miranda how his brother inveigled his way to power, concluding: 'that now he was/The ivy which hid my princely trunk,/And suck'd my verdure out on't' (1.2.85–7). This imagery is singularly apt in its exposure of the sinister nature of political guile and manipulation – and the feeling of impotency experienced by the victim.

(C) Coope (1986) links the inside-outside space of **galleries** with the use of green internal decoration, citing as an example Henry VIII's temporary palace for the Field of the Cloth of Gold. In his aptly named *Interior Landscapes*, Rees (1993) gives the practical and decorative history of the use of tapestries, including those with verdure subjects. Henderson (2005) details Burghley's great chamber at Theobalds which was decorated with artificial trees covered with real **bark**, so real that birds were said to fly in and nest in the artificial greenery. Noble (2005) notes that before the sixteenth century it was rare for plants to be depicted in any realistic way on tapestries, so that this represented a new visual experience. Adams (2008) comments that in masques it was often the *ver perpetuum*, the permanent green of spring, that provided the settings.

vine, vineyard (A) *Vitis vinifera* L. is a naturalized, probably Roman, introduction, a mass of such **plants** being a vineyard. Viticulture in Britain possibly died out in the fifth century, but modern scholarship suggests it may have survived in royal and monastic **gardens**. Vine can designate any trailing plant of the genus *Vitis*, or any trailing or climbing plant **grown** for decorative purposes. Personification of the vine derives from John's gospel, where it represents Christ. An analogy was drawn between the vine and a wife, seen to be supported by her husband, in the same way as the **elm** supported the vine. Both vines and vineyards symbolized possession, productivity and **fruitfulness**, often in contrast to **barren** land and infertile **crops** or people.

(B) The plant is used emblematically by Adriana in *ERR*. Deploying elaborate imagery she upbraids her husband for neglecting her: 'Thou art an elm, my husband, I a vine,/Whose weakness, married to thy stronger state,/Makes me with thy strength to communicate' (2.2.174–6). As the tempo of the festivities increases on Pompey's galley the revellers dance to a celebratory song, beginning: 'Come, thou monarch of the vine,/Plumpy Bacchus with pink eyne!' (*ANT* 2.7.113–14). The vine as the emblem of fruitfulness and security is employed by Cranmer in his prophecy, at the christening of the baby Elizabeth, that these blessings will be her legacy: 'In her days every man shall eat in safety/Under his own vine what he plants, and sing/The merry songs of peace to all his neighbors' (*H8* 5.4.33–5). The Archbishop returns to the image when anticipating Elizabeth's successor, James I: 'Peace, plenty, love, truth, terror,/That were the servants to this chosen infant,/Shall then be his, and like a vine grow to him' (5.4.47–9). Another promise of plenty, this time by the goddess Ceres, occurs in Prospero's masque: 'Vines with clust'ring bunches growing' (*TMP* 4.1.112). The status of the vine as a central image of peace and security is present in Richmond's indictment of Richard III prior to the battle of Bosworth. Encouraging his supporters, he exclaims, 'The wretched, bloody, and usurping boar,/That spoil'd your summer fields and fruitful vines,/Swills your warm blood like wash and makes his trough/In your embowell'd bosoms' (*R3* 5.2.7–10). The significance of the vine as the emblem of **fertility** and therefore prosperity is also evidenced in *TIM* where the protagonist beseeches **Nature** to withhold her bounty from ungrateful humanity: 'Dry up thy marrows, vines, and plough-torn leas' (4.3.193). Anticipating his body's decay the dying Mortimer draws on a vine analogy: 'And pithless arms, like to a withered vine/That droops his sapless branches to the ground' (*1H6* 2.5.11–12). The depredations inflicted on French agriculture by the English invasion is brought home by Burgundy: 'Her vine, the merry cheerer of the heart,/Unpruned dies' (*H5* 5.2.41–2). Lear, introducing Cordelia's suitors, anticipates a **fruitful** marriage for his youngest daughter: 'Now, our joy,/Although our last and least, to whose young love/The vines of France and milk of Burgundy/Strive to be interess'd' (*LR* 1.1.82–5).

Vineyards are present in four plays. Describing the place designated by Angelo for an illicit assignation, Isabella uses the word three times: 'He hath a garden circummur'd with brick,/Whose western side is with a vineyard back'd;/And to that vineyard is a planched gate' which 'from the vineyard to the garden leads' (*MM* 4.1.28–33). Laying out his utopian vision, Gonzalo lists those things to be held in common: 'contract, succession,/Bourn, bound of land, tilth, vineyard, none' (*TMP* 2.1.152–3). Delineating the activities over which Ceres, the goddess of fertility presides, Iris refers to 'thy pole-clipt vineyard' (4.1.68). Suggested interpretations for 'pole-clipt' or 'poll-clipt' includes having been **pruned**, or 'poles entwined with vines' (Riverside 1679). Presenting his case for mounting resistance against Henry V, the Constable of France cites surrender of French vineyards as the ultimate indignity: 'And if he be not fought withal, my lord,/Let us not live in France; let us quit all,/And give our vineyards to a barbarous people' (*H5* 3.5.2–4). Later, when Henry has overwhelmed the French, Burgundy describes the consequences for agriculture: 'And all our vineyards, fallows, meads, and hedges,/Defective in their natures, grow to wildness' (5.2.54–5). Fleeing the invading English a Frenchman describes, 'cities all on fire,/Cornfields and vineyards burning like an oven' (*E3* 3.2.56–7).

(C) McLean (1981) records many finds relating to vineyards near the sites of Roman villas in Britain. Voights (1979) comments on post-Roman viticulture in England; vines were ordered for Queen Eleanor's **garden** at Leeds Castle at the end of the thirteenth century (Batey and Lambert 1990). In the sixteenth century a vineyard is documented at Thornbury Castle, Gloucestershire. Harrison (1587) concurs with Holinshed who thinks viticulture had effectively ceased: 'Of wine I have written alreadie elsewhere sufficientlie ... yet at this present have we none at all or else verie little to speake of growing in this Island: which I impute not unto the soile, but the negligence of our countrimen' (1577: 530). Colonna (1499), Sidney (1580) and Spenser (1596) link the vine and the elm. Webster's Francisco suggests the contradiction and unreliability of growing vines in a cold country:

> As in cold countries husband-men plant Vines,
>   And with warme bloud manure them. Even so
> One summer she will beare unsavoury fruite,
> And ere next spring wither both branch and roote.
>
> *(1612, The White Devil 3.2.185–8).*

In siting the *MM* vineyard to the west, Shakespeare followed the advice of Heresbach (trans. Googe, 1596). **Grapes** were a ready visual image to reproduce in needlework and embroidery: Trevelyon (1608) includes a considerable number of patterns which could also have been translated into plasterwork and internal decoration. Arnold (1988) notes that the Queen's jewels included the image of a fruitful vine growing over dead elm set in gold, diamonds and rubies. Palter (2002) writes of grapes, and at length of wine, with an extensive range of literary references. Christianson (2005) provides details of vines growing in the royal gardens of the Tower of London in the thirteenth century, and at Bridge House beside Tower Bridge a century later. See **grape.**

viola (A) *Viola tricolor* L. is the wild **pansy**, also named 'heartsease'. The modern **garden** pansy has diverged much further from its wild precursor than those found in Elizabethan gardens.

(B) Although the **flower** is present as 'love-in-idleness' (2.1.168), as 'Cupid's flower' (4.1.73) in *MND,* and as 'pansies' in *HAM* (4.5.176), its name is not used except as the central character in *TN.* Names are highly significant in *TN* as the letters of Viola are contained in Olivia and in Malvolio and it is not necessary to resort to the deceived Steward's endeavour to 'crush this a little' (2.5.140) to be aware of further alphabetical mutations. Viola – in her role as Orsino's ambassador of love, Cesario – plays on the botanical association of Olivia's name when promising, 'I bring no overture of war, no taxation of homage; I hold the olive in my hand; my words are as full of peace as of matter' (1.5.208–11). Just as Viola, disguised as Cesario, inhabits a duality, the wild pansy is related to the violet. Celebrated in the opening speech of the play the violet is likened to 'the sweet sound/That breathes upon a bank of violets/Stealing and giving odor' (1.1.5–7).

(C) Gerard (1597: 853–5) begins his discussion of the **plant** under the heading 'Of Hearts-ease, or Pansies'. Associating it with the **violet** he notes that the wild pansy 'differs from the garden pansy' and that 'Hearts-ease is named in Latin *Viola tricolour,* or the three coloured Violet'. Mabey (1996: 129) points out that 'Pansies are as muddled – and muddling – a group as the violets proper. The most frequent species, the little field pansy, *v. arvensis*, … can be difficult to tell from the wild pansy, *v. tricolor*.' Fisher (2011: 139–40) observes that 'Heartsease or wild pansies are one of the main flowers decorating the magnificent red backgrounds of the *Lady and the Unicorn* tapestries' and provides a fine illustration of this remarkable work. She also notes 'Pansy was the courtly name for viola, deriving as it does from the French word meaning thought'. Ophelia provides the most significant symbolism when declaring 'there is pansies, that's for thoughts' (*HAM* 4.5.176–7), but the flower also represented love and sometimes betrayal. Heilmeyer (2001: 48) points out that viola 'for most Romans could be both the violet and stock' and notes their presence in the Zeus-Io myth.

violet (A) Several **plants** of the family *Violaceae* including violet and **pansy** were called 'violet', the most common being *Viola odorata* L., the native sweet violet, and *V. tricolor* L., the wild pansy, heartsease or **love-in-idleness**. The name was also given to plants with violet-coloured **flowers**; the true violet can be purple, blue or white in colour. Violets were particularly valued for their sweet **scent**. Seen as emblematic of spring because they can flower in March, they symbolized humility, faithfulness and gentleness, and as such were associated with the Virgin Mary. The **leaves** and flowers were used widely in cooking. Violet was used as a soporific, to improve the sight, and to provide an antidote to anger.

(B) With 18 mentions the violet is the most frequently cited flower after the **rose** and the **lily**. The harbinger of spring, it is particularly associated with scent and delicacy. A beguiling use arises in the opening speech in *TN*. Commanding a replay of a strain of music, Orsino exclaims, 'O, it came o'er my ear like the sweet sound/That breathes upon a bank of violets,/Stealing and giving odor' (5–7). Riverside adopts F's 'sound' without comment; Arden 2 (5) also retains F's 'sound' supported by extensive commentary; Arden 3 (162) adopts Pope's emendation, 'south' meaning 'south wind': 'South' has the clearer meaning: a gentle breeze draws out the delicate scent and spreads it on the ambient air, thus '*stealing* and *giving* odor'. This little flower also animates the name of the play's central character, **Viola**. Grieving at the loss of Adonis, Venus chides Death: 'what dost thou mean/To stifle beauty, and to steal his breath?/Who when he liv'd, his breath and beauty set/Gloss on the rose, smell to the violet' (*VEN* 933–6). Opposing the King's intended second coronation Salisbury contends that it would be 'To throw perfume on the violet' (*JN* 4.2.12).

The violet's distinctive colour also attracts attention. The song which draws *LLL* to a close begins, 'When daisies pied, and violets blue' (5.2.894). Attempting to draw Adonis into a more vulnerable position, Venus reassures him, 'These blue-vein'd violets whereon we lean/Never can blab, nor know not what we mean' (*VEN* 125–6). They become a darker shade in *PER* as Marina strews the grave of her nurse Lychorida: 'The yellows, blues,/The purple violets and marigolds,/Shall as a carpet hang upon thy grave/While summer days doth last' (4.1.14–17). Perdita's celebration of the exuberance of spring delineates the colours and characteristics of the various flowers, including, 'violets, dim,/But sweeter than the lids of Juno's eyes,/Or Cytherea's breath' (*WT* 4.4.120–2). Arden 2 (96) posits, 'probably the white violet praised by Bacon ('Of Gardens') as the flower with the sweetest smell. "Dim" because the hanging head is also usually concealed or partly concealed'. Arden 3 (267) suggests dim implies '"homely" (compared with bright daffodils); modest (heads of violets hang down, half-hidden)'. The idiosyncratic movement of the flower is signified twice. Oberon's description of Titania's bower refers to a place where 'the nodding violet grows' (*MND* 2.2.250). Belarius provides a delicate simile when reflecting on the princely nature of Arviragus and Guiderius: 'They are as gentle/As zephyrs blowing below the violet,/Not wagging his sweet head' (*CYM* 4.2.171–3). The violet as the expression of both spring and favour is cleverly implied by the Duchess of York. Questioning her son on the political alignment in the regime of the newly crowned Bolingbroke, she asks: 'Who are the violets now/That strew the green lap of the new-come spring?' (*R2* 5.2.46–7).

HAM is distinguished by three separate mentions of this flower. Laertes cautions Ophelia:

> For Hamlet, and the trifling of his favor,
>
> Hold it a fashion and a toy in blood,
>
> A violet in the youth of primy nature,
>
> Forward, not permanent, sweet, not lasting,
>
> The perfume and the suppliance of a minute –
>
> No more.

> *(1.3.5–10)*

It is the precocity and evanescence of the violet that is drawn on in this passage. Laertes is probably the would-be recipient when Ophelia distributes the symbolically significant **herbs** and flowers: 'I would give you some violets, but they all wither'd when my father died' (4.5.184–5). 'Fidelity' seems to be implied here. Remarkably, the siblings are again linked with the flower when Laertes expresses contempt for the cleric who has denied Ophelia full burial rites: 'Lay her i'th'earth,/And from her fair and unpolluted flesh/May violets spring!' (5.1.238–40). Gentleness, humility and purity may all be implicated here. The strongest use is in *MM* where Angelo's shocked interrogation of his newly discovered lust leads him to contemplate the nature of contagion even when innocence and beauty are present: 'it is I/That, lying by the violet in the sun,/Do as the carrion does, not as the flow'r,/Corrupt with virtuous season' (2.2.164–7). Arden 2 (49) has a long footnote.

(C) Colonna (1499) demonstrates their universal appeal when he writes of a **wreath** of fragrant violets, of the ground covered with flowers including four kinds of violet, and of their use in **knot-gardens**. Langham (1597) gives 47 different medicinal uses for violets. He appears generally to use them as **simples** rather than in compounds. Mabey (1996) details the range of native violets and their associations. McLeod (2008) and Fisher (2011) give the flower's associations with the Virgin Mary. Heath (2003) also notes its Marian associations. Armstrong (1946: 78–81) emphasizes the dual associations of the violet – love and death – and considers its relationship to wind and swallows. Tigner (2012: 103) comments on Ophelia's violets. The observations of Heilmeyer (2001: 84) are especially pertinent to *HAM* and *WT* : 'Even in antiquity, violets were planted on graves because the fragrant flowers had a mythological connection with the hereafter. Persephone was strolling across a meadow of violets when Hades carried her off to the underworld. The violet thus became the symbol of the mortal soul and of resurrection and spring.'

walk (A) Paths or informal ways through the early modern **garden**, walks offered opportunities for exercise, recreation and conversation. Walks, sometimes called **forthrights**, offered a means of exploring the constructed landscape beyond the formal garden out into the **woodland** or **wilderness**. Such paths could be informal and open to the elements, covered as long **arbours** or **alleys**, **grassy** or laid out more formally with a hard surface for walking in all weathers.

(B) There are many garden and woodland walks in the plays. Meeting the wives for their assignation in the wood, Falstaff likens himself to a stag: 'Divide me like a brib'd-buck, each a haunch. I will keep my sides to myself, my shoulders for the fellow of this walk – and my horns I bequeath your husbands' (*WIV* 5.5.24–7). The 'fellow of this walk' is the **forester** responsible for the upkeep of this part of the wood. More crisply, Maria's, 'Get ye all three into the box-tree; Malvolio's coming down this walk' (*TN* 2.5.15–16) is the overture to the conspirators' gulling of their antagonist. The walk as a convenient place for secret conversations is intimated by York's invitation to Salisbury and Warwick: 'Our simple supper ended, give me leave/In this close walk to satisfy myself/In craving your opinion of my title' (*2H6* 2.2.2–4). Determined that Bottom will be constantly entertained, Titania commands her fairies, 'Hop in his walks and gambol in his eyes' (*MND* 3.1.165). Returning from the Athenian wood to Theseus' palace, the Duke wishes the young lovers 'joy and fresh days of love/Accompany your hearts!'. Lysander reciprocates: 'More than to us/Wait in your royal walks, your board, your bed!' (5.1.29–31). Alexander Iden's delight and ease is palpable: 'Lord, who would live turmoiled in the court/And may enjoy such quiet walks as these?' (*2H6* 4.10.16–17). As he lies dying Warwick is aggrieved at the loss of his worldly goods: 'My parks, my walks, my manors that I had,/Even now forsake me' (*3H6* 5.2.24–5). Advising Chiron and Demetrius on a strategy to ensnare Lavinia, the mischievous Aaron co-mingles the carefully contrived beauty of the setting with the vileness of their intention: 'The forest walks are wide and spacious,/And many unfrequented plots there are,/Fitted by kind for rape and villainy' (*TIT* 2.1.114–16). This play, more than any other, juxtaposes the delicacy of the landscape with lurking menace. Walks in a city are unique to *JC*. Attempting to entice Brutus into the conspiracy, Cassius asks rhetorically, 'When could they say, till now, that talk'd of Rome,/That her wide walks encompass'd but one man?' (1.2.154–5). This is the only play in which grounds and walks are bequeathed to the community. Antony reports to the people that Caesar in his will, 'hath left you all his walks,/His private arbors and new-planted orchards,/On this side Tiber' (3.2.247–9).

(C) Hill (1577: 47) writes of framing 'seemly walks and allies' to facilitate the practical work in the garden and for recreation, commenting that 'the commodities of these Allies and walkes, serve to good purposes, the one is, that the owner may diligently view the prosperity of his **herbs** and **flowers**, the other for the delight and comfort of the wearied mind'. Parkinson (1629) implies walks are an integral part of garden design and can be open or closed, public or private. Jacques (1989) documents the garden at Gray's Inn where there were walks lined with **trees** out into the **fields** before 1568; they were enclosed to create the garden in the 1590s, when the laying out of formal walks was overseen by Francis Bacon in 1597–9. Henderson (2005) provides the most comprehensive overview of walks in early modern gardens. She includes Sir Thomas Tresham's instructions from prison on the precise laying out and surface material for the paths at Lyveden New Bield.

wall (A) A structure of bricks, stones or similar material laid in courses, the purpose of which was to enclose a **garden**, or other property. Within a garden, a wall could protect **fruit** from exposure to wind or separate defined parts of the garden. Walls offered privacy from the wider world, and safety in keeping intruders out. Small banqueting- or **garden-houses** could be built into or on top of walls, serving as informal dining places. Symbolically in Christian art the Virgin Mary was often depicted as inviolate in a walled garden, a *hortus conclusus*.

(B) A garden surrounded by a wall is described in *MM* as 'circummur'd with brick' (4.1.28). The best remembered garden wall in the plays is not a wall at all: this wall in *MND* is a comic improvization that separates the lovers Pyramus and Thisbe in the entertainment for Theseus' wedding. The first of the play's 27 mentions arises when Peter **Quince** informs his troupe of actors 'we must have a wall in the great chamber' (3.1.62–3). The wall as protection is illustrated by the desperate Jack Cade who, driven by hunger, muses, 'Whereof, on a brick wall have I climb'd into this garden, to see if I can eat grass, or pick a sallet' (*2H6* 4.10.6–8). Another interloper is Romeo who is observed by Benvolio: 'He ran this way and leapt this orchard wall' (*ROM* 2.1.5.). There are numerous references to city walls and a few proverbial uses such as those exchanged by Samson and Gregory in the opening scene: 'I will take the wall of any man' meaning to gain precedence or dominance, and 'the weakest goes to the wall' (1.1.12–14).

(C) Markham (1613) and Lawson (1618) write of the importance of a walled **orchard**. Jacques (1989) documents Francis Bacon's design for the garden at Gray's Inn, developed in the late 1590s with the walling in of earlier **fields**. The plans for Cecil House in the Strand show brick walls dividing some sections of the garden in place of the more usual **hedges** (Husselby and Henderson 2002). Henderson (2005) examines the walls in the gardens of some of the royal palaces and at Hatfield and discusses contemporary plans showing how they could be used decoratively. She lists contemporary surviving structures, of which the banqueting-houses or **garden-houses** are the most common survivors. Christianson (2005) comments on the walls surrounding

Thomas More's house at Chelsea, fragments of which still survive. McLeod (2008) gives details of the *hortus conclusus.*

walnut (A) *Juglans regia* L. is a slow-maturing **tree**, a naturalized Roman introduction, grown for its **nuts**. The unripe nuts were used whole for pickling as a savoury and spicy snack, or preserved with sugar as a sweetmeat or sucket. The tree is grown for its valuable timber; oil from the nuts serves to dress **salads**. It flourishes in or close to cultivation; because it does not attract insects it provides shelter for livestock in summer.

(B) Allusions to the 'walnut' and the 'walnut-shell' are purely playful. Sure in the knowledge that Falstaff cannot have escaped from his house, Ford is willing to invite mockery: 'Let them say to me, "As jealous as Ford that search'd a hollow walnut for his wife's leman"' (*WIV* 4.2.162–4). The choice of the archaic term 'leman' for 'lover' may suggest some elusive connection with walnut. Arden 3 (251) points out that the nut was 'proverbially the most unlikely hiding place; cf. *HAM* 2.2.254: "I could be bounded in a nutshell"'. The cap that delights Kate in *SHR* is disparaged by Petruchio with such spurious comments as, 'Why, 'tis a cockle or a walnut-shell' (4.3.66).

(C) Langham (1597) recommends walnuts for a considerable range of ailments. Gerard (1597: 1252–3) records the oil as a hair restorative, recommends the **leaves** and small **buds** as having 'a certaine binding qualitie'; he also notes its cosmetic use as body lotion. Webster's Flamineo uses the walnut proverbially: 'Why do you kicke her? Say/ Do you thinke that she's like a walnut-tree?/Must she be cudgel'd ere shee beare good fruite?' (1612, *The White Devil* 5.1.179–181), reminding the reader of the proverb: 'A woman, an asse, and a walnut tree,/Bring the more fruit, the more beaten they bee'.

warden An old, late-maturing variety of **pear**, valued particularly when other **fruit** was scarce, the warden was largely cultivated for baking. It was said to be named after Warden Abbey in Bedfordshire where the variety was sent from Burgundy in the twelfth century. The warden is generally listed separately from other pears; Elizabethan books often referred to 'pears and wardens'. Wardens were used in fruit pies, as a preserve or syrup; they were also thought to be efficacious against the plague. There is only one mention of this fruit, and it appears in the list of Perdita's requirements for the sheep-shearing feast. She entrusts the task to the young shepherd, designated 'Clown', who rehearses, 'I must have saffron to color the warden pies' (*WT* 4.3.45–6). This would imply easy availability of the pears; it is the complementary **saffron** that has to be purchased. Although Boorde (1547) does not recommend pears, he says wardens are good, whether roasted, stewed or baked, and the best food in time of plague. Peacham (1612) calls it the 'winter-warden', reflecting its powers of keeping. Vaughan (1617: 100, 137) says 'they are excellent food to strengthen decayed nature', and that together with 'carnall copulation' they have particular value in winter. Savage (1923) notes the three pears on the escutcheon of the Cistercians at Warden, and that of the county of Worcestershire. Campbell-Culver (2001) includes the historical journey of the warden from Burgundy to the Cistercian Abbey at Warden.

weed (A) Many **plants** now categorized as weeds were cultivated in early modern times for their medicinal and culinary virtues: primacy was generally given to profitability and customary use rather than appearance or novelty, at least outside the trophy **garden**. Technically a weed is a herbaceous plant not valued for use or beauty, growing wild and **rank**, thought to contaminate the **ground** and hindering the **growth** of superior vegetation. The idea of something unwanted or polluting led to a metaphorical use of weed in proverbs. Weeding in the **garden** context was often the role of women who were cheaper to employ than men. Weeds were regarded symbolically as a postlapsarian phenomenon, not appearing until after man's fall. Figuratively they can have unwanted characteristics and evil itself can be described as a weed, to be **rooted** out and destroyed. Weed, more common in the plural, could also refer to garments. The verb, to weed, means to clear the ground.

(B) Literal references are few; the dominant metaphorical field is political. Typical is Bolingbroke's pledge to pursue 'Bushy, Bagot, and their complices,/The caterpillars of the commonwealth,/Which I have sworn to weed and pluck away' (*R2* 2.3.165–7). Signifying 'parasite', '**caterpillar**' is a key word in the political lexicon. This closely wrought sentence also employs 'commonwealth' which encompasses the body politic in its most socially inclusive sense. The **Gardener** condemns Richard's neglect of the realm, 'the whole land,/Is full of weeds, her fairest flowers chok'd up', and then elaborates on the cause: 'The weeds which his broad-spreading leaves did shelter,/That seem'd in eating him to hold him up,/Are pluck'd up root and all by Bullingbrook' (3.4.43–52). Having outlined his plans to remove their ambitious rivals, Suffolk confides in Queen Margaret, 'So one by one we'll weed them all at last,/And you yourself shall steer the happy helm' (*2H6* 1.3.99–100). The Queen deploys the same image when endeavouring to persuade King Henry to remove Buckingham: 'Now 'tis the spring, and weeds are shallow-rooted;/Suffer them now, and they'll o'ergrow the garden,/And choke the herbs for want of husbandry' (3.1.31–3). More brutally, Bishop Gardiner expresses his hatred of Cranmer and his determination to remove him: 'He's a rank weed, Sir Thomas,/And we must root him out' (*H8* 5.1.52–3). During his quarrel with Queen Elizabeth, Richard Gloucester catalogues his past services to the King: 'I was a pack-horse in his great affairs:/A weeder-out of his proud adversaries' (*R3* 1.3.121–2).

Other aspects of human behaviour are also framed in terms of weeds. Anxious about the wayward Prince Hal, Henry IV ruefully confides, 'Most subject is the fattest soil to weeds,/And he, the noble image of my youth,/Is overspread with them' (*2H4* 4.4.54–6). Reflecting on Angelo's hypocrisy, the Duke exclaims: 'Twice treble shame on Angelo,/To weed my vice, and let his grow!' (*MM* 3.2.269–70). Forging an alliance with his former enemy, Aufidius addresses Caius Martius with unfeigned admiration: 'O Martius, Martius!/Each word thou hast spoke hath weeded from my heart/A root of ancient envy' (*COR* 4.5.101–3). Instructing his secretary Lodowick to compose a love missive to the Countess of Salisbury, Edward III proposes, 'Bid her be free and general as the sun,/Who smiles upon the basest weed that grows,/As lovingly as on the fragrant rose' (*E3* 2.1.163–5). Weeds are pervasive in *HAM*. Hamlet reflects, '"tis an unweeded garden/That grows to seed, things rank and gross in nature/Possess it merely' (1.2.135–7). The Ghost's bitterness is evident when responding to Hamlet's pledge to exact revenge: 'I find thee apt,/And duller shouldst thou be than the fat weed/ That roots itself in ease on Lethe Wharf,/Wouldst thou not stir in this' (1.5.31–4). Advising his mother not to compound her past errors, Hamlet pleads: 'Confess yourself to heaven,/Repent what's past, avoid what is to come,/And do not spread the compost on the weeds/To make them ranker'(3.4.149–52). With more references to weeds than any other play it has the only mention of 'weedy'. Describing **Ophelia's** drowning, Gertrude portrays the critical moment: 'There on the pendant boughs her crownet weeds/Clambring to hang, an envious sliver broke,/When down her weedy trophies and herself/Fell in the weeping brook' (4.7.172–5).

(C) Tusser (1573) writes of **thistle, vetch, brake** and **cockle** as the weeds threatening to overwhelm the **crops** in May saying they should be burnt to protect the **harvest**. Webster's Conjurer sees a parallel between weeds flourishing and the capacity for good or evil in man: 'Both flowers and weedes spring when the Sunne is warm,/As great men do great good, or else great harm' (1612, *The White Devil* 2.2.56–7). Spurgeon (1935) notes that the most constant running metaphor of growth in Shakespeare is seen in garden and **orchard**, the ignorance of a gardener being demonstrated by untended weeds, pests, lack of **pruning** and the untimely cutting of trees. Christiansen (2005) provides details of weeding women at Hampton Court and other royal palaces. Tigner (2012: 13) observes that 'In the period, weeds carry great metaphorical weight, as sermons, polemics, and poetry all employ the image as an emblem of the fallen world.' For a more benign view of weeds see Mabey (2010).

wheat, wheaten (A) The cultivation of *Triticum* L. is as old as civilization. While wheat is closely related to **barley** and **rye**, both were regarded as inferior constituents for bread-making; pure wheat bread was a luxury. Wheat can also designate the threshed **grain** which is the main ingredient of bread-flour in temperate countries. It was a symbol both of **fertility** and the bounty of the **earth**. The passing of the year was marked by the **growth** of wheat, and its **greening** was a sign of spring.

(B) The engagingly discursive and domestic conversation in Justice Shallow's **orchard** includes the question: 'shall we sow the hade land with wheat?'. Shallow assents and specifies what kind of wheat should be sown: 'With red wheat, Davy' (*2H4* 5.1.14–16). Moving from the bucolic comfort of Gloucestershire to the world of international politics, Pompey, addressing Octavius Caesar, rehearses the conditions embodied in the peace agreement proposed by the triumvirate: 'You have made me offer/Of Sicily, Sardinia; and I must/Rid all the sea of pirates; then, to send/Measures of wheat to Rome' (*ANT* 2.6.34–7). There can be no doubting the strategic role of wheat in this global economy. Its vulnerability to disease emerges tangentially in *LR*. Edgar/Mad Tom vociferates against the devil's destructive antics: Flibbertigibbet 'mildews the white wheat' (3.4.118). Cautioning Troilus to be patient in his pursuit of Cressida, Pandarus begins his extended metaphor: 'He that will have a cake out of the wheat must tarry the grinding' (*TRO* 1.1.14–15). Its association with spring emerges during Helena's complaint to Hermia: 'Your eyes are lodestars, and your tongue's sweet air/More tuneable than lark to shepherd's ear/When wheat is green, when hawthorn buds appear' (*MND* 1.1.183–5). The wheaten **garland** is mentioned three times. Responding to the Queen's appeal, Theseus recalls her marriage day: 'Your wheaten wreath/Was then nor thresh'd nor blasted' (*TNK* 1.1.64–5). The comment could refer to the wedding chaplet itself, her virginal state or to a life untouched by misfortune. The play has another reference to the wheaten garland which is both literal and emblematic. Approaching the altar of Diana wearing the wheaten garland or **wreath**, Emilia appeals to the goddess to determine her destiny: 'He of the two pretenders that best loves me/And has the truest title in't, let him/Take off my wheaten garland' (5.1.158–60). In contrast to matrimonial garlands the emblem of peace takes on a sinister significance in the political sphere. Hamlet's account of the circumstances of his escape includes mimicry of the contents of Claudius' letter to the English King: 'As love between them like the palm might flourish,/As peace should still her wheaten garland wear/And stand a comma 'tween their amities'. Here in the language of diplomacy is the threat that compliance is a prerequisite for the continuance of peaceful relations. The conclusion to the letter is stark: 'He should those bearers put to sudden death,/Not shriving time allow'd' (*HAM* 5.2.40–7).

(C) Langham (1597) lists nearly 100 different medicinal uses for wheat. Hoskins (1964) emphasizes the economic effects of the cost of wheat particularly in the 1590s, with the annual price at a one hundred year high in 1596. Sim (1997) comments that in times of famine and rising prices, lesser grains such as rye, **oats** and barley were used in place of wheat.

wilderness (A) A term possessing two contrasting meanings: wild or uncultivated **land** often **woodland**, untamed by man and uninhabited except by wild animals; a carefully constructed landscape forming an integral part of the **gardens** of great houses facilitating **hunting** and other leisure activities. In religious terminology wilderness can be contrasted with heaven.

(B) All references are to places distant and uncivilized, hence the precision of Titus' oxymoron: 'dost thou not perceive/That Rome is but a wilderness of tigers?' (*TIT* 3.1.53–4). The same speaker is the only character to refer to the sea as 'a wilderness'. Encountering his mutilated daughter, Lavinia, he cries: 'For now I stand as one upon a rock,/Environ'd with a wilderness of sea' (3.1.93–4). While Titus makes a startling metaphorical leap, Lucrece transmutes the sophisticated hunting **park** into a savage environment. Accosted by the remorseless Tarquin she appears, 'Like a white hind under the gripe's sharp claws' and 'Pleads in a wilderness where are no laws' (*LUC* 543–4). The 'gripe' could be a griffin or a powerful bird of prey such as the vulture or the eagle. Despite the 'white hind' hinting at a hunting **ground** the last phrase suggests somewhere isolated from civilization. Remoteness is implied by Fitzwater when responding to Surrey's challenge: 'I dare meet Surrey in a wilderness' (*R2* 4.1.74). *MM* has a metaphorical example that contrasts what is civilized and controlled with what is rude and unrestrained. Isabella is appalled by her brother's plea to sacrifice her virginity to save his life: 'Heaven shield my mother play'd my father fair!/For such a warped slip of wilderness/Ne'er issu'd from his blood' (3.1.140–2). Shylock expresses horror that Jessica has exchanged Leah's gift of a turquoise for a monkey: 'I would not have given it for a wilderness of monkeys' (*MV* 3.1.122–3).

(C) Colonna's dream (1499) starts in a true, rather than constructed, wilderness and ends in an architectural paradise. Markham (1613, ch. 1) contrasts **husbandry** with a literal wilderness, saying the former 'is most necessary for keeping the earth in order, which else would grow wilde, and like a wildernesse, brambles and weeds choaking up better plants, and nothing remaining but a Chaos of confusednesse'. Bacon's wilderness (1625) is a very controlled space, and one of the three parts of his ideal garden, which progressed from the green garden near the house to the main garden and to the wilderness beyond. He calls it a **heath**, which he wishes 'to be framed, as much as may be, to a natural wildness'; he includes artificial molehills, **alleys**, arbours with seats, and details the planting and **pruning**, saying that the trees and shrubs should 'be kept with cutting, that they grow not out of course'. Henderson (2005) provides the most comprehensive overview of the Tudor wilderness, often linking it with the park; Taylor (2008) analyses the development and meaning of the early modern wilderness. See also **nature.**

willow (A) Any plant of the extensive genus *Salix* L., willow includes several native **plants growing** near water. While precise identification is impossible, it could not refer to the now common weeping willow, a later hybrid not introduced until the seventeenth century. *S. fragilis* L. is known as the crack willow from the readiness of its **twigs** and **branches** to break without warning. *S. viminalis* L. provides **osiers,** much used in basket and fence-making, willow and osier being employed interchangeably for this purpose. Willows also have a soft, smooth, pliable **wood**. They have an astringent medicinal **bark**, which contains salicin, the source of modern aspirin, so its treatment of fevers could have worked. Willow was associated with contraception and reduced **fertility** because it bears no **fruit**; it was an ancient symbol of mourning, and to wear the willow suggests grieving for lost love. Willow was often cut on Palm Sunday to provide the **palm** branches for church processions.

(B) Present in seven plays, the 'willow' as the emblem of forsaken love is felt acutely in *OTH* and *HAM.* Communing with Emilia on the night she is murdered, Desdemona recalls the cruel fate of another young woman: 'She had a song of "Willow",/An old thing 'twas, but it express'd her fortune,/And she died singing it. That song to-night/Will not go from my mind' (*OTH* 4.3.28–31). Singing snatches of the song, she gives rise to the most frequent use of the word. Ophelia is doubly associated with the willow: she is deserted by Hamlet – making numerous references to betrayal during her songs (*HAM* 4.5.48–66) – and it is the literal cause of her death. Gertrude's elegiac account of her drowning is intensified by the tree's visual and symbolic presence:

> There is a willow grows askaunt the brook,
> That shows his hoary leaves in the glassy stream
>
> ...
>
> There on the pendant boughs her crownet weeds
> Clamb'ring to hang, an envious sliver broke,
> When down her weedy trophies and herself
> Fell in the weeping brook.

(HAM 4.7.166–75)

The sorrow or an accumulation of sorrows carries Gertrude to a new level of articulacy and sensitivity. A resonant allusion, recalled by Lorenzo in a notably lyrical scene, pertains to the Carthaginian queen deserted by Aeneas: 'In such a night/Stood Dido with a willow in her hand/Upon the wild sea-banks, and waft her love/To come again to Carthage' (*MV* 5.1.9–12).

Smarting from the indignity of Edward IV's sudden withdrawal of his marriage proposal, Lady Bona responds with biting irony: 'Tell him, in hope he'll prove a widower shortly,/I'll wear the willow garland for his sake' (*3H6* 3.3.227–8). These precise words, later communicated by the messenger to the King (4.1.98–100), provide the only case where the willow is exclusively an emblem of mourning. Two emblems – death and forsaken love – are conflated in *TNK* where the Wooer reports the Jailer's Daughter's anguish: 'Then she sung/Nothing but "Willow, willow, willow", and between/Ever was, "Palamon, fair Palamon"' (4.1.79–81). Like Ophelia she makes a 'wreath' and adorns herself with a 'Thousand fresh-water flowers' (84). Only in *ADO* is the willow used playfully. It also has the single mention of 'willow-tree'. Benedick teases the disappointed Claudio by proposing his friend accompany him 'Even to the next willow, about your own business, County. What fashion will you wear the garland of?' (2.1.187–9). He then reports to Don Pedro, 'I off'red him my company to a willow-tree, either to make him a garland, as being forsaken, or to bind him up a rod, as being worthy to be whipt' (217–20). Only **Viola** refers to a 'willow-cabin'. As Cesario, she professes to Olivia that rejection would not deter her, pledging she would rather, 'Make me a willow cabin at your gate,/And call upon my soul within the house' (*TN* 1.5.268–9).

(C) Turner provides early evidence of the substitution of willow for palm on Palm Sunday, and argues that this was effectively idolatrous (Knight 2009: 63). Langham (1597) includes the most comprehensive list of its medicinal uses, as an abortifacient, a contraceptive, to treat eye problems, and as a soporific. Ault (1949) includes Heywood's 1545 song which is said to be the earliest of the willow songs: '*All a green willow, willow, willow,/All a green willow is my garland*'. It features the unkindness of the girl, the breaking of promises, an inability to forget, and death. Heath (2003) considers the willow in the context of all Ophelia's plants.

wither (A) To dry up, become shrivelled; a withered **plant** is one that loses moisture and dies. Wither is indicative of loss of vitality, and suggestive of the effects of age, disease and decay. All its meanings appear poetically, often figuratively of people suggesting a loss of physical powers, energy and vigour, pining away, shrinking and becoming wrinkled.

(B) Plants figure strongly in perceptions of desiccation and of decay. The few literal uses are outweighed by figurative applications. Fearing bad omens, the Welsh Captain declines to wait any longer for the return of Richard II from Ireland: 'we will not stay,/The bay-trees in our country are all wither'd,/And meteors fright the fixed stars of heaven' (*R2* 2.4.7–9). The consideration in *TMP* is culinary. Prospero threatens Ferdinand, 'thy food shall be/The fresh-brook mussels, wither'd roots, and husks' (1.2.463–4). Anticipating permanent imprisonment, Arcite uses finely-tuned imagery: 'Here we are,/And here the graces of our youths must wither/Like a too-timely spring' (*TNK* 2.2.26–8). Old Capulet initially rejects Paris' marriage proposal on the grounds that Juliet is too young: 'Let two more summers wither in their pride,/Ere we may think her ripe to be a bride' (*ROM* 1.2.10–11). In Enobarbus' estimation Cleopatra is immune to the depredations of time: 'Age cannot wither her, nor custom stale/Her infinite variety' (*ANT* 2.2.234–5). As Antony dies, Cleopatra exclaims, 'O, wither'd is the garland of the war' (4.15.64). A world apart from the tragic grandeur of Egypt, Falstaff complains, 'I am wither'd like an old apple-John' (*1H4* 3.3.4). Demoralized by the strife between the houses of Lancaster and York, Henry VI pleads to heaven: 'Wither one rose, and let the other flourish;/If you contend, a thousand lives must wither' (*3H6* 2.5.101–2).

(C) Callimachus compares youth and age: 'Would you have me spend the flower of my youth as you do the withered race of your age? Can the fair blood of my youth creep into the ground as it were frost-bitten?' (1580, Lyly *Euphues*, 178). Webster's Cornelia rejects a withered plant even for the grave, suggesting regeneration from the decaying body there: 'This rosemarie is wither'd, pray get fresh;/I would have these herbes grow up in his grave/When I am dead and rotten' (1612, *The White Devil*, 5.4.60). Ault's anthology (1949) includes suggestions that the **tree** will wither away without the sun, that age is all-withering, and that winter's wind or breath can cause withering; also included is the love of a fickle woman which can be like a **flower** that 'buds and spreads, and withers in an hour'.

wood (A) **Tree**-covered country, a wood can be the trees of such a wood collectively, and signifies trees growing naturally and relatively thickly together rather than planned planting in a **plantation**; wood suggests a larger group than a **grove** or **copse** but smaller than a **forest**. It can be the substance of the trees, **root**, trunk, and **branches,** whether growing or cut down as wood or ready for use as fuel or timber. Wood also suggests the head of a tree, **branch**-wood, primarily the **leaf**-bearing rather than the **fruiting** part; it may indicate the material of which something is made, and by extension the substance of the human body. Though woods offered sanctuary they could be threatening wild places beyond the rule of law.

(B) There is a fairly even distribution between 'wood' as living trees, densely or lightly grouped, and timber as firewood or for manufacture. Mentions of wood in *MND*,

MAC and *TNK* are frequent. There is a clear distinction between woods managed on an **estate** and natural woodland. Confronting Richard's acolytes for the part they played in confiscating and despoiling his property, the indignant Bolingbroke claims they have, 'Dispark'd my parks and fell'd my forest woods' (*R2* 3.1.23). Wildness is not always a feature of natural woodland. When Benvolio reports that Romeo gave him the slip, the impression gained is of a small wood on the edge of Verona. Observed, 'underneath the grove of sycamore/That westward rooteth from this city side' the lovesick young man 'stole into the covert of the wood' (*ROM* 1.1.121–5). Bringing provisions to his cousin who has escaped jail, Arcite asks, 'Is't not mad lodging/Here in the wild woods, cousin?' (*TNK* 3.3.22–3). Contradictory perceptions of woods are present in *TIT*. The iniquitous Aaron claims, 'The woods are ruthless, dreadful, deaf, and dull' (2.1.128) – ideal for entrapment, mutilation and rape. Moments later Titus welcomes the morning: 'The hunt is up, the morn is bright and grey,/The fields are fragrant and the woods are green' (2.2.1–2). After the brutal assault on Lavinia, Titus asks whether she was ravished in 'the ruthless, vast, and gloomy woods?' (4.1.53). Timon chooses the wood as a place of retreat from humanity: 'Timon will to the woods, where he shall find/ Th'unkindest beast more kinder than mankind' (*TIM* 4.1.35–6).

In *MND* the wood outside Athens is a sanctuary for young people to share intimacies, but at night it is mysterious, confusing and intimidating. Hermia reminds Helena of their meeting place 'in the wood, where often you and I/Upon faint primrose beds were wont to lie,/Emptying our bosoms of their counsel sweet' (1.1.214–16). Later, Lysander has to confess to Hermia, 'Fair love, you faint with wand'ring in the wood;/And to speak troth I have forgot our way' (2.2.35–6). An arena for rustic rehearsals, fairy conflicts, games, lovers' quarrels, fears and confusions, the Athenian wood celebrates the benign influence of other-worldly creatures and the trepidation occasioned by night. The Forest of Arden, though light on provision for interlopers, acquires a homeliness that makes *AYL* a woodland play which is almost Arcadian. Despite such intrusive fauna as a lion, it comes as something of a surprise when Duke Frederick's arrival is described: 'And to the skirts of this wild wood he came' (5.4.159). Duke Senior while acknowledging the discomforts of cold in the forest asks, 'Are not these woods/More free from peril than the envious court?' (2.1.3–4). A wood is the presiding feature in *MND* and *AYL*; in *MAC* its shadowy presence, strangely atmospheric, is palpable and inescapable. Macbeth's musing saturates the imagination: 'Light thickens, and the crow/Makes wing to th'rooky wood;/Good things of day begin to droop and drowse,/Whiles night's black agents to their preys do rouse' (3.2.50–3). The name of 'Birnam wood' resounds throughout the last two acts, until the eponymous hero vows to fight on 'Though Birnan wood be come to Dunsinane'(5.8.30). Wood as timber is used for the manufacture of simple objects and for such impressive structures as ships and the theatre itself. Richard II enumerates the exchange of his royal accoutrements for simple things: 'My figur'd goblets for a dish of wood' (*R2* 3.3.150). In *H5* the Prologue asks, 'Or may we cram/ Within this wooden O the very casques/That did affright the air of Agincourt?' (12–14). Contrasting meanings of 'woodman' arise in *CYM* and *MM*. Belarius praises his son's achievement as a hunter: 'You Polydore, have prov'd best woodman, and/Are master of the feast' (*CYM* 3.6.28–9). Lucio implies 'hunter of women' when he confides, 'Friar, thou knowest not the Duke so well as I do; he's a better woodman than thou tak'st him for' (*MM* 4.4.161–2). Falstaff, anticipating a successful meeting with the wives in the **forest** is probably conflating the two meanings when he boasts, 'Am I a woodman, ha? Speak I like Herne the hunter?' (*WIV* 5.5.27–8).

(C) Holinshed (1577) comments on the variety of trees in woods and **hedges**, noting the navy's need for **oak**. He bemoans the destruction of woods leading to the predomi-nance in some places of such useless **plants** as **brakes**, **furze**, **sedge** and **rush**. Spenser (1596) writes of individual trees in a friendly wood, of the wood as desolate, terrifying, savage, threatening, wasteful and uncultivated. He describes it as a place of fear, the home of wild woodmen, of savage game, of briers and brakes, of thieves and wolves. He also sees a wood as a home, a hiding place, the source of healing **herbs**. Walsham (2011) points out the function of woods as places of refuge and sites of religious activity, an association which led to their consequent destruction by the Puritans. Thomas (1983: 204) charts the changing attitudes to woodland and the varying fortunes of these areas between 1500 and 1800. Young (1972) provides a richly suggestive exploration of Shakespeare's world of pastoral.

woodbine (A) It is impossible to provide a precise identification for woodbine, or woodbind. In some uses it is conflated with **honeysuckle**, *Lonicera periclymenum* L., while in others it may refer either to *Convolvulus arvensis* L., the **field** bindweed, or to *Calystegia silvatica* (Kit) Griseb, the large bindweed the **growth** habits of which is consistent with the description in *MND* (2.1.249–52). There are some suggestions that woodbine was used to designate climbing plants while honeysuckle indicated those that are **fragrant**. The uses for honeysuckle and woodbine are largely but not entirely complementary, and both were used in early modern medical practice.

(B) Two of its three mentions are in *MND*; the other is in *ADO*. This **plant** is memorable for the role it plays in Oberon's evocation of the Athenian **wood**:

> I know a bank where the wild thyme blows,
> Where oxlips and the nodding violet grows,
> Quite over-canopied with luscious woodbine,
> With sweet musk-roses and with eglantine;
>
> *(MND 2.1.249–52)*

Two aspects of woodbine are indicated: its propensity to climb and clamber, 'over-canopied', and its profuse growth, 'luscious', an adjective which may also relate to its **scent**. This description invites the perception that it is the honeysuckle. Later Titania deploys the image of this plant to naturalize her erotic embracement of Bottom: 'So doth the woodbine the sweet honeysuckle/Gently entwist; the female ivy so/Enrings the barky fingers of the elm' (4.1.42–4). Riverside (273) comments 'Obviously not the honeysuckle here'. However, placing commas after 'woodbine' and 'honeysuckle' might imply a single plant. Arden 2 (88) resists this interpretation: 'No attempt to explain Shakespeare's image in terms of a single plant is satisfactory; not Joseph Hunter's that "woodbine" and "honeysuckle" are in apposition, and entwist is intransitive.' No such difficulty exists in *ADO* as Ursula signifies Beatrice's hiding place in the **garden**: 'who even now/Is couched in the woodbine coverture' (3.1.29–30). This is a cultivated **bower** for providing **shade** and the scent of honeysuckle.

(C) Honeysuckle and woodbine were often used interchangeably. Peacham (1612) writes of the lessons to be learned from plants and says that woodbine means that friendship will hold, suggesting it is a climbing plant. Markham (1631) appears to indicate two separate plants by including woodbine and honeysuckle in one remedy. Ryden (1978: 81–3) suggests parallel symbolism, that in *ADO*, 'honeysuckles' might indicate the scented flower and 'woodbine' the **woody** structure of the plant; no equivalent early modern usage has been found. Jacques (1989) gives the planting lists for Bacon's garden at Gray's Inn of the late 1590s which show that he ordered 1,600 woodbines, which are described as **shrubs**, at a cost of six pence per hundred; although this seems a large number, it is completely dwarfed by the plants ordered for Henry VIII, including almost thirteen thousand 'woodbyne **slips**' (Christiansen 2005). Mabey (1996: 348) maintains that any climbing plant might have been called woodbine and provides a thorough analysis of the ambiguities present in *MND* (4.1.42–4). *MND* Arden 2 (88) has an extensive footnote on this debate.

worm (A) Specifically a member of the genus *Lumbricus*. Worm can suggest an earthworm, any crawling animal or insect, a serpent, snake or dragon, or the larva, grub or **caterpillar** of an insect especially one that feeds on or destroys **fruit**, flesh, **leaves**, **flowers** and textiles. Worms were food for birds, bait for fish; wood-worm damaged or destroyed furniture. Parasites breeding and living in human beings or animals and the diseases caused by them were also called worms, as were ticks or mites living in the hand, foot or other parts of the body. Worms or maggots were thought to eat dead bodies in the grave; by extension worm could apply to a grief or passion that gnaws at the conscience or torments the heart. Someone described as a worm was the subject of scorn, pity, a miserable creature, while with an affectionate qualification it could indicate tenderness or commiseration.

(B) Nowhere is there an indication that Shakespeare, who takes particular interest in the minutiae of **nature**, is aware of this creature's importance in the garden. Ignored as workmen of the **soil** they are frequently presented as the devourers of dead bodies – generally in an obnoxious way. The 'worm' can refer to a weak or vulnerable person, to the grub or 'canker worm' that destroys plants, and to a snake. 'Worm-eaten' describes something made ragged by time or holed by nibbling, and the single use of 'wormy' refers to the nocturnal residence of ghosts, their 'wormy beds' (*MND* 3.2.384). The silk-worm is mentioned twice. Elucidating on the mystique of the lost handkerchief, Othello claims, 'The worms were hallowed that did breed the silk' (*OTH* 3.4.73). As *OTH* Arden 3 (245) observes, 'T. Moffett's *The Silkwormes* was published in 1599' and asks 'A matter of topical interest?'. The idea that the silkworms were consecrated is strange and arresting, but striking too is the phrase *'breed* the silk'. Observing the half-naked Mad Tom, Lear ponders, 'Is man no more than this? Consider him well. Thou ow'st the worm no silk, the beast no hide, the sheep no wool, the cat no perfume' (*LR* 3.4.103–5). The image of the **canker**-worm is present in Cesario/Viola's narration to the Duke of her imaginary sister's 'history': 'she never told her love,/But let concealment like a worm i'th'bud/Feed on her damask cheek' (*TN* 2.4.110–12). Henry VI intervenes with a homily to restrain the quarrelling factions: 'Civil dissention is a viperous worm/That gnaws the bowels of the commonwealth' (*1H6* 3.1.72–3). Arden 3 (198) observes: '"viper", the only poisonous snake native to the British Isles. According to Pliny (10.82) the female was killed by the young gnawing their way out of her body, an error which here creates a homology for the *commonwealth* destroyed by those nurtured within itself'. Observing Miranda's love for Ferdinand, Prospero sighs, 'Poor worm, thou art infected!' (*TMP* 3.1.31). During the final humiliation of Falstaff, when surrounded by the 'fairies' at Herne's Oak, the disguised Pistol mocks him as contemptible,'Vild worm', and bewitched, 'thou wast o'erlook'd even in thy birth' (*WIV* 5.5.83). The worm as pitiable and inconsequential emerges in *LLL* when Berowne mocks Navarre: 'Good heart, what grace hast thou to reprove/These worms for loving, that art most in love?' (4.3.151–2). Kate refers to women as weak and vulnerable when proclaiming the duties a wife owes to her husband: 'Come, come, you froward and unable worms!' (*SHR* 5.2.169). An unusually gentle representation of man as food for worms is conveyed by the disguised Duke while preparing Claudio for death: 'Thou'rt by no means valiant,/For thou dost fear the soft and tender fork/Of a poor worm' (*MM* 3.1.15–17). Hamlet's comment on the dead Polonius is both witty and brutal: 'a certain convocation of politic worms are e'en at him. Your worm is your only emperor for diet: we fat all creatures else to fat us, and we fat ourselves for maggots'. Pressed by Claudius, Hamlet explains, ' A man may fish with the worm that hath eat of a king, and eat of the fish that hath fed of that worm', illustrating 'how a king may go a progress through the guts of a beggar' (*HAM* 4.3.19–31).

(C) Greene uses the image of strength as invulnerability to an attack made by worms: 'As the sappy Myrtle tree wil quickly rotte: so the hard Oake will never be eaten with wormes' (1580–3,vol. 2, *Mamillia:* 61). Most contemporary writers include worms in their lists of **garden** pests. Hill (1577) writes of canker worms and earth worms, and includes 'remedies and secrets' which survived from Greek writers, not all of which were appropriate to an English garden. Markham (1613) recommends 'swine's dung, sage and lime' beaten together to destroy worms in the **bark** of **fruit trees**.

wormwood (A) Of the several hundred **plants** in the *Artemesia* genus, also known as mugworts or mother-worts, and thought of as the 'mother' of all other **herbs**, among the most common is wormwood, *A. absinthium* L. Proverbially bitter to taste, the **leaves** and tops had medical applications, provided a tonic and vermifuge, and feature in the making of vermouth and absinthe. Wormwood was thought to protect clothes and bedding from moths and fleas. From its alternative name of motherwort, and from its association with Artemis the protector of pregnancy, it was long associated with women's health, and with childbirth. Wormwood was also used as a contraceptive and an abortifacient.

(B) Before accepting Berowne's proposal of marriage, Rosaline insists he undertake penance by visiting 'the speechless sick' for a year, 'To weed this wormwood from your fructful brain' (*LLL* 5.2.847–51). The bitterness is his propensity for unrestrained mockery or 'wounding flouts' (844). Threatening Tarquin, Lucrece deploys transformation to illuminate the abomination of his vile intent:

> Thy secret pleasure turns to open shame,
> Thy private feasting to a public fast,
> Thy smoothing titles to a ragged name,
> Thy sug'red tongue to bitter wormwood taste;

> *(LUC 890–3)*

Hamlet revels in the plant's bitterness when assessing the Player Queen's lines – 'In second husband let me be accurs'd!/None wed the second but who kill'd the first' – 'that's wormwood!' (*HAM* 3.2.179–81). Edward III responds to the insults of the French King with irony: 'If gall or wormwood have a pleasant taste,/Then is thy salutation honey-sweet' (*E3* 3.3.72–3). The Nurse's calculation of Juliet's age in *ROM* leads her to describe how the plant is used for weaning children from the breast: 'When it did taste the wormwood on the nipple/Of my dug and felt it bitter, pretty fool,/To see it teachy and fall out wi'th'dug!' (1.3.30–2).

(C) The use of wormwood from ancient times, and in medieval gynaecology, as a contraceptive and abortifacient is explored in Riddle (1992, 2010), who notes that this use continues in modern India and that recent trials suggest its efficacy for malaria, some gynaecological conditions, and as an insecticide. Rowland (1981) gives specific uses of wormwood in medieval gynaecology. Langham (1597) lists nearly 200 medicinal uses for wormwood, including as purgative, for eyes and sight, to prevent or treat **worms** in various parts of the body, and to ameliorate gynaecological problems. Jonson's Tucca comments on 'one of their wormwood comedies' obviously being particularly acerbic (1603, *Poetaster* 1.2.48). It features regularly in Hall's medical notebook with uses in pregnancy, for hysteria and melancholy, and as a purgative (Lane 1992). Bloom (1903) and Savage (1923) suggest it may be a candidate for **Dian's bud** which is generally identified by commentators as an *Artemesia,* probably *A. absinthum,* L., wormwood.

wreath (A) A circular ornament, a wreath was generally bound, twisted or coiled into shape. Made of precious metal or as a chaplet or **garland** of **flowers** or **leaves**, it could be purely decorative, or symbolic of victory or success; figuratively it represents a crown. 'Wreath' was employed poetically to suggest celebration, ceremonial and crowning.

(B) Wreaths woven for maidens' coronets appear twice; on several occasions wreaths symbolize chivalry or victory; there are two interesting figurative examples. *TNK* is the dominant source. Responding positively to the First Queen's request for aid, Theseus recalls her wedding day: 'Your wheaten wreath/Was not then thresh'd nor blasted; Fortune at you/Dimpled her cheek with smiles' (*TNK* 1.1.64–6). Here the literal and figurative appear to coalesce. The Wooer paints a compelling picture of the Jailer's Daughter pining for Palamon: 'her careless tresses/A wreath of bulrush rounded; about her stuck/Thousand fresh water-flowers of several colors' (4.1.83–5). In the same play, Palamon prays to Venus before the contest: 'Take to thy grace/Me thy vow'd soldier, who do bear thy yoke/As 'twere a wreath of roses, yet is heavier/Than lead itself, stings more than nettles' (5.1.94–7). Although Arcite triumphs in the contest he is thrown from his horse in the victory procession: 'His victor's wreath/Even then fell off his head' (5.4.79–80). As *3H6* draws to a close King Edward expresses satisfaction: 'Thus far our fortune keeps an upward course,/ And we are grac'd with wreaths of victory' (5.3.1–2). Richard Gloucester opens *R3* with a celebration of the Yorkist triumph: 'Now are our brows bound with victorious wreaths' (1.1.5).

(C) Wreaths, usually made of flowers, are found throughout Colonna (1499). Drayton (1622) writes of wreaths that beautify the spring, of being crowned with wreaths, of a wreath-imperial, and of river **banks** bedecked with wreaths. He describes **beech woods** as beechen wreaths, wreaths of **wheat** in the fields, wreaths of quivering **reeds**, and the victorious wreaths of the Yorkists.

Y

yew (A) *Taxus baccata* L. is a native **tree** with dense **wood**, and dark evergreen poisonous foliage which is fatal for man and animals; its **seeds** are also poisonous though their red casing is not. Traditionally a symbol of mourning, it was planted in churchyards; sprigs or **branches** were **strewn** on corpses. Emblematically yew represented death and mourning; it also suggested the possibility of death by poisoning. The wood was often said to provide the best material for longbows. As an evergreen, yew was brought inside to decorate houses and churches at Christmas. Yew is a candidate for the **hebona** of *HAM* (1.5.62).

(B) In all its six appearances the yew betokens death. The melancholy Orsino requests a second rendition of Feste's song about a deserted lover longing for death:

> Come away, come away, death,
> And in sad cypress let me be laid.
> Fly away, fly away, breath,
> I am slain by a fair cruel maid.
> My shroud of white, stuck all with yew,
> > O, prepare it!
> My part of death, no one so true
> > Did share it.

(TN 2.4.51–8)

A scene that the vengeful Tamora has described as appealing, suddenly changes to one that is sinister. Inciting her sons to murder Bassianus and Lavinia she dissembles, 'they told me they would bind me here/Unto the body of a dismal yew,/And leave me to this miserable death' (*TIT* 2.3.106–8). The single phrase, 'dismal yew' is powerful enough to transform the atmosphere. Approaching the Capulet tomb, Paris instructs his page to extinguish his torch and to remain alert: 'Under yond yew trees lay thee along,/Holding thy ear close to the hollow ground/So shall no foot upon the churchyard tread' (*ROM* 5.3.3–5). The subsequent episode is recounted by Romeo's servant Balthasar: 'As I did sleep under this yew tree here,/I dreamt my master and another fought,/And that my master slew him' (137–9). Yet again the yew exercises a darkening effect on an already tragic scene. In *MAC* fragments of this ominous plant form part of the ingredients of the Witches brew: 'Gall of goat, and slips of yew/Sliver'd in the moon's eclipse' (4.1.27–8). A weapon fashioned from the wood of the tree acquires mythic potency in *R2*, its lethal potential allied to its traditional association with death. Scroop warns Richard of widespread opposition: 'Thy very beadsmen learn to bend their bows/Of double-fatal yew against thy state' (3.2.116–17). When the besieged English forces run out of arrows, the Black Prince responds, 'command our bows/To hurl away their pretty-color'd yew,/And to it with stones' (*E3* 4.6.14–16). The editor of New Cambridge (155) notes 'the long bows were polished in orange, red, or brown finish (Lapides)'.

(C) Elizabethan writers agree on its toxicity and medicinal uselessness. Dekker emphasizes the association of yew with death and mourning; he comments that when the plague struck 'all the pavement should instead of green rushes be strewed with blasted rosemary, withered hyacinths, fatal cypress and yew' (1603, *The Wonderful Year*). Drayton supports the idea of imported yew and thinks that Robin Hood and his men carried bows made of Spanish yew (1622, *Polyolbion* 26.327). Parkinson (1629: 606) suggests the tree is planted in domestic situations to provide both **shade** and ornament as an evergreen and to deck houses in winter. He notes that from ancient times it has been thought 'to be dangerous at the least, if not deadly'. Macht (1918) argues that there are only two serious candidates for hebona: henbane and yew. He points out that the hebona of Marlowe's *Jew of Malta* (3.4.103) and Spenser's *Faerie Queene* (I.vii.37; II.vii.52) both indicate yew rather than henbane, but maintains that Shakespeare's hebona is more likely to have been henbane because of the means of administration. Colonna (1499: 295–6) refers to 'the bitter yew, most welcome and apt for making Cupid's lethal weapons'.

Shakespeare's Works Index

All's Well that Ends Well

branch, brier, chase, crop, distil, ear, earth, estate, field, flower, fruit, grace (herb of), graft, grape, grass, ground, grow, hedge, herb, hive, honey, iris, kernel, knot, land, leaf, limb, lime, lodge, manor, marjoram, marrow, music, nature, nut, onion, palm, pear, plant, pomegranate, root, rose, rot, rush, saffron, sallet, seed, slip, smell, straw, strew, thorn, twig, wither, wood.

A Lover's Complaint

aloe, blossom, earth, flower, fountain, grain, ground, hive, knot, land, lodge, nature, orchard, pine, plant, posy, rank, rose, scythe, stalk, straw.

A Midsummer Night's Dream

acorn, apple, apricock, bank, bark, barren, bean, berry, blow, bower, brake, brier, brook, broom, bud, bur, bush, canker, chase, cherry, corn, cowslip, crab, crop, Cupid's flower, dew, dewberry, Dian's bud, distil, earth, eglantine, elm, estate, field, fig, flower, forest, fountain, fragrant, frost, fruit, garlic, grape, grass, green, ground, grove, grow, hawthorn, hemp, herb, honey, honeysuckle, hunt, ivy, knot-grass, land, leek, lily, lime, love-in-idleness, maze, mead, mulberry, music, musk-rose, Mustardseed, nature, nosegay, nut, oak, oat, onion, orange, oxlip, park, pea, peascod, Peaseblossom, plough, primrose, quince, ripe, rose, rot, rush, shade, squash, straw, thistle, thorn, thyme, turf, violet, walk, wall, weed, wheat, wither, wood, woodbine, worm.

Anthony and Cleopatra

balm, bark, barren, berry, blossom, blow, branch, bud, crop, dung, ear, earth, estate, fertile, field, fig, flag, flower, fruit, garden, garland, grain, grape, green, ground, grow, harvest, hedge, hunt, knot, land, laurel, leaf, lodge, mandragora, music, myrtle, narcissus, nature, olive, onion, palm, perfume, pine, pink, plant, pleached, plough, rank, reed, ripe, root, rose, rot, rush, salad, sap, scythe, seed, simple, smell, statue, strew, tree, vine, walk, weed, wheat, wither, worm.

As You Like It

acorn, bark, blossom, bough, bramble, branch, brier, brook, bur, bush, chase, chestnut, cod, corn, crop, damask, distil, dunghill, earth, estate, field, flower, forest, fountain, frost, fruit, graft, grape, green, ground, grow, harvest, hawthorn, holly, honey, hunt, husbandry, husk, land, limb, lodge, medlar, moss, music, mustard, nature, nut, oak, olive, orchard, osier, palm, peascod, perfume, plant, prune, rank, ripe, root, rose, rot, rush, rye, shade, simple, slip, smell, soil, thorn, tree, turf, walk, wall, weed, wood, worm, wreath.

Coriolanus

ash, balm, barren, bower, bowls, brier, canker, cedar, chaff, chase, cockle, corn, crab, cypress, damask, dew, dove-cote, earth, estate, field, flower, frost, fruit, garland, garlic, graft, grain, grape, ground, grove, grow, harrow, harvest, hew, hunt, husbandry, knot, land, leaf, limb, mulberry, nature, nettle, oak, orange, palm, plant, plough, rake, rank, reek, ripe, root, rot, rush, shade, smell, sow, statue, stock, strew, walk, wall, weed.

Cymbeline

bank, barren, bee, bough, bowls, branch, bud, bush, cedar, chaff, chase, chimney-sweeper, cowslip, crop, daisy, dew, dig, distil, earth, eglantine, elder, estate, field, flower, fruit, garden, ground, grow, harebell, harvest, herb, hunt, knot, land, leaf, lily, lodge, lop, mary-bud, moss, music, nature, oak, park, perfume, pine, pond, pool, primrose, prune, rank, reed, reek, ripe, root, rose, rot, rush, savory, shade, smell, sow, stock, strew, tree, turf, vine, violet, walk, wall, weed, wither, wood, worm.

Edward III

ash, arbour, bank, barren, bee, blossom, blow, bough, bower, branch, bud, canker, chase, cherry, corn, crop, drone, earth, estate, fertile, field, fig, flower, flower-de-luce, fragrant, frost, fruit, garden, grain, grass, green, ground, grove, grow, hay, harvest, hazel, herb, honey, laurel, leaf, lily, land, meadow, nature, oak, orchard, ordure, pine, plough, ripe, rose, root, rot, sap, seed, sickle, smell, soil, strew, thorn, tree, turf, vineyard, weed, wilderness, wither, wood, wormwood, yew.

Hamlet

alley, apple, bark, barren, blossom, blow, bough, branch, brook, buttons, canker, chase, cockle, columbine, compost, crab, crow-flower, daisy, dead men's fingers, dew, dig, distil, earth, estate, fennel, fertile, field, flax, flower, forest, frost, fruit, garden, gardener, garland, grace, (herb of), grain, grass, green, ground, grow, harrow, hebona, hedge, herb, honey, hunt, husbandry, knot, land, leaf, limb, lime, lodge, long purples, marrow, mildew, music, nature, nettle, nut, orchard, palm, pansy, perfume, plum, posy, primrose, rank, ripe, root, rose, rosemary, rot, rue, sallet, savory, scent, seed, simple, slip, smell, soil, spade, stalk, stock, straw, strew, tennis, thorn, tree, turf, violet, walk, wall, weed, wheat, willow, wither, wood, worm, wormwood.

Henry IV, Part 1

apple-john, bank, barren, bean, blackberry, bower, bud, camomile, canker, caterpillar, chase, crop, draff, earth, fern-seed, fertile, field, flower, forest, frost, fruit, garland, garlic, ginger, graft, green, ground, grove, grow, harvest, hedge, honey, husk, knot, land, leaf, limb, lime, lop, moss, music, nature, nettle, oat, park, peach, pease, pepper, perfume, plant, pomegranate, prune, radish, rank, reed, ripe, rose, rot, rush, sedge, shade, smell, soil, speargrass, thorn, tree, walk, wither, wood, worm.

Henry IV, Part 2

aconitum, apple-john, arbour, aspen, balm, bank, barren, bee, blossom, branch, bud, canker, caraway, chaff, corn, covert, dew, dig, dunghill, earth, ebony, elder, elm, estate, fennel, fertile, field, fig, flower, forest, frost, fruit, garland, gooseberry, graft, green, green-sickness, ground, grow, hade, hemp, hermit, hive, honey, honeysuckle, hunt, husbandry, imp, land, leaf, leathercoat, limb, lodge, mandrake, manure, mast, music, mustard, nature, nut-hook, olive, orchard, palm, peach, peascod, perfume, pippin, plough, pond, pruin, radish, rank, ripe, root, rose, rot, rush, seed, smell, soil, sow, straw, tennis, till, walk, wall, weed, wheat, wilderness, wither, worm.

Henry V

apple, balm, barley, berry, bough, branch, bud, bur, burnet, carnation, chase, clover, coulter, cowslip, darnel, deracinate, dew, dig, distil, dock, drone, dunghill, earth, elder, estate, femetary, fertile, field, fig, flower, flower-de-luce, fluellen, frost, fruit, furrow, garden, gardener, ginger, graft, grain, grass, green, ground, grow, hedge, hemlock, hemp, hew, honey, hunt, husbandry, husk, imp, kecksies, knot, land, leek, limb, lodge, mead, music, nature, nettle, nutmeg, ordure, pavilion, pear, plant, plow, rake, rank, reek, ripe, root, rose, rot, rush, scion, scythe, seed, shade, smell, sow, spray, stock, straw, strawberry, tennis, thistle, turf, twig, vine, vineyard, violet, walk, wall, weed, wither, wood, worm.

Henry VI, Part 1

bee, bloom, blossom, branch, brier, canker, chase, corn, crop, darnel, dew, dunghill, earth, estate, fertile, field, flower, flower-de-luce, fruit, gallery, garden, ground, grow, harvest, hedge, hermit, hew, hive, knot, labyrinth, land, leaf, limb, lop, maze, music, nature, park, pine, plant, ripe, root, rose, rot, rue, rush, sap, shade, soil, statue, stock, thorn, tree, vine, walk, wall, wither, wood, worm.

Henry VI, Part 2

apothecary, bank, barren, bee, blossom, brook, bud, bush, canker, caterpillar, cedar, chase, corn, country, crab, cypress, damson, dew, dig, drone, dunghill, earth, estate, fertile, field, fig, flax, flower, flower-de-luce, frost, fruit, garden, gardener, graft, grass, green, ground, grove, grow, harvest, hedge, hemp, herb, hew, hive, hunt, husbandry, iris, land, leaf, limb, lime, lodge, lop, mandrake, music, nature, palm, perfume, pine, plum, primrose, rose, rue, sallet, shade, slip, smell, soil, sow, spray, statue, stock, thorn, tree, walk, wall, weed, wilderness, wither, wood, worm.

Henry VI, Part 3

balm, brake, branch, brook, bush, cedar, chase, corn, covert, crop, dig, earth, estate, field, flower, forest, fountain, fruit, garland, ground, grow, harvest, hawthorn, hew, hunt, knot, land, laund, laurel, leaf, limb, lime, lodge, lop, manor, marrow, mast, nature, nettle, oak, olive, park, plant, root, rose, rot, rue, shade, shrub, spray, straw, thicket, thorn, tree, walk, wall, weed, willow, wither, wood, worm, wreath.

Henry VIII

apple, bark, blossom, brake, branch, broom, bud, cedar, chaff, cherry, corn, crab, dew, earth, estate, field, flower, fountain, frost, fruit, gallery, garden, garland, grain, ground, grow, hedge, honey, hunt, land, leaf, lily, limb, lime, lodge, lop, manor, maze, music, nature, pink, plant, rake, rank, reek, ripe, root, rose, sap, shade, soil, sow, stock, straw, strew, tennis, thorn, tree, vine, walk, weed, worm.

Julius Caesar

arbour, bank, barren, bee, chase, covert, dew, earth, field, flower, forest, fountain, garland, ground, grow, hedge, hew, honey, hunt, knot, land, leaf, limb, lodge, music, nature, oak, orchard, palm, rank, reek, ripe, rose, rush, smell, soil, statue, straw, strew, tree, walk, wall, wood, wreath.

King John

bank, bloom, bud, canker, chase, cherry, dew, dunghill, earth, estate, field, fig, fruit, grain, green, ground, grow, hedge, hunt, knot, land, lily, limb, lime, nature, orchard, palm, perfume, plum, rank, ripe, rose, rot, rue, rush, smell, soil, stalk, straw, strew, thorn, violet, walk, wall, worm.

King Lear

apothecary, apple, balm, branch, burdock, bush, canker, centaury, corn, costard, covert, crab, cuckoo-flower, darnel, dunghill, earth, estate, femiter, field, flax, forest, fruit, furrow-weeds, garden, germain, green, ground, grow, hardock, hawthorn, hedge, hemlock, hunt, knot, land, lily, lodge, marjoram, mast, mead, mildew, music, nature, nettle, oak, oat, peascod, perfume, pine, plant, pool, rake, rank, reek, ripe, rose, rosemary, rot, sallet, samphire, sap, simple, smell, soil, stock, straw, tree, vine, walk, wall, weed, wheat, wither, wood, worm, wreath.

Love's Labour's Lost

apple, bark, barren, blossom, blow, bowls, branch, bud, bush, carnation, carrot, cedar, chimney-sweeper, clove, cockle, columbine, coppice, corn, costard, crab, cuckoo-bud, daisy, damask, dew, dunghill, earth, ebony, elder, estate, field, flower, forest, frost, fruit, garden, gingerbread, grass, green, ground, grow, harvest, hedge, hermit, honey, hunt, imp, lady-smock, land, leaf, lemon, lily, limb, lodge, manor, meadow, mint, music, nature, nutmeg, oak, oat, osier, palm, park, pease, pine, plant, plantain, plough, pomewater, pumpion, prune, reek, ripe, rose, rot, scythe, shade, smell, soil, sow, straw, strew, sycamore, thicket, thorn, tree, turf, violet, walk, wall, weed, wither, wood, worm, wormwood, wreath.

Macbeth

balm, bank, barren, bough, chestnut, corn, cyme, dew, distil, earth, estate, field, flower, forest, fountain, fruit, germain, graft, grain, green, ground, grove, grow, harvest, heath, hemlock, hew, hunt, husbandry, insane root, knot, land, leaf, lily, lime, lodge, marrow, nature, perfume, pine, plant, primrose, rank, reek, rhubarb, ripe, root, rue, rush, seed, shade, slip, smell, tree, walk, wall, weed, wither, wood, worm, yew.

Measure for Measure

bark, birch, blossom, brake, bur, circummur'd, corn, covert, crab, earth, flower, fountain, fruit, garden, garden-house, garlic, ginger, grain, grape, ground, grow, husbandry, limb, medlar, music, myrtle, nature, oak, peach, planched, pond, postern, pruin, rank, ripe, rose, rot, seed, slip, smell, soil, sow, straw, strew, tilth, twig, vineyard, violet, walk, wall, weed, wilderness, wood, worm.

Much Ado about Nothing

alley, arbour, bloom, bower, branch, bud, canker, carduus benedictus, covert, distil, dogberry, earth, frost, garden, garland, green, ground, grow, harvest, hedge, holy-thistle, honeysuckle, leaf, limb, lime, lodge, music, nature, oak, oat, orange, orchard, Padua, perfume, plant, pleached, ripe, root, rose, rot, sedge, smell, soil, stalk, statue, tennis, thistle, walk, weed, willow, woodbine, worm.

Othello

Arabian tree, balm, blossom, chase, coloquintida, dew, earth, fertile, field, fig, fountain, fruit, garden, gardener, garland, grain, grape, green, ground, grow, herb, honey, hunt, hyssop, knot, land, lawn, lettuce, locust, lodge, mandragora, manure, music, nature, nettle, oak, palm, perfume, plant, poppy, rank, ripe, root, rose, rot, rush, scion, smell, sow, strawberry, sycamore, thyme/time/tine, tree, twig, walk, weed, willow, wither, worm.

Pericles

balm, bank, bay, bee, berry, blow, branch, bud, caterpillar, cherry, corn, crop, dig, drone, earth, estate, field, flower, fruit, gallery, graft, green, ground, grove, grow, harvest, herb-woman, honey, husbandry, knot, land, lodge, lop, marigold, mast, music, nature, pine, plant, plough, apothecary, ripe, root, rose, rosemary, rot, rush, sapling, seed, simple, smell, stalk, statue, stock, strew, strow, tennis, thorn, tree, vegetive, violet, walk, weed, wither, wood, worm, wreath.

Richard II

apricock, balm, bank, bark, barren, bay, bough, bowls, branch, caterpillar, chase, corn, crop, dew, ear, earth, Eden, estate, fertile, field, flower, forest, fountain, frost, fruit, furrow, garden, gardener, graft, grass, green, ground, grow, hedge, herb, imp, knot, land, leaf, limb, lime, lodge, lop, manor, manure, music, nature, nettle, palm, park, pine, plant, plough, postern, ripe, root, rose, rot, rue, rush, sap, shade, soil, spray, strew, strow, thorn, tree, twig, violet, walk, wall, weed, wilderness, wither, wood, worm, yew.

Richard III

balm, bank, barren, branch, cedar, chase, cherry, costard, covert, crop, dew, earth, estate, field, flower, fruit, garden, garland, graft, green, ground, grow, harvest, herb, honey, hunt, knot, land, leaf, limb, lodge, mast, music, nature, plant, ripe, root, rose, rot, rue, rush, sap, sapling, shade, soil, stalk, statue, stock, straw, strawberry, strew, tree, vine, walk, wall, weed, wither, worm, wreath.

Romeo and Juliet

angelica, apothecary, bitter sweeting, bower, bud, canker, chase, covert, date, dew, distil, dove-house, earth, estate, fennel, field, flower, fountain, frost, fruit, green, ground, grove, grow, hazel, herb, honey, hunt, knot, leaf, limb, lodge, mandrake, marchpane, mattock, medlar, music, nature, nut, orchard, osier, palm, pear, pepper, pine, pink, plant, plantain, pomegranate, poperin, apothecary, quince, rank, reek, ripe, root, rose, rosemary, rot, rush, seed, shade, simple, smell, spade, statue, stock, strew, sycamore, thorn, tree, walk, wall, weed, wither, wood, worm, wormwood, yew.

Sir Thomas More

(The non-Shakespearean words are in brackets.)
(arbour), bank, (bay, branch), country, dung, earth, (estate, fig, frost, fruit, garden, green, ground), grow, (holly, hunt, labyrinth, land, may, music), nature, (oak), parsnip, (plant), pumpion, (ripe), root, (shade, slip, tree, turnip).

Sonnets

apple, balm, bank, barren, bough, bower, bud, canker, chase, damask, dig, distil, ear, earth, field, flower, forest, fountain, fragrant, frost, fruit, furrow, garden, green, ground, grow, harvest, honey, hunt, husbandry, land, leaf, lily, limb, lodge, marigold, marjoram, meadow, music, nature, olive, perfume, pine, plant, rank, reek, ripe, root, rose, rot, sap, scythe, shade, sickle, simple, smell, soil, statue, thorn, tillage, tree, violet, walk, wall, weed, wither, wood, worm.

The Comedy of Errors

alley, balsamum, barren, branch, brier, chase, cherry, cicely, earth, elm, field, grain, grass, ground, grow, ivy, land, mast, moss, music, nature, nut, palm, prune, rot, rush, saffron, sap, vine, walk, wall.

The Merchant of Venice

apple, bank, barren, branch, brook, chaff, chase, dew, drone, earth, estate, field, frost, fruit, ginger, grain, grass, green, ground, grow, hedge, herb, hermit, hive, husbandry, land, limb, lodge, music, nature, Padua, park, pine, plant, pond, posy, rank, reed, ripe, rot, rush, seed, slip, smell, stock, tree, walk, wall, wheat, wilderness, willow, worm.

The Merry Wives of Windsor
balm, bilberry, bowls, brook, Bucklersbury, bud, bush, buttons, cabbage, carrot, chase, costard, distil, draff, dunghill, earth, elder, eringo, fertile, fico, field, flower, forest, fragrant, gourd, green, ground, grow, harvest, hawthorn, hedge, hunt, knot, land, limb, lime, lodge, manor, meadow, nature, nut-hook, oak, park, pear, pepper, pippin, posy, potato, prune, pumpion, rank, reek, ripe, root, rose, rot, rush, shade, simple, smell, stock, strew, tree, turnip, walk, walnut, wither, wood, worm.

The Passionate Pilgrim
blossom, brake, brook, bud, crab, damask, dew, earth, field, flower, fragrant, green, ground, grove, grow, hedge, ivy, leaf, lily, music, myrtle, oak, osier, plant, plum, posy, rose, shade, smell, straw, thorn, tree, wither.

The Phoenix and the Turtle
Arabian tree, grow, music, nature, simple, tree.

The Rape of Lucrece
balm, bank, bark, barren, bee, branch, bud, bush, cedar, chase, corn, crop, daisy, dew, drone, earth, estate, field, flower, fountain, frost, fruit, graft, grape, grass, green, ground, grove, grow, harvest, hive, honey, hunt, land, lawn, leaf, lily, lime, lodge, marigold, maze, mead, narcissus, nature, oak, palm, pine, plant, plough, reed, reek, root, rose, rot, rush, sap, seed, shade, shrub, simple, smell, stalk, stock, straw, thorn, vine, walk, wall, weed, wilderness, wither, wood, worm, wormwood, wreath.

The Taming of the Shrew
apple, balm, brook, bud, bush, chestnut, cockle, crab, cypress, dew, distil, earth, estate, field, flower, fountain, frost, fruit, garden, green, ground, grove, grow, hazel, hedge, honey, hunt, kernel, knot, land, lodge, maze, mead, music, mustard, nature, oat, onion, orchard, Padua, park, parsley, perfume, pimpernel, pine, plant, rose, rot, rush, scent, sedge, smell, stock, straw, strew, thorn, turf, walk, wall, walnut, wither, wood, worm.

The Tempest
acorn, apple, Arabian tree, bank, bark, barley, barren, bee, berry, blossom, bosky, bough, brier, brook, broom, bush, canker, cedar, chase, corn, cowslip, crab, dew, dig, dock, earth, estate, fertile, fetch, filbert, flower, forthright, frost, furrow, furze, gorse, grass, green, ground, grove, grow, harvest, heath, honey, hunt, husk, ivy, kernel, knot, land, lime, line-grove, lodge, long heath, mallow, mast, maze, mead, mushrumps, music, nature, nettle, nut, oak, oat, pease, perfume, pignut, pine, pioned, plant, plantation, pool,

rank, reed, ripe, root, rot, rye, saffron, shrub, smell, sow, stover, straw, thorn, tilth, tree, turf, twilled, verdure, vine, vineyard, walk, wall, weed, wheat, wither, wood, worm.

The Two Gentlemen of Verona
bee, blow, bud, canker, chase, crab, earth, flower, forest, garland, ground, grow, honey, hunt, knot, land, lily, lime, lodge, music, nature, pine, postern, rake, ripe, root, rose, sedge, smell, statue, stock, thicket, verdure, walk, wall, weed, wilderness, wood, wreath.

The Two Noble Kinsmen
apricock, arbour, balm, bank, barley, bay, beech, birch, bloom, blossom, blow, bough, bowls, brake, brier, brook, broom, bud, bulrush, bush, buttons, cedar, chaff, chase, cherry, chestnut, cockle, corn, daffodil, daisy, damask, dew, ear, earth, estate, fescue, field, flax, flower, forest, fruit, garden, garden-house, garland, glade, grain, grape, green, ground, grow, hawthorn, hunt, iris, ivy, knot, land, larks'-heels, leaf, lodge, marigold, marrow, mead, mulberry, music, narcissus, nature, nettle, nosegay, oak, oat, oxlip, perfume, pink, plane, plant, plantain, plough, plum, posy, primrose, reed, ripe, root, rose, rot, rush, scythe, sedge, seed, shade, smell, soil, sow, strew, tennis, thicket, thyme, tree, vine, walk, weed, wheat, willow, wither, wood, wreath.

The Winter's Tale
bank, bark, barren, blossom, bough, bowls, branch, brier, bud, carnation, chaff, chase, covert, crab, crown imperial, cypress, daffodil, damask, dew, dibble, dungy, earth, estate, fertile, flax, Flora, flower, flower-de-luce, gallery, garden, garland, garlic, gillyvor, ginger, graft, grain, green, ground, grow, hedge, honey, hunt, ivy, kernel, land, lavender, lawn, lily, lodge, mace, marigold, marjoram, mint, music, nature, nettle, nosegay, nutmeg, oak, oxlip, palm, perfume, pine, plant, pomander, pond, postern, primrose, pruin, rank, ripe, root, rose, rosemary, rot, rue, rush, saffron, sap, savory, scion, seed, slip, smell, squash, statue, stock, straw, strew, thorn, violet, walk, warden, weed, wither.

Timon of Athens
balm, balsom, berry, bough, brier, bush, canker, chase, composture, crop, earth, estate, fertile, field, forest, fruit, grape, grass, green, ground, grow, hep, hew, hunt, husbandry, knot, land, leaf, limb, marrow, mast, medlar, music, nature, oak, olive, palm, perfume, plough, rank, reek, ripe, root, rose, rot, slip, smell, soil, sow, spade, tree, vine, walk, wall, wither, wood, worm.

Titus Andronicus
aspen, bark, barren, bee, berry, blossom, bough, branch, brier, bush, cedar, chase, corn, dew, dig, distil, earth, elder, field, flower, forest, fountain, fragrant, frost, fruit, grass, green, ground, grove, grow, herb, hermit, hew, honey, honey-stalk, hunt, knot, land,

laurel, leaf, lily, limb, lodge, lop, mattock, mead, meadow, mistletoe, moss, music, nature, nettle, park, perfume, plant, plough, ripe, root, rose, rot, rue, rush, sapling, shade, shrub, slip, smell, spade, stock, straw, tree, walk, wall, weed, wilderness, wither, wood, wreath, yew.

Troilus and Cressida

almond, balm, bank, barren, blackberry, blow, bur, chaff, crop, date, deracinate, dew, distil, earth, field, flower, forthright, fountain, fruit, grain, green, grow, hedge, hermit, hive, honey, hunt, husbandry, husk, iris, kernel, knot, labyrinth, land, laurel, leaf, lily, limb, lime, lodge, mint, music, nature, nettle, nut, oak, orchard, palm, pine, plough, potato, rank, ripe, root, rose, rot, rush, sap, seed, shade, soil, stalk, statue, straw, strew, thicket, toadstool, walk, wall, weed, wheat, wither, wood.

Twelfth Night

apple, bank, barren, bower, box-tree, branch, bud, caper, chase, cherry, codling, cypress, damask, earth, ebony, estate, fertile, field, flax, flower, fruit, garden, ginger, grain, green, ground, grow, harvest, hermit, hunt, knot, land, limb, lime, lodge, mast, mint, music, nature, olive, orchard, peascod, pepper, pine, plant, rank, ripe, rose, scent, smell, sow, squash, stock, strow, viola, violet, stock, walk, wall, weed, willow, worm, yew.

Venus and Adonis

Adonis flower, balm, bank, barren, berry, bough, brake, bramble, brier, brook, bud, bush, canker, caterpillar, cedar, chase, cherry, copse, crop, dew, dig, distil, earth, ebony, field, flower, fountain, frost, fruit, garden, grape, grass, green, ground, grove, grow, hedge, herb, honey, hunt, labyrinth, laund, lawn, leaf, lily, limb, marrow, mead, mulberry, music, myrtle, narcissus, nature, palm, park, perfume, pine, plant, plum, primrose, rank, reek, ripe, root, rose, rot, rush, sap, scent, seed, shade, slip, smell, stalk, statue, thorn, tree, violet, walk, weed, wither, wood, worm, wreath.

Bibliography

Editions of Shakespeare's works

Bate, Jonathan, ed., *Titus Andronicus*, London and New York: Arden Shakespeare, Third Series, 1995.

Bevington, David, ed., *Troilus and Cressida*, London and New York: Arden Shakespeare, Third Series, 1998.

Blakemore Evans, G., ed., *The Sonnets*, Cambridge: Cambridge University Press, 1996.

—ed., *The Riverside Shakespeare*, second edn, Boston: Houghton Mifflin, 1997.

Brockbank, Philip, ed., *Coriolanus*, London: Arden Shakespeare, Second Series, 1976.

Brooks, Harold F., ed., *A Midsummer Night's Dream*, London and New York: Arden Shakespeare, Second Series, 1979.

Brown, John Russell, ed., *The Merchant of Venice*, London and New York: Arden Shakespeare, Second Series, 1955.

Burns, Edward, ed., *King Henry VI, Part 1*, London and New York: Arden Shakespeare, Third Series, 2000.

Carroll, William C., ed., *The Two Gentlemen of Verona*, London and New York: Arden Shakespeare, Third Series, 2004.

Clark, Sandra and Mason, Pamela, *Macbeth*: Arden Shakespeare, Third Series, 2015.

Cox, John D. and Rasmussen, Eric (eds), *King Henry VI, Part 3*, London and New York: Arden Shakespeare, Third Series, 2001.

Craik, T. W., ed., *King Henry V*, London and New York: Arden Shakespeare, Third Series, 1995.

Daniell, David, ed., *Julius Caesar*, London and New York: Arden Shakespeare, Third Series, 1998.

David, Richard, ed., *Love's Labour's Lost*, London and New York: Arden Shakespeare, Second Series, 1951.

Dawson, Anthony B. and Minton, Gretchen E. (eds), *Timon of Athens*, London and New York: Arden Shakespeare, Third Series, 2008.

Dorsch, T. S., ed., *Julius Caesar*, London and New York: Arden Shakespeare, Second Series, 1955.

Drakakis, John, ed., *The Merchant of Venice*, London and New York: Arden Shakespeare, Third Series, 2010.

Duncan-Jones, Katherine, ed., *The Sonnets*, London and New York: Arden Shakespeare, Third Series, 1997.

Duncan-Jones, Katherine and Woudhuysen, H. R. (eds), *Poems*, London and New York: Arden Shakespeare, Third Series, 2007.

Dusinberre, Juliet, ed., *As You Like It*, London and New York: Arden Shakespeare, Third Series, 2006.

Elam, Keir, ed., *Twelfth Night*, London and New York: Arden Shakespeare, Third Series, 2008.

Foakes, R. A., ed., *Henry VIII*, London and New York: Arden Shakespeare, Second Series, 1957.

—ed., *The Comedy of Errors*, London and New York: Arden Shakespeare, Second Series, 1962.

—ed., *King Lear*, London and New York: Arden Shakespeare, Third Series, 1997.

Forker, Charles R., ed., *King Richard II*, London and New York: Arden Shakespeare, Third Series, 2002.

Gibbons, Brian, ed., *Romeo and Juliet*, London and New York: Arden Shakespeare, Second Series, 1980.

Gossett, Suzanne, ed., *Pericles*, London and New York: Arden Shakespeare, Third Series, 2004.

Hammond, Antony, ed., *Richard III*, London and New York: Arden Shakespeare, Second Series, 1981.

Hoeniger, F. D., ed., *Pericles*, London and New York: Arden Shakespeare, Second Series, 1963.

Hogdon, Barbara, ed., *The Taming of the Shrew*, London and New York: Arden Shakespeare, Third Series, 2010.

Holland, Peter, ed., *Coriolanus*, London and New York, Arden Shakespeare, Third Series, 2013.

Honigmann, E. A. J., ed., *King John*, London and New York: Arden Shakespeare, Second Series, 1967.

—ed., *Othello*, London and New York: Arden Shakespeare, Third Series, 1997.

Humphreys, A. R., ed., *King Henry IV, Part 1*, London and New York: Arden Shakespeare, Second Series, 1960.

—ed., *King Henry IV, Part 2*, London and New York: Arden Shakespeare, Second Series, 1966.

Hunter, G. K., ed., *All's Well That Ends Well*, London and New York: Arden Shakespeare, Second Series, 1959.

Jenkins, Harold, ed., *Hamlet*, London and New York: Methuen, Arden Shakespeare, Second Series, 1982.

Jowett, John, ed., *Sir Thomas More*, London and New York: Arden Shakespeare, Third Series, 2011.

Kastan, David Scott, ed., *King Henry IV, Part 1*, London and New York: Arden Shakespeare, Third Series, 2002.

Kermode, Frank, ed., *The Tempest*, London and New York: Arden Shakespeare, Second Series, 1964.

Klein, Karl, ed., *Timon of Athens*, Cambridge and New York: Cambridge University Press, New Cambridge Shakespeare, 2001.

Knowles, Ronald, ed., *King Henry VI, Part 2*, London and New York: Arden Shakespeare, Third Series, 2000.

Latham, Agnes, ed., *As You Like It*, London and New York: Arden Shakespeare, Second Series, 1975.

Leech, Clifford, ed., *The Two Gentlemen of Verona*, London and New York: Arden Shakespeare, Second Series, 1969.

Lever, J. W., ed., *Measure for Measure*, London and Cambridge, MA: Arden Shakespeare, Second Series, 1965.

Lothian, J. M. and Craik, T. W. (eds), *Twelfth Night*, London and New York: Arden Shakespeare, Second Series, 1975.

Maxwell, T. C., ed., *Titus Andronicus*, London and New York: Arden Shakespeare, Second Series, 1953.

McEachern, Claire, ed., *Much Ado About Nothing*, London and New York: Arden Shakespeare, Third Series, 2006.

McMullan, Gordon, ed., *King Henry VIII*, London and New York: Arden Shakespeare, Third Series, 2000.

Melchiori Giorgio, ed., *King Edward III*, Cambridge and New York: Cambridge University Press, The New Cambridge Shakespeare, 1998.

—ed., *The Merry Wives of Windsor*, London and New York: Arden Shakespeare, Third Series, 2000.

Morris, Brian, ed., *The Taming of the Shrew*, London and New York: Arden Shakespeare, Second Series, 1981.

Muir, Kenneth, ed., *Macbeth*, London and New York: Arden Shakespeare, Second Series, 1951.

—ed., *King Lear*, London and New York: Arden Shakespeare, Second Series, 1972.

Nosworthy, J. M., ed., *Cymbeline*, London and New York: Arden Shakespeare, Second Series, 1955.

Oliver, H. J., ed., *Timon of Athens*, London: Arden Shakespeare, Second Series, 1969.

—ed., *The Merry Wives of Windsor*, London: Arden Shakespeare, Second Series, 1971.

Orgel, Stephen, ed., *The Tempest*, Oxford and New York: Oxford University Press, The World's Classics, 1994.

Pafford, J. H. P., *The Winter's Tale*, London and New York: Arden Shakespeare, Second Series, 1966.

Palmer, Kenneth, ed., *Troilus and Cressida*, London and New York: Arden Shakespeare, Second Series, 1982.

Pitcher, John, ed., *The Winter's Tale*, London and New York: Arden Shakespeare, Third Series, 2010.

Potter, Lois, ed., *The Two Noble Kinsmen*, London and New York: Arden Shakespeare, Third Series, 1997.

Prince, F. T., ed., *Poems*, London and New York: Arden Shakespeare, Second Series, 1969.

Ridley, M. R. ed., *Othello*, London and New York: Arden Shakespeare, Second Series, 1958

—ed., *Antony and Cleopatra*, London and New York: Arden Shakespeare, Second Series, 1965.

Sams, Eric, ed., *Shakespeare's Edward III: An Early Play Restored to the Canon*, New Haven and London: Yale University Press, 1996.

Sanders, Norman, ed., *Othello*, Cambridge and New York: New Cambridge Shakespeare, 1984.

Siemon, James R., ed., *Richard III*, London and New York: Arden Shakespeare, Third Series, 2009.

Thompson, Ann and Taylor Neil (eds), *Hamlet*, London and New York: Arden Shakespeare, Third Series, 2006.

Ure, Peter, ed., *Richard II*, London and New York: Arden Shakespeare, Second Series, 1956.

Vaughan, Virginia Mason and Vaughan, Alden T., *The Tempest*, London and New York: Arden Shakespeare, Third Series, 1999.

Warren, Roger, ed., *Edward III*, London: Nick Hern Books in association with the Royal Shakespeare Company, 2002.

Weis, Rene, ed., *Romeo and Juliet*, London and New York: Arden Shakespeare, Third Series, 2012.

Wilders, John, ed., *Antony and Cleopatra*, London and New York: Arden Shakespeare, Third Series, 1995.

Woudhuysen, H. R., ed., *Love's Labour's Lost*, London and New York: Arden Shakespeare, Third Series, 1998.

Shakespeare's contemporaries

Bawcutt, N. W., ed., Christopher Marlowe, *The Jew of Malta*, Manchester and New York: Manchester University Press, 1978 and 1997.

Bowers, Fredson, ed., Beaumont and Fletcher, *Dramatic Works*, Cambridge: Cambridge University Press, 1976.

Campbell, Lily B., ed., Thomas Sackville, *The Mirror for Magistrates* (1559), Cambridge: Cambridge University Press, 1938, (reprinted by Barnes and Noble, 2011).

Corbin, Peter and Sedge, Douglas, eds, Anon, *Thomas of Woodstock*, The Revels Plays, Manchester: Manchester University Press, 2002.

Craik, T. W., ed., Philip Massinger, *The City Madam*, London: Ernest Benn Ltd, 1964.

Cunliffe, J. W. ed., George Gascoigne, *The Posies* (1575), London: Cambridge University Press, 1907.

David, Walter R., ed., *The Works of Thomas Campion*, London: Faber and Faber, 1969.

Gill, Roma, ed., *The Complete Works of Christopher Marlowe*, Oxford: Clarendon Press, 1995.

Grosart, Alexander B., ed., *The Life and Works of Robert Greene* (1584–92), 15 vols, The Huth Library: private circulation.

Gunby, David, ed., John Webster, *Three Plays*, Harmondsworth and New York: Penguin Books, 1972.

Hamilton, A. C., ed., Edmund Spenser, *The Faerie Queen* (1596), London: Longman, 1997.

Hebel, J. William, ed., Michael Drayton, *The Complete Works*, 5 vols, Oxford: Blackwells, 1933.

Henderson, Philip, ed., Edmund Spenser, *The Shepherd's Calendar and Other Poems*, London: Dent, Everyman's Library, 1932; 1965.

Jamieson, Michael, ed., Ben Jonson, *Three Comedies*, Harmondsworth: Penguin Books, 1966.

Kidnie, Margaret J., ed., Ben Jonson, *The Devil is an Ass and other plays*, Oxford: Oxford University Press, 2000.

Marcus, Leah, S., ed., John Webster, *The Duchess of Malfi*, London and New York: Arden Shakespeare, Third Series, 2009.

McCabe, Richard A., ed., Edmund Spenser, *The Shorter Poems*, Harmondsworth: Penguin Books, 1999.

McDonald, James H. and Brown, Nancy Pollard (eds), Robert Southwell, *Poems*, Oxford: Clarendon Press, 1967.

Phelps, William Lyon, ed., George Chapman, *All Fools*, London: T. Fisher Unwin Ltd, 1895.

Rhys, Ernest, ed., *The Plays of Christopher Marlowe*, London: J. M. Dent & Sons Ltd, 1931.

Robbins, Robin, ed., *The Poems of John Donne*, 2 vols, Harlow: Pearson Longman, 2008.

Robertson, Jean, ed., Philip Sidney, *The Countess of Pembroke's Arcadia* (1580), Oxford: Clarendon Press, 1973.

Scragg, Leah, ed., John Lyly, *Euphues: The Anatomy of Wit, and Euphues and His England* (1580), Manchester: Manchester University Press, 2003.

Smith, Emma, ed., Thomas Kyd, *The Spanish Tragedie*, Harmondsworth: Penguin Books, 1998.

Taylor, Gary and Lavagnino, John (eds), *Thomas Middleton, the Collected Works*, Oxford: Oxford University Press, 2007.

Primary sources

Adams, Thomas, *A Divine Herball*, London: George Purslow, 1616.

Anon, *England's Helicon* (1600), ed. Bullen, A. H., London: John C. Nimmo, 1887.

Bacon, Francis, 'Of Gardens: An Essay' (1625), Memphis, Tennessee: General Books, 2010.

Baldwin, William, *The Mirror for Magistrates* (1559–87), ed. Campbell, Lily B., Cambridge: Cambridge University Press, 1938.

'Calendar of Letters and Papers Foreign and Domestic, Henry VIII' vol. 21 part 2, September 1546–January 1547, (eds) James Gairdner and R. H. Brodie 1910.

Camden, William, *Remaines of a Greater Worke Concerning Britaine* (1605), in The English Emblem Tradition, ed. Daly, Peter M., vol. 4., Toronto: University of Toronto Press, 1998.

Campion, Thomas, *The Works of Thomas Campion*, ed. David, Walter R., (1969). London: Faber and Faber.

Coles, William, *The Art of Simpling. An Introduction to the Knowledge and Gathering of Plants* (1656), St Catherine's, Ontario: Provoker Press, 1968.

Colonna, Francesco, (1499), *Hypnerotomachia Poliphili. The Strife of Love in a Dream*, trans. Godwin, Joscelyn, London: Thames and Hudson, 1999.

Culpeper, N., *Complete Herbal* (1653), introd. Vowles, D., London: Arcturus, 2009.

Elizabeth I, *Selected Works*, ed. May, Steven W., New York: Washington Square Press, 2004.

Erasmus, Desiderius, *Collected Works* (1536), translated and annotated by Mynors, R. A. B., Toronto: University of Toronto Press, 1989.

Gerard, John, *The Herbal or General History of Plants:* revised and enlarged by Thomas Johnson, New York: Dover Publications, 1633.

Harrison, William, *The Description of England* (1587), ed. Eleden, Georges, Ithaca, New York: Cornell University Press, 1968.

Hawkins, Henry, *Partheneia Sacra* (1633), Introd. Höltgen, Karl Josef, Aldershot, England: Scolar Press, 1993.

Hentzner, Paul, *Travels in England* (1598), translated by Walpole, Horace, Strawberry Hill Press, 1757.

Hill, Thomas, *The Gardener's Labyrinth* (1577), ed. Mabey, R., Oxford: Oxford University Press, 1988.

Hoby, Margaret, *The Private Life of an Elizabethan Lady. The Diary of Lady Margaret Hoby 1599–1605* (1605), ed. Moody, Joanna, Gloucestershire: Sutton Publishing Ltd, 1998.

Holinshed's Chronicles of England, Scotland, and Ireland in 6 vols, (1577), London: printed for Johnson, J.; Rivington, F. C. and J.; Payne, T.; Wilkie and Robinson; Longman, Hurst, Rees, and Orme; Cadell and Davies; and Mawman, J, 1807.

Johnson, Thomas, *Iter Plantarum; Descriptio Itineris Plantarum* (1629, 1632), ed. Gilmour, J. S. L., Pennsylvania: Hunt Botanical Library, 1972.

Lambarde, William, *The Perambulation of Kent* (1576), ed. Church, Richard, Bath: Adams and Dart, 1970.

Laneham, R. *Kenilworth Festivities, comprising Laneham's description of the Pageantry and Gascoigne's Masques, Represented before Queen Elizabeth at Kenilworth Castle* (1575), John Merridew: Warwick and Leamington, 1825.

Lawson, William, *The Country Housewifes Garden*, London, 1617.

—*A New Orchard and Garden*, 1618.

Lyte, Henry, trans., *A Niewe Herball*, by Rembert Dodoens, London, 1578.

Markham, Gervase, *The English Husbandman* (1613), Charleston, S. Carolina: Bibliobazaar, 2008.

—(1615), *The English Housewife*, ed Best, Michael, (1986), Kingston and Montreal: McGill-Queens University Press.

Maunsell, Andrew, *The Catalogue of English Printed Books* (1595), London: Gregg Press Ltd, 1965.

Moryson, Fynes, *An Itinerary, containing his ten yeeres travell through the twelve dominions of Germany, Bohmerland, Sweitzerland, Netherland, Denmarke, Poland, Italy, Turky, France, England, Scotland and Ireland* (1605–17). ed. MacLehose, James, Glasgow, 1907.

Neckam, Alexander *De Naturis Rerum* (c. 1190), ed. Wright, Thomas, (Rolls Series), London: Longman, Green, Longman, Roberts and Green, 1863.

Norden, John, *The Surveyor's Dialogue* (1618), ed. Netzloff, Mark, Farnham: Ashgate Publishing Ltd, 2010.

Ovid, *Metamorphoses* (1567), trans. Golding, Arthur, ed. Bate, Jonathan, Philadelphia: Paul Dry Books, 2000.

Paradin, Claudius, *The Heroical Devises of M. Claudius Paradin [and] the Purtratures or Emblems of Gabriel Simeon, a Florentine* (1591), in The English Emblem Tradition, Daly, Peter M. and Duer, Leslie T. (eds), vol. 2., Toronto: University of Toronto Press, 1993.

Peacham, Henry, *Minerva Britanna* (1612), Leeds: Scolar Press, 1966.

Peele, George, Speeches to Queen Elizabeth at Theobalds, in *The Works of George Peele*, ed. Bullen, A. H., London: John C. Nimmo, 1888.

Plat, Hugh, *The Jewell House of Art and Nature* (1594), Early English Books Online Reprint, London, 2011.

Platter, Thomas, *Travels in England* (1599), ed. Williams, C., London: Jonathan Cape, 1937.

Porta, Giambattista Della, *Natural magic*, London, 1658.

Puttenham, George, (1589), *The Art of English Poesy*, ed. Whigham, Frank and Rebhorn, Wayne, (2007). Ithaca, New York: Cornell University Press.

Robinson, Clement, *A Handful of Pleasant Delights* (1584), ed. Arber, Edward, London: English Scholar's Library of Old and Modern Works, 1880.

Rowland, Beryl, trans. *Medieval Women's Guide to Health. The First English Gynecological Handbook*, London: Croom Helm Ltd, 1981.

Spenser, Edmund, (1579), *The Shepheardes Calendar*, ed., Smith, J. C. and De Selincourt, E., Oxford, Oxford University Press, 1989.

—(1596), *The Faerie Queene*, ed., Hamilton, A. S., London, Longman, 1997.

Stern, William Thomas, 'William Turner's *Libellus*, 1538, and *Names of Herbs*, 1548', *Libellus de Re Herbaria (1538) and The Names of Herbes (1548): Facsimiles.* By William Turner, London: Ray Society, 1965: 3–9.

Stow, John, *A Summerie of the Chronicles of England, Diligently Collected, Abridged, and Continued unto this present Yeare of Christ (1604)*, ed. Beer, Barrett L. Lewiston, New York: Edwin Mellen Press, 2007.

Stow, John, *A Survey of London written in the Year 1598* (1598), introd. Fraser, Antonia, Stroud: Sutton Publishing, 1994.

Tottel, Richard, *Songes and Sonettes* (1557), ed. Marquis, Paul A., Arizona: Renaissance English Text Society, 2007.

Trevelyon, Thomas, The Embroidery Patterns of Thomas Trevelyon (1608), ed. Nevinson, J. L., *The Walpole Society*, vol. 41, 1–35. 1966–8.

Turner, William, *Libellus de Re Herbaria* (1538). *The Names of Herbes* (1548), ed. Britten, James, Daydon Jackson, B., Stearn, W. T., London: The Ray Society, 1965.

—*A New Herball*, (Parts I, II & III: 1551-68), eds. Chapman, Tweddle, McCombie & Wesencraft, Cambridge University Press, 1995.

Tusser, Thomas, (1557), *A Hundred Good Pointes of Husbandrie*. Kessinger Publishing, (2010), from the 1810 London text. Montana, U.S.A.

Tusser, Thomas, *Five Hundred Pointes of Good Husbandrie* (1573), ed. Payne, W., Herrtage, Sydney, J., London: Trubner & Co., 1878.

Waldstein, Baron, *The Diary of Baron Waldstein. A Traveller in Elizabethan England* (1600), trans Groos, G. W., London: Thames and Hudson, 1981.

Whitney, Geffrey, *A Choice of Emblems*, London, 1586.

Web sources

Albertus Magnus, *The Boke of Secretes* (c. 1279), London, 1565. http://0–eebo.chadwyck.com. libsys.wellcome.ac.uk (accessed 22/9/2011).

Bacon, Francis, *Of Gardens*, in *The Essayes or counsels, civill and moral*, London, 1625. http://0–eebo.chadwyck.com.libsys.wellcome.ac.uk (accessed 8/3/2013).

—*Sylva Sylvarum or a Natural History*, London, 1627. http://0–eebo.chadwyck.com.libsys. wellcome.ac.uk (accessed 8/3/2013).

Bartholomaeus Anglicus, *Batman upon Bartholome. His Booke De Proprietatibus Rerum, 1582.* http://0–eebo.chadwyck.com.libsys.wellcome.ac.uk (accessed 23/9/2011).

Boorde, Andrew, A compendious regiment or a dietary of helth, London, 1542. http://0–eebo. chadwyck.com.libsys.wellcome.ac.uk (accessed 7/3/2013).

Brasbridge, Thomas, *The Poore mans Jewel, that is to say, a Treatise of the Pestilence*, London, 1578. http://0–eebo.chadwyck.com.libsys.wellcome.ac.uk (accessed 16/6/2011).

Bright, T., *A Treatise of Melancholy*, London, 1586. http://0–eebo.chadwyck.com.libsys. wellcome.ac.uk (accessed 30/6/2011).

Browne, William, *Britannia's Pastorals*, London, 1613–16. http://0–eebo.chadwyck.com.libsys. wellcome.ac.uk (accessed 7/3/2013).

Brunschwig, Hieronymus, The Vertuose boke of Dystillacyon, London, 1525. http://0–eebo. chadwyck.com.libsys.wellcome.ac.uk (accessed 4/7/2011).

Bullein, William, *A Dialogue bothe pleasaunte and pietifull wherein is a Goodly Regimente against the Feuer Pestilence with a Consolacion and Comfort against Death*, London, 1564 http://0–eebo.chadwyck.com.libsys.wellcome.ac.uk (accessed 3/4/2011). *The Government of Health*, London, 1595. http://0–eebo.chadwyck.com.libsys.wellcome.ac.uk (accessed 2/4/2011).

Cogan, Thomas, *The Haven of Health*, London, 1584. http://0–eebo.chadwyck.com.libsys. wellcome.ac.uk (accessed 23/4/2011).

Davies, John, *Hymns to Astraea*, London, 1599. http://0–eebo.chadwyck.com.libsys.wellcome. ac.uk (accessed 7/3/13).

Dekker, Thomas, *The Wonderful Year*, London, 1603. http://0–eebo.chadwyck.com.libsys. wellcome.ac.uk (accessed 7/3/13).

Dodoens, Rembert, *A Niewe Herball, or Historie of Plantes* (1578) translated from French to English by Henry Lyte., London: Gerald Dewes. http://0–eebo.chadwyck.com.libsys. wellcome.ac.uk (accessed 13/7/2011).

Elyot, Thomas, *The Castel of Helth* (1541), Miami: Hardpress Publishing, 2011. —*The Boke named The Governour*, London, 1565. http://0–eebo.chadwyck.com.libsys.wellcome.ac.uk (accessed 15/4/2011).

Estienne, (Stevens), Charles, and Liebault, John, *The Countrie Farme* (1616), translated by Surflet, Richard, newly reviewed, corrected and augmented by Markham, Gervase, London. http://0–eebo.chadwyck.com.libsys.wellcome.ac.uk (accessed 7/3/13).

Fitzherbert, John, *The Boke of Husbandry*, 1533. http://0–eebo.chadwyck.com.libsys.wellcome. ac.uk (accessed 7/3/13).

Fowler, Deborah, *The Natural Alternative*, 2011, www.livingfood.co.uk (accessed 3/9/11).

Gerard, John, *The Herball or Generall Historie of Plantes*, London, 1597. http://0–eebo. chadwyck.com.libsys.wellcome.ac.uk (accessed 8/9/2011).

Heresbach, Conrad, *The Whole Art of Husbandry, Gardening, Graffing and Planting* (1596), trans. Googe, Barnabe, London. http://0–eebo.chadwyck.com.libsys.wellcome.ac.uk (accessed 31/7/2011).

Hill, Thomas, *The Profitable Art of Gardening*, London, 1568. http://0–eebo.chadwyck.com. libsys.wellcome.ac.uk (accessed 31/8/2011).

Langham, William, *The Garden of Health*, London, 1597. http://0–eebo.chadwyck.com.libsys. wellcome.ac.uk (accessed 21/10/2011).

Lawson, William, *A New Orchard and Garden, with The Country Housewifes Garden, and the Husbandry of Bees*, London, 1618. http://0–eebo.chadwyck.com.libsys.wellcome.ac.uk (accessed 14/6/2011).

Lightfoot, John, *Flora Scotica*, London, 1777. http://0–eebo.chadwyck.com.libsys.wellcome. ac.uk (accessed 30/4/2011).

Lodge, Thomas, *An Alarum against Usurers* (1584), London: Early English Books Online, Arizona State University Library, 2010. http://0–eebo.chadwyck.com.libsys.wellcome.ac.uk (accessed 11.1.13).

Manwood, John, *A Treatise and Discourse of the Lawes of Forrests*, London, 1598 http://0–eebo.chadwyck.com.libsys.wellcome.ac.uk (accessed 2/4/2012).

Markham Gervase., *Markham's maister-peece*, London, 1610. http://0–eebo.chadwyck.com. libsys.wellcome.ac.uk (accessed 22/9/2011).

—*The English Housewife* (1631), London. http://0–eebo.chadwyck.com.libsys.wellcome.ac.uk (accessed 24/7/2011).

Mascall, Leonard, *The Countryman's Recreation, or the Art of Planting, Graffing, and Gardening in 3 Bookes*, London, 1640. http://0–eebo.chadwyck.com.libsys.wellcome.ac.uk (accessed 25/4/2011).

Miller, Philip, *The Gardeners Dictionary*, London, 1754. http://0–eebo.chadwyck.com.libsys. wellcome.ac.uk (accessed 4/7/2011).

Nichols, John, *The Progresses and Processions of Queen Elizabeth*, London, 1788. http://0–eebo.chadwyck.com.libsys.wellcome.ac.uk (accessed 26/3/11).

Overbury, Thomas, *His Wife, with New Elegies upon his now Knowne Untimely Death*, London, 1616. http://0–eebo.chadwyck.com.libsys.wellcome.ac.uk (accessed 18/5/2011).

Parkinson, John, *Paradisi in Sole Paradisus Terrestris*, London, 1629. http://0–eebo.chadwyk. com.libsys.wellcome.ac.uk. (accessed 21/4/2011).

—*Theatrum Botanicum*, 1640. http://0–eebo.chadwyk.com.libsys.wellcome.ac.uk (accessed 7/4/2011).

Plat, Hugh, *Floraes Paradise*, London, 1608. http://0–eebo.chadwyk.com.libsys.wellcome. ac.uk (accessed 30/9/2011).

—*Delights for Ladies*, London, 1609. http://0–eebo.chadwyk.com.libsys.wellcome.ac.uk (accessed 7/3/13).

—*The Garden of Eden*, London, 1654. http://0–eebo.chadwyk.com.libsys.wellcome.ac.uk (accessed 30/6/2011).

Stubbes, Philip, *The Anatomie of Abuses*, 1585. http://0–eebo.chadwyk.com.libsys.wellcome. ac.uk (accessed 7/3/13).

Taylor, John, *A New Discovery by Sea with a Wherry from London to Salisbury*, London, 1623. http://0–eebo.chadwyk.com.libsys.wellcome.ac.uk (accessed 11/6/11).

Tusser, Thomas, *A hundreth good poynts of husbandry lately maried to a hundreth good poynts of huswifery*, London, 1570. http://0–eebo.chadwyk.com.libsys.wellcome.ac.uk (accessed 1/10/11).

—*Five Hundred Points of Good Husbandry*, London, 1573. http://0–eebo.chadwyk.com.libsys. wellcome.ac.uk. (accessed 7/8/2011).

Vaughan, William, *Directions for Health*, London, 1617. http://0–eebo.chadwyk.com.libsys. wellcome.ac.uk. (accessed 9/4/2011).

Virgil, *Eclogues and Georgics*, London: Oxford University Press, 1921. http://0–eebo.chadwyk. com.libsys.wellcome.ac.uk. (accessed 9/4/2011).

Secondary sources

Ackroyd, Peter, *The Life of Sir Thomas More*, London: Chatto and Windus, 1998.

Adams, Christine, 'Francis Bacon's Wedding Gift of "A Garden of a Glorious and Strange

Beauty" for the Earl and Countess of Somerset.' *Garden History* (2008), vol. 36, no. 1, 36–58.

Alford, Stephen, *Burghley. William Cecil at the Court of Elizabeth I*, New Haven and London: Yale University Press, 2008.

Allen, D. C., Donne on the Mandrake, *Modern Language Notes*, vol. 74, no. 5 (1959): 393–7

Allen, D. E., and Hatfield, G., *Medicinal Plants in Folk Tradition. An Ethnobotany of Britain and Ireland*, Portland, OR and Swavesey: Portland Press, 2004.

Alpers, Paul, *What is Pastoral?*, Chicago and London: The University of Chicago Press, 1996.

Amherst, Alicia, 'A fifteenth century treatise on gardening, by "Mayster Ion Gardener"', *Archaeologia*, vol. 54.i (1894): 157–72.

—*A History of Gardening in England*, London: Bernard Quaritch, 1895.

Anders, Henry R. D., *Shakespeare's Books; A Dissertation on Shakespeare's Reading and the Immediate Sources of His Works (*1904), Memphis, TN: General Books, 2010.

Anderson, Frank J., *An Illustrated History of the Herbals*, New York: Columbia University Press, 1977.

Andrews, Martin, 'Theobalds Palace: The Gardens and Park', *Garden History* 21.2 (1993): 129–49.

Appelbaum, Robert, *Aguecheek's Beef, Belch's Hiccup, and Other Gastronomic Interjections: Literature, Culture and Food Among the Early Moderns*, Chicago: University of Chicago Press, 2006.

Arber, Agnes, *Herbals. Their Origin and Evolution*, Cambridge: Cambridge University Press, 1938.

—*Medieval Herbalism to Modern Botany*, in *Science, Medicine and History*, ed. Ashworth Underwood, E., London: Oxford University Press, 1953.

Archer, Jayne E., Goldring, Elizabeth and Knight, Sarah (eds), 'The Progresses, Pageants, and Entertainments of Queen Elizabeth I', Oxford: Oxford University Press, 2007.

Armstrong, Edward A., *Shakespeare's Imagination. A Study of the Psychology of Association and Inspiration*, London: Lindsay Drummond Ltd, 1946.

Arnold, Janet, ed., *Queen Elizabeth's Wardrobe Unlock'd. The Inventories of the Wardrobe of Robes prepared in 1600 edited from Stowe MS 557 in the BL, MS LR2/121 in the PRO, London, and MS V.b.72 in the Folger Shakespeare Library, Washington DC*, Leeds: W. S. Maney & Son Ltd, 1988.

Asquith, Clare, *Shadowplay. The Hidden Beliefs and Coded Politics of William Shakespeare*, New York: Public Affairs, 2005.

Aughterson, Kate, ed., *The English Renaissance: An Anthology of Sources and Documents*, London and New York: Routledge, 1998.

Ault, Norman, *Elizabethan Lyrics*, London: Longmans, Green & Co., 1949.

Bacon, Josephine, 'Oranges and Orangeries', *Connoisseur*, vol. 208, no. 836 (October 1981): 101–3.

Baker, Margaret, *Discovering the Folklore of Plants*, Oxford: Shire Publications, 2008.

Baldwin, T. W., *William Shakspere's Small Latine and Lesse Greeke*, University of Illinois: Urbana Press, 1994.

Barber, C. L., *Shakespeare's Festive Comedy*, Princeton: Princeton University Press, 1959.

Bate, Jonathan, 'A Herb by any other Name', *Shakespeare Quarterly*, vol. 33 (1982): 336.

—*Shakespeare and Ovid*, Oxford: Clarendon Press, 1993.

—*The Song of the Earth*, London: Picador, 2000.

—*The Genius of Shakespeare*, London: Picador, 2008.

—*Soul of the Age. The Life, Mind and World of William Shakespeare*, Harmondsworth: Penguin Books, 2009.

Batey, Mavis, *Oxford Gardens. The University's Influence on Garden History*, Amersham: Scolar Press, 1986.

Batey, Mavis, and Lambert, David, *The English Garden Tour*, London: John Murray, 1990.

Beck, Thomasina, 'Gardens in Elizabethan Embroidery', *Garden History*, vol. 3, no. 1 (1974): 44–56.

—*Gardening with Silk and Gold. A History of Gardens in Embroidery*, Newton Abbot: David and Charles, 1997.

Beisley, Sidney, *Shakespere's Garden* (1864), Memphis, TN: General Books, 2009.

Bending, Stephen, and McRae, Andrew, *The Writing of Rural England 1500–1800*, London: Palgrave Macmillan, 2003.

Bernstein, W., *A Splendid Exchange: How Trade shaped the World*, London: Atlantic Books, 2009.

Berry, Edward, *Shakespeare and the Hunt. A Cultural and Social Study*, Cambridge: Cambridge University Press, 2001.

Biddle, Martin, 'The Gardens of Nonsuch: Sources and Dating', *Garden History*, vol. 27, no. 1 (1999): 145–83.

Black, Virginia, 'Beddington – "The best Orangery in England"', *Journal of Garden History*, vol. 3, no. 2 (1983): 113–20.

Blake, N. F., 'Do the Green Sour Ringlets Make?', *Notes and Queries*, vol. 238, (June 1993): 201–2.

—*Shakespeare's Non-Standard English: A Dictionary of his Informal Language*, London and New York: Continuum, 2004 (second edn, 2006).

Blench, J. W., *Preaching in England in the late Fifteenth and Sixteenth Centuries. A Study of English Sermons 1450–c. 1600*, Oxford: Basil Blackwell, 1964.

Bloom, J. H., *Shakespeare's Garden*, London: Methuen, 1903.

Blunt, Wilfrid and Stearn, *The Art of Botanical Illustration*, London: Collins, 1950 and Woodbridge, 1994.

Booth, F. E. M. and Lucas, G. L., 'The Role of Botanic Gardens in Economic Botany' in Swaminathan, M. S. and Kochar, S. L. (eds), *Plants and Society*, London: Macmillan, 1989.

Boyle, Harry H., 'Elizabeth's Entertainment at Elvetham: War Policy in Pageantry', *Studies in Philology*, vol. LXVIII, no. 2, (April 1971): 146–66.

Bradbrook, M. C., *Shakespeare: The Poet in his World*, London: Methuen, 1978.

Bradford, F. C., 'Shakespeare and Bacon as Horticultural Prophets', *Modern Language Notes*, vol. 48 no. 2 (1933): 108–10.

Brenner, Robert, *Merchants and Revolution: Commercial Change, Political Conflict and London's Overseas Traders*, 1550–1653, Princeton: Princeton University Press, 1993; London and New York: Verso, 2003.

Britten, James and Holland, Robert, *A Dictionary of English Plant Names*, London: Trubner & Co., 1886.

Brotherston, R. P., '*Speargrass' The Gardener's Chronicle* no. 819, (6/9/1902), 169.

Brotton, J., *The Renaissance Bazaar: From the Silk Road to Michelangelo*, Oxford: Oxford University Press, 2002.

Bruckner, Lynne and Brayton, Dan (eds), *Ecocritical Shakespeare*, Farnham: Ashgate Publishing Ltd, 2011.

Bryson, Bill, *Shakespeare: The World as Stage*, London: Harper Collins, 2008.

Buccolar, Regina and Hopkins, Lisa (eds), *Marian Moments in Early Modern British Drama*, Burlington, VT and Farnham: Ashgate Publishing Ltd, 2007.

Bucknill, John Charles, *The Medical Knowledge of Shakespeare*, London: Longman and Co., 1860.

Bushnell, Rebecca, *Green Desire: Imagining Early Modern English Gardens*, Ithaca: Cornell University Press, 2003.

Calderwood, James, L., *A Midsummer Night's Dream*, Hemel Hempstead: Harvester Wheatsheaf, 1992.

Campbell-Culver, Maggie, *The Origin of Plants*, London: Headline, 2001.

Cantor, Leonard, *The Changing English Countryside 1400–1700*, London: Routledge and Kegan Paul, 1987.

Chancellor, John, *The Flowers and Fruits of the Bible*, Exeter: Webb and Bower, 1982.

Chartres, John and Hey, David (eds), *English Rural Society: 1500–1800: Essays in honour of Joan Thirsk*, Cambridge: Cambridge University Press, 1990.

Cheney, Patrick, ed., *Shakespeare's Poetry*, Cambridge: Cambridge University Press, 2007.

Chernaik, Warren, *The Myth of Rome in Shakespeare and his Contemporaries*, Cambridge: Cambridge University Press, 2011.

Christianson, C. P., *The Riverside Gardens of Thomas More's London*, New Haven and London: Yale University Press, 2005.

Chute, M., *Shakespeare of London*, London: Four Square, 1962.

Cirillo, Albert R., 'As You Like It: Pastoralism Gone Awry', *English Literary History*, vol. 38.1 (1971): 19–39.

Clapham, A. R., Tutin, T. G. and Warburg, E. F., *Flora of the British Isles*, Cambridge: Cambridge University Press, 1952.

Clarke, Catherine A. M., *Literary Landscapes and the Idea of England, 700–1400*, Cambridge: D. S. Brewer, 2006.

Clemen, Wolfgang, *The Development of Shakespeare's Imagery*, London: Methuen, 1951; revised edn, 1977.

Cloake, John, *Palaces and Parks of Richmond and Kew*, Chichester: Phillimore, 1995.

Coats, Alice, *Flowers and their Histories*, London: A & C Black, 1968.

Collins, Minta, *Medieval Herbals: The Illustrative Traditions*, London: British Library, 2000.

Comito, Terry, 'Renaissance Gardens and the Discovery of Paradise' in *Journal of the History of Ideas* 32, 1971: 483–506.

—*The Idea of the Garden in the Renaissance*, New Brunswick, NJ: Rutgers University Press, 1978.

Considine, John, 'Thy bankes with pioned, and twilled brims: A Solution to a Double Crux', *Shakespeare Quarterly*, vol. 54 (2003): 160–6.

Coope, Rosalys, 'The Long Gallery: Its Origins, Development, Use and Decoration', *Architectural History*, vol. 29 (V): 43–72, 74–84.

Croft, Pauline, ed., *Patronage, Culture, and Power: The Early Cecils*, New Haven: Yale University Press, 2002.

Crystal, David, and Crystal, Ben, *Shakespeare's Words: A Glossary and Language Companion*, Harmondsworth: Penguin Books, 2002.

Daley, A. Stuart, 'Where are the Woods in As You Like It?', *Shakespeare Quarterly*, vol. 34 (1983): 172–80

Danby, J. F., *Shakespeare's Doctrine of Nature. A Study of King Lear*, London: Faber and Faber, 1969.

De Bray, Lys, *The Wild Garden*, London: Weidenfeld and Nicholson, 1978.

—*Fantastic Garlands. An Anthology of Flowers and Plants from Shakespeare*, Dorset: Blandford Press, 1982.

—*Elizabethan Garland: The Flowers and Plants which Inspired Shakespeare*, London: Brockhampton Press, 1997.

—*The Art of Botanical Illustration*, Royston, Hertfordshire: Eagle, 2002.

De Luze, Albert, *A History of the Royal Game of Tennis*, Warwick: Roundwood Press, 1979.

Debus, Allen G, *Man and Nature in the Renaissance*, Cambridge: Cambridge University Press, 1978.

Dendle, Peter, and Touwaide, Alain, *Health and Healing from the Medieval Garden*, Woodbridge: The Boydell Press, 2008.

Dent, R. W., *Shakespeare's Proverbial Language. An Index*, Berkeley: University of California Press, 1981.

—*Proverbial Language in English Drama Exclusive of Shakespeare*, 1595–1616, Berkeley: University of California Press, 1984.

Dolan, Frances E., 'Taking the Pencil out of God's Hand: Art, Nature and the Face-Painting Debate in Early Modern England', *PMLA*, vol. 108, no. 2 (March 1993): 224–39.

Doring, Tobias and Greiner, Norbert (eds), *Shakespeare Jahrbuch 2009*, Germany: Verlag und Druckkontor Kamp Gmbh Bochum, 2009.

Duncan-Jones, Katherine, 'Much Ado with Red and White: The Earliest Readers of Shakespeare's Venus and Adonis' (1593), *Review of English Studies*, vol. 44, no. 176, (1993): 79–501.

—'Deep-Dyed Canker Blooms: Botanical References in Shakespeare's Sonnet 54', *Review of English Studies*, vol. 46, no. 184 (1995): 521–5.

—*Ungentle Shakespeare. Scenes from his Life*, London: Arden Shakespeare, 2001.

Dunlap, A. R., 'What Purgative Drug?', *Modern Language Notes*, vol. 54, no. 2 (1939): 92–4.

Dutton, Richard, Findlay, Alison and, Wilson, Richard (eds), *Theatre and religion. Lancastrian Shakespeare*, Manchester: Manchester University Press, 2003.

Eburne, Andrew, 'The Passion of Sir Thomas Tresham: New Light on the Gardens and Lodge at Lyveden', *Garden History*, vol. 36, no.1, (2008): 114–34.

Eburne, Andrew and Taylor Richard, *How to Read an English Garden*, London: Ebury Press, 2006.

Egan, Gabriel, *Green Shakespeare*, London and New York: Routledge, 2006.

—*Greening Shakespeare: From Ecopolitics to Ecocriticism*, New York and London: Routledge, 2006.

Eliason, Norman E., 'Shakespeare's Purgative Drug Cyme', *Modern Language Notes*, vol. 57, no. 8 (1942): 663–5.

Ellacombe, Henry N., *The Plant-Lore and Garden-Craft of Shakespeare*, London: Edward Arnold, 1896.

Ellerbeck, Erin, 'Adoption and the Language of *All's Well that Ends Well*', *Studies in English Literature*, vol. 51, no. 2 (Spring, 2011): 305–26.

Estock, Simon, *Ecocriticism and Shakespeare: Reading Ecophobia*, New York and Basingstoke: Palgrave MacMillan, 2011.

Eyler, Ellen C., *Early English Gardens and Garden Books*, Ithaca: Cornell University Press for the Folger Shakespeare Library, 1963.

Fahey, Maria Franziska, *Metaphor and Shakespearean Drama*, Basingstoke: Palgrave-Macmillan, 2011.

Ferber, Michael, *A Dictionary of Literary Symbols*, Cambridge: Cambridge University Press, 1999.

Ferguson, George, *Signs and Symbols in Christian Art*, Oxford: Oxford University Press, 1961.

Ferguson, L. and Yachnin, P., 'The Name of Juliet's Nurse', *Shakespeare Quarterly*, vol. 32, no. 1 (Spring, 1981): 95–6.

Ferguson, Margaret W., Quilligan, Maureen and Vickers, Nancy J. (eds), *Rewriting the Renaissance*, Chicago and London: University of Chicago Press, 1986.

Fisher, Celia, *Flowers of the Renaissance*, London: Frances Lincoln, 2011.

Fisher, F. J., *London and the English Economy, 1500–1700*, Corfield, P.J . and Harte, N. B. (eds), London: Hambledon, 1990.

Fitzpatrick, Joan, *Food in Shakespeare. Early Modern Dietaries and the Plays*, Farnham: Ashgate Publishing Limited, 2007.

—*Shakespeare and the Language of Food. A Dictionary*, London: Continuum, 2011.

Fleming, Laurence and Gore, Alan, *The English Garden*, London: Michael Joseph, 1979.

—*The English Garden*, London: Spring Books, 1988.

Fletcher, John, *Gardens of Earthly Delight. The History of Deer Parks*, Oxford: Windgather Press, 2011.

Foakes, R. A., *Shakespeare and Violence*, Cambridge: Cambridge University Press, 2003.

Fox, Charles O., 'A Crux in "The Tempest"'. *Notes and Queries*, vol. 202 (1957): 515–6.

Francis, Jill, 'Order and Disorder in the Early Modern Garden, c. 1558–1630', *Garden History*, vol. 36, no.1 (2008): 22–35.

Fraser, Antonia, *The Weaker Vessel. Woman's Lot in Seventeenth-Century England*, London: Phoenix, 2002.

Frazer, *The Golden Bough*, 1890, reprinted New York: Macmillan 1922.

Freeman, Margaret B., *The Unicorn Tapestries*, New York: Metropolitan Museum of Art, 1983.

Freeman, Rosemary, *English Emblem Books*, London: Chatto and Windus, 1948.

Friedman, Donald M., 'John of Gaunt and the Rhetoric of Frustration', *English Literary History*, vol. 43, no. 3 (1976): 279–99.

Fry, Carolyn, 'How to make a Meadow', *Royal Botanic Gardens Kew Magazine* (Autumn 2011).

Gent, Lucy, *Picture and Poetry 1560–1620*, Leamington Spa: James Hall Publishing Ltd, 1981.

—ed, *Albion's Classicism: The Visual Arts in Britain, 1550–1660*, New Haven and London: Yale University Press, 1995.

Gessert, George, 'Bastard Flowers', *Leonardo*, vol. 29, no. 4 (1996): 291–8.

Gillespie, Stuart, *Shakespeare's Books*, London: Continuum, 2004.

Gillies, John, *Shakespeare and the Geography of Difference*, Cambridge: Cambridge University Press, 1994.

Girouard, Mark, *Hardwick Hall*, London: The National Trust, 1976.

—*Life in the English Country House. A Social and Architectural History*, London: Book Club Associates, 1978.

Goody, Jack, *The Culture of Flowers*, Cambridge: Cambridge University Press, 1993.

Grattan, J. H. G., and Singer, Charles, *Anglo-Saxon Magic and Medicine, illustrated specially from the semi-pagan Text 'Lacnunga'*, London: Oxford University Press, 1952.

Graves, Michael A. R., *Burghley: William Cecil, Lord Burghley*, New York: Longman, 1998.

Graves, Robert, *The Greek Myths*, London: The Folio Society, 2000.

de Grazia, Margreta, *'Hamlet' Without Hamlet*, Cambridge: Cambridge University Press, 2007.

Green, H., *Shakespeare and the Emblem Writers*, London: Trübner and Co., 1870.

Green, M., *Wriothesley's Roses in Shakespeare's Sonnets, Poems and Plays*, Baltimore, MD: Clevedon Books, 1993.

Greenblatt, Stephen, *Renaissance Self-Fashioning: From More to Shakespeare*, London and Chicago: University of Chicago Press, 1980/2005.

Greene, Thomas M., 'Pitiful thrivers: failed husbandry in the sonnets' in Parker, Patricia and Hartman Geoffrey (eds), *Shakespeare and the Question of Theory*, New York and London, Methuen, 1985.

Grieve, M., *A Modern Herbal*, London: Jonathan Cape, 1931; Harmondsworth: Penguin Books, 1978.

Grigson, Geoffrey, *The Englishman's Flora*, London: Readers Union, 1958.

Bibliography

—*A Dictionary of English Plant Names*, London: Allen Lane, 1974.

Grindon, L., *The Shakspere Flora*, Manchester: Palmer and Howe, 1883.

Hackett, Helen, *Virgin Mother, Maiden Queen*, London: Macmillan, 1995.

—*Shakespeare and Elizabeth*, Princeton: Princeton University Press, 2009.

Hadfield, Andrew, *The English Renaissance: 1500–1620*, Oxford: Blackwell, 2001.

Hall, James, *Hall's Dictionary of Subjects and Symbols in Art*, London: John Murray, 1974.

Hall, Marie Boas, *The Scientific Renaissance 1450–1630*, London: Collins, 1962.

Hankins, J. E, *Backgrounds of Shakespeare's Thoughts*, Hassocks: Harvester Press, 1978.

Hannet, John, *The Forest of Arden*, London: C. Lowe, 1863.

Harkness, Deborah E., *The Jewel House: Elizabethan London and the Scientific Revolution*, New Haven: Yale University Press, 2007.

Harris, Jonathan Gil, *Sick Economies: Drama, Mercantilism, and Disease in Shakespeare's England*, Philadelphia: University of Pennsylvania Press, 2004.

Harrison, G. B., *An Elizabethan Journal. Being a Record of Those Things Most Talked About During the Years 1591–1603*, 3 vols., London: George Routledge and Sons, 1938.

Harrison, Robert Pogue, *Forests: The Shadow of Civilisation*, Chicago: Chicago University Press, 1992

—*Gardens: An Essay on the Human Condition*, Chicago: Chicago University Press, 2008.

Harrison, Thomas P., 'A Note on The Tempest: A Sequel', *Modern Language Notes*, vol. 58, no. 6 (June 1943): 422–6.

Harvey, John, *Early Gardening Catalogues*, Phillimore & Co. Ltd: Chichester, 1972.

—'Mediaeval Plantsmanship in England: The Culture of Rosemary', *Garden History*, vol. 1, no.1 (1972): 14–21.

—'Turkey as a Source of Plants', *Garden History*, vol. 3 no. 4 (1976): 21–2.

—'Gillyflower and Carnation', *Garden History*, vol. 6, no. 1 (Spring 1978): 46–57.

—*Mediaeval Gardens*, London: P. T. Batsford, Ltd, 1981.

—'The First English Garden Book: Mayster Jon Gardener's Treatise and Its Background', *Garden History*, vol. 13, no.2 (1985): 83–101.

—'Henry Daniel: A Scientific Gardener of the Fourteenth Century', *Garden History*, vol. 15 no.2 (1987): 81–93.

—'Garden Plants of around 1525: The Fromond List', *Garden History*, vol. 17 no. 2 (1989): 122–34.

—'Westminster Abbey: The Infirmarer's Garden.' *Garden History*, vol. 20, No. 2 (1992), 97–115

Hatfield, Gabrielle, *Hatfield's Herbal*, London, Allen Lane, Penguin, 2007

Hattaway, Michael, *Renaissance and Reformations: An Introduction to Early Modern English Literature*, Oxford: Blackwell, 2005.

Hearn, Karen, ed., *Dynasties. Painting in Tudor and Jacobean England 1530–1630*, London: Tate Publishing, 1995.

Heath, James, *Botanical References in Shakespeare: Some resonances of Ophelia's Gifts and Garland Flowers for Early Modern Auditors and Readers*, unpublished MA Dissertation, University of London (Birkbeck), and also in the Shakespeare Centre Library, 2003.

Heilmeyer, Marina, *The Language of Flowers: Symbols and Myths*, Munich, London and New York: Prestel, 2001.

Henderson, Paula, 'Sir Francis Bacon's Water Gardens at Gorhambury', *Garden History*, vol. 20, no. 2 (1992): 116–31.

—*The Tudor House and Garden*, New Haven and London: Yale University Press, 2005.

—'Sir Francis Bacon's Essay "Of Gardens' in context"', *Garden History*, vol. 36, no.1 (2008): 59–84.

390

Hillman, Richard, 'The Gillyfors' Exchange in *The Winter's Tale'*, *English Studies in Canada*, *1*, (1979): 16–23.

Hobhouse, Penelope, *Plants in Garden History*, London: Pavilion Books Ltd, 1992.

Hockey, Dorothy C., 'Wormwood, Wormwood!', *English Language Notes* (1964–5): 174–7.

Hoeniger, F. David, *How Plants and Animals were Studied in the Mid-Sixteenth Century* (1985), in Shirley, John W. and Hoeniger, F. David (eds), *Science and the Arts in the Renaissance*, Washington: The Folger Library, 1985.

——*Medicine and Shakespeare in the English Renaissance*, Newark: University of Delaware Press, 1992.

Hopkins, Lisa, *Shakespeare on the Edge: Border-crossing in the Tragedies and the Henriad*, Farnham: Ashgate Publishing Ltd, 2005.

Hoskins, W. G., *The Making of the English Landscape*, London: Hodder & Stoughton Ltd, 1955.

——'Harvest Fluctuations and English Economic History, 1480–1619', *The Agricultural History Review*, vol. 12, no. 1 (1964): 28–46.

Hoyles, Martin, *The Story of Gardening*, London and Concord, MA: Journeyman Press, 1991.

Hulme, Hilda M., *Explorations in Shakespeare's Language*, London: Longmans, 1962.

Hulton, Paul, *The Work of Jacques Le Moyne de Morgues. A Huguenot Artist in France, Florida and England*, London: British Museum Publications Ltd, 1977.

Hunt, John Dixon, *Greater Perfections: The Practice of Garden Theory*, London: Thames and Hudson, 2000.

Hunt, Maurice, ed., *The Winter's Tale: Critical Essays*, New York and London: Routledge, 1995.

Hunt, Tony, *Plant Names of Medieval England*, Woodbridge: D. S. Brewer, 1989.

Husselby, Jill and Henderson, Paula, 'Location, Location, Location! Cecil House in the Strand', *Architectural History*, vol. 45 (2002): 159–93.

Iyengar, Sujata, *Shakespeare's Medical Language: A Dictionary*, London: Continuum, 2011.

Jacques, David, 'The Chief Ornament of Gray's Inn: The Walks from Bacon to Brown', *Garden History* vol. 17, no. 1 (Spring 1989): 41–67.

——'The Compartment System in Tudor England' *Garden History*, vol. 27, no. 1 (Summer 1999): 32–53.

Jack, Belinda, *The Woman Reader*, New Haven and London: Yale University Press, 2012.

Jardine, Lisa, *Worldly Goods: A New History of the Renaissance*, Basingstoke: Macmillan, 1996.

Jardine, Nicholas, Secord, James and Spary, Emma (eds), *Cultures of Natural History*, Cambridge: Cambridge University Press, 1996.

Jones, Whitney R. D., *William Turner: Tudor Naturalist, Physician and Divine*, London and New York: Routledge, 1988.

Kaden, Vera, *The Illustrations of Plants and Gardens 1500–1850*, London: V & A Museum, 1982.

Kail, A, *The Medical Mind of Shakespeare*, Balgowlah: Williams and Wilkins, 1986.

Karim-Cooper, Farah, *Cosmetics in Shakespearean and Renaissance Drama*, Edinburgh: Edinburgh University Press Ltd, 2006.

Kaufmann, Thomas DaCosta, *The Mastery of Nature: Aspects of Art, Science, and Humanism in the Renaissance*, Princeton: Princeton University Press, 1993.

Keay, John, *The Spice Route: A History*, London: John Murray, 2005.

Kerr, Jessica, *Shakespeare's Flowers*, Harmondsworth: Kestrel Books, 1969.

Kinny, Arthur, F., *Shakespeare's Webs: Networks of Meaning in Renaissance Drama*, New York and London: Routledge, 2004.

Kingsbury, Noel, *Hybrid: The History and Science of Plant Breeding*, Chicago and London: University of Chicago, 2009.

Knight, Leah, *Of Books and Botany in Early Modern England: Sixteenth Century Plants and Print Culture*, Farnham: Ashgate Publishing Ltd, 2009.

Kolin, Philip C., ed., *Venus and Adonis: Critical Essays*, New York and London: Garland Publishing, 1997.

Kyle, Fiona, *Women's Medicine in Early Modern Herbals*, unpublished dissertation, London University, 1998.

Labarge, Margaret Wade, *Medieval Travellers. The Rich and Restless*, London: Hamish Hamilton Ltd, 1982.

Landsberg, Sylvia, *The Medieval Garden*, London: The British Museum, 1998.

Lane, Joan, *John Hall and his Patients: The Medical Practice of Shakespeare's Son-in-Law*, Stratford-upon-Avon: Shakespeare Birthplace Trust, 1996.

Laroche, Rebecca, *Medical Authority and Englishwomen's Herbal Texts, 1550–1650*, Farnham: Ashgate Publishing Ltd, 2009.

Leapman, Michael, *The Ingenious Mr. Fairchild: The Forgotten Father of the Flower Garden*, London: Headline, 2000.

Lees-Jeffries, Hester, *England's Helicon. Fountains in Early Modern Literature and Culture*, Oxford: Oxford University Press, 2007.

Leggatt, Alexander, *Shakespeare's Tragedies: Violation and Identity*, Cambridge: Cambridge University Press, 2005.

Lehner, Ernst and Johanna, *Folk-lore and Symbolism of Flowers, Plants and Trees*, New York: Tudor Publishing Co., 1960.

Leith-Ross, Prudence, *The John Tradescants. Gardeners to the Rose and Lily Queen*, London: Peter Owen, 2006.

Le Strange, Richard, *A History of Herbal Plants*, London: Angus & Robertson (UK) Ltd, 1977.

Leslie, Michael and Raylor, Timothy (eds), *Culture and Cultivation in Early Modern England: Writing the Land*, Leicester: Leicester University Press, 1992.

Lever, J. W., 'Three Notes on Shakespeare's Plants' *Review of English Studies, New Series*, vol. 3, no. 10 (April 1952): 117–29.

Levin, Harry, *The Myth of the Golden Age in the Renaissance*, London: Faber and Faber, 1970.

Livingston, Mary, 'The Natural Art of *The Winter's Tale*', *Modern Language Quarterly*, 30/3 (1969): 340–55.

Long, Michael, *The Unnatural Scene: A Study in Shakespearean Tragedy*, London: Methuen, 1976.

—*Macbeth*, Hemel Hempstead: Harvester Wheatsheaf, 1989.

Lyons, Bridget Gellert, 'The Iconography of Ophelia', *English Literary History*, vol. 44, no. 1 (1977): 60–74.

Mabberley, D. J., *Mabberley's Plant Book*, Cambridge: Cambridge University Press, 2008 (third edn).

Mabey, Richard, *Flora Britannica*, London: Reed International Books Ltd, 1996.

—*Weeds*, London: Profile Books Ltd, 2010.

Macht, David I., 'A Pharmacological Appreciation of S's Hamlet: on Installation of Poisons into the Ear', *Johns Hopkins Hospital Bulletin*, XXIX, no. 329 (July 1918): 165–70.

—'A Physiological and Pharmacological appreciation of Hamlet Act 1, scene 5, lines 59–73', *Bulletin of the History of Medicine*, XXIII (1949): 186–94.

—'Calendula or Marigold in Medical History and in Shakespeare', *Bulletin of the History of Medicine*, XXIX (1955): 491–502.

Mackenzie, Elizabeth, 'The Growth of Plants: A Seventeenth-Century Metaphor', *English Renaissance Studies: Presented to Dame Helen Gardner in honour of her Seventieth Birthday*, Oxford: Clarendon, 1980.

Maddison, F., Pelling, M. and Webster, C., *Essays on the Life and Work of Thomas Linacre*, Oxford: Clarendon Press, 1977.

Madelaine, R. E. R., 'Oranges and Lemans: *Much Ado about Nothing*, IV.i.31', *Shakespeare Quarterly*, vol. 33, no. 4 (Winter, 1982): 491–2.

Mahood, M. M., *The Poet as Botanist*, Cambridge: Cambridge University Press, 2008.

Martindale, Charles and Taylor, A. B. (eds), *Shakespeare and the Classics*, Cambridge: Cambridge University Press, 2004.

Martyn, Trea, *Elizabeth in the Garden: A Story of Love, Rivalry and Spectacular Design*, London: Faber and Faber, 2008.

Marvell, Andrew, 'The Mower Against Gardens', Frank Kermode and Keith Walker (eds), Oxford: Oxford University Press, 1990.

—'The Garden' in Wilcher, Robert ed., *Selected Poetry and Prose*, London: Methuen, 1986: 47–9.

Mason, Laura, and Brown, Catherine, (2006), *The Taste of Britain*. London: Harper Press.

Matar, Nabil, *Turks, Moors and Englishmen in the Age of Discovery*, New York: Columbia University Press, 1999.

McCombie, Frank, 'Garlands in Hamlet and King Lear', *Notes and queries*, vol. 226 (1981): 132–4.

McLay, Catherine M., 'The Dialogues of Spring and Winter: A Key to the Unity of *Love's Labour's Lost, Shakespeare Quarterly*, vol. 18, no. 2 (Spring 1967): 119–27.

McLean, Teresa, *Medieval English Gardens*, London: William Collins Sons & Co., 1981.

McLeod, J. A., *In a Unicorn's Garden. Recreating the Mystery and Magic of Medieval Gardens*, London: Murdoch Books Pty. Ltd, 2008.

McRae, Andrew, *God Speed the Plough: The Representation of Agrarian England, 1500–1660*, Cambridge: Cambridge University Press, 1996.

—*Literature and Domestic Travel in Early Modern England*, Cambridge: Cambridge University Press, 2009.

Meek, Richard, *Narrating the Visual in Shakespeare*, Burlington, VT and Farnham: Ashgate Publishing Ltd, 2009.

Merridew, John, *Pageantry and Gascoigne's Masques, Represented before Queen Elizabeth at Kenilworth Castle, Anno 1575*, Warwick and Leamington, 1825.

Miola, Robert, *Shakespeare's Reading*, Oxford: Oxford University Press, 2000.

Montrose, Louis Adrian, 'Of Gentlemen and Shepherds: The Politics of the Elizabethan Pastoral Form', *English Literary History*, vol. 50, no. 3 (1983): 415–59.

Moore, Arthur K., 'Mixed Tradition in the Carols of Holly and Ivy', *Modern Language Notes*, vol. 62, no. 8 (1947): 554–6.

Morgan, Joan and Richards, Alison, *The New Book of Apples*, London: Ebury, 2002 (first edn 1993).

Morrall, Andrew and Watt, Melinda (eds), *English Embroidery from the Metropolitan Museum of Art, 1580–1700*, New Haven: Yale University Press, 2008.

Morton, A. G., *History of Botanical Science: An Account of the Development of Botany from Ancient Times to the Present Day*, London: Academic, 1981.

Mosser, Monique and Teyssot, Georges (eds), *The Architecture of Western Gardens: A Design History from the Renaissance to the Present Day*, Cambridge: Massachusetts Institute of Technology, 1991.

Munroe, Jennifer, *Making Gardens of Their Own: Gardening Manuals for Women, 1550–1750*, Farnham: Ashgate Publishing Ltd, 2007.

—*Gender and the Garden in Early Modern English Literature*, Farnham: Ashgate Publishing Ltd, 2008.

Nares, Robert, *A Glossary in the Works of English Authors*, London: John Russell Smith, 1859.

Neely, Carol Thomas, '"Documents in Madness": Reading Madness and Gender in Shakespeare's Tragedies and Early Modern Culture', *Shakespeare Quarterly*, vol. 42 (1991): 314–38.

Newman, Lucile F., 'Ophelia's Herbal', *Economic Botany*, 33[2], New York: New York Botanical Garden, 1979, 227–32.

Nicholson, Adam, *Arcadia: The Dream of Perfection in Renaissance England*, London: Harper Perennial, 2009.

—*When God Spoke English*, London: Harper Press 2011.

Noble, William, 'Garden Plants Depicted on the Mid-sixteenth Century Ferrante Gonzaga Tapestries', *Garden History* (2005) vol. 33, no.2, 294–7.

Noel, E. B., and Clark, J. O. M., *A History of Tennis*, London: Gerald Duckworth and Co. Ltd, 1991.

Nuttal, a. d., *Timon of Athens*, Hemel Hempstead: Harvester Wheatsheaf, 1989.

—*Shakespeare the Thinker*, New Haven: Yale University Press, 2007.

Olsen, Kirstin, *All Things Shakespeare: A Concise Encyclopaedia of Shakespeare's World*, Oxford and Westport, CT: Greenwood World Publishing, 2007.

Onions, C. T., *A Shakespeare Glossary*, Oxford: Clarendon, 1911.

Osborne, June, *Entertaining Elizabeth I, The Progresses and Great Houses of her Lifetime*, London: Bishopsgate Press Ltd, 1989.

Otten, Charlotte F., 'Ophelia's "Long Purples" or "Dead Men's Fingers"', *Shakespeare Quarterly*, vol. 30, no. 3 (Summer, 1979): 397–402.

Painter, Robert and Parker, Brian, 'Ophelia's Flowers Again' *Notes and Queries* 41, no. 1 (1994): 42.

Palfrey, Simon, *Late Shakespeare: A New World of Words*, Oxford: Oxford University Press, 1997.

Pallister, D. M., *The Age of Elizabeth: England Under the Later Tudors, 1547–1603*, London and New York: Longman, 1983.

Palter, Robert, *The Duchess of Malfi's Apricots, and Other Literary Fruits*, Columbia: University of South Carolina Press, 2002.

Parker, Patricia and Hartman, Geoffrey (eds), *The Question of Theory*, London: Methuen, 1985.

—'(Peter) Quince: Love Potions, Carpenter's Coigns and Athenian Weddings', *Shakespeare Survey*, 56 (2003): 39–54.

Patrick, J. Max, 'The Problem of Ophelia' in Matthews, Arthur D. and Emery, Clark M. (eds), *Studies in Shakespeare*, Coral Gables, FL: University of Miami Press, 1953.

Pavord, Anna, *The Tulip*, London, Bloomsbury, 1999.

—*The Naming of Names: The Search for Order in the World of Plants*, London: Bloomsbury, 2005.

Peltonen, Markku, ed., *The Cambridge Companion to Bacon*, Cambridge: Cambridge University Press, 1996.

Perlin, John, *A Forest Journey: The Story of Wood and Civilization*, New York: W. W. Norton, 2005.

Peterson, Kaara L., *Popular Medicine, Hysterical Disease, and Social Controversy in Shakespeare's England*, Farnham: Ashgate Publishing Ltd, 2010.

Pettegree, Andrew, *Foreign Protestant Communities in Sixteenth-Century England*, Oxford: Clarendon, 1986.

—*Europe in the Sixteenth Century*, Oxford: Blackwell, 2002.

Phillips, John and Burnett, 'Nicholas: The Chronology and Layout of Francis Carew's Garden at Beddington, Surrey', *Garden History*, vol. 33, no. 2 (2005): 155–88.

Prest, John, *The Garden of Eden. The Botanic Garden and the Re-Creation of Paradise*, New Haven: Yale University Press, 1981.

Pollard, Tanya, *Drugs and Theatre in Early Modern England*, Oxford: Oxford University Press, 2005.

Potter, Jennifer, *Strange Blooms: The Curious Lives and Adventures of the John Tradescants*, London: Atlantic Books, 2006.

—*The Rose*, London: Atlantic Books Ltd, 2010.

Prest, John, *The Garden of Eden. The Botanic Garden and the Re-Creation of Paradise*, New Haven: Yale University Press, 1981.

Quest-Ritson, Charles, *The English Garden. A Social History*, London: Penguin Books, 2001.

Raber, Karen, 'Recent Ecocritical Studies of English Renaissance Literature' *English Literary Renaissance*, 37/1 (2007): 151–71.

Rackham, Oliver, *Trees and Woodland in the British Landscape*, London: J. M. Dent & Sons, Ltd, 1981.

Raven, Charles, E., *English Naturalists from Neckam to Ray*, Cambridge: Cambridge University Press, 1947.

Raven, Sarah, *Wild Flowers*, London: Bloomsbury, 2011.

Rawcliffe, Caroline, '"Delectable Sightes and Fragrant Smelles": Gardens and Health in Late Mediaeval and Early Modern England', *Garden History*, vol. 36, no. 1 (2008): 3–21.

Rea, John D., 'Notes on Shakespeare', *Modern Language Notes*, vol. 35, no. 6 (June 1920): 377–8.

Reader, John, *The Untold History of the Potato*, London: Vintage, 2009.

Rees, Ronald, *Interior Landscapes. Gardens and the Domestic Environment*, Baltimore: Johns Hopkins University Press, 1993.

Rendall, Vernon, *Wild Flowers in Literature*, London: Scholartis Press, 1934.

Riddle, John M., *Conception and Abortion from the Ancient World to the Renaissance*, Cambridge, MA and London: Harvard University Press, 1992.

—*Eve's Herbs. A History of Contraception and Abortion in the West*, Cambridge, MA and London: Harvard University Press, 1997.

—*Goddesses, Elixirs, and Witches. Plants and Sexuality throughout Human History*, Basingstoke: Palgrave-Macmillan, 2010.

Roberts, Judith, 'The Gardens of the Gentry in the Late Tudor Period', *Garden History*, vol. 27, no.1 (1999): 89–108.

Rohde, Eleanour S., *A Garden of Herbs*, London: Herbert Jenkins Ltd, 1925.

—*The Old English Gardening Books*, London: Martin Hopkinson and Co. Ltd, 1924.

—*Shakespeare's Wild Flowers, Fairy Lore, Gardens, Herbs, Gatherers of Simples and Bee Lore*, London: The Medici Society, 1924.

—*The Old English Herbals*, London: Longmans, Green and Co., 1922.

Rootsey, Samuel, 'Medicinal Plants mentioned by Shakespeare. Observations upon some of the Medical Plants mentioned by Shakespeare', *Transactions of the Medico-Botanical Society of London*, 1832; 1833, 83–96.

Ross, Lawrence J., 'The Meaning of Strawberries in Shakespeare', *Studies in the Renaissance*, vol. 7 (1960): 225–40.

Ryden, Mats, *Shakespearean Plant Names: Identifications and Interpretations*, Stockholm: Almquist and Wicksell International, 1978.

Sackville-West, Robert, *The Inheritance. The Story of Knole and the Sackvilles*, London: Bloomsbury Publishing plc, 2011.

Samson, Alexander, ed., *Locus Amoenus: Gardens and Horticulture in the Renaissance*, Chichester: Wiley-Blackwell, 2012.

Sanders, Wilbur, *The Winter's Tale*, Hemel Hempstead: Harvester Wheatsheaf, 1987.

Sanecki, Kay, *History of the English Herb Garden*, London: Ward Lock, 1994.

Saunders, Gill, *Picturing Plants: An Analytical History of Botanical Illustration*, Berkeley: University of California Press in association with the V & A Museum, 1995.

Savage, Frederick G., *The Flora and Folk Lore of Shakespeare*, Cheltenham: Ed J. Burrow and Co. Ltd, 1923.

Schiebinger, Londa and Swan, Claudia (eds), *Colonial Botany: Science, Commerce, and Politics in the Early Modern World*, Philadelphia: University of Pennsylvania Press, 2005.

Scholl, John William, 'The Gardener's Art in The Winter's Tale', *Modern Language Notes*, vol. 27, no. 6 (1912): 176–8.

Seager, H. W., *Natural History in Shakespeare's Time: Being Extracts Illustrative of the Subject as he knew it*, London: Elliot Stock, 1896; La Vergne, TN: Kessinger, 2010 reprint.

Sebek, Barbara and Deng, Stephen, *Global Traffic: Discourses and Practices of Trade in English Literature and Culture from 1550 to 1700*, New York and Basingstoke: Palgrave, 2008.

Shaheen, Naseeb, *Biblical References in Shakespeare's Plays*, London: Associated University Presses, 1999.

Sharpe, J. A., *Early Modern England. A Social History, 1550–1760*, London: Edward Arnold, 1987.

Shaw, John, 'Fortune and Nature in As You Like It', *Shakespeare Quarterly*, vol. 6 (1955): 45–50.

Sherwood, Shirley, *A New Flowering: 1000 Years of Botanical Art*, Oxford: Ashmolean Museum, 2005.

Sim, Alison, *Food and Feast in Tudor England*, Stroud: Sutton Publishing Ltd, 1997.

Simoons, Frederick J, *Plants of Life, Plants of Death*, London: University of Wisconsin Press, 1998.

Simpson, Robert R., 'How did Hamlet's Father Die?', *The Listener*, 17 (April 1947): 581–2.

—*Shakespeare and Medicine*, Edinburgh and London: E. & S. Livingstone Ltd, 1959.

Sims, James H., 'Perdita's "Flowers O' Th' Spring" and "Vernal Flowers" in *Lycidas*', *Shakespeare Quarterly*, vol. XXII (1971), 87–90.

Singleton, Esther, *The Shakespeare Garden*, New York: Century, 1922.

Smith, Pamela H. and Findlen, Paula (eds), *Merchants and Marvels: Commerce, Science and Art in Early Modern Europe*, New York: Routledge, 2002.

Smith, Roland M., 'Macbeth's Cyme Once More', *Modern Language Notes*, vol. 60, no. 1 (January 1945): 33–8.

Smith, William, and Marindin, G.E., *Classical Dictionary*, London: John Murray, 1932.

Sokol, B. J., *Art and Illusion in the Winter's Tale*, Manchester: Manchester University Press, 1994.

Spier, Robert F. G. and Anderson, Donald K. Jr., 'Shakespeare and Farming: The Bard and Tusser', *Agricultural History*, vol. 59, no. 3 (July 1985): 448–461.

Sprinkle-Jackson, Kathryn, 'King Lear IV.iv.4: A Proposal for Emendation', *English Language Notes*, vol. 26, (1989): 15–23.

Spurgeon, C. F. E., 'Shakespeare's Iterative Imagery', *Proceedings of the British Academy*, vol. XVII The Proceedings of the British Academy, London: Humphrey Milford, 1931.

—*Shakespeare's Imagery and what it tells us*, Cambridge: University Press, 1935.

Stace, Clive, *New Flora of the British Isles*, Cambridge: Cambridge University Press, 2010.

Stanivukovic, Goran V., ed., *Remapping the Mediterranean World in Early Modern English Writings*, Basingstoke: Palgrave Macmillan, 2007.

Steane, J. M., 'The Development of Tudor and Stuart Garden Design in Northamptonshire', *Northamptonshire Past and Present*, vol. 5, no. 5, (1977).

Strong, Roy, *The Cult of Elizabeth. Elizabethan Portraiture and Pageantry*, London: Thames and Hudson, 1977.

—*The English Renaissance Miniature*, USA: Thames and Hudson, 1983.

—*Henry, Prince of Wales and England's lost Renaissance*, London: Thames and Hudson, 1986.

—*Royal Gardens*, London: BCA, 1992.

—*The Renaissance Garden in England*, London: Thames and Hudson, 1998.

—*The Artist and the Garden*, New Haven and London: Yale University Press, 2000.

Stuart, David, *The Plants that shaped our Gardens*, London: Frances Lincoln Limited, 2002.

Stuart, David, and Sutherland, James, *Plants from the Past. Old Flowers for New Gardens*, London: Viking, 1987.

Sullivan, Frank, 'Cyme, a Purgative Drug', *Modern Language Notes*, vol. 56, no. 4 (April 1941): 263–4.

Tannahill, Reay, *Food in History*, Harmondsworth: Penguin Books, 1988.

Taylor, Kristina, 'The earliest wildernesses: their meanings and developments', *Studies in the History of Gardens and Designed Landscapes*, vol. 28, no. 2 (April-June 2008): 237–51.

Tayler, Edward William, *Nature and Art in Renaissance Literature*, New York and London: Columbia University Press, 1966.

Tchikine, Anatole, 'Giochi d'acqua: Water effects in Renaissance and Baroque Italy', *Studies in the History of Gardens and Designed Landscapes*, vol. 30.1 (2010): 57–76.

Terwen-Dionisius, Else, M., 'Date and design of the botanical garden in Padua', *Journal of Garden History*, vol. 14, no. 4 (1994): 13–35.

Theis, Jeffrey, *Writing the Forest in Early Modern England: A Sylvan Pastoral Nation*, Pittsburg: Duquesne University Press, 2010.

Thirsk, Joan, ed., *The Agrarian History of England and Wales, vol. IV, 1500–1640*, Cambridge: Cambridge University Press, 1967.

—ed., *Land, Church, and People*, Essays presented to Professor H. P. R. Finberg, Reading: British Agricultural History Society, 1970.

—*Economic Policy and Projects. The Development of a Consumer Society in Early Modern England*, Oxford: Clarendon Press, 1978.

—*The English Rural Landscape*, Oxford: Oxford University Press, 2000.

Thistleton Dyer, T. F., *The Folk-Lore of Plants* (1889), Felinfach, Dyfed: Llanerch Publishers, 1994.

—T. F., *Folklore of Shakespeare* (1883), New York: Kessinger Publishing, 2004.

Thomas, Graham S., *The Old Shrub Roses*, London: Phoenix Press, 1955.

Thomas, Keith, *Religion and the Decline of Magic*, London: Weidenfeld and Nicolson, 1971; Harmondsworth: Penguin Books, 1973.

—*Man and the Natural World: Changing Attitudes in England 1500–1800*, London: Allen Lane, 1983. Penguin, 1984.

Thomas, Vivian, *The Moral Universe of Shakespeare's Problem Plays*, Kent: Croom Helm, 1987; London and New York: Routledge, 1991.

—*Shakespeare's Roman Worlds*, London and New York: Routledge, 1989.

—'Translations, Transformations and Intertextuality in *Julius Caesar*' in Zander, Horst, ed., *Julius Caesar: New Critical Studies*, New York and London: Routledge, 2005.

—*Shakespeare's Political and Economic Language: A Dictionary*, London: Continuum, 2008.

Thompson, C. J. S., *The Mystic Mandrake*, London: Ryder & Co., 1934.

Thorne, Alison, *Vision and Rhetoric in Shakespeare: Looking Through Language*, Hampshire: Macmillan Press and New York: St Martin's Press, 2000.

Thurley, Simon, *The Royal Palaces of Tudor England: Architecture and Court Life 1460–1547*, New Haven and London: Yale University Press, 1993.

Tigner, Amy L., 'The Winter's Tale: Gardens and the Marvels of Transformation', *English Literary Renaissance* (2006): 114–34.

—*Literature and the Renaissance Garden from Elizabeth I to Charles II: England's Paradise*, Farnham: Ashgate Publishing Ltd, 2012.

Till, E. C., 'The Development of the Park and Gardens at Burghley', *Garden History*, vol. 19, no. 2 (1991): 128–45.

Tilley, Morris Palmer, *A Dictionary of the Proverbs in England in the sixteenth and seventeenth centuries*, Ann Arbor: University of Michigan Press, 1950.

Todd, Kim, *Tinkering with Eden: a natural history of exotics in America*, New York: W. W. Norton, 2001.

Trease, George Edward, and Evans, William Charles, *Pharmocognosy*, Eastbourne: Ballière Tindall, 1983.

Vickery, Roy, *A Dictionary of Plant-Lore*, Oxford: Oxford University Press, 1995.

—*Garlands, Conkers and Mother-Die. British and Irish Plant-Lore*, London: Continuum, 2010.

Voights, Linda E., 'Anglo-Saxon Plant Remedies and the Anglo-Saxons', *Isis*, vol. 70, no. 2 (1979): 250–68, Chicago: The University of Chicago Press.

Walsham, Alexandra, *The Reformation of the Landscape*, Oxford: Oxford University Press, 2011.

Watkins, W. B. C., *Shakespeare and Spenser*, Princeton: Princeton University Press, 1950.

Watts, Cedric, *Romeo and Juliet*, Hemel Hempstead: Harvester Wheatsheaf, 1991.

Watts, D. C., *Elsevier's Dictionary of Plant Lore*, Burlington, MA: Academic Press, 2007.

Wentersdorf, Karl P., '*Hamlet*: Ophelia's Long Purples', *Shakespeare Quarterly*, vol. 29, no. 3 (Summer 1978): 413–17.

Whalley, Robin, and Jennings, Anne, *Knot Gardens and Parterres*, London: Barn Elms Publishing, 1998.

White, R. A., *The Merry Wives of Windsor*, Hemel Hempstead: Harvester Wheatsheaf, 1991.

Wilders, J., *The Lost Garden: A View of Shakespeare's English and Roman History Plays*, London and Basingstoke: Macmillan, 1978.

Willes, Margaret, *The Making of the English Gardener*, New Haven and London: Yale University Press, 2011.

—*The Gardens of the British Working Class*, New Haven and London: Yale University Press, 2014.

Williams, Gordon, *Shakespeare's Sexual Language: A Glossary*, London: Continuum, 2006.

Williamson, Elizabeth M. ed., *Potter's Herbal Cyclopaedia*, Saffron Walden: C. W. Daniel Co. Ltd, 2003.

Willis, Kathy and Fry, Carolyn, *Plants: from Roots to Riches*, London, John Murray, 2014.

Wilson, Richard, '"Like the old Robin Hood"; As You Like It and the Enclosure Riots', *Shakespeare Quarterly*, vol. 43 (1992): 1–19.

—*Secret Shakespeare. Studies in theatre, religion and resistance*, Manchester: Manchester University Press, 2004.

Woodhouse, Elisabeth, 'Spirit of the Elizabethan Garden', *Garden History*, vol. 27, no.1 (Summer 1999): 10–31.

Woodhouse, Elisabeth, 'Kenilworth, the Earl of Leicester's Pleasure Grounds following Robert Laneham's Letter', *Garden History*, vol. 27, no. 1 (Summer 1999): 127–44.

—'"Propaganda in Paradise": The Symbolic Garden created by the Earl of Leicester at Kenilworth, Warwickeshire'. *Garden History*, (2008), vol. 36, no. 1, 94–113.

Wrightson, Keith, *English Society: 1580–1680*, London: Hutchinson, 1982; London and New York: Routledge, 2003.

Yates, Frances A., *Astraea: The Imperial Theme in the Sixteenth Century*, London: Pimlico, 1975.

Yates, Sarah, ed., *Rushton Triangular Lodge*, London: English Heritage, 2004.

Young, Andrew, *A Prospect of Flowers*. London: Jonathan Cape, 1945.

Young, David, *The Heart's Forest: A Study of Shakespeare's Pastoral Plays*, New Haven and London: Yale University Press, 1972.

Zirkle, Conway, *The Beginning of Plant Hybridization*, Philadephia: University of Pennsylvania Press, 1935.

Online resources

www.apothecaries.org (accessed 12/4/12).

www.british-history.ac.uk (accessed 8/5/12).

www.kew.org/plant-cultures/plants (accessed 13/8/11).

Oxford English Dictionary, consulted frequently online, via www.richmond.gov.uk

Index